THE
SIERRA CLUB
GUIDE TO
THE
NATURAL AREAS
OF IDAHO,
MONTANA, AND
WYOMING

THE SIERRA CLUB GUIDE TO THE NATURAL AREAS OF IDAHO, MONTANA, AND WYOMING

JOHN PERRY

AND

JANE GREVERUS PERRY

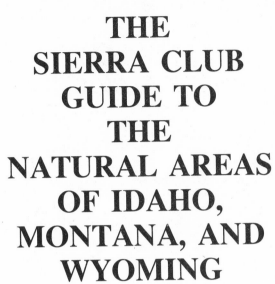

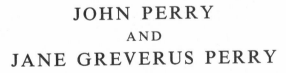

SIERRA CLUB BOOKS   SAN FRANCISCO

The Sierra Club, founded in 1892 by John Muir, has devoted itself to the study and protection of the earth's scenic and ecological resources—mountains, wetlands, woodlands, wild shores and rivers, deserts and plains. The publishing program of the Sierra Club offers books to the public as a nonprofit educational service in the hope that they may enlarge the public's understanding of the Club's basic concerns. The point of view expressed in each book, however, does not necessarily represent that of the Club. The Sierra Club has some sixty chapters coast to coast, in Canada, Hawaii, and Alaska. For information about how you may participate in its programs to preserve wilderness and the quality of life, please address inquiries to Sierra Club, 730 Polk Street, San Francisco, CA 94109.

Library of Congress Cataloging in Publication Data

Perry, John, 1914–
The Sierra Club guide to the natural areas of
Idaho, Montana, and Wyoming.

Includes index.
1. Natural areas—Idaho—Guide-books.
2. Natural areas—Montana—Guide-books.
3. Natural areas—Wyoming—Guide-books.
I. Perry, Jane Greverus. II. Sierra Club.
III. Title
QH76.5.I2P47   1988   917.96'0433   87-26312
ISBN 0-87156-781-4 (pbk.)

Production by Felicity Luebke

Cover design by Gael Towey

Book design concept by Lilly Langotsky

Illustrations by Nancy Warner

Printed in the United States of America on acid-free paper containing a minimum of 50% recovered waste paper, of which at least 10% of the fiber content is post-consumer waste
10 9 8 7 6 5 4 3 2

TO THE RANGERS,
FORESTERS, NATURALISTS,
WILDLIFE BIOLOGISTS,
AND OTHER MEN AND WOMEN
WHO CARE FOR OUR FORESTS,
PARKS, AND PRESERVES

CONTENTS

INTRODUCTION

This is a guide to one of North America's most magnificent and diverse regions. Here are towering, snow-capped mountain ranges, deep canyons, blowing sand dunes, volcanic badlands, caves, buttes, mesas, deserts, and seemingly endless prairies. Here are great lakes, crystal-clear ponds in high cirque basins, roaring mountain streams, lazily meandering rivers, potholes, and marshes. The many plant communities range from desert scrub and valley wetlands up through splendid conifer forests to alpine tundra. Wildlife is abundant and as diverse as the habitats, not only the big game and sport fish that have long attracted hunters and fishermen from around the world but an array of creatures great and small.

John saw this region first in 1929 and returned with camping gear in 1930. We have visited it often since we met. At first, like most tourists with limited vacation days, we had eyes only for the Rocky Mountains. We hastened across the plains and prairies, eager for the first glimpse of peaks that assured us we would soon be in Yellowstone or Glacier National Park. The Rockies dominate northwestern Wyoming, western Montana, and northern Idaho. Most mountain land is within the 46 million acres of National Forests. The Forests have more than 10 million acres of Wildernesses and as many more in roadless areas with Wilderness qualities. A lifetime would not be long enough to hike the countless trails that follow mountain streams to the high country.

People find the plains and prairies dull in part because highways are designed to follow the easiest routes, avoiding escarpments, chasms, and marshes—in effect avoiding the best scenery. Leaving the interstate highways to explore is richly rewarding. In our final field trip to gather data for this book, we traveled 11,000 miles, bypassing places we knew, making fascinating discoveries every day. At a time when National Park campgrounds were full, we were alone most nights, usually on the shore of a lovely lake or river. In days exploring desert canyons, wilderness trails, and waterfowl marshes, we seldom saw other visitors.

One of the places we visited has been proposed as a National Park. Given the name and the publicity it would attract crowds, and they would not be disappointed. Few people go there now.

Many attractive but little-known places are within these states' 38 million acres of federal public domain. Local hunters and fishermen know them, as they know the state wildlife management areas and fishing access sites, but few outsiders do. We were alone, or nearly so, on most of our visits to the National Wildlife Refuges of the region. In season, and especially on weekends, State Parks may be crowded, but several parks with attractive natural areas had few if any other visitors when we were there.

This is a guide to the quiet places. People sometimes ask if our writing about them attracts crowds. It doesn't happen. We omit a few sites so small, unique, and vulnerable that any traffic could be damaging. People congregate by choice. We write for those who enjoy solitude and who, if they know about quiet places, will support efforts to protect them.

CHANGES

By the time this book is published, the Reagan Administration will be in its final months. Since 1981 the President and his men have striven to tear down the environmental protections built since the time of Theodore Roosevelt. Except when blocked by Congress or the courts, they have succeeded. Much of the damage they have inflicted on the nation's natural resources cannot be healed for decades. Some precious assets are lost forever.

The foresters, wildlife managers, rangers, and others who gave us warm and generous help are, by and large, angry men and women. Dedicated professionals, they have been forced to witness or even participate in the ravaging. We join them in hoping the next Administration will begin the long task of reconstruction.

As conservation activists, we write and speak about these issues. This book is not an appropriate forum. Here we note only what visitors should know: that the Administration has been dismantling the facilities and support for public recreation on the public lands. Visitors may encounter these and other changes:

Potholes unrepaired in National Park roads

Trails impassable, obstructed, or in poor condition for lack of maintenance

Campgrounds closed, open for shorter seasons, or turned over to concessioners

Trash accumulating in backcountry campgrounds

Toilets, tables, and other facilities unrepaired

Recreation staff specialists assigned to other duties

Campfire programs and other ranger naturalist activities discontinued

Publications discontinued

At times the hiker who wants to avoid crowds may find it hard going. The most heavily used trails have first claim on maintenance. We found one of our favorite trails blocked by trees blown down a year before.

Budgets have been cut while the number of visitors increases. The deterioration is cumulative.

HOW WE SELECT SITES

We use the term *natural area* broadly. We look for places where a visitor can enjoy nature. Many are roadless areas, some truly pristine, but we do not reject a logged, grazed, or otherwise disturbed site if the healing processes of nature are working. Nor do we reject a wildlife refuge because its impoundments are man-made and feed crops are planted. When thousands of waterfowl and shorebirds assemble, we accept their endorsement.

National Forests, National Parks, and National Wildlife Refuges are automatic selections. City parks are not entries. We don't include a State Park designed for intensive recreation unless it includes or adjoins a substantial natural area.

Most entries describe lands owned by the state or federal government. We have entries for floatable rivers with a mixture of private, state, and federal riparian lands.

We do not include historical or archeological sites. This has been a difficult policy to sustain, especially in this region where the pioneer trails are shown on highway maps and wagon ruts can still be seen. Including such sites would make this guidebook unmanageable.

THE PUBLIC DOMAIN

Of the original public domain, 12 million acres remain in Idaho, 8 million in Montana, 18 million in Wyoming. These lands are administered by the U.S. Bureau of Land Management (BLM). They are not subdivided into named units, as are National Forests and National Parks. They include some fascinating natural areas.

No previous guidebooks describe these public lands. No posted signs identify them. They are widely scattered, sometimes in huge blocks, often intermixed with private and state landholdings, sometimes with private and federal lands alternating in a checkerboard of one-mile squares.

Our review of the BLM lands was facilitated by the Wilderness Act, which required all federal land-holding agencies to identify and describe all roadless areas of 5,000 or more acres. Each was given a name, usually that of a prominent feature. We spent many hours reading the field notes of BLM specialists who had studied these areas and recorded hours of interviews with them. They recommended the sites they considered most attractive to outdoorsmen, and we visited as many as we could.

Before the Reagan Administration, BLM was developing a public recreation program. Campgrounds were built, most of them primitive. Some trails and river access sites were developed and marked. Some BLM districts we visited had their recreation budgets cut to zero for fiscal 1988.

Except for signs identifying recreation sites, BLM lands are unmarked. Most BLM land has been leased for grazing, mining, or other purposes.

Leased lands are often fenced. Nevertheless, it is all public land, all yours to enjoy. Whether leased or not, you can drive, hike, backpack, hunt, fish, and camp on BLM land. Legally, the fences don't shut you out, although you're expected to close gates.

Sometimes BLM land is separated from public roads by private land. Unless BLM has negotiated an easement, you can't cross the private land without permission. We don't include sites that lack legal access.

The roads to some BLM tracts require high-clearance or 4-wheel-drive vehicles. We include these hard-to-get-to sites only if they have exceptional qualities.

How can you know when you're on public land? Most of our BLM entries describe substantial blocks of public land. Every BLM office has excellent land ownership maps, which also show many backcountry roads highway maps don't.

A rancher who has leased public land for years often comes to regard it as his own and may resent "intruders." It doesn't happen often, but you might be asked to leave. Go quietly. The BLM office would like to know about the incident, but don't expect any action.

WILDERNESS AREAS

How does a wilderness become a Wilderness? Only by a lengthy procedure prescribed by the Wilderness Act and elaborated by books of regulations. Roadless areas of 5,000 or more acres are studied, recommended, and reviewed. Hearings are held. The sites surviving this process (a minority) are recommended to Congress. Only by Congressional action does a wilderness become a Wilderness. It is then given special protection. Unless Congress makes other provisions, it is thereafter closed to all mechanical vehicles, to logging, and to other intrusions that would alter its natural condition.

The political forces aligned against Wilderness designations are formidable: timber and mining companies, off-road vehicle operators and manufacturers, frequently hunters and outfitters. Few BLM sites have been recommended to Congress.

We describe many sites that have Wilderness qualities, even though they presently lack the full legal protection.

Land managers have divergent views on how Wildernesses should be presented to visitors. One National Forest provides excellent Wilderness maps, detailed descriptions of trails, and other information. Another provides nothing except its Forest map, which includes everything inside Forest borders.

"A wilderness should be a place of discovery and testing," the wilderness specialist told us. "People should have a real wilderness experience, finding their own way. Sure, we'll always answer questions. But we don't mark trails and we don't hand out maps."

ROADS AND MAPS

America's most interesting roads aren't on highway maps. Many county roads aren't shown. The National Forests have more miles of road than the state and federal highways. BLM has a road system. Then there are ranch roads, mine roads, and roads on timber company lands.

Each State Preface describes the maps we found most useful in the field. More detailed maps, such as the U.S. Geological Survey's (USGS) 7.5-minute topo quadrangles, are great for local use, but a set for an entire state such as Montana would fill a file drawer.

Maps showing unpaved roads label them in various ways: "improved," "graveled," "all-weather," "graded," "unimproved," "primitive," "jeep trail." Most maps are several years old, and beyond the pavement conditions can change drastically with a single storm. A road that's passable in dry weather can become a quagmire when wet. A road that's a delight just after a grading can be a hellish washboard a few weeks later.

Federal and state agencies advise that certain roads require high-clearance or 4-wheel-drive vehicles. In dry weather, a carefully driven passenger car might get through. We've driven our motor home many a mile on primitive roads, but occasionally we've had to turn back. Only by getting local information can you learn about the bridge that washed out Sunday night.

A general rule for backcountry travel: don't drive in farther than you're prepared to walk out.

STATE WILDLIFE MANAGEMENT AREAS

All three states have Wildlife Management Areas (WMAs). Their usual purpose is helping maintain populations of one or more species. Elk, for example, spend their summers on high ground, often in a National Forest. When snow falls, they descend to the valleys. Many WMAs are winter feeding grounds for elk that might otherwise feast on farmers' haystacks.

Hunting is permitted on many, not all, WMAs, as well as fishing if fishable streams or lakes are present. Support for state wildlife agencies comes largely from sale of hunting and fishing licenses, so a bias toward hunters and fishermen is logical. However, wildlife departments are giving increasing attention to nongame species, and the "nonconsumptive user"—the hiker, birder, camper, etc.—is increasingly welcome when such visits don't conflict with the principal mission.

We spent time at each state wildlife agency reviewing their files and management plans and consulting with staff members. They were invariably helpful in suggesting which WMAs would be of interest to the general visitor. We visited as many as we could. The wildlife agencies also administer fishing access sites, which are often attractive to boaters and overnight campers.

These agencies govern hunting and fishing in their states, including hunting and fishing on federal land.

CONTINENTAL DIVIDE NATIONAL SCENIC TRAIL CORRIDOR

The Continental Divide extends from the Canadian border in Glacier National Park to the Mexican border S of Lordsburg, NM. Most of Montana and Wyoming are E of the Divide, draining to the Gulf of Mexico. All of Idaho is W of the Divide, part of which lies on the ID-MT border.

With the examples of the Appalachian Trail and Pacific Crest Trail as inspiration, the idea of a Continental Divide Trail gathered advocates. In 1978 Congress approved, but without specifying a route, setting a time goal, or providing funds.

For most of its 3,000 mi., the Divide is on federal land: National Forests, National Parks, and public domain. Even a mountain goat would be challenged to follow the precise line of the Divide along its more rugged crests. A hikeable trail will necessarily approximate the route. In many places, the crests are boundaries between National Forests. In the summer of 1987, working parties from several Forests were developing a plan to divide responsibility for trail layout and construction.

Sections of some existing trails will be included. Each year a few people hike or ride the route, using these trails, bushwhacking, detouring when they must. More sections will be blazed or built from time to time, but the Trail won't be completed in this century.

WEATHER

Driving from Red Lodge to Yellowstone National Park, we saw people skiing in June. Two weeks later, crossing from Montana into Idaho over Lost Trail Pass, we were caught in a blizzard. On occasion we've hiked in shirt-sleeve weather by day and found snow on our tent next morning. Many high trails are not snow-free until after July 1.

The great majority of visitors to this region come between June 15 and Sept. 1, because of climate as well as school vacations. One way to avoid crowds is to come earlier or later. Unless you want snow, this requires planning.

The three states have a wide range of climates. In general, of course, temperatures decline with increasing altitudes; the peaks are colder than the valleys. Local conditions vary; some valleys collect cold air that flows down from the mountains at night. In Wyoming, the average number of days without a killing frost ranges from 40 to 140, with most of the state between 80 and 120 days. Montana also has the 40–140 range, but the great majority of the state, east of the Rockies, has 100 to 140 frost-free days. The range is more extreme in Idaho, where the western valleys have up to 200 days with no killing frost; most of the state is in the 60- to 100-day range.

Visitors who enjoy the river valleys, lakes, deserts, canyons, and lower slopes can anticipate temperate weather beginning in May and continuing into October.

The prospect of rain shouldn't dampen plans. Annual precipitation is highest at high elevations, where most of it falls as snow. For most of the region, the wettest months are in late spring and early summer, but even then more than two-thirds of the daytime hours are sunny. In the mountains, afternoon thunderstorms are common in summer, but they usually pass quickly.

HOW WE GATHER INFORMATION

Roughly a third of the information assembled here is available somewhere in print: technical reports, Environmental Impact Statements (EISs), management plans, computerized biological records, maps, pamphlets, hearing transcripts, etc. We assembled 26 shelf-feet of documents.

Another third was gathered from the files of state and federal agencies, chiefly in local and district offices. Many field reports are accompanied by color photographs that never get beyond field offices. When our friends imagined we were enjoying long hikes in the mountains, we were often combing through dozens of file drawers.

The final third was gathered by interviews and first-hand field observation. While we visited most sites, becoming familiar with the backcountry of a single National Forest would take months. We interviewed foresters who had known the country for years.

The task would have been far more difficult had we not known the region from many previous visits and impossible without the generous help of dozens of federal and state employees.

This help was renewed when we sent each entry out for checking at the source. With few exceptions, they came back with evidence of careful checking, often with fresh material for us to add.

HOW TO USE THIS BOOK

Each state is divided into zones. A zone map precedes each state chapter. At the beginning of each zone section is a map and list of sites. Entries are arranged alphabetically within zones. Once you have a destination in mind, the map will show what other sites are nearby or on your way.

Information in entries is presented in a standard sequence:

SITE NAME

Parks, federal and state, are for people. Most parks have formal entrances. National Parks and most State Parks are closed to hunting and logging. Parks have more facilities, more supervision, more rules, and more visitors than forests or refuges. National Parks and Monuments were established "to conserve the scenery and the natural and historic objects and the wild life therein and to provide for the enjoyment of same. . . ."

National Forests are managed for wood, water, wildlife, and recreation, although critics charge imbalance. Campgrounds are less elaborate than those in National Parks and often less congested. Further, one can camp almost anywhere in a National Forest. Fishing and hunting are regulated by state laws.

National Recreation Areas give more emphasis to recreation, less to strict preservation.

National Wildlife Refuges are for birds and beasts. Some have visitor facilities, such as auto tour routes. Hunting is usually permitted, often in a part of a refuge and with special rules.

Public lands administered by BLM have many uses, including grazing, mining, forestry, and geothermal development. Most areas are open to public use.

State Wildlife Management Areas are also for birds and beasts. Few have visitor facilities except, in some cases, parking areas and latrines for hunters. Visitors are welcome, with some restrictions; but some WMAs have seasonal closures. Camping is often permitted.

ACREAGE

Many National Forests and some other sites have "inholdings," land owned by others, within their boundaries. Entries note this when significant.

Acreages given for BLM sites do not measure the limits of public ownership. They refer to selected areas, often surrounded by other public land.

HOW TO GET THERE

Routings begin from points easily found on highway maps. For large sites, entries describe main access routes.

Don't rely on our directions. You need maps. If the routing leaves paved roads, inquire locally.

OPEN HOURS

Mentioned only if unusual. Most National Parks are open 24 hours.
Some State Parks close their gates at night.
National Forests have no gates.
Most National Wildlife Refuges are open from sunrise to sundown.

SYMBOLS

Symbols designate the principal activities available. Most have obvious meanings:

 Without the pack, day hiking; with it, backpacking opportunities

 Flatwater boating, with or without motors

 Whitewater rafting; may also include kayaking

DESCRIPTION

Each site is briefly characterized: landform, principal physical features, vegetation. Beyond this, data resources varied. For some sites we could obtain weather data; others are far from any weather station. Some have detailed accounts of their flora and fauna; most areas have never been studied.

One can infer the presence of species from studies of similar sites. We chose not to do this, inviting readers to do it for themselves. We provide rather full accounts of flora and fauna for sites that have such data. If Douglas-fir grows on a N-facing slope at 8,500 ft. elevation in one location, one can expect to find it on a similar slope not far away. The reader who studies entries will soon recognize common patterns and associations.

We provide rather full lists of birds and mammals where checklists are available. Such lists usually classify species as Abundant, Common, Uncommon, or Rare. We list the abundant and common species, those most likely to be found over a broader area. Some lists note seasonality and habitat preferences, too much data for our entries to include.

We judged some checklists unreliable, including species long since vanished, obvious misidentifications, "common" applied to species that aren't common anywhere. Use of obsolete Latin and common names dated a few lists. On the whole, however, patterns were consistent and illuminating. We deleted only the most improbable items.

FEATURES

Noted first are Wilderness Areas and other large, natural portions of sites, followed by mentions of such outstanding features as canyons, waterfalls, rivers, and lakes.

Major recreation centers are noted.

ACTIVITIES

Camping: Entries report the number of campgrounds accessible by road and the total number of sites. Auto camping in parks is generally limited to campgrounds. For details, see a standard campground guide.

One can camp almost anywhere in a National Forest or on the public domain.

Hiking, backpacking: Before undertaking anything more ambitious than a day hike on marked trails, we strongly recommend visiting the appropriate Forest, Park, or BLM office. They can recommend routes and destinations. Trail conditions can change overnight. Once, not taking our own advice, we hiked for half a day, found a landslide across the route, and had to turn back.

Horse riding: Some ranches and outfitters offer pack trips, with and without guides. Lists are usually available from state tourist offices, chambers of commerce, National Forest headquarters, etc.

Hunting: Prohibited in National Parks. Regulated in wildlife areas. Always subject to state laws.

Fishing: Subject to state laws. Protected fish species occur in some waters; taking one subjects the fisherman to a heavy fine.

Boating: Flatwater, rivers and lakes, motor or hand-propelled. Most ramps are suitable for launching with passenger cars, not all.

Rafting: Rivers offer floating from Class I to Class VI. Entries have general descriptions only.

HAZARDS

Many site managers urged us to warn you about local hazards: giardia, hypothermia, rattlesnakes, poison ivy, grizzly bears, and so on. They weren't consistent; other managers ran up no red flags. Should we warn of rattlesnakes in every place where they occur? With that policy, entries would be burdened with repetitive warnings.

Local federal and state offices have leaflets about giardia and other local problems, and there's always someone there to offer advice. People who act sensibly seldom have difficulties.

RULES AND REGULATIONS

All sites have some. Parks have the most.

Pets are regulated in much the same way everywhere. They must be leashed (and usually attended) in National and State Parks and National Wildlife Refuges. They are usually barred from beaches and public buildings. In most National and State Parks, pets are prohibited on trails. In National Forests, the leash rule applies in campgrounds, picnic areas, and other recreation sites. Trails are seldom posted, but we wouldn't let our dog run free in bear country.

PUBLICATIONS

Listed are the maps, pamphlets, trail guides, and other printed matter available when we last inquired. Changes are frequent, especially now that budgets have been cut. Some items won't be reprinted when stocks are gone.

You can write for these publications, but responses may not be quick. We suggest sending a stamped, self-addressed envelope (SASE) with your request.

REFERENCES

General

Riley, Laura and William. *Guide to the National Wildlife Refuges.* New York: Doubleday, 1979.

Tilden, Freeman. *The National Parks.* New York: Knopf, 1976.

Carstensen, Vernon (ed.). *The Public Lands: Studies in the History of the Public Domain.* Madison: University of Wisconsin Press, 1968.

Shanks, Bernard. *This Land Is Your Land.* San Francisco: Sierra Club Books, 1984.

Geology

Alt, David, and Donald Hyndman. *The Roadside Geology of the Northern Rockies.* Billings: Falcon Press, 1984.

Plants

Craighead, John J., Frank Craighead, and Roy J. Davis. *A Field Guide to Rocky Mountain Wildflowers.* Billings: Falcon Press, 1974.

Dannen, Kent and Donna. *Rocky Mountain Wildflowers.* Estes Park; CO: Tundra Publications, 1981.

Preston, Richard J. *Rocky Mountain Trees.* New York: Dover Publications, 1968.

Birds

Ulrich, Tom. *Birds of the Northern Rockies.* Missoula, MT: Mountain Press, 1985.

Mammals

Ulrich, Tom. *Mammals of the Northern Rockies.* Missoula, MT: Mountain Press, 1986.

Camping

National Forest Campground Guide. Aberdeen, SD: Tensleep Publications, 1985.

THE
SIERRA CLUB
GUIDE TO
THE
NATURAL AREAS
OF IDAHO,
MONTANA, AND
WYOMING

IDAHO

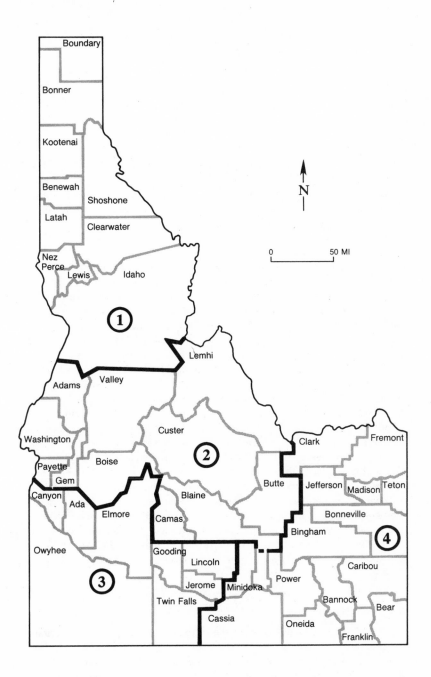

Boundary

Bonner

Kootenai

Benewah

Shoshone

Latah

Clearwater

Nez
Perce

Lewis   Idaho

①

N

0   50 MI

Lemhi

Adams   Valley

Washington   Custer

Payette   Boise   Clark   Fremont

Gem

②

Canyon   Butte   Jefferson   Madison   Teton

Ada   Elmore   Blaine   Bonneville

Camas   Bingham   ④

Owyhee   Gooding   Lincoln   Power   Caribou

③   Jerome   Minidoka   Bannock   Bear

Twin Falls   Cassia   Oneida   Franklin

IDAHO

Like many summer tourists, we had crossed Idaho several times, on I-84 following the Snake River in the S, on I-90 making the briefer passage in the N. Once we had driven S from Missoula to Craters of the Moon before turning E toward the Tetons, once taken the Sawtooth Scenic Route. Once we camped overnight at Bear Lake, en route from the Tetons to Salt Lake City.

We liked what we saw. We understood why someone seeing Coeur d'Alene for the first time might rush home, sell his business, and come back to stay. Nonetheless, the two years this book was in preparation were full of delightful surprises and discoveries. Idaho has far more than we had suspected.

The state has been attractive to generations of hunters and fishermen from other parts of America and other continents. Attractive to skiers, especially since the development of Sun Valley. Attractive to whitewater adventurers, for the state has famous rafting routes, including the River of No Return. But each of these groups has known just one aspect of a complex state.

Most sightseeing tourists head for National Parks: Yellowstone, Grand Teton, Glacier, Bryce, Zion. Idaho has none, although several sites have been proposed. Many of the state's outstanding natural features are in areas the highway map shows as roadless blanks. To find them takes study and a spirit of adventure.

One afternoon we stopped to camp on an attractive lake shore. A few fishermen were nearby. They noticed our out-of-state license plate. "How did you find this place?" they asked. They live nearby, come to the lake often, and rarely see strangers. More often we had no company, driving for hours without seeing another vehicle, camping in solitude beside a lake or river, enjoying a magnificent canyon that is seen by fewer than 500 people in a year.

It's changing. More people discover Idaho each year. The Sawtooth National Recreation Area now draws more visitors than some National Parks. But for years to come there will be quiet places.

THE LAND

Idaho is mountainous. Most of the state is over a mile high. Mountain ranges dominate the entire E side of the state and most of its central portion. Highest peak is 12,662-ft. Mt. Borah. Craters of the Moon National Monument is at the center of a huge area of recent volcanism. The SW portion of the state is high desert.

Average annual precipitation ranges from less than 8 in. to well over 50 in. Most precipitation falls as snow. Summers tend to be dry, with occasional intense storms. Summer in the desert can be too hot for comfort, while high-country hikers may experience nighttime frost in July. Lost Trail Pass on US 93 is only 6,995 ft. high, but we once met a blizzard there in June.

Countless streams descending from melting snowfields gather in ID's great rivers: the Snake, Salmon, Selway, Clearwater, Payette, St. Joe, Coeur d'A-lene, and others, more than 16,000 mi. of streams that support fish. The rivers have cut canyons as much as a mile deep into mountains and plateaus. The state's lowest point, 610 ft. elevation, is where the Snake exits. Dam-builders covet canyons, and the state has many large and small reservoirs. Pend Oreille, covering 125 square miles, is the largest of many lakes in the valleys. Many more, most too small to appear on highway maps, dot the high country.

National Forests occupy 38% of ID's area. Another 22% is public domain managed by BLM. State lands and other federal holdings bring the total public ownership to more than two-thirds of the state. Most private holdings are lands that were attractive to settlers: farmers, ranchers, and miners. In general, the mountainous regions are National Forests; the deserts and can-yonlands are public domain, while many valleys are a mix of BLM and private holdings.

MAPS AND ROADS

National Forest and BLM road networks far exceed the mileage of public highways, and they're not shown on highway maps. For most of ID, National Forest maps are the most useful. They usually show much detail outside Forest boundaries. National Forest maps differ in age and quality.

BLM published a 1:500,000 Surface Responsibility Map for the entire state. Imposed on a contour map are colors showing land ownerships. Also shown are the principal roads.

When you want detail about an area not covered by a National Forest map, BLM's 1:100,000 maps are useful. They're available at BLM District Offices.

Most Forest Service and BLM roads were built for utilitarian purposes, not recreation. A road built to open an area for logging has served its purpose when logging ends. Popular recreation routes are maintained if budgets per-mit, but many roads in the backcountry are virtually abandoned, washouts and bridges left unrepaired. We often see trees growing between old tire tracks.

Maps don't tell you which unpaved roads can be traveled by an ordinary car. Conditions change too quickly. At BLM offices and Forest Service Ranger Districts you'll find people who know. Local information is helpful. More than once we've been flagged and warned about an obstacle or hazard ahead.

The state highway map shows the Lewis and Clark, Nez Perce, Oregon, California, and other historical trails. Highway markers call attention to them. BLM is marking trail sections on public land. Some parts of the old trails can be hiked.

TRAILS

Idaho's trails could satisfy a hiker for a lifetime of long backpacks in wildernesses, early-season hikes up canyons to snowfields, easy strolls along lake shores, scrambles through canyons and across lava lands, walks to observe big game, waterfowl, or wildflowers.

The route of the Continental Divide Scenic Trail enters Idaho in Yellowstone National Park. It follows the ID-MT border along the Centennial and Bitterroot Mountains, turning E into MT at Lost Trail Pass, where US 93 crosses. Jim Wolf's *Guide to the Continental Divide Trail* describes the route and the existing trails that approximate portions of it.

FEDERAL AGENCIES

NATIONAL PARK SERVICE

It is not strictly correct to say ID has no National Park, because it has a small strip of Yellowstone with no road access. We do have an entry for Craters of the Moon National Monument.

U.S. FOREST SERVICE

The National Forests in ID are
Bitterroot
Boise
Cache
Caribou
Challis
Clearwater
Idaho Panhandle (Kaniksu, Coeur d'Alene, St. Joe)
Kootenai
Nez Perce
Payette
Salmon
Sawtooth
Targhee

The entry for the Bitterroot is in Montana. The Cache is predominantly in Utah, and we did not provide an entry for the ID portion.

The Sawtooth National Recreation Area is administered by the Sawtooth National Forest but has a separate entry.

U.S. Bureau of Land Management
3380 Americana Terrace
Boise, ID 83706
(208) 334-1401

BLM manages about 12 million acres of public domain in ID, land no one took when it was available for the taking. Only a few scattered tracts are in the N third of the state. In the central region, BLM lands are generally in valleys where mountain ranges are in National Forests. By far the largest BLM areas are in the southern desert and lava lands. Fifty-seven roadless tracts larger than 5,000 acres each were identified as Wilderness Study Areas. With the advice of BLM staff members, study of file documents, and our own field notes, we selected sites of special interest, often combining WSAs that are separated only by roads.

U.S. FISH AND WILDLIFE SERVICE

Four *National Wildlife Refuges*, Bear Lake, Camas, Grays Lake, and Minidoka, are included in the Southeast Idaho Refuge Complex. Deer Flat NWR is on the Snake River W of Boise. Kootenai NWR is in the far N of the state.

U.S. ARMY CORPS OF ENGINEERS

We have entries for two Corps projects: Albeni and Dworshak.

STATE AGENCIES

Idaho Department of Parks and Recreation
2177 Warm Springs Ave.
Boise, ID 83720
(208) 334-2154

We have entries for 7 of the 19 State Parks. Others we visited are attractive and well designed for their intended purposes, but are not natural areas.

PUBLICATIONS

Idaho State Parks. Booklet.
Idaho Adventure Guide. Booklet.

Idaho Department of Fish and Game
600 S. Walnut
Boise, ID 83707
(208) 334-3700

ID has 23 Wildlife Management Areas totaling about 170,000 acres, ranging in size from 275 to 50,000 acres. Fish and Game also manages about 200 public access areas on streams and lakes. Some are state-owned, some leased. Some are federal lands for which Fish and Game provides management.

This language appears in their five-year management plans: "Nonconsumptive uses of wildlife (and the production of shorebirds and songbirds) will be accommodated as funds and time permit. . . . All nonwildlife oriented uses will be discouraged. If they conflict with planned uses, they will be prohibited." Our translation: "Fish and game is our prime responsibility, and the budget is tight. We'll support nongame management as much as we can. Birders and others interested in wildlife viewing are welcome if they don't disturb animals or get in hunters' way. But we don't want ORVers tearing up the place."

Fair enough! We were given excellent help in selecting WMAs, and they reviewed our entries.

We stopped at most of the Public Access Areas along our route and parked overnight at several. They range in size from a third of an acre to several thousand acres. All but a few have graveled parking areas. A majority have latrines. More than a third have boat ramps. Most of those we saw were attractive. A few were littered. The published list of these areas was out of date when we visited, including only 147 sites, but a new list was planned.

PUBLICATIONS

Idaho Wildlife. Bimonthly. $10/yr. July–Aug. 1986 is the *Official Fishing Guide.*
Public Access Areas. List, locations, map.
General Fishing Seasons and Regulations.
Big Game Regulations.
Nongame Wildlife Leaflet 2. Idaho's Water Birds: the Colony Nesters.

OUTFITTERS AND GUIDES

Idaho Outfitters and Guides Association
P.O. Box 95
Boise, ID 83701
(208) 342-1438

PUBLICATION: *Outdoor Idaho Experiences.* Annual directory.

REFERENCES

GENERAL
Sunset Travel Guide to Idaho. Menlo Park, CA: Lane Books, 1969.
Conley, Cort. *Idaho for the Curious.* Cambridge, ID: Backeddy Books, 1982. (Highly recommended! 704 pages; all about Idaho.)

GEOLOGY
Fiero, Bill. *Geology of the Great Basin.* Reno: University of Nevada Press, 1986.

TREES AND SHRUBS
Lanner, Ronald M. *Trees of the Great Basin.* Reno: University of Nevada Press, 1984.

Mozingo, Hugh N. *Shrubs of the Great Basin.* Reno: University of Nevada Press, 1986.

FLOWERING PLANTS
Boren, Robert R., and Marjorie D. Boren. *Wildflowers of the Sawtooth Mountain Country.* Boise: Sawtooth Publishing, 1975.

BIRDS
Ryser, Fred A., Jr. *Birds of the Great Basin.* Reno: University of Nevada Press, 1985.

MAMMALS
Larrison, Earl Jr. *Mammals of Idaho.* Moscow: University Press of Idaho, 1981.

HIKING
Idaho Recreation Trails. Boise: Idaho State Parks and Recreation, 1980.
Maughan, Jackie Johnson. *The Hiker's Guide to Idaho.* Billings, MT: Falcon Press, 1984.
Bluestein, S. R. *Hiking Trails of Southern Idaho.* Caldwell, ID: Caxton Printers, 1981.
Bluestein, S. R. *North Idaho Hiking Trails.* Boise: Challenge Expedition Co., 1982.
Fuller, Margaret. *Trails of the Sawtooth and White Cloud Mountains.* Edmonds, WA: Signpost Books, 1979.
Fuller, Margaret. *Trails of Western Idaho, from Sun Valley to Hells Canyon.* Edmonds, WA: Signpost Books, 1982.
Mitchell, Ron. *50 Eastern Idaho Hiking Trails.* Boulder, CO: Pruett, 1979.
Wolf, James R. *Guide to the Continental Divide Trail: Southern Montana and Idaho.* Bethesda, MD: Continental Divide Trail Society, 1986.

BOATING
A River Runner's Guide to Idaho, Boise, 1980: U.S. Bureau of Land Management and Idaho Department of Parks.
Garren, John. *Idaho River Tours.* Beaverton, OR: Touchstone Press, 1980.
Carrey, John, and Cort Conley. *The Middle Fork and the Sheepeater War.* Cambridge, ID: Backeddy Books, rev. 1980.

CAVES, CAVING
Ross, Sylvia A. *Introduction to Idaho Caves and Caving.* Moscow: Idaho Bureau of Mines and Geology, 1969.

STATE PARKS
State Parks of Idaho. College of Forestry, Wildlife, and Range Sciences, University of Idaho, 1980.

ZONE 1

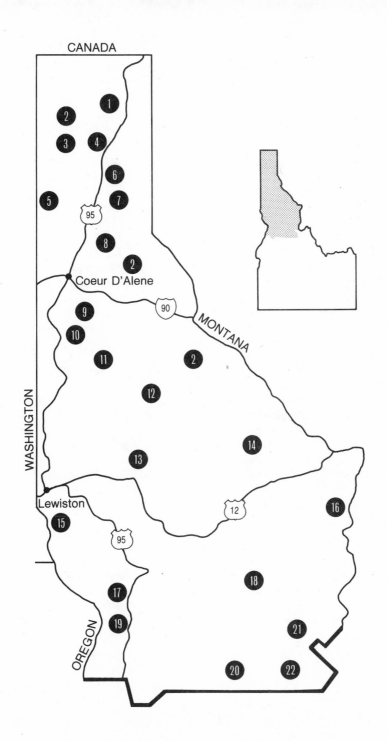

CANADA

1

2

3   4

6

5   95

7

8

2

Coeur D'Alene

9

10

11   2

12

14

13

Lewiston

15

95

17

19

18

21

20   22

WASHINGTON

MONTANA

12

16

OREGON

ZONE 1

Includes these counties:

Boundary	Bonner	Latah
Shoshone	Benewah	Lewis
Clearwater	Nez Perce	
Idaho	Kootenai	

Zone 1 is northern Idaho. Well over half of it is National Forest land: the Idaho Panhandle and Nez Perce National Forests, the N portion of the Payette, and the W portion of the Bitterroot, most of which is in Montana. Forest land extends from Canada along the E boundary in a strip that widens until, at the S end of the zone, it reaches from border to border, interrupted only by the corridor of US 95.

The SE portion of the zone is wilderness. Here are the Selway-Bitterroot and Gospel Hump Wildernesses, a part of the Frank Church - River of No Return Wilderness, and several Wild and Scenic Rivers.

The central portion of the zone has major lakes: Priest, Pend Oreille, and Coeur d'Alene, plus Dworshak, other reservoirs, and many smaller water bodies. The zone includes portions of the Salmon, Clearwater, Selway, Coeur d'Alene, and St. Joe rivers, with their forks and tributaries. From the mountains flow hundreds of fishable streams. All these rivers run to the Snake, which flows deep in Hells Canyon on the SW boundary of the zone, bordered by another Wilderness. The rivers offer adventures from raft trips on challenging whitewater to placid drifting through quiet woods.

Most of the zone is mountainous. Rivers flow mostly in canyons rather than meandering over plains. It is not Idaho's highest country, however; only a few isolated peaks rise above the 7,000-ft. contour.

Wildlife is abundant, attracting hunters and fishermen from far away. Hikers have their choice of scenic day trips, backpackers as much wilderness as they can handle. Only a few major highways traverse the zone, but there are several thousand miles of unpaved roads, some suitable for ordinary cars, some requiring high clearance or 4-wheel drive. Sightseeing by car is the principal visitor activity.

ALBENI FALLS PROJECT; PEND OREILLE RIVER
U.S. Army Corps of Engineers
4,215 acres.

The dam is on US 2, 2 1/2 mi. from the Washington border. Corps recreation sites are on both sides of the river, accessible from US 2 and US 95.

Idaho's largest lake, Pend Oreille, was further enlarged when the Albeni Falls Dam was built in the 1950s to provide hydroelectric power. The dam is on the Pend Oreille River, 25 mi. downstream. This stretch of the river has become, in effect, an arm of the lake.

The Corps necessarily acquired some of the lands that would be inundated or affected by the higher lake level. Some of these riparian lands are managed by the Idaho Fish and Game Department. The Corps operates six recreation areas along the river, at Trestle Creek, Springy Point, Priest River, Riley Creek, Albeni Cove, and the Vista area.

Plants: About 70% of the Corps-owned land is floodplain wetlands. Slopes above the plain are forested with ponderosa and lodgepole pine, western larch, Douglas-fir, western redcedar, grand fir, and western white pine. An old-growth stand of redcedar is at Albeni Cove. Understory species include alder, hawthorn, snowberry, dogwood, blackberry, thimbleberry. Flowering species include wild rose, oceanspray, ninebark, lupine, western trillium, huckleberry, fireweed.

Birds: See entry for Pend Oreille Wildlife Management Area.

Mammals: Species reported include mink, weasel, marmot, muskrat, beaver, river otter, fox, coyote, black bear, elk, moose, whitetail deer.

ACTIVITIES

Camping: At 4 recreation areas; 141 sites. Earliest open May 1; latest close Oct. 1. No reservations. 14-day limit. May be full on summer weekends. Campground at Farragut State Park. Informal camping on Fish and Game lands.

Fishing: Kokanee salmon; kamloops rainbow, Dolly Varden, and cutthroat trout; whitefish, perch, largemouth bass, crappie.

Boating: Ramps at 5 recreation areas. The main lake is subject to high winds. Fall drawdown may limit access.

PUBLICATION: Folder with color map of lake and river, showing federal and state sites.

HEADQUARTERS: Albeni Falls Project Office, P.O. Box 310, Newport, WA 99156-0310; (208) 437-3133.

BITTERROOT NATIONAL FOREST
U.S. Forest Service
464,165 acres in ID.

Most of the Forest is in Montana. The entry is in MT Zone 1.

The ID acreage is in the Selway-Bitterroot Wilderness (see entries, Nez Perce and Clearwater NFs, ID Zone 1) and Frank Church - River of No Return Wilderness (see entry, ID Zone 2).

CLEARWATER NATIONAL FOREST
U.S. Forest Service
1,831,374 acres; 1,975,889 acres within boundaries.

NE Idaho. Crossed by US 12.

On the N, the Clearwater adjoins the Idaho Panhandle National Forests; on the E, the Lolo and Bitterroot National Forests in Montana; on the S, the Nez Perce National Forest. The Bitterroot Range extends along the entire E side of the Forest. Highest point in the range is 8,817 ft. Lowest elevation in the Forest is 1,600 ft., on its W boundary. The land between is mountainous, heavily forested, deep canyons separated by high, rugged ridges. The terrain offers few natural travel routes. Lewis and Clark crossed the Bitterroots at Lolo Pass, where US 12 now crosses. US 12 follows the Lochsa River across the Forest to the SW.

Few roads penetrating the Forest were built until the 1930s. Road building increased with timber sales in the 1950s and later, but even today two-thirds of the Forest is roadless and undeveloped.

About 4,300 mi. of roads are on or adjacent to the Forest. Only 63 mi. are paved, 1,172 graded and graveled. About 3,100 mi. of dirt roads are maintained as logging requires. Many of these can be driven in summer in dry weather, but it's wise to inquire. About 1,140 mi. are subject to seasonal closures; these are shown on the Forest map.

Principal rivers are the Lochsa and the North and Middle Forks of the Clearwater. The Forest has 364 significant fishing streams totaling 5,018 mi. It also has 172 subalpine lakes, the largest only 117 acres. Dworshak Reservoir (see entry), formed by a dam on the Clearwater River, is 53 mi. long but backs up into the Forest only 3 to 4 mi. from its western border.

Less than one-fifth of the visitor-days are spent at developed sites, camping and picnicking. Hiking, backpacking, horse riding, and backcountry camping are often associated with hunting and fishing. Except during the fall hunting season, hikers, backpackers, and other nonconsumptive users will encounter few others on the trails. We were told no trails or destinations are overused. Some lake shores have been trampled by pack and saddle horses, but visitors are now asked to camp at least 200 ft. from a shoreline.

Climate: The summer season usually extends from May through Sept., although trails at high elevations may be blocked by snow until mid-July. Nights are cool even after a hot day. Average annual precipitation is about 45 in., with a range from 30 in. at the lowest elevations to 100 in. along the Bitterroot Divide. Snow makes up about 40% of the precipitation at low elevations, 80% on high slopes. Snow cover sufficient for snowmobiling and ski touring is common Dec.–Mar. Although summer is the dry season, spectacular lightning, often dry lightning, is seen July–Aug., and thundershowers are frequent at high elevations.

Plants: In about one-third of the Forest, vegetation has been altered by logging and road building. Clearcutting is practiced. In the other two-thirds, influences such as fire and disease have created a mosaic of brushfields, dense stands of conifers, and scattered old growth and snag patches. Great fires burned large parts of the Forest in the late 1800s and early 1900s. Some burned-over areas are still in the shrub stage of recovery. At elevations below 4,000 ft., these are fine winter range for elk, deer, and some moose.

The Forest has three principal forest communities: *cedar/hemlock/white pine,* generally below 5,000 ft. elevation, is the Forest's largest plant community and has the greatest diversity of flora and fauna. It is also the most productive, and nine-tenths of the timber harvest is here. Tree species include western redcedar, white pine, grand fir, western hemlock, western larch, and Douglas-fir. Common shrubs include false huckleberry, ninebark, oceanspray, ceanothus, juneberry, huckleberry, pachistima, snowberry. In riparian areas, red alder, devil's club, ladyfern, birch. In the *spruce/fir* community, generally above 5,000 ft. elevation, burned-over areas support large pure and mixed stands of Engelmann spruce, mountain hemlock, lodgepole pine, and subalpine fir, with representations of grand fir, western larch, Douglas-fir, and western white pine. The shrub community includes beargrass and huckleberry; at higher elevations, mountain heather, mountain phlox, grouse whortleberry. The *ponderosa pine/grand fir/Douglas-fir* association, in the western portion of the Forest, is heavily timbered.

Birds: The available bird list is for the Selway-Bitterroot Wilderness; it's applicable to most other Forest areas. Although the Forest has diverse habitats, birders will note the general absence of waterfowl and shorebirds. Species include goshawk; sharp-shinned, Cooper's, and red-tailed hawks; golden eagle, osprey, prairie falcon, merlin, kestrel. Owls: screech, flammulated, great horned, pygmy, long-eared, boreal, saw-whet. Blue, Franklin's, and ruffed grouse; gray and Steller's jays, black-billed magpie, common raven, Clark's nutcracker; black-capped, mountain, chestnut-backed, and white-breasted chickadees; red-breasted and pygmy nuthatches, brown creeper, dipper. Wrens: house, winter, canyon, and rock. Catbird, American robin; varied, hermit, and Swainson's thrushes; veery, western and mountain blue-birds, Townsend's solitaire, golden-crowned and ruby-crowned kinglets, cedar waxwing, warbling vireo. Warblers: orange-crowned, yellow, yellow-rumped, Nashville, Townsend's, Wilson's, yellow-breasted chat, American redstart. Northern oriole, Brewer's blackbird, brown-headed cowbird, common nighthawk, Vaux's swift; violet-green and tree swallows; broad-tailed, rufous, and calliope hummingbirds; belted kingfisher. Woodpeckers: northern flicker, pileated, Lewis', hairy, downy, black-backed and northern three-toed, yellow-bellied and Williamson's sapsuckers. Flycatchers: Traill's, Hammond's, dusky, olive-sided, western wood-pewee. Black-headed, evening, and pine grosbeaks; lazuli bunting, Cassin's and house finches, pine siskin, American goldfinch, red crossbill, rufous-sided towhee. Sparrows: savannah, chipping, Brewer's, white-crowned, fox, Lincoln's, song, Oregon junco.

Mammals: Elk are the principal big game species. Populations increased after wildfires created more extensive forage areas. Whitetail deer occur through much of the area, with smaller numbers of mule deer. A few hundred moose are present. Mountain goat occur; no estimate of numbers. Black bear population is estimated at over 1,000, mountain lion about 100.

The mammal list for the Selway-Bitterroot Wilderness applies to most other Forest areas. Included are various shrews, voles, and bats; porcupine, muskrat, beaver, yellowbeily and hoary marmots, pika, mountain cottontail, snowshoe hare, Columbian ground squirrel, golden-mantled and red squirrels, northern flying squirrel, least and yellow pine chipmunks, northern pocket gopher, deer mouse, bushytail woodrat, coyote, badger, fisher, spotted and striped skunks, lynx, bobcat, otter, wolverine, pine marten, shorttail and longtail weasels.

Reptiles and amphibians, also listed for the Wilderness, include salamanders: Pacific giant, blotched tiger, northern long-toed, Coeur d'Alene; western toad, Pacific tree frog, tailed and spotted frogs. Snakes: Rocky Mountain rubber boa; Great Basin, valley, and western garter snakes; western rattlesnake. Western skink.

FEATURES

Selway-Bitterroot Wilderness. 259,165 acres of its 1,337,910 acres are in the SE portion of the Clearwater NF. Other portions are in the Nez Perce and Bitterroot National Forests of ID, and the Bitterroot and Lolo NFs in MT. One of the largest Wildernesses, it lies on both sides of the Bitterroot Range. Elevations range from about 1,600 ft. on the Selway River to over 10,131 ft. on Trapper Peak. It is considered one of the roughest of all mountain regions, with alternating deep, sharp, narrow canyons and high barren peaks. Except for barren areas along the high ridges, the Wilderness is forested, forest areas in various stages of succession following old and more recent fires. Present policy is to suppress man-caused fires but to allow lightning-caused fires to burn if they stay within the limits of wilderness management policies.

The Wilderness boundary is generally 3 to 6 mi. S of US 12 but borders the highway for about 7 mi. along rugged Lochsa River Canyon. Access to the Wilderness is from a number of trailheads along the highway and side roads. 358 mi. of established trails are in the Clearwater NF portion, ranging from easy to challenging for either foot or horse travel. Several lakes are reached by trails.

The Selway-Bitterroot isn't a pure Wilderness where even foot-propelled bicycles are outlawed. The Act establishing it includes compromises that permit prospecting and mining, continued operation of airstrips, and outfitter activities. It allows the President to authorize water and power projects. The Forest Service is allowed limited use of motorized equipment for maintenance and emergencies—an infrequent occurrence. Some Wilderness advocates deplore the compromises, but you're not likely to be aware of them on a visit unless you camp near an airstrip.

Middle Fork Clearwater Wild and Scenic River System. US 12 follows the river. Along the way are camp and picnic grounds, rest areas, and trailheads. 93 mi. of the Lochsa and Middle Fork of the Clearwater River are classified as a Recreational River under the Wild and Scenic Rivers Act. The strip of land includes 25,540 acres. The classified river system includes adjacent river portions in the Bitterroot and Nez Perce NFs. These rivers have opportunities for whitewater boating: 70 mi. on the Lochsa to Lowell, 23 mi. on the Middle Fork from Lowell to Kooskia. The Lochsa is reputed to be one of the most difficult whitewater runs, potentially dangerous even to the experienced. 5 outfitters offer trips during the April–July 4 runoff.

Lochsa Face, 73,027 acres, lies between the Lochsa River and the Selway-Bitterroot Wilderness. Steep, rocky cliffs, hot springs, good trout streams, large elk and moose populations, trails.

Mallard-Larkins Pioneer Area, 30,500 acres, straddles the border of the Clearwater and Idaho Panhandle NFs. A roadless area on the high divide between the North Fork and the Little North Fork of the Clearwater River, it can be reached by secondary roads from US 12, 10, and 95A. Elevations from 2,600 to over 7,000 ft. Trails radiate from road endings. The Heritage Cedar Grove of ancient cedars is at the S edge. Many small lakes in glacial cirques. Wildlife includes mountain goat, elk, deer, black bear. Camping, hiking, hunting, fishing, horse riding.

Elk Creek Falls Recreation Area, 960 acres, includes a 300-ft. 3-step waterfall, local trails. Groomed ski and snowmobile trails nearby. Access by SR 8.

Lewis and Clark National Historical Trail crosses the Forest. The 150-mi. Lolo Motorway, Forest Road 500, is narrow, single-lane, often rough and rutted, usually open from mid-July to Nov. In places it follows the Trail; in others one can hike portions of the Trail. No developed campgrounds on the way, but suitable informal sites. Two outfitters offer horseback trips over the route.

Other scenic drives include North Fork Drive, 160 mi. (Forest Roads 247 and 250); White Pine Drive, a 6-mi. drive E of Potlatch along SR 6, 2 mi. N of the Laird Park turnoff, through majestic white pines; Elk Creek Road, for about 10 mi. N from Elk River.

Austin Ridge, Weitas Butte, and Castle Butte lookouts, no longer used for spotting fires, can be rented for stays of two or more days in summer. The Walde Mountain lookout cabin can be rented by skiers and snowmobilers in winter.

INTERPRETATION

Lolo Pass Visitor Center, on US 12 at the MT border, has exhibits, literature, information. 8 A.M.–5 P.M., Memorial Day–Labor Day. Winter season: Nov. 1–Apr. 1, depending on snow conditions. Groomed ski and snowmobile trails. Snow information: (208) 942-3113.

Colgate Licks Nature Trail, a 0.6-mi. loop past natural mineral spring where deer, elk, and moose are often seen. At Mile 147 on US 12. Interpretive signs.

Major Fenn Nature Trail, 0.6 mi. At picnic area, mile 108 on US 12. Interpretive signs. A National Recreation Trail.

White Pine Trail, 5 mi. with shortcuts, in variety of forest settings. At Giant White Pine Campground on US 95A.

ACTIVITIES

Camping: 19 campgrounds, 308 sites, all on or near streams. Some are closed in winter; most open before Memorial Day. Some campgrounds can be used in winter, without services. Camp anywhere unless posted; many delightful informal sites.

Hiking, backpacking: 1,182 mi. of maintained trails, most of them following streams or divides. Trail conditions vary greatly. Trail maintenance on side trails is minimal, and some little-used trails are difficult to follow. Before undertaking more than a short day hike, check with a Ranger Station. Simple guides and maps are available for some trails.

Hunting: Chiefly elk, deer, and black bear. 30 licensed outfitters offer guide services.

Fishing: Most lakes, rivers, and streams have native or stocked game fish: cutthroat, bull, and rainbow trout; whitefish. Several streams, such as Kelly and Cayuse creeks, are nationally known. Steelhead and salmon spawn in certain Forest streams, but fishing for them has been prohibited in Forest waters.

Horse riding: Many trails are available, but mountainous terrain and difficult trail conditions are demanding on stock. A list of outfitters is available.

Rafting: Floating season on the Lochsa is usually May to early July. Commercial outfitters offer river trips. Most rapids are Classes II–IV, one Class V. Heavy equipment and technical skill are needed; at high water the professionals cancel trips or reroute. The North Fork of the Clearwater has sections of whitewater comparable to those on the Lochsa; no commercial outfitters are permitted. The Middle Fork is suitable for lighter equipment and open boats, including canoes. It can be floated later in the season. During late July to early Sept., conditions on the Clearwater invite relaxed rafting and tubing.

Ski touring: Groomed trails at Lolo Pass winter sports area and Elk River. Intermittently groomed trails at North/South ski area. Hundreds of mi. of unplowed Forest roads.

PUBLICATIONS
Visitor map. $1.
Forest visitor guide.
Lolo Pass winter sports area map. $1.
Selway-Bitterroot Wilderness map. $1.
Visitor Guide.
Information pages:
List of outfitter guides.
Selway-Bitterroot Wilderness.
Leaflets:
Austin Ridge Lookout.
Weitas Butte Lookout.
Castle Butte Lookout.
Plant guide, Major Fenn National Recreation Trail.
Following Lewis and Clark Across the Clearwater National Forest.
Lochsa White Water Rafting.
Lochsa Historical Ranger Station.
The Western Larch.
Elk Creek Falls Recreation Area.

REFERENCE:
Maughan, Jackie J. *The Hiker's Guide to Idaho.* Billings, MT: Falcon Press, 1984. Pp. 29–36.

HEADQUARTERS: 12730 Highway 12, Orofino, ID 83544; (208) 476-4541.

RANGER DISTRICTS: Pierce R.D., Kamiah, ID 83536; (208) 935-2513. Palouse R.D., Route 2, Box 4, Potlatch, ID 83855; (208) 875-1131. Moscow Information Office, 1221 S. Main, Moscow, ID 83843; (208) 882-1152. North Fork R.D., P.O. Box 2139, Orofino, ID 83544; (208) 476-3775. Lochsa R.D., Route 1, P.O. Box 398, Kooskia, ID 83539; (208) 926-4275. Powell R.D., Lolo, MT 59847; (208) 942-3113.

CRAIG MOUNTAIN WILDLIFE MANAGEMENT AREA
Idaho Department of Fish and Game
24,200 acres.

Boat access. On the Snake River 10 mi. S of Lewiston. County Road P2 near Waha leads to a riverside road to the site, but this crosses private property.

The site extends 14 mi. S along the Snake River, between Lewiston and Hells Canyon National Recreation Area. Boat excursions to the NRA pass this way, and there is considerable private boat traffic. Here the canyon is not quite as dramatic as it is further upstream, but it's impressive. From the river at 800 ft. elevation, the land rises steeply to 5,200 ft. at the rim. Most of the area consists of steep (40 to 64%) slopes.

Hunting is the leading visitor activity, followed by river fishing. Camping, swimming, and picnicking attract significant numbers.

Plants: Three-fourths of the site is perennial grasslands, principal species being bluebunch wheatgrass, Sandberg bluegrass, and prairie junegrass, with balsamroot, biscuitroot, pricklypear, and wild carrot. Overgrazing by cattle on the gentler slopes caused considerable damage, but where soils permit the climax grasses are returning. The upper elevations along the rim and the adjacent plateau support second-growth ponderosa pine, with Douglas-fir on S-facing slopes, Douglas-fir, grand fir, and a few larch on N-facing slopes.

Birds: The area has one of the state's largest populations of chukar partridge. Partridge is the chief game species, with small populations of valley quail, blue grouse, and pheasant. Merriam's turkeys were released and have established a breeding flock. 152 bird species have been recorded, but few are rated as abundant. Included are many waterfowl, shorebirds, and birds of prey.

Mammals: Bighorn sheep have been reintroduced on both sides of the river. Mule deer are the leading big game species, followed by elk. Only a few whitetail deer are resident, with others present in winter. Black bear and mountain lion have been sighted. Common species include cottontail, coyote, river otter, mink, striped and spotted skunks, badger, and bobcat.

ACTIVITIES
Camping: Boat camping on sand bars, alluvial fans.
Hunting: On the increase, chiefly for partridge and deer.
Fishing: Steelhead, smallmouth bass, channel catfish, rainbow trout. Catch-and-release area for sturgeon.

HEADQUARTERS: Region 2, 1540 Warner Ave., Lewiston, ID 83501; (208) 743-6502.

DWORSHAK RESERVOIR
U.S. Army Corps of Engineers
19,764 water acres at full pool; 27,360 land acres.

From Orofino on US 12, 5 mi. E on SR 7.

The 717-ft. high dam has backed up a narrow pool 53 mi. long in the canyon of the North Fork Clearwater River. This steep-walled canyon winds its way through the lower western slopes of the Bitterroot Mountains, the upper end extending into the Clearwater National Forest. Most of the shoreline is steep and rugged, the N-facing slopes heavily timbered, and much of it is roadless, accessible only by boat. Scattered along the 184 mi. of shoreline, 75 locations offer 140 camping and picnicking sites, some on the main lake, others on secluded creeks. Road-access recreation sites are larger, with boating facilities, swimming beaches, hiking trails, and large campgrounds.

Elevation at the reservoir is about 1,000 ft. Upland areas rise to 3,555 ft. Annual precipitation ranges from 17 to 54 in., about 40% of that as snow. July–Aug. are dry.

Upland areas are accessible by road and from some lakeshore points. Designated trail mileage is limited, but off-trail hiking is feasible in some areas. One trail connects with a Forest Service trail along the Clearwater River.

Plants: About 90% of the upland is forested. Forest types include cedar/hemlock, Douglas-fir, western spruce/fir. Western redcedar mingles with firs in bottomlands. Understory includes red alder, willow, cottonwood, ceanothus, ninebark, oceanspray, thimbleberry, mountain huckleberry. Spring and early summer wildflowers include shootingstar, angel slippers, bluebells, followed by Indian paintbrush, wood rose, monkshood, fireweed, monkeyflower, and syringa. An extensive list of flora is available at the visitor center.

Birds: Lists of waterfowl, upland game birds, and birds of prey are available at the visitor center; abundance is not noted. Species often seen include bald and golden eagles, osprey, spruce and ruffed grouse, mourning dove, Canada goose, mallard, American wigeon, northern shoveler, common merganser, red-tailed hawk, northern harrier, and undoubtedly many more.

Mammals: More than 10,000 acres were acquired near the upper end of the reservoir for development as winter elk range, to mitigate for inundated land. A zone of deer browse was planned. Black bear are common, as are coyote, shorttail weasel, bobcat, beaver, porcupine, yellowbelly marmot.

INTERPRETATION
Visitor center at dam has exhibits, films, talks, literature. Open daily in summer, weekends spring and fall.

Nature trail near visitor center.
Campfire programs June–Sept. at developed campgrounds.

ACTIVITIES
Camping: 3 major campgrounds with 162 sites; May 1–Sept. 30. Also 140 scattered sites.
Hiking: 25 mi. of designated trails. No trail map.
Hunting: Chiefly whitetail deer, elk.
Fishing: Rainbow and cutthroat trout, kokanee salmon, smallmouth bass.
Boating: Marina, 6 ramps, other facilities, rowboat and power boat rentals. Reservoir usually ices over in Nov.–Mar. Maximum drawdown in fall and winter is 155 ft., which isolates some pools in upper reaches.

PUBLICATION: *Recreation Guide.*

HEADQUARTERS: Dworshak Project Office, Corps of Engineers, P.O. Box 48, Ahsahka, ID 83520; (208) 476-3294.

FARRAGUT STATE PARK
Idaho Department of Parks and Recreation
4,000 acres.

From Coeur d'Alene, 20 mi. N on US 95, then 4 mi. E on SR 54.

Believe it or not, three months before Pearl Harbor, in 1941, the U.S. Navy decided to train sea-going sailors at this remote lake in Idaho. Land was taken from private owners, using power of eminent domain. Construction required 22,000 workers. Six camps were built, each accommodating 5,000 recruits, each with a gigantic drill hall, swimming pool, rifle range, medical center, and other facilities. Three years later, almost before construction was completed, the Farragut Naval Training Center was decommissioned, and the site is now a State Park and Wildlife Management Area. A museum at the park's visitor center tells the story. Park officials said the exhibits were assembled from private sources; most official records had been destroyed.

On the S shore of Lake Pend Oreille, the Park is one of the busiest in the ID system. When we visited at the beginning of a Fourth of July weekend, the visitor center was full of campers, some claiming reservations, others hoping for vacancies. Those without reservations were shunted to an overflow area.

Camping, including group camping, is the principal visitor activity. Most visitors come from the region. Fishing and boating are next in popularity. The park offers a variety of other activities: bicycling, horse riding, model airplane flying, target shooting, and winter sports.

Much of the site is heavily forested with mature trees. Park terrain is gently rolling, its highest point about 400 ft. above the lake. About 1,000 acres have been set aside as a nature reserve, with no development other than trails.

Lake Pend Oreille is Idaho's largest lake: 68 mi. long, up to 6 mi. wide, covering 80,000 acres, with a maximum depth of 1,150 ft. A natural lake, it was enlarged by the Albeni Falls Dam (see entry). Most of the shoreline is privately owned, but the Idaho Panhandle National Forest has some shoreline tracts, as does the Idaho Fish and Game Department. The Park has 5 mi. of waterfront.

INTERPRETATION

Visitor center has a museum, talks, literature. Open May 24–Sept. 8.

Campfire programs, guided hikes, summer months.

ACTIVITIES

Camping: 2 campgrounds, 138 sites. Open May 1–Sept. 30. Reservations recommended for busy weekends.

Hiking: 6 to 8 mi. of trails, viewpoints, and lake shore. Trailhead for Bernard Peak in the National Forest.

Horse riding: About 7 mi. of trails.

Fishing: Brown, kamloops, cutthroat, and Dolly Varden trout; kokanee, perch, largemouth bass.

Boating: Ramp and docks.

Ski touring: Although most Park facilities are closed in winter, ski trails and a snowmobile parking area are available.

PUBLICATIONS

Leaflet with map.
Facilities information page.
Ski trail map.
Snowmobile trail map.
Nature trail booklet.
Bicycle route map.

HEADQUARTERS: P.O. Box F, Athol, ID 83801; (208) 683-2425.

FRANK CHURCH - RIVER OF NO RETURN WILDERNESS

U.S. Forest Service
2,230,300 acres.

Access from US 93 on the E, US 95 and SR 55 on the W, SR 21 on the S. By boat on the N.

This is the largest Wilderness in the Lower 48, 90 mi. long, 56 mi. wide. Although the River of No Return is in Zone 1, the majority of the acreage is in Zone 2, and our entry is there.

GRANDMOTHER MOUNTAIN
U.S. Bureau of Land Management
17,129 acres.

12 mi. E of SR 3 at Clarkia. One trailhead is at a BLM campsite on Freezeout Saddle Road, Forest Road 301, unpaved but OK for ordinary cars in dry weather. Access to the trail system is also from Forest Road 321 at Marble Creek, NE from Clarkia.

A block 12 mi. W–E, 6 mi. N–S, is a mix of BLM and National Forest land, with bits of state and private land. The St. Joe National Forest (of the Idaho Panhandle National Forests) is on the N, E, and S. This is the center of the Marble Creek Trail System, a 45-mi. complex of trails, jointly maintained by BLM and the National Forest; 27 mi. are included in the National Recreation Trail System.

Terrain includes heavily forested drainages and bare peaks. Elevations range from 4,800 ft. to 6,369 ft. on Grandmother Mountain, 6,307 ft. on Grandfather Mountain. Dominant tree species are subalpine fir, mountain hemlock, and grand fir, with scattered western white pine, Engelmann spruce, lodgepole pine, Douglas-fir, western larch, and ponderosa pine. Approximate age of timber is 120 years. Annual precipitation averages 50 in. per year. Heavy snow in winter. The area includes several streams and small lakes with populations of cutthroat and Dolly Varden trout. Crater Lake is stocked with grayling.

Wildlife is abundant. The area includes both summer and winter elk range. Mule deer and black bear are often seen. Also present are moose, whitetail deer. Upland game birds include forest grouse.

Recreation use is estimated at about 2,500 visitor-days per year. Hunting is the chief use, many elk hunters using horses. Trailbikers use the area. Backpacking is on the increase, as is fishing.

Some of the trails follow high ridges offering panoramic views. Other sections follow creeks, meander through deep woods. All trails are rated Moderate in degree of difficulty.

PUBLICATIONS
Hiking; Horse/Pack Saddle. Marble Creek Trail System.
Freezeout Mountain Snowmobile Trail.
(Leaflets with maps, available from BLM or St. Maries R.D., Idaho Panhandle National Forests.)
REFERENCE: Maughan, Jackie J. *The Hiker's Guide to Idaho.* Billings, MT: Falcon Press, 1984. Pp. 21–29.

HEADQUARTERS: BLM, Coeur d'Alene District, 1808 Third St., Coeur d'Alene, ID 83814; (208) 765-7356.

HELLS CANYON NATIONAL RECREATION AREA
U.S. Forest Service
131,000 acres in Idaho, 392,308 acres in Oregon.

On the ID side, SR 71 from Cambridge follows the shore of Hells Canyon Reservoir to the Dam at the S end of the NRA, but there's no riverside road or trail beyond that point on the ID side. Access to the Canyon rim from US 95 is by county and Forest roads from near Council, Lucile, and Riggins. From White Bird a gravel road goes to Pittsburg Landing; the last part is rough and steep.

Hells Canyon, on the Snake River between ID and OR, is the deepest gorge in North America. In 1975 Congress established the National Recreation Area, combining parts of the Wallowa-Whitman National Forest in OR and the Nez Perce and Payette National Forests in ID. The same Act designated 31 1/2 mi. of the Snake River, from Hells Canyon Dam to Pittsburg Landing, as a Wild River, and 36 mi. from Pittsburg Landing to the Wallowa-Whitman boundary as a Scenic River. The two forks of the Rapid River, SW of Riggins, were also added to the Wild and Scenic River system. A total of 215,233 acres on both sides of the Snake River corridor were designated Wilderness. Another 15 roadless units including 320,000 acres are in the Wilderness planning process.

Access to the Canyon isn't easy. Walls of granite and basalt rise 5,000 to 6,000 ft. above the river. On the OR side, steep slopes alternate with large, open benches; on the ID side, steep walls rise without interruption. From the ID side there are several ways to visit the NRA. *On foot or horseback:* From Pittsburg Landing a trail runs S beside the river for 31 mi., stopping about 3 mi. short of the dam. From a trailhead at Windy Saddle, near Heavens Gate, a trail circles the Seven Devils Mountains. A branch drops down into the Canyon. Another extends S to the campground on Black Lake. *Sightseeing from overlooks:* Most roads are narrow, crooked, and steep. Some can be traveled in a passenger car, at least in dry weather; others require 4-wheel drive. Some aren't snow-free until July. The most popular and probably the most accessible is Heavens Gate. About 2 mi. N of Riggins on US 95, left on Squaw Creek Road then left on Papoose Creek Rd. about 16 mi. to parking lot; trail to overlook. We tried the road in from Lucile and were flagged by a local resident who warned that a motor home couldn't make it. *Floating:* From Hells Canyon Dam, by raft or kayak, through Class IV rapids. Below Pittsburg Landing, canoes can be used by experts. Floating may be difficult during spring runoff in high-water years. *By power boat:* Outfitters operate jet boats. Private power boats are also used. A cruise boat from Lewiston visits the lower reaches of the Canyon.

In its long journey from Wyoming, the Snake has been imprisoned behind many dams. Another was proposed for Hells Canyon, but the 1975 Act scotched it, and once past Hells Canyon Dam the river flows freely for a hundred miles. The National Recreation Area includes spectacular wild terrain, from the depths of the Canyon to the alpine peaks of the Seven Devils Mountain, a rise of about 8,600 ft.

Some canyons, like the Grand Canyon of the Colorado, are cut through plateaus. Not this one. It has no continuous flat rim to invite construction of a scenic drive or trail. The surrounding country is ruggedly mountainous, slopes cut by many V-shaped canyons, often separated by knife edges. The canyon averages 10 mi. from rim to rim. It is being slowly widened by rock falls, debris flows, and slumps. Three-fourths of the NRA's land area slopes at 30% or more.

Recreation use of the river corridor is about 66,200 visitor-days per year, in the Seven Devils area about 19,000 visitor-days.

As on the upper Salmon River, there is friction between floaters and power boaters. Floaters and wilderness advocates have urged that power boats capable of ascending the rapids be barred from the NRA. Thus far they have not been barred.

Climate: Within the Canyon, winters are relatively mild, summers hot, daily maximums often exceeding 100°F. Spring and fall are the optimum seasons for activity. It's usually about 20° cooler along the rim in summer, 10° cooler in winter. Above 6,000 ft., subalpine climate prevails, with cold winters and the possibility of frost on any night. Annual precipitation at low elevations is about 10 in. The highest slopes receive 50 in. and more, most of it as snow. Roads back of the canyon rim are usually closed by snow from mid-Nov. through mid-June or later.

Plants: Streamside communities include Douglas hackberry with occasional ponderosa pine, and white alder associations with box elder and water birch. Chokecherry and bittercherry are common components of the understory. Lower slopes are usually bunchgrass associations. Midslopes have a variety of associations, depending on exposure and fire history. Douglas-fir is common on N-facing slopes. Brushfields and grasslands are common. Upper slopes are often forested, primarily with grand fir, adding subalpine fir at higher elevations. The *Guide to the Common Plants of Hells Canyon* (see Publications) provides a more detailed account of these associations and descriptions of flowering species.

Birds: No checklist is available. 249 species have been recorded, an unusually high total that reflects the great diversity of habitats on both sides of the river. Game birds include blue and ruffed grouse (and Franklin's in OR), chukar. Canada goose, mallard, and goldeneye are common.

Mammals: No checklist is available. 76 species recorded. Mentioned are Idaho ground squirrel, fisher, bobcat, wolverine, Rocky Mountain elk, mule deer, Rocky Mountain bighorn sheep, mountain goat.

Fishes: Dam construction on the Snake and Columbia rivers blocked salmon and chinook from their spawning grounds. Hopes of restoring the fishery above Hells Canyon Dam were abandoned in the 1960s, and the 100-mi. section of the Snake from Lewiston to Hells Canyon Dam is the last remaining spawning ground on the river for fall chinook. Access from the sea around downstream dams is now possible, and the Snake River receives significant runs of salmon and steelhead.

White sturgeon inhabit the Snake; any caught must be released. Other game species in the NRA include black crappie, smallmouth bass, channel catfish. The Rapid River and tributaries have salmon and steelhead runs, as well as populations of rainbow, Dolly Varden, and eastern brook trout, mountain whitefish, sculpin.

FEATURES

Hells Canyon Wilderness, 215,233 acres. About 40% of the area is on the ID side, extending downstream about 18 mi. from a point near the dam. It includes all of the ID portion of the NRA S of Low Saddle Viewpoint. Seven Devils Mountains are within this region. Chief trail access is from the trailhead at Windy Saddle. Road access from the S by a 40-mi. combination of county and Forest roads from Council on US 95 NW past Bear to a campground on Black Lake. This road, not recommended for low-clearance vehicles or trailers, is often blocked by snow through July.

Seven Devils Mountains rise nearly 8,000 ft. above the river, a number of rocky spires, often snowy, the slopes a maze of V-shaped drainages with strings of vegetation. The area has about 32 small lakes. Good hiking.

Heavens Gate Scenic Trail is a short walk from parking lot to an observation tower at 8,429 ft. elevation, the Heavens Gate Lookout. The road W from US 95 gains over 6,500 ft. in 18 mi. It's usually open July–Oct. The road continues 2 mi. to the Windy Saddle campground (tents only) and trailhead.

Snake River National Recreation Trail extends S along the river 31 mi. from

Pittsburg Landing. Open all year, but sections may be flooded at high water. Campsites are used by boaters and backpackers.

INTERPRETATION: Visitor center with exhibits, literature, etc., is at Lewiston, adjacent to Hells Gate State Park, on the river.

ACTIVITIES

Camping: In ID, 2 campgrounds, 8 sites, accessible by road.

Hiking, backpacking: In ID, maintained trails include the riverside route and trails radiating from Windy Saddle, two of which descend to the river.

Hunting: Elk, deer, upland game.

Fishing: River, mountain lakes.

Boating: Use of power boats between Hells Canyon Dam and Pittsburg Landing is limited by the rapids. Most private boaters cruise near the ramps at these two points. Several commercial operators make upstream runs from Pittsburg Landing.

Rafting, kayaking: From near Hells Canyon Dam to Pittsburg Landing is a 2-day trip, 32 mi. River is boatable all year. Floating may be difficult in spring runoff in high-water years. Rapids to Class IV. Reservations are required from Fri. before Memorial Day through Sept. 15. Launches are presently limited to 5 per day, 2 of these for commercial operators. Outfitter-guides offering float or power boat trips are licensed.

PUBLICATIONS

A Guide to the Hells Canyon National Recreation Area.
Folder with map, list of campgrounds, etc.
Information pages, mimeo:
  Rim to Rim, visitor guide. 13 pp.
  River permit system.
7 Devils Hiking Map.
Leaflets:
  Heritage.
  Renewable Resources.
  Wildlife.
  Wilderness.
  Fishing.
  River Guide.
Guide to the Common Plants of Hells Canyon. Pamphlet, 56 pp.

HEADQUARTERS: Wallowa-Whitman National Forest, P.O. Box 490, Enterprise, OR 97828; (503) 426-3151. *Subheadquarters, ID:* 3620-B Snake River Ave., Lewiston, ID 83501; (208) 743-3648. [For river information: (208) 743-2297.] At Riggins: P.O. Box 832, Riggins, ID 83549; (208) 628-3916.

HEYBURN STATE PARK
Idaho Department of Parks and Recreation
7,826 acres.

From Plummer on US 95, 6 mi. E on SR 6.

The Park is unusual in several respects, the most puzzling one best seen from the air. What appears to be a large lake is crossed by parallel embankments with a channel between them. A river channel, indeed; we saw a boat towing a log raft. It's the St. Joe River, at 2,307 ft. elevation said to be the world's highest navigable stream.

And it's not one lake but four. Years ago they were ponds. When a dam raised the level of Lake Coeur d'Alene in 1906, the ponds became lakes, merging. Round Lake is now elongated.

Established in 1908, it is one of the oldest state parks. It was developed in the 1930s by the Civilian Conservation Corps. Completion of the Dworshak Reservoir (see entry) in the early 1970s caused a drop in Park attendance. In 1980 the Mt. St. Helens eruption buried the Park in ash, closing it for a year. Attendance is on the increase, but the campgrounds are seldom full. June–Aug. are the busiest months, Nov.–Apr. the quietest. Although the lakes are the primary attraction, more than 5,000 acres are undeveloped. Foot and equestrian trails lead to viewpoints. The Park is open all year.

We saw what looked like private cottages on the lake shore; in fact, the Park owns and leases 160 cabins and 28 houseboats. Also unusual is that waterfowl hunting is permitted. "That's part of our history," the Park Manager explained. "When the hunters come in the fall, few others are here, so there's no conflict." Wild rice is grown in the lakes. Some is harvested commercially, more than half left for the waterfowl.

The Park's NE boundary extends to the center of the river channel. Fish and Game owns part of the other embankment as well as tracts on Round Lake. Part of the embankment was also inundated when the water level was raised, so boats from Park waters can cross into Round Lake or cruise the river into Lake Coeur d'Alene or upstream to the E.

The lakes are surrounded by forested rolling hills. Highest point is 3,320-ft. Shoeffler Butte. Annual precipitation is about 29 in. July–Sept. is the dry season. Snowfall is often sufficient for ski touring, reaching depths of several feet, but seldom remaining through the winter.

Plants: 80% of the land area is forested. Principal tree species are Douglas-fir, grand fir, ponderosa and lodgepole pines, western redcedar, western larch, western white pine. Principal understory species are ninebark, oceanspray, snowberry, bunchberry, blueberry, thimbleberry, honeysuckle, false Solomon's-seal, western paper birch, red maple, red osier dogwood. The fall colors, we were told, are "fantastic."

Wildflowers include trout and checker lilies, trillium, heartleaf arnica, windflower, shootingstar, bluebells, wild strawberry, collomia, wild rose, clarkia, yarrow, buttercup, yellow evening primrose, yellow violet, pearly everlasting, syringa, pink spirea, twinflower, blue-eyed Mary.

Birds: 228 species recorded. Large population of wood ducks, about 200 pairs nesting. Area claims the largest nesting population of osprey in North America. Several hundred whistling swan stop off in spring and fall, as well as 10 to 15 pairs of trumpeter swan. Great blue heron rookery. Also seasonally common: mallard, western grebe, Canada goose, ruffed grouse, ring-billed gull, great horned and barred owls, red-tailed hawk, northern flicker; pileated, hairy, and downy woodpeckers; rufous hummingbird, American robin, varied and Swainson's thrushes, red-winged blackbird, red crossbill, American goldfinch, pine siskin, red-breasted nuthatch, cedar waxwing, yellow and MacGillivray's warblers, brown-headed cowbird, evening grosbeak, song sparrow, Oregon junco.

Mammals: 79 species recorded. Often or occasionally seen: pine squirrel, chipmunk, snowshoe hare, raccoon, muskrat, beaver, badger, skunk, otter, coyote, black bear, mountain lion, bobcat, whitetail deer, elk. Present but rarely seen: flying squirrel, pine marten, wolverine.

Reptiles and amphibians: Often or occasionally seen: western toad, tree frog, bullfrog, leopard frog, red-legged frog, tiger salamander, rubber boa, garter snake.

FEATURES

The lakes cover about 1,300 acres, with access to an extensive system of waterways.

Indian Cliffs, reached by a hiking trail, offer views of the lower St. Joe River and lower Lake Coeur d'Alene.

Plummer Creek estuary is a prime birding area.

INTERPRETATION

Information and literature at HQ. 7:30 A.M.–4 P.M.; Mon.–Fri. in winter, every day in summer.

Campfire programs and *guided hikes,* Memorial Day–Labor Day or on request.

Naturalist on site all year.

Junior Ranger program for children ages 8–12, summer weekends.

ACTIVITIES

Camping: 3 campgrounds, 130 sites. All year, but no water in winter.

Hiking: 12 mi. of trails. Trail map.

Horse riding: 15 mi. of trails. No stable on site.

Hunting: Waterfowl only.

Fishing: Largemouth bass, perch, crappie, bullhead, catfish, cutthroat trout, kokanee salmon, chinook salmon.
Boating: 3 ramps.
Swimming: Lake Chatcolet, June–Aug.
Ski touring: Depending on snow, usually Dec.–Feb.

PUBLICATIONS
Park leaflet with map.
Indian Cliffs Nature Trail guide.

HEADQUARTERS: Route 1, Box 139, Plummer, ID 83851; (208) 686-1308.

IDAHO PANHANDLE NATIONAL FORESTS
U.S. Forest Service
2,479,245 acres.

Northern ID. Crossed by US 2, US 95, I-90, SR 200.

"Forests," not "Forest." In 1973 most of the Kaniksu and St. Joe National Forests were combined with the Coeur d'Alene National Forest, forming the Idaho Panhandle National Forests. Together they occupy almost half of northeastern ID, extending S for 150 mi. from the Canadian border.

Much of their E boundary is on the W slopes of the Bitterroot Rocky Mountains. They have an abundance of handsome mountain scenery, from the Selkirk, Purcell, and Cabinet mountains in the N and the Coeur d'Alene Mountains of the center to the St. Joe Mountains in the SE. Highest point in the Forests is only 7,600 ft., but this is more than a mile above the lowest elevation.

The mountains are high enough to intercept moist air carried by westerlies from the Pacific. Annual precipitation averages 30 in. at low elevations, 80 in. on high slopes. Three-fourths of this falls as winter snow, from 220 in. up high to 40 in. below. This ample supply of moisture produces a rich array of plant and animal species and many lakes, rivers, and streams. The Forests have large parts of the shorelines of Priest Lake, Upper Priest Lake, and Lake Pend Oreille. The Upper Coeur d'Alene, Priest, and St. Joe rivers offer whitewater rafting. Snow and relatively low elevations make the Forests a winter playground.

The names of the three Forests persist. The available Forest maps are for the Kaniksu, St. Joe, and Coeur d'Alene. Many local residents use the old names, as do some Forest employees. Indeed, the combination was an administrative, not a legislative, action. Unless and until Congress makes the change, much official data must be kept and reported for the separate Forests.

The Forest has been profoundly altered by three major forces: heavy logging, which began in the 19th century; wildfires, notably the great fire of 1910; and white pine blister rust, an introduced disease. Today's managed Forest is productive and attractive, but not the same.

On maps, the Forests appear fragmented, pocked with inholdings. Some parts have mile-square checkerboarding of private ownerships. The maps show over a hundred scattered tracts of 1 square mile or less, some smaller than 100 acres. Since the maps were made, many tracts have been exchanged to consolidate ownerships. Driving on one of the many scenic highways, one seldom notices where Forest land ends and private ownerships begin.

Because the larger blocks of Forest land are widely separated, Forest maps are essential in trip planning. Logging and mining created a network of roads. Only a few areas offer opportunities for extensive backcountry experience. One third of the Forests is roadless and undeveloped, but the roadless tracts are scattered. The Selkirks in the N and Mallard-Larkins in the S are the largest roadless areas. Four smaller areas—including present and proposed wild river corridors—were recommended to be managed to retain their wilderness status.

To aid trip planning, the IPNF offers visitors the most comprehensive Recreation Opportunities Guide (ROG) we saw anywhere in ID. These great looseleaf volumes can be used at Forest HQ or any Ranger District. There's a section for each Ranger District, prefaced by a description of the District and its principal attractions, including historical and archeological sites. Following are sections on every conceivable activity: camping, hiking, motorized sightseeing, horsepacking, hunting, fishing, birding, climbing, spelunking, rafting, canoeing, bicycling, mushroom gathering, berry picking, ski touring, snowshoeing, etc.

For example, the user is told the Sandpoint Ranger District has 90 trails totaling over 300 mi., with opportunities for day hikes to mountain lakes or extended backpacking. There's a page for each trail with a sketch map and profile, driving directions to the trailhead, trail length, elevations, features and attractions, season of use, degree of difficulty, popularity, and hazards, plus a narrative describing scenery, vegetation, etc. Choose your trail and the page will be photocopied for you. Similarly detailed information is provided on each campground, lake, and river.

The Forests have almost 2,000 mi. of summer trails, 70 percent reported to be in good condition, although maintenance budgets are inadequate. Hunters are among the principal trail users, as are fishermen interested in the many high mountain lakes. The most popular hiking and horsepacking areas are the Selkirks and Mallard-Larkins. Except in hunting season, hikers can find many secluded trails in scenic, natural settings complete with lakes and rushing streams. Some riverside trails are available when the high country is deep in snow.

Plants: The Forest has four principal life zones: valley, midslope, upper slope, and alpine. Prominent tree species include ponderosa, lodgepole, and white pines, western redcedar, hemlock, Douglas-fir, Engelmann spruce, and western larch. Understory trees and shrubs include mountain ash, yew, willow, dogwood, snowberry, ninebark, and huckleberry. Wildflower lists for the several life zones weren't available. Species mentioned include glacier and sego lilies, western trillium, cinquefoil, buttercup, lupine, twinflower, goldenrod, yarrow, salsify, Indian paintbrush, dogtooth violet, lady slipper, shootingstar.

Wildlife: No lists were available. 380 species are said to inhabit the Forests, but we could obtain no details.

Birds: Those mentioned in staff documents include mallard, pintail, wood duck, canvasback, redhead, common goldeneye, lesser scaup, bufflehead, American wigeon, merganser, Canada goose; blue-winged, green-winged, and cinnamon teals; golden and bald eagles, goshawk; Cooper's, rough-legged, and red-tailed hawks; American kestrel, osprey, northern harrier, common nighthawk; spruce, ruffed, and Franklin's grouse; mountain bluebird, dipper, northern flicker, pileated woodpecker.

Mammals: Include elk, whitetail and mule deer, caribou, moose, mountain lion, coyote, grizzly and black bear, mountain lion, lynx, mountain goat, snowshoe hare, marmot, porcupine, badger, mink, striped skunk, beaver, pine squirrel, pack rat, chipmunk.

KANIKSU NATIONAL FOREST
Bonners Ferry, Priest Lake, and Sandpoint Ranger Districts.

Its largest block is an unbalanced, inverted U, the bigger arm extending from Canada almost to US 2 at Priest River, the E side on Priest Lake, the W extending to the Washington border. The lesser arm is separated from the E side of the lake by Priest Lake State Forest. The Selkirk Mountains run N–S across its middle. Much of its S end is fragmented. Other blocks occupy most of ID's E boundary from Canada to E of Lake Pend Oreille. The Selkirk, Purcell, Bitterroot, and Cabinet mountains provide a scenic background for the region's 74 lakes, many of them in glacial cirques, and 500 mi. of streams.

The Forest has had long use, for logging and other purposes, as evidenced by its network of roads. Few miles of road are paved; most are primitive.

FEATURES
Selkirk Crest, 26,000 acres, about 15 mi. NW of Bonners Ferry, has wilderness qualities, 24 mountain lakes. Peaks at the N and S ends are 7,670 and 7,355 ft. Most of the area is forested with spruce, subalpine fir, lodgepole pine,

and larch; the highest slopes have alpine tundra with colorful wildflowers and lichens. "Trails," says the Forest leaflet, "are where you find them . . . much travel requires cross-country routes." Access is by unimproved Forest roads. Current road conditions should be ascertained.

Priest Lake, 23,680 acres, 19 mi. long, is a primary recreation area. 12 campgrounds are on the W shore and nearby islands. Units of the Priest Lake State Park are on the E shore. Many summer homes occupy lakeshore land by permit.

Hanna Flats Cedar Grove, on SR 57 near Kalispell Bay on Priest Lake, is a remnant of the original forest that escaped axe and fire. Nature trail.

Upper Priest Lake Scenic Area, 6,400 acres, can be reached only by boat or on foot or horseback. The Area surrounds Upper Priest Lake, with National Forest land on the W shore, state forest land on the E.

Lower Priest River can be floated for the 44 mi. from Priest Lake to the Pend Oreille River. For most of this distance the river is the boundary between the Forest and Priest Lake State Forest. Rapids to Class III, riffles, pools, slack water, and slow meandering flow. Suitable for canoes, but hazardous at high water. A few developed campgrounds along the way.

Roosevelt Grove of Ancient Cedars Scenic Area, 138 acres, and *Granite Falls* are about 8 mi. W of Upper Priest Lake, near the Stagger Inn Campground, on an all-weather road.

Tepee Creek Natural Area, near the N end of Priest Lake, has about 660 acres of western white pine, the species that once dominated the forest here.

Priest River Experimental Forest and *Canyon Creek Research Natural Area,* between Priest Lake and the community of Priest River, illustrate the processes of forest regeneration.

Robinson Lake, Smith Lake, and *Brush Lake* in the NE block are among the small, less busy water bodies of the Kaniksu.

Pend Oreille Lake, 80,000 acres, is the largest lake in the Panhandle. Most of the shoreline is privately owned and much of it developed. Parts of the National Forest shoreline have steep banks, making access difficult. The Forest Service has 4 lakeside campgrounds with a total of 97 sites. Farragut State Park is at the S end of the lake.

COEUR D'ALENE NATIONAL FOREST
Fernan and Wallace Ranger Districts

The Forest lies between the Kaniksu NF on the N, the St. Joe NF on the S. On the W is the Rathdrum Prairie, on the E the rugged Bitterroot Mountains. The Coeur d'Alene Mountains are an intricately dissected highland. Elevations range from 2,100 ft. at Coeur d'Alene Lake to 6,826 ft. at Stevens Peak. Mountain slopes are generally steep.

As in the Kaniksu, the mountains here intercept moist air moving E from the Pacific, chiefly in winter, but annual precipitation is slightly less than farther N: about 26 in. at Coeur d'Alene, 92 in. on the highest slopes. Snow makes up 65 to 75 percent of the annual precipitation; accumulations range from a few in. at Coeur d'Alene to 83 in. up high. This ample moisture supplies 425 mi. of fishable streams and 16 lakes.

Like the Kaniksu, the Coeur d'Alene has been logged since the 19th century. As for mining, it is considered the richest silver, lead, zinc, and antimony area in the United States. The resulting road network has opened most of the Forest to motorized sightseeing, hunting, camping and picnicking, fishing, other water-based activities, and winter sports.

The Forest has a variety of riverside and mountain lake trails, attractive to hiker or horse rider, and not heavily used. Snowmobiling is popular throughout the Forest, with several hundred miles of groomed trails.

The two largest lakes of the area, Coeur d'Alene and Hayden, are outside the National Forest boundaries, although the Forest has small tracts on the shoreline of each. Within the Forest are a number of high mountain lakes along the Coeur d'Alene-St. Joe and ID-MT divides. Most are accessible by trail.

Most of the Forest's 425 mi. of fishable streams are tributary to the Coeur d'Alene River. The upper river can be floated by raft or canoe for 55 mi. from Senator Creek to Cataldo. During runoff, rapids are Class II with spots of Class III. In summer it's all Class I, but flow diminishes; after July, floating is best below Shoshone Creek.

From Cataldo to the lake, the river flows in a wide corridor of private, state, and federal land. This is a splendid complex of river, lakes, and wetlands, fine for birding and canoeing. (See entry, Lower Coeur d'Alene River.)

The North Fork is within the Forest. About 55 mi. can be floated by raft or canoe from late spring until water levels are too low.

The South Fork of the Coeur d'Alene River flows W, paralleling I-90 in a wide corridor between portions of the Forest. Land in the corridor is mostly private, with some BLM tracts. An extensive network of Forest trails is on both sides of this corridor. Longest, 22 mi., is the St. Joe Divide trail.

The road network makes most of the Forest easily accessible, thus requiring careful game management. Whitetail and mule deer were the principal game species until recently. Elk transplants began in 1925; the first hunting was in 1949; and elk is now the principal big game attraction.

Winter sports attract increasing numbers of visitors. Two major ski areas are on or adjacent to the Forest; ski touring is popular; snowmobilers enjoy unplowed Forest roads.

Settler's Grove of Ancient Cedars, 183 acres, protected as a Botanical Area, is shown on the state highway map, N of I-90, near the MT line.

ST. JOE NATIONAL FOREST
St. Maries and Avery Ranger Districts

The Forest boundaries extend from MT to WA, but most of the Forest land is in the E, a relatively solid block on the W slopes of the Bitterroot Range. The central portion is a checkerboard of 1-mi. squares. A smaller solid block adjoins the Clearwater NF on the S. The W half is fragmented.

Annual precipitation is less than in the Kaniksu and Coeur d'Alene: up to 60 in. at the higher elevations, enough to maintain lively streams. Major drainages are the St. Joe and St. Maries rivers, the Little North Fork of the Clearwater, and the Palouse. At high elevations, two-thirds of the annual precipitation falls as winter snow, often accumulating to well over 100 in., a snowpack that maintains streamflow through late summer.

Like the Forests to the N, the St. Joe was heavily logged for its white pine, and the original forest was also altered by major fires. Mining has also disturbed the landscape, though less extensively than in the Coeur d'Alene.

Wildlife species are affected by these changes in different ways. Large wildfires created excellent habitat and browse for elk and deer. Hunting is second only to camping in recreation activity.

The central feature of the Forest is the St. Joe River, said to be the world's highest navigable stream. Above Avery the river is part of the Wild and Scenic River system. It flows 133 mi. from St. Joe Lake to Coeur d'Alene Lake, 72 mi. of this inside Forest boundary. Near the headwaters is a 17-mi. whitewater wilderness canyon, which only the most experienced kayakers should run. The last 31 mi. are meandering, deep, slow-moving, and scenic. In between are rapids varying from Class I through Class IV. (See entry, Heyburn State Park.)

Fishing is described as "quality as opposed to quantity," with 560 mi. of fishable streams and 17 high mountain lakes where fish populations depend on stocking.

A ski area is on the Palouse Divide. Ski touring and snowmobiling have been increasing.

FEATURES

Mallard-Larkins Pioneer Area, 13,975 acres in the St. Joe, 18,356 acres in the Clearwater NF, is a roadless subalpine area with wilderness qualities, straddling a high divide. It includes 12 high mountain lakes. Access to the boundary is by unpaved road or trail.

ACTIVITIES (FOR ALL IDAHO PANHANDLE NATIONAL FORESTS)

Camping: 47 campgrounds; 652 sites. Some open all year, others for various periods, May–June to Sept.–Oct. Many attractive, informal sites throughout the Forests.

Hiking, backpacking: The Forests have over 2,000 mi. of foot trails, of which 70% are reported to be in good condition. Thirteen trails totaling 199 mi. have been designated National Recreation Trails. Trail use is generally moderate to light. Access to most trails is easy. Many offer attractive day hikes to lakes, beside streams. Excellent trail descriptions are in the Recreation Opportunities Guide.

Hunting: The Coeur d'Alene and St. Joe areas are nationally known for elk hunting. Deer and elk hunting throughout the Forests. Other big game includes black bear, mountain goat, moose. Waterfowl hunting on the larger lakes. Upland birds throughout the Forests.

Fishing: The Forests offer some of the finest fishing in this part of the world. The variety includes large lakes, high mountain lakes, swift streams, and slow-moving rivers. Cutthroat, rainbow, Dolly Varden, brook, lake, and golden trout; kokanee, whitefish.

Horse riding: Mostly by private owners. Outfitters serve fall hunters.

Boating: On large and small lakes, flatwater sections of major rivers.

Rafting, kayaking: On sections of the Coeur d'Alene, Priest, St. Joe, Moyie, and Pack rivers. Outfitters offer float trips on the Lower Priest and Moyie.

Skiing: At Lookout Pass. Other ski areas near the Forests.

Ski touring: 85 mi. of trails. Also on miles of unplowed roads.

PUBLICATIONS
Forest maps, one for each Forest. $1 each.
(We were told a consolidated St. Joe-Coeur d'Alene map would be issued in 1988.)
Travel plan map.
Campground and Picnic Area Directory.
An Introduction to the Kaniksu National Forest.
An Introduction to the Coeur d'Alene National Forest.
An Introduction to the St. Joe National Forest.
"Summertime Recreation Opportunities" Status Report, 1984.
Leaflets:
Visitor Information: Summertime.
Visitor Information: Snowtime.
Selkirk Crest.
Priest Lake Recreation Area.
Emerald Creek Garnet Area.
Hanna Flats/Cedar Grove Interpretive Trail.
South Fork Coeur d'Alene River Trails.
Independence Creek Trail System.
Bigfoot Ridge Trail.
Marble Creek Trail System.
Big Creek Trail System.
St. Joe River Float Trips.
Floating the Upper Coeur d'Alene River.
Priest River Float Trips.

Avery Ranger Station.
Magee Ranger Station.

REFERENCE:
Maughan, Jackie J. *The Hiker's Guide to Idaho*. Billings, MT: Falcon Press, 1984. Pp. 12–21, 24–32.

HEADQUARTERS: 1201 Ironwood Dr., Coeur d'Alene, ID 83814; (208) 765-7223.

RANGER DISTRICTS: Priest Lake R.D., Route 5, Box 207, Priest River, ID 83856; (208) 443-2512. Bonners Ferry R.D., Route 1, Box 390, Bonners Ferry, ID 83805; (208) 267-5561. Sandpoint R.D., 1500 Highway 2, Sandpoint, ID 83864; (208) 263-5111. Fernan R.D., 2502 Sherman Ave., Coeur d'Alene, ID 83814; (208) 765-7381. St. Maries R.D., P.O. Box 407, St. Maries, ID 83861; (208) 245-2531. Wallace R.D., P.O. Box 14, Silverton ID 83867; (208) 752-1221. Avery R.D., HC, Box 1, Avery, ID 83802; (208) 245-4517.

KOOTENAI NATIONAL WILDLIFE REFUGE
U.S. Fish and Wildlife Service
2,775 acres.

Far N ID. At Bonners Ferry on US 95, on the S end of the Kootenai River bridge, turn W on paved dike road, 5 mi. to refuge.

This small refuge has a diversity of wildlife, something to see at any season, although spring and fall are best. Most of the Refuge was part of the Kootenai River floodplain until a 37-ft. dike was built in the 1920s. Now the lowlands are a mix of managed ponds, marsh, grassland, and grainfields, extending to the base of the Selkirk Mountains.

Visitors are welcome during daylight hours. They can drive the 4 1/2-mi. auto tour route and hike on several foot trails, notably the Island Pond trail. Visitor travel is restricted during the Oct.–Dec. hunting season.

March–May is the spring waterfowl migration season, Apr.–June for songbirds. In summer the waterfowl produced on the Refuge can be seen. The fall migration of waterfowl, shorebirds, and raptors begins in Aug., continues through Oct. Winter is quiet as waterfowl move to the ice-free river, though they still feed in the grainfields. Visitor travel in the Refuge may be blocked by snow.

Birds: Checklist of 210 species available. Seasonally common or abundant species include red-necked and pied-billed grebes, great blue heron, tundra swan, Canada goose, mallard, gadwall, pintail; green-winged, blue-winged, and cinnamon teals; American wigeon, northern shoveler, redhead, ring-necked duck, common goldeneye, bufflehead, ruddy duck, common merganser. Red-tailed and rough-legged hawks, bald eagle, northern harrier, osprey, American kestrel, ruffed grouse, American coot, killdeer, common snipe, spotted sandpiper, greater and lesser yellowlegs, long-billed dowitcher, ring-billed gull, black tern, mourning dove, great horned owl, common nighthawk. Rufous hummingbird, northern flicker, eastern kingbird; willow, alder, and Hammond's flycatchers; western wood-pewee. Swallows: violet-green, tree, bank, barn, cliff. Steller's jay, common raven, American crow, Clark's nutcracker, black-capped chickadee, long-billed marsh wren, American robin, varied and Swainson's thrushes, mountain bluebird, golden-crowned kinglet, European starling, red-eyed vireo, yellow and yellow-rumped warblers, common yellowthroat, western meadowlark, red-winged and yellow-headed blackbirds, brown-headed cowbird, pine siskin, American goldfinch; savannah, chipping, and song sparrows; dark-eyed junco.

Mammals: Include various shrews and bats, snowshoe hare, yellow pine and redtail chipmunks, yellowbelly marmot, red squirrel, beaver, muskrat, coyote, mule deer, whitetail deer. Present but seldom seen: moose, elk, black bear, raccoon, weasel, striped skunk, river otter.

ACTIVITIES
Hiking: 4 mi. of trails, restricted in hunting season.
Hunting: Waterfowl, Oct.–Dec. Big game, Sept.–Dec. Special rules.

PUBLICATIONS
Refuge leaflet with map.
 Wildlife checklist.
 Island Pond Nature Trail leaflet.
 Hunting and fishing information.

HEADQUARTERS: HCR 60, Box 283, Bonners Ferry, ID 83805; (208) 267-3888.

LAKE PEND OREILLE
Mixed ownerships
153 mi. long, up to 6 mi. wide.

Near Sandpoint on US 95.

Idaho's largest lake is fed by several rivers. The Albeni Falls Dam, a hydro-electric project, raised the natural lake level, which is now up to 1,225 ft. deep.

The lake is a popular resort area with many shoreline developments, but it retains much of its natural appearance. Around the lake are numerous public lands administered by the U.S. Army Corps of Engineers, U.S. Bureau of Land Management, Idaho Department of Fish and Game, and Idaho Department of Parks and Recreation.
See entries for
Albeni Falls Project; Pend Oreille River
Pend Oreille Wildlife Management Area
Farragut State Park

LOWER COEUR D'ALENE RIVER
Idaho Department of Fish and Game and other agencies
28 river miles; 5,166 acres, plus 2,226 acres of leased and cooperative lands. Also National Forest and BLM tracts.

Along the Coeur d'Alene River, between I-90 at Cataldo and Lake Coeur d'Alene. Principal land access by SR 3, SW from Cataldo.

For one who enjoys wetlands, a map of this area is an irresistible invitation. The WMA includes all or portions of 12 small to moderate-size, mostly shallow lakes with extensive adjacent marshlands,· 16 separate marshland tracts, and meandering channels, all on floodplain. Around the wetlands is a willow, cottonwood, and birch riparian zone, beyond which the land rises to a forest of lodgepole pine, western larch, Douglas-fir, and grand fir. On the N side of the Coeur d'Alene River, the land rises to the Coeur d'Alene National Forest.

Cave Lake is the largest, about 600 acres. Killarney, 500 acres, is considered the most scenic. Thompson Lake, 400 acres, has large floating islands. Others are Blue, Anderson, Hidden, Swan, Black, Medicine, Rose, Bull Run, and Porter. Three former lakes are now sloughs or marshes.

Water level of Coeur d'Alene Lake and the lower rivers is controlled by a dam. Near-optimum level is maintained June–Sept., but it is then drawn down to maintain power generation, reducing the carrying capacity of the marshes. However, the once-deadly pollution of the river has been abated, and the river area is healthy again.

Exploring these wetlands by land isn't easy, even though SR 3, designated a Scenic Route, parallels the Coeur d'Alene River. Public and private lands are intermixed and mostly unposted. Side roads are often unsigned and of uneven quality. Launching places aren't easy to find without the site map. We saw a few informal campsites, all occupied. When we return, we'll explore by boat.

Canoeing and boating are the chief visitor activities, followed by fishing and waterfowl hunting. Spring and fall are best for fishing. Some lakes become weed-choked in midsummer.

Birds: The habitat supports a major breeding population of wood ducks. Fish and Game has put up several hundred nest boxes. Few Canada geese nest here because of spring flooding. Mallards are more successful, and the area also produces several hundred pintail, baldpate, green-winged teal, and other ducks.

97 species have been recorded, a total that seems low. Seasonally common species include American coot, whistling swan, killdeer, California gull, black tern, great blue heron, American bittern, red-tailed hawk, bald eagle; violet-green, barn, and cliff swallows; black-capped chickadee, American robin.

Mammals: Common species include muskrat, chipmunk, western red squirrel, whitetail deer.

ACTIVITIES

Camping: No campgrounds. (The Rainy Hill unit shown on the site map is a Forest Service picnic ground and boat ramp.) We saw two small lakeside areas where people camp in RVs, several others used for boat camping.

Hunting: Good waterfowl hunting, chiefly mallard, during the early weeks of the season, but hunting has declined in recent years. A few elk and whitetail deer are taken.

Fishing: Largemouth bass, bullhead, crappie, yellow perch, northern pike.

Boating: Ramps near the river mouth at Harrison, and on or near Thompson, Black, Cave, Killarney, and Rose lakes.

PUBLICATION: *Waterways of the Lower Coeur d'Alene River.* Folder with map, bird list, etc. Issued jointly by Fish and Game, BLM, Idaho Department of Parks and Recreation, Idaho Panhandle National Forests.

HEADQUARTERS: Region 1, 2320 Government Way, Coeur d'Alene, ID 83814; (208) 765-3111.

MCARTHUR LAKE WILDLIFE MANAGEMENT AREA
Idaho Department of Fish and Game
1,208 acres.

On the W side of US 95 at the Boundary-Bonner county line, just S of Naples.

The site includes a 600-acre shallow lake, peat bog, sedge marsh, and willow-cottonwood riparian zone, grading up to cedar-hemlock and a fringe of Douglas-fir.

Most visitors come to fish, few to hunt. The site produces Canada geese, mallards, teals, and wood ducks. Opening of the fishing season is delayed until after waterfowl nesting.

It isn't a popular birding spot, but 103 species have been recorded, including a variety of waterfowl and shorebirds. If you're traveling on US 95, pause for a look around.

ACTIVITIES

Camping: Permitted. No facilities except latrines. Some travelers make this an overnight stop.

Fishing: Perch, sunfish.

Boating: Dock. Chiefly fishermen with small craft.

HEADQUARTERS: Region 1, 2320 Government Way, Coeur d'Alene, ID 83814; (208) 765-3111.

NEZ PERCE NATIONAL FOREST
U.S. Forest Service
2,218,333 acres; 2,247,082 acres within boundaries.

Access by local roads E and W from US 95. SR 14 penetrates the Forest.

The Nez Perce extends across central Idaho from Oregon to Montana, part of a huge area of National Forest land. The Forest's principal mass lies E of US 95. The Clearwater NF is on its N boundary, Payette NF on the S, Frank Church - River of No Return Wilderness and Bitterroot NF on the S and E. The smaller portion W of US 95 adjoins Hells Canyon National Recreation Area.

The Forest's terrain is rough: mountain ranges separated by foothills and valley floors, cut by deep canyons. The Selway, South Fork Clearwater, Salmon, and Snake rivers and their tributaries drain the W slopes of the Bitterroot Mountains, cutting a maze of peaks and ridges. On the W, the Snake River Canyon is 9,000 ft. deep; on the S, that of the Salmon is about 5,000. Steep canyon walls make river access difficult. The Clearwater Mountains extend through the Forest from the N. Elevations range from 1,104 ft. at the Snake River to 9,393 ft. Except in the canyons, most of the Forest is over 5,000 ft.

Two-thirds of the Forest is roadless. About 935,000 acres are included in the Wildernesses and the corridors of Wild and Scenic Rivers. Over 100,000 acres of the Nez Perce are included in the Frank Church - River of No Return Wilderness, for which we have a separate entry, 34,000 acres in the Hells Canyon Wilderness, described in the entry for Hells Canyon National Recreation Area. Over 500,000 acres are in 16 roadless areas, some of which may eventually be designated as Wildernesses.

From US 95 near Grangeville, a paved road, SR 14, penetrates to the only large inholding, a 6-by-6-mi. square at the heart of the Forest. About a third of this square is private land, including Elk City, population under 500. The rest is mostly BLM and state land. A number of resident miners work claims. Elk City is a base for outfitter-guide services. Beyond Elk City, a secondary road runs S for about 22 mi. into a broad dead-end corridor formed by the Gospel Hump Wilderness on the W and the River of No Return Wilderness on the S and E. From this road, the famous Nez Perce Trail runs E. Another secondary road extends for a few miles from US 12 at Lowell along the Selway River to Selway Falls.

The Forest has about 2,000 mi. of roads, but most others are unpaved, usually single-lane. Many, built for logging service and not maintained thereafter, aren't suitable for passenger cars, especially in wet weather. About 200 mi. have use restrictions, seasonally or all year; these are shown on the Forest Visitor and Travel Plan map.

About 5,000 mi. of trails were built before 1940, chiefly for fire detection and control, not recreation. As more logging roads were built, about half the trails were abandoned. Budget constraints limit maintenance of those remaining. Many are in poor condition, so it's advisable to check routes with a Ranger before an extended trip, especially during snowmelt. Four National Recreation Trails are in the Forest, with designation of a fifth pending.

Prevailing westerly winds give the Forest a milder climate than is usual at this latitude. At middle elevations, 120 to 140 days are frost-free. The warmest weather is in the valleys of the principal rivers, the coldest on high slopes. Annual precipitation ranges from less than 18 in. in the Salmon and Snake river valleys, to over 60 in. in the high country, most of the latter falling as snow.

Recreation in the Forest totals about 900,000 visitor-days per year. Only 17% of this is recorded at the 28 campgrounds and other developed sites, 14% in Wildernesses. More than two-thirds of the activity is in undeveloped non-Wilderness areas, most of this in the 16 roadless units. Many of these units are defined by Forest roads on their boundaries, and most have trails. Hunting and fishing are major activities. Camping, hiking, and horse riding are often linked to hunting and fishing.

Plants: Vegetation ranges from bunchgrass in canyon bottoms to subalpine communities on high mountains. Most of the area is forested, over a million acres classified as suitable for commercial timber production. Subalpine fir is the dominant species at high elevations, with an understory of Sitka alder, Utah honeysuckle, menziesia, and blue huckleberry. Douglas-fir and ponderosa pine predominate on lower, drier slopes, with understories including mountain maple, serviceberry, creambush, oceanspray, ninebark, white spirea, snowberry, black hawthorn, black chokecherry. Grand fir and western redcedar stands occur on moister slopes, with mountain maple, thimbleberry, snowberry, baldhip rose, prickly currant, Pacific yew, serviceberry. Seasonally flowering species on high slopes include twinflower, broadleaf arnica, prince's-pine, greencup beadlily, louseworts, false-hellebore, darkwoods violet, common beargrass. At lower elevations: heartleaf arnica, largeleaf sandwort, arrowleaf balsamroot, false Solomon's-seal, American trailplant, Pacific trillium, common yarrow, western rattlesnake plantain, western meadowrue.

Birds: Checklist of 228 species available. Seasonally abundant or common species include great blue heron, trumpeter swan, Canada and snow geese, mallard, gadwall, pintail; green-winged, blue-winged, and cinnamon teals; American wigeon, northern shoveler, wood duck, common goldeneye, common merganser, turkey vulture; sharp-shinned, red-tailed, and rough-legged hawks; golden and bald eagles, northern harrier, prairie falcon, American kestrel. Blue, spruce, and ruffed grouse; chukar, gray partridge, killdeer, common snipe, spotted sandpiper, Wilson's and red-necked phalaropes, rock and mourning doves. Owls: western screech, great horned, short-eared, northern saw-whet. Common nighthawk; black, Vaux's, and white-throated swifts; rufous and calliope hummingbirds, belted kingfisher. Woodpeckers: northern flicker, yellow-bellied sapsucker, pileated, Williamson's, hairy, downy. Eastern and western kingbirds, Say's phoebe; Hammond's, dusky, and olive-sided flycatchers; western wood-pewee, horned lark. Swallows: violet-green, tree, bank, cliff. Steller's and gray jays, black-billed magpie, common raven, American crow, Clark's nutcracker, black-capped and mountain chickadees, red-breasted and pygmy nuthatches, brown creeper, dipper. Wrens: house, winter, marsh, canyon, rock. American robin; varied, hermit, and Swainson's thrushes; western and mountain bluebirds, Townsend's solitaire, golden-crowned and ruby-crowned kinglets, water pipit, cedar waxwing, northern shrike, European starling, solitary vireo. Warblers: orange-crowned, Nashville, yellow, yellow-rumped, Townsend's, MacGillivray's. Western meadowlark, red-winged and Brewer's blackbirds, northern oriole, brown-headed cowbird, western tanager; black-headed, evening, and pine grosbeaks; lazuli bunting, house finch, pine siskin, American goldfinch, red crossbill, rufous-sided towhee, dark-eyed junco. Sparrows: savannah, vesper, lark, chipping, white-crowned, song.

Mammals: No checklist. Elk is the principal big game species. The current winter population is about 12,000, two-thirds of them in Wildernesses. The Forest has one of the largest concentrations of moose in ID, about 740 individuals. Other big game species include mule deer, whitetail deer, bighorn sheep, black bear. Sightings of gray wolf have not been confirmed. Other species reported include raccoon, marten, fisher, longtail and shorttail weasels, mink, river otter, wolverine, badger, spotted and striped skunks, coyote, red fox, mountain lion, lynx, bobcat, marmot, Columbian ground squirrel, golden-mantled squirrel, yellow pine chipmunk, northern flying squirrel, bushytail woodrat, muskrat, beaver, porcupine, pika, snowshoe hare, mountain cottontail.

Fishes: The Forest has about 1,368 mi. of fishing streams and 1,194 acres of lakes, with populations of coldwater and warmwater fish species. Summer steelhead and spring chinook salmon return to the Snake, Salmon, and Clearwater rivers each year to spawn.

FEATURES

Hells Canyon Wilderness and National Recreation Area (see entry in Zone 1) include about 117,000 acres of the Nez Perce, now separately administered.

Selway-Bitterroot Wilderness, 1,340,681 acres, lying across the Bitterroot Range, in Idaho and Montana. 560,088 acres are within the Nez Perce NF at its NE corner. The Wilderness extends into the Clearwater NF on the N. The Nez Perce portion ends at the ID-MT boundary on the Bitterroot crest. Access in the Nez Perce is by Forest roads from Elk City or along the Selway River to Selway Falls. The Selway Wild and Scenic River cuts across the Wilderness. Terrain is rugged, with spectacular steep-walled canyons. The Wilderness map shows numerous trails, but the interior has large areas with no trails. Visitation is light except along the Selway River corridor and trails to the Selway Crags. Hunting is the principal activity, camping second, followed by hiking and backpacking.

This Wilderness is the second largest in the Lower 48. It is separated from the Frank Church - River of No Return Wilderness (the largest Wilderness) by the Nez Perce Trail.

Nez Perce Trail, a traditional Indian route, now offers a 113-mi. backcountry experience to adventurous motorists. We know of no other road that traverses a narrow corridor between such vast Wildernesses. Driven carefully and slowly, an ordinary car can travel the route in summer; 4-wheel drive is needed in wet weather. Cars with low clearance, motor homes, and trailers aren't suitable. Don't try it without checking at the Red River Ranger Station just before the turnoff.

From SR 14 near Elk City, turn E on the Red River-Dixie road, Forest Road 222, for 14 mi., then left on the Trail. 36 mi. are within the Nez Perce NF, the final 65 mi. within the Bitterroot NF.

The route is scenic, beside water much of the way, with excellent opportunities for camping, hunting, fishing, hiking.

Selway Wild and Scenic River rises in the Bitterroot Range on the Bitterroot NF, crosses the Selway-Bitterroot Wilderness. 62 mi. are within the Nez Perce NF. Rafting from Paradise in the Bitterroot NF to Selway Falls, 47 mi., requires advanced skills and suitable equipment; launches by permit are limited, assigned by a drawing. (For information and list of licensed outfitters, ask the West Fork Ranger Station.) Except for a riverside trail and several airstrips, this portion of the river is isolated. From below Selway Falls to Lowell, the river is suitable for most boats except at high water. Trips up to 20 mi. A road follows the river.

Frank Church - River of No Return Wilderness. See entry in Zone 2. Of its 2,230,300 acres, the Nez Perce portion is 105,736. The S boundary is 66 mi. of frontage on the Salmon River. N boundary is the Nez Perce Trail. The area is mountainous with peaks over 8,000 ft. and several dozen mountain lakes. It lies within the Red River Ranger District. Permits are required for private floaters and power boaters on the 79-mi. river stretch from Corn Creek to Long Tom Bar, 25 mi. E of Riggins. Outfitters offer trips. The Nez Perce has numerous campgrounds along the river.

Gospel Hump Wilderness, 200,464 acres, is in the S central portion of the Forest, adjoining the Salmon Wild and Scenic River. Access from the W is by Forest Road 444 to Square Mountain; other access points are on the N, E, and SW. All access roads are low standard. Elevations range from 1,970 ft. at the river to 8,940 ft. on Buffalo Hump. Landforms include a heavily forested area with moderate slopes in the N, the glaciated divide between the Clearwater and Salmon river drainages, and the steep Salmon River Breaks. Roads and trails in the high country are generally snow-free from mid-July to mid-Sept. Trails range from moderate to "extremely challenging." Some have had no recent maintenance. Fishing is good, for resident and anadromous species. (Anadromous species are those that ascend rivers from the sea to spawn.) Big game includes elk, mule and whitetail deer, black bear, mountain lion, moose, mountain goat, bighorn sheep. Also chukar and grouse hunting.

Middle Fork Clearwater Recreational River begins at the confluence of the Lochsa and Selway rivers, at Lowell, extending W along the Nez Perce boundary for 11 mi. and continuing beyond the Forest for 12 mi. to Kooskia. Suitable for rafts, canoes, all summer. The Lochsa, in the Clearwater NF, is part of the Wild and Scenic River system.

South Fork Clearwater River, the route of SR 14 for about 50 mi. to the Elk City inholding, is best known as a fishing stream. Salmon and steelhead spawned here until 1912, when a dam blocked their passage upstream from the sea. In 1962 the dam was removed, and both species are now well established.

Rapid Wild River is W of US 95. One fork enters the Nez Perce from the Payette NF, flowing N, another from Hells Canyon Wilderness. The river flows within the Nez Perce for 12 mi. before joining the Little Salmon River S of Riggins. A scenic trail follows the river; trailhead is at the Rapid River Fish Hatchery 2 mi. off US 95.

Selway Falls, a cascade, is 19 mi. from Lowell up the dead-end road beside

the Selway River. Several campgrounds are along the river, as well as trailheads for the Selway-Bitterroot Wilderness. A popular destination is *Selway
Crags,* a region of high peaks and cirque lakes.

Other roadless areas include *Rackcliff-Gedney,* 90,173 acres, bounded by
the Lochsa River on the N, Selway River on the S, the Selway-Bitterroot
Wilderness on the E. The Coolwater Ridge bisects the area W–E, and the
northern 34,710 acres are in the Clearwater NF. US 12 follows the N side of
the Lochsa River; a pack bridge at Split Creek provides access. A low-
standard road penetrates from US 12 near the rivers' junction. Slopes are
steep, terrain rugged, rising from the river canyons to 6,926 ft. The area has
several streams and a few small lakes. Vegetation is a mix of forest, brush,
and grass. The area is winter range for elk.

The Forest map shows the East Boyd-Glover Roundtop National Recreation Trail circling Round Top Mountain from and returning to the Selway
corridors, but we were advised that the few trails in the area are in poor
condition, receiving little or no maintenance. Recreation use is light: chiefly
hunting, some berry picking and day hiking.

Meadow Creek, 201,715 acres. Two adjacent areas lie between the Elk City
mining area and the Selway-Bitterroot Wilderness. To the S, a road corridor
separates this area from the Frank Church - River of No Return Wilderness.
The Selway-Bitterroot Wilderness is the area's N and E boundary. Access is
from a trailhead near Selway Falls. A trail follows Meadow Creek, the first
15 mi. designated a National Recreation Trail. The Anderson Butte National
Recreation Trail is on the W. Other trailheads are at campgrounds along the
Nez Perce Trail.

The area includes almost all the drainage of Meadow Creek, which flows
N to the Selway. Elevations from 1,800 ft. near Selway Falls to 8,196 ft. on
Burnt Knob. In terrain and vegetation, it has characteristics similar to those
of the adjacent Wildernesses, but it is more accessible than much of the
RONR.

Present recreation uses are reflected in conflicting recommendations for the
area's future. Pro-wilderness groups urge adding the area to the Selway-
Bitterroot Wilderness, or at least that part of it E of Meadow Creek. Backpackers, who enjoy the Meadow Creek Trail when the high country is still
snowed in, favor Wilderness designation in part because it would exclude trail
cyclists, who oppose such designation. Hunting is probably the chief activity.
Outfitters would like to keep the country wild, because of its abundant big
game; the Idaho Outfitters and Guides Association is among those advocating
Wilderness designation. Timber companies want the area to remain open to
road building and logging.

ACTIVITIES

Camping: 28 campgrounds, 198 sites. Only two of the campgrounds have
10 or more sites; some have only 2 or 3. Seasons differ, according to elevation.

Some are all year. Some boat access. Camping is permitted almost anywhere, and most camping is informal, not in campgrounds.

Hiking, backpacking: The Forest has over 2,300 mi. of trails, chiefly in the Wildernesses and other roadless areas. Some are in poor condition. The 4 National Recreation Trails include a short path to a scenic overlook and 3 backcountry trails, from a 14 1/2-mi. round trip to one which is 15 mi. one way. Most campgrounds are at or near trailheads.

Forest HQ acknowledged that available information on trails is "insufficient, fragmented." Trail information in the ROG is spotty. There are no printed descriptions of the National Recreation Trails. However, there's almost always someone at HQ or the Ranger District office who can be helpful.

Hunting: One of the principal activities. Big game and upland birds. 32 commercial outfitters provide services; list available at HQ and Ranger Districts.

Fishing: Although the Forest has many miles of streams, productivity of resident sport fish is only fair. Fish over 12 in. are uncommon except in some high mountain lakes. The cutthroat and cutthroat-rainbow hybrid are most abundant, with brook trout and Dolly Varden also present. About 130 mountain lakes support a goodly number of fish. Steelhead fishing is best in Mar.–Apr.

Horse riding: All trails and roads are open to horses. Most horse use is in conjunction with hunting, but 16 outfitters offer summer fishing and pack trips.

Rafting: Chiefly on the Salmon and Selway rivers. 40 commercial outfitters provide service. List available at HQ.

Ski touring: Ample snowfall provides good opportunities. Most Forest roads are unplowed. A trail is laid out near Fish Creek Meadows S of Grangeville.

INTERPRETATION

A tourist booth at the W end of Grangeville has Forest information. Other information at HQ and Ranger District offices.

PUBLICATIONS

Forest map. $1.
Selway-Bitterroot Wilderness map. $1.
Forest visitor and travel plan.
Information pages:
   Gospel Hump Wilderness.
   Selway-Bitterroot Wilderness.
   Floating the Selway River.
South Fork Clearwater River: A New Beginning for Anadromous Fish.
Bird checklist.
Gospel Hump. Pamphlet.

REFERENCES
Arkava, Morton L. and Leone K. *Hiking Trails of the Bitterroot Mountains.* Boulder, CO: Pruett, 1983.
Bluestein, S. R. *Hiking Trails of Southern Idaho.* Billings, MT: Caxton Printers, 1981. Pp. 86–88.
Carrey, John, and Cort Conley. *The Middle Fork and the Sheepeater War.* Cambridge, ID: Backeddy Books, rev. 1980.
Conley, Cort. *Snake River of Hells Canyon.* Cambridge, ID: Backeddy Books, 1979.
Maughan, Jackie J. *The Hiker's Guide to Idaho.* Billings, MT: Falcon Press, 1984. Pp. 36–45, 48–54, 76–80, 115–19.
A River Runner's Guide to Idaho. Boise: U.S. Bureau of Land Management and Idaho Department of Parks and Recreation, 1980. Pp. 40–41.

HEADQUARTERS: Route 2, Box 475, Grangeville, ID 83530; (208) 983-1950.

RANGER DISTRICTS: Salmon River R.D., HCO1, Box 70, White Bird, ID 83554; (208) 839-2211. Clearwater R.D., Route 2, Box 475, Grangeville, ID 83530; (208) 983-1963. Red River R.D., P.O. Box 23, Elk City, ID 83525; (208) 842-2255. Moose Creek R. D., P.O. Box 464, Grangeville, ID 83530; (208) 983-2712. Selway R.D., HCR1, Box 91, Kooskia, ID 83539; (208) 926-4258. Elk City R.D., P.O. Box 416, Elk City, ID 83525; (208) 842-2255.

PAYETTE NATIONAL FOREST
See entry in Zone 2.

PEND OREILLE WILDLIFE MANAGEMENT AREA
Idaho Department of Fish and Game
About 4,300 acres.

Ten tracts on the N shore of Pend Oreille Lake, along the Pend Oreille River, and in the Clark Fork River delta. Most adjoin the W side of SR 200.

The tracts are on extensive, marshy floodplains, through which river channels meander to Lake Pend Oreille, 143 mi. long, Idaho's largest. Most of the land in these tracts is submerged for part of the year, as the lake level fluctuates. The tracts include about 500 acres on the lake that remain above water all year, providing opportunities for boat launching, camping, and picnicking.

Much of the area can be seen from the highway, but it's best explored by canoe or other small craft.

Most visitors come to fish, some to camp, boat, water ski, or swim. It's a significant waterfowl area. Fish and Game's management objectives are headed by Canada goose production, duck production, and migratory waterfowl feeding and resting, followed by public hunting, fishing, and wildlife appreciation.

The main body of the lake doesn't freeze, but the sloughs and marshes do by mid-Nov., remaining frozen until Mar. or early Apr. Annual precipitation here is 33 in., half of it in winter, when snow depths average about 2 ft.

Birds: 115 species have been recorded. The fall-winter migrant count of redhead duck can reach 23,000, almost the entire Idaho population, concentrated in Oden Bay. Canada geese are resident in the Clark Fork area, Denton Slough, and Pack River. Nesting occurs in mid-Mar., and the first broods are seen after mid-Apr.

Spring migrants average 60,000 ducks, 15,000 Canada geese, 2,000 whistling swans. Migrant waterfowl species include—in descending order—baldpate, redhead, mallard, Canada goose, American merganser, coot, pintail, lesser scaup, bufflehead, ringneck.

A great blue heronry is near the mouth of Clark Fork River, another on private land near Morton Slough. Ospreys nest. Bald eagles arrive in winter; 123 were counted in 1981.

Mammals: Trappers take beaver, mink, and muskrat from the Pack and Clark Fork rivers. Populations of other species are small. Elk, moose, black bear, mule deer, and whitetail deer have been observed occasionally, as well as coyote, bobcat, badger, porcupine, raccoon, and other species.

ACTIVITIES

Camping: About 500 camping parties per year, mostly fishermen and hunters, some transients stopping overnight. No facilities except latrines.

Hunting: Waterfowl.

Fishing: Yellow perch, crappie, bullhead, largemouth bass. Kokanee in the main lake.

Boating: Several ramps.

HEADQUARTERS: Region 1, 2320 Government Way, Coeur d'Alene, ID 83814; (208) 765-3111.

PRIEST LAKE STATE PARK

Idaho Department of Parks and Recreation
463 acres.

On the E side of Priest Lake, off SR 57.

The Park consists of 3 campgrounds:

Dickensheet, 4 mi. S of Coolin on the Priest River. 46 acres. Summer only.

Indian Creek, 11 mi. N of Coolin, on the lake. 295 acres. All year.

Lion Head, 23 mi. N of Coolin, on the lake. 122 acres. Summer only.

The campgrounds are attractive bases for water-based recreation and for activities in the Idaho Panhandle National Forests (see entry), which occupy most of the W side of the lake. Most of the E side is occupied by the Priest Lake State Forest. Priest Lake, 26 mi. long, 23,680 acres, appears almost pristine, with only modest shoreline development. Several islands are in the lake. Upper Priest Lake can be reached only by foot trail or boat.

The Park is popular in summer. Campgrounds were full when we visited.

ACTIVITIES

Camping: 110 sites. Reservations can be made for Indian Creek and Lion Head.

Boating: Ramp and dock at Indian Creek. Small-craft ramp at Lion Head.

Rafting: On Lower Priest River. See Idaho Panhandle National Forests entry.

HEADQUARTERS: Coolin, ID 83821; (208) 443-2200.

SALMON RIVER, LOWER
U.S. Bureau of Land Management
112 river miles.

From Riggins to the Snake River.

See also Salmon River, Zone 2.

The Lower Salmon River, below the Wild and Scenic River section described in Zone 2, has rapids to Class IV, with stretches of smooth water. Turning N near Riggins, it flows beside US 95 in the Salmon River Canyon. This is high desert, with many points of road access. Public and private land are intermixed. About half is BLM, and there are some state holdings. Sandbars offer good campsites. The Forest Service has a campground upstream from Riggins.

Near White Bird the river turns W toward its junction with the Snake, into a series of steep-walled canyons 2,000 to 3,000 ft. deep. The next 20 mi. is a strip of BLM land averaging less than 1/2 mi. in width. Only at Mahoney Creek, near the halfway point, does the public land extend as much as 1 mi. S.

Both sections have been proposed for inclusion in the Wild and Scenic River system: Recreation River from Long Tom Bar, upstream from Riggins, to White Bird; Scenic River from White Bird to the Snake.

Outfitters and private parties float the river from Riggins or put in at White Bird. The section beside US 95 is popular for day trips. Floater use of the final canyon portion, usually involving an overnight camp, is estimated to be 12,000 visitor-days per year, outfitter parties making up slightly more than half of the total. The river can be floated all year except for about 6 weeks during the runoff: June and a period just preceding or following.

BLM has an excellent river guide to Lower Salmon, detailed information on the river and the environment.

Sections of the canyon bottom can be hiked, but others are impassable.

PUBLICATION: *Lower Salmon River Guide.* 20 pp. $2.

HEADQUARTERS: BLM, Cottonwood Resource Area, Route 3, Box 181, Cottonwood, ID 83522; (208) 962-3245.

SALMON RIVER, UPPER
U.S. Forest Service

From North Fork to Riggins.

See entries: Frank Church - River of No Return Wilderness and Salmon River, both in Zone 2.

ST. MARIES WILDLIFE MANAGEMENT AREA
Idaho Department of Fish and Game
13,022 acres.

5 mi. S of St. Maries. Access from SR 3.

SR 3, the White Pine Scenic Route, cuts across a curve of the St. Maries River. The WMA lies within that curve, with the river on its N, W, and S. At its center is 4,695-ft. Lindstrom Peak. On the N and W, slopes drop sharply to the river at 2,130-ft. elevation. S and E slopes are gentler, interspersed with abrupt rolling hills.

Most of the land was purchased or leased in the 1940s, to be managed for big game. Public hunting and production of big game and forest grouse are still the principal Fish and Game priorities, but nonconsumptive users far outnumber hunters except in the first 2 weeks of the big game season. Except in hunting season, the site offers opportunities for uncrowded camping, hiking, and fishing.

Spring and fall are cool and wet, summers moderate and dry, winters long with periods of severe and moderate weather. Annual precipitation is about 30 in., about half in winter, much of this as snow. Snow depths of 2 to 3 ft. are normal for lowlands, 3 to 4 ft. higher up, with depths of 6 ft. recorded.

The site has 25 mi. of improved access and loop roads, several leading to the river. Some spur and secondary roads have been closed to vehicles. These roads and 12 mi. of foot trails serve as hiking routes.

Plants: Lowlands are primarily in the cedar-hemlock zone. Most uplands and moister mid-elevations are a highly productive Douglas-fir/grand fir community. Ponderosa pine predominates on drier SW slopes and bluffs above the river. Riparian wet meadows support alder, bog birch, and sedges, with some redcedar. Understory includes oceanspray, ninebark, snowberry, shinyleaf ceanothus, willow, redstem ceanothus, elderberry, boxwood.

Birds: Ruffed grouse are common, blue grouse declining. Only 45 bird species have been recorded, which is surely low, and almost none are called abundant.

Mammals: The most abundant big game species is whitetail deer, with smaller populations of mule deer, elk, and black bear.

ACTIVITIES

Camping: No facilities, but many attractive sites.

Hiking, backpacking: The longest loop route is about 12 mi., including river bank and ascent of Lindstrom Peak.

Hunting: Deer, elk, grouse, squirrel.

Fishing: Rainbow and cutthroat trout, kokanee salmon.

HEADQUARTERS: Region 1, 2320 Government Way, Coeur d'Alene, ID 83814; (208) 765-3111.

ZONE 2

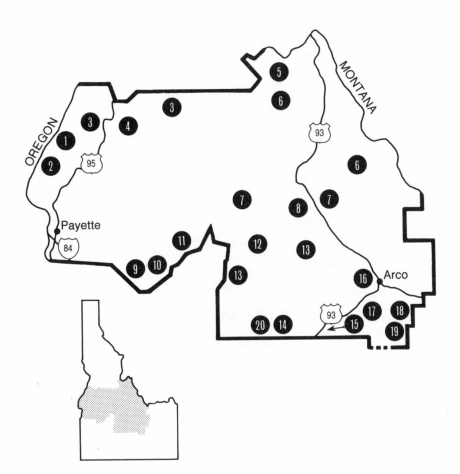

ZONE 2

Includes these counties:

Adams	Valley	Lemhi
Washington	Payette	Gem
Boise	Custer	Camas
Blaine	Butte	

Zone 2 is central Idaho, border to border. Well over half of the zone is occupied by National Forests: the Boise, Challis, Payette, and Sawtooth, including the Sawtooth National Recreation Area. The zone is almost entirely mountainous, with the state's highest and most spectacular peaks and ridges. It includes the major part of the Frank Church - River of No Return Wilderness and the N half of the Sawtooth Wilderness. A bit of the Seven Devils Wilderness is in the far NW corner.

On the E are parallel ranges: the Beaverhead Mountains on the MT border and the Lemhi and Lost River ranges. The valleys between are a mix of private and public land, with good fishing sites and access roads to the Forests. The Salmon River rises in the S of the zone, flowing past Stanley, Challis, and Salmon, turning W where it joins its North Fork, meeting its Middle Fork near the zone boundary. The Payette River drains the W portion of the zone, dammed to form Cascade Reservoir. The Payette basin includes the Payette Lakes and numerous small lakes, many of them favorites of fishermen and campers. On the W boundary are the Hells Canyon, Oxbow, and Brownlee reservoirs on the Snake River. The S central portion of the zone also has small lakes seldom seen except by local fishermen.

The state's most dramatic scenery, many visitors say, is in the Sawtooth National Recreation Area. Here mountains, rivers, and lakes offer an almost infinite range of recreation opportunities, from water skiing to wilderness backpacking. The Sawtooth Scenic Route and Ponderosa Pine Scenic Route meet at the N side of the NRA.

In the SE corner of the zone, the mountains give way to a far younger volcanic landscape. Craters of the Moon National Monument is the best introduction to an extensive region of lava formations.

APPENDICITIS HILL
U.S. Bureau of Land Management
21,900 acres.

From Arco, 8 mi. NW on US 93 to Moore, then 1 mi. W on local roads. The site occupies most of the triangle between Darlington, Lost River, and Arco.

It's not pristine wilderness, but it is a scenic and accessible area for day hikes and weekend backpacking. Lower elevation hills are generally rounded, sage-brush-grassland areas used for cattle grazing. Vehicle ways used by ranchers penetrate these lower areas, and livestock watering sites have been developed. But from Antelope Valley at 2,900 ft. elevation the terrain rises to 8,523-ft. Crawford Peak. The high ridges and peaks offer fine vistas. The mountain mass is cut by 15 canyons, many of them natural hiking routes, with impressive rock outcrops and several caves. N-facing slopes have good stands of Douglas-fir. Chokecherry and mountain-mahogany occur in the canyons, with some stands of aspen and willow. There are no perennial streams.

Few visitors use the area except in hunting season. Most hunters use motorized vehicles, but these are restricted to roads and trails.

Wildlife: Mule deer and pronghorn range the site all year. It's winter range for about 100 elk and over 1,000 mule deer. BLM reports numerous birds and small mammals, but no lists are available. Principal game species are elk, mule deer, chukar partridge, and sage grouse.

HEADQUARTERS: BLM, Idaho Falls District, 940 Lincoln Rd., Idaho Falls, ID 83401; (208) 529-1020.

BIG SOUTHERN BUTTE
U.S. Bureau of Land Management
586 acres.

From the SW end of Atomic City, off US 26, 15 mi. on dirt road. The butte is shown on the highway map.

If you like sweeping views from high places, this is the highest place for miles around: 7,550 ft. elevation, half a mile above the surrounding Snake River plain. It's a National Natural Landmark now, and it was a landmark for pioneers, who paused at Frenchman Springs at its base.

The condition of the road to the foot depends on when it was last bladed and when rain fell. The 2 1/2-mi. road to the lookout on the top is for 4-wheel-drive vehicles and hikers. Most of the surrounding land is public domain. A 586-acre tract including the butte was proposed as a Research

Natural Area. Vegetation is primarily sagebrush-grassland with some Douglas-fir, lodgepole pine, and limber pine.

Deep snows and high winds keep visitors away in winter. Hang gliders soar from the top in summer despite treacherous air currents.

HEADQUARTERS: BLM, Idaho Falls District, 940 Lincoln Road, Idaho Falls, ID 83401; (208) 529-1020.

BOISE FRONT
Multiple ownerships
43,600 acres.

NE of Boise. Extends from Lucky Peak Reservoir NW about 12 mi. to Bogus Basin Road on the W. Crossed by several unpaved roads.

Boise's elevation is about 2,700 ft. The land rises to about 6,000 ft. on Boise Ridge on the N border. The slope between the city and Boise National Forest, about 4 mi. away, is generally called the Boise Front. Ownership is a patchwork. About 11,800 acres are BLM land. About 5,700 acres are administered by Idaho Fish and Game Department, 4,800 acres by Idaho Department of Public Lands. Almost half the area is in private ownerships.

These hills and peaks are a scenic backdrop for the city. Its popularity as a recreation area has grown with the city's population. Protecting this watershed is essential to Boise's water supply. The area is significant wildlife habitat.

Summers are hot and dry, winters mild with cold spells. Annual precipitation is 10 to 20 in., most falling as snow in the higher elevations.

Intensive recreational use began to cause unacceptable damage to the resource. Most destructive was the tremendous increase in use by off-road vehicles. Destruction of vegetation exposed large areas of soil to wind and water erosion. The increased runoff turned ruts into ever-deepening gullies.

All the concerned agencies have joined in adopting travel restrictions. Motorized vehicles are now restricted to designated roads and trails. Some low-standard roads and trails have been closed to vehicles. Several are closed seasonally, either to prevent harassment of wildlife in winter or to prevent erosion when roads are muddy. The regulations and closures are described in BLM's publication. The Boise National Forest also has regulations, described in its Travel Plan (see entry).

The map in BLM's publication shows access routes, hiking trails, and contours.

No campgrounds are on state or federal land.

Eighth Street Road is closed to vehicles in wet weather, because of erosion. Hikers are welcome.

INTERPRETATION
Hulls Gulch Environmental Trail, a National Recreation Trail, begins on Eighth Street Road, a continuation of North Eighth Street in Boise. From end of pavement: 3 1/2 mi. to lower trailhead, 6 1/2 to upper trailhead. Options are a 3 1/2-mi. one-way hike or a 2 1/2-mi. loop trail from the upper trailhead. Interpretive signs. The bottom of the gulch is lined with Rocky Mountain maple, hawthorn, water birch, chokecherry. Spring flowers include arrowleaf balsamroot, phlox, lupine, larkspur. Idaho's state flower, the syringa, is common. Birding is good. Mammals often seen include squirrel, rabbit, mule deer, skunk, porcupine, badger, coyote.

PUBLICATIONS
Off-Road Vehicles on the Boise Front. Leaflet with map.
Hulls Gulch Environmental Trail. Leaflet.

HEADQUARTERS: BLM, Boise District, 3948 Development Ave., Boise, ID 83705; (208) 334-1582.

BOISE NATIONAL FOREST
U.S. Forest Service
2,612,000 acres; 2,959,719 acres within boundaries.

E and NE of Boise. Crossed by SR 21, SR 55.

The Boise attracts three times as many visitors as the adjacent Challis National Forest, eight times as many to campgrounds and other developed sites. Most visitors to the Challis seek the backcountry. On the Boise, they gather at lakes, reservoirs, ski areas, and picnic grounds as well as campgrounds. One reason is the Boise's proximity to Idaho's most populous counties. Another is the accessibility of its primary attractions.

The Boise is part of the huge mass of National Forest land in central Idaho. On its boundaries are the Payette, Sawtooth, and Challis National Forests, the Frank Church - River of No Return Wilderness, and the Sawtooth National Recreation Area. Between the Forest boundary and Boise is the Boise Front (see entry), an area of mixed public and private lands. The 380,000 acres of inholdings within the Forest boundaries are chiefly NE of

Boise, on both sides of SR 21, and to the E, between Boise and the Anderson Ranch Reservoir. Principal uses of the private lands are forestry, recreation homes, and recreation-oriented businesses. A disjunct portion of the Forest is N of Boise, extending S along the West Mountains from Cascade Reservoir to the Payette River.

Terrain is mountainous, the Salmon River Mountains in the N, Boise Mountains in the S, West Mountains in the W. Elevations range from 2,800 ft. to 9,730-ft. Steel Mountain. Most of the Forest is over a mile high. The land has been sculptured by glaciers and streams. There are over 1,400 mi. of fishing streams, over 250 fishing lakes.

Climate is moister than in E central ID. Most areas receive 25 to 50 in. of annual precipitation; the extremes are 15 and 70 in. Temperatures are warmer in the SW, near Boise, declining to the NE. Winters are cold in the mountains, with ample snow for skiing and snowmobiling. Most campgrounds open in June, a few not until July.

Plants: Forest ecosystems range from riparian to subalpine. About 85% of the land area can support trees. About 80% of the forested area is in three cover types: ponderosa pine, lodgepole pine, and Douglas-fir. Moister slopes support grand and subalpine fir and Engelmann spruce. Lower elevations have open grassland and brush. Many brushy areas are an aftermath of fire. Brush types include ninebark, snowberry, ceanothus, willow, twinberry, bitter cherry, chokecherry, alder, bitterbrush, sagebrush, and rabbitbrush.

Birds: 213 species recorded. The list we received doesn't note abundance or seasonality, but it was marked for species of "special interest." These include blue-winged, green-winged, and cinnamon teals; mallard, gadwall, shoveler, Canada goose, goshawk, ferruginous hawk, peregrine and prairie falcons, bald eagle, osprey; blue, ruffed, and spruce grouse; chukar, wild turkey, sandhill crane. A remarkable 12 owl species were listed, with boreal and great gray owls underscored. Pileated woodpecker was underscored, but none of the many passerines. Comparing this list with *Birds of the Challis and Salmon National Forests,* differences include the greater number of waterfowl and shorebird species in the Boise, more species of birds of prey, and more woodpecker species.

Mammals: 70 species recorded. Estimates of big game populations are mule deer (30,000), elk (4,070), black bear (2,190), mountain goat (210), and white-tail deer (210). Species marked "special interest" include river otter, fisher, mink, Canada lynx, beaver, marten, coyote, mountain lion, bobcat, pika. Population of the endangered gray wolf is estimated at between 4 and 9. About 638,000 acres in the NE are potential wolf habitat, and the national Wolf Recovery Team is developing plans to restore the species.

FEATURES

Frank Church - River of No Return Wilderness, an area of 2,361,767 acres, includes 63,594 acres managed by the Boise NF. See entry in Zone 2. The

Boise portion is bounded on the W and S by Landmark Stanley Road, along which are several Forest campgrounds.

OTHER ROADLESS AREAS. The Boise NF has 38 roadless areas, the largest 198,283 acres, totaling about 1,209,000 acres. Nine adjoin roadless areas in adjacent Forests; in seven cases, the other Forests have responsibility for evaluation. The Boise is responsible for two:

Red Mountain, 111,316 acres, plus 4,685 acres in the Challis NF. Access is from SR 21 at Lowman or Stanley by dirt roads, or by any of several trails. Elevations range from 4,500 along the South Fork Payette River to 8,722 ft. at Red Mountain. Lower elevations have steep slopes and canyons; higher are glacial troughlands and alpine lakes in cirque basins. Vegetation in the South Fork Payette River drainage includes open sagebrush-grasslands and moderate to dense stands of ponderosa pine and Douglas-fir. The Clear Creek and Bear Valley areas have scattered to dense stands of lodgepole pine, Douglas-fir, and subalpine fir, with scattered stands of Engelmann spruce in moister areas. Wildlife includes deer, elk, and mountain goat. A section of the South Fork Payette River is being considered for study and possible inclusion in the Wild and Scenic River system.

Recreation activity includes hunting, fishing, hiking, horse riding, and trailbike riding. Recreation use is moderate around the Red Mountain lakes, Warm Spring Canyon, Eightmile Mountain, and trails near Bull Trout Lake, low elsewhere.

Ten Mile; Black Warrior, 138,866 acres between the Middle Fork Boise River and the South Fork Payette River, adjoins the Sawtooth Wilderness. Access is by Forest roads and SR 21, or by trails from the Johnson Creek and Deer Park campgrounds. (The Deer Creek-Johnson Creek trail is not maintained.) Elevations range from 4,700 ft. at the Middle Fork Boise River to 8,765 ft. on Goat Mountain. Borders a section of the South Fork Payette River, also a possible candidate for the Wild and Scenic River system. Terrain sculptured by streams and glaciers. Largely forested, with scattered to dense stands of ponderosa pine or Douglas-fir, dense to open stands of lodgepole pine and subalpine fir interrupted by avalanche paths. Wildlife includes mule deer and elk. Black Warrior and West Warrior creeks have rainbow and Dolly Varden trout. Although the area offers opportunities for hunting, fishing, and backpacking, recreation use is low, about 250 visitor-days per year.

Peace Rock, 198,607 acres between the Middle Fork Payette River and Deadwood River. Road access by South Fork Payette River Road, between Banks on SR 55 and Lowman on SR 21. Also access by trails from the several campgrounds on both sides of the area. Elevations range from 3,600 ft. along Middle Fork to 8,696 ft. on Rice Peak. Steep, highly dissected slopes with sharp ridgetops. Includes sections of the Deadwood River, South Fork Salmon River, and South Fork Payette River, all candidates for the Wild and

Scenic River system. The area adjoins Deadwood Reservoir; 8,139-ft. Peace
Rock is 3 mi. W of the reservoir. Lower elevations have scattered to dense
stands of Douglas-fir and ponderosa pine. Higher slopes have moderate to
dense stands of subalpine fir, scattered stands of lodgepole pine. Wildlife
includes mule deer, elk, bobcat. Despite opportunities for hunting, fishing,
and backpacking, annual recreation use is light, about 850 visitor-days.

Sheep Creek, 93,735 acres, S of the Middle Fork Boise River, about 40 mi.
E of Boise. Road access by the unpaved Middle Fork Boise River Road.
Several campgrounds are along this road and on the Trinity Lakes SE of the
area. The area is bisected by the William H. Pogue Trail, a National Recreation Trail. Elevations range from 3,500 ft. at the Middle Fork to over 8,000
ft. in the Trinities. 8,211-ft. Sheep Mountain is near the E boundary, 8,177-ft.
Rattlesnake Mountain in the SW corner. Steep, forested slopes rise above dry,
rolling hills. Several small lakes are along the southern divide. Opportunities
are good for primitive recreation: hunting, backpacking, horse riding, ski
touring. Present recreation use is about 1,200 visitor-days per year.

Information about the 34 other roadless areas can be obtained at HQ and
Ranger District offices.

PRINCIPAL RECREATION AREAS INCLUDE

Lucky Peak Reservoir, 2,850 acres (see entry), on SR 21 near Boise. Heavily
used for fishing, boating, swimming.

Arrowrock Reservoir, 4,000 acres, on the Middle Fork Boise River Road
near Lucky Peak Reservoir. Fishing, boating, swimming. Campgrounds on
the lake and upstream.

Anderson Ranch Reservoir, 5,000 acres, on the South Fork Boise River.
Camping, fishing, boating, swimming. The South Fork Boise River Canyon
is scenic, with sheer lava walls, overlooks along the road. River has good
fishing but difficult access.

Trinity Lakes, N of Anderson Ranch Reservoir, has several small alpine
lakes, 4 campgrounds.

Ponderosa Pine Scenic Route, SR 21, has several campgrounds, trailheads,
other features.

Middle Fork Payette River has several campgrounds, trailheads, on dirt
roads.

Payette River Scenic Route, SR 55, isn't scenic from Boise almost to Banks,
where it runs in the valley of the Payette River. It's within the Forest for only
about 12 mi. N of Banks, and this is indeed attractive. Riverside campgrounds
are in this area. SR 55 is also access to Forest land on the W side of 30,000-
acre Cascade Reservoir; 3 campgrounds, ramps. (Bureau of Reclamation
campgrounds are also on Cascade Reservoir.)

Warm Lake Area, 26 mi. E of SR 55 at Cascade, is a resort with summer
homes, organization camps, lodges, etc., as well as campgrounds. More isolated campgrounds are on Forest roads radiating from this area.

Sagehen Reservoir, W of Smiths Ferry on SR 55, has 4 campgrounds.

185 ZONE 2

Bogus Basin, 16 mi N of Boise, a ski area.

ACTIVITIES

Camping: 78 campgrounds, 684 sites. Openings generally June or July, closings Sept. or Oct.

Hiking, backpacking: Over 1,000 mi. of trails, including 4 National Recreation Trails. Trail use has been increasing, while budget cuts have sharply reduced trail maintenance. Many trails are in poor condition. Some may be difficult or impassable during snow melt.

Hunting: Chief big game species are mule deer, elk, mountain goat, black bear, mountain lion. Game bird species include blue and spruce grouse, chukar, gray partridge.

Fishing: 1,400 mi. of fishing rivers and streams; over 250 fishing lakes and reservoirs. Chinook salmon and steelhead are returning to the Salmon River basin, under careful management. Principal game species include brook, brown, Dolly Varden, and rainbow trout, kokanee and coho salmon, mountain whitefish, largemouth and smallmouth bass, perch, bluegill, bullhead and channel cat.

Horse riding: Trails are open. Most horse use is incidental to hunting. Fewer outfitters serve the Boise than National Forests to the N and E.

Swimming: Only one designated swimming site (at Warm Lake) but visitors swim in lakes and reservoirs during a short season.

Boating: Chiefly on the larger reservoirs.

Rafting, kayaking: Rivers above the dams are high and dangerous in runoffs, too low later in summer. Part of the Middle Fork Boise is intermediate canoe water after the runoff.

Skiing: Bogus Basin winter sports area has lifts, tows. Season: late Nov.–mid-Apr.

Ski touring: 100 mi. of designated ski trails. Some grooming. Many other opportunities.

PUBLICATIONS

Forest map. $1.
Information pages:
    Fact sheet.
    Recreation sites.
    Scenic areas.
    Historical sites.
    Area history.
    Ghost towns.
    For each Ranger District: trails, campgrounds, boating areas.

REFERENCES

Bluestein, S. L. *Hiking Trails of Southern Idaho.* Caldwell, ID: Caxton Printers, 1981. Pp. 27–42, 46–51, 101–04, 101–26.

Carrey, John, and Cort Conley. *The Middle Fork of the Salmon River and the Sheepeater War.* Cambridge, ID: Backeddy Books, rev. 1980.

Fuller, Margaret. *Trails of Western Idaho.* Edmonds, WA: Signpost Books, 1982. Pp. 92–129.

Maughan, Jackie J. *The Hiker's Guide to Idaho.* Billings, MT; Falcon Press, 1984. Pp. 217–19.

Mitchell, Ron. *50 Eastern Idaho Hiking Trails.* Boulder, CO: Pruett, 1979. Pp. 84–87.

HEADQUARTERS: 1750 Front St., Boise, ID 83702; (208) 334-1516.

RANGER DISTRICTS: Mountain Home R.D., 2180 American Legion Blvd., Mountain Home, ID 83647; (208) 587-7961. Boise R.D., 5493 Warm Springs Ave., Boise, ID 83712; (208) 334-1572. Idaho City R.D., Highway 21, Idaho City, ID 83631; (208) 392-6681. Cascade R.D., Highway 55, Cascade, ID 83611; (208) 382-4271. Lowman R.D., Highway 21, Lowman, ID 83637; (208) 259-3361. Emmett R.D., 1648 N. Washington, Emmett, ID 83617; (208) 365-4382.

BROWNLEE RESERVOIR
Idaho Power Company
15,000 water acres; impoundment 58 mi. long.

Brownlee Dam is on SR 71 at the OR border. Other access from Weiser on US 95.

Brownlee Dam on the Snake River has backed up a narrow pool 58 mi. to a point W of Weiser. Brown, rounded, largely treeless mountains are on both sides, rising from 2,077 ft. at the dam to 5,748-ft. McChord Butte. The ID side has cliffs, slide, boulders, a few sand dunes. Brownlee was completed in 1959. Downstream, Oxbow Dam was completed in 1961, Hells Canyon Dam in 1968. All three are in Hells Canyon, although the term is popularly understood to mean the section within the Hells Canyon National Recreation Area (see entry).

On the OR side, Snake River Road follows the shoreline N from I-84. BLM has a campground on this road, and we saw several informal camping and launch sites. Farewell Bend State Park is 4 mi. SE of Huntington, off old highway 30; it is used by fishermen, boaters, and picnickers as well as campers.

Access on the ID side is more limited. The Power Company maintains Woodhead Park, for camping and water-based recreation site, near the dam.

The ID highway map shows no access at the S end, but an unimproved road runs from near Weiser to a shoreline trailer park.

Fishing: Rated excellent for rainbow trout. Also coho, largemouth and smallmouth bass, bluegill, channel cat, crappie, perch, pumpkinseed.

NEARBY: Oxbow Reservoir (see entry).

PUBLICATIONS: Leaflets.

HEADQUARTERS: 807 W. Idaho, Boise, ID 83721.

CAREY LAKE WILDLIFE MANAGEMENT AREA
Idaho Department of Fish and Game
1,001 acres.

From Carey, 1 mi. NE on US 20/26/93; turn right into parking area.

The highway is the site's NW boundary from a point about 1/2 mi. from Carey to the parking access. Much of the W and S portion is irrigated cropland. The E side, extending S from the parking lot, is wetland: a marsh, a shallow lake, and a deep channel that passes the parking area. The best way to see the area is by canoe, raft, or rowboat.

About 2 mi. of deep channel have been dredged. One of several water sources is a hot spring in the NE section, which flows into the channels. The lake generally freezes over in mid-Nov. except for a small area at the spring.

Fishing is the site's primary use, about 5,000 visits per year, for bass and bluegill. We saw half a dozen fishermen in the channel, wearing waders attached to flotation rings. But the site's primary mission is waterfowl production. Hunter visits are less than 1,000 per year, about 300 of those for dove hunting. An almost equal number of visits were for nonconsumptive purposes, such as birding and hiking.

Birds: About 15,000 waterfowl have been seen at one time, in Dec., just before freeze-up. Seasonally abundant species include coot, pied-billed grebe, spotted sandpiper, California gull, mallard, green-winged teal, Canada goose; red-winged, yellow-headed, and Brewer's blackbirds; mourning dove.

HEADQUARTERS: Idaho Department of Fish and Game, Region 4, 868 E. Main St., Jerome, ID 83338; (208) 324-4350.

CHALLIS NATIONAL FOREST
U.S. Forest Service
2,516,191 acres.

The largest block is N of Stanley and SR 75, W of Challis and US 93. Other blocks on the Lost River Range E of US 93 and on the W side of the Lemhi Range.

Most of central Idaho is National Forest land, with much BLM-managed land in the valleys. The 2 1/2 million acres includes parts of the Salmon, Sawtooth, and Boise National Forests that are administered by the Challis. Several parts of the Challis are administered by the Salmon and the Sawtooth National Recreation Area. The Frank Church - River of No Return Wilderness includes parts of 6 National Forests, but each administers its own. Don't bother trying to sort that out. It's all your land. Choose your area, and the nearest National Forest or BLM office will help.

The Challis offers outstanding opportunities for big game hunting, fishing, and backpacking in a scenic, uncrowded environment. It includes four rugged mountainous areas, including the 25 highest peaks in ID:

Salmon River Mountains, including 782,255 acres of the Frank Church - River of No Return Wilderness. Numerous peaks over 9,000 ft. The Challis administers the Middle Fork of the Salmon River, part of the Wild and Scenic River system.

Lemhi Range, W side, up to the crest. This range, shared with the Salmon and Targhee NFs, has numerous peaks over 10,000 ft.

Lost River and *Pahsimeroi* mountains, parallel to the Lemhi, include 12,662-ft. Mt. Borah, highest in the state, others over 12,000 and 11,000 ft.

Boulder, Pioneer, and *White Knob* mountains, with peaks over 10,000 ft. In addition to its share of the River of No Return Wilderness, the Challis has 28 other roadless areas totaling 1,392,135 acres, bringing the unroaded total to 2,174,390 acres, almost 90% of the Forest. These areas range from 5,000 to 169,420 acres. Most have Forest roads at their boundaries. Of the 28, three were recommended for Wilderness designation: Borah Peak, White Clouds, and Pioneer Mountains.

Climate: Varies with altitude and terrain but is relatively dry, annual precipitation ranging from 6 in. to 30 in. per year. Snowfall averages from 6 in. in valleys and on sheltered slopes to 96 in. at high elevations. The hiking season is May–Nov. at moderate elevations. The high country may be blocked by snow in June.

Forest HQ was unable to supply information on miles of streams and number of lakes, data that most National Forests include in their Environmental Impact Statements. An old document reported 900 mi. of streams. The Forest map shows an extensive dendritic stream pattern with most streams seasonal until they gather near the principal drainages: the Salmon and its Middle Fork, Loon Creek, Pahsimeroi, Garden Creek, Marsh Creek, Big and Little Lost rivers. The map also shows a few widely scattered small lakes.

The only paved highway on Forest land is a 13-mi. V-shaped section of SR 21, the Ponderosa Pine Scenic Route from Stanley to Boise, usually closed in winter. Forest system roads total 1,705 mi., but few are rated all-weather. Maintenance of many miles hasn't kept up with increasing use. Headquarters calls the road system "deteriorating." Drive with caution. Ask about road conditions before venturing far into the backcountry.

Recreation use of the Forest is relatively light, about 600,000 visitor-days per year. Only about 15% of this occurs at developed sites. People seeking campgrounds and other facilities are likely to stop at the adjacent Sawtooth National Recreation Area. Developments on the Challis are concentrated in two accessible areas near the NRA: 6 campgrounds on or near SR 21 W of Stanley, 15 in the Yankee Fork District, about 11 mi. E of Stanley. The only other areas receiving much visitor impact are the Middle Fork of the Salmon River, where the growing popularity of rafting has required quotas, and the Trail Creek-Copper Basin area E of Sun Valley, reached by SR 75 from Ketchum.

Outfitters, other than those offering rafting on the Middle Fork, do most of their business with hunters. A few provide guide service to fishermen. No doubt some would provide pack trips in summer, but the demand is small.

Borah Peak and Soldier Lakes are popular with backpackers. Otherwise, backpacking activity is light and widespread, though usually associated with streams and lakes.

The Forest has 1,600 mi. of foot and horse trails, half within the River of No Return Wilderness. Like the roads, many trails are deteriorating. Some, little used for recreation, aren't maintained. Some popular trails, especially those leading into the Wilderness and to lake basins, need more maintenance than they get. Hikers are most likely to encounter problems during the runoff from melting snow.

Plants: Principal Forest habitats are alpine tundra, above timberline; Douglas-fir, lodgepole pine, sagebrush, grasses, and riparian. Less than half of the non-Wilderness area is forested. Only 340,000 acres are deemed suitable for commercial timber production, and well over half of these are on slopes so steep as to make logging difficult. The most extensive habitat, at lower elevations, is sagebrush-grassland.

Birds: 247 species reported. A checklist of 230 species is available: *Birds of the Salmon and Challis National Forests.* See the Salmon NF entry for abundant and common species.

Mammals: 63 species recorded. Big game species include elk, mule deer,

IDAHO 66

mountain goat, bighorn sheep, pronghorn, black bear, moose. The list provided by the Salmon NF is applicable here.

FEATURES

Frank Church - River of No Return Wilderness, 2,361,767 acres, largest Wilderness in the Lower 48. Includes portions of 6 National Forests, including 782,255 acres on the Challis. Each Forest administers its own portion, within the framework of a management plan. See entry in Zone 2.

The Challis portion lies N of SRs 21 and 75 and W of US 93. The nearest highway approach to the Wilderness boundary is W of Stanley, at the tip of the arc in SR 21. Here there are campgrounds and trailheads. Beyond, unpaved Forest roads lead along the Wilderness perimeter and into a large mining area excluded from the Wilderness. Other access roads are through the Yankee Fork area off US 93 E of Stanley and others W of Challis. The Challis portion is within three Ranger Districts: Challis, Middle Fork, and Yankee Fork.

Middle Fork, Salmon River is a National Wild River for 104 mi. from its source to its confluence with the Salmon—except for a 1-mi. Scenic River segment near Dagger Falls that has the only road access and two campgrounds. A popular whitewater stream requiring advanced skills. A permit system limits the number of private parties. Permits are awarded to qualified persons by lot. A number of licensed commercial outfitters offer float trips of 5 to 6 days. For permit information: Middle Fork Ranger District. For outfitter information, write

Idaho Outfitters and Guides Association
P.O. Box 95
Boise, ID 83701

Western River Guides Association
994 Denver St.
Salt Lake City, UT 84111

OTHER ROADLESS AREAS:

Borah Peak, 129,581 acres in the Lost River Range, a proposed Wilderness. 34 mi. S of Challis. Access from US 93 by Double Springs Pass Road and other roads. Several hundred people come here each year to climb Borah Peak, 12,662 ft., highest in the State. Steep slopes, large cirque basins, narrow canyon bottoms. The alpine zone has plant species typical of tundra 2,400 mi. to the N. Below, forest species include subalpine fir, whitebark pine, Engelmann spruce, and Douglas-fir. Sagebrush-grassland on the lower slopes. Several small high mountain lakes, some with fish. Wildlife includes elk, mule deer, bighorn sheep, pronghorn. Recreation activity includes fishing, hunting, and camping, in addition to climbing. Total is 13,000 visitor-days per year, high for the region. Because of snow, most climbing is in July–Aug. There is no maintained trail, but the route is mapped and easy to see. The round-trip hike takes about 12 hours, ascending 5,000 ft. in 3 mi. It requires cleated boots but no climbing gear, unless snow or ice are present. As on any high mountain, hikers should be prepared for any kind of weather and know what to do.

Pioneer Mountains, 169,420 acres, plus 116,350 acres in the Sawtooth National Forest. A proposed Wilderness. 20 mi. SW of Mackay; 6 mi. E of Ketchum. Access by local and Forest roads from US 93 and SR 75, some Forest roads penetrating the area. The Pioneer Range is Idaho's second highest, with elevations to 12,000 ft. Alpine meadows under barren summits. Basins, flats, and benches; steep, rocky walls topped by peaks. Some glacial cirques have vertical relief of 3,000 to 4,000 ft. Numerous streams and mountain lakes. Western spruce-fir forest, with sagebrush steppe below. Mule deer, pronghorn, and elk summer in the area. Mountain goat are year-round residents. Bighorn sheep are seen occasionally. Blue and spruce grouse are common. Recreation activity includes hunting, backpacking, climbing, fishing, some ski touring, snowmobiling.

Pahsimeroi Mountains, 72,107 acres. Also in the Lost Peak Range, N of the Borah Peak area. 11 mi. SE of Challis. Access from jeep roads and Forest system roads along US 93 and county roads in the Pahsimeroi River Valley. Terrain and vegetation are similar to the Borah Peak area, with peaks at about 10,000 ft. Perhaps because better-known areas are nearby, this one has little recreational use, although there are good opportunities for hunting, fishing, hiking, climbing, ski touring, and snowmobiling.

Hanson Lakes, 13,719 acres, plus 54,574 acres in the Sawtooth and Boise NFs and Sawtooth National Recreational Area. 9 mi. W of Stanley, it is S of and adjacent to SR 21. The Sawtooth Mountain Range runs NW through the area, ending near SR 21. The W side has heavily timbered U-shaped valleys, canyons, and moraines that drop steeply to Canyon Creek. 12 high mountain lakes are in cirque basins. Forest species are ponderosa pine with Douglas-fir on lower slopes, Engelmann spruce and subalpine fir up to timberline. On the colder E side is a large morainal area of rolling terrain, wet meadows, small pocket lakes, and dry benches. Lower slopes on this side are dominated by lodgepole pine with intermixed Douglas-fir, subalpine fir, and Engelmann spruce, with whitebark pine and subalpine fir in open stands up to timberline.

Recreation activity is relatively low in comparison with the adjoining Sawtooth Wilderness: about 8,000 visitor-days per year. Most activity is in the NRA portion: camping, fishing, and hiking, favored destinations being Bridal Veil Falls; Hansen, Marten, Elizabeth, Kelly, and Zumwalt lakes; and Bench Lakes.

Information about other roadless areas is available at HQ and Ranger Districts.

Yankee Fork District is a principal recreation area. The Custer Motorway loop connects US 93 at Challis and SR 75 at Sunbeam. High, rugged peaks, alpine lakes, cirque basins, conifer forest, sagebrush-grasslands. Elevations from the Salmon River to above 10,000 ft. Numerous streams and lakes. Two abandoned mining towns; Custer Museum, Yankee Dredge exhibit. Opportunities for camping (15 campgrounds), backpacking (9 major trailheads), hunting, fishing, horse riding.

INTERPRETATION

Custer Museum in the Yankee Fork area has exhibits, talks, information. The Forest has no nature trails, campfire programs, or other naturalist activities.

ACTIVITIES

Camping: 32 campgrounds, 279 sites. June–Sept. Most camping is at informal sites.

Hiking, backpacking: 15 of the 24 principal trailheads are in the Lost River and Yankee Fork areas. Half of the 1,600 mi. of trails are in the Frank Church - River of No Return Wilderness. The most-used trails are those leading to the Wilderness. The Knapp Creek-Loon Creek and Mill Creek Lake trails have been designated National Recreation Trails.

Hunting: Elk, mule deer, black bear, mountain goat, bighorn sheep, pronghorn, grouse. Most out-of-state hunters use professional guides.

Fishing: Chinook salmon and steelhead are returning to the Middle Fork; restrictions. Many streams and mountain lakes. Brook, cutthroat, rainbow, and Dolly Varden trout; whitefish.

Horse riding: All trails open. List of outfitters available.

Rafting: Middle Fork, June–Sept. Rapids to Class IV. Outfitters offer float trips. Private parties must have permits, awarded by lot, and show competence.

Ski touring: Dec.–Apr. Many possible routes, but no groomed trails.

PUBLICATIONS

Forest map. $1.
Borah Peak hiking guide; leaflet.
Birds of the Challis and Salmon National Forests.

REFERENCES

Bluestein, S. R. *Hiking Trails of Southern Idaho.* Caldwell, ID: Caxton Printers, 1981. Pp. 135–46, 160–62, 167–68.
Carrey, John, and Cort Conley. *The Middle Fork and the Sheepeater War.* Cambridge, ID: Backeddy Books, rev. 1980.
Fuller, Margaret. *Trails of Western Idaho.* Edmonds, WA: Signpost Books, 1982. Pp. 180–219.
Maughan, Jackie J. *The Hiker's Guide to Idaho.* Billings, MT: Falcon Press, 1984. Pp. 67–70, 89–95, 134–45, 148–79, 184–97, 211–14.
Mitchell, Ron. *50 Eastern Idaho Hiking Trails.* Boulder, CO: Pruett, 1979. Pp. 20–25, 30–35.

HEADQUARTERS: P.O. Box 404, Challis, ID 83226; (208) 879-2285.

RANGER DISTRICTS: Middle Fork R.D., Box 750, Challis, ID 83226; (208) 879–4321. Challis R.D., Box 337, Challis, ID 83226; (208) 879-5204. Yankee Fork R.D., H/C 67, Box 650, Clayton, ID 83227; (208) 838-2201. Lost River R.D., P.O. Box 507, Mackay, ID 83251; (208) 588-2224.

CHALLIS AREA
U.S. Bureau of Land Management
Indeterminate acreage.

From Challis, SW on SR 75 or SE on US 93.

S of Challis, the land opens into a broad sagebrush-grassland valley. E of US 93 are the Lost River Range and Pahsimeroi Mountains, including Borah Peak, 12,662 ft., highest point in ID. SR 75, the Sawtooth Scenic Highway, branches off to the SW and W, following the Salmon River with the Salmon River Mountains on the N. The area between the two routes is hilly to mountainous, with no well-defined ridgelines. The valleys are at elevations between 5,200 and 6,000 ft. Highest point in the land between is 9,652-ft. Lone Pine Peak, about 11 mi. S of Challis.

This triangle, about 30 mi. N–S, 25 mi. wide at its base, is mostly BLM-managed land. The mountains to the E and W are in the Challis National Forest.

The principal recreation feature of the area is the Upper Salmon River, 100 mi. of it within BLM's Salmon District, much of it close to the highway. BLM maintains 15 campgrounds and river access points. The Scenic Highway continues into the Sawtooth National Recreation Area (see entry).

BLM has both developed and primitive campsites at Herd Lake and Upper Lake Creek. Roads to these and several other BLM campsites don't appear on the highway map but are shown on a BLM map available at Salmon. The Upper Lake Creek site adjoins a large BLM Wilderness Study Area.

Most visitors drive the Sawtooth Scenic Highway, perhaps camping, fishing, or boating. For campers, hikers, hunters, or fishermen interested in the backcountry, we suggest stopping at the BLM's Salmon office for a detailed map.

NEARBY: Mackay Reservoir, 1,000 water acres, is further S on US 93, about 3 mi. N of Mackay. BLM has a campground on the reservoir. Fishing, boating, swimming. Two BLM Wilderness Study Areas are nearby as well as the Challis Wild Horse Area and canyon access to the National Forest.

ACTIVITIES
Camping: 7 developed campgrounds, 3 primitive sites, many informal sites.
Hiking, backpacking: Primitive roads and jeep tracks.
Fishing: River and small lakes.
Canoeing, rafting, kayaking: River conditions vary from section to section and seasonally. Some portions are suitable for open canoe. Some others are considered unrunnable at high water. Consult BLM office.

PUBLICATION: *Challis Planning Unit; Off-Road Vehicle Travel Plan.*

HEADQUARTERS: BLM, Salmon, District, P.O. Box 430, Salmon, ID 83467; (208) 756-2201.

CHINA CUP BUTTE
U.S. Bureau of Land Management
1,940 acres.

About 17 mi. SE of Craters of the Moon National Monument. 8 mi. S of Big Southern Butte. Access by BLM roads; BLM map and high-clearance vehicle needed.

We don't include sites not accessible by car unless they have exceptional qualities. An aerial photo persuaded us to mention this one.
It's an almost perfect circle, a volcanic crater 1,260 ft. across, 100 ft. deep, surrounded by a moatlike depression.
The surrounding area has other volcanic features, including smaller and less regular craters.

HEADQUARTERS: Idaho Falls District, BLM, 940 Lincoln Rd., Idaho Falls, ID 83401; (208) 529-1020.

CRATERS OF THE MOON NATIONAL MONUMENT
National Park Service
53,545 acres.

On US 20/26/93, 18 mi. SW of Arco.

The Monument is part of a much larger area of lava flows that began about 15,000 years ago and continued intermittently. Of the eight major periods of activity, the most recent occurred about 2,000 years ago. Geologists expect the eruptions to resume some day.

The entire area covers hundreds of square miles, but in much of it the visitor may not recognize the signs of volcanism. Most of the older flows are now covered with vegetation. The Monument is in a more recent area that displays a great variety of volcanic phenomena. This is the place to learn about cinder cones and spatter cones, aa and pahoehoe, lava tubes and ice caves, rafted blocks, lava bombs, and tree molds. At first it appears to be a black, forbidding wasteland. Then one sees patches of wildflowers growing on beds of cinders, others rooted in crevices. The dark landscape is broken by vegetated kipukas, oases where a lava flow was diverted around part of an older one.

About 15,000 years ago, a great fissure opened, 65 mi. long. When a fissure first opens, there is usually an outpouring of lava and a "curtain of fire." Soon, as the eruptions diminish, sections of the fissure close, leaving fire fountains around which cinder cones form. Here one can see a chain of cinder cones extending to the SE. (See entry, Great Rift, in Zone 4.)

The Monument is open all year. Most visitors come in summer. The campground is sometimes full. Almost all visitors drive the loop road, stopping at the several parking areas on the loop and spur roads. From here short trails lead to major features: cinder cones, caves, etc. Visitors who have spent the night elsewhere seldom arrive before 9:30 A.M. From dawn until 9:30 few people are on the trails.

Elevation at HQ is 5,900 ft.

Climate: Average annual precipitation is 17 to 19 in., most of it falling as winter snow. Spring weather is unpredictable: daytime temperatures ranging from the 30s to the 60s; nights often below freezing; strong winds; sometimes a late snowstorm. Summer days are warm, daytime temperatures sometimes peaking in the 90s, more often in the 80s and 70s; summer nights are cool. Strong afternoon winds are common in summer, with occasional thunderstorms. (Visitor: "Does the wind always blow like this?" Ranger: "No, sometimes it's worse.") Fall days and nights are cooler. Winters are cold, average daytime temperatures near freezing, nights often below zero. Blizzards occur. The loop road is closed by snow from about Nov. 15 to Apr. 15.

Plants: Checklist available. More than 200 species identified. The limber pine is the most prominent of the few trees growing in this environment; it grows chiefly on N-facing slopes of cinder cones and where moisture conditions favor growth. Shrubs include big sagebrush, antelope bitterbrush, rubber rabbitbrush, syringa.

The wildflowers fascinate the visitor, especially the "cinder gardens." Open cinder slopes are covered with masses of low-growing herbs that blossom colorfully in season. Plants of the cinder slopes include eriogonum, bitterroot lewisia, and dwarf monkeyflower. Other flowering plants seen include scabland penstemon, Anderson larkspur, dusty maiden, scorpionweed, blazing-star, arrowleaf balsamroot.

Birds: Checklist available. Seasonally common species include Brewer's blackbird, mountain bluebird, black-capped and mountain chickadees, chukar, American crow, mourning dove, golden eagle, American kestrel, house finch, northern flicker, dusky and olive-sided flycatchers, American goldfinch, black-headed and pine grosbeaks, blue and sage grouse, northern harrier, red-tailed and sharp-shinned hawks, dark-eyed junco, horned lark, black-billed magpie, western meadowlark, common nighthawk, red-breasted nuthatch, great horned and long-eared owls, gray partridge, western wood-pewee, Say's phoebe, poor-will, common raven, American robin, pine siskin, Townsend's solitaire. Sparrows: black-throated, Brewer's, chipping, fox, lark, song, vesper, white-crowned. European starling, violet-green swallow, western tanager, sage thrasher, green-tailed and rufous-sided towhees, warbling vireo, MacGillivray's and Wilson's warblers, hairy and Lewis' woodpeckers; house, rock, and winter wrens.

Mammals: Common species include little brown bat, Great Basin pocket mouse, deer mouse, mountain vole, bushytail woodrat, pika, whitetail jackrabbit, pygmy rabbit, porcupine, red squirrel, yellow pine chipmunk, shorttail weasel, red fox, coyote, badger, mule deer.

Reptiles and amphibians: Common species include western toad, western skink, gopher snake, rubber boa, western rattlesnake.

FEATURES

Wilderness Area, 43,243 acres, adjoins BLM's 322,450-acre Great Rift area proposed for Wilderness designation (see entry). That's impressive, but few people have ever tried to cross the area. Indeed, fewer than 200 people a year spend a night in the Monument's wilderness. They may not get much sleep; finding a spot to lie down is difficult.

Only three trails enter the area, and those for short distances. Beyond that the going is rough. "Aa" is Hawaiian for "hard on the feet," an understatement for the jumble of jagged, abrasive lava. Deer trails are travel routes—if you can find them and want to go their way. Skiing and snowshoeing when snow blankets the area is more feasible, but not without hazards.

All Wilderness hikers are asked to register. Overnighters must have permits.

Caves: When we visited years ago, we entered one cave by descending a long ladder, coming nose-to-beak with a perched raven on the way; we were told there's now a stairway. In the Boy Scout Cave, we walked and slipped on a floor of ice. Several other caves can be entered, some requiring flashlights and a bit of scrambling and ducking.

Spatter and cinder cones are prominent features. Trails ascend several, offering fine views.

Trails to many other features: tree molds, Devils Orchard, etc.

INTERPRETATION

Visits should begin at the *visitor center* near the entrance. Exhibits and a film show how eruptions formed the many features of the area. Rangers answer questions. Literature.

Guided walks are offered morning and evening in summer. Also *campfire programs* near the campground.

Loop drive, 7 mi., passes many of the Monument's features. Spurs to parking at special areas.

Nature trails at the Caves, Devils Orchard, North Crater Flow.

ACTIVITIES

Camping: One campground, 51 sites. We suggest registering for a site on arrival. Winter camping is permitted, but the area isn't plowed and snow may be a problem.

Hiking, backpacking: 8 mi. of trails, plus open hiking in the Wilderness Area.

Ski touring: Chiefly on the unplowed Loop Road, Dec.–Mar. In the Wilderness as conditions permit.

PUBLICATIONS

Leaflet with map.
Guide. (Newsprint leaflet.)
Plant checklist.
Wildlife checklist.
Schedule of walks and tours.
Leaflets:
  The Cave Trail.
  Devils Orchard Trail.
Mimeo pages:
  General information.
  Wilderness travel.
  Climate data.
  Skiing information.
  Bibliography.
  Publications list.

REFERENCES:

Around the Loop. Guide to roads and trails. Publication of the Craters of the Moon Natural History Association. Pamphlet, 20 pp. $3.

HEADQUARTERS: Box 29, Arco, ID 83213; (208) 527-3257.

FRANK CHURCH - RIVER OF NO RETURN
WILDERNESS

U.S. Forest Service

2,230,300 acres.

Access from US 93 on the E, US 95 and SR 55 on the W, SR 21 on the
S. By boat on the N.

This is the largest Wilderness in the Lower 48, 90 mi. long, 56 mi. wide. It
was established by the Idaho Wilderness Act of 1980, which also brought
portions of the Salmon River into the Wild and Scenic River system. The
Wilderness includes portions of 6 National Forests: the Payette, Challis,
Salmon, Boise, Bitterroot, and Nez Perce. Each administers its own portion
within the framework of a master plan.

The best and most current information about any part of the Wilderness
can be obtained from the Forest HQ and Ranger District responsible for that
area. What we provide here is an overview.

It is a Wilderness with unique and peculiar qualities. Despite its huge size,
no interior point is really remote. Although Wildernesses are supposedly
closed to motor vehicles, the legislation specifically allows jet boats to operate
on the Salmon River, and continued use of airstrips that have over 4,000
landings and takeoffs per year. Although the Wilderness has relatively few
visitors, limiting river traffic has become a serious concern, and trash, trampling, and sanitation are growing problems at some campsites. Nonetheless,
it's easy to find beauty and solitude.

With a few exceptions, no main highway approaches closer than 5 mi. to
the Wilderness boundary. A Wilderness is, by definition, roadless, so roads
are often the boundaries, in this case unpaved Forest roads. When the Wilderness boundary was drawn, existing dead-end roads that penetrated the area
were accommodated by "cherry-stemming," drawing the Wilderness boundary around them. Accommodation also had to be made for a few private and
state landholdings, including several resorts, and for existing mines and
claims. Also accommodated were 24 airstrips used by outfitters to transport
clients and supplies and by State and Forest personnel for firefighting and
other functions. More than half of these airstrips are on private inholdings.

Elevations range from 2,200 ft. on the Salmon River to over 10,000 ft. in
the Big Horn Crags. Terrain is rugged and mountainous, cut by deep canyons.
The Salmon River Canyon is the second deepest gorge in the United States,
its steep walls sharply limiting access or escape.

Annual precipitation ranges from 14 in. at low elevations to nearly 60 in.
in the high country, most of the latter falling as snow. Summers are generally

dry. Temperatures often exceed 100°F at low elevations. Winters are long and severe.

The Wilderness has over 400 lakes and 685 streams. We could find no estimate of total stream mileage, but it is clearly in the thousands. The map shows almost all streams as perennial. Efforts are gradually succeeding to restore populations of chinook salmon and steelhead to the Salmon and its tributaries. Steelhead runs now attract fishermen from throughout the United States. Fish productivity of high wilderness lakes and streams is variable but, in sum, not high. Most lakes require stocking.

Principal game fish species include rainbow and cutthroat trout, mountain whitefish, chinook salmon, and steelhead. Smallmouth bass and white sturgeon are also present.

Campgrounds, trailheads, and outfitter bases are on peripheral and cherry-stemmed roads. Access from main routes is by unpaved Forest roads, some of them low standard.

Only about 35,000 visitors per year come here, 40% of them from nearby. The principal activities, camping, hiking, and horse riding, are often incidental to fishing and hunting. The most concentrated visitor activity is rafting on the Salmon and Middle Fork; demand has made it necessary to limit the number of floaters. Thus far no limits have been placed on backpackers and horsepackers, but trampling and trash at popular mountain lakes and outfitter camps are becoming a problem. Many backcountry campsites can be visited and cleaned only once each year or two. Regulations are in the making.

Hunters and fishermen unfamiliar with the area are often advised to hire an outfitter-guide. More than 88 licensed outfitters operate here, offering float trips, jet boat excursions, hunting and fishing expeditions, camping, backpacking, horsepacking, camera safaris, and ski touring. Their services have made many outings pleasant and successful. As Wilderness use increases, Forest managers are receiving complaints from private parties about conflicts with outfitters over campsites and other facilities.

Trails: Wilderness access is from 66 recognized trailheads. Over 2,500 mi. of trails were present before the Wilderness was established. Some were travel routes of native Indians. Some evolved from game trails. Some served mines. Many were built for firefighting and other services. Few were planned and built with recreation in mind.

Two trail categories remain in the system. *Main trails* are primary routes into or through the area. Usually they are in drainages of large rivers or creeks or along major ridgetops. Serving both foot and horse traffic, they lead to popular hunting, fishing, and camping sites. Efforts are made to keep them in service. *Primitive trails* are less-used secondary routes. Within this network are 23 trailless areas of more than 10,000 acres each, totaling 588,000 acres. Boundary configuration is such, however, that no point in the Wilderness is more than 12 mi. from a trailhead.

Each Forest is responsible for the trails in its portion, as well as its other trails. Popular trails have first claim on limited maintenance funds, and most such trails are outside the Wilderness. Maintenance of Wilderness trails is generally limited to clearing downed trees and repairing impassable sections of the most-used trails. Some trails in remote areas have been abandoned, no longer maintained, signed, or mapped.

Plants: Each of the six National Forests has information characterizing its plant communities. In the Wilderness, these range from ponderosa pine/ bluebunch wheatgrass or Idaho fescue, and Douglas-fir/ninebark or snowberry at lower elevations to subalpine fir types above 5,000 ft., near-alpine conditions on the highest slopes. Wildfires have created brushfields, large stands of lodgepole pine, and extensive snag patches. Most are lightning-caused and limited to less than an acre. Present policy is to allow naturally occurring wildfires to burn if conditions are favorable. The annual total burned is less than 6,000 acres. Prescribed burning has been urged as necessary to maintain the natural ecosystem.

Birds: 242 species have been recorded. For the birder entering the Wilderness, the most useful list can be provided by the National Forest responsible for the area to be visited. See entries.

Mammals: 75 species recorded. Principal big game species are mule and whitetail deer, elk, bighorn sheep, mountain goat, black bear, mountain lion, moose. Common mammal species include various bats, coyote, yellowbelly marmot, Columbian ground squirrel, golden-mantled and red squirrels, least and yellow pine chipmunks, northern pocket gopher, deer mouse, beaver, bushytail woodrat, meadow and mountain voles, pika, snowshoe hare, blacktail jackrabbit. Numerous wolf sightings indicate the presence of this endangered species.

FEATURES

Salmon River: See entries, Salmon River, Salmon National Forest. 91 mi. of the Salmon Wild and Scenic River are within the River of No Return Wilderness. A scenic road parallels the river from North Fork to Corn Creek. This section is floated by kayaks and small rafts. The next 79 mi. are in a deep canyon through rugged and roadless terrain, with rapids and other hazards demanding high skill and good equipment. Rafting this section has become so popular as to create problems of litter and sanitation at campsites. Forest policy is to limit the number of permits issued to outfitters and private parties. Jet boats are permitted to travel upstream in this section, with inevitable complaints from floaters about noise and near-misses inconsistent with a Wilderness experience.

Middle Fork Salmon River is also a popular whitewater stream requiring high skill and good equipment. See entries, Salmon River and Payette National Forest. 105 mi. are within the Wild and Scenic River system. Floating is restricted by permits, divided between commercial and private users. Jet boats do not operate here.

Selway River: 18 1/2 mi. within the River of No Return Wilderness are part of the Wild and Scenic River system. See entry, Bitterroot National Forest.

PUBLICATIONS
Wilderness maps: N and S halves; 2-sided; 1:100,000 scale; multicolored; contour lines; waterproof paper. $1 each.
A User's Guide. Frank Church - River of No Return Wilderness. Pamphlet, 42 pp.
Information page.
The Middle Fork of the Salmon River. Map. $1.

REFERENCES
Bluestein, S. R. *Hiking Trails of Southern Idaho.* Caldwell, ID: Caxton Printers, 1981. Pp. 56–84.
Maughan, Jackie J. *The Hiker's Guide to Idaho.* Billings, MT: Falcon Press, 1984. Pp. 54–87, 84–95, 100–10.
Mitchell, Ron. *50 Eastern Idaho Hiking Trails.* Boulder, CO: Pruett, 1979. Pp. 80–87.

HEADQUARTERS: HQ and Ranger District offices of the Nez Perce NF (Zone 1); Boise, Payette, Challis, and Salmon NFs (Zone 2); and Bitterroot NF (Montana Zone 1).

HELLS CANYON RESERVOIR
Idaho Power Company
2,400 water acres; impoundment 25 mi. long.

Between Oxbow Dam and Hells Canyon Dam on the Snake River, at the Oregon border. Principal access to the ID side is from OR by a bridge below Oxbow Dam. From here a paved shoreline road at the foot of the Seven Devils Mountains leads to Hells Canyon Dam. A secondary road in ID at the S end of Hells Canyon National Recreation Area drops down to the shoreline road. This is shown on the highway map as "Kleinschmidt Grade; inquire locally."

Hells Canyon Dam has backed up a narrow pool about 25 mi. to Oxbow Dam in a canyon nearly 8,000 ft. deep. Slopes on both sides are steep and relatively treeless.

The Power Company maintains Copperfield Park on the OR side at Oxbow Dam; camping and boat launch. The Forest Service has trails and boat launch below Hells Canyon Dam on the OR side.

On the ID side, the Power Company maintains Hells Canyon Park, 10 mi.

N of the bridge. Camping and boat launching. Beyond Hells Canyon Dam is a fishing and backpacking trail into the National Recreation Area.

NEARBY: Oxbow Reservoir; Hells Canyon National Recreation Area (see entries).

PUBLICATIONS: Leaflets.

HEADQUARTERS: 1220 W. Idaho, Boise, ID 83721.

LUCKY PEAK RESERVOIR
U.S. Army Corps of Engineers
2,850 water acres.

From Boise, 10 mi. SE on SR 21.

An overlook near the dam gives an extensive view of the reservoir, surrounded by rolling to steep hills with scanty vegetation, basalt cliffs. We saw it on a summer weekend, crowded with boats, swimmers lounging on rafts anchored along the shore. It's popular for water-based recreation, but it doesn't resemble a natural area. We weren't tempted to launch our small boat, but perhaps there are quieter, more natural spots on the upper arms of the impoundment.

Lucky Peak State Park, near the dam, is for day use only.

MAGIC RESERVOIR
U.S. Bureau of Land Management
Indeterminate acreage.

From Shoshone, N about 18 mi. on SR 75. Left to dam and Magic Reservoir.

We turned off the highway along the Big Wood River, which flows from the reservoir below the dam. Along the river are two or three informal shaded campsites used mostly by fishermen. The road turns N along the W side of the reservoir. After driving about 8 mi. from the highway on good road, we saw a cluster of RVs at the shore and took the next right turn, marked "West Magic Reservoir Recreation Club," which led to a small resort: a few dozen buildings and an airstrip. Before entering this settlement we turned right again on a rutted but passable dirt track. In less than a mile, it took us to the RVs we'd seen.

All belonged to fishermen from Bellevue, Shoshone, and other nearby communities. They said fishing is usually good. Our out-of-state tags aroused polite curiosity. The amenities consisted of a latrine and a boat ramp. Later we saw several rough tracks leading to other shoreline points. BLM has other sites with ramps and latrines, but one can camp almost anywhere.

We saw but didn't investigate a larger resort development, Magic City, on the E side, where boats can be rented. The shortest access from a main highway is on the N, where Hot Springs Landing is only 1/2 mi. off US 20.

The main body of the reservoir is 6 mi. long, up to 2 1/2 mi. wide, with a mean depth of 114 ft.

The surrounding land, much of it public domain, is flat to rolling, semiarid. The most attractive area we saw is in the N, where a narrow arm of the lake lies between steep bluffs.

Not great scenery, but it's quiet and uncrowded. Few people are here on weekdays, and one can always find a weekend campsite.

Birds: Hiking for several miles along the shore, we saw marshy stretches with abundant waterfowl and shorebirds. Several hundred Canada geese with many goslings were in a cove. Myrtle Point was white with a mass of gulls. Also seen: short-eared owl, willet, killdeer, American avocet, meadowlark, yellow-headed and Brewer's blackbirds, brown-headed cowbird, western grebe, mallard, redhead, kestrel, American robin, American crow, and a prairie falcon seizing a snake. Our BLM advisor said Seagull Point, not named on the map but signed on the road, is the best area for viewing waterfowl.

Fishing: Rainbow and brown trout, yellow perch, whitefish, sucker.

REFERENCE: *Magic Reservoir Fishing and Recreation Map.* Includes informa-
tive text. Intermountain Geographics, P.O. Box 324, Boise, ID 83701.
$5.50.

HEADQUARTERS: Shoshone District Office, BLM, 400 W. F St., Shoshone, ID
83352; (208) 886-2206.

OXBOW RESERVOIR
Idaho Power Company
1,200 water acres; impoundment 13 mi. long.

Between Brownlee Dam and Oxbow Dam on the Snake River, at the OR border. Principal access points are on the OR side. The Idaho Power Company maintains Woodhead Park, a campground with boat launch on the ID side, off SR 71, just upstream from Brownlee Dam.

Oxbow Dam has backed up a narrow pool 13 mi. to Brownlee Dam. Brown, rounded, largely treeless mountains are on both sides, rising from 1,820 ft. at the dam to 5,748-ft. McChord Butte. The ID side has cliffs, slide, boulders, a few sand dunes. Brownlee, Oxbow, and Hells Canyon impoundments are all within Hells Canyon, although the term is popularly understood to mean the section within the Hells Canyon National Recreation Area (see entry).

NEARBY: Brownlee Reservoir; Hells Canyon National Recreational Area (see entries).

ACTIVITIES
Camping: McCormick Park.
Fishing: Rainbow trout, coho, largemouth and smallmouth bass, bluegill, channel cat, crappie, perch, pumpkinseed.

PUBLICATIONS: Leaflets.

HEADQUARTERS: 1220 W. Idaho, Boise, ID 83721.

PAYETTE NATIONAL FOREST
U.S. Forest Service
2,314,436 acres; 2,425,773 acres within boundaries.

Two principal portions. The larger lies E of US 95; the Salmon River is its N boundary. NW boundary of the smaller is on or near the Snake River; it extends SE from Hells Canyon across US 95 and S to the vicinity of Cascade Reservoir.

This country is wild, rugged. The main body of the Forest lies on the Salmon River Mountains. Its E portion, 781,717 acres, is within the Frank Church - River of No Return Wilderness, for which we have a separate entry in Zone 2. 21 other roadless areas including 1,079,269 acres bring the roadless total to 80% of the Forest.

Its N boundary is the Salmon Wild and Scenic River, not accessible by road within the Payette. The Nez Perce National Forest is across the deep canyon. The Salmon National Forest is on the SW boundary of the Forest, the Boise NF on the S. On the NW is the Snake Wild and Scenic River, the Hells Canyon National Recreation Area, and the Wallowa-Whitman National Forest. Within the Payette are portions of two other Wild and Scenic Rivers, the

Middle Fork Salmon and Rapid rivers. Portions of French Creek, South Fork Salmon River, and Secesh River are proposed for inclusion in the Wild and Scenic system, their corridors totaling over 40,000 acres. The Forest has over 1,500 miles of fishing streams, over 150 fishing lakes.

Most of the Payette's roadless areas are divided by roads, and many roadless area boundaries have been drawn to exclude or "cherry-stem" roads. There are 2,500 mi. of roads. 90% of the W side and 40% of the E side are within 3 mi. of a road. However, many of these roads were built for logging service and, no longer needed, are closed permanently or seasonally. A few light-duty roads provide passenger car access to some of the principal campgrounds, trailheads, and fishing waters.

Total recreation use of the Forest is about 628,000 visitor-days per year. Less than one-fourth of this usage is in developed sites. Several popular resort areas are close by. The town of McCall is at the foot of Payette Lake. Little Payette Lake is nearby, Cascade Reservoir 35 mi. S. Summer homes and other recreation developments are along US 95, which parallels the Little Salmon River. Many Forest users sleep outside, come in to hike or hunt or fish by day.

Elevations range from 1,500 ft. in Hells Canyon to over 9,500 ft. in the River of No Return Wilderness. Most of the Forest is above 6,000 ft. It has four principal drainage basins: the Snake, Salmon, Payette, and Weiser. Winters are cool and moist, summers hot and relatively dry. Annual precipitation ranges from 12 in. at low elevations to over 60 in. in the high country. Above 4,000 ft. most precipitation is snow. Some areas are snow-covered 8 months a year. At high elevations, the frost-free period may last less than 30 days.

Plants: Habitats range from riparian and sagebrush-grasslands to high mountain meadows and subalpine forests. Almost 90% of the area is forest land, in various stages of succession. About 850,000 acres are termed suitable for timber production. Principal species are ponderosa pine, Douglas-fir, western larch, and Engelmann spruce. Subalpine fir and whitebark pine on high ridges. Cottonwood in stream bottoms. Shrubs include huckleberry, snowberry, mountain-mahogany, willows, ninebark, and sagebrush. Bluebunch wheatgrass and Idaho fescue on open sideslopes. Wildflowers include lupine, Indian paintbrush, shootingstar.

Birds: 214 species have been recorded. We obtained a list which doesn't note relative abundance or seasonality. *Birds of the Challis and Salmon National Forest* (see Challis NF entry, Zone 2) is generally applicable, although the Payette appears to have a greater variety of waterfowl and shorebirds.

Mammals: 101 species recorded. Big game species include bighorn sheep, elk, moose, mule and whitetail deer, black bear, mountain goat. Gray wolf have been sighted. The Gray Wolf Recovery team has recommended a corridor of critical habitat from the Boise through the Payette and north. Grizzly bear have been sighted, but very rarely.

FEATURES

Goose Lake-Hazard Lake is a popular recreation area N of McCall: camping, boating, fishing. Beyond Hazard Lake is a region of small lakes with attractive hiking trails.

Frank Church - River of No Return Wilderness. See entry in Zone 2. Includes 781,717 acres of the Payette, almost one-third of the Forest. The area extends S from the Salmon River, occupying the E half of the Forest's largest block. Best access from the Payette side is the road E from McCall to Big Creek. A car can make it, but it's slow going and the snow-free season is short. Most people would look elsewhere for weekend backpacking. Outfitters use the area, chiefly in the hunting season.

Salmon Wild and Scenic River. See entry. The Salmon River Gorge forms the N boundary of the main body of the Forest. The gorge is one of America's deepest, with steep walls. No road approaches the rim, and only a few trails. No trail follows the rim. Rafting parties put in above the Payette boundary and take out below it, although they may camp overnight in the gorge.

South Fork Salmon River flows N from the Boise National Forest to the main Salmon River, the lower 10 mi. within the River of No Return Wilderness. Forest roads cross or parallel portions of river upstream. Downstream, the canyon becomes progressively deeper, the surroundings more rugged, access more difficult. The river may be studied for Wild and Scenic River status. The river is important spawning ground for chinook salmon and steelhead. Fishing for mountain whitefish, rainbow and Dolly Varden trout. Two campgrounds are accessible by roads.

Hells Canyon National Recreation Area includes 24,200 acres of the Payette. See entry. The legislation establishing the NRA also designated a section of the Rapid River as part of the Wild and Scenic River system.

Hells Canyon-Seven Devils Scenic Area, 33,956 acres. On Hells Canyon Reservoir (see entry), S from Hells Canyon Dam, adjoining the Hells Canyon National Recreation Area, extending to the tops of the Snake River Breaks. Access is by SR 71 NW from Cambridge, which follows the river to the dam. Hells Canyon, America's deepest gorge, is the dominant feature. Elevations from 1,500 ft. at the river to 8,355 ft. Upland recreation is limited by the steep, rugged topography; hunting, hiking, and sightseeing account for about 1,350 visitor-days per year. Use of the reservoir has been modest.

OTHER ROADLESS AREAS INCLUDE:

Cottontail Point to Pilot Peak, 98,532 acres, extends from the Marshall Mountain mining area, an inholding, for about 25 mi. SE, along the boundary of the Frank Church - River of No Return Wilderness, crossing the South Fork Salmon River. Although the boundaries are accessible by primitive Forest roads, the area is extremely rugged: the river's steep breaks and canyons, craggy peaks E of the river. Much of the area is heavily timbered. Fishing, hunting, backpacking, and ORV travel make up about 2,400 annual visitor-days.

French Creek-Patrick Butte, 168,215 acres. An irregularly shaped site, so fitted among Forest roads that one is never far away, extends from N of Payette Lake to the Forest boundary. A campground at Hazard Lake is at the center of the area. Crossed by several trails. Rugged terrain, steep river breaks, high alpine meadows, glacial cirque basins, over 50 lakes. Backpacking, hunting, fishing, and horse riding total an annual 12,000 visitor-days.

Secesh, 259,682 acres, largest of the roadless areas lacking Wilderness designation, occupies most of the area between French Creek-Patrick Butte and Cottontail Point, the center of the Forest. The McCall-Warren-Elk Creek Road on the N and Lick Creek Road on the S are boundaries and principal access routes. On the Salmon River Mountains, elevations from 3,400 to 9,200 ft. Mostly forested, but with some open ridges and slopes. The scenic Secesh River and the deep South Fork Salmon River Canyon cut through the middle of the area. Several high mountain lakes. Abundant wildlife. Backpacking, hunting, fishing, trailbiking, ski mountaineering; camping and boating on lakes just outside the roadless area.

Rapid River, 53,114 acres, plus 23,300 acres in the Nez Perce NF. The area surrounds the Wild and Scenic Rapid River corridor and adjoins the Hells Canyon Wilderness. Easiest access is to the Nez Perce portion, by several roads and trails. Elevations from 2,200 to 8,747 ft. Craggy peaks, glacial cirques, hanging valleys, steep forested slopes, deep river canyons. Backpacking and hiking, hunting, fishing, climbing, ski mountaineering, and limited trailbiking make up about more than 26,000 visitor-days per year, most of it in the Nez Perce portion.

ACTIVITIES

Camping: 25 campgrounds, 213 sites. Openings May–July, closings Sept.–Nov. Budgets have placed some restraints on maintenance and repairs.

Hiking, backpacking: Over 1,400 mi. of trails, plus little-used primitive roads. The Forest maintains 500 mi. of trails on a 3-year cycle. Other trails are likely to be in poor condition, some virtually abandoned. Many opportunities for day hikes to backcountry lakes such as Loon, Josephine, Snowslide, Louie, Boulder, Box, Hum, and Duck, round trips from 1 mi. to 14 mi. The Lava Ridge Trail and Sheep Rock Overlook Trail are National Recreation Trails. Lava Ridge Trail, 7 mi. long, is part of a complex totaling 60 mi., much of it in the French Creek-Patrick Butte roadless area. Sheep Rock Overlook Trail is a small loop from a trailhead to an overlook on Hells Canyon.

Hunting: Mostly big game, some upland game birds. Hunters frequently use outfitter-guides, usually on the rugged E side of the Forest and in the Frank Church - River of No Return Wilderness.

Fishing: Most fishing is in the more accessible lakes and streams: cutthroat and rainbow trout, chars, grayling, catfish, sunfish. South Fork Salmon River is spawning ground for chinook salmon and steelhead, both under careful management. Outfitter-guides are often used for salmon and steelhead fishing in the main Salmon River near Riggins.

Skiing: Two ski areas are near McCall.
Ski touring: Many opportunities for ski touring and mountaineering.
Groomed trails are in the McCall area, outside the Forest.

PUBLICATIONS
Forest map. $1.
Information pages:
General information.
Geology.
Cultural history.
Flora and fauna (general, no lists).
Short hikes.
Cross-country skiing.
List of outfitters.
Hiking guides:
Lava Ridge Trail.
Sheep Rock Overlook Trail.

REFERENCES
Bluestein, S. R. *Hiking Trails of Southern Idaho.* Caldwell, ID: Caxton
Printers, 1981. Pp. 55–99.
Fuller, Margaret. *Trails of Western Idaho.* Edmonds, WA: Signpost Books,
1982. Pp. 56–93.
Maughan, Jackie J. *The Hiker's Guide to Idaho.* Billings, MT: Falcon
Press, 1984. Pp. 57–67, 96–114.

HEADQUARTERS: P.O. Box 1026, McCall, ID 83638; (208) 634-8151.

RANGER DISTRICTS: Council R.D., P.O. Box 567, Council, ID 83612; (208)
253-4215. Weiser R.D., 275 East 7th St., Weiser, ID 83672; (208) 549-
2420. New Meadows R.D., P.O. Box J, New Meadows, ID 83654; (208)
347-2141. McCall R.D., P.O. Box 1026, McCall, ID 83638; (208) 634-8151.
Big Creek/Krassel R.D., P.O. Box 1026, McCall, ID 83638; (208) 634-
8151.

PONDEROSA STATE PARK
Idaho Department of Parks and Recreation
1,487 acres.

From McCall, follows signs E from city center.

McCall, a popular resort community, is at the foot of Payette Lake. The lake,
glacier-carved and originally filled with glacial melt, was once higher than it

is now. A dam was built on the North Fork Payette River to maintain its present level. About 7 mi. long, with a surface area of 1,000 acres, the lake lies between forested hillsides. The Payette National Forest is on the W, N, and E, but the Forest boundary is 1/2 mi. or more from the lake shore. Resort cottages are scattered along the shoreline, but the lake still retains a pleasantly natural appearance.

The State Park has two units. The principal unit occupies a 2 1/2-mi.-long peninsula extending N into the lake. The 640-acre North Beach tract is at the head of the lake.

The main unit, artfully planned, seems much larger than it really is. The entrance road plunges into deep woods. Most of the peninsula is forested, with a magnificent stand of old-growth ponderosa pine, some specimens 400 to 500 years old, rising to 150 ft. and more. Although the peninsula is only a half-mile wide, the lake isn't visible from the heart of the forest.

Elevations range from 5,020 to 5,400 ft. In addition to the forest, habitats include two marshes, sagebrush flats, grassy hillsides, and basalt cliffs. Average annual precipitation is 28 in., annual snowfall about 150 in. July–Aug. are dry months.

Plants: Tree species, in addition to the dominant ponderosa, include grand fir, Douglas-fir, lodgepole pine, western larch, cottonwood, aspen, and Engelmann spruce. Shrubs include thinleaf and Sitka alder, Rocky Mountain ash, bitter cherry, ceanothus, chokecherry, currant, dogwood, huckleberry, rabbitbrush, bitterbrush, twinberry, serviceberry. Wildflowers include sunflower, arrowleaf balsamroot, asters, yellow bell, glacier lily, yarrow, many more.

Birds: Annotated checklist of 112 species available. 139 species have been recorded. Seasonally abundant or common species include common loon, eared grebe, snow goose, mallard, wood duck, redhead, ring-necked duck, lesser scaup, bufflehead, red-tailed hawk, osprey, spotted sandpiper, common nighthawk, Vaux's swift, rufous and calliope hummingbirds, northern flicker; pileated, hairy, and downy woodpeckers; western wood-pewee; violet-green, tree, and barn swallows; gray and Steller's jays, common raven, American crow, Clark's nutcracker, mountain chickadee, red-breasted and white-breasted nuthatches, brown creeper, Swainson's thrush, American robin, cedar waxwing, yellow-rumped and yellow warblers, western tanager, evening grosbeak, Cassin's finch, lazuli bunting, red crossbill, pine siskin, chipping and song sparrows, dark-eyed junco.

Mammals: Species observed include mountain beaver, muskrat, red fox, porcupine. Present but seldom seen: bobcat, otter, black bear, mink, whitetail deer.

FEATURES

North Beach area, at the head of the lake, has an extensive sand beach. Boaters from the peninsula often picnic here, and a few boat-camp. The Payette River offers good canoeing. No facilities except latrines.

Meadow Marsh has a 1.7-mi. self-guiding nature trail. Lily Marsh is larger, 305 acres, has been nominated as a National Natural Area; trails and viewpoint.

Overlooks are at the N tip of the peninsula, Porcupine Point on the NW, and Pilgrim Cove on the E.

INTERPRETATION

Visitor center has wildflower specimens, publications.

Evening programs are held in summer in the amphitheater.

Guided hikes in summer.

Newsletter is published by the Park's Natural History Association.

ACTIVITIES

Camping: 170 sites. Memorial Day to mid-Sept. Half are available by reservation. Reservations are recommended for weekends, end of June to Aug.

Hiking: Trails within the Park. No links with National Forest trails.

Fishing: Rainbow, brook, and lake trout; kokanee.

Boating: Ramps. Mostly June–Oct. Canoes or small rafts on the North Fork S of McCall, outside the Park; 8 mi. of Class I and II until flow diminishes after mid-July.

Swimming: Unsupervised; July–Aug.

Ski touring: 7 1/2 mi. of groomed trails.

PUBLICATIONS

Leaflet with map.

Bird checklist.

Trees and Shrubs of Ponderosa State Park.

Nature Notes. (We have No. 26, describing the Columbian ground squirrel.)

Meadow Marsh nature trail guide.

NEARBY: Packer John's Cabin State Park, 16 1/2 acres, is on SR 55 9 mi. W of McCall. Limited camping.

HEADQUARTERS: P.O. Box A, McCall, ID 83638; (208) 634-2164.

SALMON NATIONAL FOREST

U.S. Forest Service

1,776,994 acres; 1,800,882 acres within boundaries.

Principal access is by US 93; also SR 28.

The great mass of the Forest, rugged and largely roadless, lies W of US 93. Other portions are E of US 93 and SR 28 on the W slopes of the Bitterroot Range and between the two routes on the Lemhi Range. The area is mountainous, with elevations from 2,800 ft. on river bottoms to 11,350 ft. Principal physical features are the Salmon Mountains on the W, the Bitterroots on the N, the Beaverhead Mountains on the E, and the Lemhi Range on the S. Principal drainage is by the Salmon River and its tributaries. 550 named streams extend 2,040 miles. 322 mountain lakes, with areas of 1 to 200 acres, have a total surface of 1,400 acres. The Forest is surrounded by the Challis, Payette, Bitterroot, and Beaverhead National Forests.

The Frank Church - River of No Return Wilderness includes portions of 6 National Forests, including 427,258 acres on the Salmon. We have a separate entry for it in Zone 2. Other roadless areas include 830,469 acres, bringing the total unroaded acreage to 70% of the Forest.

In the other 30%, system roads total 1,600 mi., but only a few short stretches are rated all-weather. An additional 1,000 mi. of temporary roads will eventually be obliterated. A high-clearance vehicle is recommended for most Forest roads. A passenger car can travel on most of them, including routes to campgrounds, in dry weather, if driven cautiously.

In many National Forests, trail maintenance budgets have been cut far below need, sometimes to zero. We were pleasantly surprised to be told here that 1986 had been "one of our best years" for trail work, with sufficient funds to maintain 450 mi., about one-third of the system. Forest management says new roads have made many other trails redundant, and that even a reduced trail system would accommodate demand "for the foreseeable future." About 520 mi. of trail are in the River of No Return Wilderness.

A trail is being planned for the Continental Divide. About 80 mi. of the Divide are on the crest dividing the Salmon and Beaverhead NFs. Terrain will force many stretches to be built below rather than on the crest, perhaps using bits of existing roads and trails. An interagency meeting was to be held soon after our visit to lay out a route and assign responsibilities. Groups of volunteers stand ready to help build the trail once a route is decided.

The Salmon has 18 campgrounds, remarkably few for a National Forest of its size. Developed sites account for less than one-fifth of the visitor-days. The principal activities are fishing, hunting, river floating, and hiking. Except in the river corridor, visitor use is light. Only a few popular sites show signs of overuse. River traffic has become so heavy as to require control. Rafting parties, we were told, keep their campsites remarkably clean, even picking up trash left by others. By contrast, steelhead fishermen left 10 tons of trash for Forest personnel to remove.

Hunters and fishermen unfamiliar with the vast backcountry of this region are advised to use professional guides if they hope for success. Backpackers should have good maps, advice on trail conditions, and be equipped for whatever weather conditions or emergencies they may encounter.

Climate: Varying elevations and terrain make for different climates. Annual precipitation averages range from 10 in. in the lower foothills to 50 in. on the highest slopes. Most precipitation occurs from late fall to early spring, but short, intense storms are common in summer. Annual snowfall in some areas exceeds 150 in. Snow cover begins to accumulate in late fall and persists until late June at high elevations. Winters are cold, summers generally mild. June–Oct. bring the most visitors, although winter sports are on the increase.

Plants: Plant communities are diverse, from lowland riparian to alpine. 75% of the area is forested. Douglas-fir is the dominant tree species in somewhat more than half of the forested acres, lodgepole pine and subalpine fir in most of the rest. North-facing slopes are generally forested, while the drier southern exposures are likely to be vegetated with bunchgrasses and such shrubs as curlleaf mountain-mahogany, rabbitbrush, and big sagebrush.

Riparian zones, in all the drainages, have a rich diversity of plant species. Open parks and wet meadows are common in the lodgepole pine zone, usually small but valuable to wildlife. Alpine zone vegetation, at 9,500 to 10,000 ft., is chiefly low-growing matlike plants.

Birds: Checklist of 230 species available. Seasonally abundant or common species include great blue heron, Canada goose, mallard, northern shoveler, common goldeneye, bald eagle, American kestrel, blue and sage grouse, ring-necked pheasant, chukar, gray partridge, American coot, killdeer, common snipe, spotted sandpiper, Wilson's phalarope, mourning dove, common nighthawk, northern flicker, Lewis' woodpecker, alder flycatcher, horned lark. Swallows: violet-green, tree, rough-winged, barn, cliff. Black-billed magpie, common raven, American crow, Clark's nutcracker, black-capped and mountain chickadees, red-breasted nuthatch, sage thrasher, American robin, hermit thrush, veery, mountain bluebird, ruby-crowned kinglet, Bohemian and cedar waxwings, European starling, yellow and yellow-rumped warblers, western meadowlark; yellow-headed, red-winged, and Brewer's blackbirds; western tanager, lazuli bunting, evening grosbeak, house finch, gray-crowned rosy finch, pine siskin, dark-eyed junco. Sparrows: house, vesper, chipping, Brewer's, white-crowned, song.

Mammals: 77 species recorded. Elk, mule deer, bighorn mountain sheep, mountain goat, and pronghorn are the principal big game species. Others include black bear, moose, mountain lion, and whitetail deer. Fur-bearers include coyote, bobcat, beaver, and pine marten. Sightings of gray wolf and grizzly bear have been reported but not confirmed. Other species include various shrews, voles, and bats, red squirrel, northern flying squirrel, Great Basin pocket mouse, Ord kangaroo rat, deer mouse, northern grasshopper mouse, bushytail woodrat, wolverine, badger, striped skunk, red fox, mountain lion, lynx, yellowbelly and hoary marmots, Columbian ground squirrel, golden-mantled squirrel, least and yellow pine chipmunks, mountain cotton-tail, pygmy rabbit, muskrat, western jumping mouse, porcupine, pika, white-tail and blacktail jackrabbits, snowshoe hare, black bear, raccoon, pine marten, longtail and shorttail weasels, mink, river otter.

Reptiles and amphibians: Species reported include long-toed and tiger salamanders, tailed frog, western toad, Pacific tree frog, spotted frog. Also western skink, rubber boa, western yellow-bellied racer, Great Basin gopher snake, common and western terrestrial garter snakes, western rattlesnake.

FEATURES

Frank Church - River of No Return Wilderness. See entry in Zone 2. The Salmon NF portion extends from the Continental Divide on the Bitterroot Mountains to the Salmon River at Corn Creek. Because of the North Fork-Corn Creek road, the Wilderness boundary is on the S side of the river E to Panther Creek. Here it turns S to the Challis NF boundary. This large area S of the Salmon River includes about 30 mi. of the Middle Fork Salmon River, a Wild and Scenic River; and the Bighorn Crags, a mountainous region with dozens of glacial lakes, outstanding scenery, hunting, and fishing.

Principal access to this portion of the Wilderness is from the Panther Creek Road. Forest roads lead to the Crags and Yellowjacket Lake campgrounds at the Wilderness boundary.

The area is within the North Fork and Cobalt Ranger Districts.

Bighorn Crags is the most popular area in the Salmon portion of the Wilderness, with outstanding scenery, hunting, and fishing. On the W side of the Salmon River Mountains, it has many high mountain lakes. Forest roads lead to the Crags and Yellowjacket Lake campgrounds on the Wilderness boundary.

Salmon Wild and Scenic River. One of the most popular whitewater streams. An all-weather road parallels the main river from North Fork to Shoup, a passable dirt road continuing to Corn Creek. Before Corn Creek the river is joined by the N-flowing Middle Fork, also a popular rafting-kayaking stream. 104 mi. are part of the Wild and Scenic River system. Floating the 46 mi. of the main river from North Fork to Corn Creek takes 1 to 2 days. Many parties raft from Corn Creek to Riggins, a 6-day journey. The gorge is the nation's second deepest, the scenery magnificent. We drove and hiked part of the route, sighting bighorn sheep and other wildlife. Many of the kayakers we saw were out for the day, using car shuttles between parking areas. The Middle Fork and the main river below Corn Creek flow through Wilderness. (See entries: Frank Church - River of No Return Wilderness, Salmon River.)

After years of decline caused chiefly by dams, anadromous fish—steelhead trout and chinook salmon—are again in the Salmon River drainage. Fishing is under strict management.

OTHER ROADLESS AREAS: The Forest has 30 roadless areas, ranging from 490 acres to 154,498 acres, totaling 830,469 acres, almost half of the entire Forest. Nine of these areas adjoin roadless areas in other National Forests. The following are brief descriptions of four areas:

Camas Creek, 34,887 acres, plus 63,949 acres in the Challis NF. 7 mi. NW of Challis. Accessible by road. Adjoins the Frank Church - River of No Return Wilderness. Elevations from 5,200 to 10,196 ft., topography including gentle slopes and near-vertical headwalls in cirque basins. Largely forested, with lakes and streams. Hunting, fishing, backpacking, and horse riding total about 6,700 visitor-days per year.

Taylor Mountain, 48,280 acres, plus 14,940 acres in the Challis NF. System roads are on the boundaries. Elevations range from 5,500 ft. along Panther Creek to 9,000 ft. on Taylor Mountain. Recreation uses include hunting, fishing, backpacking, and horse riding. The scenic Hat Creek Lakes in the S of the area attract the most visitors.

Lemhi Range, 154,498 acres, plus 149,629 acres in the Challis NF. This is most of a disjunct portion of the Forest extending for 50 mi. along the Lemhi Range, from 15 mi. S of Salmon. Access is by Forest roads from SR 28 in the Lemhi Valley, or into the Challis portion from the Pahsimeroi Valley. Barren, rocky peaks and ridges rise above forest slopes, the highest point 11,300 ft. This high country was shaped by glaciers, leaving lakes in cirque basins at the heads of many drainages. Numerous lakes and streams have fish populations. Wildlife is abundant. Mountain goats are common near the crest. Black bears inhabit the major canyons and lower forest fringes. Many elk. Unconfirmed sightings of gray wolf. Recreation use exceeds 20,000 visitor-days per year, chiefly hunting, fishing, backpacking, and trailbike riding. Big Timber Creek has the heaviest use, with moderate to light fishing action at Basin, Bear Valley, and Buck lakes.

West Big Hole, 81,068 acres. About 10 mi. NE and E of Salmon. Its E boundary is the Continental Divide, where it adjoins the Beaverhead National Forest in Montana. Access is from unpaved roads leading from US 93 N of Salmon and SR 28 SE of Salmon. Most of these roads cross BLM lands adjoining the Forest. Elevations along the Divide range up to 10,200 ft. The area includes important big game range and a key migration corridor for elk and mule deer herds. Black bear and mountain lion are numerous in the Sheep Creek area, a pristine stream that is habitat for anadromous fish. Bighorn sheep are seen occasionally. Although trout fishing in a number of streams is rated fair to good, fishing pressure is light. The principal attraction is the Continental Divide and its developing crest trail. Recreation use is about 3,000 visitor-days per year, chiefly for hunting and backpacking.

INTERPRETATION: Maps and information are available at HQ and Ranger District offices. The Forest has no visitor center, campfire programs, or other naturalist activities.

ACTIVITIES

Many outfitters and guides are available for hunting, fishing, rafting, pack trips. Many are ranchers in the off season.

Camping: 18 campgrounds, 152 sites. Open June–Oct.

Hiking, backpacking: 1,164 mi. of trails. Trail map available. Permits are not required for Wilderness travel. Hiking season is generally Apr.–Nov., but high country may be blocked by snow into June.

Hunting: Mule deer, elk, mountain sheep, mountain goat, mountain lion, black bear, upland game birds.

Fishing: Restrictions on chinook salmon and steelhead protect recovering populations. Salmon River, major tributaries, many streams, high mountain lakes. Brook, cutthroat, rainbow, and Dolly Varden trout; whitefish.

Horse riding: All areas are open. Saddle and pack animals available from outfitters.

Rafting, kayaking, canoeing: Private parties must have reservations and permits during the control season, June 20–Sept. 7, to float the Salmon between Corn Creek and Long Tom Bar. Permits are allotted by computer drawing in early Feb., to qualified and experienced boatmen only. For information, write to North Fork Ranger District. Professional guides and outfitters can be contacted through

Western River Guides Association
994 Denver St.
Salt Lake City, UT 84111

Idaho Outfitter and Guides Association
P.O. Box 95
Boise, ID 83701

The Middle Fork of the Salmon River is managed by the Challis National Forest (see entry, Zone 2).

Ski touring: Mapped trails. An extensive trail system begins at Williams Creek Summit, on Williams Creek Road, W of US 93, 7 mi. S of Salmon. Also at the Lost Trail Winter Sports Area, in the far N of the Forest, off US 93 at Lost Trail Pass.

PUBLICATIONS

Forest map. $1.

Frank Church - River of No Return Wilderness maps (2). $1 each.

General area description.

Main Salmon River rafting information

Birds of the Salmon and Challis National Forests.

Vascular Plants of the Lower Salmon River. Pamphlet.

Salmon National Forest Ski Trails.

A User's Guide. Frank Church - River of No Return Wilderness.

Salmon Valley Recreation Guide. (Salmon Valley Chamber of Commerce, 315 Highway 93 North, Salmon, ID 83467.)

REFERENCES

Carrey, John, and Cort Conley. *The Middle Fork and the Sheepeater War.* Cambridge, ID: Backeddy Books, rev. 1980.
Maughan, Jackie J. *The Hiker's Guide to Idaho.* Billings, MT: Falcon Press, 1984. Pp. 70–76, 80–84, 87–89, 114–16, 119–22, 128–34, 139–42, 150–52.
Mitchell, Ron. *50 Eastern Idaho Hiking Trails.* Boulder, CO: Pruett, 1979. Pp. 90–105.
Wolf, James R. *Guide to the Continental Divide Trail,* vol. 2, *Southern Montana and Idaho.* Bethesda, MD: Continental Divide Trail Society, 1976. Pp. 103–49.

HEADQUARTERS: Box 729, Salmon, ID 83467; (208) 756–2215.

RANGER DISTRICTS: Cobalt R.D., Box 729, Salmon, ID 83467, (208) 756-2240 (winter); 756-3221 (summer). North Fork R.D., Box 780, North Fork, ID 83466; (208) 865-2383. Leadore R.D., Box 180, Leadore, ID 83464; (208) 768-2371. Salmon R.D., Box 729, Salmon ID 83467; (208) 756-3724.

SALMON RIVER
National Forests and BLM lands
425 river miles.

Principal upstream access points from SR 75 and US 93, downstream from US 95.

The Salmon, with its many tributaries, drains a huge complex of high mountains and deep canyons. It is the longest river in the Lower 48 contained within a single state, 425 mi. to its confluence with the Snake River. From its headwaters above the Sawtooth Valley at 8,000 ft. elevation, it drops to 905 ft. It flows through BLM and private lands and several National Forests. The following description provides an overview.

Within the Sawtooth National Recreation Area, the river is a popular fishing stream. It turns E at Stanley into a scenic forested gorge with several National Forest campgrounds. We talked with campers who came to raft this section.

Beyond the NRA the river flows N, draining the Pahsimeroi and Lemhi valleys, part of the time in a valley bordered by sagebrush-covered hills, then into a gorge with cliffs, talus slopes, and rock outcrops. For most of this section US 93 is close to the river. Valley land is BLM and private, with the Challis and Salmon National Forests on either side. We saw two Fish and Game Sportsman Access Sites, both adequate for overnight camping, and two BLM campgrounds. The river is suitable for small rafts and canoes, with some shallows.

N of Salmon, at the town of North Fork, it is joined by its S-flowing North Fork and turns W. From here westward the river is one of the nation's best whitewater streams, part of the Wild and Scenic River system. Its principal tributary, the Middle Fork, joins it 39 mi. from North Fork. 104 miles of the Middle Fork are also Wild and Scenic River, flowing through rugged wilderness, dropping over many dangerous rapids and falls.

From North Fork to Corn Creek, 46 river miles, a scenic road parallels the river. The next 79 mi. are rugged wilderness, virtually inaccessible except by boat. Most of this section lies between the Nez Perce and Payette National Forests. The Salmon River Gorge is second deepest in the United States. The whitewater of this 79 mi. gave the river its other name: River of No Return. Regrettably, the name is no longer apt, because jet boats are allowed to ascend the river.

At Riggins, having emerged from the Forests, the Salmon joins the Little Salmon River and turns N, close to US 95 in a narrow V-shaped canyon flanked by desert hills. 30 mi. later it turns W toward its junction with the Snake.

When Lewis and Clark passed this way, salmon and steelhead were abundant in the Salmon and its tributaries, swimming upstream hundreds of miles from the Pacific Ocean to spawn in their native streams. Construction of dams blocked their return, and both species vanished from the spawning grounds. Great efforts have been made by state and federal agencies to restore the species: construction of fish ladders and weirs to bypass the dams, planting hatchery-raised fish in streams with the hope that they would eventually return. It's working. The salmon and steelhead are returning, not in such great numbers as in the past, but sufficient for an important sport fishery.

Floating has become increasingly popular. At Riggins and elsewhere a bewildering number of roadside shops advertise float and jet boat tours. Many outfitters offer 1- to 6-day float trips on the Salmon and its Middle Fork. Some of the more accessible sections of the river can be floated by kayak or open canoe, except perhaps at high flow. Others, especially the roadless portions, require good equipment and high skills. A permit system limits river traffic in the busy season. Permits are issued by lot, but only to the qualified.

For further information about river conditions and permits, write to

North Fork Ranger District
Salmon National Forest
P.O. Box 780
North Fork, ID 83466
(208) 865-2383

Middle Fork Ranger District
Challis National Forest
P.O. Box 337
Challis, ID 83226
(208) 879-5204

For outfitter information, write to

Idaho Outfitters and Guides Association
P.O. Box 95
Boise, ID 83701

Western River Guides Association
994 Denver St.
Salt Lake City, UT 84111

The Lower Salmon River, from below the W and S section to the Snake River, has rapids to Class IV with some stretches of smooth water. See entry, Salmon River, Lower, in Zone 1.

HEADQUARTERS: See entries: Sawtooth National Recreation Area, Frank Church - River of No Return Wilderness, Salmon National Forest, Challis National Forest (all Zone 2).

SAWTOOTH NATIONAL FOREST
U.S. Forest Service
1,347,422 acres, excluding acreage in the Sawtooth National Recreation Area.

The Northern Division surrounds Ketchum on 3 sides, crossed by SR 75. The Southern Division includes 5 smaller blocks on or near Idaho's southern border, one of them in Utah; all are S of the Snake River between Twin Falls and American Falls, in our Zone 4 but described here.

When the Sawtooth National Recreation Area was established in 1972, it combined over 300,000 acres of the Sawtooth National Forest, including the Sawtooth Wilderness, with portions of the Boise and Challis NFs. The SNRA is administered by the Sawtooth National Forest. We describe it in a separate entry.

For scenic splendor and recreation opportunities, the SNRA has the best of it. The layout could hardly be improved: one main highway traverses the Sawtooth Valley with spur roads and trails leading to attractions on both sides. The rest of the Forest is in six scattered blocks with no unifying theme. Needless to say, the SNRA has more visitors, but the rest of the Forest isn't far behind, with 83% as many.

There would be many fewer visitors were it not for the resorts in the Wood River Valley just S of the SNRA: Sun Valley, Ketchum, Hailey, and Bellevue. What began as the Sun Valley ski area fifty years ago is now a bustling all-year vacation and retirement complex, with private homes and condos sprawling everywhere. At Ketchum and Sun Valley, the Forest boundary is close. Residents and visitors make much use of nearby Forest areas in all seasons.

Most visitors to other parts of the Forest come from communities nearby. They know and enjoy places few outsiders see. Hunting and fishing are their chief activities.

Northern Division

This is the largest of the six blocks and the most popular, because of the Ketchum-Sun Valley area. Excluding the SNRA, it measures about 68 mi. W–E, from 5 to 30 mi. N–S. More than four-fifths lies W of Ketchum. It has a common boundary with the Boise NF on the W, the SNRA on the N, the Challis NF on the NE. The entire area is mountainous, with numerous peaks over 9,000 ft. The Soldier Mountains are in the SW. The Smoky Mountains extend SE, bisecting the Division. The Pioneer Mountains are on the boundary with the Challis NF. Highest point in the Forest is 12,009-ft. Hyndman Peak in the Pioneers.

On the W side of the Smoky Mountains, most drainage is to the W-flowing South Fork of the Boise River. From the E side of the Smokies and the SW side of the Pioneers, principal drainage is toward the Big Wood River.

Annual precipitation in the Northern Division ranges from 17 to about 45 in., most falling as snow, although intense local storms are common in summer and early fall. Summers are pleasantly warm, although frost can occur at high elevations. Winters are long and cold. Forest types are primarily Douglas-fir and lodgepole pine, with lesser amounts of ponderosa pine, Engelmann spruce, subalpine fir, other conifers, and aspen, with areas of mountain brush and meadows.

Several hundred thousand acres, chiefly on the principal mountain ranges, are roadless. Topography is broken: numerous steep slopes and talus slides, glaciated granite peaks, rocky cirques, U-shaped valleys. Many springs and perennial streams. Scattered stringers of Douglas-fir, subalpine fir, limber and lodgepole pines, occasional Engelmann spruce; moderate to dense timber stands at lower elevations on the W.

Wildlife populations include elk, mule deer, a few mountain goat, wolverine, various small mammals. Recreation use has been increasing. Activities include camping, backpacking, horse riding, trailbike riding, ski touring, hunting, and fishing.

Ketchum Ranger District administers the area E of the Smokies, surrounding Ketchum and Sun Valley. Bald Mountain, one of the principal ski areas, is on Forest land. Other features of the District include:

Baker Creek Lakes, a group of small mountain fishing lakes 14 mi. N of
Ketchum, reached by hiking trails.

Penny and Dollar Lakes, 3 mi. W of Ketchum on a canyon road; fishing
and swimming.

Warm Springs Creek, a canyon with many hot sulfur springs.

Prairie Creek Lakes, 3 mi. up the Prairie Creek Road, then 4 mi. of trail.
Small, but good fishing.

East Fork of Wood River extends 12 mi. E to the base of the Pioneer
Mountains. Trails lead into the Pioneers, which have some of Idaho's
highest peaks, rugged cliffs, cirque lakes, magnificent vistas. Trails
cross talus and avalanche paths, and maintenance is questionable.
Rough but splendid country for backpackers.

Trail Creek Summit can be reached by a somewhat breathtaking mountain road, requiring care in driving. The last 4 miles of road are cut
into a canyon wall. Trail Creek Falls is a mile down a rough, steep
trail.

Camping: Small campgrounds, the largest with 7 units, several with only
1, are scattered along the various creeks. Camp anywhere except along the Big
Wood River and in Trail Creek Canyon, where only designated sites may be
used.

Fairfield Ranger District is W of the Smoky Mountains. Principal access
is by secondary roads N from Fairfield or E from Featherville.

North of Fairfield are:

Soldier Mountain Ski Area.

Little Smoky Winter Play Area.

Little Smoky Creek has a Forest road leading to campgrounds near the
center of the District. The Smoky Mountains roadless area is on the
N.

E from Featherville, a Forest road follows the South Fork of the Boise
River upstream to the confluence with Little Smoky Creek. Several hot
springs are along the river, as are 7 campgrounds. Trails lead up side drainages. Good fishing.

Southern Division

(Most of this area is in our Zone 4.)

Five scattered blocks are on small mountain ranges. They are somewhat
drier than the Northern Division, but high areas receive much snow. They
have no major streams and only a few small lakes, but some areas of outstanding interest.

Twin Falls Ranger District. The *Cassia unit* is the largest block in this
Division, about 22 mi. square, 14 mi. S of Twin Falls. Highest point here is
8,060 ft. Mountain slopes are moderate rather than steep. Center of recreation
activity is the deep valley of Rock Creek, which has several campgrounds,

cross-country ski trails, and a ski area. Much of this recreation is ORV activity, including snowmobiling. Hunting is popular. This unit is criss-crossed by many low-standard roads, but the Third Fork of Rock Creek and Cottonwood Canyon offer good hiking away from roads.

Burley Ranger District. The *Albion Mountain unit* is about 12 mi. SE of Burley. 20 mi. N–S, 4 to 8 mi. W–E, its highest point is 10,335 ft. Cache Peak, in the S. Principal development is the Howell Canyon road in the NE leading to campgrounds, a ski area, and summer homes. Good access has promoted considerable recreation use: hiking, trail cycling, snowmobiling, horse riding, and hunting. Fishing is only fair.

Silent City of Rocks, a famous rock climbing area partially within this unit, is managed cooperatively; see entry in Zone 4. The outstanding roadless area in this division is Cache Peak, which contains Independence Lakes within a subalpine forest environment. 9,265-ft. Mt. Harrison is in the N central part of the unit, most of which is roadless.

The *Black Pine unit,* on the UT border between SR 81 and I-84, is on a small N–S mountain range, the highest point 9,385 ft. Access from all sides by Forest roads, but a 40,140-acre tract is roadless. There is little recreation use, mostly hunting in the fall: deer and upland game birds.

Furthest E is the *Sublett unit,* occupying part of the N–S Sublett Range. Principal access is an all-weather road E from I-84 at Sublett. Sublett Reservoir, at the SW corner, partially in the unit, is noted for its fishing. Two campgrounds are nearby.

The *Raft River unit* is entirely in UT.

INTERPRETATION: The SNRA visitor center on SR 75, 7 mi. N of Ketchum, serves the entire Forest. Information on flora and fauna available here is generally applicable to most Forest areas. See SNRA entry.

ACTIVITIES

A recorded message on (208) 737-3250 reports current road and trail conditions, campground openings, etc.

Camping: Campgrounds are widely scattered, often on unpaved roads. In the Northern Division: 17 campgrounds, 121 sites. Southern Division: 19 campgrounds, 272 sites. A few are open all year, some June–Sept. Many attractive informal sites.

Hiking, backpacking: More than 850 mi. of trails. More than two-thirds are substandard, receiving little or no maintenance. Many mi. of little-used Forest roads are also available. For extensive backpacking, the Smoky Mountains roadless area offers an experience comparable to the Sawtooth Wilderness or White Cloud Peaks with far fewer people. Hiking season in the high country may begin in June, but snowfields may remain and stream crossings can be dangerous. Both divisions offer attractive opportunities for day hikes in lightly used areas. Get advice from a Ranger District office, especially before an extended trip. Hikers at high elevations should be prepared for storms and freezing weather at any season.

Hunting: Mule deer are in both divisions. Elk and bighorn sheep are in northern areas. Upland birds include sage and forest grouse, partridge.

Fishing: Best fishing opportunities are in the SNRA. Several streams and small lakes in the Northern Division have good trout fishing.

Horse riding: A number of outfitter-guides offer a variety of summer pack trips. Horses may also be rented by the day.

Skiing: Ski areas at Bald Mountain near Ketchum, Soldier Mountain N of Fairfield, Magic Mountain in the Cassia unit, Pomerelle in the Albion unit.

Ski touring: Many opportunities on groomed trails and unplowed Forest roads. Set trails include the Wood River Trail near Ketchum, upper Rock Creek Canyon in the Cassia unit, upper Howell Canyon in the Albion unit.

PUBLICATIONS

Forest maps: Fairfield and Ketchum Ranger Districts (Northern Division); Twin Falls and Burley Ranger Districts (Southern Division). $1 each.

Travel Plan Map.

A Guide to the Ketchum Ranger District. Leaflet with map.

Information page: Visitor information. (Includes SNRA.)

REFERENCES

Bluestein, S. R. *Hiking Trails of Southern Idaho.* Caldwell, ID: Caxton Printers, 1981. Pp. 43–45, 52–54, 163–73, 175–77.

Maughan, Jackie J. *The Hiker's Guide to Idaho.* Billings, MT: Falcon Press, 1984. Pp. 203–4.

Miller, Ron. *50 Eastern Idaho Hiking Trails.* Boulder, CO: Pruett, 1979. Pp. 12–17, 26–29, 38–39, 44–47, 78–79.

HEADQUARTERS: 2647 Kimberly Rd. E., Twin Falls, ID 83301; (208) 737-3200.

RANGER DISTRICTS: Fairfield R.D., P.O. Box 186, Fairfield, ID 83327; (208) 764-2202. Ketchum R.D., P.O. Box 2356, Sun Valley Rd., Ketchum, ID 83340; (208) 622-5371. Twin Falls R.D., 2647 Kimberly Rd. E, Twin Falls, ID 83301; (208) 737-3200. Burley R.D., 2621 S. Overland Ave., Burley, ID 83318; (208) 678-0430.

SAWTOOTH NATIONAL RECREATION AREA
U.S. Forest Service
754,000 acres.

Crossed N–S by SR 75, the Sawtooth Scenic Route.

Why go anywhere else? People who discover the spectacular Sawtooth Valley often return again and again. Three mountain ranges with more than 50 peaks over 10,000 ft.; more than a thousand high mountain lakes; a thousand miles of rivers and streams; deep forests, mountain meadows. Although most visitors come in summer, many enjoy the quiet trails and bright colors of autumn. Winter offers ski touring, snowshoeing, snowmobiling, and ice fishing. Wildflowers brighten the slopes as snowfields melt in spring.

In 1911 a group of Idaho clubwomen proposed the area as a National Park. Several legislative efforts failed, but in 1972 Congress established the SNRA, combining contiguous portions of the Sawtooth, Challis, and Boise National Forests into one National Forest unit. The mandate from Congress is "to assure the preservation and protection of the natural, scenic, historic, pastoral, and fish and wildlife values and to provide for the enhancement of the recreation values associated therewith." Timber can still be harvested, sheep and cattle grazed, and mining claims worked if compatible with the mandate. The Act also provided for compatible management of the 25,000 acres of private landholdings within the boundaries, chiefly in a strip along the highway.

Most visitors arrive from the south. Newcomers should stop at the visitor center just inside the boundary at the SE corner and spend some time with the exhibits. In addition to a helpful staff, the center has a Recreation Opportunities Guide (ROG) with an immense amount of information about every aspect of recreation. For example, each principal trail has a page in the ROG with sketch map, profile graph, difficulty rating, description of the trail and destinations, and more. Photocopies are available on request.

At the visitor center, the Sawtooth Scenic Route turns NW in the valley of the Big Wood River, with the Boulder Mountains to the N, several peaks over 11,000 ft. After climbing to Galena Summit, 8,701 ft., the route descends into the Sawtooth Valley, following the Salmon River northward. To the E are the White Cloud Peaks, to the W the jagged Sawtooth Range. On the W, not far from the highway, are the largest lakes: Alturas, Pettit, and Redfish. Just beyond is the roadless Sawtooth Wilderness.

At Stanley, the Scenic Route turns E along the SNRA boundary, still following the Salmon River, meeting US 93 at Challis. From Stanley the Ponderosa Pine Scenic Route, SR 21, runs NW, then SW through the Boise National Forest to Boise. This route is often closed in winter because of slides.

Climate: Summers are short, bright, and cool, winters long and cold. At the visitor center, the average high daytime summer temperature is 72°F, nighttime average below 40°. The average daytime winter high is just about freezing, nights dropping to about 6°. The Sawtooth Valley is a bit cooler, the high slopes lower still. Most precipitation is winter snow, and it arrives in a few scattered storms. Brief afternoon thundershowers are common in summer.

Plants: The SNRA has four major plant communities: *Great Basin Sagebrush,* in lower valley bottoms and exposed hillsides. Here is a fine wildflower display in early summer, when the ground is still moist. Common species include scarlet gilia, lupine, arrowleaf balsamroot, fireweed, shrubby cinquefoil, sulfur flower. Later come sego lily, Indian paintbrush, and buttercup. River bottoms support black cottonwood, aspen, and a few Engelmann spruce, Douglas-fir, and lodgepole pine. *Subalpine Forest* is above the sagebrush, beginning higher on W and S-facing slopes. Lodgepole pine and Douglas-fir are dominant, with some subalpine fir. Aspen in fire-caused forest openings. Small wet openings and streamsides display bluebells, columbine, skunk cabbage, occasional larkspur. Still higher within this subalpine community are whitebark pine and limber pine. *Alpine Community* is above timberline, about 10,000 ft. elevation. This is not an extensive community in the SNRA. Marked by low-growing shrubs and forbs with short blooming seasons, some flowers appearing through melting snow. *Riparian Community* includes such streamside species as willow, alder, aspen, tufted hairgrass, Indian paintbrush, alpine timothy, wild rose, buttercup.

Birds: These diverse habitats attract nearly 200 species, most of them migratory. Checklist notes seasonality but not abundance. Another publication lists birds by habitats, noting abundance. Those rated high or medium include the following: *Water:* dipper, killdeer, spotted sandpiper, common merganser, mallard, lesser scaup, belted kingfisher, cinnamon and green-winged teals, eared grebe, great blue heron. *Meadow-Willow:* American robin, northern harrier, yellow warbler. *Sagebrush:* western meadowlark, chipping sparrow, red-tailed hawk, vesper sparrow, American kestrel, northern shrike, Brewer's sparrow, house wren, Swainson's hawk. *Timber:* gray jay, Clark's nutcracker, common raven, black-billed magpie, tree swallow, song sparrow, yellow-bellied sapsucker, downy woodpecker, red-breasted nuthatch, hermit thrush. *Alpine:* horned lark.

Mammals: No checklist. The listing by habitats rates only 15 species as having high or medium abundance, so we include those with low abundance, but not the rarities. *Water:* beaver, river otter, muskrat, mink. *Meadow-Willow:* Unspecified bats, deer mouse, spotted and striped skunks. *Sagebrush:* Columbian ground squirrel, badger, coyote, pronghorn, northern pocket gopher, western harvest mouse. *Timber:* yellow pine chipmunk, red squirrel, golden-mantled squirrel, porcupine, mule deer, elk, snowshoe hare, shorttail and longtail weasels, red fox, black bear, flying squirrel, pine marten, bushytail woodrat. *Alpine:* pika, yellowbelly marmot, mountain goat, bighorn sheep.

Fishes: Three species of anadromous fish travel upstream more than 800 mi.

from the Pacific Ocean to the upper Salmon River to spawn. Sockeye salmon travel to Redfish Lake, the only remaining population of their species in ID. Chinook and steelhead migrate to the upper Salmon and its tributaries.

Wildlife watch: Visitors are asked to report sightings of pileated woodpecker, sage grouse, goshawk, screech owl, boreal owl, great gray owl, common loon, peregrine falcon, bald eagle, wood duck, lynx, bobcat, gray wolf, wolverine.

FEATURES

Sawtooth Wilderness, 217,088 acres of mountain lakes and meadows, with many peaks over 10,000 ft., lies W of the Sawtooth Scenic Route. The mountain terrain extends 32 mi. N–S, a long line of jagged peaks giving the area its name. Sculptured by glaciers are countless U-shaped valleys and basins with more than 300 alpine lakes. Four rivers have their headwaters here.

Wildlife is abundant. Lake fishing depends on stocking. Streams are too steep to provide fishing opportunity.

More than 350 mi. of mapped trails provide hiking routes. Many of the lake basins are reached by off-trail hiking. The hiking season is relatively short. High passes may not be snow-free until mid-July, and earlier travel is often impeded by soft snow and high water. Some lower trails can be hiked by July 1.

Of roughly a million visitor-days spent in the SNRA each year, only about 50,000 are in the wilderness. However, because of the short season, the most popular trails are heavily used from mid-July through Aug. Ask at visitor centers about less-used trails.

Hikers are asked to register at trailheads. Permits are required for groups of 10 or more (maximum is 20) and for overnight use with pack and saddle stock.

White Cloud-Boulder Mountains. The area, more than half of the SNRA, includes everything E of the Sawtooth Scenic Route. Unlike the Sawtooth peaks, most in this area are too distant to be seen from the valley. But they're impressive, five of them higher than any in the Sawtooth Range. The area has about 125 lakes, many in spectacular cirques. The glaciers have melted, but snowfields remain well into summer. The White Clouds are home to a third of the mountain goat population of ID. However, wildlife in general is not overly abundant.

The area, a candidate for Wilderness status, is managed as "backcountry." Primitive and rough roads provide vehicle access to the perimeter. Two-wheeled vehicles are permitted on several trails. Trails lead to the high country and the many lakes. In general, trails are not heavily used, but there are exceptions. One drawback, for hikers and horsemen, is that motorized trailbikes are permitted on several trails. Visitor center staff can recommend quiet routes. Travelers are asked to register at trailheads.

The lakes. The 6 largest lakes are W of the highway, accessible by auto.

Power boats can be used on Alturas, Pettit, Redfish, and Stanley. Campgrounds are on 5 of the lakes. All of the lakes have trailheads for the Wilderness.

The Salmon River, longest and largest in the SNRA, parallels the Sawtooth Scenic Route. Headwaters of the Upper, Main, and East forks are in the SNRA. Several campgrounds are along the river E of Stanley. The river is floatable for 33 mi. from Redfish Lake Creek. The river and its tributaries offer good fishing.

Scenic drives include Valley Road, E of and parallel to SR 75, skirting the White Cloud foothills; trailheads. High-clearance vehicles are advised for Pole Creek from Valley Road into the heart of the mountains; trailheads. Boulder Creek, a drive-and-hike route to a high lake and deserted mining town; high-clearance vehicles are recommended beyond the stream crossing, 4-wheel drive or trailbike beyond the trailhead.

INTERPRETATION

Visitor center near the S entrance has exhibits, maps, literature, the ROG, and a well-informed staff. Open daily, except weekends only during Apr. and Nov.

Visitor center at Redfish Lake is open daily, late June–Labor Day weekend. *Stanley Ranger Station* is open daily in summer, otherwise weekdays. Similar services.

Cassette tapes for a self-guided tour are available free at visitor centers.

Evening programs in summer at Redfish and Wood River campgrounds.

Nature trails at Redfish visitor center and Wood River campground.

Nature walks and other programs, as scheduled; information at visitor centers.

Old Valley Creek Ranger Station Museum at Stanley has information and exhibits; sponsored by the Sawtooth Interpretive Association.

ACTIVITIES

Camping: 37 campgrounds, 667 sites. Campgrounds open when weather permits in late May or early June, remain open until mid-Sept. Campgrounds may be used when accessible. Camping is permitted anywhere in the SNRA except in posted areas.

Hiking, backpacking: Over 750 mi. of trails. Many day hikes are possible. The leaflet listed under Publications describes some popular routes. Hiking season in the high country begins about July 15. Hikers should be prepared for subfreezing nights, sudden rain or snow, high winds. Insect repellent is essential in summer.

Hunting: The extensive information file provided to us by the SNRA contained nothing about hunting, which is permitted in National Forests and wasn't prohibited in the legislation creating the SNRA. We asked for clarification and received only this reply: "Occurs in the SNRA and is regulated by permit from the Idaho Department of Fish and Game. Several outfitters and guides offer hunting services."

Fishing: Opportunities range from excellent to poor. Many of the mountain lakes are unproductive, and fishing depends on stocking. Many mountain streams lack nutrients to provide good fishing. The newsprint visitor guide listed under Publications has a schematic map dividing the SNRA into 10 zones, describing the fishing opportunities in each. Occasional open seasons on steelhead; none recently on chinook.

Horse riding: Most trails are suitable for riding. Visitor centers have list of outfitters. Permit is required for overnight use in the Wilderness, and special rules apply. Insect repellent is recommended for horses as well as riders.

Boating: Power boats permitted on Alturas, Redfish, Pettit, and Stanley lakes. Power boat and canoe rentals at Redfish Lake Lodge. Guide boat tours and boat shuttle to trailhead is available at Redfish. Perkins, Yellowbelly, and Little Redfish lakes, accessible by car, are reserved for nonmotorized craft.

Rafting, kayaking: On 33 mi. of the Salmon River. Outfitters offer trips. Rapids to Class IV, but extremely hazardous during high flows, usually in June. An 18-mi. section is mostly gentle water. For current conditions, check Stanley Ranger Station.

Ski touring: Designated areas suitable for beginners, intermediates, and experts. Equipment rentals and instruction available from nearby centers. Some routes on unplowed roads also used by snowmobiles. Avalanche hazard forecast is available.

PUBLICATIONS
Visitor guide. (20 pp., newsprint)
Leaflet with map.
Pictorial brochure.
Information guide and map.
Folders with maps:
   Sawtooth Wilderness.
   White Cloud-Boulder Mountains.
Mimeo pages:
   Sawtooth Wilderness.
   Wilderness regulations.
   Geology.
Publications list, Sawtooth Interpretive and Historical Association.
Bird checklist.
Leaflets *(these are being replaced by information in the newsprint visitor guide):*
   General description.
   Trees (not a checklist).
   Wildflowers (not a checklist).

Wildlife (not a checklist).
Birds (not a checklist).
Geology.
Day hikes.
Backpacking.
Fishing.
Horseback riding.
Boating.
Cross-country skiing.
Mountaineering.
Snowmobiling.
Trailbike riding.

REFERENCES

The Sawtooth Mountain Star. General guide, locally sponsored, available at visitor centers.

Bluestein, S. R. *Hiking Trails of Southern Idaho.* Caldwell, ID: Caxton Printers, 1981. Pp. 34–39, 127–29, 147–57.

Fuller, Margaret. *Trails of the Sawtooth and White Cloud Mountains.* Edmonds, WA: Signpost Books, 1979.

Linkhart, Luther. *Sawtooth National Recreation Area.* Berkeley, CA: Wilderness Press, 1981.

Maughan, Jackie J. *The Hiker's Guide to Idaho.* Billings, MT: Falcon Press, 1984. Pp. 197–203, 208–11.

Mitchell, Ron. *50 Eastern Idaho Hiking Trails.* Boulder, CO: Pruett, 1979. Pp. 40–43, 48–51, 60–77.

HEADQUARTERS: Star Route, Ketchum, ID 83340; (208) 726-8291.

RANGER DISTRICT: Stanley R.D., Stanley, ID 83278; (208) 774-3681.

THORN CREEK RESERVOIR
U.S. Bureau of Land Management
80 water acres when full. Indeterminate land acreage.

From Gooding, N on SR 46. At about 20 mi., pass Flattop Butte and turnoff for Gooding City of Rocks on left (see entry). Take next right turn; about 4 mi. to reservoir on dirt road.

We include this small site because of our BLM advisor's comment: "Beautiful!"

It's small, out of the way, seldom visited by other than local fishermen. The reservoir is set in the rolling Mount Bennett Hills. The shoreline is made scenic by lava outcrops. It's a productive trout fishery. Facilities consist of a latrine.

HEADQUARTERS: Shoshone District Office, BLM, 400 W. F St., Shoshone, ID 83352; (208) 886-2206.

ZONE 3

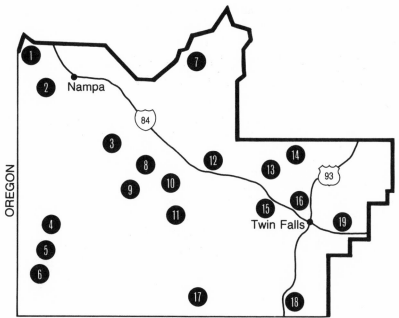

OREGON

1

2 Nampa

84

7

3

8

12

14

13

93

9

10

15

16

19

11

Twin Falls

4

5

6

17

18

NEVADA

ZONE 3

Includes these counties:

Canyon	Ada	Elmore
Camas	Owyhee	Gooding
Lincoln	Jerome	Twin Falls

This is SW Idaho, a region dramatically different from the rest of the state. The SW half of the zone is desert, flat to gently rolling land cut by deep and rugged canyons. The plateaus are hot and dry, with scanty vegetation, but many canyon bottoms have perennial streams bordered by green strips of riparian vegetation. The canyon walls provide nesting sites for large numbers of raptors. The Snake River Birds of Prey Area on the Snake River Canyon provides raptors with nesting sites and hunting grounds.

The highway map is of limited use in exploring this SW region. Most of it is roadless, but there are many primitive roads the map doesn't show. We used BLM's 1:100,000 series, with caution, asking about road conditions when we could, and had no disasters, although the dishes rattled. Most of the area is BLM land, with the state owning two sections in each township of 36.

For a good introduction to the Snake River-Bruneau River area, stop at Bruneau Dunes State Park. The visitor center has a capable staff, exhibits, and literature, the only such resource in the canyon country.

Most of the area drains to the Snake. The far SW is Owyhee country, several branches of the Owyhee River flowing into Oregon where they assemble, flowing N through a spectacular whitewater canyon to Owyhee Reservoir and then the Snake.

Few people visit this canyon country. Twice we drove all day without passing another vehicle. Pave a few roads, call it a National Monument, and crowds would come.

The N central portion of the zone includes mountainous terrain typical of Zone 2, including part of the Sawtooth Wilderness. The NE corner is hilly, with many bizarre and dramatic rock formations.

BOISE NATIONAL FOREST
U.S. Forest Service
2,612,000 acres; 2,959,719 acres within boundaries.

E and NE of Boise. Crossed by SR 21, SR 55.

A majority of the Forest is in Zone 2. See entry.

BRUNEAU DUNES STATE PARK
Idaho Department of Parks and Recreation
4,800 acres.

From Mountain Home, 18 mi. S on SR 51 to Snake River crossing, then 2
mi. E on SR 78.

The exceptionally large live dunes here are surrounded by gently rolling
sagebrush-grassland, including many old, vegetated dunes. According to Park
literature, one dune is the largest in North America, rising 470 ft. from its
base. Most dunefields form at the edges of natural basins, but these have
formed at the center, in a natural trap. The two principal dunes cover about
600 acres.

The three small lakes are surprising. They appeared in the 1950s when dams
built on the Snake River raised the surrounding water table. The largest
covers 150 acres and is up to 20 ft. deep. Introduction of water has added
aquatic, riparian, and wetlands habitats to the desert dunes and prairies, with
consequent additions to the species of plants and animals.

Geologists attribute the dunes to the Bonneville flood 30,000 years ago, a
meander scar forming a trap for sand carried from hundreds of miles away.
Among other unusual features is the "crater" in the center of the largest dune,
a wind-formed funnel that dips down to ground level.

It's hot! It was 110°F on the June afternoon when we arrived, too hot for
much exploring. The evening was pleasantly cool, and it was cool enough for
hiking early next day. Spring and fall would be best for a visit. Most visitation
is Apr.–June. Annual precipitation is about 7 in.

Plants: About 90 species have been recorded. Desert species include sagebrush, rabbitbrush. Flowering plants include sand lily, rusty lupine, pale
evening primrose, sharpleaf penstemon, sunflower, mustard, white sand ver-
bena, Russian thistle, rush-pink, yellow beeplant, arrowleaf balsamroot. Cattail and bulrush grow along the shoreline with occasional cottonwood stands.
No plant list is available, but the visitor center has an excellent photographic
display.

Birds: The Park is within the boundary of the Snake River Birds of Prey
Area (see entry). No checklist is available. Species noted include yellow-
headed blackbird, meadowlark, avocet, black-necked stilt, curlew, great blue
heron, ruddy duck, mallard, coot, other migratory waterfowl. Birds of prey

include northern harrier, red-tailed hawk, burrowing owl, bald and golden eagles. A black-billed magpie joined us at our table, unalarmed by the interest of our black Labrador.

Mammals: Often or occasionally seen: muskrat, coyote, cottontail, black-tail jackrabbit, Ord kangaroo rat, Great Basin pocket mouse, deer.

Reptiles and amphibians: Often or occasionally seen: Great Basin whiptail; leopard, desert horned, side-blotched, and western fence lizards; leopard frog, Great Basin spadefoot; Great Basin gopher snake, striped whipsnake. Great Basin rattlesnake is present but seldom seen.

Arthropods: Scorpion, black widow spider.

INTERPRETATION

The excellent *visitor center* has exhibits, literature, and a well-informed, enthusiastic staff prepared to discuss not only the Park but also nearby areas. The evening slide talk was on birds of prey. Open Mar.–Oct.

Big Dunes Nature Trail.

ACTIVITIES

Camping: 48 sites. All year.

Hiking: 5 mi. of mapped trails.

Fishing: Largemouth bass, bluegill, channel cat.

Boating: Electric motors only. Lake freezes Nov.–Feb.

Swimming: Permitted. Swimmer's itch is a problem in vegetated areas.

NEARBY: Bruneau Canyon, Snake River Bird of Prey Area, C. J. Strike Wildlife Management Area. See entries.

PUBLICATIONS

Leaflet with map.

Hiking trail map.

Nature trail map.

The Geology of Bruneau Dunes. $.75.

HEADQUARTERS: HC 85, Box 41, Mountain Home, ID 83647; (208) 366-7919.

BRUNEAU RIVER; BRUNEAU CANYON

U.S. Bureau of Land Management

134,062 acres.

From Mountain Home, 21 mi. S on SR 51 to Bruneau, then SE through Bruneau Hot Springs. Bruneau Canyon overlook is about 18 mi. from Bruneau.

This roadless area is shown clearly on the highway map: between SR 51 and the county road SE from Bruneau, its heart about 15 mi. NE of Grasmere. About 37 mi. long, up to 13 mi. wide, the area is a relatively flat volcanic tableland with a sparse cover of desert shrub, dissected by deep canyons. Driving SE from Bruneau, one first passes through an irrigated valley but soon climbs to dry, open grassland plateau. Some visitors are fascinated by this brown expanse. The main attractions here are the canyons of the Bruneau River and Sheep Creek.

The first few miles from Bruneau are blacktop. Then comes gravel, with enough washboard to rattle dishes in our motor home, but no problem. The canyon overlook is well signed. From the county road, it's 3 mi. of somewhat rutted but passable dirt to the edge, where BLM has provided parking and a guardrail. We met no other cars.

The canyon is spectacular, cut about 800 ft. deep through the plateau. It is exceptionally narrow for such depth, in places only 30 ft. wide, seldom as much as a quarter-mile. Below the overlook, it seemed to be about 100 ft. wide. The walls are almost vertical, a series of cliffs, ledges, and steep slopes, with occasional spires, columns, and other formations. The exposed rock layers are chiefly in shades of brown. Sheep Creek and the Jarbidge River, both in deep canyons, are the chief tributaries of the Bruneau. The canyon ends where the surrounding land drops down to the Snake River plain.

BLM's site evaluation found the canyons suitable for primitive recreation, including whitewater rafting and kayaking, backpacking, camping, sightseeing, nature photography, rockhounding, hunting, fishing, and wildlife viewing, with "significant mental and physical challenge." Both the Bruneau and Sheep Creek have been recommended to Congress for inclusion in the Wild and Scenic River system. The canyonlands and adjacent plateaus are under wilderness study.

Birds: Birds of prey are present, but the area doesn't support raptors in numbers comparable to the Snake River Birds of Prey Area. The cliffs have suitable nesting sites, but the plateaus lack a high density of prey species. Soils here are thinner, and most native shrubs have been lost to fire and crested wheatgrass seeding. Shrubs are essential to the squirrels and jackrabbits on which raptors prey.

ACTIVITIES

Camping: Nearest developed campground is Bruneau Dunes State Park (see entry). Campgrounds also at C. J. Strike WMA. On BLM land, camp almost anywhere, but it's hot, dusty, and without potable water.

Hiking, backpacking: There are few points of access from the plateau to the canyon bottom. Descending from the rim from anywhere near the overlook would be impossible except by rope. There is a trail into the canyon 3 mi. upstream, the trailhead reached by a dirt road. Travel through the canyon on foot would be a scenic adventure, but with much rock scrambling, occasional deep water crossings, and poison ivy. At the BLM office we were told a few people do hike the canyon in summer, sometimes taking an inner tube to float deep sections. Hiking the rim would be easy, if a bit warm.

Rafting: BLM's evaluation said the Bruneau is "nationally known for its excellent whitewater boating." *The River Runners Guide to Idaho* calls these rivers "difficult and demanding for boaters." Access is poor, rapids are tough, and portages are difficult. Rattlesnakes and poison ivy are common. The Bruneau and its tributaries are best run only by expert boaters in kayaks and small rafts. Put-in for the West Fork Bruneau is below Rowland, NV, for the Main Bruneau at Indian Hot Springs, ID. From the latter it's 40 mi., 2 to 3 days, to take-out 8 mi. S of Bruneau. Class II to V rapids. The floating season usually ends in early June. Boaters are asked to register.

NEARBY: Bruneau Dunes State Park; Snake River Birds of Prey Area; C. J. Wildlife Management Area. See entries.

PUBLICATIONS

The State Park visitor center gave us a useful map:
Owyhee County-Bruneau Area.
A River Runner's Guide to Idaho. BLM pamphlet.

HEADQUARTERS: BLM, Boise District, 3948 Development Area., Boise, ID 83705; (208) 334-1582.

C. J. STRIKE WILDLIFE MANAGEMENT AREA
Idaho Department of Fish and Game
8,345 acres.

From Mountain Home, S 20 mi. on SR 51.

The WMA borders the C. J Strike Reservoir, which extends 26 mi. up the Snake River and 12 mi. up the Bruneau River from the dam. The reservoir is long and relatively narrow. It was constructed in the 1950s for power generation. The surrounding land is flat to rolling, with elevations from 2,400 to 2,900 ft., not scenic.

Climate is arid, annual precipitation about 8 in. Snow seldom remains on the ground. Summers are warm, average high temperatures from 92° to 100°F. Boaters should be aware that strong winds are common in spring and early summer.

Vegetation is sparse, with low sagebrush dominant. The surrounding area has large irrigated farms.

Public use is low to moderate for a reservoir of this size. Fishing is the chief activity, about 30,000 user-days per year. Visitors who come for picnicking, sightseeing, boating, camping, and swimming outnumber hunters more than 2 to 1. Recreational developments, chiefly at the lower end of the reservoir, include two campgrounds, marina, and ramps. We passed several dirt roads leading to the water's edge from the highway. We took one that ended at an unimproved parking area. The only structure was a latrine. Fire rings, litter, and other signs showed use by fishermen, picnickers, and campers. Apparently one can usually find a solitary, primitive, waterside campsite.

The HQ area is at the mouth of the Bruneau River. Wildlife management developments include duck ponds and goose nest platforms.

Birds: The area is a major wintering ground for waterfowl. Duck counts average 30,000 to 90,000, mallard predominating. Canada goose counts are from 1,000 to 10,000, and many geese nest. Other wintering waterfowl include American wigeon, green-winged teal, northern shoveler, pintail, redhead, canvasback, lesser scaup, ringneck duck, common goldeneye, bufflehead, ruddy duck. Most waterfowl arrive in Nov. and leave in early Jan. Upland game bird populations are moderate to low.

Mammals: Species most often seen include muskrat, cottontail, blacktail, jackrabbit, whitetail, antelope squirrel, pocket gopher, kangaroo rat, coyote, raccoon.

ACTIVITIES

Camping: Two campgrounds and primitive sites.

Hunting: Waterfowl and pheasant.

Fishing: Fair to good all year. Rainbow trout, bluegill, black crappie, perch, channel catfish, large and smallmouth bass. Fishing is heaviest May–June.

Boating: Marina, ramps.

NEARBY: Bruneau Dunes State Park (see entry).

HEADQUARTERS: Idaho Department of Fish and Game, Region 3, 109 W. 44th St., Boise, ID 83704; (208) 334-3725.

DEER FLAT NATIONAL WILDLIFE REFUGE (LAKE LOWELL)

U.S. Fish and Wildlife Service

11,585 acres, including 9,500-acre lake.

The Refuge also includes 86 islands in the Snake River, from the Ada-Canyon county line to Farewell Bend, OR. See entry, Fort Boise Wildlife Management Area.

From I-84 at Nampa, exit 36, Karcher Rd., SR 55. Karcher Rd. to Lake Ave., then S.

The Boise Valley is an important waterfowl wintering area on the Pacific Flyway. Migrants begin arriving in Sept. By Dec. up to 8,000 geese and 400,000 ducks may be present.

The Refuge is in the lowlands, its elevation about 2,500 ft. Average annual precipitation is about 10 in., most of it Nov.–Apr. Snow falls but seldom remains long. The lake margins are seasonally flooded marsh and brush. The 2,000 acres of dry land, most of it on the N side, are sagebrush-grass complex and cropland.

It's popular, not just for hunting, fishing, and wildlife observation but also for picnicking, swimming, boating, and water skiing. Some activities interfered with the primary mission, and the lake has now been zoned to separate uses. Much of the Refuge is closed to all access Oct. 1–Apr. 14 to protect wintering waterfowl.

We asked if this closure handicaps birding during spring and fall migrations. There's sufficient open area for good birding in the HQ area, was the reply, and birders who inquire at HQ will be directed to the best areas.

Birds: Wintering population is principally Canada geese and mallards. Migrant geese join a resident population of about 5,000. Small numbers of pintail, American wigeon, green-winged teal, wood duck, common merganser, and shoveler also winter here. Also bald and golden eagles, American kestrel, northern harrier, prairie falcon, goshawk, and red-tailed, Cooper's, sharp-shinned, and rough-legged hawks. Peregrine falcon have been seen. Species nesting in spring include eared and western grebes, great blue heron, black-crowned night-heron. Resident game birds include ring-necked pheasant, bobwhite, California quail, gray partridge.

Checklist of 190 species is available. Other seasonally abundant or common species include double-crested cormorant, blue-winged and cinnamon teals, common goldeneye, American coot, killdeer, common snipe, long-billed dowitcher, western sandpiper, American avocet, Wilson's phalarope, California and ring-billed gulls, Caspian and black terns, mourning dove, barn and burrowing owls, common nighthawk, northern flicker, downy woodpecker, eastern and western kingbirds. Swallows: violet-green, bank, cliff, rough-winged, barn. Black-billed magpie, American crow, American robin, ruby-crowned kinglet, cedar waxwing, European starling, yellow and yellow-rumped warblers, western meadowlark; red-winged, yellow-headed, and Brewer's blackbirds; northern oriole, western tanager, lazuli bunting, evening grosbeak, house finch, American goldfinch, dark-eyed junco; house, white-crowned, and song sparrows.

INTERPRETATION

Exhibits and *literature* at HQ, W end of upper dam, intersection of Lake and Lake Lowell avenues.

Nature trail, 1 mi., at HQ.
Films, talks, tours can be arranged, usually for groups and by advance reservations.

ACTIVITIES
Hiking: About 10 mi. of patrol road can be hiked Apr. 15–Sept. 30.
Hunting: Ducks, pheasant, partridge, quail.
Fishing: Large and smallmouth bass, crappie, perch.
Boating: Ramp. Motorboats and sailboats allowed Apr. 15–Sept. 30; no horsepower limit. Hand-propelled craft permitted all year, with Oct.–Jan. area restriction. The lake freezes 3 winters in 5.

PUBLICATIONS
Refuge leaflet with map.
Bird checklist.
Hunting, fishing, and boating information.

HEADQUARTERS: P.O. Box 448, Nampa, ID 83653; (208) 467-9278.

FORT BOISE WILDLIFE MANAGEMENT AREA; DEER FLAT NATIONAL WILDLIFE REFUGE (ISLANDS)
Idaho State Department of Fish and Game/U.S. Fish and Wildlife Service
1,444 acres; 110 river miles.

The WMA straddles the mouth of the Boise River where it flows into the Snake at the ID–OR line, just W of Parma. The entrance road is paved. The NWR includes 86 islands in the Snake, from a point S of Nampa, at the Canyon-Ada county line, to Farewell Bend, OR. (The main portion of the Deer Flat National Wildlife Refuge is at Lake Lowell, S of Caldwell. See entry.)

The WMA occupies the delta of the Boise River and extends down the Snake for over 2 mi. The area is generally flat, with many meanders and oxbows. The WMA also includes 330-acre Gold Island. Six smaller islands of the NWR complex surround Gold Island. All the federal islands are conspicuously posted. Islands are accessible only by boat.

Management priorities for the WMA, in order, are public hunting, pheasant and waterfowl production, other wildlife production, public fishing, and "wildlife appreciation." Most hunting is for pheasant, with duck hunting close behind. Visitors who come for fishing, birding, sightseeing, and other purposes outnumber hunters. Birding is good all year.

Plants: Riparian trees and shrubs in swales and on stream banks. Sagebrush-grassland on well-drained soils, grading into greasewood, saltgrass, and rabbitbrush. About 150 acres is ponded, producing emergent vegetation. 175 acres on the delta and 90 on Gold Island are irrigated cropland and pasture.

Birds: Habitats are favorable for pheasant and quail production, but hunting pressure is such that several hundred farm-raised pheasants are released each year. Canada goose nesting on the islands declined in the late 1970s, then recovered when the hunting season was shortened. Wild turkeys have been released and appear to be established.

A resident Canada goose population nests on the WMA and NWR islands, and along the Boise and Payette rivers. Other nesting species include ducks, herons, and gulls. Migrants begin to arrive in Sept., and by Dec. the area has a large concentration of mallards, with small numbers of goldeneye, lesser scaup, redhead, canvasback, bufflehead, ruddy duck, wood duck, and green-winged teal.

Other species common to the area include mourning dove, white pelican, dowitcher, American avocet, killdeer, marbled godwit, various hawks and owls, black-billed magpie, European starling, Brewer's blackbird, song and white-crowned sparrows.

Mammals: Mammals on the WMA include cottontail, muskrat, pocket gopher, porcupine, red fox, raccoon, weasel, and striped skunk. 30 to 40 mule deer move between islands and mainland.

ACTIVITIES

Hunting: Hunting is generally permitted on both WMA and NWR, subject to the usual federal and state regulations, plus local closures and rules about use and occupancy of blinds.

Fishing: On the WMA, designated sites. On both WMA and NWR some areas may be off limits during nesting and hunting seasons. Channel catfish, smallmouth and largemouth bass, black crappie.

Boating: The WMA has gravel ramps and floating docks. Installation of concrete ramps has been opposed, to discourage use of big boats and water skiing.

PUBLICATIONS: See Deer Flat NWR entry for publications.

HEADQUARTERS: *WMA:* Idaho Department of Fish and Game, Region 3, 109 W. 44th St., Boise, ID 83704; (208) 334-3725. *NWR:* Box 448, Nampa, ID 83651; (208) 467-9278.

GOODING CITY OF ROCKS

U.S. Bureau of Land Management
21,030 acres.

From Gooding, about 18 mi. N on SR 46. Turn left on gravel road at

Flattop Butte, an unmistakable landmark. A small sign (if it's still there) says, "City of Rocks—9 miles."

See entry for Little City of Rocks. You may wish to sample the area there before venturing further. The gravel road here ends after 3 mi. The dirt road beyond is likely to be rough in dry weather, treacherous when wet.

In the Mount Bennett Hills, the area consists of high plateaus cut by deeply eroded stream channels. The differing resistance to erosion by rock layers has produced a landscape of rhyolite columns and other striking shapes, to some viewers suggesting a ruined city. Others see ghosts and goblins. Formations are chiefly in the central area.

The area is semiarid, plant communities dominated by sagebrush except in drainages, most of which run N–S.

Wildlife: Elk graze the N portion of the area in summer. A few mule deer are present in summer, more in the S portion during the winter. Black bear have been seen. Chukar occur in canyons where water is available. Nesting raptors include golden eagle, prairie falcon, red-tailed hawk, great horned owl.

Sightseers and picnickers are more likely to visit the more accessible Little City of Rocks. Some hunting in the fall. Camping and horse riding are often associated with hunting. Some ORV activity occurs in spring and fall, snowmobiling in winter. Hiking use is moderate, chiefly in spring and fall when the Sawtooth area to the N is blocked by snow.

HEADQUARTERS: Shoshone District Office, BLM, 400 W. F St., Shoshone, ID 83352; (208) 886-2206.

HAGERMAN WILDLIFE MANAGEMENT AREA
Idaho Department of Fish and Game
880 acres.

From Hagerman, 2 mi. E on US 30. US 30 is the SW boundary, Snake River on the S and SE.

The entrance road leads to a state fish hatchery. The site has about 460 acres of sagebrush-grassland and includes cropland, ponds, marshes, irrigation ditches, Riley Creek, seeps, springs, and cottonwood-willow riparian strips.

The wetlands, closed to waterfowl hunting, hold over 100,000 mallard during the hunting season, from the end of Nov. into Jan. The site produces significant numbers of pheasant and valley quail.

Fishing is the principal public use. Visitors interested in wildlife are welcome at times and places that do not conflict with the site's mission. Project personnel give talks and tours as their duties permit.

Birds: Mallards outnumber all other waterfowl by more than 100 to 1. Nesting waterfowl include Canada goose, cinnamon teal, lesser scaup, ringneck duck, ruddy duck. Most common migrants include redhead, ringneck duck, pintail, gadwall, American wigeon, green-winged teal.

Other seasonally common species include coot, black-crowned nightheron, American bittern; red-winged, yellow-headed, and Brewer's blackbirds. Hawks: northern harrier, rough-legged, American kestrel. Also mourning dove, meadowlark, barn and bank swallows, black-billed magpie, European starling, American robin.

Mammals: Include muskrat, beaver, mink, raccoon, longtail and shorttail weasels, river otter, fox squirrel, yellowbelly marmot, sagebrush and longtail voles, striped skunk, porcupine, coyote, mountain cottontail, mule deer.

ACTIVITIES

Hunting: Pheasant, quail. Special rules.

Fishing: Largemouth bass, bluegill, rainbow and brown trout, yellow perch.

HEADQUARTERS: Region 4, Idaho Department of Fish and Game, 868 E. Main St., Jerome, ID 83338; (208) 324-4350.

JACKS CREEK
U.S. Bureau of Land Management
122,878 acres.

S of Grand View, SW of Bruneau. About 2 mi. S of Bruneau, SR 51 is just E of the creek, about 1 mi. from the confluence of Big and Little Jacks creeks. The roadless areas are to the W and SW

The principal feature of this region is its many spectacular canyons. The terrain is mostly gently rolling, sloping NE from about 5,000 ft. down to 2,455 ft. at the C. J. Strike Wildlife Management Area. The predominant sagebrush-grassland plant community is near-pristine in some parts of the area, free from the characteristic signs of prolonged overgrazing. The streams in most of the canyons are perennial. Annual precipitation is about 14 in. The canyon and surrounding plateau are Wilderness Study Areas.

The Little Jacks Creek roadless area has two major canyon systems separated by a sagebrush-covered basalt dome. Little Jacks Creek Canyon is 1,000 ft. deep, with steep, multitiered walls, 27 mi. long. 5 mi. to the NW, Shoofly Creek has cut a 600-ft.-deep canyon, the walls not as sheer as those of Little Jacks Creek but comparably scenic. Shoofly Creek is perennial.

Big Jacks Creek and 6 major tributaries have more than 50 mi. of rugged, sheer-walled, meandering canyons up to 700 ft. deep. The tributary canyons divide the surrounding plateau into narrow fingers. In an adjoining roadless area to the S, Duncan Creek has a 10-mi., 500-ft.-deep, meandering canyon linked to the Big Jacks Creek complex.

The canyons, near-pristine environment, and accessibility have made this region attractive to hikers and backpackers as well as hunters. In the Little Jacks Creek Canyon area, they are almost equally divided: hikers and backpackers active for about 800 visitor-days in the spring, hunters for 850 visitor-days in the fall. Most hiking is in the canyon bottom. Fishermen use the mouth of the canyon but few hike up it. In the Big Jacks Creek-Duncan Creek area, hunters make up 80% of the recreational use.

According to our BLM advisor, the best hiking is in Big Jacks Canyon in the vicinity of the Parker Trail. BLM's Boise office can provide maps and directions. The Wickahoney-Battle Creek Road, off SR 51, provides good auto access to the E side of Big Jacks Creek and to Duncan Creek. Wear tennis shoes, because the meandering creeks must be waded 20 or more times per mi. Hiking in the adjacent Little Jacks Creek is very difficult because of dense riparian vegetation, beaver ponds, and rock rubble.

None of the canyons have sufficient water for rafting or kayaking.

Wildlife: Visitors to the Little Jack Creek Canyon may see California bighorn sheep, reestablished there some years ago and now totaling more than 150. Mule deer are the principal big game species. Pronghorn are present all year, but scattered. Sage grouse are relatively common, as are chukar. Golden eagle are often seen.

REFERENCE: *A River Runners Guide to Idaho.* (BLM pamphlet.)

HEADQUARTERS: BLM, Boise District, 3948 Development Ave., Boise, ID 83705; (208) 334-1582.

JARBIDGE RIVER
U.S. Bureau of Land Management
75,000 acres.

Upstream access 2 mi. N of Murphy Hot Springs. On the official highway map, this settlement is at the airport symbol near the NV border, on the road W from US 93 at Rogerson, beyond Three Creek.

The Jarbidge River flows for 31 mi. in a deep canyon from the NV border to its confluence with the Bruneau River. The canyon has been cut through flat high plateau, a region receiving about 12 in. of precipitation yearly. One road crosses the river, about 2 mi. N of Murphy Hot Springs. Floaters put in here.

Strangers to this desolate region would do well to visit the Bruneau River Canyon first, because it is more accessible. (See entry.) BLM's Sheep Creek Quadrangle map shows a few roads coming close to the Jarbidge Canyon, but caution suggests inquiring about their condition before exploring.

Most of the surrounding area has been used for grazing, as indicated by various fence lines, small reservoirs, and dirt tracks. The canyon is scenic, meandering, and deep. Walls are often vertical. Riparian vegetation on the canyon bottom includes juniper, willow, tall shrubs, and grasses. Water, vegetation, and isolation make this prime habitat for bighorn sheep and winter range for mule deer. Otter and redband trout inhabit the river.

According to BLM's evaluation, the canyon offers opportunities for camping, backpacking, floating, nature photography, sightseeing, fishing, and hunting. The area has been recommended to Congress for inclusion in the Wild and Scenic River system.

ACTIVITIES

Hiking, backpacking: Hiking the canyon may be difficult or impossible during the runoff, Apr.–June, and very hot in midsummer. At other times it would require rock scrambling and wading. Some adventurers float with inner tubes during midsummer to avoid rock scrambling and poison ivy.

Rafting, kayaking: Suitable for small rafts and kayaks Apr.–June. Several outfitters have offered trips. Rapids to Class IV and logjams require expert boating skills. There is one portage. It's a 2- to 3-day trip to Indian Hot Springs on the Bruneau River, with no good exit en route. Boaters are asked to register.

PUBLICATION: *A River Runners Guide to Idaho.*

HEADQUARTERS: BLM, Boise District Office, 3948 Development Ave., Boise, ID 83705; (208) 334-1582.

LITTLE CAMAS RESERVOIR
Idaho Fish and Game Department
1,250 acres.

From US 20 about 20 mi. E of Mountain Home, 1 mi. N.

We saw the Sportsman Access sign and turned off the highway. We liked the site. It's a small reservoir, just big enough to be shown on the highway map, not big enough for Fish and Game to include it in the Official Fishing Guide. We mention it as a sample of ID's Sportsman Access sites.

The reservoir is surrounded by low sagebrush hills, with mountains in the distance. Adjoining wetlands offer good birding. There is an informal campground with latrines and trash receptacles, unpaved ramp, and dock. Like most such sites, it is visited chiefly by local residents. That day no one was there.

LITTLE CITY OF ROCKS
U.S. Bureau of Land Management
5,875 acres.

From Gooding, about 14 mi. N on SR 46. Look for dirt road on left.

Technically a Wilderness Study Area, it's really a children's playground. We hiked in from the highway, about a mile, but a car can make it easily in dry weather, taking care at a few rutted spots.

The road ends at the base of low hills, almost an amphitheater, with several hundred fascinating rock formations: columns, hoodoos, arches, spires, suggesting the ruins of some ancient city. They invite and inspire activity, from hide-and-seek to more imaginative play, and small feet have worn tracks among the formations. We saw signs of picnics and camping.

This is the most accessible part of an extensive roadless area in the Mount Bennett Hills, a rolling foothills belt between the Sawtooth Mountains to the N and the Snake River Plains to the S. A larger portion is the Gooding City of Rocks, the adjoining area to the W. (See entry.)

The area is semiarid, sparsely covered with sagebrush, grasses, and forbs. It offers opportunities for spring and fall hiking, when the Sawtooth trails are still snowbound.

HEADQUARTERS: Shoshone District Office, BLM, 440 W. F St., Shoshone, ID 83352; (208) 886-2206.

NIAGARA SPRINGS WILDLIFE MANAGEMENT AREA
Idaho Department of Fish and Game
957 acres.

On the Snake River W of Twin Falls, 6 1/2 mi. S of Wendell, by local roads.

The site is 1/2 mi. wide, with 3 1/2 mi. frontage on the Snake River. Most of it is at the base of a 400-ft. canyon wall. It includes a variety of wildlife habitats: ponds, wetlands, a stream, sagebrush-grassland, and cropland, in addition to the river, canyon wall, and talus. It also includes 8 islands in the river. This diversity supports resident and transient populations of waterfowl, upland game birds, many nongame birds, mule deer, and small mammals.

Management priorities are headed by upland game bird and waterfowl production, pheasant and waterfowl hunting, and fishing access. Visitors are welcome if they don't conflict with those priorities.

Birds: This is not a winter concentration area for mallards, as is the Hagerman WMA (see entry). Otherwise, its species inventory is similar. A noteworthy addition is wild turkey, released here in 1982 and apparently established.

Mammals: The species inventory is similar to Hagerman's. The talus slope here is habitat for a large population of yellowbelly marmot. Mule deer population is estimated at 30 to 50, increasing.

ACTIVITIES
Hunting: Waterfowl and pheasant.
Fishing: Bank, in the Snake. Rainbow trout, channel catfish, brown trout. Some trout fishing in ponds and stream.

HEADQUARTERS: Region 4, Idaho Department of Fish and Game, 868 E. Main St., Jerome, ID 83338; (208) 324-4350.

OWYHEE RIVER
U.S. Bureau of Land Management
240 river miles in 3 states.

No main highway crosses the river in ID. US 95 crosses in OR. Most of the land adjoining the river canyons is roadless, approached by unpaved roads.

This is an overview. See other entries for more detail.

The Owyhee River rises in northern Nevada, flows through the Duck Valley Indian Reservation into Idaho, exits at the NW corner of the Reservation, and flows WNW, joining its South Fork about 5 mi. from the Oregon border. The portion below the Reservation can be floated Apr.–June. The area offers attractive but demanding backpacking.

(The official ID highway map calls the river before the confluence the "East Fork Owyhee River." So does BLM. The U.S. Geological Survey calls it the "Owyhee.")

The South Fork also arises in NV flowing NNW into ID through a scenic canyon about 45 mi. long cut into desert terrain. This portion offers attractive but demanding backpacking. About 45 mi. can be floated Apr.–June, continuing into ID.

About 11 mi. to the W, the Little Owyhee flows N from NV, joining the South Fork about 12 mi. N of the border, 7 mi. E of OR. 7 air miles further N, the meandering South Fork joins the Owyhee. (One popular atlas calls it "South Fork Owyhee River" *after* the confluence. This nonsense is abandoned a few miles into OR.)

This SW corner of ID is high desert, relatively flat below the Owyhee Mountains and foothills, cut by many steep-walled canyons. The highway map shows no roads. BLM has a quadrangle map covering most of the area, showing several primitive roads.

See entry: Owyhee Canyonlands.

The Owyhee flows W into OR, then turns N, soon to be joined by its Middle Fork and North Fork at Three Forks. Here it is a famous, spectacular, and dangerous whitewater stream until it enters the long, narrow Owyhee Reservoir.

The Middle Fork rises in an ID spring about 5 mi. E of the border. In that short distance it is joined by several tributaries. The North Fork rises on the S side of the Owyhee Mountains in ID, collecting streams from several other drainages before entering OR. This area is characterized by canyons and the forested Juniper Mountains.

See entry: Owyhee River: North and Middle Forks.

Most of the land surrounding the Owyhee and its many tributaries in ID is public domain. The state owns 2 sections in each 36-section township, and ranchers own a few tracts.

The entire 240-mi. route of the main river from the Indian Reservation to the reservoir was proposed for inclusion in the Wild and Scenic River system. The OR section has been included. The South Fork is proposed for study to determine its suitability for inclusion.

OWYHEE RIVER: NORTH AND MIDDLE FORKS
U.S. Bureau of Land Management
93,610 acres.

On the Oregon border SW of Mountain Home. The highway map shows a secondary road from Grand View to the Border, crossing the North Fork.

This area differs from the Owyhee River Canyonlands (see entry) in several respects. The terrain is mountainous rather than flat, although the range of elevations is little more than 1,500 ft. Vegetation includes dense juniper forest as well as sagebrush meadows. Annual precipitation is greater, about 16 in. per year. Somewhat more private land, together with low-standard roads, separates BLM roadless areas into two large blocks about 4 mi. apart.

These roadless areas are on the northern and western flanks of Juniper Mountain, a southern extension of the Owyhee Mountains, rising to 6,775 ft. The rough, broken terrain of the slopes is cut by V-shaped canyons 100 to 300 ft. deep. Below are sagebrush-covered basins and plateaus. To the N of Juniper Mountain is the scenic canyon of the North Fork, about 30 mi. long, narrow, meandering, 300 ft. deep, with sheer walls and rock pinnacles. The canyon bottom has a mix of wet meadows, grasses, willows, and shrubs. The shorter Middle Fork drains the W side of Juniper Mountain. Both streams flow W into OR, there joining the main Owyhee at Three Forks.

Our BLM advisor wrote, "The North Fork is one of the most beautiful areas of the southwest Idaho desert, particularly during the spring flower season. It is very accessible by a gravel road on the south side."

Most of the visitors who come here are hunters. It is estimated that hunting in the Juniper Mountain area totals about 4,500 visitor-days per year. BLM's wilderness studies attracted a few backpackers, but only about 180 visitor-days per year in the North Fork area. River flow is generally insufficient for floating, but we were told a few expert kayakers have floated the lower portion of the North Fork in OR.

Wildlife: Mule deer is the primary big game species, although the habitat is rated poor to fair. Pronghorn are thinly scattered in sagebrush expanses. Sage grouse are on the increase. Some waterfowl use the area for resting and nesting. Beaver and otter are present. Fishing for native redband trout is rated poor to fair.

HEADQUARTERS: BLM, Boise District Office, 3948 Development Ave., Boise, ID 83705; (208) 334-1582.

OWYHEE CANYONLANDS
U.S. Bureau of Land Management
225,650 acres in ID.

Ask BLM about access. No all-weather road touches the canyon rims in ID. Floaters have a few established put-in sites. Campers, hikers, hunters, and fishermen have other options. Low-standard approach roads may be impassable when wet.

We are selective about sites with difficult access. This region couldn't be omitted. It's scenic, colorful, dramatic, wild, isolated. It is under Wilderness study. Most who come here are boaters in the spring floating season, hunters in fall and winter. Not many of either.

The Canyonlands complex extends for about 240 river miles in NV, ID, and OR, including almost 450,000 acres. The ID acreage, more than half the total, is made up of 7 contiguous roadless areas on the East and South Forks, the East Little Owyhee, and tributaries.

This is a region of a mile-high desert plateau, flat to gently rolling with a sparse cover of sagebrush and bunchgrass and scattered western juniper. Blue, yellow, and white flowers spangle the land in spring. Winters are long and cold. Only about 100 days a year are frost-free. Summers are hot, at least by day, and dry.

Cut into the plateau is a network of meandering, narrow canyons, from 200 to 1,200 ft. deep. In many areas, sheer walls rise from river to rimrock. Often there are talus slopes between cliffs and the river, or talus above the cliffs, or several terraces of cliffs and talus. In places the rock has been eroded into columns and spires. Most of the rock colors are shades of brown and red, but lichens and small plants add green, yellow, and orange to the landscape. Canyon bottoms support a rich, often dense plant community: grasses, rushes, sedges, willow, aspen, and cottonwood.

In many places, a hiker can scramble up a talus slope to the canyon rim. Hiking on the plateau is easier than below, and it offers fine views of both the canyon and almost limitless open space, sometimes with snow-capped peaks visible on the horizon.

Birds: The upper river attracts many migratory waterfowl for nesting and resting. 22 species have been reported. Golden eagle, red-tailed hawk, American kestrel, prairie falcon, and owls nest in the canyons. The canyons are winter habitat for bald eagle. Sage grouse are abundant on the plateau, with chukar along canyon bottoms and lower slopes. Mountain quail are found in the canyon of the South Fork.

Mammals: Mule deer are the most abundant big game species. California bighorn sheep were introduced in the 1960s and have multiplied. Pronghorn are scattered across the plateau. Other mammal species include mountain lion, river otter, bobcat, beaver.

ACTIVITIES

Camping: No developed campgrounds, but campsites are everywhere. No potable water, unless you know where to find a spring. The few campers who know the best springs and swimming holes may share their knowledge with people they trust.

Hiking, backpacking: Hiking conditions in the canyons range from passable to impassable, often calling for rock scrambling and wading. Advisable to visit BLM and talk with someone who has been there and can suggest an access route and hiking objective.

Hunting: Big game, upland birds.

Fishing: Not outstanding. Small trout populations; smallmouth bass increasing.

Horse riding: On the plateau; not much opportunity in the main canyon, but in tributaries.

Rafting: Float parties are required to register. Above Three Forks, beginning about 30 mi. below the confluence of East and South Forks, rafts, kayaks, and canoes can be used. The East Fork has two hard portages, more if the trip begins in the Duck Valley Indian Reservation, but otherwise mostly Class I and II whitewater. No portages on the South Fork; mostly Class II and III. Class IV and V rapids below the East Fork-South Fork confluence and below Three Forks may require portages.

Most current rafting on the Owyhee is below Three Forks, chiefly in OR, and most commercial outfitters operate there. A few offer trips on South Fork and East Fork. Ask BLM.

PUBLICATION: *Boating on the Owyhee River.*

HEADQUARTERS: BLM, Boise District Office, 3948 Development Ave., Boise, ID 83705; (208) 334-1582.

SALMON FALLS CREEK AND RESERVOIR
U.S. Bureau of Land Management
34,000 water acres at full pool; land acres indeterminate.

From Rogerson on US 93, 21 mi. S of Twin Falls, W about 7 mi. to dam.

This out-of-the-way area is known chiefly to nearby residents. Upper Salmon Falls Creek flows N in a canyon N from Nevada. The dam W of Rogerson backs up a pool about 12 mi. long to within 7 mi. of the border. Elevation at the dam is about 5,000 ft. Below the dam, the creek is in Lower Salmon Falls Canyon. Most of the surrounding land is public domain, but the principal opportunities for recreation are within the canyons and on the reservoir. Canyon hikers are estimated to be fewer than 500 per year. Upstream rafting and canoeing attract perhaps 1,000. Many more come to the reservoir for camping and water-based recreation. The reservoir is subject to heavy drawdowns.

Best access is the road to the dam. Here BLM has a campground and boat ramps. For routing to the canyons, we suggest consulting the BLM office or seeking local information.

Upstream: A roadless area of 5,977 acres in ID, 11,790 acres in NV, was not recommended for wilderness study because the land surrounding the canyon didn't meet the naturalness criteria. The canyon, however, is scenic and offers opportunities for camping, hiking, canoeing, rafting. Cottonwood Creek, a tributary canyon in NV, has similar characteristics. The canyons are incised in flat to rolling terrain. Several unimproved roads, not shown on highway maps, run to or near the canyon rim from US 93. The meandering canyons have sheer walls and talus slopes. Broad bottoms have dense willow stands and grassy meadows.

Downstream: Below the dam, the meandering river canyon is up to 400 ft. deep with only a few points of access. An area of 3,500 acres, including 16 mi. of the canyon, was recommended for wilderness study. Several unimproved roads not shown on highway maps lead to both E and W sides of the canyon rim. Riparian vegetation on the canyon bottom includes willow, juniper, and grasses. The canyon offers opportunities for backpacking, hunting, fishing.

ACTIVITIES

Camping: Chiefly at the BLM site near the dam. Informal camping along unimproved roads.

Hiking, backpacking: In the canyons, upstream and downstream.

Fishing: Trout fishing is said to be good for 10 mi. below the dam. In the reservoir: walleye, perch, landlocked salmon, trout, carp, suckers. Ice fishing in winter.

Rafting, canoeing: Said to be moderately good upstream, with a floating season extending from spring through much of the summer.

HEADQUARTERS: Burley District Office, BLM, Rt. 3, Box 1, Burley, ID 83318; (208) 678-5514.

SNAKE RIVER BIRDS OF PREY AREA

U.S. Bureau of Land Management
482,000 acres.

From I-84, exit 44. S 8 mi. to Kuna, then S on Swan Falls Road. The area begins 5 mi. S of Kuna. Canyon parking areas are between 12 and 15 mi. S.

We're delighted it's there, but it's no place for a casual visit. One should consider both when and where to go. We drove from Kuna in summer, before visiting the BLM office, knowing it was not the season to see the raptors.

Road signs point the way and tell when you've entered the area. One said BLM plans to build an overlook. Otherwise we saw nothing but open sagebrush-grassland until we arrived at the access road for Swan Falls Dam. From the top we got our first view of the canyon, above and below the dam. Descending, we found ourselves in a power company complex, with much construction under way. Signs admonished us not to stop, park, or camp. No sign told us what, if anything, we could do. BLM has no information station or bulletin board in the area.

The site map in BLM's folder shows roads in the canyon above and below the dam. Access to the upstream road was gated. Access to the downstream road was at least temporarily blocked. Neither was signed. From above, we saw jeep tracks and trails on both sides of the canyon.

Later, at the Boise District Office, we were told an on-site information program would soon be in place. A nature trail-interpretive site is being built at Dedication Point. A nature trail suitable for wheelchairs will lead from Swan Falls Road to the overlook.

The area's primary mission is preserving birds of prey, not providing public recreation. The deep canyon of the Snake River attracts more nesting raptors than any known location of comparable size in North America. 14 species of raptors have been observed. Golden eagle and prairie falcon are most abundant. An estimated 6 to 10% of the entire nesting population of prairie falcon in the United States assembles in this area.

In addition to nesting sites offered by canyon ledges, the birds need an abundant food supply. This is why the site includes so many acres of surrounding fields and desert, ideal hunting grounds for birds of prey. Ten years of research defined the support requirements. Except for a few sections of state and private land, almost the entire area was in the public domain. The purpose of establishing the Snake River Birds of Prey Natural Area in 1971 was to protect essential nesting habitat along a portion of the canyon. Legislation protecting the surrounding area was adopted in 1980. Permitted activities such as cattle grazing were not outlawed.

The time to come here is mid-Mar. through June. In the first weeks of this period, birds are courting and establishing nesting territories, then laying and incubating eggs. After hatchings, the adults are busy hunting for food and caring for the young. By July—which is when we came—most raptors have departed. Elevation along the rim is about 2,500 ft. Spring weather is unpredictable. High winds are common. Summer temperatures often exceed 100°F.

Raptor viewing is best from the two parking areas adjacent to the canyon rim. Visitors are warned to exercise caution near the rim. Climbing the cliffs isn't allowed. Viewing birds on the nests and ledges requires good binoculars or, better still, a spotting scope on tripod. For photography, a long telephoto lens is necessary. Birds can often be seen riding the updrafts out of the canyon, then soaring out across the desert.

Canoeing or rafting the canyon is also a good way to observe the birds. The put-in site at Black Butte, near Grand View, is used both by private parties and outfitters. There are no rapids in the 20 mi. to the take-out at Swan Falls Dam, and this section is suitable for rafts and canoes. Boaters should plan to spend one night camping en route. Boaters can float below the dam for 10 mi. to Guffey Railroad Bridge, and to Walters Ferry 6 mi. further by paddling. Several Class II rapids below the dam require some skill.

Most of the land near the dam belongs to the Idaho Power Company. The gate to the upstream road is kept closed, but visitors are welcome to pass through. A new boat ramp is replacing the one we saw on the upstream side; another is below the dam. Canyon visitors may use the downstream road, although it's in poor condition, suitable only for 4-wheel drive. BLM and the power company have been discussing road improvements.

Birds: Checklist of 210 species is available at the Boise office. Raptors include prairie falcon, American kestrel, golden and bald eagles, northern harrier, osprey. Hawks: red-tailed, ferruginous, Swainson's, rough-legged, northern goshawk, Cooper's, sharp-shinned. Owls: great horned, long-eared, short-eared, western screech, common barn-owl, burrowing, saw-whet. Also turkey vulture, common raven, western meadowlark, horned lark.

Mammals: Include Townsend ground squirrel and blacktail jackrabbit, both important prey species. Also cottontail, yellowbelly marmot, antelope ground squirrel, kangaroo rat, pocket gopher, coyote, badger, mule deer.

ACTIVITIES

Camping: Camp anywhere except near nesting areas. Pack out all refuse. Bury human waste but not unburned food (which would be dug up, making a mess).

Hiking: We saw no trail along the canyon rim, but limited hiking is possible. From above the dam, we saw jeep tracks and trails on both sides of the canyon. Hikers must not scramble on cliff walls.

Boating, rafting: Power boats, rafts, and canoes are suitable both above and below the dam. Downstream whitewater requires some experience. All boaters must register in advance. Forms can be obtained from BLM's Boise office and at the Black Butte put-in. BLM has a list of outfitters offering float trips.

NEARBY: C. J. Strike Wildlife Management Area, Bruneau Dunes State Park. See entries.

Hazards: Scorpions and rattlesnakes are common. So is poison ivy.

PUBLICATIONS
Leaflet with road map.
Folder with color illustrations of raptors.
Snake River Birds of Prey. Booklet, 52 pp., color illustrations.

HEADQUARTERS: BLM, Boise District Office, 3948 Development Ave., Boise, ID 83705; (208) 334-1582.

SNAKE RIVER, MURTAUGH SECTION
U.S. Bureau of Land Management
14 river miles.

Put-in is 1/2 mi. N of Murtaugh at the Murtaugh Bridge.

BLM calls it "the best big whitewater day run in the United States." In BLM's Shoshone office, we watched a film of two intrepid kayakers running the Murtaugh and the even more hazardous Milner section just upstream. The kayaks were hurled about, submerged, pitchpoled, rolled, but somehow came through.

The Murtaugh Run has numerous Class III, IV, and V rapids. Pair of Dice rapids is a dangerous Class VI; floaters are advised to portage or at least scout the rapid before trying it. The Murtaugh can usually be run spring and fall. The only take-out is above Twin Falls Dam on the S side.

The rapids can be seen from a place of safety. The Hansen Bridge is less than a mi. S of I-80 on US 30. Pair of Dice rapids is upstream, Let's Make a Deal rapids downstream.

BLM's leaflet says the Milner section is shown on the map "as a warning to boaters." The Milner Run is upstream from the Murtaugh, take-out just above Star Falls. According to the leaflet the Milner has "continuous Class V rapids, huge hydraulics and suck holes and very few eddies."

We were told that an outfitter had tested the Murtaugh by raft. The raft was demolished and hauled out at the bridge. Kayaks seem to be the only suitable craft.

Among the many admonitions to those contemplating the run: One member of the party should have had experience on this run.

NEARBY: Star Falls, between the Milner and Murtaugh, is one of the last remaining free waterfalls on the Snake, spectacular in high-flow periods. From the Murtaugh Bridge, continue N, E on the first gravel road; in about 1/2 mi. turn S on the first dirt road. Road improvements were impending when we visited, but if it's still a dirt road, have a look before descending into the canyon.

PUBLICATION: Leaflet and map, Murtaugh and Milner sections.

HEADQUARTERS: BLM, Shoshone District Office, 400 West F St., Shoshone, ID 83352; (208) 886-2206.

ZONE 4

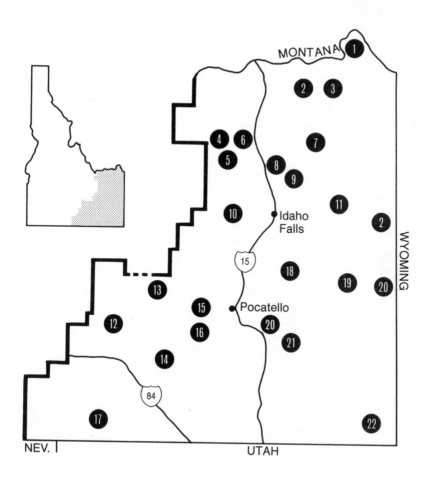

ZONE 4

Includes these counties:

Clark	Fremont	Bonneville
Madison	Teton	Blaine (S tip)
Bingham	Minidoka	Caribou
Power	Bannock	Franklin
Cassia	Oneida	
Bear Lake	Jefferson	

Zone 4, in SE Idaho, has extraordinary variety. In its N are the Centennial Mountains, the W edge of Yellowstone National Park, Henrys Lake and Henrys Fork, the splendid Harriman State Park, and the W side of the Teton Range.

The central portion of the zone has a volcanic wilderness and other volcanic features on its W. On the E, the Targhee National Forest surrounds Palisades Reservoir. Below the dam, the Snake River South Fork offers scenic floating through plains and canyons.

The S has basin-and-range topography. Most of the small ranges are in the Sawtooth and Caribou National Forests, providing opportunities for day hiking, fishing, and hunting. In the valleys are streams and lakes, including a complex of National Wildlife Refugees: Grays Lake, Bear Lake, Camas, and Minidoka.

BEAR LAKE NATIONAL WILDLIFE REFUGE
Southeast Idaho Refuge Complex
U.S. Fish and Wildlife Service
17,605 acres.

From Montpelier, 7 mi. S on county road through Dingle.

Bear Lake is a large body of water lying across the ID-UT line. A county road cuts across the N tip. The Refuge lies N of this road. An area of marsh, open water, and grasslands, it is not, as the map suggests, on the Bear River; however, it receives a regulated supply of water from the river. Part of the

E boundary is along the steep, rocky, brush-covered slopes of Merkley Mountain.

It isn't arranged for visitors. Up to 85% of the area is flooded at high water, and travel is restricted during the nesting and rearing season. However, the Salt Meadow wildlife observation route at the N end of the site is open, with good viewing of shorebirds and waterfowl. If you're passing this way in May–June or Sept., turn E at Paris on the Paris-Dingle road, then S along the Refuge outlet canal. This provides a 7-mi. round trip.

Birds: Checklist of 130 species notes seasonality and abundance. The Refuge is a primary nesting ground for Great Basin Canada goose. Other nesting species include mallard, gadwall, pintail, shoveler, redhead, western grebe, double-crested cormorant, great blue heron, snowy egret, white-faced ibis, American bittern, American avocet, Franklin's and California gulls, Forster's and black terns, red-winged and yellow-headed blackbirds.

Several years of high runoff have raised the level of Great Salt Lake, inundating state waterfowl refuges around the lake and the Bear River National Wildlife Refuge in Utah—which we understand has been abandoned. We asked if the Bear Lake Refuge had experienced any consequent changes. The only marked change that seems attributable is a large increase in nesting population of white-faced ibis.

Spring migrants usually start arriving in Mar.; Apr.–May are the peak months. Fall migration begins in Aug. By mid-Oct., waterfowl are the most numerous birds present. There are few winter residents.

Hunting: Designated areas. Special rules.

PUBLICATIONS
Leaflet with map.
Bird checklist.

HEADQUARTERS: 370 Webster St., Montpelier, ID 83254; (208) 847-1757.

BIRCH CREEK VALLEY
U.S. Bureau of Land Management
Indeterminate acreage.

From I-15 N of Idaho Falls, W on SR 33 to Mud Lake, then NW 20 mi. to campground.

SR 28 is in the Birch Creek Valley. On the NE are the Beaverhead Mountains of the Bitterroot Range, with the Continental Divide at their crest. The valley is at about 7,000 ft. elevation. Scott Peak, in the Beaverheads, is 11,393 ft. The

Lemhi Range on the SW also has peaks over 11,000 ft. The valley-side slopes of both ranges are in the Salmon National Forest.

Much of the valley land is BLM-managed public domain, although there are many scattered blocks of private land. BLM also has a 24,922-acre Wilderness Study Area on the slope below the Continental Divide from Baldy Mountain S to Eighteenmile Peak. Numerous deep creek valleys drain to the Birch Creek Valley. The WSA adjoins a National Forest area considered for Wilderness status. The Lemhi Range, over 70 mi. long, is Idaho's longest uncrossed by any public road.

ACTIVITIES

Camping: BLM's John Day campground has 12 sites, tables, grills, latrines, a convenient base.

Fishing: Birch Creek is a blue-ribbon trout stream.

HEADQUARTERS: Idaho Falls District, BLM, 940 Lincoln Road, Idaho Falls, ID 83401; (208) 529-1020.

BLACKFOOT RIVER
U.S. Bureau of Land Management
Indeterminate acreage; about 50 river miles.

From US 91, 2 mi. S of Firth, turn W on Wolverine Creek Road. 9 mi. to Wolverine Creek. 30 mi. of gravel road parallels the river to Blackfoot Reservoir.

Blackfoot Reservoir, about 12 mi. long, 6 mi. wide, is a locally popular site for water-based recreation: boating, water-skiing, fishing, swimming, camping. Most of the shoreline is public domain. BLM has a campground at the S end. A state Fishing Access Site is at the N end.

From the reservoir, the river flows W, then loops around the N boundary of the Fort Hall Indian Reservation, entering the Snake River near Blackfoot. About 80% of the riparian land is public domain. The Blackfoot Mountains rise on the NE. Elevation of the reservoir at full pool is 6,118 ft.; elevation at Blackfoot is 4,504 ft.

The river is little known, unpublicized. The big guidebook *Idaho for the Curious* doesn't mention it. The Bureau of Land Management's *Recreational Rivers* doesn't either. River outfitters don't advertise it. When we planned our field work, nothing flagged the Blackfoot River.

Our BLM advisor at Idaho Falls told us about it. Beautiful country, he said, fairly dry, but a greenbelt of riparian vegetation along the river, colorful in the fall. The river canyon is broad below the dam, narrow and steep-walled further downstream. Good fishing, good camping. Not a well-known whitewater stream, but there is a good 12-mi. run that outfitters use.

NEARBY: Wolverine Creek Canyon drains to the Blackfoot River near the N tip of the Indian Reservation. (From Firth, S on US 91 for 1 1/2 mi. Turn E into Wolverine Canyon. E about 9 1/2 mi.; stay left; about 4 mi. to BLM's Wolverine Creek campground. 3 sites; no latrines.)

ACTIVITIES

Camping: BLM has 3 small campgrounds: Graves Creek, Cutthroat Trout, and Sagehen Flat.

Hiking: In side drainages.

Rafting, canoeing: From the dam down to BLM's Cutthroat Trout campground, it's Class I and II water, good canoeing. The 12 mi. from the campground to Trail Creek have Class II and III rapids, approaching IV. Several outfitters offer trips on this stretch. Below Trail Creek, the river drops as much as 100 ft. per mi., with some Class V and VI rapids; "Not suitable for boating," says *A River Runner's Guide to Idaho.*

Flows are controlled at the dam. Outside the irrigation season, when the reservoir level is being raised, the river may be dewatered.

HEADQUARTERS: Idaho Falls District, BLM, 940 Lincoln Rd., Idaho Falls, ID 83401; (208) 529-1020.

CAMAS NATIONAL WILDLIFE REFUGE
Southeast Idaho Refuge Complex
U.S. Fish and Wildlife Service
10,578 acres.

From Idaho Falls, 30 mi. N on I-15. Exit E at Hamer. N 3 mi. on frontage road, W across freeway; see Refuge sign.

Of the refuges in the SE complex, this offers the best opportunities for birding. About half of the area is occupied by scattered lakes, ponds, and marshes. The two largest lakes occupy 600 and 700 acres. Camas Creek flows for 8 mi. across the area. The rest is sagebrush, uplands, meadows, and cropland. Unpaved roads border most of the lakes and marshes and along the creek. Visitors can drive these roads, with the warning that some are impassable in wet weather. One can also hike.

Birds: Checklist of 177 species notes seasonality and abundance. During migrations, up to 100,000 ducks and 3,000 geese may be present. Peaks occur in Mar.–Apr. and Oct.–Nov. Most numerous in migrations: mallard, northern pintail, gadwall, American wigeon, Canada goose. Principal nesting species: redhead, mallard, northern shoveler, lesser scaup, blue-winged and cinnamon teals. Trumpeter swans have begun nesting recently.

Other seasonally common or abundant species include pied-billed, eared, and western grebes; double-crested cormorant, American bittern, great blue heron, snowy egret, black-crowned night-heron, white-faced ibis, tundra swan, green-winged teal, canvasback, ring-necked duck, common goldeneye, bufflehead, common and red-breasted mergansers, ruddy duck. Hawks: northern harrier, Swainson's, red-tailed, rough-legged. Golden and bald eagles, American kestrel. Ring-necked pheasant, sage grouse, American coot, sandhill crane, killdeer, black-necked stilt, American avocet, willet, long-billed curlew, Wilson's phalarope. Franklin's, ring-billed, and California gulls; black tern, mourning dove, great horned and short-eared owls, common nighthawk, northern flicker, eastern and western kingbirds, horned lark, bank and barn swallows, black-billed magpie, American crow, common raven, black-capped chickadee, marsh wren, American robin, sage thrasher, European starling, yellow and MacGillivray's warblers, vesper and savannah sparrows, dark-eyed junco; red-winged, yellow-headed, and Brewer's blackbirds; western meadowlark, brown-headed cowbird, house finch, American goldfinch, house sparrow.

Mammals: Include mule deer, pronghorn, moose, muskrat, beaver, jackrabbit, coyote.

ACTIVITIES
Hiking: On Refuge roads at any time. Off roads except Mar. 1–July 15.
Hunting: Designated areas; special rules.
Boating: Small boats; no motors; except Mar. 1–July 15.
Ski touring: On Refuge roads; off roads to Mar. 1.

NEARBY: Market Lake and Mud Lake Wildlife Management Areas (see entries).

PUBLICATIONS
Refuge leaflet with map.
Bird checklist.

HEADQUARTERS: HC 69, Box 1700, Hamer, ID 83425; (208) 662-5423.

CARIBOU NATIONAL FOREST
U.S. Forest Service
1,080,322 acres in ID; 6,948 acres in WY; 6,956 acres in UT.

Several blocks in SE ID. Two large blocks are W and E of US 30. US 89 crosses the S tip of the largest.

139 &v ZONE 4

Here is no vast, unspoiled wilderness. Although about 72% of the Forest is unroaded, the largest roadless area is just over 100,000 acres. At no point can a hiker be more than 4 mi. from a road. To the dismay of some conservationists, Forest management recommended only 2 of 34 roadless areas, 30,600 of 775,251 roadless acres, for Wilderness designation.

Its attractions and accessibility make it a popular Forest, recording about 500,000 visitor-days per year. Next to sightseeing, camping is the principal activity, followed by hunting and fishing. Activity is year-round: hiking in summer, horse riding in summer and fall; skiing, ski touring and snowmobiling in winter.

Most of these visitors come from nearby. Travelers seeking a Forest experience are likely to go to the larger and wilder National Forests in central and northern ID, or just over the border in WY or UT. Forest HQ provided us with a mountain of excellent information, including descriptions of each roadless area and ecological unit, annotated lists of fauna, and much more. Together with our field notes, this could have made one of our longest entries. We decided a summary would be more appropriate.

The blocks of Forest land are on N–S mountain ranges. They include both timber and rangeland. The mountains rise steeply from semiarid sagebrush plains or agricultural valleys.

The largest block is on the WY border, extending N from just E of Montpelier to a point W of Palisades Reservoir. Most of it is in the Soda Springs Ranger District; the southern 22 mi. is in the Montpelier R.D. The N portion is on the Caribou Range; in the S is the Webster Range and several lesser ranges. The block is an irregular oblong about 64 mi. N–S, 7 to 21 mi. W–E. Peaks over 8,000 ft. are scattered throughout the block. The Forest's highest point is 9,953-ft. Meade Peak in the far S of this block. US 89 crosses the S tip through Montpelier Canyon, in which are three Forest campgrounds.

Second largest is the block extending 45 mi. N from the UT border just W of Bear Lake, along the N end of the Wasatch Range. It is the remaining three-fourths of the Montpelier R.D. Average width is about 9 mi. Small canyons cut into the range on both sides. The block's best-known feature is Minnetonka Cave.

Four smaller, irregularly shaped blocks lie between the Fort Hall Indian Reservation and the UT border. They are generally mountainous, on small ranges: the Portneuf, Bannock, and Malad. The two northern blocks are the Pocatello R.D., the two southern blocks the Malad R.D., which also administers the Curlew National Grassland.

The Forest has 2,437 mi. of roads. About 500 mi. are all-weather. Others, unpaved, range from good to poor. The 1,200 mi. of trails also range in condition from good to poor.

The Forest has almost 1,500 mi. of fishable streams. Two lakes and two reservoirs with a combined area of 437 acres also support fisheries. Both reservoirs are subject to heavy drawdowns. The Forest map, issued in 1963, shows frontage on Palisades Reservoir and the Snake River, but this area, in the far NE, is now administered by the Targhee NF. The Blackfoot River, NE of Soda Springs, is formed by the joining of two creeks. It flows through a steep-walled canyon, then out into a valley. Only 2.2 mi. of the canyon are within the Forest, but it's scenic and accessible by road.

Climate. Summers are hot, winters moderately cold. Total annual precipitation ranges from 12 to 50 in. Except in the mountains, little rain falls in summer. Much of the annual total falls as snow.

Plants: Sagebrush dominates the lower elevations, with rabbitbrush, bitterbrush, chokecherry, serviceberry, horsebrush, maple, juniper, aspen, and grasses. Higher elevations are forested, with lodgepole pine, Douglas-fir, Engelmann spruce, aspen, and mountain-mahogany. Aspen and lodgepole pine usually replace the original species following fire. About 35% of the Forest is timberland, less than half of it suitable for intensive timber management.

Birds: The Forest's Environmental Impact Statement lists 248 bird species, noting the Ranger Districts in which they were observed but without indication of abundance. It's a remarkably long list for any Forest, especially one with few areas of open water and wetlands. We assume many of the species would be classified as Rare or Occasional.

Mammals: The list of 63 species notes the Districts in which they were observed and those which reproduce in the Forest. Two of those listed, kit fox and ringtail, are outside their normal ranges, but both are listed as reproducing.

FEATURES

Stump Creek Roadless Area, 100,965 acres, is the largest roadless unit. About 20 mi. NE of Soda Springs, it is in the Caribou and Webster mountain ranges, with elevations from 6,000 to 9,131 ft. It has about 85 mi. of developed trails. Important habitat for deer, elk, and moose, as well as sandhill crane and grouse. Light to moderate recreational use includes hunting, fishing, snowmobiling, hiking, ski touring.

Worm Creek Roadless Area, 41,565 acres, is about 8 mi. W of St. Charles. 16,000 acres have been proposed for Wilderness status. The area is penetrated by several roads, including one in St. Charles Canyon. Included are foothills, high basins, and steep, rocky peaks, several about 9,000 ft. elevation. It also includes a small lake. The area has about 32 mi. of trails.

St. Charles Canyon is the Forest's most popular recreation area. The road W from St. Charles runs through the scenic canyon to *Minnetonka Cave,* Idaho's largest developed cavern, 1/2 mi. long. Three campgrounds are in the canyon.

Curlew National Grassland, 47,600 acres, is 16 mi. W of Malad on SR 37.

Like other National Grasslands, this an area where, in the 1930s, the federal government acquired degraded farmland unable to yield adequate returns to its owners. The purpose was to rebuild the range and serve as a demonstration area for nearby landowners. Grasslands are good birding sites.

High Line Trail extends about 40 mi. N from near Minnetonka Cave. A National Recreation Trail, it is one of the Forest's longest and most scenic.

INTERPRETATION

Cherry Springs Nature Area, on the Bannock Highway about 10 mi. S of Pocatello. Self-guiding trail. Facilities for the handicapped.

The Forest has no visitor center.

Some *campfire programs* were offered in the Pocatello area in 1986 and may be continued.

ACTIVITIES

Camping: 24 campgrounds; 288 sites. 13 are May–Oct., 11 June–Sept.

Hiking, backpacking: 1,200 mi. of trails. Most are open to motorized vehicles under 40 in. wide. Funds for trail maintenance have been curtailed. Some lightly used trails are vanishing.

Hunting: Big game hunting, chiefly for deer and elk, is popular, but it represents only 6% of the visitor-days. Hunting for small game and upland birds represents less than one-third as many.

Fishing attracts about as many visitors as big game hunting. Chiefly trout.

Horse riding is slightly more popular than hiking. Most horse use is associated with hunting.

Skiing: The Pebble Creek Ski Area is 15 mi. SE of Pocatello. Normal season: Christmas through Mar.

Ski touring: On trails and unplowed roads. Access to groomed trails near Pocatello is from Park "N" Ski areas requiring permit. Trail map available at Pocatello R.D. office.

PUBLICATIONS

Forest map (1963 edition). $1.

Travel Plan map.

Recreation Information. Pamphlet.

Minnetonka Cave leaflet.

Guide to the Lander Cut-Off Oregon Trail.

REFERENCE: Maughan. Jackie J. *The Hiker's Guide to Idaho.* Billings, MT: Falcon Press, 1984. Pp. 254–58, 261–63.

HEADQUARTERS: Federal Building, 250 S. 4th, Pocatello, ID 83201; (208) 236-6700.

RANGER DISTRICTS: Soda Springs R.D., 140 E. 2nd S., Soda Springs, ID 83276; (208) 547-4356. Montpelier R.D., 431 Clay, Montpelier, ID 83254;

(208) 847-0375. Malad R.D., 75 S. 140 E., Malad, ID 83252; (208) 766-4743. Pocatello R.D., Federal Building, 250 S. 4th, Pocatello, ID 83201; (208) 236-6700.

GRAYS LAKE NATIONAL WILDLIFE REFUGE
Southeast Idaho Refuge Complex
U.S. Fish and Wildlife Service
18,575 acres; 32,825 acres within boundaries.

From Soda Springs, N 27 mi. on SR 34. The route then turns E, skirting the S end of the Refuge. In about 9 mi., turn N on local road to HQ, 5 mi. N of Wayan.

The Refuge has the world's largest nesting population of greater sandhill cranes, over 200 pairs. They begin arriving in early Apr. More sandhills gather here in the fall before migrating to Arizona, New Mexico, and Mexico.

Grays Lake was chosen as the site for an attempt to establish a second wild breeding population of the critically endangered whooping crane. Eggs taken from wild birds in Canada and captive birds at Patuxent, MD, are placed in sandhill nests here. The first hatchings occurred in 1975. When we visited in 1986, the first phases of the experiment had been successful: eggs hatched, sandhills reared the whooper nestlings, the fledged whoopers joined the sandhill migration, and a significant number return to this region. None had mated and nested, presumably because there are as yet few females of breeding age.

If you want to see whooping cranes, this may not be the best place to try. The interior of the Refuge is closed to visitors from about mid-Apr. to Oct. Cranes are easily spooked. An observation site is on a small hill near HQ, and cranes can sometimes be seen from the public road. Cranes may be out in the open, in the grain fields, in Sept. Earlier they are more likely to be out in the marsh, and, after June, hidden by vegetation.

Winters are severe. Snow covers the Refuge Nov.–Apr. Few birds remain, and the public roads are likely to be impassable.

The "lake" is a large, shallow marsh with little open water and dense vegetation, chiefly bulrush and cattail, surrounded by wet meadows, grasslands, and cultivated fields.

Birds: There's more to be seen than cranes, and the observation areas can be rewarding, especially with binoculars or scope, May–June and Sept. A checklist of 174 species notes seasonality and abundance. Common nesting species include mallard, cinnamon teal, canvasback, lesser scaup, redhead, Canada goose. Typical production is 5,000 ducks, 2,000 geese.

Hunting: Permitted in specified areas, with special rules.

PUBLICATIONS
Refuge leaflet with map.
Bird checklist.
Hunting information.

HEADQUARTERS: HC 70, Box 4090, Wayan, ID 83285; (208) 574-2755.

GREAT RIFT
U.S. Bureau of Land Management
322,450 acres.

Two large lava flows, S of the Craters of the Moon National Monument. The Arco-Minidoka road, not shown on the highway map, parallels the E boundary of the larger unit, then turns SW between the two units. From this road, numerous dirt roads lead to the site boundary. High-clearance vehicle and BLM map recommended.

Few people have ever crossed this vast and difficult area. There are places of special interest on or accessible from the perimeter. It would be frustrating to seek them without a BLM map and advice.

Visit the National Monument before you consider coming here. The larger of the BLM units is part of the Craters of the Moon lava flow. The Monument's visitor center provides a quick education in volcanology. The Monument has the same volcanic features. Hiking the Monument's trails suggests what off-trail travel is like in this rough, abrasive terrain. The Monument's Wilderness adjoins this BLM site.

The Great Rift is a tremendous fissure extending 65 mi. NW–SE, up to 800 ft. deep. It opened about 15,000 years ago, inaugurating a period of lava flows that ended only 2,000 years ago. Successive flows cooled into a landscape of thick, jagged blocks, with many spatter cones, ice tubes, caves, and other formations. The Rift is marked by a long line of cinder cones. One could follow this line from the Monument down through the BLM area, but it would be a long walk. The Great Rift is more accessible from the perimeter.

The climate is hot and dry in summer, cold in winter. Annual precipitation is 10 to 14 in., most falling in winter and spring.

Of the few visitors who enter this forbidding area, about 200 per year, many are attracted by the kipukas. (Most dictionaries ignore the Hawaiian words for volcanic phenomena, although there are no English equivalents. *Kipukas* are vegetated islands of older lava surrounded by newer flows.) The area has over 450 kipukas, ranging in size from less than one acre to over 2,200 acres. Few of them have water, but intermittent pools gather in some depressions. Botanists are interested because over 300 plant species are found in the areas, and because most kipukas are isolated and undisturbed habitats. Pioneer plants such as mosses and lichens are found in small crevices. The oldest plants are junipers, some up to 750 years old. Kipukas also have a distinctive wildlife. One BLM visitor was surprised to find bear tracks.

Some kipukas are accessible by unpaved roads, such as Wood Road in the SW of the smaller unit, but you should have advice on routing and whether high clearance is needed.

Also attractive are the many caves. In summer, the caves are cool; a few have ice. Artifacts indicate that Indians used them.

Lava lands, like deserts, are an acquired taste, but some find them fascinating. Two BLM staff members talked enthusiastically about places they've visited in the Great Rift. It helps to know what you're looking at, how to read the history of the lava flows and interpret the succession of plant life.

The lava flows extend far beyond this site. Most areas of exposed lava remain in the public domain. Our BLM advisors thought few readers would want to see more volcanism than the Monument and Great Rift, but those with special interest may wish to ask about these:

ADJACENT AND NEARBY

Crystal Ice Cave, commercially operated under BLM permit, is within the area and accessible. From I-86, exit at American Falls; N on SR 39 6 mi. to North Pleasant Valley Rd. Follow signs for 23 mi. 1,200-ft. tunnel. Open May 1–Oct 1. Office of concession: (208) 226-2465.

Raven's Eye, 67,110 acres. The N tip is near the town of Carey on US 20. (See entry for Carey Lake Wildlife Management Area.) The N portion is part of the Craters of the Moon flow, with a rough, broken surface. Features include pressure ridges, lava cascades, subsidence craters, lava blisters. Older flows in the S portion are soil-covered and vegetated. This area is marked by 3 volcanic cones.

Sand Butte, 20,792 acres, adjoins the S end of Raven's Eye, separated from it by a dirt road. Its principal feature, the butte, is a maar crater, formed by a great explosion when erupting magma met groundwater. Our BLM advisor said it looks like a football stadium ready for installation of seats.

Hiking, backpacking: If you've been to Craters of the Moon and want to see an undeveloped area of lava flow, by all means visit the BLM office first. Traversing areas of aa—the tumbled blocks of abrasive lava—is next to impossible. But there are extensive areas of pahoehoe, ropy and smoother; you'll need to know where they are. A few ORV routes penetrate the flow area. Get a map; decide on a route; and leave word. Don't enter the area without a resourceful companion and ample water.

HEADQUARTERS: Idaho Falls District, BLM, 940 Lincoln Rd., Idaho Falls, ID 83401; (208) 529-1020.

HARRIMAN STATE PARK
Idaho Department of Parks and Recreation
4,700 acres.

Off US 20 at Island Park.

One of the most magnificent and unusual State Parks to be found anywhere. The setting is splendid: the floor of a huge caldera, more than 20 mi. across, crater of an ancient volcano. Henrys Fork of the Snake River cut through the walls of the caldera long ago and now meanders across lush meadows. Park elevations range from 6,200 to 6,600 ft.

For 75 years this was the site of the Railroad Ranch, a private hunting reserve and cattle ranch. The ranch buildings stand on a promontory overlooking river and meadows, backed by the forested caldera wall, with the snow-capped Centennial Mountains beyond.

In 1961 the ranch owners, Mr. and Mrs. E. Roland Harriman and W. Averell Harriman, offered to the state of Idaho the ranch headquarters site in the caldera plus more than 10,000 acres of other ranch lands. To accept, the state had to meet conditions guaranteeing preservation of the natural environment. The Park land plus 10,000 acres of adjoining National Forest land, must be managed as a wildlife refuge, with no hunting or trapping; this interagency agreement was a precursor of the Greater Yellowstone plan now taking shape. The state must maintain a year-round waterfowl sanctuary, permit fly fishing only, make payments to Fremont County in lieu of property taxes, and retain all grazing and other fees for use on site. Furthermore, the state must establish a professionally staffed park service. Meeting these conditions took time. The Department of Parks and Recreation was established in 1965. It was 1977 before ownership was transferred. The Park opened to the public in 1982.

The 27 log ranch buildings are still in place, some open to the public, others housing Park personnel and services. Habitats include *Forest,* chiefly lodgepole pine with some Douglas-fir and aspen; *sage meadows* at forest edges, green and dotted with colorful wildflowers in summer, brown in fall; and *wetlands* well populated with waterfowl. *Water bodies* include 150-acre Silver Lake, 50-acre Golden Lake, numerous ponds. Habitat for waterfowl, fish, and small mammals. *The river,* one of the finest fly fishing streams in the West, attracts moose, fishing birds such as bald eagle and osprey. 6 mi. of Henrys Fork are within the Park.

Plants: Only 600 acres within the Park are forested, although extensive forests are nearby. Common flowering plants include snowberry, rosy pussytoes, Canadian buffalo berry, kinnikinnick, umbrella plant, serviceberry, mountain laurel, Oregon grape, woolly daisy, false dandelion, dandelion, salsify, common yarrow, aster, false Solomon's-seal, sego lily, fireweed, Indian paintbrush, lupine, brodiaea, common camas, arrowleaf balsamroot, dogtooth violet, starflower, larkspur, milkvetch, heartleaf arnica, groundsel, meadow goldenrod.

Birds: Checklist of 171 species available. Seasonally common species include common loon, eared and western grebes, great blue heron, trumpeter swan, Canada goose, mallard, gadwall, pintail; green-winged, blue-winged, and cinnamon teals; ring-necked duck, lesser scaup, common goldeneye, ruddy duck, bufflehead, common merganser, turkey vulture, bald eagle, northern harrier, osprey, red-tailed hawk, American kestrel, great horned owl, ring-billed gull, Caspian tern, mourning dove, blue grouse, sandhill crane, American coot, killdeer, common snipe, long-billed curlew, northern flicker, Lewis' woodpecker, Wilson's phalarope, downy woodpecker, eastern kingbird, belted kingfisher, western wood-pewee, olive-sided flycatcher; rough-winged, barn, and cliff swallows; gray jay, common raven, dipper, marsh wren, American robin, mountain bluebird, yellow warbler, house sparrow, western meadowlark; yellow-headed, red-winged, and Brewer's blackbirds; pine siskin, vesper and sage sparrows, dark-eyed junco.

Mammals: Checklist of 62 species available. Common species include little brown and Yuma myotis, least chipmunk, yellowbelly marmot, Uinta ground squirrel, northern pocket gopher, beaver, deer mouse, western jumping mouse, muskrat, porcupine, coyote, longtail weasel, striped skunk, river otter, elk, mule deer, moose.

Reptiles and amphibians: Checklist of 13 species available. Common species include tiger salamander, leopard frog, common garter snake.

The town of Island Park, on US 20, is within the caldera, and here one sees evidence of the cooperative relationship between Park and National Forest. Henrys Fork is W of the highway. Short access drives lead to parking areas for fishermen. At the highway is a sign: "Welcome to Harriman State Park and Targhee National Forest. Recreation Area next 20 miles." Other signs give fishing information.

INTERPRETATION

Reception center has information, publications, and a walk with several outstanding kiosk exhibits. For example, one exhibit explains that sagebrush traps snow in winter, so it lasts longer in spring, slowly releasing moisture. Where ranchers remove sagebrush, most of the snow blows off, and these areas are drier in summer. There is also a river overlook with exhibits.

Jones House visitor center has slide shows, swan observation in winter. *Guided nature walks and wagon rides.*

ACTIVITIES

Camping: Harriman is for day use only. Campgrounds in the Targhee National Forest and at Henrys Lake State Park.

Hiking: Excellent trail map, posted at the reception center and reproduced in a leaflet. 9 mi. of trails through the several habitats. We found the lakeshore and pond-side trails excellent for wildlife observation and photography.

Horse riding: 4 mi. of horse trails. Stable. Riders must be accompanied by a guide.

Fishing: Rainbow, eastern brook, and native cutthroat trout; whitefish. Fly fishing with barbless hooks only. Fishing season is shortened to avoid disturbance to nesting waterfowl.

Ski touring: On 9 mi. of trails. 2 to 3 mi. groomed. Jones House is warming center. Snowpack of 4 to 6 ft. is normal. Temperatures below −40°F occur occasionally.

Pets are permitted in parking area only, on leash.

NEARBY

Targhee National Forest (see entry). Box Canyon campground is near the Park. A 14-mi, scenic drive is E of US 20 between Island Park and Ashton. Warm River Campground on this route is exceptionally attractive.

Island Park Reservoir, 7,000 acres. Fishing, boating.

Upper and Lower Mesa Falls.

Big Springs, headwaters of Henrys Fork.

Henrys Lake State Park. Camping, boating.

PUBLICATIONS

Leaflet with map.
Area map. $.35.
Hiking trail map.
Ski trail map.
Equestrian trail brochure.
Historical guide. $.25.
Checklists of flowering plants, birds, mammals, reptiles, and amphibians.
Nature notes on various species.

HEADQUARTERS: Star Route, Box 33, Ashton, ID 83420; (208) 558-7368.

HELL'S HALF ACRE
U.S. Bureau of Land Management
66,200 acres.

From Idaho Falls, about 20 mi. W on S 20. On left, Twenty-Mile Rock and a sign noting that 44,000 acres S of here are a National Natural Landmark.

BLM map and high-clearance vehicle are needed for travel on interior roads.

Many of the features of this 4,100-year-old lava flow can be explored on foot. Boy Scouts and school groups come here. One can hike in to the source vent, a shield cone, explore caves, tunnels, and kipukas. Volcanic features include deep crevices, fissures, ridges, depression, spatter cones. Much of the surface is pahoehoe, ropy and billowing, easier for walking than are the shattered blocks of aa.

Pioneer plants such as lichens and mosses cling to lava surfaces. Ferns are among the plants rooted in small crevices. Kipukas are islands of vegetation of diverse species, including junipers.

Sage grouse and mourning dove are hunted near the boundary. Mammals include mule deer, pronghorn, coyote, rabbit.

Don't venture far from the perimeter without water, strong shoes, and a companion.

HEADQUARTERS: Idaho Falls District, BLM, 940 Lincoln Rd., Idaho Falls, ID 83401; (208) 529-1020.

HENRYS LAKE STATE PARK
Idaho Department of Parks and Recreation
586 acres.

From the Island Park bridge on US 20, 10 mi. N; W 2 mi. at sign. Park is 15 mi. W of the West Gate of Yellowstone National Park.

Henrys Lake, a natural water body enlarged by a dam, has a surface area of 6,200 acres, at 6,472 ft. elevation. The lake is at the foot of the Henrys Lake Mountains. Except for the Park, the lake is surrounded by private land. The Targhee National Forest is nearby.

ACTIVITIES

Camping: 32 sites. Closed by snow in winter. Some visitors to Harriman State Park (see entry) camp here.

Fishing: Brook and cutthroat trout; rainbow-cutthroat hybrids.

Boating: Ramp.

HEADQUARTERS: Macks Inn, ID 83433; (208) 558-7532.

MARKET LAKE WILDLIFE MANAGEMENT AREA
Idaho Department of Fish and Game
4,876 acres.

From I-15 about 20 mi. N of Idaho Falls, take Roberts exit. From Roberts, N on old highway parallel to I-15, about 2 mi. This road cuts across the site.

A fine area for birding. Marshes are on both sides of the old highway. 15 mi. of interior roads. The SE corner, near HQ, has 3/4 mi. of frontage on the Snake River. The Butte-Market Lake Canal crosses this corner. The site includes 3 large marshes totaling 1,580 acres, 12 springs and artesian wells, 6 mi. of channels and drains.

Birders and general sightseers are the principal visitors, far outnumbering hunters. However, the site is not well known except to nearby residents, and crowding is no problem.

Terrain is relatively flat, elevation 4,780 ft. Summers are warm, winters cold. Annual precipitation is about 11 in. Marshes usually freeze in mid-Nov., thaw in late Mar. or early Apr. Average winter snow depth is 8–12 in., with drifts.

Birds: Up to 750,000 waterfowl use the area for 2 or 3 weeks in the spring migration, fewer in the fall. In one recent year, this included 500,000 pintails, 200,000 mallards, 10,000 snow geese, 500 Canada geese. Other seasonally common species include snowy egret, black-crowned night-heron, white-faced ibis, gadwall; green-winged, blue-winged, and cinnamon teals; American wigeon, shoveler, golden and bald eagles, American coot, Franklin's gull, horned lark, bank swallow, black-billed magpie, American crow, American robin, house sparrow, yellow-headed blackbird.

Mammals: Mule and whitetail deer, moose, and elk inhabit the nearby Snake River corridor, some wintering on the site. Common species include cottontail, blacktail and whitetail jackrabbits, chipmunk, marmot, raccoon, beaver, muskrat, mink, otter, weasel, badger, porcupine, spotted skunk, bobcat.

NEARBY: Camas National Wildlife Refuge; Mud Lake Wildlife Management Area. See entries.

ACTIVITIES
Camping: Permitted, but few visitors camp. Mostly overnight parking of ORVs.

Hunting: Chiefly waterfowl, pheasant, jackrabbit.
Fishing: Marshes and river. Rainbow trout, bass, bluegill, crappie, perch. Some spring cutthroat fishing in the river.

HEADQUARTERS: Region 6, 1515 Lincoln Rd., Idaho Falls, ID 83401; (208) 522-7783.

MASSACRE ROCKS STATE PARK
Idaho Park and Recreation Department
565 acres.

Off I-84, 12 mi. W of American Falls.

The Park is on a bluff overlooking the Snake River, downstream from American Falls Dam. The landscape is volcanic. Layers exposed by erosion show both a variety of volcanic rocks and the deposits of ancient lakebeds. Vegetation is juniper-sagebrush.

Birds: Checklist of 200 species. The uplands, bluffs, riparian area, and river islands provide an attractive environment and good birding. Many waterfowl, shorebirds, and raptors.

Mammals: Visitors may see marmot, beaver, coyote, muskrat, badger, cottontail.

INTERPRETATION
Visitor center has geological and historical displays, publications.
Campfire programs, Fri.–Sat. in summer.
Nature trail with brochure, emphasizing geological and botanical features.
Devil's Garden displays unique geological features.
Register Rock is in a picnic area just off the highway, 2 mi. W. Oregon Trail travelers scratched their names on the rock.

ACTIVITIES
Camping: 52 sites, all year.
Fishing: River. Chiefly trout.
Boating: Launching ramp on the river.

PUBLICATIONS
Park leaflet with map.
Information page; things to do.
Bird checklist.
Nature trail guide.

Historical leaflet.
The Geology of Massacre Rocks State Park. 12 pp. $.26.

HEADQUARTERS: HC 76, Box 1000; American Falls, ID 83211; (208) 548-2672.

MENAN BUTTES
U.S. Bureau of Land Management
340 acres.

3 mi. S of SR 33 at a point 9 mi. W of Rexburg, visible from the highway.
Easy foot access along ORV tracks.

The site is near the confluence of Henrys Fork and the South Fork of the
Snake River. When lava erupted through a fissure about 30,000 years ago, it
met cold river water. The result was a violent explosion, hurling great blocks
of basalt. The sudden chilling solidified two cones of glassy tuff, 500 and 800
ft. high. The cones are a National Natural Landmark. Most of the surrounding land is public domain, although the southern butte is private.

340 acres have been designated a Research Natural Area because of the
unique geological features and the variety of range vegetation types. Sagebrush-grassland types are dominated by Basin big sagebrush, black sagebrush,
and three-tip sagebrush, with scattered Utah juniper. Understory dominants
are bluebunch wheatgrass, Sandberg bluegrass, and needle-and-thread grass.

HEADQUARTERS: BLM, Idaho Falls District, 940 Lincoln Rd., Idaho Falls,
ID 83401; (208) 529-1020.

MINIDOKA NATIONAL WILDLIFE REFUGE
Southeast Idaho Refuge Complex
U.S. Fish and Wildlife Service
20,721 acres.

From Rupert, 6 mi. NE on SR 24, then 6 mi. E on County 400 North.

The Refuge surrounds 11,000-acre Lake Walcott Reservoir, formed by
Minidoka Dam on the Snake River. The reservoir is narrow, 25 mi. long, with
many small bays and inlets and an abundance of aquatic vegetation. Sur-

rounding uplands are chiefly sagebrush and grassland, with sand dunes and stands of juniper.

Great concentrations of waterfowl occur during spring and fall migrations, numbers sometimes reaching 100,000 in the fall. Seeing them isn't easy. The road to Refuge HQ is well maintained, but other roads aren't suitable for cars. Boating is permitted but restricted to the W end of the reservoir, to protect waterfowl from disturbance. One can hike, but 25 miles is a long walk.

Birds: Checklist of 201 species notes seasonality and abundance. In migration, large populations of redhead, lesser scaup, ruddy duck, and canvasback are common. Mallard and pintail are prominent, with numerous gadwall, American wigeon, northern shoveler, ring-necked duck, bufflehead, and green-winged, blue-winged, and cinnamon teals. Tundra swan are seen in spring. Nesting species include Canada goose, mallard, gadwall, pintail, ruddy duck, redhead. Also great blue heron, black-crowned night-heron, snowy egret, double-crested cormorant, grebes, white-faced ibis, long-billed curlew, American avocet. White pelican appear in summer but haven't nested.

ACTIVITIES

Hiking: The shoreline is long, so ask at HQ where the action is.

Hunting: Waterfowl, upland game birds, cottontail. Designated areas; special rules.

Fishing: State regulations plus designated areas and special rules.

Boating: Ramp near HQ. Restricted to a 4,400-acre area at the W end of the reservoir. Season: Apr. 1–Sept. 30. Motors permitted.

PUBLICATIONS

Refuge leaflet with map.
Bird checklist.
Hunting and fishing information.

HEADQUARTERS: Route 4, Box 290, Rupert, ID 83350; (208) 436-3589.

MUD LAKE WILDLIFE MANAGEMENT AREA
Idaho Department of Fish and Game
8,853 acres.

From I-15 about 23 mi. N of Idaho Falls, left on SR 33 about 14 mi. Site is N of the highway.

The site almost surrounds 2,000-acre Mud Lake. The area was once desert with wet meadow supplied by Camas Creek. Building dikes confined the water in the present shallow lake. The S boundary is close to the lake shore, with public roads just outside. HQ is at the SW corner. Internal roads give access to the N shore. Boat docks are on both N and S shores.

The lake is used to accumulate and dispense water for irrigation. Fish and Game doesn't control lake levels. High water often inundates waterfowl nests, curtailing production, and fluctuations of the lake level have drastically reduced trout population. However, the site is an important stopover for migratory birds. Hunting, fishing, birding, and general sightseeing are the chief visitor activities. Most visitors come from nearby, the largest number on opening day of the waterfowl season. Visitation at other times is light, often zero on weekdays.

Birds: 28 species of waterfowl and 34 species of shorebirds have been recorded. Spring use is highest, with up to 150,000 ducks, 50,000 snow geese, and 5,000 geese arriving, numbers peaking in Mar.–Apr. Fall migrants begin arriving in late Aug., up to 90,000 ducks, 60,000 coots, 2,500 Canada geese, few snow geese. Pheasant populations crashed in the 1970s; game farm birds are released just before hunting season. The site's bird list closely resembles that for Market Lake WMA (see entry).

Mammals: Pronghorn and mule deer use the area in winter. Cottontail, jackrabbit, muskrat, and beaver are common. Also occurring: mink, raccoon, fox, bobcat.

ACTIVITIES

Camping: Permitted, but few people camp, chiefly hunters with RVs.

Hunting: Chiefly waterfowl and pheasant.

Fishing: Chiefly perch. Stocking of trout and other species has had little success.

Boating: A few fishermen use cartoppers.

NEARBY: Camas National Wildlife Refuge; Market Lake WMA. See entries.

HEADQUARTERS: Region 6, 1515 Lincoln Rd., Idaho Falls, ID 83401; (208) 522-7783.

PETTICOAT PEAK
U.S. Bureau of Land Management
11,298 acres.

From US 30 at Lund, 18 mi. W of I-15, N on road toward Bancroft. The site is on the left. One access road is about 1 mi. N, into Rindlisbacher Canyon.

A place for day hiking and hunting. At over 8,000 ft., Petticoat Peak is the highest of several in the small Fish Creek Range, rising half a mile from its base, offering sweeping vistas. Terrain is steep. Many canyons and ridges radiate from the peak. The S and E sides are heavily forested with limber pine, lodgepole, and Douglas-fir. On the W side, juniper, sagebrush, and mountain shrubs, including maple. Aspen groves in the moist draws.

Fall is the most scenic time, with the bright colors of maple and aspen, but hikers may prefer to keep out during the deer and grouse hunting seasons.

Most visitors come from nearby, and recreational use has been light. The growing resort community of Lava Hot Springs is only a mile away, so visitation will probably increase.

HEADQUARTERS: Idaho Falls District, BLM, 940 Lincoln Rd., Idaho Falls, ID 83401; (208) 529-1020.

PIPELINE RECREATION AREA
U.S. Bureau of Land Management
23 acres.

From I-86, exit at American Falls. About 1 1/2 mi. S on frontage road. Right at BLM sign.

This small picnic site provides public access to the Snake River below American Falls Dam. Chief use is by fishermen, many of whom use small boats with motors. Some people use small rafts. We were told there are rapids both above and below the site, but not major whitewater. The current is often swift and the channel is rocky.

Good birding. Bald eagles often fish nearby.

ACTIVITIES
Camping: Informal.
Fishing: Rainbow and cutthroat trout. BLM said up to 25 pounds.
Boating: Ramp.

HEADQUARTERS: Burley District Office, BLM, Rt. 3, Box 1, Burley, ID 83318; (208) 678-5514.

SAND CREEK WILDLIFE MANAGEMENT AREA
Idaho State Department of Fish and Game
26,914 acres.

SANDS MOUNTAIN WILDERNESS STUDY AREA

ST. ANTHONY SAND DUNES SPECIAL RECREATION MANAGEMENT AREA
U.S. Bureau of Land Management
21,740 acres; 36,900 acres.

From St. Anthony, 4 mi. W on North Parker Rd., then 2 mi. N on Red Road. Or, from Parker, 3 mi. W to Egin Lakes area.

These three units are within a huge 430,000-acre area encompassed by the Sands Habitat Management Plan. This HMP sprawls from just S of SR 33, W of Rigby to within a few miles of the Continental Divide. Land ownership is a checkerboard. BLM is the largest owner. The Plan is a cooperative undertaking of federal, state, and private landowners. It gives priority to wildlife.

The WMA's main HQ is 2 mi. N of Parker, a sub-HQ 17 mi. N of St. Anthony. Its N boundary is on the SW slope of Big Bend Ridge, which rises to 6,200 ft. The unit extends SW into semiarid rangeland. Topography is rolling hills with broken lava reefs and 15 mi. of live sand dunes. Several large dunes are in the S, where elevation is about 5,200 ft.

Most of the area is sagebrush-grassland, with scattered bitterbrush, choke-cherry, shinyleaf ceanothus, snowberry, and other shrubs. Aspen, lodgepole pine, and Douglas-fir grow on the slopes of Big Bend Ridge.

BLM's WSA is part of a 45,000-acre area of live sand dunes, the highest rising about 500 ft. The Recreation Area is 6 mi. W of St. Anthony. Most visitors come to ride ORVs on the dunes.

Summers are warm, winters long and cold, with temperatures of −40°F not uncommon. Annual precipitation ranges from 8 in. in the S to 16 in. in the N. Average snow depths range from 2 ft. in the S to 6 ft. on the ridge. Wind speeds up to 50 mph are common Mar.–May.

Big game management is the primary theme of the cooperative scheme and Fish and Game's priorities. The chief concern is elk introduced in this region in the 1940s, thereafter increasing to substantial numbers. They summer N of here, gather on the W end of the Big Bend Ridge in the fall, then move S and W, their movements depending on the severity of the winter.

Many threats cloud their future, chiefly agricultural encroachment on their winter range and the proposed Egin-Hamer road. A narrowing corridor between Egin (not on the highway map; W of St. Anthony) and Hamer is winter home for about 2,000 elk. The Fremont and Jefferson county commissions, at the behest of a few landowners, asked BLM for permission to build an 8-mi. all-weather road through the heart of this corridor. It would have devastating effects on the herd. Local officials committed to the Habitat Management Plan were preparing to say no when they were pushed aside by BLM's Washington office. The issue seems likely to be taken to court. The Reagan Administration may have departed before a final decision.

Next to elk, Fish and Game's priorities relate to mule deer and moose wintering, sage and sharp-tailed grouse production, and public hunting. Public fishing ranks fifth among the priorities, but it's the primary attraction for visitors; fishermen outnumber hunters 3 to 1. The only fishing is in 5 small ponds, totaling 165 acres, constructed by Fish and Game and stocked with rainbow trout. Camping ranks third behind hunting, but many campers come to fish. Hiking, picnicking, horse riding, and snowmobiling are also attractions. The sand dunes attract ORVs. As in other WMAs, most visitors are from nearby.

Birds: Sharptailed and sage grouse occur over most of the WMA. Waterfowl, mourning dove, sandhill crane, and trumpeter swan are also common. 115 bird species have been recorded.

Mammals: Deer were scarce in the 1930s, have since increased, with occasional setbacks. About 2,000 are now on the winter range. About 100 moose winter on or near the WMA. Pronghorn occur in small numbers. Coyote, marmot, and muskrat are common. Whitetail and blacktail jackrabbit are abundant, as well as ground squirrel, pocket gopher, and other small mammals.

Camping: On the WMA, a campground with minimum facilities is located near the ponds. A camping area without facilities is on the E side of the BLM area.

Sand tracks make treacherous routes for passenger cars in summer, when the sand is dry and blowing.

HEADQUARTERS: Fish and Game, Region 6, 1515 Lincoln Rd., Idaho Falls, ID 83401; (208) 522-7783. *BLM,* Idaho Falls District, 940 Lincoln Rd., Idaho Falls, ID 83401; (208) 529-1020.

SAWTOOTH NATIONAL FOREST
U.S. Forest Service
1,347,422 acres, excluding acreage in the Sawtooth National Recreation Area.

Most of the acreage is in Zone 2. The Southern Division includes 5 smaller blocks on or near Idaho's southern border, one of them in Utah; all are S of the Snake River between Twin Falls and American Falls. See entry in Zone 2.

SILENT CITY OF ROCKS
Mixed federal, state, and private ownerships
6,800 acres.

From I-84 at Rupert, S 23 mi. on SR 77. SW 16 mi. to Almo. Then W 4
mi., the last part on dirt road.

In 1972 the National Park Service recommended that this area become a
National Monument. When we visited in 1986, NPS, BLM, the U.S. Forest
Service, the Idaho Department of Parks and Recreation, and Idaho Department of Fish and Game were developing a joint plan for the area. No facilities
were in place except a picnic site with no water. Some visitors came to see
the spectacular rock formations, not as many as the "National Monument"
label would attract. Others came to climb.

The area has hundreds of towers, pinnacles, and other rock structures, the
tallest of them more than 600 ft. above their bases, some pointed, some
mushroom-shaped. It was first described by pioneers on the California Trail,
which crossed the site; portions of it are still visible.

The tallest pinnacles are the Twin Sisters, at the picnic site. One, we were
told, is 2 1/2 billion years old, the other 250 million. We must have misunder-
stood.

The access road passes through the formations. Several drainages converge
in Circle Creek, which flows most of the year. Vegetation is a mixture of trees,
notably juniper, pinyon pine, and aspen; shrubs such as serviceberry and
mountain-mahogany; grasses and wildflowers. Wildlife includes a variety of
birds, ground squirrel, cottontail, jackrabbit, coyote, badger, mountain lion,
bobcat, and mule deer.

The site is on part of the Albion Range. It adjoins and includes a portion
of the Albion Division of the Sawtooth National Forest.

PUBLICATION: Leaflet with map.

FOR FURTHER INFORMATION: Burley District Office, BLM, Rt. 3, Box 1,
Burley, ID 83318; (208) 678-5524; or Idaho Department of Parks and
Recreation, 2177 Warm Springs Ave., Boise, ID 83720; (208) 334-2154.

SOUTH FORK SNAKE RIVER
U.S. Bureau of Land Management; U.S. Forest Service; Idaho Department
of Fish and Game
64 river miles.

E of Idaho Falls. Various access points from US 26, from Palisades Dam downstream to Menan.

On many maps it's just "Snake River," but BLM prefers to add "South Fork" for the segment between Palisades Reservoir and the junction with Henrys Fork. Whatever the label, it's splendid, a candidate for Wild and Scenic River status, but with easy access. Flatwater, no rapids, it can be floated in almost any kind of craft, though skill is required to avoid hazards. There's hiking along the canyon rim and up side canyons. Boaters can camp on islands, backpackers along the trail.

For 9 mi. below the dam, the river flows just S of US 26 in a narrow channel. It then broadens and meanders among 39 large and small islands. Until US 26 crosses to the S side, the river is close to the N edge of the Caribou National Forest. Both the Forest and BLM have some river frontage, but most of the valley is private farmland.

After the bridge, the river turns N, and for several miles the BLM-managed lands include both the islands and a riparian strip. Then the river enters a scenic canyon with vertical walls several hundred feet high. The tall cottonwoods growing on the banks and islands are considered a unique ecosystem. The canyon is at the boundary of the Targhee National Forest, at the foot of the Snake River Range. A fine trail follows the canyon rim. Side trails ascend Dry Canyon, Black Canyon, and Table Rock Canyon. For about 10 mi., Forest Road 206 also follows the river. The Cottonwood Access, marked on the *Boater's Guide* (see Publications) is on 206.

Near Heise the river emerges from the canyon onto a flood plain, once again close to US 26. From here to its confluence with Henrys Fork, there's farmland on both sides, but the dense cottonwood forest along the banks provides a sheltered avenue.

The South Fork is one of the few remaining free-flowing stretches of the Snake. It's a famous fishery, a blue ribbon cutthroat trout stream. Motorboats use the river, and trailbikes operate on the trails. Up to now these have been minor disturbances.

Cress Creek nature trail is near Heise. From US 26, take the Heise road; just across the river, turn left on gravel road, 1 1/4 mi. to parking lot. Good birding, seasonal wildflowers.

Wildlife: Bald eagles and a few golden eagles nest in the large cottonwoods and winter throughout the corridor. Large numbers of ducks and geese winter and nest. Several great blue heron rookeries are in treetops. Grouse and over 80 species of nongame birds have been observed. Big game animals include mule and whitetail deer, moose, occasional mountain goat; in 1985 bighorn were sighted above Heise Hot Springs, the first ever recorded here. Also present: river otter, beaver, bobcat, mountain lion.

ACTIVITIES

Camping: Boaters have their choice of islands and some shoreline sites. Hikers, too, can find overnight spots. For motorists there's a Forest Service site near the highway bridge at Falls Creek, and a BLM campground on Kelly's Island near Heise.

Hiking, backpacking: South Fork trail parallels the river for about 6 mi.

Fishing: Chiefly cutthroat trout and whitefish. Also German brown, rainbow, and lake trout.

Boating, rafting: Ramps at Palisades Dam, Irwin, Spring Creek, and Conant Valley on upper segment; Byington and Twin Bridges below the canyon. Hand-carried craft can be launched and retrieved at many points.

River is floatable at all seasons, but swiftness of current depends on release at dam. Several diversion structures are major hazards; boaters must know where they are, how to avoid them. Other hazards include standing waves, whirlpools, rocks, overhanging brush, fallen trees.

PUBLICATIONS

South Fork of the Snake River Boater's Guide. Folder with map. Available from all 3 agencies.

Targhee NF: Forest map, Island Park, Ashton, Teton Basin and Palisades Ranger Districts. $1. Travel map, Palisades R.D.

HEADQUARTERS: Idaho Falls District, BLM, 940 Lincoln Rd., Idaho Falls, ID 83401; (208) 529-1020. Targhee National Forest, 420 N. Bridge St., St. Anthony, ID 83445; (208) 624-3151. Idaho Department of Fish and Game, 1515 Lincoln Rd., Idaho Falls, ID 83401; (208) 522-7783.

SOUTHEAST IDAHO REFUGE COMPLEX

U.S. Fish and Wildlife Service

In 1978 these four Refuges were placed under common management (see the individual entries):

Grays Lake National Wildlife Refuge
Bear Lake National Wildlife Refuge
Camas National Wildlife Refuge
Minidoka National Wildlife Refuge

Information is available at the Pocatello HQ.

More recently, the complex has acquired a Waterfowl Production Area:

Oxford Slough

1,890 acres.

From Pocatello, S on I-15 to US 91, SE on US 91 12 mi., then 8 mi. S on county road to Oxford.

The site adjoins the town. No interior roads, but good viewing from public roads on the perimeter. Good area for shorebirds in spring and late summer. It won't be publicized.

HEADQUARTERS: Federal Building, 250 South Fourth Ave., Pocatello, ID 83201; (208) 236-6833.

TARGHEE NATIONAL FOREST
U.S. Forest Service
1,557,792 acres in ID, 296,448 acres in WY.

Adjoins Yellowstone and Grand Teton National Parks. US 20 crosses the N portion. US 26 is near the S boundary.

The Targhee has, very roughly, the form of an inverted L. Its widest point is 30 mi. across, its narrowest less than 2 mi. Although about half the Forest is unroaded, the largest roadless tract is just over 200,000 acres. Studying the map, we could find no point more than 5 mi. from a road.

The Forest occupies the mountains framing the NE end of the Snake River plain. A disjunct portion in the far W, on the the Lemhi Range, is administered by the Salmon NF. The W–E crossbar of the L begins on the E side of Birch Creek Valley. Its N boundary lies on the Continental Divide, the crest of the W–E Centennial Mountains.

At the corner of the L, the Henrys Lake Mountains surround Henrys Lake. The common boundary with Yellowstone begins at the ID-MT border, extending S, then E for about 14 mi. into WY. Here begins the common boundary with Grand Teton National Park, along the Teton Range.

The resemblance to an L ends in the S of the Forest, where two large blocks extend NW from opposite sides of Palisades Reservoir, separated by the Snake River, US 26, and Swan Valley.

Forest topography ranges from stream valleys and rolling foothills to steep, rugged mountains, from 5,500 ft. to 12,000 ft. Summers are warm and dry, winters cold and snowy. Annual precipitation is about 10 in. at low elevations, 40 in. on high slopes, most of the latter falling as winter snow.

Recreation use of the Targhee is relatively high, over 1.8 million visitor-days per year. The pattern of activities reflects the Forest's special characteristics: easy accessibility, splendid scenery, proximity to Yellowstone and the Tetons, rivers and streams, lakes and reservoirs, an extensive trail network. The most popular activities are motorized sightseeing, family camping, and backcountry visits.

The Forest has about 300 mi. of rivers and streams. Included are four candidates for the Wild and Scenic River system: the Snake River from Palisades Dam to its confluence with Henrys Fork; Henrys Fork from Big Springs to its confluence with Warm River, excepting Island Park Reservoir; Warm River from Warm Springs to the Forest boundary, just above the confluence; and Falls River from its source to the Forest boundary.

The Forest surrounds but has no frontage on Henrys Lake. The S shore of 7,000-acre Island Park Reservoir is Forest land, as is the N shore near the dam. 16,000-acre Palisades Reservoir is surrounded by Forest land. Numerous lakes and wetlands are in the area S of Yellowstone, including Lake of the Woods, Grassy Lake, and Indian Lake.

The Forest has 1,776 mi. of roads, more than half of which can be driven in passenger cars, at least in dry weather. About 300 mi. of roads were built after 1970 to facilitate timber harvest. Some redundant roads are being closed. Restricted budgets have curtailed needed maintenance.

The Forest now has 1,185 mi. of trails. Several hundred mi. were eliminated from the system in recent years, being replaced by new roads or judged redundant. Most trails are in poor condition. Maintenance funds have been less than half of the requirement. When lodgepole blowdowns block trails, hikers detour around the obstacles, beating new paths that often cause environmental damage. Most heavily used trails such as Palisades Creek and Teton Canyon are in need of extensive reconstruction.

Some of the principal trailheads are along or near WY route 22, which enters the Forest at Teton Pass, becoming Idaho route 33. These trailheads are access for the Jedediah Smith Wilderness by popular canyons such as Moose Creek, Fox Creek, Darby, and Teton canyons, and both North and South Leigh creeks.

Plants: Visitors see large areas of dead trees. 1.4 million acres are forested. Lodgepole pine is the most abundant species. An estimated 85% of the lodgepole pines have been killed in an epidemic of mountain pine beetle. This is said to be part of a natural cycle: an overmature forest succumbs, burns, and is renewed. When efforts to control the beetle failed, the chosen strategy was removal of dead timber as an alternative to uncontrollable wildfires. Most stands with commercial value have been taken. Firewood is offered free or for $2.50 a cord to those who will cut and haul it. Clearing is followed by replanting.

Plant zones begin with the highest: alpine tundra, characterized by low-growing species adapted to a short growing season. The subalpine zone is generally dominated by subalpine fir with interspersed shrub and sagebrush meadows. Next lower is the montane zone, with Douglas-fir dominant. Following fire, however, both Douglas-fir and subalpine fir may be replaced by lodgepole pine. Aspen is dominant just below the montane zone, with some areas of mountain brush. Along the plain of the Snake River, sagebrush-grass communities extend into the foothills. Beside many streams are wet meadows with sedges, grasses, and willows.

Flowering species of the higher zones include cow parsnip, aster, groundsel, bitterroot, sandwort, buttercup, cinquefoil, lupine, fireweed, Indian paintbrush, goldenrod, penstemon, heartleaf arnica, bluebell, death camas, phlox. At lower elevations: yarrow, geranium, heartleaf arnica, pussytoes, bluebell, violets, spirea, larkspur, arrowleaf balsamroot.

Birds: A checklist of 145 species doesn't indicate abundance. Elsewhere it is stated that 156 species nest on the Forest. Blue and ruffed grouse are the most common upland game birds. One of the largest known winter concentrations of trumpeter swan is here. Prominent nesting species include sandhill crane, bald eagle, and osprey. Common species noted include Clark's nutcracker, gray and Steller's jays, mountain chickadee. Other species mentioned as interesting to birders include great gray owl, white-faced ibis, three-toed woodpecker.

Mammals: No checklist. 50 to 60 species occur. Elk is the most abundant big game species, with a Forest population of about 9,000. Others include mule deer, moose, pronghorn, black bear. Less common are mountain goat and bighorn sheep. Grizzly bear are seen occasionally, most often in areas adjoining Yellowstone. Wolf sightings have been reported near the Continental Divide. Present, but in unknown numbers, are coyote, mountain lion, bobcat, lynx, porcupine, beaver, otter, martin, wolverine, and fisher. Pika and marmot are often seen on rocky slopes.

FEATURES

Jedediah Smith Wilderness, 116,500 acres, entirely in WY. Visitors to Grand Teton National Park often wonder what's on the other side of the mountains. This is—a roadless area on the W slopes, extending from Lake of the Woods, near the Yellowstone National Park boundary, almost to Teton Pass. None of the famous peaks that dominate the eastern skyline are in the Forest, but the Wilderness has Table Mountain, 11,101 ft., 4 peaks higher than 10,000, others exceeding 9,000 ft. Trail systems of Wilderness and Park interconnect. A popular destination for Teton backpackers and horsepackers has been Alaska Basin, so popular that outfitter parties and others with horses can no longer camp here. Granite Basin Lakes, Green Lakes, and Moose Falls are also popular and, at times, heavily used. For those who seek solitude in wilderness, there are several trailless areas.

Winegar Hole Wilderness, 10,600 acres, is on the S boundary of Yellowstone National Park, separated from the Jedediah Smith Wilderness by a narrow corridor. Primary access is from Cave Falls campground at the end of Forest Road 582. Terrain is relatively flat. Numerous lakes, streams, wetlands, with extensive stands of lodgepole pine. Trailless except for one unmaintained trail. Grizzly bear habitat.

Palisades Reservoir and adjoining lands, 448,435 acres, including 91,380 acres in WY. This is the total acreage of 8 adjacent or proximate roadless areas surrounding Palisades Reservoir and extending NW on both sides of the Snake River and Swan Valley. Palisades Dam was built on the Snake River in 1958, backing up a pool 16 mi. long, up to 3 mi. wide, covering 16,000 acres. It is one of the Targhee's principal recreation areas, with 9 campgrounds on or near the lake shore, three boat ramps, and a marina. US 26 is close to the NE shore. Except near the two ends of the reservoir, the SW shore is roadless, with a lakeshore trail.

The reservoir and South Fork of the Snake River are said to offer outstanding native cutthroat trout fishing. Other species include whitefish, brown and rainbow trout.

Below the dam is an easy 8-hour float to Heise, suitable for rafts, canoes, and kayaks, open to motor craft. From Jackson Lake in Grand Teton National Park to the reservoir is a 3-day float. Several access points permit shorter trips. The lower section has whitewater requiring skill and good equipment.

The Palisades Ranger District lists more than two dozen named and marked trails, from 2 to 12 mi. long, beginning at trailheads near campgrounds or on Forest roads. Destinations include waterfalls, scenic valleys, and other points of interest.

The reservoir and valley are framed by the Snake River Range on the NE, the Caribou Range on the SW. Several roadless areas on these ranges have been considered for Wilderness designation. The Forest map shows many trails, most following drainages. Before an extended backcountry trip, ask at the Ranger District about trail conditions.

Centennial Mountains, 64,600 acres, are a W–E range on the ID-MT boundary. This roadless area is E of I-15, W of US 20. Access is from a secondary road extending E from Spencer on I-15. At the E end, Forest Road 024 runs from US 20 NW to 9,866-ft. Sawtell Peak, site of a radio beacon. Elevations range from 7,000 ft. to above 10,000 ft. Gradients range from gentle to moderately steep.

This area will include a segment of the projected Continental Divide Trail. The Forest map shows no present trail approximating the Divide, and the Island Park Ranger District mentions none in its list of hiking trails. Each summer a few people travel on foot or horseback as close to the Divide as feasible. Most present use is hunting.

Island Park on US 20 is the center of a major recreation area. The Park is an old caldera, a plain within a large crater that subsided. Only portions of the walls remain. Henrys Fork, a famous trout stream, crosses the caldera, passing close to US 20. 7,000-acre Island Park Reservoir, 11 mi. long, was formed by a dam built in 1938. It has a population of kokanee salmon that spawn in tributary streams. Big Springs, headwaters of Henrys Fork, is 5 mi. E of Macks Inn. Big Springs National Recreation Waterways Trail is a 2- to

4-hour float trip, no rapids, offering good fishing and birding. 7 mi. S of Island Park is a scenic drive past Mesa Falls, returning to US 20 at Ashton. Harriman State Park and Henrys Lake State Park are nearby (see entries).

ACTIVITIES

Camping: 33 campgrounds, 741 sites. The official camping season is Memorial Day–Labor Day, but openings can be delayed by snow. Campgrounds can be used after Labor Day without water or services. July–Sept. are the best months, although insects may be a problem in July. One can camp almost anywhere. We saw many attractive informal sites, including one we had to ourselves on Henrys Fork.

Hiking, backpacking: The information page *This Is the Targhee* lists the principal trails in each Ranger District, noting gradients, mileages, use, and whether each is marked. The Forest map shows the principal trailheads. It also shows many other trails, but some are virtually abandoned, perhaps impassable. Off-trail hiking is feasible and attractive in some areas, including parts of the two Wildernesses.

Hunting: Principal big game species are elk, mule deer, moose, pronghorn. Blue and ruffed grouse are the chief upland game birds.

Fishing: Wide range of opportunities: reservoirs, lakes, over 600 named creeks and streams; 300 mi. are state-classified trout streams. Henrys Fork is a famous trout fishery. Island Park Reservoir has populations of kokanee salmon, coho; brook, cutthroat, and rainbow trout; whitefish.

Horse riding: About 1,200 mi. of trails are available. No stables in the Forest. Several outfitters operate in the Forest. Information from Idaho Outfitters and Guides Association, P.O. Box 95, Boise, ID 83701; (208) 342-1438.

Boating: On the principal reservoirs, portions of the Snake River. (See entry: Snake River, South Fork.)

Rafting, kayaking: Chiefly on Henrys Fork (N) and South Fork of the Snake River. Some sections are suitable for small rafts, open canoes. Some have dangerous rapids, and Henrys Fork has 3 impassable falls. Inquire. Some outfitters offer trips.

Skiing: Grand Targhee ski resort is in the WY portion of the Forest, access from ID. Also at Kelly Ski Canyon, Bear Gulch. Season: Nov.–Apr.

Ski touring: Many opportunities, as on unplowed Forest roads. Island Park is a center for ski touring with groomed trails.

INTERPRETATION

Information and literature at all District offices.

Nature trail at Big Springs, planned for handicapped.

Cross-country interpretive ski trail, 6 mi., Ashton-Mesa Falls.

Campfire programs at Buffalo Campground, Island Park, July–Aug.

165 &• ZONE 4

PUBLICATIONS
Forest map. $1.
Travel map.
Preliminary map, Jedediah Smith and Winegar Hole Wildernesses.
Recreation map: Palisades Reservoir.
Palisades backcountry map.
Information pages, mimeo:
This Is the Targhee. 14 pp.
Wildlife on the Targhee.
Bird checklist.
Peregrine falcon.
Herbaceous plants.
Regulations for grizzly bear habitat.
Brimstone and Buffalo River cross-country ski trails.

REFERENCES
Lawrence, Paul. *Hiking the Teton Backcountry.* San Francisco: Sierra Club Books, rev. 1979. Pp. 127–45.
Maughan, Jackie J. *The Hiker's Guide to Idaho.* Billings, MT: Falcon Press, 1984. Pp. 122–26, 145–48, 219–28, 232–54.
Mitchell, Ron. *50 Eastern Idaho Hiking Trails.* Boulder, CO: Pruett, 1979. Pp. 2–3, 10–11.

HEADQUARTERS: P.O. Box 208, St. Anthony, ID 83445; (208) 624-3151.

RANGER DISTRICTS: Dubois R.D., P.O. Box 46, Dubois, ID 83423; (208) 374-5422. Island Park R.D., Island Park, ID 83429; (208) 558-7305. Ashton R.D., P.O. Box 228, Ashton, ID 83420; (208) 652-7442. Palisades R.D., Route 1, Box 398-B, Idaho Falls, ID 83401; (208) 523-1412. Teton Basin R.D., P.O. Box 127, Driggs, ID 83422; (208) 354-2312.

MONTANA

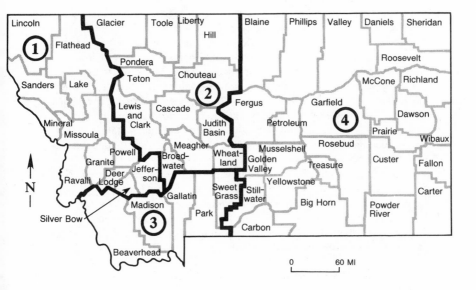

Lincoln

Glacier Toole Liberty

Hill

Blaine Phillips Valley Daniels Sheridan

① Flathead

Roosevelt

Pondera

Sanders Lake

Teton

Chouteau

McCone Richland

Lewis Cascade

② Fergus

Garfield

and

Clark

Judith
Basin

Dawson

Mineral

Petroleum ④ Prairie

Missoula

Rosebud

Wibaux

Powell

Meagher

Musselshell

Granite

Broad- Wheat- Golden Treasure Custer Fallon

water land Valley

Deer Jeffer- Yellowstone

Ravalli Lodge son

Carter

Sweet Still-

Madison Gallatin Grass water Big Horn Powder

Silver Bow

③ Park River

Carbon

Beaverhead

N

0   60 MI

MONTANA

Montana ranks fourth among the 50 states in area, but only Alaska and Wyoming have fewer residents per square mile. The magnificent Rocky Mountains dominate the W, ranges separated by valleys with great rivers and handsome lakes. The SW is a dramatic region of high desert plateaus cut by deep canyons. The E half is largely prairie, with some low and isolated mountain ranges chiefly in the S. Elevations range from 1,800 ft. where the Kootenai River enters Idaho to 12,850 ft. on Granite Peak, N of Yellowstone National Park. Half the state is more than 4,000 ft. above sea level.

Federal agencies own most of the western half of the state. The largest blocks are in 9 National Forests and Glacier National Park. The public domain is administered by the U.S. Bureau of Land Management (BLM). Other federal sites include several National Wildlife Refuges. State landhold-ings include Fishing Access Sites, Wildlife Management Areas, State Recrea-tion Areas, and State Parks.

The Continental Divide traverses the W half of the state in a generally N–S direction, although it is by no means straight. Someday there will be a Continental Divide Trail, although it cannot precisely follow the Divide; only a mountain goat could cope with the jagged peaks. Many sections of the Divide are the boundary between two National Forests. In 1986 Forest re-presentatives were meeting to decide what route could best approximate the Divide and who should build each section. Each year a few people hike the Divide route, following existing trails where they can.

W of the Divide, MT is drained by the Kootenai, Clark Fork, and Flathead rivers through the Columbia to the Pacific Ocean. E of the Divide, the Gallatin, Madison, and Jefferson rivers join to form the Missouri, to which all streams flow except St. Marys River, which finds its way from Glacier NP to Hudson Bay.

Public lands in the state's E half are generally smaller and more widely scattered. The largest federal holdings are the Charles E. Russell National Wildlife Refuge and the Custer National Forest, but the total of BLM-administered lands is greater. Although most of this region receives less than 14 inches of precipitation per year, many of its most interesting natural features are rivers and wetlands. State lands include riparian Fishing Access Sites and State Recreation Areas, as well as Wildlife Management Areas and a few State Parks.

Montana has long been world famous for big game hunting and trout fishing. We were told of outfitters whose principal clients come from Europe. Quotas govern the issuance of hunting licenses, and for some species applications outnumber licenses by 10 or 25 to 1. Many Montana sportsmen have their favorite hunting and fishing grounds, isolated lakes and streams and unmarked trails into canyons and basins, places unknown to outsiders.

Glacier National Park was the first major site to attract the general traveler. The Park was established in 1910, but the cross-park road wasn't built until the 1930s. Later the Bob Marshall Wilderness gained such a reputation that outdoorsmen boast of having hiked in "the Bob."

In comparatively recent times, Montana has attracted growing numbers of campers, backpackers, birders, trail riders, floaters, climbers, spelunkers, and other outdoorsmen. Today some campgrounds fill early on summer weekends; some lake shores show the scars of too many feet; some trails are heavily used. Such impacts affect a small fraction of MT's splendid natural areas. In midsummer we could always find a quiet campsite for our motor home. Hiking, we could easily find solitude.

Climate: W of the Continental Divide, winters are milder, precipitation spread more evenly over the year, summers are cooler, and winds are lighter. At elevations below 4,000 ft. E of the Divide, hot weather is common in summer. Winter cold waves are often followed by mild but windy weather. Most MT lakes freeze in winter. Annual precipitation is highest around the mountain ranges, lowest in the eastern plains, but the highest average in any region is less than 35 in. May–July is generally the wettest season.

MAPS

Montana's official highway map shows the paved roads, the principal graveled roads, and a few unsurfaced roads. The map and tourist information are available from

Montana Promotion Division
Department of Commerce
Helena, MT 59620
1-800-548-3390

Between 1978 and 1983 BLM published a series of 42 Public Lands maps covering all but the NW corner of the state, showing all roads and land ownerships. Unfortunately they aren't being reprinted as stocks are depleted. We were able to obtain 34, but several were among the last. They and other maps can be seen at BLM offices. We were told a new series is in preparation but not when it might appear.

For the western portion of the state, we rely chiefly on National Forest maps. These show not only Forest roads but many county and local roads in the surrounding area.

FEDERAL AGENCIES

NATIONAL FOREST SERVICE
Montana's ten National Forests cover 16.8 million acres.

Zone 1	Bitterroot NF
	Deerlodge NF
	Flathead NF
	Kootenai NF
	Lolo NF
Zone 2	Helena NF
	Lewis & Clark NF
Zone 3	Beaverhead NF
	Gallatin NF
Zone 4	Custer NF

The Bitterroot, Kootenai, and Custer NFs extend into other states.

U.S. BUREAU OF LAND MANAGEMENT
222 N. 32nd St.
Billings, MT 59107
(406) 657-6462

BLM administers 8.1 million acres of public land in MT. The largest concentration of these lands is N and S of the Missouri River in the E half of the state, including 149 mi. of the Missouri Wild and Scenic River. Other lands, including some relatively large blocks, are scattered statewide except in the NW.

BLM's first entry in the national Wilderness system is Bear Trap Canyon on the Madison River.

MT is divided into 3 BLM Districts: Butte, the western third; Lewistown, the N central area; and Miles City, the S central and NE. Addresses appear in entries.

U.S. FISH AND WILDLIFE SERVICE
Montana has 20 National Wildlife Refuges including 1.1 million acres. Some of these are combined for administrative purposes and in our entries. Most are maintained primarily for waterfowl, but the largest, 900,000-acre Charles M. Russell, serves chiefly for upland game.

STATE AGENCIES

Montana Department of Fish, Wildlife & Parks
1420 E. Sixth St.
Helena, MT 59620
(406) 449-2535

Everyone who travels Montana should have the Department's *Montana Recreation Map*, which shows and lists 500 campsites and recreation areas, state and federal. Each listing tells how to get there, whether the site has camping, toilets, water, and boat ramp, and whether it offers fishing, swimming, and trails, as well as its open season.

When we last looked, the state sites included the following:

	Sites	Acres
State Parks	11	15,370
State Monuments	20	6,495
State Recreation Areas	80	10,686
Fishing Access Sites	224	18,399

Some are not entries here; we do not include urban or historical sites or sites without natural qualities.

The Department is organized in a number of divisions, including Fisheries, Wildlife, and Parks. Services are unified, and site categories are sometimes blurred. We were puzzled to find sites called "SRA" (State Recreation Area) in one listing, "FAS" (Fishing Access Site) in another, but we soon found it doesn't greatly matter.

State Parks: Those we visited are attractive, but few could be called natural areas. We have entries for those.

Fishing Access Sites; State Recreation Areas: The array of Fishing Access Sites is splendid and unique. We've seen nothing like it in other states. As the name implies, an FAS provides access to a river or a lake. In some states, access may be a rough dirt track to a littered, muddy parking area. We saw many Montana FASs that are attractive, well-maintained parks with shaded campsites, latrines, picnic tables, and concrete boat ramps. We camped in several of them, usually alone.

On the average, FASs are smaller than SRAs, but some are larger than many SRAs, having several hundred acres. Most SRAs are also on rivers or lakes. We found no conspicuous differences and enjoyed both.

We have written entries for many of MT's rivers and lakes, to which these sites are the keys.

Wildlife Management Areas: Few WMAs are listed in the Recreation Map. They total almost 300,000 acres. Many were acquired to provide winter range for elk, which would otherwise prey on farmers' haystacks when they come down from the mountains. Because they are natural areas, we looked over their management plans and talked with Division staff members who know them well.

"In summer, the elk aren't there, and it's just another place at the bottom of a hill," was the comment on one. And "That's a neat canyon! You'll want to see it," we were told about another site.

With such advice and help, we identified several WMAs that are attractive for hiking, birding, and camping. The Division's 7 regional offices can provide information on these and other WMAs.

Region 1 618 Leisure Dr., Kalispell, MT 59901   (406) 755-5505
Region 2 210 39th St., Missoula, MT 59801   (406) 721-5808
Region 3 104 Sunset Blvd., Bozeman, MT 59715   (406) 994-3553
Region 4 Millegan Route, Great Falls, MT 5940   (406) 454-3441
Region 5 1418 Janie St., Billings, MT 59105   (406) 252-4654
Region 6 437 Sixth Ave. N, Glasgow, MT 59230   (406) 228-9347
Region 7 2004 Main, Miles City, MT 59301   (406) 232-4365

REFERENCES

GENERAL

Montana, Last of the Big Time Splendors. Helena, MT: Department of Highways, 1973.

Peterson, Martin. *The Complete Montana Travel Guide.* Ronan, MT: Lake County Press, 1979.

Turbak, Gary. *The Traveler's Guide to Montana.* Billings, MT: Falcon Press, 1983.

Cunningham, Bill. *Montana's Continental Divide.* Billings, MT: Falcon Press, 1986.

Meloy, Mark. *Eastern Montana Mountain Ranges.* Billings, MT: Falcon Press, 1986.

Gildart, Bert. *Montana's Flathead River Country.* Billings, MT: Falcon Press, 1986.

Brooks, Charles E. *The Henry's Fork.* Billings, MT: Falcon Press, 1986.

Woodruff, Steve, and Don Schwennesen. *Montana Wilderness—Discovering the Heritage.* Kansas City, MO: Missoulian and Lowell Press, 1984.

MAMMALS

Hoffman, Robert S. *A Guide to Montana Mammals.* Missoula: University of Montana, 1968.

HIKING

Schneider, Bill. *The Hiker's Guide to Montana.* Billings, MT: Falcon Press, 1983.

Wolf, James R. *Guide to the Continental Divide Trail, Northern Montana.* Bethesda, MD: Continental Divide Trail Society, 1979.

Wolf, James R. *Guide to the Continental Divide Trail, Southern Montana and Idaho.* Bethesda, MD: Continental Divide Trail Society, 1979.

FISHING

Burk, Dale A. *Montana Fishing.* Stevensville, MT: Stoneydale Press, 1982.

Konizeski, Richard L. *The Montanans' Fishing Guide.* Vol. 1: *West of the Continental Divide.* Missoula: Mountain Press Publishing, rev. 1986.

FLOATING/CANOEING

Fischer, Hank. *The Floater's Guide to Montana.* Helena, MT: Falcon Press, 1979.

Fischer, Hank. *River Mile Index of the Columbia River Basin.* Helena: Water Resources Division, Montana Department of Natural Resources and Conservation, 1984.

NORDIC SKIING

Sedlack, Elaine. *The Nordic Skier's Guide to Montana.* Billings, MT: Falcon Press, 1981.

ROCKHOUNDING

Feldman, Bob. *The Rockhound's Guide to Montana.* Billings, MT: Falcon Press, 1980.

CAVES/CAVING

Campbell, Newell P. *Caves of Montana.* Butte: Montana College of Mineral Science and Technology, 1978. (For sale by Montana Bureau of Mines and Geology.)

ZONE 1

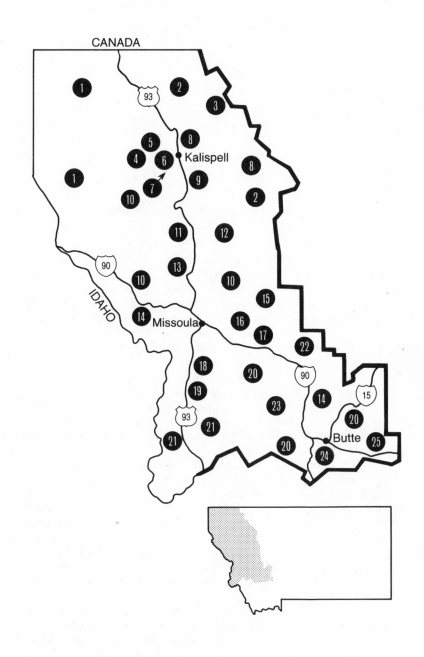

ZONE 1

Includes these counties:

Lincoln	Flathead	Sanders
Lake	Mineral	Missoula
Powell	Deer Lodge	Ravalli
Granite	Jefferson	Silver Bow

Zone 1, western Montana, is dominated by the Rocky Mountains, high, rugged ranges trending NW–SE. The mountains, more than three-fifths of the zone, are occupied by five National Forests and Glacier National Park. Another large block of land, in the central part of the zone, is the Flathead Indian Reservation. The Forests and the National Park offer a wide range of recreation opportunities, from easy driving on scenic highways to backpacking and horsepacking in remote wildernesses.

Most of the privately owned land is in the broad river valleys, but here, too, is much of interest to outdoorsmen. State Recreation Areas and Fishing Access Sites are scattered along most of the rivers, which have miles of challenging whitewater as well as long stretches for lazy drifting. Fishing is good in the rivers and in the many lakes. Flathead, Hungry Horse, and Koocanusa are the largest water bodies, but there are hundreds of others, from road-access lakes not far from main highways to sparkling ponds in high glacial cirques reached only by trail.

Wildlife is abundant, hunting and fishing second only to sightseeing and camping in popularity. Those who prefer to do their hunting with binoculars and cameras have excellent viewing opportunities in Glacier NP, the National Bison Range, the Swan River and Lee Metcalf National Wildlife Refuges.

The zone's most crowded places in summer are the Going-to-the-Sun Road in Glacier NP and the developed areas at each end. Some lakeshore campgrounds fill up quickly on summer weekends, especially those on the major lakes. But throughout this vast zone are 10 million uncrowded acres, little-used roads and trails. In midsummer, we often camped alone beside delightful lakes and streams.

The season in the high country is short. Trails may not be snow-free until July, and snow may fall again in Sept. Spring and fall are delightful in the valleys, and there are attractive hiking opportunities in the foothills and on the lower slopes.

The Swan and Clearwater river valleys along SR 83 have many natural features. Valley wetlands attract great numbers of waterfowl. Some of the lakes are heavily used by campers, fishermen, and boaters, while others are more isolated and quiet. Trails lead up into the Bob Marshall Wilderness and other scenic high country.

ASHLEY LAKE
Montana Department of Fish, Wildlife & Parks
3,200 acres of water, 32 of land.

From Kalispell, 16 mi. W on US 2, then 13 mi. N on county road. Not recommended for trailers.

The lake is about 5 mi. long, surrounded by private and timber company land. A popular fishing lake, visited chiefly by local residents. The campground is usually full on weekends. The surrounding area is forested. Deer, moose, and black bear are sometimes seen.

ACTIVITIES
Camping: 12 sites. May 15–Sept. 15.
Fishing: Cutthroat trout, kokanee, a few large cutthroat-kokanee hybrids.
Boating: Ramp.

NEARBY: Little Bitterroot Lake (see entry).

BITTERROOT NATIONAL FOREST
U.S. Forest Service
1,113,838 acres in MT; 463,985 acres in ID.

From US 93.

The Forest has the shape of a large, lopsided U, surrounding the broad Bitterroot Valley S of Missoula. (See entry, Bitterroot River.) On the W are the peaks of the Bitterroot Range, on the E the less rugged shapes of the Sapphire Mountains. The Forest is part of the huge complex of National Forests in this region. In MT it adjoins the Lolo, Beaverhead, and Deerlodge NFs, in ID the Clearwater, Nez Perce, and Salmon NFs.

A glance at the Forest map shows only two areas, in the S and SE, with the can-of-worms road pattern indicative of timber harvesting. Almost half of the Forest is in three Wildernesses; another quarter is roadless and un-developed. All three Wildernesses extend into adjacent National Forests.

By comparison with other National Forests of the region, recreation on the Bitterroot is light, less than half a million visitor-days per year, and this includes motorists on US 93. Camping and other uses of developed sites make up about one-quarter of the visitor-days. Much of the camping is associated with hunting, the chief backcountry activity. One reason for the light use is the lack of large road-access lakes with good fishing, a major attraction elsewhere in the region. Another is that many of the Forest's clear, cold streams are not highly productive of fish because they run through rather sterile granitic soil.

Hunters have long been attracted to the Bitterroot by its elk herd and other game. Hiking and backpacking are gradually increasing because of the easy access to Wilderness trailheads and the spectacular country beyond.

The Bitterroot Valley is about 60 mi. long, 4 to 10 mi. wide. On the W the Bitterroot Range rises sharply, 5,000 ft. in 3 to 4 air miles. The front is cut at intervals of 1 to 3 mi. by 30 deep, rocky canyons. On the E, grassy foothills provide a more gradual transition to the Sapphires, rising about 3,000 ft. above the valley floor. About 70% of the non-Wilderness portion of the Forest has slopes ranging from moderate to very steep, making it costly to cut timber. Elevations range from 3,200 ft. at the N end of the valley to 10,157-ft. Trapper Peak in the southern mountains.

Lakes and streams: The MT portion of the Forest has 86 lakes, most of them small mountain lakes accessible only on foot or horseback. Two road-access lakes have boat ramps. The larger, Lake Como, is 3 mi. long and has a campground with 12 sites. The Forest has about 1,600 mi. of streams in MT.

Climate: The valley is semiarid, with annual precipitation less than 14 in. Precipitation increases with altitude, to 50 in. on the Sapphire Divide, to 100 in. on the highest slopes of the Bitterroots. Snow accumulations begin in Oct. and reach 2 to 6 ft. on the Sapphires, 4 to 10 ft. on the Bitterroots, often lasting into July. Summer temperatures in the valley average 60° to 70°F by day, 40° to 50° at night. The high country is at least 10 degrees cooler, and nighttime frost is always possible.

Roads: From US 93, secondary roads, mostly paved, provide access to the principal drainages, including East Fork, West Fork, Skalkaho, Lake Como, Sleeping Child, Threemile, Ambrose, and Burnt Fork. These connect with 3,500 mi. of Forest roads and logging spurs, most single-lane dirt roads built for logging. Of these, 2,000 mi. are maintained. Those leading to camp-grounds are usually serviceable for ordinary cars in dry weather, but it's always useful to inquire.

By far the longest and most interesting backcountry route is the Nez Perce Trail, Forest Road 468, which follows Deep Creek to the Selway River at Magruder Crossing, then the East Fork into the Nez Perce NF. This route is the boundary between the Selway-Bitterroot Wilderness and the Frank

Church - River of No Return Wilderness. Built by the Civilian Conservation Corps in the 1930s, it is narrow, rough, winding, only occasionally maintained, not advised for passenger cars. It offers access to wild backcountry, isolation, some scenic views.

Trails: Of the 1,600 mi. of trails, 940 are in Wildernesses, 660 outside. About one-fourth of the trails are in poor condition, requiring rebuilding or relocation, for which funds aren't available. Most trails receive some degree of maintenance. The system includes 4 National Recreation Trails. Parts of the Continental Divide and Lewis & Clark trails are in the Forest.

Plants: Three-fourths of the area is forested. Areas receiving less than 20 in. of moisture won't support continuous forest cover. At these lower elevations, S- and W-facing slopes are generally grasslands, while N- and E-facing slopes have scattered trees and stands, chiefly Douglas-fir and ponderosa pine. Douglas-fir remains dominant up to about 5,000 ft., with increasing amounts of ponderosa and lodgepole pine and grand fir, pine grass, beargrass, and huckleberry prominent in the understory. Pure stands of lodgepole pine are common from 5,000 to 6,800 ft., with subalpine fir, Engelmann spruce, larch, and Douglas-fir on moister sites. Above 6,800 ft., lodgepole pine gradually gives way to whitebark pine and subalpine fir, with some larch and Engelmann spruce.

The Forest has an abundance of seasonal wildflowers. A special Wild Flower Area is described under Features.

Birds: Checklist of 223 species is unusually well annotated, with information on status (summer breeding, permanent resident, winter resident, migrant), abundance, and occurrence in 8 habitat types. Seasonally abundant or common species include eared and pied-billed grebes, great blue heron, Canada goose, mallard; green-winged, blue-winged, and cinnamon teals; shoveler, redhead, ruddy duck, common merganser, red-tailed and rough-legged hawks, northern harrier, American kestrel, ruffed grouse, ring-necked pheasant, American coot, killdeer, common snipe, spotted sandpiper, Wilson's phalarope, ring-billed gull, rock and mourning doves, great horned and short-eared owls, common nighthawk, rufous and calliope hummingbirds, belted kingfisher, northern flicker; Lewis', hairy, and downy woodpeckers; house wren, American robin, Swainson's thrush, ruby-crowned kinglet, eastern and western kingbirds; tree, bank, and barn swallows; black-billed magpie, common raven, black-capped chickadee, Bohemian waxwing, European starling; solitary, red-eyed, and warbling vireos; yellow, yellow-rumped, and MacGillivray's warblers; common yellowthroat, American redstart, western meadowlark, red-winged and Brewer's blackbirds, western tanager, evening grosbeak, Cassin's finch, pine siskin, dark-eyed junco. Sparrows: savannah, vesper, chipping, song.

Mammals: No checklist published, but the following species are recorded in a listing that doesn't note abundance and appears to include occasional sightings: masked, northern water, and vagrant shrews; big brown, hoary, silver-haired, and western big-eared bats; fringed, little brown, long-eared, long-legged, small-footed, and Yuma myotis; black and grizzly bear, raccoon, fisher, marten, bobcat, wolverine, badger, gray wolf, coyote, red fox, lynx, mountain lion, shorttail and longtail weasels, mink, river otter, striped and western spotted skunks, hoary and yellowbelly marmots, Columbian and Richardson ground squirrels, golden-mantled and red squirrels, northern flying squirrel, northern pocket gopher, redtail and yellow pine chipmunks, beaver, bushytail woodrat, deer mouse, western jumping mouse; boreal red-back, longtail, meadow, mountain, and Richardson vole; muskrat, porcupine, pika, snowshoe hare, whitetail jackrabbit, mountain cottontail, mule and whitetail deer, elk, moose, bighorn sheep.

FEATURES

Frank Church - River of No Return Wilderness, 2,364,334 acres, all in ID, of which 193,703 acres are in the Bitterroot NF. The Wilderness, which includes portions of 6 National Forests, is described in a separate entry in ID Zone 2. Principal access from the Bitterroot is by the Nez Perce Trail, Forest Road 438, the N boundary of the Wilderness. The S boundary of the Bitter-root's portion is on the Salmon River, but the accessible section of the river is on the Salmon NF. Riverside campsites are used by floaters. Recreation use of the area is light, except at the river. Most use occurs during the big game hunting season.

Selway-Bitterroot Wilderness, 1,340,681 acres, of which 511,547 acres are in the Bitterroot, just under half of this in MT, the rest in ID. Straddling the Bitterroot Range, the Wilderness is characterized by rugged terrain, with spectacular, steep-walled, rocky canyons dropping into the Bitterroot Valley. Many barren peaks are in the 7,000- and 8,000-ft. range. The Selway-Bitter-root is separated from the River of No Return Wilderness only by the 600-ft. corridor of the Nez Perce Trail. Where the Trail meets the Selway River at Magruder Crossing, Forest Road 6223 extends N along the river for about 10 mi. to the Paradise campground, a cherry-stem penetrating the Wilderness. The E boundary of the Wilderness is as close as 5 mi. to US 93 in the vicinity of Darby. Although there are trailheads along both Forest roads and near US 93 and many trails, the Selway-Bitterroot has large areas with no mapped trails. Most recreational use is in the principal canyons accessible from US 93 and along the Selway River corridor. Hunting is the leading use, followed by camping, hiking, and horse riding. The Selway elk herds are nationally known. Most lakes and streams have trout.

Selway Wild and Scenic River provides a whitewater wilderness adventure. Launching at Paradise, floaters begin a 47-mi. journey through almost contin-uous rapids, many of them Class IV, to Selway Falls in the Nez Perce NF (see entry in ID Zone 2). Floating is by permit, only one issued per day. River information at the West Fork Ranger Station.

Anaconda-Pintler Wilderness, 158,516 acres, 41,162 acres on the Bitterroot, in the Forest's far SE corner. Access from US 93 at Sula by a paved secondary road, shown on the highway map, which follows the East Fork Bitterroot River almost to the Wilderness boundary. The Bitterroot NF portion lies on the NW side of the Anaconda Range, on the Continental Divide. Other portions are in the Deerlodge and Beaverhead NFs. Elevations are from 5,100 to 10,793 ft. Terrain includes peaks with perpetual snow, steep canyons with rushing streams, cirque basins, high mountain lakes, and glacial moraine. Here a section of the Continental Divide Trail is already in place. Recreational use is light, overnighters about equally divided between backpackers and horsepackers. Wildlife includes deer, elk, moose, mountain goat, black bear. Most lakes and streams have trout.

Bitterroot Wild Flower Area, from Woodside, on US 93 4 mi. N of Hamilton, W 2 1/2 mi. on County Road 54, then 1/2 mi. N, 1/2 mi. W, 1/4 mi. N. This puts you on a logging road where walking is the best way to see the flowers and enjoy the view of the valley. Seasonal wildflowers include bitterroot, fritillary, trillium, glacier lily, beargrass, pasqueflower, clematis, 27 species of lupine, stonecrop, fairy slipper, Oregon grape, 50 species of beardtongue, false hellebore, St. Johnswort, twinflower, rhododendron, wintergreen, columbine, monkeyflower, elephanthead, little larkspur, mountain heath, kinnikinnick, Indian paintbrush, death camas.

INTERPRETATION

The Forest maintains a looseleaf Recreation Opportunity Guide (ROG) for each Ranger District. Pages provide detailed information on each principal campground and hiking trail, hunting, fishing, boating, skiing and ski touring, horse riding, snowmobiling, snowshoeing, identification and gathering, and more. Each trail page provides a small sketch map, profile, narrative description, and information on access, attractions, length, season, degree of use, difficulty, etc. Each ROG also includes an extensive bibliography on outdoor activities and skills.

The Forest has no visitor center or naturalist programs.

ACTIVITIES

Camping: 20 campgrounds, 173 sites. Campgrounds are generally open Memorial Day–Labor Day. Some are kept open through hunting season though water may be off.

Hiking, backpacking: The ROGs provide the best information for selection of trails. There are 4 National Recreation Trails, 6 to 23 mi. long. Such trails are usually selected for their scenic values and general interest and often are given some maintenance priority. High trails are usually snow-free by mid-July.

Hunting: The Forest is noted for its elk herds and other big game. Each Ranger District has a list of the permitted outfitter-guides.

Fishing: Cutthroat and rainbow trout are present in most lakes and streams.

Horse riding: More horsemen than hikers in the backcountry. Mostly in conjunction with hunting. Some outfitters offer summer pack trips.

Boating: Lake Como and Painted Rocks Lake. Ramps. No hp limitation.

Rafting: On the Selway River from Paradise Campground, by permit; one permit per day.

Skiing: Lost Trail ski resort, Sula R.D.; Thurs.–Sun. in season, usually Dec. 1–Mar. 31.

Ski touring: No special trails, but many opportunities on unplowed Forest roads. Also in meadows along the Continental Divide near Lost Trail Pass.

PUBLICATIONS

Forest map. $1.

Maps: Frank Church - River of No Return Wilderness; Selway-Bitterroot Wilderness; Anaconda-Pintler Wilderness. $1 each.

Information pages:

Selway-Bitterroot Wilderness.

Anaconda-Pintler Wilderness.

Brochures:

Information about the Bitterroot National Forest.

Bird checklist.

Selway-Bitterroot Wilderness Primer.

REFERENCES

Rudner, Ruth. *Bitterroot to Beartooth.* San Francisco: Sierra Club, 1985. Pp. 121–52.

Schneider, Bill. *The Hiker's Guide to Montana.* Billings, MT: Falcon Press, 1983. Pp. 53–68.

HEADQUARTERS: 316 N. Third St., Hamilton, MT 59840; (406) 363-3131.

RANGER DISTRICTS: Stevensville R.D., Box 169, Stevensville, MT 59870; (406) 777-5461. Darby R.D., Box 266, Darby, MT 59829; (406) 821-3913. Sula R.D., Sula, MT 59871; (406) 821-3201. West Fork R.D., Darby, MT 59829; (406) 821-3269.

BITTERROOT RIVER

Montana Department of Fish, Wildlife & Parks

80 river miles.

Parallels US 93 N to Missoula.

The river flows N through a broad valley between the Bitterroot and Sapphire ranges, joining the Clark Fork (see entry) near Missoula. It is seldom more than a mile or two away from US 93. The valley land is predominantly private. Some owners of riparian land have abused the river banks, but the float is generally pleasant, with mountain views, a screening of trees and brush, and enough wildlife to attest to its natural virtues.

The Department of Fish, Wildlife & Parks has 10 Fishing Access Sites along the river, half of them larger than 20 acres, providing opportunities for camping, picnicking, fishing, and boat launching, allowing boaters to tailor float trips to their taste. The full 80-mi. trip takes 5 or 6 days.

The river has no great rapids, but there are hazards potentially disastrous to the uninformed, inexperienced, or unwary. Canoes and rafts are both used. Some sections are suitable for beginners.

Just N of Stevensville, the river skirts the Lee Metcalf National Wildlife Refuge (see entry).

Fishing is said to be outstanding, for rainbow and brown trout, some Dolly Varden, cutthroat, largemouth bass.

HEADQUARTERS: Region 2, 210 39th St., Missoula, MT 59801; (406) 721-5808.

BLACKFOOT-CLEARWATER WILDLIFE MANAGEMENT AREA
Montana Department of Fish, Wildlife & Parks
49,459 acres.

From Missoula, E on SR 200. Entrance on left, 6 mi. beyond SR 83.

On the W, the WMA adjoins SR 83, including the lower half of Salmon Lake and the lower portion of the Clearwater River. On the N is Lolo National Forest, on the S SR 200 and the Blackfoot River. The area has been a popular fishing and hunting site for years. The Department acquired it to provide winter range for elk.

Elevations range from 3,800 ft. on the lower Clearwater to nearly 7,000 ft. on Ovando Mountain, on the NF boundary. The lower portion is mostly grassy flats and rolling hills. The higher slopes are conifer forest, chiefly ponderosa pine, Douglas-fir, and larch.

The site provides habitat for mule and whitetail deer, elk; blue, ruffed, Franklin's, and sharp-tailed grouse. Salmon Lake, the Clearwater River, Cottonwood Creek, Harpers Lake, and potholes provide habitat for waterfowl, beaver, muskrat, and mink. There's good trout fishing in the lakes and streams.

Black bear are common, as are coyote, bobcat, skunk, and badger. Small mammals include meadow, white-footed, and jumping mice; bushytail woodrat, snowshoe hare, whitetail jackrabbit, red and golden-mantled squirrels, yellowbelly marmot, flying squirrel, pocket gopher, Columbian ground squirrel.

The Range is open to hunters and fishermen. Other visitors interested in wildlife are welcome, for hiking and camping, subject to game management needs.

The area is closed to all human use Dec. 1–May 15.

HEADQUARTERS: Montana Department of Fish, Wildlife & Parks, Missoula Regional Office, 3201 Spurgin Rd., Missoula, MT 59801; (406) 721-5808.

BLACKFOOT RIVER
Mixed public and private ownerships
100 river miles.

Flows W along or near SR 200 from the Continental Divide at Rogers Pass to Bonner, near Missoula.

This was the route of the Lewis & Clark Trail. SR 200 is a scenic drive, descending gradually through the river valley from 5,610 ft. elevation at the Pass to 3,210 ft. at Missoula. Much of the scenic grandeur is provided by the mountains of the Helena and Lolo National Forests, although the river and road touch Forest land only briefly. SR 200 crosses the river three times, and a few local roads also cross. Although there are frequent access points—we counted 16 Fishing Access Sites—much of the river is quiet and undeveloped. Many streams rush down from the mountains to join the river. The river crosses several tracts of BLM land.

The river can be floated for most of the 100 mi., but the character of the stream differs from section to section and season to season. No one should try it without knowing downstream conditions. High in the drainage one can sometimes enjoy a quiet canoe trip, possibly hauling the canoe around occasional bars and logjams. Upstream areas are the least floated, and the canoeist is often alone.

Some downstream sections have whitewater calling for good information, good equipment, and high skill. Downstream sections are also the most popular, and the final section before Bonner is heavily used.

Camping: Available at most Fishing Access Sites and two National Forest riverside campgrounds, for highway travelers as well as boaters.

REFERENCE: Fischer, Hank. *The Floater's Guide to Montana.* Billings, MT: Falcon Press, 1986. Pp. 23–26.

HEADQUARTERS: Montana Department of Fish, Wildlife & Parks, Region 2, 210 39th St., Missoula, MT 59801; (406) 721-5808.

CLARK FORK RIVER
Montana Department of Fish, Wildlife & Parks
200 river miles.

Generally follows I-90 from near Warm Springs to St. Regis, then SRs 135 and 200 to the ID border.

For almost its entire length, Clark Fork flows through private land, at times in a corridor through the Lolo National Forest. Nonetheless, it has many sections with natural qualities, including splendid scenery and plentiful wildlife. Although I-90 was built in the Clark Fork valley and crosses the river occasionally, it's often out of floaters' sight and hearing.

At first glance, the highway map seems to show the river staying with I-90 all the way to ID. But it's the SE-flowing St. Regis River that parallels the highway from the border for 30 mi. to a confluence at St. Regis. Here the Clark fork turns E for 21 mi., then NW along SR 200. For motorists, this is the most scenic part of the river's course, in the valley between the Cabinet Mountains on the N, the Bitterroot and Coeur d'Alene ranges on the S. Fed by many tributaries, the river is now carrying more water than any other in MT.

The river can be floated for almost its entire 200 mi. Each section has its own characteristics, changing from season to season. Far upstream are canoe waters, winding through forest and brush, often shallow, usually too shallow after midsummer. Alberton Gorge, downstream from Missoula, has 20 mi. of whitewater, with rapids to Class IV. Along SR 200 the river is backed up by Noxon Dam into a long reservoir.

From the headwaters to St. Regis, access is chiefly at the state's Fishing Access Sites. We counted 14 of them. Half of these are near Missoula, and along here the heaviest use of the river occurs. We saw improvised small-boat access points along SR 200.

Once the river was too polluted for people or fish. Some problems remain, but the fish are back, and fishing is generally good.

ACTIVITIES
Camping: At most Fishing Access Sites.
Fishing: Brown, rainbow, cutthroat, and Dolly Varden trout.

Boating: Chiefly flatwater sections above Noxon and other dams.
Rafting, kayaking: Most of the river, varying conditions. Get information
before launching.

REFERENCE: Fischer, Hank. *The Floater's Guide to Montana.* Billings, MT:
Falcon Press, 1986. Pp. 26–30, 113–17.

HEADQUARTERS: Region 2, 210 39th St., Missoula, MT 59801: (406) 721-5808.

DEERLODGE NATIONAL FOREST
U.S. Forest Service
1,195,771 acres of Forest land; 1,355,783 acres within boundaries.

Access by local roads from I-90 and I-15; US 10, 10A, and 91.

The several blocks of the Forest are arranged in two clusters, one surrounding
Butte, the other, a few miles W, surrounding Philipsburg. Anaconda approximates the geographic center. The blocks are on mountain ranges separated
by flat valley floors and foothills. The Forest is part of the huge complex of
National Forests occupying most of western MT. It adjoins the Bitterroot NF
on the W, the Helena on the N and NE, the Beaverhead on the S.

The mountains rise from valley floors at 4,500 to 5,000 ft. elevation to
heights generally in the 8,000-ft. range, a few peaks exceeding 9,000 and
10,000 ft. Highest is 10,641-ft. Mt. Evans. Slopes are generally moderate;
almost three-fourths of the land has less than a 40% slope. The Continental Divide follows a looping course along the mountains N, E, and S
of Butte.

The mountain slopes are cut by deep, often narrow canyons or gorges. The
work of glaciers is seen in numerous cirque basins, many with lakes. In all,
the Forest has about 100 lakes and 1,033 mi. of fishable streams. Four lakes—
Georgetown, East Fork and Whitetail reservoirs, and Silver Lake—are the
largest water bodies. W of the Divide, drainage is to Clark Fork and Rock
Creek, E of the Divide to the Boulder and Jefferson rivers, all outside Forest
boundaries.

No point in the Forest is more than 8 mi. from the boundary, and only
44,000 acres are defined as Primitive settings, at least 3 mi. from a road. The
only Wilderness is a 43,629-acre portion of the Anaconda-Pintler Wilderness.
However, 17 roadless areas of 5,000 or more acres, the largest with 72,414
acres, have varying Wilderness qualities, and several may acquire Wilderness
status.

Recreational use of the Forest is over 1 million visitor-days per year, about one-fourth of this at campgrounds, picnic areas, boat launch sites, and ski areas. Half of the activity at developed sites is in the Georgetown Lake-East Fork Reservoir area. The dispersed uses making up the other three-fourths include hiking, camping, hunting, fishing, motorcycle riding, driving for pleasure, ski touring, and snowmobiling.

Climate: Summers are warm and dry, winters cold. Most precipitation falls as snow, augmented by rainy periods in June and Sept. Total annual precipitation varies from 10 to 14 in. in valley bottoms to over 40 in. at higher elevations, where snowfall is about 150 in.

Plants: Foothill grasslands extend from the broad valley bottoms, giving way to timber as moisture increases. Trees cover 83% of the Forest. On the highest slopes, the tree cover is broken by talus and rock outcroppings, with stunted trees. Two-thirds of the timbered area is dominated by lodgepole pine. Douglas-fir is dominant in one-fifth of the area, mixed conifers such as subalpine fir and spruce in the remainder. Also present are limber pine and subalpine larch. Typical understory components are grouse whortleberry, pinegrass, Idaho fescue, bluebunch wheatgrass, glacier lily, elk sedge, menziesia, snowberry, twinflower. Areas of alpine tundra are present on the Flint, Tobacco Root, and Anaconda ranges.

Seasonal wildflowers include lupine, glacier lily, pasqueflower, phlox, heartleaf arnica, arrowleaf balsamroot, sego lily, musk thistle, prairie flax, Indian paintbrush, elk thistle, shootingstar, little larkspur, fireweed, yellow bells, bluebells, monkeyflower, elephant head, camas, shrubby cinquefoil, beargrass, arrowleaf groundsel.

Birds: Recent checklist of 260 species notes seasonality and habitats. Common species include pied-billed, horned, red-necked, eared, and western grebes; great blue heron, tundra swan, snow and Canada geese; green-winged, blue-winged, and cinnamon teals; mallard, pintail, shoveler, gadwall, American wigeon, canvasback, redhead, ring-necked duck, lesser scaup, common and Barrow's goldeneyes, bufflehead, common merganser, ruddy duck. Also osprey, northern harrier, red-tailed and rough-legged hawks, golden eagle, American kestrel, prairie falcon, gray partridge; spruce, blue, and ruffed grouse; sora, American coot, sandhill crane, killdeer, American avocet, greater and lesser yellowlegs, solitary and spotted sandpipers, long-billed curlew, long-billed dowitcher, common snipe, Wilson's phalarope; Franklin's, ring-billed, and California gulls.

Also rock and mourning doves, great horned and short-eared owls, common nighthawk, rufous and calliope hummingbirds, belted kingfisher, downy and hairy woodpeckers, northern flicker, western wood-pewee, willow flycatcher, eastern kingbird, horned lark. Swallows: tree, violet-green, rough-winged, bank, cliff, barn. Gray and Steller's jays, Clark's nutcracker, black-billed magpie, American crow, common raven, black-capped and mountain chickadees, red-breasted nuthatch, rock and marsh wrens, dipper, ruby-crowned kinglet, mountain bluebird, Townsend's solitaire, Swainson's thrush,

American robin, Bohemian and cedar waxwings, northern shrike, European starling, yellow and yellow-rumped warblers, western tanager, lazuli bunting. Sparrows: tree, chipping, vesper, savannah, song, white-crowned, house. Dark-eyed junco, snow bunting, bobolink; red-winged, yellow-headed, and Brewer's blackbirds; western meadowlark, brown-headed cowbird, northern oriole, Cassin's finch, pine siskin, American goldfinch, evening grosbeak.

Mammals: List provided from administrative document. Abundant and common species include vagrant shrew; little brown, big brown, and silver-haired bats; badger, coyote, yellowbelly marmot, Columbian ground squirrel, golden-mantled squirrel, yellow pine chipmunk, pine squirrel, northern pocket gopher, beaver, western deer mouse, bushytail woodrat; red-backed, meadow, and longtail voles; porcupine, snowshoe hare, elk, mule deer, moose. Grizzly bears occur occasionally on the Deerlodge.

FEATURES

Anaconda-Pintler Wilderness, 44,175 acres, plus 113,699 acres in the Bitterroot and Beaverhead NFs. Access by local and Forest roads from US 10A and SR 38. The Wilderness lies across about 30 mi. of the Continental Divide on the Anaconda Range. Elevations from 5,100 ft. at the foothills to 10,793 ft. on West Goat Peak. High, rugged, splendid mountain scenery. Soils are thin and rocky. The mountains have spectacular cirques, many lakes, U-shaped valleys, glacial moraines, steep canyons, cascading streams. The highest slopes have bare talus, tarns, and snowfields, with vegetation limited to lichens, mosses, and low-growing hardy plants.

Winters are cold, the snow-free season short. Lakes usually remain frozen until the first week of July.

Wildlife includes deer, elk, moose, mountain goat, and black bear. Cutthroat and rainbow trout are in most lakes and streams.

Several road-access trailheads are on the N Wilderness boundary. Trails follow drainages to a number of high lakes and to the Hi-Line Trail along the Divide. 15,000 visitor-days per year feature hunting, fishing, and backpacking.

Sapphire Roadless Area, 72,614 acres in the Deerlodge, plus 44,416 acres in the Bitterroot NF. On the crest of the Sapphire Mountains, about 27 mi. W of Anaconda, the area adjoins the N boundary of the Anaconda-Pintler Wilderness. Access from the E by various Forest roads. About 25 mi. N–S, the area is 2 to 10 mi. wide. It is penetrated by the Copper Creek road, which passes Copper Creek campground. Most of the area is above 7,000 ft. Highest point is about 9,000 ft. Along the crest are steep, rocky cirque basins and trough walls, with 15 small lakes and numerous potholes. Terrain in the W and around the Ross Forks of Rock Creek is rolling hills with flat creek bottoms. Copper Creek and the West and Ross Forks of Rock Creek are nationally known trout fisheries. The area has a network of 17 trails. Current use of the area is very light, including hunting, fishing, camping, hiking, and horse riding.

Flint Range-Dolus Lakes Roadless Area, 60,297 acres. 10 mi. W of Deer Lodge. Access by local and Forest roads, one popular route being to Rock Creek Lake, on the E edge of the area. Several 4-wheel-drive roads penetrate the area. It includes all of the highest peaks of the Flint Range: 10,300-ft. Mt. Powell, others over 9,000 ft., with steep timbered and talus slopes, U-shaped canyons, large cirque basins. The Dolus Lakes—a chain along Dolus Creek, just W of Rock Creek Lake—are popular for walk-in fishing. Many other lakes are backpacking destinations. The Trask Lakes, 5 mi. from the trailhead at Rock Creek Lake, are a scenic area with good fishing. Visitor use is light.

Whitetail-Haystack Roadless Area, 71,429 acres. NE of Butte. The area lies between Butte and Boulder, its boundary within 4 or 5 mi. of each city. From Butte, access is from the S by local roads; a 4-wheel-drive road penetrates to Whitetail Reservoir in the heart of the area. Slopes are moderate, with broad ridges, the highest point 8,862 ft. The landscape includes forest, wet meadows, and mountain grasslands. Large boulder fields limit ORV activity. Recreation includes fall elk hunting, fishing, backpacking, and ski touring.

Middle Mountain-Tobacco Roots Roadless Area, 37,761 acres in the Deerlodge, 59,701 acres in the Beaverhead NF. The N boundary is about 10 mi. S of Whitehall. Principal access is from the NE by Forest Road 107 along the South Boulder River. This is the central portion of the isolated Tobacco Range. The area is rugged and diverse, with many peaks over 10,000 ft., cirque basins, and glacial lakes. One of the most scenic is Lake Louise, reached by a steep National Recreation Trail.

Georgetown Lake, 3,000 acres, is the Forest's busiest recreation site. About 14 mi. W of Anaconda on US 10A, it is said to have the heaviest per-acre fishing pressure of any MT lake. About half of the recreation at developed sites occurs here and at nearby East Fork Reservoir. On the shore are a marina, docks, boat ramps, picnic sites. The scenery is splendid, with the Flint Range on the N, the Pintlers on the S. Campgrounds here are used as base camps for many hunters and hikers heading for the high country. Fishing is said to be excellent for kokanee salmon, rainbow, brook, and Dolly Varden trout.

Sheepshead Mountain Recreation Area, 156 acres, was designed for people with disabilities. From I-15, 13 mi. N of Butte, left 6 mi. at the Elk Park exit. The setting is a 15-acre lake, meadow, range, brushland, and three streams surrounded by forest. Facilities include a specially designed campground and 2 1/2 mi. of paved trails. A day-use area open to all includes a fishing pier, wading pond, picnic area, and playground. It has been called one of the nation's outstanding handicapped-accessible recreation sites.

INTERPRETATION

A looseleaf Recreation Opportunity Guide (ROG) can be seen at HQ and all Ranger Stations. Pages of information on trails, campgrounds, fishing, etc., are photocopied on request.

The Forest has no visitor center, campfire programs, or other naturalist activities.

ACTIVITIES

Camping: 22 campgrounds, 356 sites. Open May–Oct.

Hiking, backpacking: 600 mi. of trails. 300 mi. were maintained in the year preceding our last visit. New bridges were built in the Anaconda-Pintler Wilderness, some trails relocated.

Hunting: Chiefly elk. Also moose, mule deer, black bear, blue grouse.

Fishing: Lakes and streams. Chiefly trout; kokanee in Georgetown Lake.

Boating: Power boating chiefly on Georgetown Lake.

Horse riding: Mostly in conjunction with hunting. A list of outfitter-guides serving the area is available.

Skiing: Discovery Basin, N of Georgetown Lake.

Ski touring: On Forest roads and trails. No groomed trails.

PUBLICATIONS

Forest map. $1.

Anaconda-Pintler Wilderness topo map. $1.

Trail map. $1.

Bird checklist.

Sheepshead Mountain Recreation Area leaflet.

Cross-country ski trail maps.

REFERENCES

Schneider, Bill. *The Hiker's Guide to Montana.* Billings, MT: Falcon Press, 1983. Pp. 74–76, 86–90.

Turbak, Gary. *The Traveler's Guide to Montana.* Billings, MT: Falcon Press, 1983. Pp. 65–69, 147–48.

HEADQUARTERS: Federal Building, Box 400, Butte, MT 59703; (406) 496-3352.

RANGER DISTRICTS: Deer Lodge R.D., 91 Frontage Rd., Deer Lodge, MT 59722; (406) 846-1770. Jefferson R.D., 403 W. Legion, P.O. Box F, Whitehall, MT 59759; (406) 287-3223. Philipsburg R.D., P.O. Box H, Philipsburg, MT 59858; (406) 859-3211. Butte R.D., 2201 White Blvd., Butte, MT 59701; (406) 494-2147.

FLATHEAD LAKE

Montana Division of Fish, Wildlife & Parks

28 mi. long, about 6 mi. wide; over 200 sq. mi.

S of Kalispell, between US 93 and SR 35.

This is the largest natural lake in the West. Some maps suggest that the Lolo National Forest fronts on the E shore; it doesn't. Indeed, there are only a few small tracts of public land on the lake shore. The S half of the lake is within the Flathead Indian Reservation, which doesn't seem to impede development. The largest concentration of private homes and commercial establishments is near Kalispell. However, the lake is so large that a boater can find quiet waters and perhaps even an informal overnight campsite.

Wild Horse Island State Park, 2,165 acres, near Big Arm, is accessible only by boat. There is no public dock. Camping is prohibited, as are fires, hunting, and pets. The island is best known for its wildlife, notably bighorn sheep and deer. Private inholdings are 47 circular one-acre lots that include no shoreline but have easements permitting docks. Otherwise it's wilderness, and state policy is to keep it that way.

ACTIVITIES

Camping: Public campgrounds on the W shore are, N to S, West Shore State Park; Lambeth Memorial, Big Arm, and Walstad Memorial State Recreation Areas. On the E shore: Wayfarers, Woods Bay, Yellow Bay, and Finley Point SRAs.

Fishing: Called excellent. Cutthroat, lake, and Dolly Varden trout; kokanee salmon, mountain and lake whitefish, largemouth bass, perch. Fishing the S half of the lake requires a tribal permit.

Boating: Numerous marinas. Launching at state sites.

HEADQUARTERS: Region I, P.O. Box 67, Kalispell, MT 59901; (406) 755-5505.

FLATHEAD NATIONAL FOREST
U.S. Forest Service
2,350,508 acres; 2,628,745 acres within boundaries.

NW MT. Principal access from US 2 and 93.

The Flathead extends S from the Canadian border more than 130 mi. The N portion adjoins the Kootenai NF on the W, Glacier National Park on the E.

This N portion is divided by blocks of state, timber company, and private lands. The largest mass of Forest land extends S from Glacier NP, bisected by Hungry Horse Reservoir and the South Fork Flathead River. Over a million acres of this area is Wilderness.

Terrain is typical of glaciated lands: high alpine ridges and basins, broad U-shaped valleys. Mountain ranges are parallel, trending NNW to SSE. Principal ranges are the Whitefish, Salish, Flathead, Swan, and Mission. Elevation of the Flathead valley bottom is about 3,000 ft. Lower slopes are gentle, gradually steepening. Nearly half of the area outside the Wildernesses has slopes steeper than 60%. The highest peaks are just under 10,000 ft.

Weather is cool. Annual precipitation ranges from 16 in. in the valleys to over 100 in. on high ridges. In the valleys, about half of this precipitation is snow, on the ridges 80%.

The Forest has about 3,400 mi. of streams. Principal rivers are the three forks of the Flathead, the Stillwater, and the Swan. The largest water body surrounded by NF lands is the Hungry Horse Reservoir on the South Fork Flathead River. Several lakes within the Forest boundaries have mixed shoreline ownerships. On Ashley, for example, only bits of lake shore are Forest land, whereas Tally's lake shore is all Forest. Many small lakes, including high mountain lakes, are entirely within Forest land. Examples are the Chain Lakes in the N.

In the S, along SR 83, is a complex of wetlands, ponds, and lakes in a checkerboard of Forest, private, and timber company lands. Lindbergh and Holland lakes have both Forest campgrounds and private cottages on their shores. Holland Lake is a major trailhead for the Bob Marshall Wilderness.

More than half of the Forest is roadless. The Flathead's 3,900 mi. of roads were developed largely because of logging, mostly on the lower slopes. This road network provides good access to many fishing streams, small lakes, and trailheads. Most recreational use in the heavily roaded areas is by hunters, wood gatherers, fishermen, and berry pickers.

Of the 2,146 mi. of trails, more than half are in Wilderness areas, and they receive the larger portion of limited maintenance funds. High-standard maintenance is provided for over 200 mi. of Wilderness trails, less than 20 mi. of others. About one-third of the trail system is in poor condition.

Recreation use of the Flathead exceeds a million annual visitor-days, and the trend is up. Less than a third of this is at developed sites. Only about 15% is in Wildernesses. More than half is classified as "dispersed" in roaded areas, which includes hunting, fishing, climbing, snowmobiling, sightseeing, etc. Some lakeshore sites show signs of overuse, as do a few trails near the most accessible Wilderness trailheads, but there are ample opportunities to find solitude in attractive places.

Plants: Habitat types range from low-elevation ponderosa pine-bunchgrass to whitebark pine. Most of the area below 7,000 ft. is capable of supporting tree cover, except for such local settings as bogs, meadows, shrub fields, talus, rock outcrops, and avalanche chutes. The predominant plant community is subalpine fir.

Existing vegetation shows the effects of fire and logging. Because of fire, extensive stands of lodgepole pine occur in the N, and these stands have been infested by mountain pine beetle. More than four-fifths of the timber stands are mixed conifers, more than half classified as mature or over-mature.

Prominent tree species of the Flathead include Engelmann spruce, Douglas-fir, western larch, Rocky Mountain juniper, water birch, mountain ash. Seasonal wildflowers include lupine, beardtongue, mertensia, monkshood, forget-me-not, speedwell, heartleaf arnica, Indian paintbrush, fireweed, elephanthead, white bog orchid, monkeyflowers. At high elevations, alpine forget-me-not, carpet pink.

Birds: More than 200 species recorded. Checklist available. Seasonally abundant or common species include horned grebe, great blue heron, mallard, blue-winged teal, gadwall, common and Barrow's goldeneyes, common merganser, American kestrel, ruffed grouse, spotted sandpiper, common snipe, rufous hummingbird, yellow-bellied sapsucker, downy and hairy woodpeckers, tree swallow, gray and Steller's jays, common raven, black-capped and mountain chickadees, red-breasted nuthatch, brown creeper, dipper, golden-crowned and ruby-crowned kinglets, American robin, Bohemian waxwing; yellow-rumped, Townsend's and MacGillivray's warblers; northern waterthrush; chipping, vesper, and song sparrows; dark-eyed junco, red-winged blackbird, pine siskin.

Mammals: No checklist available. Big game species include elk, mule and whitetail deer, moose, Rocky Mountain goat, grizzly and black bears, mountain lion. Other species noted include badger, beaver, muskrat, skunk, hoary marmot, woodchuck, porcupine, chipmunk, snowshoe hare, pika, golden-mantled squirrel, bobcat, lynx, marten, coyote, wolverine, mink, weasel.

FEATURES

Bob Marshall Wilderness Complex includes 3 Wildernesses—Bob Marshall, Lincoln-Scapegoat, and Great Bear—in 4 National Forests. The Flathead manages 70% of the "Bob," everything W of the Continental Divide, and all of the Great Bear, almost a million acres. The Bob is probably the most famous Wilderness, named for the man most responsible for establishing the Wilderness system. It was designated Wilderness in 1964, the Great Bear in 1978.

The Bob extends about 60 mi. N–S. The Great Bear adds about 40 mi. to the NW. The area is bisected S–N by the South and Middle Forks of the Flathead Wild and Scenic River system. Elevations range from 5,000 ft. in the valleys to over 9,000 ft. on the Divide.

This is the outdoorsman's dream of wilderness: rugged peaks, alpine lakes, mountain valleys with meandering streams in flowered meadows, mountain streams with cascades and waterfalls, towering trees, abundant wildlife. The Flathead portion of the complex has 1,150 mi. of trails, most following drainages up to mountain passes. Principal access routes are off SR 83 and from the South Fork Flathead River drainage. Well-developed trails near the principal trailheads give way to primitive trails in more pristine areas. The Forest map suggests a variety of trips, from 3 to 10 days, routes from 25 to 75 mi.

Annual visitor-days in the Bob total about 100,000, in the Great Bear about a fourth as many. This isn't a day-use area; the average length of stay is over 5 days. A large share of the visitors come from out of state, especially in the fall hunting season when use is heaviest. About half of the travel is by horse. About 50 outfitter-guides serve the area.

Management is concerned about overuse in parts of the Bob, shown by overgrazing, worn trails, trampled vegetation, and tree damage. Visitors are urged to use low-impact techniques.

Unless you're traveling with an outfitter, plan your trip with advice from the Spotted Bear Ranger District. Be equipped and prepared for emergencies, including storms and injuries. It's grizzly country, so you should know how to minimize the chance of an encounter.

Mission Mountains Wilderness, 73,877 acres. We saw the Missions first on the W side, seeming to rise almost vertically to bare ridgetops. That side is Indian Reservation. The Wilderness, on the E side, is more approachable. Access is from SR 83 in the Swan Valley. The lower slopes leading to the Wilderness are a checkerboard of Forest, timber company, and private land. The Wilderness is a strip about 30 mi. N–S, from 2 to 6 mi. W–E. Most visitation is in the S half, a region of many lakes.

Most travel here is on foot. The 45 mi. of maintained trails aren't maintained to pack stock standards, and horse use is not encouraged. Average length of stay is 1.7 days, indicating a mix of backpackers and day hikers. The fishing lakes closest to trailheads show signs of heavy use. Camping is now banned within a quarter-mi. of the shores at two heavy use areas. Other areas of the Wilderness have light use.

Peaks are rugged and snow-capped, rising to 9,820 ft., with several small glaciers. Topography is rough and broken, with many near-vertical cliffs, flat boulders, talus slopes. The N portion is less rugged and more timbered. Wildlife is abundant, fishing only fair.

Flathead Wild and Scenic River, 219 river mi., including portions of the South, Middle, and North Forks. The South and Middle Forks, flowing NW, and the North Fork, flowing SE, join near West Glacier, forming the Flathead River which turns S, outside the Forest, into Flathead Lake. Major segments of the Forks are classified as "Wild," "Recreational," or "Scenic." The North Fork is part of the boundary between the Forest and Glacier NP. The lower Middle Fork follows US 2 along the base of Glacier NP. The South Fork flows into Hungry Horse Reservoir, continuing below the dam to the confluence. Sections of the South and Middle Forks are in the Bob Marshall and Great Bear Wildernesses, flowing through some of the state's wildest and most scenic areas, through narrow gorges, dense forests, and open valleys.

All three forks can be floated in appropriate seasons. Floating may be hazardous during spring runoff, and by late Aug. low water creates another set of problems in some areas. In general, the floating season begins in late May on the Middle and North Forks, not until July on the South. All three have rapids, the Middle and South Forks to Class V, the North to Class III. South and North also have Class I sections.

The river corridors also offer excellent opportunities for hiking and backpacking, camping, hunting and fishing, wildlife observation, and over-snow travel.

A birder scanning a map of the area N of Flathead Lake is sure to be fascinated by the complex of meanders, oxbows, and marshes. The Flathead River can be floated from below the confluence of the forks to the lake, not through National Forest but through Kalispell's outskirts, floated with some paddling, for this is slow-moving flatwater. As the map suggests, the birding is excellent.

The Forest has only small frontage on Flathead Lake (see entry).

Hungry Horse Reservoir is 34 mi. long, 3.5 mi. across at the widest point. It lies between the Swan Range and the Flathead Range, the mountains rising rather steeply on both sides from what had been the South Fork floodplain. Elevation at the reservoir is about 3,560, the slopes rising to over 8,000 ft. The reservoir is encircled by Forest roads, 115 mi. to make the full circuit. Almost half of the Forest's campgrounds and picnic areas are around the Reservoir, as well as 12 ramps and launch sites and swimming areas. Access to the Jewel Basin Hiking Area is on the W side. The Great Bear Wilderness is on the E.

Jewel Basin Hiking Area, 15,349 acres at the N end of the Swan Mountain Range, between Kalispell and Hungry Horse Reservoir. Access by Forest roads from SR 83, US 2, or the Hungry Horse Reservoir West Side Road. Current information on road conditions is recommended. A scenic area with 27 alpine lakes from 2 to 58 surface acres, high peaks, rushing streams, subalpine forest, open meadows, countless wildflowers. Elevations from 4,240 to 7,542 ft. Mechanized vehicles and pack animals are banned. 35 mi. of trail link most of the lakes. Hiker use of the area has increased rapidly while funds to maintain it have not. Trail maintenance is below standard. Some lake shores have been trampled. It's still gorgeous!

Other roadless areas that qualify for inclusion in the Wilderness system total 495,000 acres. Some of these are proposed additions to existing Wildernesses. Several have comparable natural qualities but are lightly used because they are little known and, in some cases, hard to reach.

INTERPRETATION

The Forest has an excellent looseleaf Recreation Opportunities Guide (ROG), available for use at HQ and Ranger Districts. It includes sections on camping and picnicking, hiking and backpacking, hunting, fishing, horse travel, cross-country skiing and snowshoeing, snowmobiling, boating, identification and gathering. Arranged by Ranger Districts, pages offer detailed information and advice. Each principal trail, for example, is described on both sides of a page, with sketch map: access, location, length, elevations, recommended season, degree of difficulty, amount of use, attractions and considerations, plus a narrative. Photocopies of individual pages are made on request.

Danny On Memorial Trail, 5 mi. nature trail, from the Big Mountain ski area parking lot N of Whitefish. The trail ascends 2,000 ft. to the upper end of the chairlift. Cutoffs permit shorter loops. Trail guide.

ACTIVITIES

Camping: 24 campgrounds, 304 sites. Most are open Memorial Day–Labor Day weekends. Most can be used out of season but have no water or services. Informal camping elsewhere.

Hiking, backpacking: 2,146 mi. of trails include 1,244 in Wildernesses. Outside Wildernesses, about 75% of trails are open to all uses; 25% are closed to motorized use, 5% to horses. About one-third of the trails are in poor condition; Wilderness trails get the most maintenance. ROG has detailed information on principal trails, including season of use and whether use is heavy or light.

The hiking season usually begins about June 15, but snow will still be encountered above 6,000 ft. at the end of June.

Hunting: Whitetail deer and elk are the principal big game species. Others include mule deer, black bear, moose, mountain goat, grizzly bear. Upland birds include spruce, ruffed, and blue grouse. HQ has a list of outfitters.

Fishing: Hundreds of mi. of fishable streams, plus large and small lakes and reservoirs. The ROG has individual pages on the principal fishing waters: how to get there, description, kind and quality of fishing. The leaflet *Fishing the Flathead* has a keyed map of lakes and streams in the Flathead Basin noting the fish in each. Most waters have varieties of trout. Some waters have perch, kokanee, bass, northern pike, whitefish, grayling.

Horse riding: Most trails are open to horse travel. Principal horse use is in Wildernesses during hunting season. HQ has list of outfitters.

Boating: Principal flatwater boating is on Hungry Horse Reservoir. Also boating on several lakes near SR 83. Motors restricted on Holland Lake. (See entry, Flathead Lake.)

Rafting, kayaking: On the three forks of the Flathead River. Mid-May to mid-Aug. 5 outfitters have permits. Excellent map-guide.

Skiing: Big Mountain Ski Area, N of Whitefish.
Ski touring: Ski trails in 4 Ranger Districts are described in the ROG. Some have sufficient snow by Thanksgiving. ROG also mentions Forest roads often used for ski touring.

PUBLICATIONS
Forest maps, N and S halves. $1 each.
Forest travel plan map. $1.
Mission Mountains Wilderness map. $1.
Jewel Basin Hiking Area map, with text. $1.
Three Forks of the Flathead River: map, floating information, other text. On waterproof paper. $2.
"Fishing the Flathead." Map, text. $1.
Information pages:
  Bob Marshall Wilderness.
  Great Bear Wilderness.
  Mission Mt. and Scapegoat Wilderness.
  List of outfitters.
  Lists of heavily used areas and trails.
Bird checklist.
Trees.
Wildflowers.
Danny On Memorial Trail folder.
Pamphlets:
  Guide to the Mission Mountains Wilderness.
  Geology of the Flathead Forest Region.
  You Are in Grizzly Country.

REFERENCES
Schneider, Bill. *The Hiker's Guide to Montana.* Billings, MT: Falcon Press, 1983. Pp. 104–24, 129–31.
Turbak, Gary. *Traveler's Guide to Montana.* Billings, MT: Falcon Press, 1983. Pp. 114–18, 166–78.
Woodruff, Steve, and Don Schwennesen. *Montana Wilderness.* Kansas City: Lowell Press, 1984. Pp. 20–37, 82–92.
Graetz, Rick. *Montana's Bob Marshall Country.* Helena: Montana Magazine Inc.

HEADQUARTERS: 1935 Third Ave., Kalispell, MT 59901; (406) 755-5401.

RANGER DISTRICTS: Talley Lake R.D., Whitefish, MT 59937; (406) 862-2508. Glacier View R.D., Columbia Falls, MT 59912; (406) 892-4372. Swan Lake R.D., Bigfork, MT 59911; (406) 837-5081. Hungry Horse R.D., Hungry Horse, MT 59919; (406) 387-5243. Spotted Bear R.D., c/o Hungry Horse R.D.; summer telephone (406) 752-7345.

FLATHEAD RIVER

The North, Middle, and South Forks are largely within the Flathead National Forest and are described in that entry. The main river, flowing S into Flathead Lake, is outside the Forest but also described in that entry.

GARNET WINTER RECREATION TRAILS

U.S. Bureau of Land Management
Indeterminate acreage.

From Missoula, 26 mi. E on I-90 to Bearmouth exit; continue 5 1/2 mi. E on US 10 then N on Bear Gulch Road to Beartown and Garnet; chains recommended.

Winter trails because they are not available for summer hiking. They cross public and private land and include unplowed roads. BLM has developed a 55-mi. system of snowmobile and cross-country skiing trails, of which 31 1/2 mi. are a National Recreation Trail. The main trail is groomed.

Garnet is a ghost town, now maintained by a nonprofit association in cooperation with BLM. The town has a visitor center. Cabins can be rented Dec.–Apr.

PUBLICATION: Folder with map.

HEADQUARTERS: BLM, Butte District Office, 106 N. Parkmont, Butte, MT 58702; (406) 494-5059,

GLACIER NATIONAL PARK

National Park Service
1,012,811 acres.

From Kalispell, NE on US 2 to West Glacier.

John Muir said it a century ago:

The time [you spend in Glacier] will not be taken from the sum of your life. Instead of shortening, it will indefinitely lengthen it and make you truly immortal. Nevermore will time seem short or long and cares will never again fall heavily on you. . . ."

We tried to keep this firmly in mind when we drove from Kalispell through an appalling, neon-lit, commercial tourist avenue. The new approach road is better, we're assured, but the Park can't control what's outside its gates. Inside, the problem is crowds, almost two million visitors in a short summer season. However, the great majority of visitors stay between West Glacier and St. Mary. The Park is huge. Most of it is roadless. There's plenty of quiet isolation.

Glacier adjoins Canada's Waterton Lakes National Park, and the two administrations cooperate. The two aren't linked by Park roads, although SR 17 cuts across a bit of Glacier's NE corner just before entering Waterton. From Canada, it's possible to cross the border by cruising S on Waterton Lake. A Glacier NP campground and Ranger Station are at Goat Haunt on the S end, but beyond is wilderness.

The entire Park is mountainous, carved by many glaciers into sharp peaks, knife-edge ridges, cirque basins, hanging valleys, and deep lakes, further sculptured by hundreds of rushing streams with countless waterfalls and cascades. It is bisected N–S by the Continental Divide on the Lewis Range, a chain of peaks and ridges, some over 9,000 ft. elevation. The highest peak, 10,448-ft. Mt. Cleveland, is E of the Divide. Indeed, there are glaciers, 50 living ones, an important element of the dramatic scenery. Snowfields, too, persist well into summer, giving many children the opportunity of making their first snowballs.

The Park has over 200 mountain lakes, substantial ones on both sides of the Divide, McDonald the largest on the W, St. Mary on the E. Valleys on the W side are at 3,000 to 4,000 ft., those on the E side about 1,000 ft. higher.

Climate: Summers are cool, winters cold. At West Glacier, the average July maximum is 80°F; at high elevations, nighttime frost is always possible. Average annual precipitation is about 29 in. at West Glacier, much more on the high slopes, where most precipitation is snow and drifts over 100 ft. deep have been recorded. The main summer travel season is June 15–Sept. 10, but some campgrounds open as early as mid-May, and two are open all year. The Going-to-the-Sun Road usually opens in early June and remains open until closed by snow, through Sept. with possible temporary closures, sometimes through Oct.

The era of hunting, trapping, prospecting, and mining ended when Glacier became a National Park in 1910. It was then a wilderness to be enjoyed only on foot and horseback. Backcountry chalets were supplied by packhorse. Horseback tours traveled from chalet to chalet. Roads now link the developed sites. Only two trail-access chalets remain. Still, most of the Park can be visited only on foot or horseback.

The character of the Park was forever changed when Going-to-the-Sun Road was completed in 1933. It's one of the world's most spectacular routes, the many overlooks providing magnificent views of mountains, glaciers, and valleys far below, and it's not to be missed, despite the crowds. The drive begins along Lake McDonald, follows a rushing stream, passes alpine meadows, then becomes a ledge blasted from solid rock, ascending to Logan Pass where there's a fine visitor center. Beyond, the road descends to St. Mary Lake and the Park's E exit. Drivers can return the same way or via US 89 and 2, which parallel the E and S boundaries just outside. This is the Glacier experience for most visitors today.

Going-to-the-Sun Road was designed for lighter traffic and smaller vehicles than use it today. Traffic is often heavy and overlook parking crowded between 10 A.M. and 4 P.M. When we passed another motor home, our mirrors cleared by inches. Vehicles and combinations over 30 ft. long are prohibited July–Aug.

Opposition to another cross-Park route would be overwhelming. Widening would require closing the road for several years, because work could be done only in the snow-free months. The simplest solution, one-way traffic, has aroused opposition, as has another remedy: banning private cars and providing ample jitney service.

Going-to-the-Sun isn't the only road. North Fork Road is a narrow, unimproved motor route just inside the Park's W boundary, providing access to Kintla and Bowman lakes and primitive campgrounds. One can return by the parallel road in the adjoining Flathead National Forest. On the E side, dead-end roads penetrate the Park to the Many Glacier, Cut Bank, and Two Medicine areas. The Chief Mountain International Highway crosses the Park's NE corner, entering Waterton Lakes National Park near the Canadian border.

Escaping from crowds is possible even in midsummer. Few visitors venture far from their cars. Less than one in a hundred spends even one night in a backcountry camp. Even the day hiker who chooses the right trail can sample the splendid solitude that moved John Muir.

Plants: Bunchgrass prairie is the most common plant community at the lowest elevations, bordered by stands of cottonwood and aspen. Stands of lodgepole pine and lodgepole-larch mark areas of past burns. Visitors see a handsome redcedar-hemlock forest in the McDonald Valley on the W side, but this is confined to a small part of the Park. By far the most extensive plant community is dominated by Engelmann spruce, subalpine fir, and Douglas-fir, which extends from about 4,000 ft. elevation to 7,000 ft. on the W side, 6,000 ft. on the E. Above this is the alpine zone, a region of stunted trees and shrubs and low-growing plants, including many flowering species that make a brilliant display as snow recedes. A 55-page checklist of vascular plants lists over a thousand species, but without relating them to habitats or blooming seasons.

Birds: Checklist of 240 species notes seasonality, abundance, and occurrence on W side, E side, or alpine zone. Seasonally abundant or common species include common loon; horned, eared, and western grebes; great blue heron, tundra swan, Canada goose, mallard, American wigeon, ring-necked duck, common and Barrow's goldeneyes, bufflehead, harlequin duck, common merganser, sharp-shinned and red-shouldered hawks, golden and bald eagles, northern harrier, osprey, American kestrel; blue, spruce, and ruffed grouse; white-tailed ptarmigan, American coot, killdeer, common snipe, spotted sandpiper, California and ring-billed gulls, mourning dove, great horned and northern pygmy owls, common nighthawk, Vaux's swift, rufous and calliope hummingbirds, belted kingfisher, northern flicker; pileated, hairy, downy, and three-toed woodpeckers; yellow-bellied sapsucker, eastern kingbird; willow, Hammond's, and olive-sided flycatchers. Swallows: violet-green, tree, bank, barn, cliff. Gray and Steller's jays, black-billed magpie, common raven, American crow, Clark's nutcracker, black-capped and mountain chickadees, red-breasted nuthatch, brown creeper, American dipper, winter wren, American robin; varied, hermit, and Swainson's thrushes; mountain bluebird, Townsend's solitaire, golden-crowned and ruby-crowned kinglets, water pipit, Bohemian and cedar waxwings, solitary and warbling vireos. Warblers: yellow, yellow-rumped, Townsend's, northern waterthrush, MacGillivray's, common yellowthroat, Wilson's, American redstart. Red-winged blackbird, western tanager, evening and pine grosbeaks, lazuli bunting, Cassin's and rosy finches, common redpoll, pine siskin, red crossbill. Sparrows: savannah, vesper, chipping, white-crowned, fox, song. Dark-eyed junco.

Mammals: Checklist of 60 species notes occurrence on E side, W side, and alpine areas. Omitting those marked rare, the list includes masked, vagrant, and northern water shrews; little brown, long-legged, big brown, silver-haired bats. Bobcat, lynx, mountain lion, black and grizzly bears, red fox, coyote, striped skunk, badger, wolverine, shorttail and longtail weasels, mink, marten, pika, snowshoe hare, porcupine, beaver, northern pocket gopher, hoary marmot; least, yellow pine, and red-tailed chipmunks; golden-mantled and red squirrels, Columbian ground squirrel, western jumping mouse, bushytail woodrat, deer mouse, muskrat. Voles: redback, montane heather, water, longtail, meadow. Whitetail and mule deer, elk, moose, bighorn sheep, mountain goat.

Glacier is grizzly country, and encounters have occurred, a very few of them fatal. A hiker was mauled by a grizzly during our last visit. Visitors are offered advice on how to avoid encounters. Hikers who discuss their plans will be warned about areas where grizzlies are active.

The North Fork corridor shared by Glacier and the Flathead National Forest is prime grizzly country and a route for wolves extending their range from Canada.

FEATURES

Our entries usually describe Wildernesses and such exceptional features as canyons and waterfalls. Except for its developed areas and a few roads, all

Glacier is Wilderness and outstanding features are everywhere. When one drives the Going-to-the-Sun Road, vistas pass too quickly to be absorbed. One pauses for five minutes to overlook a landscape that should be contemplated for a day, watching it change as the sun crosses the sky.

Almost every day hike has a notable feature as its destination: Apgar Lookout, Rocky Point, Snyder Lake, Paradise Valley, and Huckleberry Mountain, to name but a few. Backpackers and horsepackers have a far wider choice of features that can be seen in no other way, with time to enjoy them.

DEVELOPMENTS

Few National Parks have such an array of services and facilities. In addition to campgrounds they include 6 hotels, motels, and lodges; 2 backcountry chalets; 3 restaurants; 5 coffee shops or snack bars; 5 gift and book shops; 5 grocery and merchandise stores; 3 gasoline stations; a wilderness guide service; 5 boat tours; a bus tour company; 4 boat liveries; 3 horse liveries; a bicycle livery; a barber and beauty shop; and 2 laundry-shower facilities.

INTERPRETATION

Visitor centers are at Apgar (west side), Logan Pass, St. Mary, and Many Glacier.

Naturalist programs are announced in the *Waterton Glacier Guide*. They include campfire talks, guided hikes, launch tours, film programs, Junior Ranger programs. All begin in late June.

Nature trails are at the Camas Creek entrance, near the Avalanche picnic area, at the Sun Point and Many Glacier picnic areas, and at Logan Pass.

Self-guiding auto tour, 10 mi., along Camas Creek Road.

ACTIVITIES

Camping: 15 campgrounds, 1,057 sites. Openings from May 17 to June 14; closings from Sept. 2 to 28, but 2 are open all year and primitive camping is permitted until closed by snow. No reservations.

Hiking, backpacking: 750 mi. of trails. All information stations have trail information. Overnight stays in the backcountry require permits which include campsite reservations. Backcountry trips are permitted for up to 6 nights but may be extended. Campground stays are limited to 3 days at most sites, one night at some locations July–Aug. Concessioner offers guided backpacking trips.

Fishing requires a no-fee permit. Some waters are barren, so it's best to have advice.

Horse riding: Concessioner offers day rides.

Boating: Ramps on Lake McDonald, St. Mary Lake. Boat rentals at Apgar, Lake McDonald Lodge, Two Medicine, Many Glacier.

Rafting, kayaking: On the North and Middle Forks of the Flathead River. Various sections range from tame to wild, so good information is essential. Outfitters offer raft trips.

Ski touring has increased but still represents less than 5,000 visitor-days per year.

PUBLICATIONS
Waterton-Glacier leaflet with map.
Waterton Glacier Guide. Newsprint annual.
Information pages:
 Small map.
 Campground information.
 Weather information.
 Accommodations and services.
 Backcountry camping regulations.
 Day hike safety.
 Day hikes, Lake McDonald Valley.
 Bicycling.
 Boating.
 Backcountry camping.
 Auto campgrounds.
Folders:
 Day hikes.
 Backcountry.
 Fishing the Flathead.
 Grizzly.
 You Are in Grizzly Country.
Bird checklist.
Mammal checklist.

PUBLICATIONS OF THE GLACIER NATURAL HISTORY ASSOCIATION
Catalog of publications includes numerous items on the history and natural history of the Park. Included are guides: roads and trails, climbing, fishing, etc. Items can be ordered by mail: Glacier Natural History Association, West Glacier, MT 59936.

REFERENCES
Nelson, Dick. *Hiker's Guide to Glacier National Park.* West Glacier, MT: Glacier Natural History Association, 1978.
Raup, Earhart, Carrara, and Whipple. *A Guide to the Geology of the Going-to-the-Sun Road, Glacier National Park.* West Glacier, MT: Glacier Natural History Association, 1983.
Reiner, Ralph E. *Introducing the Flowering Beauty of Glacier National Park and the Majestic High Rockies.* East Glacier Park, MT: Glacier Park, Inc., 1969.
Sample, Michael S. *The Angler's Guide to Montana.* Billings, MT: Falcon Press, 1984. Pp. 217–26.

Schneider, Bill. *The Hiker's Guide to Montana.* Billings, MT: Falcon Press, 1983. Pp. 124–36.
Turbak, Gary. *The Traveler's Guide to Montana.* Billings, MT: Falcon Press, 1983. Pp. 35–40.

HEADQUARTERS: West Glacier, MT 59936; (406) 888-5441.

HOODOO MOUNTAIN; GALLAGHER CREEK
U.S. Bureau of Land Management
15,637 acres.

From Avon, on US 12 W of Helena, N on SR 141 about 16 mi. to Nevada Lake. About 2 mi. SW on primitive road.

BLM's inventory found here two candidates for Wilderness status, roadless areas in natural condition, separated by a jeep trail. Both were judged to offer good opportunities for sightseeing, camping, hiking and backpacking, and hunting, as well as fishing, ski touring, nature study, and rock climbing.

The area is an irregular block, about 6 by 6 mi., in the Garnet Range. Elevations range from 5,200 ft. to 7,438 ft. on Devil Mountain. Most surrounding land is privately owned but undeveloped.

Hoodoo Mountain, the W portion, includes densely forested areas, open grassland parks, rock outcrops, wet meadows, and small creeks. Forested areas are predominantly Douglas-fir, lodgepole pine, and some alpine fir.

Terrain in the E portion, Gallagher Creek, is somewhat more rugged, with narrow meadows, steep, rocky bluffs, and scree slopes. Most of the area is forested.

Fall hunting is the primary recreational use. The number of hunters is thought to be less than 300 a year, visitors in other seasons as few as 30. Trails were marked some years ago in the W portion. Although they are not maintained, hiking is feasible, on the old trails, in stream beds, and through open forest and meadows.

The range of habitats supports a diversity of wildlife. Although no checklist is available, birding is said to be excellent. Mammals include elk, whitetail and blacktail deer, black bear, and porcupine, with marten, fisher, and wolverine considered probable.

ACTIVITIES
Camping: No campground. Sites used by hunters, chiefly on the perimeter and jeep trail.

Hunting: Chiefly big game.

Fishing: Cutthroat trout, limited in size and abundance.

HEADQUARTERS: BLM, Butte District, 106 N. Parkmont, Butte, MT 59702; (406) 494-5059.

HUMBUG SPIRES

U.S. Bureau of Land Management

11,175 acres.

From Butte, 26 mi. S on I-15 to Moose Creek interchange. 3 mi. NE on Moose Creek Road to parking area.

The Humbug Spires are weathered granitic formations: large, well-spaced, vertical columns rise out of the forest, 9 of them to heights between 300 and 600 ft., 50 or more smaller ones. On the edge of the Big Hole River valley, the site adjoins the Deerlodge National Forest and Highland Mountains on the E. Base elevation is 6,800 to 7,000 ft. Nearby Mount Humbug in the NF is 8,265 ft.

The Spires offer what has been called the finest hard-rock climbing in MT. One spire, overhung on all sides, hasn't been climbed—or hadn't been when we inquired. Hiking opportunities range from day trips to weekend backpacks, from easy to strenuous. Moose Creek, the principal drainage, enters the area in a narrow, boulder-strewn canyon. An attractive stream with beaver ponds and minor waterfalls, it has pan-size trout. Hunting elk and mule deer is the chief fall activity. Terrain limits horse riding and ski touring.

Primary cover is Douglas-fir forest with little understory except in riparian and meadow areas. The riparian zones are usually grassy, with scattered cottonwood, aspen, and a few Engelmann spruce, dense willow and dogwood thickets at stream edges.

Most of the site has been recommended for Wilderness designation. Present use is light. BLM doubts that Wilderness designation would cause a significant increase, since far larger Wildernesses are available in the region.

PUBLICATION: Folder with map.

REFERENCE: Rudner, Ruth. *Bitterroot to Beartooth.* San Francisco: Sierra Club Books, 1985. Pp. 96–100.

HEADQUARTERS: BLM, Butte District, 106 N. Parkmont, Butte, MT 59702; (406) 494-5059.

KILA FISHING ACCESS SITE
Montana Department of Fish, Wildlife & Parks
3 acres.

From Kalispell, 7 mi. W on US 2, then 1 mi. S on county road.

We stopped here for an hour and were delighted. Kila is a fine example of Montana's unique Fishing Access Site program, a long step ahead of any others we've seen. The hillside site is on the shore of Smith Lake, a wide place in Ashley Creek, with perhaps a mile of open water and considerable marsh. The wood area has 3 camping units, latrine, parking, boat ramp, and dock, all well-maintained and clean. A fisherman said the perch were biting. The marsh offers good birding.

KOOTENAI NATIONAL FOREST
U.S. Forest Service
2,245,000 acres.

NW corner of MT. Libby is near its center. Access routes include US 2 and 93, SRs 200, 56, 37, and 508.

The Kootenai NF adjoins Idaho's Kaniksu NF on the W and S, the Lolo NF also on the S, the Flathead on the E. Although there are large inholdings, most of the Forest land is contiguous. Timber companies' lands are chiefly in the SE. Private holdings are mostly around Libby and in a broad strip near US 93 in the NE.

The region is mountainous, characterized by ranges with high, craggy peaks, including the Cabinet, Purcell, and Salish mountains and the Bitterroot and Whitefish ranges, oriented generally N–S. Highest point is 8,738-ft. Snowshoe Peak in the Cabinet Mountains. Lake Koocanusa is at 3,000 ft. elevation. Where the Kootenai River leaves the Forest and MT is the state's lowest point, 1,862 ft.

Climate is modified Pacific Maritime, more moderate than in most of MT. Average Jan. temperatures are 10 to 14 degrees higher than in the NE of the state, while July averages are slightly lower, the maximums seldom exceeding

90°F. Average annual precipitation ranges from 14 to 31 in. over most of the Forest, with totals over 100 in. recorded at the heights of the Cabinet Mountains, most of this falling as snow. Fall and winter are the wet seasons.

Two rivers, the Kootenai and Clark Fork, drain most of the Forest. Fishable streams total more than 3,000 mi. Libby Dam on the Kootenai River has formed Lake Koocanusa, 90 mi. long, less than 1 mi. wide, 48 mi. in MT, extending 42 mi. N into Canada. Other large reservoirs are Cabinet Gorge and Noxon, also long and narrow, on Clark Fork. The Forest has over 200 lakes, from small alpine ponds to 1,240-acre McGregor Lake.

Most of the Kootenai is tree-covered, 80% of it capable of producing commercial timber. Thus it has an extensive network of roads, about 6,000 mi. More roads are built each year, chiefly for logging access. 900 mi. have been closed for various reasons, and 700 mi. have seasonal closures, chiefly to protect wildlife. Studying the Forest map, we could find no point as much as 5 mi. from a road.

This is reflected in the pattern of recreation, which totals about 900,000 annual visitor-days. One-half of this number is classified as "roaded dispersed": hunters, wood gatherers, berry pickers, and sightseers using vehicles on the road network spring to fall, winter visitors driving to trailheads for winter sports. About one-third is recorded at developed recreation sites.

Cabinet Mountains Wilderness, 94,400 acres, is the only present Wilderness. Another 438,000 acres are eligible for consideration. The largest unit is 72,000 acres. The relatively small roadless units and their easy accessibility favor day use rather than extended backcountry travel. The Forest has 1,335 mi. of trails, including 5 National Recreation Trails, the three longest being 19, 22, and 23 mi.

Plants: Because of the climate, the Forest has an abundance of species common to the Pacific Coast, less common or absent elsewhere in MT. It also has a great diversity of species, from cacti to fairy slipper orchids. Habitats range from grasslands to alpine tundra, but the principal associations are Douglas-fir, hemlock, and alpine fir. Logging has been extensive, and many areas are in various stages of regeneration. Principal native tree species include western redcedar, western hemlock, western white pine, lodgepole pine, ponderosa pine, alpine and western larches, mountain hemlock, grand fir, subalpine fir, whitebark pine, Douglas-fir, Engelmann spruce, and juniper.

Common understory shrubs include huckleberry, snowberry, ninebark, mountain maple, menziesia, spirea, serviceberry, bitterbrush, chokecherry, wild rose, oceanspray, syringa, kinnikinnick, and dogwood. Seasonal wildflowers include violets, lupine, trillium, sego lily, spotted coralroot, buttercups, columbine, queencup beadlily, arrowleaf balsamroot, beargrass, clematis, pinedrops, phlox, harebell, Indian paintbrush.

Birds: 191 species recorded. Checklist available provides unusual detail on seasonal abundance and habitats. Species that, in season, "can be readily found" include common loon, horned grebe, great blue heron, Canada goose, mallard, pintail, blue-winged teal, American wigeon, common goldeneye, common merganser, American kestrel, ruffed grouse, great horned owl, common nighthawk, northern flicker, hairy and downy woodpeckers, eastern kingbird, horned lark, gray and Steller's jays, northern raven, Clark's nutcracker, mountain and black-capped chickadees, dipper, red-breasted nuthatch, winter wren, American robin, yellow-rumped warbler, western meadowlark, red-winged and Brewer's blackbirds, Cassin's finch, pine siskin, rufous-sided towhee, dark-eyed junco, chipping sparrow.

In fall and winter migration, bald eagles congregate and feed below Libby Dam.

Mammals: No checklist, but we were told the Forest has everything "from moose to mice." Elk are the chief game species, with a Forest-wide population of about 5,500; the Clark Fork herd is well known to hunters. Other game species include mule and whitetail deer, mountain goat, bighorn sheep, moose, black and grizzly bears, and mountain lion. Nongame species include coyote, weasel, mink, beaver, otter, squirrel, porcupine, chipmunk, skunk, snowshoe hare, mountain cottontail, pika, bobcat, lynx.

FEATURES

Cabinet Mountains Wilderness, 94,272 acres, S of Libby, is about 32 mi. N–S, 7 mi. W–E at its widest point. Mountainous, rugged terrain. Highest point is 8,738-ft. Snowshoe Peak, 7 others over 7,500 ft. More than 20 trails give access to dozens of small lakes, ridgetop panoramas, alpine meadows. Snowstorms as late as June and as early as Sept. limit most hiking to midsummer. Trails lead through a succession of plant communities, from giant western redcedars in moist valleys to stunted heath on ridges.

Most of the lakes are scenic, stocked with fish, and easily reached by trail. The "Wilderness" label attracts more visitors. The lake basins and their trail corridors, only 15% of the Wilderness, get most of the visitors, some destinations showing trampling, tree damage, and water pollution. Management is considering each location for such remedies as discontinuation of fish stocking, limiting use of horses, and prohibiting camping within 500 ft. of the lake shore.

Additions totaling 16,000 acres are under consideration.

Ten Lakes Scenic Area, 15,700 acres, is on the Canadian border NE of Eureka. With an adjoining 19,000 acres, it has been designated for Wilderness evaluation. Dominated by the rugged Whitefish Mountains, with peaks over 7,000 ft., it has many lakes in glacial cirque basins. Forested areas have Engelmann spruce, subalpine fir, lodgepole pine, Douglas-fir, whitebark pine, and the uncommon alpine larch. Abundant wildflowers in spring and summer. Wildlife includes bighorn sheep, moose, mule deer, elk, black bear, an occasional grizzly, pika, marmot, golden-mantled squirrel.

Access is by local and Forest roads to trailheads and to campgrounds on the Therriault Lakes, routes shown on the site leaflet. Several trails crisscross the area. Motor vehicles are prohibited except snowmobiles in winter. Here, too, destination lakes are showing damage from overuse, and management measures are designed to reduce impact.

Northwest Peaks Scenic Area, 19,100 acres, in the NW corner near Canada and Idaho. Access from US 2 via SR 508 and Forest roads. On the Selkirk Range, with peaks over 7,500 ft. and deep valleys, alpine lakes, forests. This site is lightly used because of the long access route, relatively few trails, and short hiking season.

Ross Creek Scenic Area of Giant Cedars, 100 acres. Shown on the highway map, off SR 56 SW of Libby, reached by 4 mi. of good road. A 0.9-mi. trail winds among giant western redcedars. Ferns and wildflowers on the forest floor.

Lake Koocanusa was formed by Libby Dam, an Army Corps of Engineers project. This portion of the Kootenai River was straight and narrow, and the reservoir is also. Steep, forested slopes on both sides limit access to a few picnic and boat launching sites on each side. No campgrounds are on the lake, although several are nearby. Near the Souse Gulch picnic area, on the W side near the dam, is a stand of old-growth ponderosa pine. SR 37 and Forest Road 228 provide a 100-mi. circuit of the U.S. portion of the lake, crossing at a bridge. From this route, several roads and trails extend W and E.

Scotchman Peaks, 83,700 acres, including acreage in the Idaho Panhandle National Forests. From a point near the intersection of SRs 200 and 56, the site extends N and W. Forest Road 398, W from SR 56 just S of Bull Lake, extends about 2 mi. to the Ross Creek campground and trailhead. Spar Lake is the largest of several glacial lakes, linked to Little Spar Lake by a deep canyon. Mountains, glacial cirques, creeks, forested slopes, stands of large cedar, hemlock, white pine. Because of its accessibility, this candidate for Wilderness status receives 6 times as many visitors as the Northwest Peaks, but most follow the popular trails to the more accessible lakes.

National Recreation Trails are chosen for their natural qualities, including scenic values. They are usually well maintained.

> *Trout Creek Loop,* 22 mi., in the Bitterroot Range near the town of Trout Creek
>
> *Pulpit Mountain,* 5 mi., N of Troy
>
> *Skyline Mountain,* 23 mi., from near Libby to the Yaak River Valley
>
> *Boulder-Vinal,* 19 mi.; trailhead on Forest Road 92
>
> *Backcountry route* on the flanks of Mt. Henry and Vinal Creek Canyon
>
> *Little North Fork,* a short trail off SR 37, near Lake Koocanusa, leading to a waterfall

Scenic drives: The Forest has many. Of the main highways, we enjoyed SR 200 from ID, SR 56 N past the Ross Creek Scenic Area, US 2 from Libby to Kalispell.

ACTIVITIES
Camping: 29 campgrounds, 373 sites. One is open all year; others mid-Apr. to Sept. 30.
Hiking, backpacking: 1,300 mi. of trails. Mostly day hiking. Backpackers can find scenic roadless areas for outings of 2 or 3 days, but not a vast backcountry. Good access to most trailheads.
Hunting: Elk, deer, black bear, mountain bighorn, mountain goat.
Fishing: Good fishing in over 3,000 mi. of streams and 37,000 acres of reservoirs and lakes. Lower elevation lakes have populations of lake, brook, rainbow, and cutthroat trout, yellow perch, largemouth bass, pumpkinseed sunfish, northern pike, and bullhead catfish. Kootenai Reservoir has become a good kokanee salmon fishery. High lakes have rainbow, cutthroat, and brook trout.
Horse riding: Mostly in hunting season; stock provided by outfitters and guides.
Rafting, kayaking, boating: Below Libby Dam, the Kootenai River can be floated to and beyond the ID border. The scenic course traverses narrow canyons past Libby and Troy. It can be floated in small craft, with information, caution, portages; occasional rapids, high waves. For Clark Fork River, see entry.
Swimming: Most low-elevation lakes, in summer.
Skiing: Ski area at Turner Mountain near Libby.
Ski touring: Groomed trails at Bear Creek and Flatiron Mountain near Libby. Unlimited opportunities on unplowed Forest roads.

PUBLICATIONS
Forest map. $1.
District travel plan maps.
Welcome to the Kootenai National Forest. Folder.
Kootenai Country. Pamphlet.
Cabinet Wilderness map.
Ten Lakes Scenic Area. Folder with map.
Bird checklist.
Places to Go When There's Snow.
Information pages:
  Recreation sites; campground information.
  Ross Creek Cedar Grove.

REFERENCES
Fischer, Hank. *The Floater's Guide to Montana.* Billings MT: Falcon Press, 1986. Pp. 26–30, 57–61.
Schneider, Bill. *The Hiker's Guide to Montana.* Billings, MT: Falcon Press, 1983. Pp. 12–41.
Woodruff, Steve, and Don Schwennesen. *Montana Wilderness.* Kansas City: Lowell Press, 1984. Pp. 12–19.

HEADQUARTERS: 506 U.S. Highway 2 West, Libby, MT 59923; (406) 293-6211.

RANGER DISTRICTS: Rexford R.D., P.O. Box 666, Eureka, MT 59917; (406) 296-2536. Fortine R.D., P.O. Box 116, Fortine, MT 59918; (406) 882-4451. Libby R.D., 1263 Highway 37, Libby, MT 59923; (406) 293-7741. Yaak R.D., Route 1, Troy, MT 59935; (406) 295-4717. Troy R.D., 1437 N. Highway 2, Troy, MT 59935; (406) 295-4693. Cabinet R.D., HCR 2 Box 210, Trout Creek, MT 59874; (406) 847-2462. Fisher River R.D., 12557 Highway 37, Libby, MT 59874; (406) 293-7773.

LEE METCALF NATIONAL WILDLIFE REFUGE
U.S. Fish and Wildlife Service
2,696 acres.

From US 93 at Florence, take East Side Highway S 6 mi. At Refuge sign, turn W on Wildfowl Lane.

Established primarily for waterfowl, this Refuge also displays numerous raptors, shorebirds, and passerines, something of interest at any season. The Bitterroot River (see entry) is on its W border. The Refuge occupies river bottomland, with an old oxbow, small impoundments, and a fringe of upland forest. The Bitterroot Mountains on the W and the Sapphire Range on the E provide a scenic backdrop.

Refuge HQ is on Third St. in Stevensville, and serious birders should stop for a briefing on the current situation. A county road entering from the E, then turning S, crosses the lower third of the Refuge, passing several ponds. It's always open. A half-mile foot trail in the SW corner provides access to the river. Visitors are usually excluded from the N portion of the Refuge, but ask about it.

The Bitterroot Valley is semiarid, annual precipitation ranging from 12 to 14 in. Snowfall is light and periods of snow cover are brief. May–July is the dry season, Aug.–Sept. the wettest months.

Birds: No checklist is available. HQ lists as seasonally abundant or common: snow, Canada, and Ross geese; mallard, gadwall, pintail, American wigeon, wood duck; blue-winged, green-winged, and cinnamon teals; shoveler, canvasback, redhead, scaup, common and Barrow's goldeneye, bufflehead, ruddy duck, hooded merganser, American coot, tundra swan, great blue heron, red-tailed hawk, northern harrier, pheasant. Noted as of special interest to birders: Eurasian wigeon, bald eagle, osprey, pileated woodpecker; and occasional peregrine falcon, gyrfalcon, golden eagle, great gray owl.

Visitors have also observed great horned owl, Cooper's and rough-legged hawks; Lewis', downy, and hairy woodpeckers; yellow-bellied sapsucker, Clark's nutcracker, Steller's jay, red crossbill, pine and evening grosbeaks, western tanager, mountain bluebird, pygmy and red-breasted nuthatch, marsh wren, veery; rufous, calliope, and black-chinned hummingbirds; bank, barn, cliff, rough-winged, violet-green, and tree swallows; western wood-pewee, dusky and Hammond's flycatchers.

Mammals: No checklist. Often seen: whitetail deer, muskrat, beaver, skunk, raccoon, pine squirrel. Occasionally: elk, moose, black bear, river otter.

ACTIVITIES
Hunting: Deer, waterfowl. Special regulations.
Fishing: River only.

PUBLICATION: Leaflet.

HEADQUARTERS: P.O. Box 257, Stevensville, MT 59870; (406) 777-5552.

LEWIS & CLARK CAVERNS STATE PARK
Montana Department of Fish, Wildlife & Parks
2,735 acres.

19 mi. W of Three Forks on US 10. *Open May 1–Sept 30.*

The caverns became a National Monument in 1908, then were deeded to the state in 1937. They are typical of limestone caverns, with bizarre formations decorating the labyrinth of chambers and passageways. The guided tour takes about 2 hrs.

The site, surrounded by private land, overlooks the Jefferson River. From US 10, a 3-mi. drive leads to the visitor center. We saw no trails other than the nature trail, but 4 sq. mi. is enough real estate for a casual walk.

ACTIVITIES
Camping: 35 sites.
Fishing: Access to Jefferson River.

PUBLICATION: Leaflet.

HEADQUARTERS: P.O. Box 648, Whitehall, MT 59759; (406) 287-3541.

LITTLE BITTERROOT LAKE
Montana Department of Fish, Wildlife & Parks
2,825 acres of water, 37 acres of land.

From Kalispell, 20 mi. W on US 2, then 5 mi. N on paved road.

The lake is about 3 mi. long, 2 mi. wide, surrounded by private and timber company land. Most of the area is forested.

NEARBY: Ashley Lake (see entry).

ACTIVITIES
Camping: 20 sites, May 15–Sept. 15.
Fishing: Kokanee, cutthroat and rainbow trout, perch.
Boating: Ramp.

LOLO NATIONAL FOREST
U.S. Forest Service
2,091,944 acres; 2,614,849 acres within boundaries.

W central MT. Access from I-90, US 10, 10A, 12, 93; SRs 200, 83.

A first glance at maps of the Lolo is bewildering. The Forest extends about 120 mi. NW–SE, 40 to 80 mi. wide. It has 5 irregularly shaped blocks. Inholdings, about one-fifth of the total area, are chiefly a checkerboard of timber company lands, dividing some of the blocks into fragments. Some Forest land is in isolated mile-square blocks.

A second look shows large blocks of Forest land. The Idaho Panhandle NF adjoins the Lolo on the W, the Kootenai NF on the NW, Flathead NF on the N, Helena NF on the E, Bitterroot and Deerlodge NFs on the S, Clearwater NF on the SW. The Lolo includes all or parts of 4 Wildernesses and adjoins the Bob Marshall Wilderness. It has 36 other roadless areas totaling 37% of the Forest lands, 9 of them larger than 25,000 acres. Although the Forest has many developed recreation sites for camping, boating, skiing, etc., 80% of visitor use is dispersed.

Even the checkerboard areas don't look that way on the ground. The timber companies haven't posted their lands; trails cross them; and visitors are unimpeded unless there's active logging. We thought of identifying scenic drives, beginning with Rock Creek Road, but concluded that most of the roads are scenic.

For recreation visitors, the Forest is best understood by Ranger Districts. The Forest map is in 3 sections: Seeley Lake Ranger District; Ninemile-Missoula R.D.s; and Thompson Falls-Superior-Plains R.D.s. (The latter two are on opposite sides of one map.) The Forest's Recreation Opportunities Guide (ROG) is organized by Ranger District and can be seen at each R.D. office.

The Forest is in the Rocky Mountain Region between the ID border and the Continental Divide. The prevailing landform is N–S ranges separated by flat valleys and foothills. The Missoula Valley is central to the Lolo. Radiating from it are the Bitterroot Valley to the S; Clark Fork, SE; Blackfoot, NE; and Frenchtown-Ninemile, NW. Principal drainage is the Clark Fork of the Columbia River, flowing generally NW, bisecting the area. Chief tributaries are the Bitterroot, Blackfoot, St. Regis, and Thompson rivers. The Forest has about 3,500 mi. of fishing streams, 96 lakes totaling 5,220 acres that support or could support a fishery.

Lowest point in the Forest is about 2,400 ft., on Clark Fork. Peaks over 7,000 ft. occur throughout the Forest. Highest peaks, over 9,000 ft., are in the Bitterroot Range. Terrain is typical of the glaciated region: steep, rugged, with bowllike cirque basins, U-shaped valleys separated by narrow ridges. Slopes are generally steep. About one-third of the area has slopes under 40%, the rest steeper.

The Missoula Valley is semiarid, with annual precipitation of about 14 in. The Forest-wide average is 42 in., over two-thirds of this falling as snow.

Plants: Most of the land is heavily timbered, although many S-facing slopes are open and grassy. The Lolo is an important timber producer. Principal commercial species are Douglas-fir, ponderosa and lodgepole pine, western larch. Other species present include grand fir, subalpine fir, western redcedar. Understory components include ninebark, serviceberry, chokecherry, dwarf huckleberry, elderberry, Oregon grape. Various open areas support bunchgrasses, beargrass, sedges.

Seasonal wildflowers include yarrow, field pussytoes, Alberta penstemon, false Solomon's-seal, western meadowrue, round-leafed violet, blue-eyed Mary, heartleaf arnica, showy aster, arrowleaf balsamroot, prince's-pine, queencup, fairybells, strawberries, bedstraw, hawkweed, lupine.

Birds: Five Valleys Audubon Society publishes *Birds of Western Montana,* encompassing the Lolo. The annotated checklist includes 297 species. Seasonally abundant or common species include common loon; red-necked, horned, western, and pied-billed grebes; great blue heron, whistling swan, Canada and snow geese, mallard, gadwall, northern pintail; green-winged, blue-winged, and cinnamon teals; American wigeon, northern shoveler, wood duck, redhead, ring-necked duck, canvasback, lesser scaup, common goldeneye, bufflehead, ruddy duck, hooded and common mergansers, red-tailed and rough-legged hawks, bald eagle, northern harrier, osprey, American kestrel, blue and ruffed grouse, ring-necked pheasant, gray partridge, sora, American coot, killdeer, common snipe, spotted sandpiper, greater and lesser yellowlegs; Baird's, least, and semipalmated sandpipers; long-billed dowitcher, American avocet, Wilson's and red-necked phalaropes, California and ring-billed gulls, black tern. Also rock and mourning doves, great horned and short-eared owls, common nighthawk, Vaux's and white-throated swifts, rufous and calliope hummingbirds, belted kingfisher, northern flicker, yellow-bellied sapsucker, hairy and downy woodpeckers, eastern and western kingbirds. Willow, Hammond's, dusky, and olive-sided flycatchers; western wood-pewee, horned lark. Swallows: violet-green, tree, bank, rough-winged, barn, cliff. Gray and Steller's jays, black-billed magpie, common raven, American crow, Clark's nutcracker, black-capped and mountain chickadees; white-breasted, red-breasted, and pygmy nuthatches; dipper, marsh and rock wrens, gray catbird, American robin, hermit and Swainson's thrushes, veery, mountain bluebird, Townsend's solitaire, golden-crowned and ruby-crowned kinglets, water pipit, Bohemian and cedar waxwings, European starling; solitary, red-eyed, and warbling vireos. Warblers: orange-crowned, yellow, yellow-rumped, Townsend's, MacGillivray's, northern waterthrush, common yellowthroat, Wilson's, American redstart. Bobolink, western meadowlark; yellow-headed, red-winged, and Brewer's blackbirds; northern oriole, brown-headed cowbird, western tanager, black-headed grosbeak, lazuli bunting, rufous-sided towhee. Sparrows: savannah, vesper, tree, chipping, white-crowned, song. Dark-eyed junco, evening and pine grosbeaks; Cassin's, house, and rosy finches; common redpoll, pine siskin, American goldfinch, red crossbill.

Mammals: No checklist available. Big game species include elk, deer, moose, bighorn sheep, mountain goat, black and grizzly bear, mountain lion. Gray wolf is present. Other mammals include coyote, Columbian ground squirrel, beaver, porcupine, bobcat, snowshoe hare, fisher, pika.

FEATURES

Rattlesnake National Recreation Area and Wilderness, 25,010 acres in the NRA, 31,479 acres of Wilderness.

A scenic, mountainous area only 4 mi. N of Missoula, yet lightly used. Narrow, steep-sided valleys, hanging valleys, cirque basins, 18 lakes, 11 principal streams. Elevations from 3,600 ft. at the creek entrance to 8,620 ft. on McLeod Peak near the N boundary. The creek and its watershed are Missoula's water supply, and protective measures apply. The area is forested, principally with larch, Douglas-fir, and lodgepole pine. Wildlife includes fisher, lynx, elk, mountain lion, wolverine, pine marten, mountain goat, with infrequent sightings of grizzly bear. Lakes and streams have both native and introduced fish species.

Hunting and fishing have been the principal visitor activities prior to Wilderness designation. Hiking, backpacking, horse riding, ski touring, and snowshoeing have been increasing. 98 mi. of trails in good condition.

Rattlesnake Wilderness, 33,000 acres, including 12,881 acres of private inholdings, is the N portion of the National Recreation Area, 7 mi. from Missoula, easy access. Several trails enter from Forest roads on the W, S, and E. A primitive Forest road follows Rattlesnake Creek across the NRA and into the heart of the Wilderness, ending within 2 or 3 mi. of a cluster of high alpine lakes.

Welcome Creek Wilderness, 28,184 acres, 16 mi. SE of Missoula. Principal access is by Rock Creek Road extending S along Rock Creek from I-90, 20 mi. E of Missoula. The E boundary of the Wilderness begins 5 mi. from I-90. On the E slopes of the Sapphire Mountains, the area is about 9 mi. N–S, 7 mi. W–E. Steep ridges and narrow valley bottoms offer few places level enough for campsites. Principal drainage is Welcome Creek, flowing SE. Most of the area is forested. About 25 mi. of trails follow ridges and valley bottoms. Hunting is the chief visitor activity, followed by summer day hiking.

Rock Creek Area, 570,670 acres, of which 182,756 acres are within the Lolo NF. Includes the Welcome Creek Wilderness. The Rock Creek drainage is about 54 mi. long and averages 18 mi. in width. Rock Creek enters the Clark Fork of the Columbia River about 20 mi. SE of Missoula. Several campgrounds are along Rock Creek Road, across from the Welcome Creek Wilderness. The S half of the area is bowl-shaped, abutting the Continental Divide. It narrows to the N. Elevations range from 10,456 ft. at Warren Peak on the Divide to 3,540 ft. at Clark Fork. About 280 mi. of fishable streams. The lower 51 mi. of Rock Creek are a blue-ribbon trout stream, the only such stream where National Forest land includes most of the watershed and stream banks. The area includes over 63,000 acres of winter big game range. Large populations of elk, mule and whitetail deer, bighorn sheep, and moose.

Scapegoat Wilderness, 74,832 acres in the Lolo, 165,104 acres in the Helena and Lewis & Clark NFs. 75 mi. NE of Missoula. A SE extension of the Bob Marshall Wilderness. Access from the Lolo requires driving local and Forest roads from SR 200, then hiking several mi. to the Wilderness boundary. The Wilderness straddles the Continental Divide, with the Lolo portion SW of the ridge. Highest point on the Divide is 9,204-ft. Scapegoat Mountain, whose massive limestone cliffs are an extension of the Chinese Wall in the Bob Marshall. The area includes rugged ridges, gently sloping alpine meadows, forested slopes. Trails in the Lolo portion follow drainages. Hunting and fishing are the chief visitor activities. Most of the Wilderness lakes are in the

Helena and Lewis & Clark portions, and the most popular hiking trails are on that side. Outfitter and guide services are available.

Selway-Bitterroot Wilderness. Less than 10,000 acres of this 1,341,000-acre Wilderness are in the Lolo. This portion lies 10 mi. SW of Lolo. Lolo Peak, 9,096 ft., on the Wilderness boundary, is the highest peak near Missoula. The ROG has information on trails to the Peak, a scenic hike featuring alpine vegetation and a small lake and campsite near the Peak; the round trip usually takes 2 days. A trail follows South Fork, which bisects the area. Adjacent are more than 240,000 acres of the Wilderness, also in MT, in the Bitterroot NF. This area is easily reached by local and Forest roads W from US 93. See entry for Bitterroot NF. Most of the Wilderness is in Idaho; see also entries there for Nez Perce, Bitterroot, and Clearwater NFs.

Swan River Valley (see entry) is a popular recreation area along SR 83, the Swan Forest Highway, a mixture of Forest, state, and private land. Seeley, 2 1/2 mi. long, is the largest of several lakes. The Ranger office at Seeley has trail maps. One popular trail leads to Morrell Lake and Falls, others into the Bob Marshall Wilderness.

Other roadless areas total 654,000 acres. About 212,000 acres were recommended for inclusion in the Wilderness system.

Bear-Marshall-Scapegoat-Swan is an irregular strip of over 865,000 acres in four National Forests surrounding the Bob Marshall, Great Bear, and Scapegoat Wildernesses. About 121,000 acres are in the Lolo, chiefly along the Swan Front, E of SR 83. Most trails in this strip lead into the Bob Marshall.

Great Burn, about 250,000 acres, 98,500 in the Lolo, the rest across the ID state line in the Clearwater NF. The Lolo portion lies about 30 mi. W of Missoula, between I-90 and the state line, several Forest roads leading to trailheads.

The name refers to fires that swept the area in the early 1900s, so devastating that tree stands occur only in the drainages. Otherwise the area is shrub-covered, with a thin scattering of lone or clustered trees. The area is a long, high divide about 40 mi. N–S, with peaks over 7,000 ft. The high country has subalpine characteristics: mountain meadows, rock outcrops, mountain heather and other subalpine plants. Annual precipitation ranges from 30 in. on the E border to near 100 in. on the ridge, where snow depths of 10 to 14 ft. are not uncommon and snowfields persist into July. Outstanding scenery includes 33 mountain lakes, most of them near the divide. Many mountain streams, but most are in ID, including the largest, Kelly Creek, a blue-ribbon trout stream. Most streams and lakes have populations of cutthroat and rainbow trout.

Wildlife is abundant, including elk, mule deer, and black bear, with smaller numbers of mountain goat, moose, and mountain lion. Commercial outfitters use the area for elk hunting.

The area has over 200 mi. of trails, the main ones regularly maintained.

Visitor activities include hiking, backpacking, and horse riding, as well as hunting and fishing. Summer use will doubtless increase if Wilderness designation calls attention to the area.

INTERPRETATION

No visitor center, campfire programs, other naturalist activities.

Blue Mountain Nature Trail, 1/4 mi., on Blue Mountain Road, a scenic drive beginning on the W side of Missoula.

ACTIVITIES

Camping: 27 campgrounds, 417 sites. Most open last week of May, close mid-Sept.; a few have longer or shorter seasons. Most are off I-90, Rock Creek Road, or Swan Forest Highway; others are scattered.

Hiking, backpacking: 1,823 mi. of system trails, of which only 182 mi. are in Wildernesses. The Lolo trail system is linked with those of adjacent National Forests and their Wildernesses. Included in the system are the 28-mi. Lewis & Clark National Historic Trail and 8 National Recreation Trails of 1/4 mi. to 18 mi. Each of the principal trails is described on a page of the ROG; copies at HQ and Ranger Districts.

Hunting: One of the principal elk areas in western MT. Also deer, mountain sheep, mountain goat, other big game, and upland game birds. Several outfitter-guides serve the area.

Fishing: 3,500 mi. of fishing streams, including Rock Creek, a blue-ribbon trout stream. 96 lakes that support or could support a fishery, some dependent on stocking. Principal species: cutthroat, rainbow, cutthroat-rainbow hybrid, brook, and Dolly Varden trout, mountain whitefish. The leaflet *Fishing the Flathead* has a keyed map of lakes and streams, including several in the Mission Mountains Wilderness and Swan River Valley.

Horse riding: Most trails, including trails leading into Wildernesses, are suitable for horses. Most horse riding is in conjunction with hunting.

Boating: Chiefly on Seeley and other lakes in the Swan Valley.

Rafting, kayaking: Clark Fork is floatable throughout its length, in season. It traverses the Lolo, but in a corridor of private land, chiefly paralleling I-90. No rapids, but diversion dams, fences, downed trees, and other hazards require information and skill. Rock Creek is floated, chiefly by fishermen, until flow rate declines in mid-July.

Skiing: Three commercial ski areas are partially on Forest land.

Ski touring: 150 mi. of designated cross-country ski trails. Unlimited opportunities on unplowed Forest roads.

Detailed information on locations for these activities is in the ROG.

PUBLICATIONS

Forest maps: Ninemile, Missoula, Thompson Falls, Superior, and Plains R.D.s; Seeley Lake R.D. $1 each.

Information booklet.

Information pages:
Rattlesnake Wilderness.
Scapegoat Wilderness.
Picnic and campground directory.
Bird checklist. (By Five Valleys Audubon Society.)
Fishing the Flathead. Leaflet with map.

REFERENCES

Schneider, Bill. *The Hiker's Guide to Montana.* Billings, MT: Falcon Press, 1983. Pp. 41–53, 68–74, 101–04.
Sample, Mike. *The Angler's Guide to Montana.* Billings, MT: Falcon Press, 1984. Pp. 48–58, 118–26, 168, 188–90, 192, 203–04.
Turbak, Gary. *The Traveler's Guide to Montana.* Billings, MT: Falcon Press, 1983. Pp. 41–50, 70–72, 114–18, 136–43, 179–86, 201–03.

HEADQUARTERS: Building 24, Fort Missoula, Missoula, MT 59801; (406) 329-3750.

RANGER DISTRICTS: Missoula R.D., 5115 Highway 93 South, Missoula, MT 59801; (406) 251-5237. Ninemile R.D., Hudson, MT 59846; (406) 626-5201. Plains and Thompson Falls R.D.s, P.O. Box 429, Plains, MT 59859; (406) 826-3821. Seeley Lake R.D., Drawer G, Seeley Lake, MT 59868; (406) 677-2233. Superior R.D., Superior, MT 59872; (406) 822-4233.

LONE PINE STATE PARK
Montana Division of Fish, Wildlife & Parks
171 acres.

5 mi. SW of Kalispell off Foys Lake Rd.

It's small, for day use only. Even so, the Park is too attractive to omit.

The Park occupies a hilltop overlooking the Flathead Valley and its waterways, with mountains in the distance. The site includes a forest of mature Douglas-fir, open meadows, rock outcrops, a small stream. The land was given to the state by donors who specified that it be preserved for public recreation and nature education. It took 40 years for their wishes to be fulfilled, but they have been now, admirably. The visitor center was designed for use by groups in the community, with exhibits, literature, meeting rooms, and kitchen. They use it. The nature education program is lively and imaginative. A 3/4-mi. nature trail crosses a ravine and climbs to 3 scenic overlooks.

PUBLICATION: Leaflet.

HEADQUARTERS: 225 Cemetery Rd., Kalispell, MT 59901; (406) 755-2706.

LOST CREEK STATE PARK
Montana Department of Fish, Wildlife & Parks
25 acres.

From Anaconda, 1 1/2 mi. E on US 10A, then 2 mi. N on County Road 273, then 6 mi. W.

A 25-acre site seemed too small to be an entry, but our Parks advisor objected: "This one is beautiful! It has a wilderness setting with waterfalls and wildlife, excellent mountain goat and sheep habitat . . ."

All that and campsites in 25 acres? We looked further. The site is best seen on the Deerlodge National Forest map. The narrow Park extends for more than 2 mi. along Lost Creek. A trail follows the creek upstream into the Forest.

Much of the surrounding land is in the 54,000-acre Mt. Haggin Wildlife Management Area. This was part of the 154,000-acre Mt. Haggin Ranch, which occupied land on both sides of US 10A; Mt. Haggin itself is S of the highway. Because of its outstanding qualities—rugged terrain, high valleys, rolling foothills, many lakes and ponds, and abundant wildlife—The Nature Conservancy began negotiations in 1969 to acquire portions of the site, including the area that is now a state WMA. This area ranges from 6,500 ft. to 10,000 ft. elevation. It has wet and dry meadows, grass uplands, dense timber, rich riparian vegetation. Features include Lost Creek Falls, in a deep limestone canyon with walls up to 1,500 ft. high, and Garrity Cave, which has dramatic stalactites and stalagmites.

Camping: 16 sites.

HEADQUARTERS: Montana Department of Fish, Wildlife & Parks, 1420 E. Sixth St., Helena, MT 59620; (406) 449-2535.

NATIONAL BISON RANGE
U.S. Fish and Wildlife Service
18,541 acres.

From Missoula, N on US 93 to Ravalli. W on SR 200 6 mi., then N on SR 212 to Moiese.

The primary mission of the Range is protecting a major herd of American bison. Its three principal habitats—grassland, forest, and river-bottom woodland—support an abundance of other wildlife species. It offers a fine visitor center and a 19-mi. scenic auto tour route.

The area is at the S end of the Flathead Valley, W of the Mission Range. Terrain includes steep hills, narrow canyons, rolling prairie. Elevations range from 2,585 to 4,885 ft.; the auto tour route ascends 2,000 ft. Average annual precipitation is about 13 in. Although snow is heavy on nearby mountains, here the annual snowfall is only about 4 1/2 in. Wettest months are Apr.–June, driest July–Aug.

Slaughter reduced the American bison from an estimated 50 million in the early 1800s to a known wild population of under 100 in 1900. The National Bison Range was established in 1908 and stocked with 41 bison from captive herds. Current population of about 400 is kept in balance with carrying capacity by annual sale of surplus.

We enjoyed the visitor center and the scenic views from the tour route. Except for a few birds, we saw no wildlife until near the end of the tour when we spotted a small herd of bison at a distance, out of camera range. What you see depends on weather, season, time of day, and species behavior, as well as your patience and spotting ability. This isn't a game farm or animal show.

Birds: Checklist of 187 species available. Seasonally abundant or common upland species include red-tailed and rough-legged hawks, golden eagle, northern harrier, American kestrel, ring-necked pheasant, gray partridge, killdeer, mourning dove, great horned and short-eared owls, common nighthawk, northern flicker; Lewis', hairy, and downy woodpeckers; yellow-bellied sapsucker, eastern and western kingbirds, horned lark. Swallows: violet-green, tree, bank, rough-winged, barn, cliff. Black-billed magpie, American crow, Clark's nutcracker, black-capped and mountain chickadees, red-breasted and pygmy nuthatches, house and rock wrens, American robin, mountain bluebird, Townsend's solitaire, ruby-crowned kinglet, Bohemian and cedar waxwings, European starling, red-eyed and warbling vireos. Warblers: yellow, yellow-rumped, MacGillivray's, common yellowthroat. Western meadowlark, red-winged and Brewer's blackbirds, northern oriole, brown-headed cowbird, western tanager, lazuli bunting, evening grosbeak, American goldfinch, red crossbill, dark-eyed junco. Sparrows: house, grasshopper, vesper, tree, chipping, white-crowned, song.

The list includes a number of waterfowl and shorebirds, but nearby satellite Refuges have greater variety and numbers. See entry, Ninepipe and Pablo National Wildlife Refuges.

Mammals: Descriptive list of 40 species available. Often or occasionally seen: elk, whitetail and mule deer, pronghorn, bighorn sheep, yellowbelly marmot, Columbian ground squirrel, yellow pine chipmunk. Present but rarely seen: mountain goat, coyote, bobcat, black bear, badger.

FEATURES: *Red Sleep Mountain Auto Tour Route,* 19 mi. on steep but well-maintained gravel road. On the route are overlooks and two short trails; otherwise visitors must remain at their vehicles. The drive takes about 2 hours. A short tour, Buffalo Prairie Drive, is available.

Trailers are not allowed on the 19-mi. Tour Route. Motorcycles and bicycles are prohibited on all drives.

INTERPRETATION
Broadcast received on car radio while approaching the Range provides introductory information.
Visitor center has video film, exhibits, talks, literature. Open 8 A.M.–8 P.M. June–Aug., otherwise 8 A.M.–4:30 P.M.
Nature trails totaling 3/4 mi. at day-use area on Mission Creek. Also a trail for the handicapped.

ACTIVITIES
Hiking is not permitted except as designated.
Fishing is permitted, as posted, on Mission Creek and Jocko River.

NEARBY: Ninepipe and Pablo National Wildlife Refuges are satellites. See entry.

PUBLICATIONS
Range leaflet with map.
Auto tour leaflet.
Bird checklist.
Mammals leaflet.

HEADQUARTERS: Moiese, MT 59824; (406) 644-2211.

NINEPIPE AND PABLO NATIONAL WILDLIFE REFUGES
U.S. Fish and Wildlife Service
2,022 and 2,542 acres.

Ninepipe: From Missoula, N on US 93 about 49 mi., then left on SR 212. US 93 and SR 212 are boundaries. Pablo: From US 93 near Pablo, W at KERR radio tower; follow county road to dike road entrance.

These are wetland satellites of the nearby National Bison Range. Visitors are requested to stop at the Range HQ before entering, for current information and regulations. Both Refuges are closed during the migratory waterfowl hunting season; no hunting is permitted. Certain areas are closed during the waterfowl nesting season: Mar. 1–July 15. Best times to visit are Sept. and late Mar. through early May. Good viewing from the public roads. At Pablo the dike road is open spring and summer.

Both units are near US 93. The highway crosses the E tip of Ninepipe. Both have open water, marsh, and upland grass. The area is in the Flathead Valley, bounded by spectacular mountains. Both are on Indian land and managed by the Fish and Wildlife Service.

Birds: Waterfowl numbers peak in the fall, with as many as 40,000 birds. Spring brings about half that number. A few ducks and geese winter here. Nesting begins in late Mar. Canada goose, mallard, and redhead lead in production, followed by pintail, American wigeon, northern shoveler, blue-winged and green-winged teals, ruddy duck, common merganser, American coot.

Checklist available. Seasonally abundant or common waterfowl and shore-bird species, in addition to those just listed, include red-necked and western grebes, double-crested cormorant, great blue heron, whistling swan, common goldeneye, common snipe, greater and lesser yellowlegs, American avocet, Wilson's and northern phalaropes, ring-billed and California gulls.

ACTIVITIES

Hiking: Closed in waterfowl hunting season. Pablo: N and E shorelines, as posted. Ninepipe: Entire Refuge open July 15 to hunting season.

Fishing: Tribal permit required; inquire at sporting goods stores or tribal office at Pablo. At Pablo on N and E shorelines. Ninepipe: Before July 15 on W and N shorelines as posted. Entire Refuge open July 15 to hunting season. Ice fishing on both Refuges.

ADJACENT: Ninepipe Game Management Area (Montana Department of Fish, Wildlife & Parks, 2,984 acres). Lands of the GMA adjoin and generally surround the NWR. They were acquired to provide for public hunting and upland habitat for game birds, chiefly ring-necked pheasant and gray partridge. Also waterfowl. The area includes grassland, meadow, marsh, and fields planted with wheat.

The GMA is open to visitors for birding and other recreation as well as hunting. Boundaries are fenced and posted.

PUBLICATIONS

Leaflet with maps.
Bird checklist.
Fishing regulations.

HEADQUARTERS: National Bison Range, Moiese, MT 59824; (406) 644-2211.

SWAN RIVER VALLEY; CLEARWATER RIVER VALLEY

Mixed ownerships
Indeterminate acreage.

Traversed by SR 83 between Missoula and Kalispell.

Lying between the Mission and Swan ranges, the valley has a divide. The Swan River, rising in the Missions, flows N; the Clearwater, rising in the Swans, flows S. N of the divide is the Flathead National Forest, S of it the Lolo. The valley is a mixture of Forest, state, timber company, and private land, much of it in checkerboard pattern. On the W are trails into the Mission Mountain Wilderness, on the E trails into the Bob Marshall Wilderness.

The valleys have become a popular resort area because of their many lakes, spectacular scenery, moderate climate, and easy access to high country with splendid hiking trails, hunting, and fishing. N of the divide, Swan and Lindbergh are the largest lakes, with Crystal, Pierce, Holland, Loon, and at least a hundred smaller water bodies. S of the divide, Seeley is largest, followed by Clearwater, Rainy, Alva, Inez, and others.

A few of the lakes are entirely within a National Forest. Most others have some Forest or state shoreline, providing fishing access and, in most cases, camping. Some shorelines are heavily developed, with private homes, lodges, etc.

FEATURES

The Swan River cascades from Crystal Lake into Lindbergh Lake, so named because the Lone Eagle once visited and admired it. For most of the 40 mi. to Swan Lake, the river can be floated by canoe with skilled paddlers, but not at high water. Most floating is below Swan Lake, an upper section best suited to kayaks, then a section popular for float fishing, and, below Bigfork Dam, whitewater labeled the "Mad Mile."

Swan River National Wildlife Refuge, 1,569 acres, is at the S end of Swan Lake, on the river. The best birding is from a canoe. The small area includes grassland, marsh, and wooded bottomland. An annotated bird checklist with 171 species is available. The Refuge is nesting habitat for bald eagle, great blue heron, black tern, 23 species of waterfowl. (*Refuge HQ:* Northwest Montana

Fish and Wildlife Center, 780 Creston Hatchery Rd., Kalispell, MT 59901; (406) 755-4375.)

PUBLICATIONS: The area is well shown on the Flathead NF map, S half, and Lolo NF, Seeley Ranger District map. $1 each. See entries.

ZONE 2

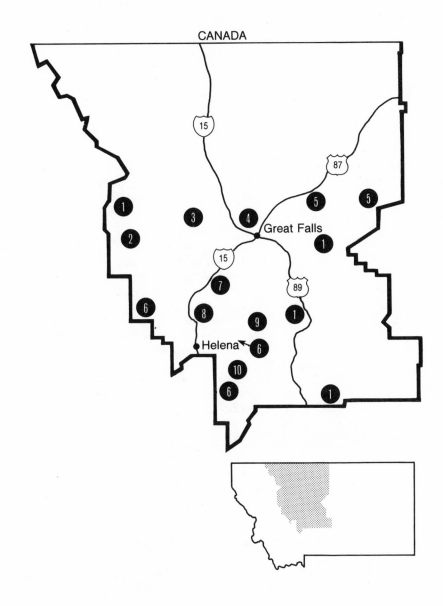

CANADA

15

87

1   3   4   ● Great Falls
                5   5

2   1

15

7

89

6

8   9   1

Helena   6

10

6   1

ZONE 2

Includes these counties:

Glacier	Toole	Chouteau
Hill	Pondera	Cascade
Teton	Lewis and Clark	Meagher
Judith Basin	Broadwater	
Wheatland	Liberty	

Zone 2 is northern Montana from the Continental Divide eastward to the state's midpoint. It includes some of the highest ridges and the E slopes of the Rockies. These are in Glacier NP and the Flathead and Lolo NFs, for which entries are in Zone 1, where they have their principal acreage. On the E are miles of rolling prairie. In the S, the Big Belt, Little Belt, and Snowy Mountains are in the Helena and the Lewis & Clark National Forests.

A principal feature of the zone is the Upper Missouri River. It flows N through Canyon Ferry and Holter Lakes, then turns NE past Great Falls and Fort Benton. Fort Benton, the head of navigation in the steamboat era, is now the gateway to the Missouri Wild and Scenic River. The Smith River, flowing N to the Missouri, attracts floaters and fishermen. The Benton Lake National Wildlife Refuge provides great birding with its multitudes of waterfowl, shorebirds, raptors, and passerines.

BENTON LAKE NATIONAL WILDLIFE REFUGE
U.S. Fish and Wildlife Service
12,383 acres.

From Great Falls, 14 mi. N on US 87 and SR 225, the Bootlegger Trail.

Established in 1929, the Refuge wasn't staffed or managed until 1961. It occupies an old glacial lake bed into which flows Lake Creek. The Mullen Trail, surveyed in the 1850s, crossed the lake bed when it was dry but detoured in wet periods. The environment is semiarid shortgrass prairie. Surrounding private land is used for small-grain farming and some cattle grazing. Immediately around the lake bed are gently rolling low hills interspersed with occasional coulees and breaks.

Beginning in 1961, dikes were built, retaining water and dividing the lake bed into 6 wetland units. The Refuge now has 5,800 acres of marsh and water surrounded by a belt of upland that averages about a half-mile wide. Water can be pumped from another creek to maintain wetland conditions even in dry years. About 600 acres of upland are planted dense cover to create additional duck nesting habitat. To encourage geese to nest, islands were built in the pools.

Can such a site be considered a "natural area"? We leave that decision to the ducks and geese, and they do approve of this Refuge. It has become one of the most productive waterfowl refuges in the system, as well as a favored resting and feeding area for over 100,000 migrants.

Visitors are welcome Mar. 1 to Nov. 30, sunrise to sunset. Viewing opportunities are excellent. In some refuges, auto tour routes are barely within binocular range of impoundments. Here an 8-mi. auto tour route offers a close look at several Refuge marshes. A 1.5-mi. hiking trail along a Refuge dike is also available.

Elevations within the boundaries are from 3,613 to 3,700 ft. Average annual precipitation is about 15 in., snowfall about 57 in. Monthly precipitation is above average in May and June, below average in July and Aug. Summers are hot.

Birds: May–June and Oct. are the best times to come, to see both the nesting waterfowl species and the migrants, the latter totaling up to 100,000 ducks, 4,500 whistling swans, 40,000 snow geese, and 1,000 Canada geese. But birding is still good later, as the broods appear. Annual duck production averages about 20,000, chiefly gadwall, shoveler, lesser scaup, and blue-winged teal, plus a growing number of Canada geese. Of the 175 species recorded in the checklist, 59 have been observed nesting.

Checklist available. Seasonally abundant or common species (excluding winter, when the Refuge is closed), in addition to those mentioned, include eared grebe, black-crowned night-heron, mallard, pintail, green-winged and cinnamon teals, American wigeon, common goldeneye, northern harrier, gray partridge, sora, American coot, killdeer, upland sandpiper, lesser yellowlegs, long-billed dowitcher, marbled godwit, American avocet, Wilson's phalarope, California and Franklin's gulls, mourning dove, short-eared owl, eastern kingbird, horned lark, barn and cliff swallows, water pipit, western meadowlark, yellow-headed and red-winged blackbirds, lark bunting; savannah, vesper, chipping, and song sparrows; chestnut-collared longspur.

Mentioned as of special interest to birders: tundra swan, McCown's longspur, white-faced ibis, black-necked stilt, European wigeon, peregrine falcon.

Mammals: Species mentioned include Richardson ground squirrel, muskrat, coyote, skunk, yellowbelly marmot, whitetail and mule deer, occasional pronghorn.

INTERPRETATION: Kiosk at beginning of tour route has map, literature.

Hunting: Waterfowl, upland game birds. Designated area; special rules.

The impoundments are too shallow to support game fish.
The Refuge has no camping or picnicking facilities.

PUBLICATIONS
Refuge folder with map.
Bird list.

HEADQUARTERS: P.O. Box 450, Black Eagle, MT 59414; (406) 727-7400.

CANYON FERRY LAKE
Montana Department of Fish, Wildlife & Parks
35,300 water acres; indeterminate land acreage.

SE of Helena, off US 12/287.

About 25 mi. long, Canyon Ferry, a reservoir on the Missouri River, is one of MT's largest and most popular water bodies. The U.S. Bureau of Reclamation built the dam, completing it in 1951. Although a narrow strip of shoreline remains in public ownership, development includes marinas, restaurants, and private homes. We saw little that would qualify the lakeside environment as natural.

This part of the Missouri Valley is broad and relatively flat. On the E, the base of the Big Belt Mountains is 6 to 12 mi. away. On the W shore, near the N end of the reservoir, the Spokane Hills rise to about 1,500 ft. above the plain for about 6 mi. Otherwise, the valley floor extends W to an area of hills and buttes. Elevation of the reservoir is 3,765 ft. at full pool. The climate is arid, average annual precipitation about 11 in. Vegetation is chiefly sparse grasses, except for some cottonwood, willow, wild rose, buffaloberry, and dogwood in riparian areas. Temperatures are generally moderate, snowfalls light.

Canyon Ferry is close to Helena and within easy reach of other population centers. The fishing is highly rated, at least until the water warms in early July.

The U.S. Bureau of Reclamation retains legal title to much of the shoreline, but management of recreation and wildlife has been given to the state of Montana.

FEATURES
State Recreation Areas. More than 20 SRAs are on the reservoir, all but 5 of them clustered at the N end. Camping is available at many; others are

for day use. Five have concrete boat ramps; others have gravel ramps or carry-in sites.

Canyon Ferry Wildlife Management Area, 5,000 acres, occupies the upper end of the reservoir, from 1 1/2 mi. N of Townsend to Garnet, Duck, and Confederate creeks.

Responsibility for wildlife management of riparian areas is with the Montana Department of Fish, Wildlife & Parks. The WMA is at the S end of the lake on the E shore, a strip extending roughly 1/4 mi. from the shore. The land is flat, sloping up from the shore at most 60 ft.

At this end of the lake, shallows periodically exposed by drawdowns were a source of windblown dust. Fortunately, the remedy adopted was construction of four impoundments along 6 mi. of lake shore, creating several hundred acres of marsh habitat. Some maps show these impoundments, labeling them "bird ponds." Waterfowl use is heaviest during spring migration.

ACTIVITIES

Camping: 9 campgrounds. Sites aren't designated; about 300 camping units can be accommodated. Most are open May 15–Sept. 15, a few all year.

Hunting: In the WMA. Waterfowl, pheasant, some sharp-tailed grouse.

Fishing: Rainbow and brown trout, whitefish, yellow perch, largemouth bass, kokanee.

Boating: Commercial marinas at N and S ends of the lake and at Goose Bay on W shore. Ramps at several SRAs.

NEARBY: *Hauser Lake,* about 14 mi. long, mostly less than 1/4 mi. wide, is just downstream from Canyon Ferry. It is crossed by SR 280. Two SRAs with campgrounds are on the lake. Boat ramp. Fishing is said to be excellent. Shoreline is mostly private land, with several BLM sections and about 1 mi. of Helena NF land at the N end.

HEADQUARTERS: Montana Department of Fish, Wildlife & Parks, 1420 E. Sixth St., Helena, MT 59620; (406) 449-2535.

FREEZEOUT LAKE WILDLIFE MANAGEMENT AREA
Montana Department of Fish, Wildlife & Parks
11,417 acres.

On the W side of US 89 between Fairfield and Choteau.

Today this is one of the best places in MT to see waterfowl. Before 1933 highway travelers had no reason to pause. The years since have seen a highly successful enrichment of a damaged environment.

The site is part of an old glacial lake bed. Prior to 1920 it was an ephemeral lake basin with no natural outlet. Then it became a sump for drainage from irrigated land, stagnant and highly alkaline. By the late 1940s the water level sometimes rose high enough to inundate the highway, railroad tracks, and nearby fields. Drainage was urged, but the wildlife managers had a better plan. In 1953 the Department of Fish, Wildlife & Parks began to acquire and develop the land. Records show purchases of 22 tracts, plus land acquired from the U.S. Bureau of Reclamation.

Water management was the prime requirement. An 8-mi. canal provided controlled drainage to the Teton River. More than 10 mi. of dams and dikes plus 26 mi. of canals and ditches retain water in impoundments at desired levels. More than 170 nesting islands were built in the impoundments. Next came extensive plantings of trees, shrubs, grasses, grain crops, and aquatic plants. The site now provides 7,000 acres of water, including 2,500 acres of marsh.

Such habitats naturally attract wildlife, but the management scheme included more than an invitation. This had not been a nesting area for Canada geese. A captive goose flock was installed and maintained for ten years, with offspring periodically released. They returned and established a permanent nesting population.

Many other species readily accepted the invitation. During spring migrations, up to a million waterfowl use the site. As many as 300,000 snow geese and 10,000 whistling swans may be present at one time. The fall migration is spread over a longer period.

Base elevation is 3,654 ft. Climate is semiarid, annual precipitation about 12 in. The lake freezes, and a few visitors use iceboats. Snowfall is generally too light for ski touring or snowmobiling.

Headquarters is on US 89. 19 mi. of gravel roads and 10 mi. of trails provide good viewing of all the impoundments. Visitor facilities include parking areas, latrines, and campground.

Birds: The spring migration, beginning in late Mar., includes hundreds of thousands of mallards and pintails. Thereafter the schedule includes the following:

April	Geese, swans, songbirds; major species duck migration; mating flights and Canada goose nesting activities
May	Ducks, shorebirds; nesting activities, goose broods appear
June–July	Broods of ducks and shorebirds
August	Songbirds, shorebirds; molting time for waterfowl
Sept.–Oct.	Migration of shorebirds, waterfowl
Nov.–Dec.	Waterfowl, hawks, eagle
Winter	Hawks, owls, pheasants, Hungarian partridge

Mammals: Muskrat are abundant. Common species include mink, raccoon, longtail weasel, fox, coyote.

ACTIVITIES
Camping: One campground, 19 sites. Most camping is by hunters in fall, but others are welcome.
Hunting: Chiefly waterfowl. Designated portion of the site.
Boating: Ramp on the main lake.

HEADQUARTERS: Freezeout Lake Wildlife Management Area, Fairfield, MT 59436; (406) 467-2646.

HELENA NATIONAL FOREST
U.S. Forest Service
976,673 acres; 1,164,289 acres within boundaries.

Surrounds Helena. Access from I-15, U.S. 12, and local roads.

The several parts of the Forest lie around Helena, nearly all within 60 mi. of the city. Its three principal units are separated by valleys and foothills. The largest unit, NW of the city, is on a 100-mi. section of the Continental Divide. At the N end of this unit is the Scapegoat Wilderness, shared with the Lolo and Lewis & Clark NFs and adjacent to the Bob Marshall Wilderness.

The unit SE of the city is on the Elkhorn Mountains. A 60-mi.-long unit on the E side straddles the Big Belt Range; the Gates of the Mountains Wilderness is at the N end.

Although the Forest is mountainous, elevations are not dramatic. Along the Forest boundaries, the land is generally between 4,500 and 5,500 ft., while ridges are generally below 8,000 ft. Only a few peaks rise above timberline. About two-thirds of the Forest has slopes of 40% or less.

One of our advisors said the Helena has "the best of both worlds." W of the Continental Divide the annual precipitation is as much as 60 in., and forests are dense. On the E slopes the average is 10 to 12 in. Here the forests are more open, with more scattered parklands, grass and timber intermingled.

Most of the 580 mi. of streams are small. The several high mountain lakes are attractive, but their total surface area is 255 acres. The Forest has about 10 mi. of frontage on the Missouri River between Hauser and Holter lakes.

Recreational use here is the lowest of any NF in the region, about a quarter-million visitor-days per year. About half of this recreational use is classified as "motorized," which includes automobile sightseeing and ORV activity. Hunting is the principal dispersed use. About one-quarter of the use is at developed sites, chiefly camp and picnic grounds. Many Forest visitors come from the local area.

The proximity of other outdoor attractions is a partial reason for the light use. Canyon Ferry Lake (see entry), 24 mi. long, lies between Helena and the Big Belt Mountains. Nearby are Hauser and Holter lakes (see Holter Lake entry). Other attractions, such as the Swan River Valley and Bob Marshall Wilderness, are within easy weekend reach.

Another reason is that outsiders aren't likely to find the most attractive, quiet places without a Forest map and advice from a Ranger District office. Access to campgrounds and trailheads isn't difficult, but it is often by a combination of local and Forest roads not shown on highway maps.

It's worth the trouble; the opportunities are substantial. Well over half of the Forest is roadless. Its 733 mi. of trails include two National Recreation Trails, portions of the Lewis & Clark National Historic Trail, and portions of the proposed Continental Divide National Scenic Trail, with links to trail systems in other Forests. Further, most of its trails are in good condition. Trails in the Scapegoat Wilderness and destinations such as Mt. Baldy and Birch Creek Basin offer the hiker and backpacker a full array of natural features and, except in hunting season, a likelihood of solitude. The Forest also has some attractive trails at lower elevations that may be snow-free before the end of Apr.

Plants: About 80% of the area is timbered. The most heavily timbered slopes are those W of the Divide. More typical is the pattern of the E slopes, where rolling grassland with scattered timber patches at the lower elevations grades into more solid forest on middle and upper slopes, with subalpine vegetation or bare ridges at the top.

Douglas-fir is the dominant tree species on almost half of the forest area, followed by lodgepole pine, with smaller amounts of whitebark and limber pine, ponderosa pine, and mixed spruce and subalpine fir. The most common understory components are beargrass, pinegrass, twinflower, snowberry, huckleberry, rough fescue, grouse whortleberry, bluebunch wheatgrass, and menziesia.

Birds: The Forest provides habitat "for at least 267 species of birds," according to its Environmental Impact Statement. No checklist has been issued by the Forest, but in our final review we learned that the Last Chance Audubon Society of Helena has published "Birding in the Helena Valley," listing 233 species.

Mammals: No checklist. Big game species include elk, mule and whitetail deer, bighorn sheep, black bear, pronghorn, moose, and mountain goat. Small game species include cottontail and snowshoe hare. Furbearers include beaver, muskrat, marten, fisher, river otter. Grizzly bear are seen occasionally in the Scapegoat Wilderness and N of SR 200.

FEATURES

Scapegoat Wilderness, 80,679 acres in the Helena, plus 84,407 acres in the Lewis & Clark NF and 74,192 acres in the Lolo. 44 air mi. NW of Helena. A SE extension of the Bob Marshall Wilderness. Access by local and Forest roads from SR 200. The Wilderness straddles the Continental Divide, with the Helena portion S of the ridge. Highest point on the Divide is 9,204-ft. Scapegoat Mountain, whose massive limestone cliffs are an extension of the Chinese Wall in the Bob Marshall. The area includes rugged ridges, gently sloping alpine meadows, forested slopes. Most trails follow drainages. Hunting and fishing are the chief visitor activities. Most of the Wilderness lakes are in the Helena and Lewis & Clark portions, and the most popular hiking trails are on this side. An example is Trail 483, from the SW corner of the Wilderness along Meadow Creek through Alpine Park to Meadow Lake and beyond. Outfitter and guide services are available.

Gates of the Mountains Wilderness, 28,492 acres, is less than 20 mi. NE of Helena. The Forest's Environmental Impact Statement says it has fewer visitors than any other MT Wilderness, despite good trailhead access and easy trails, ascribing this to "lack of water sources and few outstanding visual qualities." But Bill Schneider's hiking guide notes its "open parks, deep canyons, craggy peaks . . . steep-walled Beaver Creek Canyon with its whitish limestone cliffs and beautiful stream . . ." An unusual feature is Refrigerator Canyon, usually 12 to 20 degrees cooler than the outside. This area is among the first to open in the spring, about May 1. Midsummers are hot.

(Beaver Creek Canyon and Refrigerator Canyon are outside the present Wilderness boundary but will almost certainly be included by a pending addition.)

The Forest has several mi. of frontage on the waterways from Hauser Lake to Holter Lake (see entry, Holter Lake Area). The Wilderness boundary is set back slightly from this shoreline, a technicality the hiker won't notice. On the shoreline are two boat-access campgrounds, of which Meriwether is a Wilderness trailhead. The cruise boat stops at Meriwether.

Gates of the Mountains is a dramatic passage cut by the Missouri River through whitish rock now towering over a thousand feet above the river, the passage through which Lewis and Clark came to the Rocky Mountains. A cruise boat operates June–Sept., daily at 11 A.M. and 2 P.M., more often on weekends. Access to the dock is by paved road from I-15, a well-marked exit 16 mi. N of Helena. The area around the boat dock includes a picnic area. This is the heaviest public use area in the Forest, with the highest proportion of out-of-state visitors.

Mt. Baldy Roadless Area, 16,114 acres, 20 mi. NE of Townsend. Access from US 12 by local and Forest roads. Mt. Baldy, 9,472 ft.; is the highest point in the Forest. The area is about 7 mi. N–S, 3 to 6 mi. W–E. About 3 mi. E of Mt. Baldy is 8,400-ft. Mt. Edith. Although there's no trail, foot and horse travel is easy along the divide between them. Perhaps the most attractive feature of the area is Birch Creek Basin, a glacial cirque 2 to 3 mi. wide enclosing several mountain lakes. Big Birch Creek has two small waterfalls. This area is moister than most of the eastern Forest, receiving 30 to 40 in. of precipitation per year, even more on the highest slopes, where most of it falls as snow. Vegetation ranges from heavy forest at lower elevation to treeless peaks. Wildlife includes elk, moose, mountain goat, black bear, mule deer, grouse. Birch Creek, Gypsy Creek, and the deeper lakes have trout fishing.

Gypsy Lake, near the N tip of the area, is accessible by road and is popular with campers and fishermen in summer and fall.

Camas Creek Roadless Area, 28,286 acres, is in the Big Belt Mountains about 15 mi. NE of Townsend, on both sides of the Big Belt Divide. Near the center is Boulder Baldy, 8,942 ft., with 8,810-ft. Boulder Mountain to the SW. Boulder Lakes and Camas Lakes are in glacial cirques on these mountains. The lakes offer cutthroat and brook trout fishing. Some summer visitors come for backpacking and sightseeing. Big game hunting is the chief visitor activity.

Our Forest advisors recommended this as a lightly used area with Wilderness qualities. When we visited, access was difficult because of private land on the E and W. Since then a new trail from Blacktail Road provides improved access, and a new road up Atlanta and Mule creeks provides better access on the E side.

Electric Peak Roadless Area, 28,046 acres, plus 18,959 acres in the Deerlodge NF. The area is on the Continental Divide about 30 mi. SW of Helena, 25 mi. N of Butte. Several peaks on the Divide are above 8,000 ft. Access is from various points along Forest Road 227, the Little Blackfoot River Road, S from US 12. The Little Blackfoot River crosses the N portion. Blackfoot Meadows, at the river's head, has a number of beaver ponds; the meadows are a popular camping area. Cottonwood Lake, in the S portion, on the Deerlodge NF, is also popular. Meadows occur throughout the area, openings in forests of lodgepole pine, Engelmann spruce, Douglas-fir, and subalpine fir. Annual precipitation is 24 to 30 in.

Nevada Mountain Roadless Area, 49,530 acres, straddles the Continental Divide about 30 mi. NW of Helena. Access by local and Forest roads. Aside from hunters, this area is likely to be of interest chiefly to those wishing to hike portions of the Divide. Terrain is steep, with broad, rounded ridges. Nevada Mountain, 8,293 ft., and 8,338-ft. Black Mountain are the principal peaks. Streams are small, potable water scarce.

Other Roadless Areas, 18 of them, range from about 6,444 acres to 51,485 acres. They differ in accessibility and attractiveness, but several offer handsome scenery, a near-pristine environment, and little likelihood of meeting other visitors except in hunting season. Rangers can suggest access routes, trails, and destinations.

INTERPRETATION

The Forest is developing a looseleaf Recreation Opportunities Guide (ROG), which can be seen at HQ and Ranger District offices. We saw pages describing a number of campgrounds and attractive trails.

The Forest has no visitor center, campfire talks, other naturalist programs.

ACTIVITIES

Camping: 19 campgrounds, 175 sites. Open season is generally June 1–Sept 15, but dates may vary. Informal camping anywhere unless posted.

Hiking, backpacking: 733 mi. of trails. Minimum maintenance is performed annually on about 400 mi. Trails are reported to be in generally good condition. Maintenance problems are less in this dry climate.

While much of the Continental Divide Trail is still in planning elsewhere, the Helena's present combination of Forest roads and trails permits travel along most of the Divide. Also, the Divide is easily reached here, with three highways crossing it at passes, making short hikes feasible. Elevations of 6,000 to 7,000 ft. make the hiking season longer than on many other sections.

Hunting: Most hunters come here for elk, deer being the next most-sought big game. Others include black bear, bighorn sheep, pronghorn, moose, mountain goat. Small game includes grouse, cottontail, snowshoe hare.

Fishing: Fishing pressure inside the Forest boundaries is light, about 5,500 visitor-days per year. Excellent fishing is available nearby. None of the major rivers are within the Forest except for the Missouri at Gates of the Mountains.

Horse riding: Mostly associated with hunting. No restrictions, but some trails are steep.

Ski touring: Trails developed and marked near MacDonald Pass, one groomed by a local club. Marked and unmarked trails at Stemple Pass are popular because of reliable snow quality and quantity. Also trails in the Elkhorn Mountains.

PUBLICATION: Forest map. $1.

REFERENCES

Schneider, Bill. *The Hiker's Guide to Montana.* Billings, MT: Falcon Press, 1983. Pp. 160–82.

Rudner, Ruth. *Bitterroot to Beartooth.* San Francisco: Sierra Club Books, 1985. Pp. 73–95.

Turbak, Gary. *The Traveler's Guide to Montana.* Billings, MT: Falcon Press, 1983. Pp. 205–08.

HEADQUARTERS: 301 S. Park, Drawer 10014, Helena, MT 59626; (406) 449-5201.

RANGER DISTRICTS: Townsend R.D., 415 S. Front, Box 29, Townsend, MT 59644; (406) 266-3425. Helena R.D., 2001 Poplar, Helena, MT 59601; (406) 449-5490. Lincoln R.D., Highway 200, Box 234, Lincoln, MT 59639; (406) 362-4265.

HOLTER LAKE AREA

U.S. Bureau of Land Management; Montana Department of Fish, Wildlife
& Parks; Helena National Forest
About 45,000 acres, exclusive of National Forest land.

From I-15 between Great Falls and Helena, Wolf Creek exit, E across
bridge, then S.

Holter Dam is about 17 air miles N of Hauser Dam, the next upstream on
the Missouri River. Holter Lake, including two major oxbows of the meandering river channel, is less than 10 mi. long as the crow flies, more than 13
as the trout swims. 5 mi. of river connect it with the smaller Upper Holter
Lake, beyond which is 3 mi. of river to Hauser Dam.

The land ownership pattern is complex: mostly BLM and private land on
the W side, state and National Forest Service on the E.

On the E side of Holter Lake, ranch land is on the N, BLM on the S.

Most of the W side is in the Beartooth Wildlife Management Area. BLM
   has a small tract at the N end with a campground and boat ramp. The
   rest, including a lodge and marina, is private.

Most land on the E side of the river between the lakes is in the Helena
   National Forest.

Upper Holter Lake is largely surrounded by private land.

Between this lake and Hauser Dam, most land on the W is BLM, on the
   E National Forest.

The complexity doesn't matter to most visitors, who come here to fish, boat,
camp, and swim. All the campgrounds are on the E side. A well-maintained
BLM campground is near Holter Dam, two State Recreation Areas further
S on Holter Lake. Camping is usually permitted in the WMA. The National
Forest has two boat-access campgrounds.

Terrain is hilly to mountainous, slopes moderate, with many rock outcrops.
The area is semiarid, annual precipitation from 12 to 14 in. Average annual
snowfall is about 32 in. Plant cover is chiefly grasses with patches of timber.

Beartooth Wildlife Management Area, 32,318 acres. The W boundary is a
12-mi. shoreline on Holter Lake, including both oxbows. From here the WMA
extends E about 11 mi. Access is from the road on the E side of the lake from
Holter Dam. Gently rolling hills rise from the shore at 3,578 ft. to the steeper
mountains of upper Elkhorn Creek. The area is divided by several high, rocky
ridges. Three perennial streams drain to the lake.

Maintained roads lead to HQ and partway up the three main drainages,
beyond which are trails. Vehicles may be barred from the drainages except
in hunting season. One trail links with a trail in the adjacent Forest Service
wilderness area. Facilities include parking areas, latrines, horse corrals and

loading chutes, plus latrines and trash barrels at two shoreline points, where primitive campgrounds are located. Although game management is the primary objective, hiking, birding, horse riding, boat camping, and other nonmotorized recreation are encouraged, and the Range receives a considerable number of visitors outside hunting season. Cottonwood and Elkhorn creeks are trout and salmon spawning areas, but fishing pressure has been light on the streams; most fishermen prefer the lake.

Sleeping Giant, U.S. Bureau of Land Management, 11,000 acres. The area has about 9 mi. of lake shore, across from the WMA. Hilly to mountainous terrain, somewhat steeper than that of the WMA, rising to 6,192-ft. Beartooth Mountain, whose profile is called the "Sleeping Giant." The view from the top is well worth the climb. As in the WMA, vegetation is chiefly grasses and forbs, with timbered draws and slopes.

Public access is by a hard-to-find dirt road from the W, otherwise by water. Recreation opportunities include camping, hiking, hunting, and fishing.

Helena National Forest. See entry.

The boundary of the Gates of the Mountains Wilderness is close to the river, between the lakes.

Birds: Game birds include sharp-tailed, blue, and ruffed grouse; Hungarian partridge. A list prepared for the Wildlife Division includes only nongame species, omitting upland game birds and waterfowl. Listed as seasonally abundant or common species are turkey vulture, Cooper's and red-tailed hawks, golden and bald eagles, osprey, American kestrel, great blue heron, American coot, spotted sandpiper, California gull, mourning dove, great horned owl, common nighthawk, white-throated swift, belted kingfisher, northern flicker, Lewis' and hairy woodpeckers, yellow-bellied sapsucker, western kingbird, western flycatcher. Swallows: barn, cliff, violet-green, tree, rough-winged. Gray jay, black-billed magpie, common crow, Clark's nutcracker, black-capped and mountain chickadees, white-breasted and red-breasted nuthatches, American robin, Swainson's thrush, veery, mountain bluebird, ruby-crowned kinglet, cedar waxwing, European starling, solitary and warbling vireos. Warblers: yellow-rumped, yellow, MacGillivray's, yellowthroat, American redstart. Western meadowlark, Brewer's blackbird, northern oriole, western tanager, black-headed grosbeak, pine siskin, red crossbill, green-tailed and rufous towhees. Sparrows: vesper, lark, chipping, white-crowned.

Mammals: Abundant or common species include masked and dusky shrews, northern water shrew, little brown and long-eared myotis, marmot, beaver, coyote, bobcat, weasel, raccoon, skunk, black bear, thirteen-lined ground squirrel, pine chipmunk, red squirrel, deer mouse, meadow vole, western jumping mouse, porcupine, whitetail jackrabbit, snowshoe hare, mountain cottontail, mule and whitetail deer, elk, bighorn sheep, Rocky Mountain goat.

NEARBY: Recreation Road (see entry).

PUBLICATION: Campground leaflet (by BLM).

HEADQUARTERS: BLM, Butte District Office, 106 N. Parkment, Butte, MT 59702; (406) 494-5059. Montana Department of Fish, Wildlife & Parks, Beartooth WMA, Wolf Creek, MT 59648; (406) 235-4249.

LEWIS & CLARK NATIONAL FOREST
U.S. Forest Service
1,843,397 acres.

The Rocky Mountain Division is W of Great Falls, S of US 2, about 18 mi. W of US 89 and 287. The several blocks of the Jefferson Division are SE of Great Falls; the largest is crossed by US 89.

This became one National Forest as a matter of administrative convenience. The two Divisions are 60 mi. apart and differ in topography, climate, and the recreation opportunities they offer.

Rocky Mountain Division, a single Ranger District, comprises roughly half of the Forest. Most of it is roadless wilderness. A solid block of Forest land, it extends about 85 mi. N–S, with a width of 9 to 22 mi. On the Front Range of the Rocky Mountains, it is mostly high and rugged, with spectacular peaks and steep ridges. On the N, US 2 runs between the Forest and Glacier National Park. Its W boundary is on the Continental Divide, adjoining the Flathead National Forest (entry in Zone 1). The Scapegoat-Great Bear-Bob Marshall Wilderness complex straddles the Divide; 384,407 acres of the Wilderness are in the Rocky Mountain Division.

The mountains rise steeply from grassland at about 5,000 ft. elevation to 9,362 ft. The mountain mass has many stream-cut narrow valleys. It is divided by the broad and gently rolling N–S valley of the North Fork of the Sun River. Much of the Division drains to the Sun River, which is dammed to form Gibson Reservoir, the Forest's largest water body.

Access is by a number of improved gravel roads, shown on the highway map, from US 89, connecting with Forest roads and trailheads and serving several campgrounds. The District has more than 1,000 mi. of foot and horse trails. This is one of the few National Forests with funds to maintain its trails reasonably well. Three trail crews were at work when we visited.

Plants: Except for areas of exposed rock on peaks and ridges, most of the Division is forested. Lower elevations are dominated by Douglas-fir, with limber and ponderosa pine, lodgepole pine growing in moister areas. Lodgepole becomes dominant at mid-elevations, with aspen, Douglas-fir, and spruce, and some open grasslands. Because of strong winds, trees at higher elevations grow shorter and stouter. Species here include lodgepole and white-bark pine, spruce, Douglas-fir, and alpine fir. The Forest Plan notes that suppression of wildfires has reduced vegetative diversity. It recommends natural fire management in the Wilderness, harvesting and prescribed burning elsewhere.

Beargrass is the most conspicuous of the flowering plants. Lupine is said to be the most abundant of the blue flowers. Other seasonal wildflowers include beardtongue, tall mertensia, monkshood, forget-me-not, and speed-well, Indian paintbrush, Oregon grape, monkeyflowers, elephanthead, white bog orchid, heartleaf arnica, death camas, blue camas, queencup, false helle-bore, glacier lily, false Solomonseal, coralroot, spring beauty, anemone, meadow rue, white clematis, larkspur, cliff saxifrage, purple avens, service-berry, wild hollyhock, violets, alpine fireweed, blue gentian, phacelia, pasqueflower, purple clematis, buttercup, yellow columbine, globeflower, red stonecrop, thimbleberry, wild rose, locoweed, purple geranium, fire-weed, pipsissewa, shootingstar, penstemon, twinflower, harebell, hawk-weed, goldenrod, fleabane, balsamroot, yarrow, speedwell, aster, pussy-toes, gaillardia.

FEATURES

Bob Marshall-Great Bear-Scapegoat Wilderness, 1,535,334 acres, of which 384,407 acres are in the Lewis & Clark. An additional 46,844 roadless acres on the L & C are proposed additions to the Wilderness. This is one of the most spectacular National Forest Wildernesses, with almost limitless opportunities for backpacking, horsepacking, hunting, fishing, ski touring, snowshoeing, and climbing. Its most-photographed geological feature is the Chinese Wall, a 1,000-ft.-high escarpment that extends 22 mi. along the Continental Divide. A well-developed trail system generally follows drainages up to the high country, several trails crossing the Divide. Popular backpacking routes take from 3 to 10 days, covering 30 to 75 mi. Visitor use of this area is relatively high, about 70,000 visitor-days per year.

Several outfitters and guides serve the area, chiefly for hunting.

The entire Division, including the Wilderness, is grizzly bear country. Travelers should know how to minimize the possibility of encounters.

Sun River Game Preserve, 199,661 acres, is more than half of the L & C portion of the Wilderness. Established by the Montana legislature in 1913 in hopes of rebuilding depleted big game populations, it has since been closed to sport hunting. As in National Parks, wildlife tends to be more visible than in hunted areas. Elk have multiplied, and the area has the state's largest herd of bighorn sheep. Also present are mule and whitetail deer, mountain goat, black and grizzly bear, and moose. Game birds include blue, ruffed, and spruce grouse; wild turkey, ptarmigan, and a few waterfowl.

Gibson Reservoir, though large, has only limited recreation value because a large drawdown begins in early July to supply irrigated farms. Fishing is poor. A trail to the Wilderness follows the shore.

Sun River Wildlife Management Area, a state site open to hunting, is just outside the Forest boundary. See entry.

Jefferson Division includes one large and 4 smaller blocks of Forest land. The largest block, 30 mi. SE of Great Falls, is bisected by US 89. The smaller blocks are on the N, S, and E. All the blocks are easily accessible from US routes 89, 87, 12, or 191. This Division has three Ranger Districts: Kings Hill, Judith, and Musselshell.

Most of the Forest land is on mountain ranges. These rather short ranges have domelike shapes rather than jagged peaks. The longest range is the Little Belt Mountains, which cross the largest block. The Division has many streams, no large rivers or lakes large enough for boating. Its moderate slopes have less demanding hiking and riding trails than those of the Rocky Mountain Division.

It is also mostly forest-covered. Tree species are generally the same as on the Rocky Mountain Division, but patterns differ both because of topography and soils, and history. A higher proportion of the Jefferson lands have a history of disturbance by fire, logging, grazing, and mining.

Little Belt Mountains bisect the largest block, which is about 30 mi. N–S, up to 54 mi. W–E. The mountains are rounded, tree-covered, with numerous dry, rocky canyons. Most streams are intermittent, although some become perennial as they descend. Highest point in this block is 9,175-ft. Big Baldy. The Showdown winter sports area is on the E slope of 8,192-ft. Porphyry Peak. This area, as well as several campgrounds and trailheads, is along US 89, which traverses the area N–S. A few other maintained roads penetrate the block, but 17 tracts totaling more than 450,000 acres are roadless. The largest tract has over 90,000 acres. The area has a network of dirt roads, many of them unused and overgrown, as well as trails. Together with scattered inholdings, these are products of a history of logging, mining, and grazing. It's a spotty region, some areas essentially natural, others disturbed, and there is also much variation in the quality of scenic and other attractions. The Recreation Opportunity Guide (ROG), available at Ranger District offices, has information on trails, fishing streams, etc.

The Middle Fork Judith River, a roadless area of 92,000 acres, is well known to hunters and fishermen, not yet discovered by many backpackers. The scenery is splendid, including high viewpoints and tall cliffs along the river, fishing excellent, trails uncrowded.

The Smith River, a popular floating stream (see entry), is on the W boundary of this block, a strip with alternating Forest and private lands. The most popular float, a 60-mi. 3-day trip, begins S of the Forest and ends N of it, but there are boat camps along the Forest shoreline.

The unit has several caves. The largest, Lick Creek, has 1,500 ft. of known passageways connecting several caverns.

Castle Mountain is a block about 10 mi. N–S, 18 mi. W–E, about 6 mi. E of White Sulphur Springs. The W portion is mountainous, with peaks over

8,500 ft., noted for their castlelike tall spires. Several streams are perennial but there is no fishing. The E portion is rolling, dry, with elevations about 5,000 ft. A maintained road crosses the block N–S. Hunting, camping, hiking, and ski touring are the chief visitor activities. Use is relatively high because White Sulphur Springs is nearby. Two campgrounds are in the NW corner, and from here trails spread S and E.

Big Snowy Mountains are 14 mi. S of Lewistown, in a block about 10 mi. N–S, 16 mi. W–E. Access by local roads from US 191. The mountains rise to over 8,600 ft. from plains at about 5,000 ft. The ridge is flat-topped, surrounded by cirquelike basins. The central portion, roadless but accessible by trails, was a Wilderness Study Area; the Regional Forester recommended against Wilderness designation. One of the two campgrounds is on Crystal Lake, trailhead for the Crystal Lake National Recreation Trail. The lake offers fishing, but motorized boating is prohibited. The unit has several caves, one with perpetual ice.

Highwood Mountains, in a block about 24 mi. E of Great Falls, are a mosaic of forest, meadow, and exposed rock on steep slopes. The block is about 8 mi. N–S, 10 mi. W–E. Highwood Baldy, 7,670 ft., is the highest in this small cluster of bare-topped peaks, three others in the 7,000-ft. range, all in the western third of the unit. The unpaved South Fork Highwood Road enters near the NW corner, where there is one campground. Otherwise the block is roadless. This is the closest forested area to Great Falls, with good populations of elk and other game and several mi. of trout stream. Thus it attracts visitors for hunting, fishing, hiking, camping, horse riding, and ORV travel.

The fourth small block, on the Crazy Mountains E of Ringling, is largely a checkerboard of Forest and private land.

Climate: On the plains at the base of the mountains, Jan. average temperature is about 24°F, the July average 69°, but extremes of record are wide-ranging, from far below zero to well over 100°. Average annual precipitation is 15 in., more than half of that falling May–Aug. Higher elevations are colder, limiting plant growth to June–Aug. Annual precipitation on the Rocky Mountain ridges is 65 in., about 80% of this falling as snow. Travelers should be aware of the frequent strong winds that occur at all elevations but can be dangerous up high. Chinook winds in winter can cause a temperature drop of 50° in an hour.

Roads: Except for US 89, the Forest has only 20 mi. of paved road. Inventoried roads total 1,737 mi. Of these, 180 mi. are graveled, 441 mi. graded and drained. The other 1,096 mi. are primitive wheel tracks that receive little or no maintenance. Many of these require high clearance or 4-wheel drive.

Trails: Total trail mileage is 1,677, of which about 1,000 mi. are in the Rocky Mountain Division. The principal trails in that Division, including those in the Wilderness, are quite well maintained. The system includes seven National Recreation Trails, which usually have some maintenance priority. Two are in the Jefferson Division, others in the Rocky Mountain Division.

Birds: A bird list is available, but it does not note relative abundance or seasonality. The annotated lists available for Glacier NP and Flathead NF are generally applicable and more useful.

Mammals: A checklist without annotation is available, listing 72 species. Mule deer are the most abundant game species, with a population of about 30,000. Elk habitat capacity is 8,500, whitetail deer 4,500, bighorn sheep 1,100, mountain goat 500, black bear 1,050. Moose and pronghorn are also present. Grizzly bear occur throughout the Rocky Mountain Division; estimated population is about 85. The endangered gray wolf is represented by 4 to 8 individuals. Nongame mammals include hoary marmot, beaver, bobcat, wolverine, and lynx, as well as more common furbearers, predators, and rodents.

ACTIVITIES

Camping: In the Rocky Mountain Division, 15 campgrounds, 207 sites. In the Jefferson, 11 campgrounds, 135 sites. Season is generally from late May to mid-Sept.

Hiking, backpacking: The ROG has pages describing the principal trails: access to trailheads, sketch map, profile, hiking season, degree of difficulty, degree of use, trailside features, camping sites, etc. Photocopies on request. Most backpacking is in the Rocky Mountain Division, chiefly in the Wilderness. Hiking season is generally summer to mid-Sept., but some low-elevation trails are open in May, some high trails not until late June or early July. Trails tend to follow drainages, and the ROG identifies fishing streams.

Hunting: Mule deer is the primary game, but elk attracts greater hunter interest. Big game attracts many hunters from out of state, both to the Rocky Mountain Division and to the mountains of the Jefferson Division. Grouse are hunted Forest-wide. Licensed outfitter-guides serve both divisions.

Fishing: Of the Forest's 1,600 mi. of streams, 535 mi. are considered fish habitat. Rainbow, brook, and cutthroat trout and mountain whitefish are in all of the larger streams. Brown trout are found in a few large streams near the Forest boundary, notably in Big Spring Creek, tributary to the picturesque Judith River. The Smith River is famous for float fishing in a scenic setting.

Horse riding: Most horse riding is in conjunction with hunting and fishing, but some outfitters offer summer pack trips, chiefly into the Bob Marshall Wilderness.

Skiing: Ski areas at Teton Pass in the Rocky Mountain Division and Kings Hill in the Jefferson Division.

Ski touring: The season for ski touring, snowshoeing, and snowmobiling is relatively long. Trails have been developed in the vicinity of the downhill ski areas. Unlimited opportunities on unplowed roads.

INTERPRETATION: The Forest has no visitor center (other than HQ and Ranger District offices) and no naturalist programs such as campfire talks, guided hikes, etc.

PUBLICATIONS

The looseleaf volumes of the Recreation Opportunity Guide are available at each office. The ROG has detailed information on bicycling, boating, camping, picnicking, hunting, fishing, 4-wheel drive, hiking, horse and pack saddle, hunting, identification and gathering, motorcycling, sightseeing, photography, and winter sports.

Forest maps (2). $1 each.

Bob Marshall Wilderness map. (In preparation.)

Snowmobile trails map, Kings Hill area.

Information pages:

Topography and climate.

Recreation.

Roads and trails.

Wilderness.

Bob Marshall Wilderness.

Scapegoat Wilderness.

Checklists: birds, mammals, reptiles and amphibians, fishes.

Hiking and horse trail guide.

REFERENCES

Fischer, Hank. *The Floater's Guide to Montana*. Billings, MT: Falcon Press, 1986. Pp. 32–35, 87–92, 95–98.

Sample, Mike. *The Angler's Guide to Montana*. Billings, MT: Falcon Press, 1986. Pp. 126–31, 191, 196.

Schneider, Bill. *The Hiker's Guide to Montana*. Billings, MT: Falcon Press, 1984. Pp. 136–59, 206–07, 215–19.

Turbak, Gary. *The Traveler's Guide to Montana*. Billings, MT: Falcon Press, 1983. Pp. 130–35, 232–36.

HEADQUARTERS: 1601 Second Ave., Great Falls, MT 59403; (406) 791-7700.

RANGER DISTRICTS: Rocky Mountain R.D., Box 340, Chouteau, MT 59422; (406) 466-5341. Judith R.D., Box 484, Stanford, MT 59479; (406) 566-2292. Musselshell R.D., Box F, Harlowton, MT 59036; (406) 632-4391. Kings Hill R.D., Box A, White Sulphur Springs, MT 59645; (406) 547-3361. Augusta Information Station, Box 365, Augusta, MT 59410; (406) 562-3247. Belt Creek Information Station, Neihart, MT 59465; (406) 236-5511.

RECREATION ROAD

Montana Department of Fish, Wildlife & Parks
Indeterminate acreage.

Off I-15, between Cascade and Wolf Creek.

Driving S on I-15 about 25 mi. from Great Falls, look for an impressive mass of rock with a parking area at the foot. From the parking, an open stairway leads to a viewing platform overlooking the Missouri River Valley. The road below is Recreation Road.

What a splendid idea! This was the highway before I-15 was built. It follows the river, a quiet scenic drive. Along the way are campgrounds, fishing access sites, boat launching areas, all quite informal. Below Holter Dam is a 90-mi. dam-free section of the Missouri.

Recreation Road returns to I-15 4 mi. toward Helena from Wolf Creek. Just at the bridge, a county road continues S to Holter Lake; see that entry.

ACTIVITIES

Camping: 5 campgrounds; informal sites.

Fishing: Said to be excellent, especially just below the dam. Brown and rainbow trout.

HEADQUARTERS: Montana Department of Fish, Wildlife & Parks, 1420 E. Sixth St., Helena, MT 59620; (406) 449-2535.

SMITH RIVER
Mixed ownerships
60 river miles.

From Camp Baker, 22 mi. NW of White Sulphur Springs, to Eden Bridge on SR 330, S of Great Falls.

Fed by many tributaries, the river flows N past White Sulfur Springs, between the Big Belt and Little Belt mountains. The 60 mi. from Camp Baker to Eden Bridge offer the best floating. For most of that distance, the river crosses private land, but that hardly seems to matter; while there are some developments, most of the riparian zone is roadless and undeveloped. No public roads cross until Eden Bridge. Scenic, too, especially in the Smith's tall, rock-walled canyon. Here and there are small blocks of state land, and for a few miles in mid-course the river is on the boundary of the Lewis & Clark NF. This is enough to enable the Department of Fish, Wildlife & Parks and the Forest to provide campsites for the 3-day float trip.

There are only minor rapids, mostly riffles and pools. Swift current and eddies, plus boulders and other obstructions, require some boating skill. Rafts and canoes are both used, with some use of kayaks and wooden river boats.

The river can be dangerous; floating is not advised during the spring high-water period, usually from mid-May through early June. The principal season is June–July. There's usually too little water after July.

The river is popular with both fishermen and floaters, so there's not much solitude on weekends, when finding a campsite may be difficult. The Department of Fish, Wildlife & Parks is experimenting with a reservation system for floaters. Most visitors come from nearby, which means fewer on weekdays. Rainbow and brown trout are the principal game fish. Quiet floaters may see much wildlife, especially near dawn and dusk.

Floaters are warned not to trespass on private land.

PUBLICATION: *Smith River Guide.*

INFORMATION AVAILABLE FROM:
Montana Department of Fish, Wildlife & Parks, Region 4 Headquarters, RR 4, Box 243, Great Falls, MT 59405; (406) 454-3441. Montana Department of Fish, Wildlife & Parks, District Warden, Box 446, White Sulphur Springs, MT 59645; (406) 547-3792. Kings Hill R.D., Lewis & Clark National Forest, Box A, White Sulphur Springs, MT 59645; (406) 547-3361.

SUN RIVER WILDLIFE MANAGEMENT AREA
Montana Department of Fish, Wildlife & Parks
19,728 acres.

Adjoining the Lewis & Clark National Forest, between Augusta and Gibson Reservoir. Sun River Road 208 W from Augusta is the N boundary.

By 1890 market hunters and ranchers had virtually eliminated the buffalo in this region and deer and elk populations were depleted. In 1913 the Montana legislature established the Sun River Game Preserve, within the National Forest, hoping to protect the surviving elk in the upper Sun River drainage and promote recovery. Hunting was and is forbidden in this Preserve. (See entry, Lewis & Clark NF.) By 1925 the elk herd had so increased that overgrazing was a problem in the Preserve and ranchers were complaining about elk depredation. The Sun River WMA was acquired and fenced to provide winter range for elk. In addition to elk, big game species using the range include mule and whitetail deer, pronghorn, bighorn sheep, and black bear. Game birds include sharp-tailed and ruffed grouse, with smaller numbers of blue and Franklin's grouse and Hungarian partridge. Hunting is permitted here.

Most of the area is glacial moraine with ridges, basins, flats, terraces, small lakes, and potholes. Creeks drain to the Sun River. To the W, rugged limestone cliffs and outcroppings rise above talus slopes. Elevations range from 4,300 ft. to 8,179 ft.

Average annual precipitation is 15 to 18 in. Snow accumulations at lower elevations rarely begin before Dec., and because of prevailing SW winds periods of complete snow cover are brief.

Grass range covers 40% of the area. About 28% is forest: Douglas-fir, limber pine, alpine fir, Engelmann spruce, lodgepole and whitebark pine. About 20% is browse and meadow, the rest barren rock.

ACTIVITIES

Camping: One 4-unit campground.

Hiking: About 35 mi. of dirt roads and trails.

Fishing: About 12 mi. of fishable streams. Two ponds also have trout.

HEADQUARTERS: Montana Department of Fish, Wildlife & Parks, Sun River WMA, Augusta, MT 59410; (406) 562-3684.

UPPER MISSOURI WILD AND SCENIC RIVER

U.S. Bureau of Land Management

149 river miles; 131,840 acres.

From Fort Benton on US 87 to the US 191 bridge at the W end of the Charles M. Russell National Wildlife Refuge (see entry in Zone 4).

This is the only section of the 2,315-mi.-long Missouri River that is preserved and protected in its natural free-flowing condition. The dam builders tried to change that, but in 1976 these 149 mi. were added to the National Wild and Scenic River system. Steamboats once ascended the river as far as Fort Benton. Visitors can float the river today seeing little that has been altered from what Lewis and Clark described in 1805–1806. With some important exceptions, the boundaries set by Congress are the valley rims, or all the area that can be seen from the river. The exceptions relate to riparian land ownership. By no means all the riparian land is publicly owned.

The 42 mi. from Fort Benton to Coal Banks Landing are classified as Recreational, one of three categories in the Wild and Scenic River system. Here federal jurisdiction is limited to the river and its bed except for a few BLM tracts, including several islands. The river is broad, meandering between bluffs and high banks. Two gravel roads and a few primitive roads come to or near the river banks, but there's little or no riverside development. The first launch or take-out is Loma Ferry at Mile 21. The first campground is at Coal Banks Landing, also a put-in and take-out point.

A section designated Wild begins at Mile 51.5. Here the river is narrower and straighter, with fewer islands, flowing between the White Cliffs, light-

colored sandstone eroded into what the Lewis and Clark journal called "eli-
gant ranges of lofty freestone buildings, having their parapets well stocked
with statuary." Formations include honeycombs, windows, arches, capped
columns, spires, and monuments.

From here on the proportion of BLM-managed streamside land gradually
increases, and there are few points where even primitive roads come to the
banks. Campgrounds are at Miles 63 and 77. Judith Landing, at Mile 88, is
the next major launch and take-out point, with campground and ferry.

The final 61 miles are through the Badlands Area, the Missouri Breaks,
rough country cut by a maze of ravines and coulees. This is largely BLM land.
Various sections are classified as Wild or Scenic. McClelland Ferry at Mile
102 is the last put-in or take-out before the end. The only campground is at
Mile 125. At Mile 139 the river enters the Charles M. Russell National Wildlife
Refuge. The Wild and Scenic River area ends at James Kipp State Recreation
Area on US 191. (See entry in Zone 4.)

The management plan adopted in 1978 would safeguard the river's wild and
scenic qualities and provide for the increasing use that is sure to come. Having
only 5 campgrounds between Fort Benton and James Kipp SRA creates
problems, especially when intervals are greater than a day's floating. The plan
calls for land acquisitions to provide more campgrounds, protect significant
natural features and historic and cultural sites, and additional launch and
take-out places. Scenic easements would be obtained to exclude development
on private land within sight of the river. The interpretive program would be
based on publications, not on exhibits or signs visible from the river. Some
primitive roads on BLM lands may be closed and naturalized. Realization of
the plan depends on appropriations, which may come slowly. By the spring
of 1987, 12 tracts of private land had been purchased or easements acquired,
and a visitor contact station at Fort Benton was in use.

Most float trips begin at Fort Benton, Coal Banks Landing, or Judith
Landing. Fort Benton to Loma Ferry, 21 mi., is a popular day trip. The
average mid-summer current speed is 3 1/2 mph. Most floaters travel about
22 mi. per day.

A permit system has been considered, but it probably won't be adopted
until river traffic is heavier. In 1986 there were 2,400 floaters. Over 60,000
visitors were recorded, enjoying other forms of recreation.

In the public debate that preceded adoption of the plan, wilderness advocates urged that motorcraft be prohibited on the entire 149 mi., or at least on
the sections designated Wild. BLM's decision was to permit motorcraft but
adopt a no-wake rule in the Wild section, a rule almost impossible to enforce.
The debate continues, but experience on other rivers suggests that once
commercial outfitters begin using motorcraft, they won't be banned. In 1987,
2 of the 6 or 8 outfitters were using motorized pontoon boats. The no-wake
rule applies from Memorial Day through Labor Day; no upstream travel is
permitted during this period.

Climate: The region is generally semiarid, with annual precipitation about

14 in., half of this falling May–July. Temperatures below zero occur 5 to 10 times a year, cold periods seldom lasting more than 5 days. Annual snowfall is about 40 in., Mar. having the highest average. Summers are pleasant, daytime highs rarely exceeding 90°F. Heavy late afternoon and evening thunderstorms are common in summer, sometimes accompanied by hail.

Plants: Cottonwood groves and willow thickets are limited to sandy and wetland sites. Because they are favored as campsites, groves are shown on the Wild and Scenic maps. They are most common in the upper reaches, where the river meanders and has numerous islands. There is also a concentration at Judith Landing and up the Judith River. The vegetation on the larger islands indicates what grew on riverbanks before grazing. Above a rim of dense willows, grasses and sagebrush associate with cottonwood and boxelder. Shrubs, including rose and snowberry, are often so dense as to preclude camping. River benches above the riparian zone have a variety of patterns shaped by soil type, past use, and other factors. Blue grama, western wheatgrass, and needle-and-thread are common.

Those who float in springtime can enjoy a bright display of wildflowers, including yucca, purple prairie clover, sweetclover, scarlet globemallow, rose, pasqueflower, western yarrow, prairie coneflower, common pricklypear, Missouri goldenrod, common sunflower, broom snakeweed, rubber rabbitbrush, pincushion cactus.

Wildlife: The river corridor's many habitats attract a great variety of wildlife. 233 bird species have been identified, 60 species of mammals, 20 of reptiles and amphibians, 49 of fish. No checklists have yet been published.

Birds: Canada goose and mallard are the principal nesting waterfowl, the geese nesting almost exclusively on river islands. Migrating waterfowl are most abundant in the fall, when they feed in fields and marshes away from the river but return for nesting and cover. Shorebirds are abundant in spring and summer. Upland game birds include sharp-tailed and sage grouse, gray partridge, pheasant, and turkey. Golden eagles are common, while bald eagles winter along the river. Common hawks include red-tailed and Swainson's. Most of the passerines are year-round residents, eastern and western species often overlapping.

Mammals: The bison, black and grizzly bears, wolf, and swift fox, once resident here, are gone. Elk, once eliminated, were reintroduced in 1951 and have multiplied sufficiently for limited hunting. Mule deer are the chief big game species, whitetail present in a more restricted range. Pronghorn use the sagebrush-grasslands where terrain is open and provides easy river access.

INTERPRETATION: Visitor center at Fort Benton was opened in 1986.

ACTIVITIES

Camping: Until more campgrounds are developed, many floaters will camp on private land, especially between Fort Benton and Coal Banks Landing. Most landowners seem tolerant. BLM encourages camping on public lands only, but adds: "You are the landowner's guest if you stop on his land, and you must treat private property with respect." A landowner can prohibit entry, ask you to leave, or charge trespass.

Hiking: Upstream from Mile 66 there are few places to go ashore on public land. Thereafter, blocks of BLM land are available. One might wish to go ashore to explore the White Rocks or Badlands area. There are no trails, and the management plan recommends that none be built, but off-trail hiking is feasible in many places, and there are a few primitive roads. If one wants to hike along the Upper Missouri, however, we'd suggest trying the Charles M. Russell NWR downstream.

Hunting: Floating and hunting aren't usually combined. Hunters enter the areas from adjacent land. Hunting is, of course, limited to the public lands, a specified distance from campsites. Chiefly mule deer, waterfowl, upland game birds.

Fishing: This section of the Missouri River isn't one of MT's great fisheries, but it attracts many anglers. 35 fish species occur in the river. Fishermen are most likely to catch goldeye, drum, sauger, walleye, northern pike, channel catfish, carp, and smallmouth buffalo. The Upper Missouri has one of six remaining paddlefish populations.

Boating, rafting: The river has no rapids. Those named on the map are historical. However, floating requires preparation and care. Storms and submerged obstacles are among the hazards. Even minor mishaps can become major when help is hours away. Craft and gear should be well chosen and in good condition. It's essential to have the floaters' maps and know how to read them. Advice on current river level and a weather forecast are pre-launch musts. Everyone is asked to use the self-registration boxes.

Several outfitters operate on the Upper Missouri. BLM has a list.

PUBLICATIONS

Upper Missouri Wild and Scenic River. Two maps: set 1, 2; set 3, 4. $1.50 per set.
Float the Wild Missouri. Leaflet.
Some Hazards on the Upper Missouri National Wild & Scenic River. Pamphlet.
Highlights of the Upper Missouri National Wild & Scenic River and Lewis & Clark National Historic Trail. 32-page pamphlet includes history of the region.

REFERENCE: Fischer, Hank. *The Floater's Guide to Montana.* Billings, MT: Falcon Press, 1986. Pp. 72–81.

HEADQUARTERS: BLM, Lewistown District, Airport Road, Lewistown, MT 59457; (406) 538-7461.

ZONE 3

1 Beaverhead National Forest
2 Bear Trap Canyon Wilderness
3 Missouri River Headwaters State Park; Missouri Headwaters Wildlife Management Area
4 Gallatin National Forest
5 Ruby Mountains
6 Axolotl Lakes
7 Clark Canyon Reservoir
8 Blacktail Mountains
9 Centennial Mountains
10 Red Rock Lakes National Wildlife Refuge

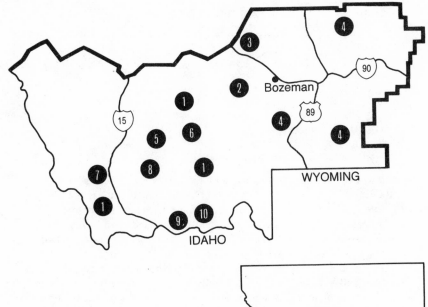

ZONE 3

Includes these counties:

Beaverhead	Madison	Gallatin
Park	Sweet Grass	

Southwestern Montana is dominated by the Rocky Mountains, which are in a less orderly array here than farther N. The Anaconda Range runs SW–NE, the Centennials W–E. Nor are the mountain ranges here so predominantly within National Forests. BLM, state, and private lands also include mountainous terrain. The NW corner of Yellowstone National Park extends into MT, and the Park's N and W entrances are in MT.

The principal rivers of the zone—the Big Hole, Beaverhead, Madison, Gallatin, and Yellowstone—flow generally N. Many Fishing Access Sites and campsites are along the Madison, Gallatin, and Yellowstone, fewer on the Beaverhead and Big Hole. All have floatable sections and good fishing. The zone has no large lakes but several provide good fishing and camping.

The Red Rock Lakes National Wildlife Refuge is part of a fine wetlands complex in the remote and scenic Centennial Valley.

AXOLOTL LAKES
U.S. Bureau of Land Management
7,804 acres.

From Virginia City on SR 287, 4 mi. SE on county road to N edge of site.

This block of public land, about 3 by 4 miles, is on the N end of the Gravelly Range. From 5,822 ft. elevation at Virginia City the land slopes up to 7,200 ft. at the site's N boundary, then to more than 9,300 ft. at the SW corner. The site's S boundary is a block of the Beaverhead National Forest, in which the ridge rises to 10,545 ft.

Open, rolling, sagebrush and grass meadows characterize the N end of the site, with aspen groves in small drainages and basins. As the land rises, Engelmann spruce appears, then forest of mixed conifers with interspersed meadows. In the still higher W and SW is a dense forest of whitebark and lodgepole pines with some subalpine fir. More than half the site is forested.

Numerous "lakes," glacial potholes, are scattered over the N portion. Most are small. Upper Axolotl Lake and Blue Lake are large enough to have names, though not enough to appear on the highway map. "Axolotl" is the name of a rare salamander found here. Before the Wilderness Act became law, BLM had recommended that the lakes and their surroundings be protected as an "Outstanding Natural Area." The lakes add much to the scenic qualities of the site, especially Blue Lake, which has a steep, forested slope as a backdrop. The site has numerous small drainages and several small perennial streams.

The Gravelly Range is excellent elk habitat, and the elk population has been increasing. Mule deer are common. The site has small seasonal populations of moose and antelope. Blue, ruffed, and spruce grouse are hunted. Golden eagles nest here. Other raptors include red-tailed and sharp-shinned hawks, northern harrier, and goshawk.

The site is scenic and readily accessible. Foot travel is easy. It offers excellent opportunities for both summer and winter camping, day hiking and backpacking, hunting, fishing, and ski touring. Even so, it has only about 300 visitors per year.

Primitive roads within the site are closed to vehicle traffic Apr. 1–July 1.

ACTIVITIES
Camping: No campground, but many attractive sites, including lakeside.
Hunting: Big game, grouse.
Fishing: Several lakes are stocked with cutthroat and rainbow trout.
Ski touring: Good open areas.

HEADQUARTERS: BLM, Butte District, 106 N. Parkmont, Butte, MT 59702; (406) 494-5059.

BEAR TRAP CANYON WILDERNESS
U.S. Bureau of Land Management
6,000 acres.

From Bozeman, about 30 mi. W on SR 84 to trailhead at N end. Floaters put in at S end, near powerhouse, 10 mi. N of Ennis by local roads.

The Lee Metcalf Wilderness, established by Congress in 1983, has 4 separate units. Three are in the Gallatin and Beaverhead NFs and are described in those entries. The fourth, Bear Trap Canyon, is the first BLM land added to the Wilderness system. Here the Madison River has cut a deep gorge through the NW end of the Madison Range, linking N and S Madison valleys. It's a spectacular gorge, 9 mi. long, with steep to vertical walls up to 1,500 ft. high. Portions of the E side adjoin the Gallatin and Beaverhead NFs.

The river, which flows W from Yellowstone NP, has several sections of interest to floaters. The rapids in the canyon are for experts. Put-in is at the S end, just below the dam. There is no trail access at this end.

Fishing has been the principal recreation activity, and it's still popular. But while the Madison River as a whole has some of MT's finest trout fishing, the quality has declined somewhat within the canyon. Ennis Lake, impounded by the dam, is filling with silt, and the water released into the canyon has been warmed, so trout tend to move further downstream. Most fishermen favor the N end of the canyon.

Hiking the canyon trail is delightful. Pets and pack animals are prohibited. BLM says the canyon is primarily a day-use area and urges visitors to use nearby campgrounds, but trailside camping in the canyon has not yet been prohibited. Summers are warm to hot, but that's when most visitors come. Winters are harsh. Snow may fall as early as late Sept., as late as May; the canyon is usually snowed in by late Nov. Average annual precipitation is about 11 in., two-thirds of this between May and Sept.

Both sides of the canyon have areas of bare rock. N slopes are forested with Douglas-fir, denser on the E side of the canyon. SW-facing slopes have scattered juniper, patches of aspen, and sagebrush.

ACTIVITIES

Camping: Red Mountain campground (BLM), off SR 84; same turnoff for campground and trailhead. 22 sites.

Hiking: 9 mi. trail on the E side of the canyon. Heaviest traffic is in summer.

Rafting: BLM has licensed two outfitters.

PUBLICATIONS

Bear Trap Canyon Wilderness. Folder with map.
Bear Trap Canyon Floater's Guide. Folder with map.

REFERENCES

Rudner, Ruth. *Bitterroot to Beartooth.* San Francisco: Sierra Club Books, 1985. Pp. 210–13.
Schneider, Bill. *The Hiker's Guide to Montana.* Billings, MT: Falcon Press, 1983. Pp. 182–84.

HEADQUARTERS: BLM, Butte District, 106 N. Parkmont, Butte, MT 59702; (406) 494-5059.

BEAVERHEAD NATIONAL FOREST
U.S. Forest Service
2,148,683 acres.

SW corner of MT. Access by local roads from I-15, US 287, and several paved state highways.

When first seen on a map, "Beaverhead" appears to be just a name applied to seven irregularly shaped blocks of land scattered over the landscape. A contour map reveals the pattern: valleys surrounded by a ring of mountains. Occupying the SW corner of MT, the Beaverhead has some of Montana's most splendid mountains, almost 40 peaks higher than 10,000 ft., several above 11,000. On the N, W, and S are the ranges of the Continental Divide, including the Anaconda, Bitterroot, Beaverhead, and Centennial; on the E the Madison and Tobacco Root ranges. Within this frame are the interior ranges: the Gravelly, Snowcrest, Fleecer, Greenwood, Tendoy, and Pioneer. These mountains with their high, glaciated peaks rise from broad valley bottoms and sagebrush foothills. In the valleys are state, BLM, and private lands, most of them in cattle and sheep ranches and hayfields.

The seven Forest blocks have Dillon as their approximate center. Largest and closest to Dillon is a block on the Pioneer Mountains, about 42 mi. long, 30 mi. wide. Next larger is a strip over 100 mi. long, mostly 6 to 10 mi. wide, on the E side of the Continental Divide; beyond a short gap it continues S and E for another 60 mi. in a strip less than 6 mi. wide. Third largest is a block on the Gravelly Range SE of Dillon. Other blocks are smaller, but each has attractions. Indeed, a remarkable quality of the Forest is that recreational opportunities are almost everywhere. Each block has high peaks, spectacular cirque basins, blue lakes, rushing streams, diverse wildlife, and inviting trails. Campgrounds are distributed throughout the Forest.

Gentle slopes characterize the mid-elevations. Although this terrain makes foot and horse travel easier, it also causes conflicts. Harvesting timber is more economical on gentle slopes, and they also encourage ORV activity, which has inflicted some damage. Still, three-fourths of the Forest is roadless and undeveloped, much of it in natural condition.

More than 1,000 mi. of fishable streams drain to the rivers in the valleys: the Beaverhead, Big Hole, Madison, Ruby, Red Rock, and Wise. Only headwaters are within the Forest, but these rivers cross BLM and state as well as private land, and along them are numerous state Fishing Access Sites. Within the Forest are 254 lakes, most of them high mountain lakes with surface areas of less than 10 acres. The largest is long, narrow Cliff Lake with 679 acres, accessible by road.

Climate: Summers are cool with brief hot spells. Winters are cold, with readings of −50°F not uncommon at high elevations. The Forest is in the rain shadow of the Continental Divide ranges. Average annual precipitation in the valleys is about 12 in., on high slopes up to 50 in. and more. Three-fourths of the moisture is received as snow between Oct. and Apr.

Plants: About one-half of the area is forested. Lower elevations are grasslands. Sagebrush dominates the gentle slopes between grassland and forest. Douglas-fir occupies the drier portions of the transition zone, lodgepole pine the sites with more moisture. Subalpine fir and whitebark pine are the principal upper-elevation species. Pinegrass and grouse whortleberry are prominent in the understory.

No wildflower list is available, but the Yellowstone NP guides can be used. A few of the many species noted were buttercup, shootingstar, pasqueflower, spring beauty, yarrow, geranium, lupine, alpine sunflower, penstemon, forget-me-not, Indian paintbrush, larkspur.

Birds: Checklist of 271 species available. The number and diversity of species is greater than we found in sites further N. The Beaverhead includes a northern component of the Greater Yellowstone Ecosystem, a region of great diversity.

Abundant or common species of the Beaverhead include eared and western grebes, white pelican, double-crested cormorant, American bittern, whistling and trumpeter swans, Canada goose, mallard, gadwall, pintail; green-winged, blue-winged, and cinnamon teals; American wigeon, northern shoveler, redhead, canvasback, greater and lesser scaup, Barrow's goldeneye, red-tailed and rough-legged hawks, golden eagle, northern harrier, American kestrel; blue, Franklin's, ruffed, and sage grouse; sandhill crane, sora, American coot, killdeer, common snipe, spotted sandpiper, willet, American avocet, Wilson's phalarope; California, ring-billed, and Franklin's gulls; Forster's tern, rock and mourning doves. Owls: screech, great horned, short-eared, saw-whet. Poor-will, common nighthawk, white-throated swift, rufous and calliope hummingbirds, belted kingfisher, northern flicker; Lewis', hairy, and downy woodpeckers; yellow-bellied sapsucker, eastern and western kingbirds, Say's phoebe. Flycatchers: Traill's, Hammond's, dusky, olive-sided. Western wood-pewee, horned lark. Swallows: violet-green, tree, bank, rough-winged, barn, cliff. Gray and Steller's jays, black-billed magpie, common raven, American crow, Clark's nutcracker, black-capped and mountain chickadees; white-breasted, red-breasted, and pygmy nuthatches; brown creeper, dipper. Wrens: house, marsh, canyon, rock. Gray catbird, sage thrasher, American robin, hermit and Swainson's thrushes, veery, mountain bluebird, Townsend's solitaire, golden-crowned and ruby-crowned kinglets, water pipit, Bohemian and cedar waxwings, European starling, solitary and red-eyed vireos. Warblers: orange-crowned, yellow, yellow-rumped, black-throated gray, Townsend's, MacGillivray's, common yellowthroat, yellow-breasted chat, Wilson's, American redstart. Western meadowlark; yellow-headed, red-winged, and Brewer's blackbirds; northern oriole, brown-headed cowbird, western tanager; black-headed, evening, and pine grosbeaks; lazuli bunting; Cassin's, house, and gray-crowned rosy finches; pine siskin, American goldfinch, red crossbill, rufous-sided towhee. Sparrows: savannah, grasshopper, vesper, lark, tree, chipping, Brewer's, white-crowned, fox, Lincoln's, song. Dark-eyed junco, lapland longspur, snow bunting.

Mammals: Checklist of 75 species available. Abundant or common species include vagrant, dusky, and Merriam shrews. Myotis: little brown, Yuma, long-eared, long-legged, small-footed. Bats: silver-haired, big brown, hoary, western big-eared. Pika, mountain cottontail, snowshoe hare, whitetail jack-rabbit, least chipmunk, yellowbelly marmot, Richardson ground squirrel, golden-mantled and red squirrels, northern pocket gopher, beaver, deer mouse, northern grasshopper mouse, bushytail woodrat. Voles: red-backed, heather, meadow, longtail, sagebrush. Muskrat, western jumping mouse, porcupine, coyote, black bear, short-tail and long-tail weasels, mink, badger, striped skunk, mountain lion, bobcat, elk, mule and whitetail deer, pronghorn, mountain goat.

Reptiles and amphibians: Checklist of 22 species available. Abundant or common species include tiger salamander, western toad; chorus, spotted, and leopard frogs. Snakes: yellow-bellied racer, gopher snake, common and western garter snakes.

FEATURES

Anaconda-Pintler Wilderness, 72,537 acres, plus 85,337 acres in the Bitterroot and Deerlodge NFs. In the far NW corner of the Forest, straddling 30 mi. of the Anaconda Range and Continental Divide. Access from SR 43 by Forest Road 185 along Pintler Creek; trailhead at Pintler campground. Elevations from 5,400 ft, to 10,793 ft. on West Goat Peak. Sagebrush, willow flats, ponderosa pine, Douglas-fir, lodgepole pine, and spruce comprise the lower elevation vegetation. These blend into aspen, subalpine fir, whitebark pine, and subalpine larch with increasing altitude, a region of forest, open parks, and lakes on both sides of the Divide. The alpine zone has high, jagged peaks, with talus slopes, rock outcroppings, tarns, and snowfields. Trails generally follow drainages. The projected Continental Divide Trail has not been constructed, but an existing trail approximates a section of the Divide. Visitor use of the area is relatively light.

Lee Metcalf Wilderness, 259,000 acres, of which 101,400 acres are in the Beaverhead NF. This is not a single block of Wilderness but 4 separate units:

Bear Trap Canyon, 6,000 acres, was included in the legislation establishing the Wilderness. It adjoins the Forest but is on BLM land. See entry.

Spanish Peaks, 78,000 acres, chiefly in the Gallatin NF, 7,640 acres on the Beaverhead. E of Ennis, on the Madison Range. Steep, rugged, glaciated peaks rising to more than 11,000 ft. Cirque basins and lakes. Access is by local roads from US 287. Jack Creek campground is a good trailhead.

Taylor-Hilgard, 93,800 acres on the Beaverhead, a strip about 30 mi. long on the crest of the Madison Range. SE of Ennis. The W boundary is largely congruent with the Forest boundary. Access by local roads from US 287. Several peaks above 11,000 ft.

Monument Mountains, the fourth block, is entirely in the Gallatin NF. See entry.

North Big Hole Roadless Area, 53,098 acres, plus 3,691 acres on the Bitterroot NF, includes most of the Forest land on the S boundary of the Anaconda

Wilderness. These are the gentle to moderately steep foothills of the Anaconda Range, including several glacial trough valleys, narrow canyons, and terminal moraines. Most of the land is forested with subalpine fir, lodgepole pine, Douglas-fir, and spruce. The area offers opportunities for camping, hiking, hunting and fishing.

East and West Pioneer Roadless Areas, 235,075 acres. This large area lies between Wisdom and Melrose, with the Big Hole River Valley on the W, N, and E. It is bisected by Forest Road 484 extending S from Wise River. This is the largest roadless area within the Forest, and the Pioneer Range has some of the Forest's highest peaks, over 11,000 ft. The chain of mountains has steep cirque headwalls, rocky cirque basins with numerous scenic mountain lakes, glacial trough valleys. As on other high ranges of the Forest, areas of grass and sagebrush are at the low elevations, conifer forests on the middle slopes, barren peaks and small alpine meadows above timberline. Access is from the highways that surround the block and from the Wise River road, along which are several campgrounds. A good trail system provides routes to many of the high lakes. Opportunities for backpacking, camping, horse riding, hunting, fishing. Some areas have considerable ORV use.

Middle Mountain-Tobacco Roots Roadless Area, 58,336 acres, plus 34,991 acres in the Deerlodge NF. The Tobacco Roots are an isolated range E of Twin Bridges on SR 41. The Middle Mountain area, the central portion of the range, is rugged and diverse, with peaks over 10,000 ft. and many glacial lakes in cirque basins. Forest Road 107 penetrates to the heart of the area from the NE, and several other roads provide access to lakes and campgrounds, dividing the area into several roadless tracts. Mill Creek Road provides access to the heavily used Branham Lakes at the fringe of the alpine zone. Opportunities for camping, hiking, hunting, fishing, and winter sports.

Snowcrest Mountain Roadless Area, 97,630 acres. The Snowcrest Range, 20 mi. long, is SW of Dillon. Access is from Forest Road 100, S from Alder on SR 287, or by the Blacktail Deer road E from Dillon. A trail along the crest is often above 9,500 ft. elevation, with splendid vistas. It may not be open until mid-July. The East Fork of Blacktail Deer Creek is a popular fishing stream. Hunting, camping, and hiking are the principal activities.

Other roadless areas. To date, only 8% of the Forest is classified as Wilderness. Another 66% is in 34 roadless areas distributed throughout the Forest. Of these, 9 adjoin roadless areas in adjoining NFs. How many of these will ultimately be given Wilderness protection is in controversy. The Forest visitor is well advised to stop at a Ranger District office for advice on where to go.

ACTIVITIES

Camping: 30 campgrounds, 246 sites. Season generally May 30–Labor Day, but most campgrounds can be used out of season, without water, if accessible.

A number of cabins used by work crews in summer are available for winter recreation use, by reservation.

Hiking, backpacking: 1,632 mi. of trails, of which 895 are considered in adequate condition. There are trails for easy day hikes and for several days of backcountry travel. Destinations such as Lake of the Woods, the Bobcat Lakes, Minneopa Lake, Ajax Lake, Divide Creek Lake, and others are attractive. Many of the trails are described in the Recreation Opportunities Guide (ROG) available at HQ and Ranger District offices.

Many trails are difficult to find because of poor marking and because use is too light to maintain a visible treadway. However, much of the country is so open that off-trail travel is relatively easy.

Hunting: Said to be excellent, big game including elk, mule deer, moose, pronghorn, black bear, mountain goat, bighorn sheep.

Fishing: The Big Hole River has been called "one of the nation's truly great fly-fishing waters for trophy grayling and brook, rainbow, and brown trout," as well as "one of the most beautiful undammed rivers." Fishermen have similar praise for the Beaverhead and Madison rivers. Many Forest lakes and streams are well supplied with grayling; cutthroat, rainbow, brook, brown, and golden trout; and mountain whitefish.

Horse riding: Most horse use is in conjunction with hunting, but summer horsepacking is increasing.

Boating: Not a major activity. Long, narrow Cliff Lake, 679 acres, is the largest. Nearby are Wade and Elk lakes. These three, in the Madison River drainage, are the only ones on which power boats can be used. Nine others are closed to gasoline motors.

Skiing: Maverick Mountain, 38 mi. NW of Dillon on SR 278. Lifts, 7 trails.

Ski touring: Marked and groomed trails in several locations. Also ski mountaineering trails.

INTERPRETATION

Information and publications are available at HQ and Ranger District offices.

The Forest has no visitor center, campfire programs, other naturalist programs.

PUBLICATIONS

Forest Visitor's Map. $1.

Visitor Information. Pamphlet.

Anaconda-Pintler Wilderness map. $1.

Self-guided Range Tour map. Auto tour guide, Ruby River-Gravelly Range.

Camping Guide.

Lake inventory.

Information pages:

Lee Metcalf Wilderness.

Checklists: birds, mammals, reptiles and amphibians, fishes.

Marked snowmobile trails.

Maverick Mountain ski area.

Elkhorn-Wise River winter sports area.

Ski touring trails.
Ski mountaineering trails.
Forest Service cabins.
Outfitter-guide list.

REFERENCES

Rudner, Ruth. *Bitterroot to Beartooth.* San Francisco: Sierra Club, 1985. Pp. 101–61, 183–88.

Schneider, Bill. *The Hiker's Guide to Montana.* Billings, MT: Falcon Press, 1983. Pp. 76–86, 91–99.

Turbak, Gary. *The Traveler's Guide to Montana.* Billings, MT: Falcon Press, 1983. Pp. 109, 222–31.

HEADQUARTERS: P.O. Box 1258, Dillon, MT 59725; (406) 683-3900.

RANGER DISTRICTS: Dillon R.D., P.O. Box 1258, Dillon, MT, 59725; (406) 683-3960. Wise River R.D., P.O. Box 86, Wise River, MT 59762; (406) 832-3178. Wisdom R.D., P.O. Box 238, Wisdom, MT 59761; (406) 689-3243. Sheridan R.D., P.O. Box 428, Sheridan, MT 59749; (406) 842-5432. Madison R.D., Rt. 2, Box 5, Ennis, MT 59729; (406) 682-4253.

BLACKTAIL MOUNTAINS
U.S. Bureau of Land Management
17,479 acres.

From SR 41 in Dillon, turn S on Blacktail County Road at the Barrett Memorial Hospital. In 26 mi., turn left into the Blacktail Elk Winter Range (well marked) and continue to the site. The county road continues S to the Centennial Valley and Red Rock Lakes National Wildlife Refuge (see entry).

The road S from Dillon, shown but not numbered on the highway map, follows the course of Blacktail Creek. The Blacktail Mountains, about 16 mi. NW–SE, rise steeply on the W side of the creek valley. Slopes on the other side of the range are gentler. Elevation at the creek is about 5,000 ft. The range has 5 peaks above 9,000 ft.

The site is about 11 mi. long, 1 to 5 mi. wide. Deep drainages from the ridge flow generally NE toward Blacktail Creek. Although these are natural access routes, a mile-wide strip between site and road is privately owned. A primitive road in Jake Canyon, about 19 mi. S of Dillon, has been used by hunters and other visitors, but the owner can close it at will. BLM is seeking legal access through Ashbough Canyon near the N end of the site.

The many deep canyons are heavily timbered with Engelmann spruce, Douglas-fir, and limber pine. Most of them rise to dramatic cliffs and head-walls, moderate to severe obstacles for hikers and horsemen. Several of the canyons have running water most of the year. The ridgetop is rolling, open, and scenic. In all, about 60% of the site is forested, the remainder rock outcrops, scree slopes, or grassland.

Recreation visits are estimated at 550 per year. Most of the visitors are hunters seeking mule deer, elk, and grouse. Moose and black bear have been sighted in the unit, but populations are small.

About 11,000 acres, the N portion of the site, have been recommended for Wilderness status.

HEADQUARTERS: BLM, Butte District, 106 N. Parkmont, Butte, MT 59702; (406) 494-5059.

CENTENNIAL MOUNTAINS
U.S. Bureau of Land Management; U.S. Forest Service
43,390 acres in MT; 45,450 acres in ID.

MT trail access from Monida on I-15 and from the road to the Red Rock Lakes National Wildlife Refuge, 28 mi. E of Monida.

Seen from the Island Park area of ID, the snow-capped Centennials are an impressive feature of the landscape. The Continental Divide runs along their crest, separating ID from MT, the Snake River plain from the Centennial Valley. The ID side is within the Targhee NF and described in that entry. The 38 mi. of hiking trails in ID are used chiefly by hunters, on foot or horseback.

Most of the land on the MT side is managed by BLM, although about 4,500 acres are in the Beaverhead NF. The entire area has been studied for Wilderness suitability. It adjoins the Red Rock Lakes National Wildlife Refuge (see entry), which has been designated a Wilderness.

The Centennials, about 34 mi. long, are one of the few W–E trending ranges in the northern Rockies. Elevations range from 6,400 ft. in the valleys to over 9,000 ft. on the summits of Mt. Jefferson and of Baldy, Slide, Taylor, and Sawtell mountains. The study area is 2 to 8 mi. wide. The ID side is character-ized by moderately steep, broad open ridges separated by forested drainages. On the MT side, the range rises abruptly along a fault zone, more than 3,000 ft. in the mile from the Refuge to the Divide.

Most of the area is forested. Predominant habitat types are Douglas-fir and western spruce-fir. The highest slopes are an alpine zone with hardy communities of grasses and stringers of scattered Douglas-fir, subalpine fir, and whitebark pine. The subalpine zone is dominated by subalpine fir interspersed with forb and grass meadows and sagebrush parks. Next lower is a zone of mature Douglas-fir, with lodgepole pine covering disturbed sites. Aspen stands occur in many of the drainages.

Average annual precipitation ranges from 15 in. in the valleys to 50 in. along the Divide, where most falls as snow. Winters are cold up there. Snow usually persists into late June or early July; we saw substantial snow patches in Aug.

More than half of the visitor use on the MT side is hunting, followed by hiking, fishing, and camping in summer, snowmobiling and ski touring in winter. The area has a few small lakes and streams. Most fishing is on the ID side, or in the Centennial Valley outside the study area. Most of the MT side is too steep for ORVs.

Our maps show a few primitive roads and trails from the valley to passes on the Divide. The proposed Continental Divide Trail hasn't been established here. Some portions of a crest trail are in place, but neither mapped nor signed. A hundred or so people hike along the Divide each summer.

Wildlife: Mule deer are common throughout the area spring to fall. Elk are also common, especially in the W half. Moose are abundant in riparian areas in summer. Black bear are also common. Game birds include blue and ruffed grouse. Other birds of interest include golden eagle, long-eared owl, and prairie falcon. Grizzly bear have been reported 16 times in a decade.

ACTIVITIES

Camping: At Red Rock Lakes NWR (see entry) or informal sites.

Hiking, backpacking: Plenty of scenery and solitude. No well-developed trail system. Ruth Rudner's *Bitterroot to Beartooth* is the best trail guide we found. Also consult BLM.

REFERENCE:

Rudner, Ruth. *Bitterroot to Beartooth.* San Francisco: Sierra Club Books, 1985. Pp. 162–72; map.

HEADQUARTERS: BLM, Butte District, 106 N. Parkmont, Butte, MT 59702; (406) 494-5059.

CLARK CANYON RESERVOIR
Montana Department of Fish, Wildlife & Parks
6,000 acres of water; 1,200 acres of land.

On I-15 about 20 mi. S of Dillon.

The reservoir is a triangle, each side 3 1/2 to 4 mi. long. Three valleys meet here. Red Rock River flows in from the S, Horse Prairie Creek from the W. Outflow is to the Beaverhead River. The U.S. Bureau of Reclamation, which built the reservoir in 1964, gave responsibility for fish and wildlife management to the state. It's a popular fishing lake. The shoreline is readily accessible, with several public use areas.

Elevation is 5,520 ft. The lake is surrounded by low grass and marshland. Beyond are sagebrush-grass foothills and low mountain ranges. The site is a nesting area for ducks, a rest stop during migrations of ducks and geese. However, early freezeup and lack of nearby grainfields discourage late migrants.

Pheasants are found on the W side, along the creek. Both tributaries have lush bottomlands and marsh, with willows, sedges, and cattails. Deer, muskrat, beaver, and ground squirrel are often seen.

NEARBY: Most of the land to the S is BLM. Limekiln Canyon, 2 mi. S, and Bell Canyon, 4 mi. S, offer attractive day hiking possibilities. Canyon walls are 300 to 700 ft. high. Douglas-fir, sagebrush, and mountain-mahogany are the main canyon vegetation.

HEADQUARTERS: Region 3, Montana State University Campus, Bozeman, MT 59715; (406) 994-3553.

GALLATIN NATIONAL FOREST
U.S. Forest Service
1,738,138 acres; 2,149,552 acres within boundaries.

On the W and N boundaries of Yellowstone NP. Access from US 287, 191, and 89.

Most of the 411,414 acres of non-Forest land is in areas of checkerboard, Forest land alternating with timber company, other private, and state landholdings in mile-square blocks. The main Forest area is in two huge and relatively unbroken blocks adjoining Yellowstone NP. This is a vast region with snowy peaks, alpine meadows, deep forest, cascading streams in scenic canyons, great rivers, large lakes and high mountain ponds, abundant fish and wildlife. It adjoins the Beaverhead NF on the W, the Custer NF on the E, the Shoshone NF at the WY boundary E of Yellowstone NP.

More than 40% of the Forest is designated Wilderness, an exceptionally high proportion. Another 30% is roadless and undeveloped. Excluding the checkerboard areas, about 90% of the Forest is roadless. The Absaroka-

Beartooth Wilderness alone has 575,000 acres on the Gallatin, plus 373,000 acres on the Custer and Shoshone NFs, with additional large roadless areas adjoining.

Despite the popularity of nearby Yellowstone, more than two million visitor-days per year are recorded in the Gallatin. One-third of this traffic is at developed sites, including camp and picnic grounds, ski areas, boat launch sites, and the visitor center at Earthquake Lake. Some lakes and the trails leading to them have relatively heavy summer use, but a Ranger District can offer advice on how to find solitude in splendid surroundings.

The Forest is in the Rocky Mountain region, where N–S mountain ranges separated by foothills and flat valley floors are the characteristic pattern. The Gallatin and Madison ranges occupy the western half of the Forest, separated by the canyon of the Gallatin River. Both have peaks over 10,000 ft. The Bridgers, N of Bozeman and Livingston, are almost as high, reaching to 9,800 ft. N of Big Timber are the Crazy Mountains, which have several peaks higher than 10,000 ft. The highest and wildest country is on the Absaroka-Beartooth ranges.

Less than half of the Forest area has slopes classified as "gentle," grades of less than 40%. These are adjacent to the larger streams and along ridges. Midslopes between streams and ridges are steep, those rising above major streams very steep.

The Forest's rivers—the Yellowstone, Gallatin, Madison, Boulder, and their tributaries—are famous among fishermen. The Forest has over 1,000 mi. of fishing streams and 18,800 acres of lakes. Largest lake is Hebgen, 8,000 acres, about 14 mi. long, near the W entrance to Yellowstone.

Climate: Available weather information is scanty, but data for the Beaverhead NF and Yellowstone NP are indicative. Summers are generally warm. In winter, subzero invasions of arctic air may be followed by warm, dry chinook winds. Apr. through June is a rainy period. High elevations receive most of their moisture as snow.

At Livingston, N of the Forest, elevation 4,489 ft., Jan. average temperature is 26°F, July's 69°; annual precipitation is 15 in. At Red Lodge, E of the Forest, elevation 5,548 ft., Jan. average is 21°F, July's 62°; annual precipitation 18 in. At Hebgen Dam, W of Yellowstone, elevation 6,548 ft., Jan. average is 12°, July's 60°; annual precipitation 23 in. The mountains receive up to 5 times as much precipitation.

Plants: More than three-fourths of the area is forested. The typical pattern begins with grasslands at the lowest elevations, changing to limber pine and/or Douglas-fir above, then a zone with lodgepole pine, followed by spruce or subalpine fir. Whitebark pine dominates the zone just below timberline, above which is alpine tundra or alpine turf.

Wildlife: No species checklists are available. The checklists for the Beaverhead NF and Yellowstone NP approximate the species occurring in the Gallatin. Wetlands along the Yellowstone, Gallatin, and Upper Madison

River tributaries provide nesting and resting habitat for a great variety of waterfowl and shorebirds. The Forest provides habitat for 14 raptor species and 9 species of owls.

The Forest is used by two large migratory herds of elk. Wintering elk population in the Forest is about 5,600, with 4,200 more on adjacent lands. Summer population of mule deer is estimated at well over 13,000. Other big game includes moose, bighorn sheep, mountain goat, black bear, and whitetail deer. The areas adjoining Yellowstone are occupied grizzly bear habitat, and visitors are advised to take precautions.

Common mammals include beaver, porcupine, marmot, golden-mantled squirrel, gopher, chipmunk, coyote.

FEATURES

Absaroka-Beartooth Wilderness, 574,721 acres, plus 345,589 acres in the Custer NF and 27,750 acres in the Shoshone NF (WY). The Wilderness is based on two quite different ranges. On the W are the Absarokas, a chain of mountains with rugged peaks above 9,000 ft. elevation, Mt. Cowan rising to 11,200 ft. Although the terrain includes rocky ridges, the Absarokas are gentler than the Beartooths, with rolling mountains and foothills and broad, forested valleys. Three-fourths of the Absaroka is below timberline, and precipitation is greater than in the Beartooth.

On the E the Beartooth Mountains, so named for their white limestone cliffs, have some of Montana's most rugged country. Elevations range from 5,200 ft. on the Stillwater River to 12,799 ft. on Granite Peak, highest in the state; more than two dozen others top 12,000 ft. Here are glaciers, high, broad tundra plateaus, deep canyons, and hundreds of high lakes. One Forest publication claims "more than 5,000 waterfalls," no doubt an exaggeration, but there are a great many. Timberline is at about 9,000 ft.

We walked over one of the tundra plateaus in early June. Snow still covered about half of it; hundreds of glacier lilies and globeflowers were in bloom above the melting snow. Snowmelt here is a primary source of 14 major streams, including the Boulder, Stillwater, and Clark's Fork of the Yellowstone.

Access is easy. From Big Timber on I-90, an all-weather cherry-stemmed road shown on the highway map runs S along the Boulder River into the heart of the Wilderness. Campgrounds and trailheads are along the way. Other access routes run from US 89 on the W side, and by trail from Yellowstone NP.

Wildlife is abundant in the forested valleys. Few mammals appear on the barren ridges except pika and mountain goat. The Wilderness has a resident population of grizzly bear.

Trout fishing is said to be excellent in some of the streams and lakes, but the fisherman should know where to go. Some fishing waters are best reached by packhorse. Outfitter-guide services offer both hunting and fishing expeditions.

The Wilderness has an extensive trail network, most trails following drainages. Because of easy access, it is MT's most-used Wilderness. Some trails show the signs of heavy use, especially by horses, and some lake shores have been degraded. Visitors are advised to obtain the current regulations, as changes are in prospect.

Beartooth Plateau. US 212 from Red Lodge to the NE entrance of Yellowstone NP is as scenic a route as one can find anywhere. It dips into WY, climbs to Beartooth Pass at 10,947 ft., returns to MT near Colter Pass, and is in the Gallatin NF for about 8 mi. before the Yellowstone entrance. N of US 212, on both sides of the MT-WY line, is a tree-covered plateau at about 8,200 ft. elevation with an incredible number of lakes. (Although the MT portion is in the Gallatin NF and the WY portion in the Shoshone NF, the area is best seen on the Custer NF map.) Much of the Gallatin portion is in the Absaroka-Beartooth Wilderness. Jeep roads in the non-Wilderness portion provide access to a number of popular lakes.

Lee Metcalf Wilderness, 140,594 acres, plus 108,350 acres in the Beaverhead NF, has three parts. Outdoorsmen who knew this region before 1983 will remember the Spanish Peaks Primitive Area; that's now the Spanish Peaks Unit. It's just W of US 191 about 16 mi. S of Gallatin Gateway. The Taylor Hilgard Unit is just N of the Madison River Canyon Earthquake Area on US 287. These two larger units are separated by a checkerboard area of timber company and private land. The Monument Mountain Unit, smallest of the three, has a common boundary with Yellowstone NP extending S from the point where US 191 enters the Park from the N.

Congress also designated the Cabin Creek Wildlife and Recreation Management Area, 36,759 acres, which lies between the Taylor Hilgard and Monument Mountain units. Congress gave first priority to wildlife management in this area, which is elk winter range and grizzly bear habitat, but permitted continued use of the Big Sky Snowmobile Trail, as well as some management practices not allowed in Wildernesses. Hiking trails link all these areas.

The region encompasses almost the entire length of the Madison Range. The glaciated landscape includes rocky peaks and ridges, U-shaped valleys, and many cirque basins. Major streams draining the area flow E into Yellowstone NP or the Gallatin River, S and W to the Madison River.

The Spanish Peaks area has been most attractive to visitors, and some trails are heavily used. The scenery is spectacular, with many high peaks and cirque lakes. It's accessible, and it has a well-developed trail system. Hunters favor the area, in part for its population of mountain sheep.

Access to the Taylor-Hilgard area, chiefly from US 287, isn't quite as easy, but there are good trails and fine scenery. Hilgard Basin is splendid, subalpine meadows and lakes surrounded by snow-capped mountains.

The Monument Mountain unit is less accessible and lightly used. It's a likely place to meet a grizzly.

Hyalite-Porcupine-Buffalo Horn area, 155,000 acres. The Wilderness Study Act required that this and eight other National Forest areas be studied for Wilderness suitability. Forest management recommended that no part of this area be so designated, but that 23,100 acres in the Hyalite Peaks area be reserved for public recreation and that a National Recreation Trail be established along the Gallatin Crest. The area is on the Gallatin Range, extending about 36 mi. from the Hyalite Peaks to the NW corner of Yellowstone NP. The Hyalites are a cluster of peaks in the 10,000-ft. range about 18 mi. S of Bozeman, a fine scenic area with cirque basins, lakes, and waterfalls. Access to the Hyalites is by Hyalite Canyon Road from Bozeman. Forest campgrounds and trailheads are near Hyalite Reservoir, just N of the study area boundary. Access to trailheads in the S of the area is by Forest and local roads from US 89 and 191. The southern portion has moderately rolling terrain.

This is a checkerboard area. The 155,000 acres include 42,700 acres of timber company and other private land, 6,650 acres of state and city land. Although few developments have altered the natural qualities of the landscape, such mixed ownership was a major obstacle to Wilderness designation.

Recreational use is about 45,000 visitor-days per year, chiefly for hiking, camping, snowmobiling, fishing, hunting, trailbike riding, ski touring, and climbing.

Bridger Range is N of Bozeman, and access is by local roads from there. This is an isolated block of Forest land, about 22 mi. N–S, 4 to 6 mi. W–E. We overlooked it, but Ruth Rudner in *Bitterroot to Beartooth* (see References) wrote that these mountains deserve mention "partly because of their beauty and partly because they offer marvelous and little-used ridge walks that provide a good alternative to the crowds in the Lee Metcalf Wilderness or in Hyalite, both just a few miles away." Highest peak is Sacajawea, 9,665 ft.; several others are above 9,000 ft. Fishing in two lakes and several streams. Bridger Bowl ski area is on the E side of the area.

Crazy Mountains Roadless Area, 107,647 acres, plus 28,900 acres in the Lewis & Clark NF 20 mi. NE of Livingston, between US 89 and 191, although several miles from either. The map shows it as a checkerboard of Forest and private land, detached from the main Forest area. Despite the inholdings, the landscape is nearly pristine. This isolated range rises abruptly from rolling ranchlands on the E and S, overlooking the broad Shields River Valley on the W. Crazy Mountains, 11,214 ft., is highest of several in a central core. High cirque basins surround cold lakes. Streams cascade down through mountain meadows and deep forest. People who know the area come for hiking, backpacking, fishing, hunting, horse riding, and snowmobiling.

Madison River Canyon Earthquake Area. From West Yellowstone, 8 mi. W on US 287. On the night of 17 August 1959, a major earthquake caused a great landslide at the W end of Madison Canyon, so forceful that great boulders were carried far up the opposite hillside. A Forest Service campground was buried, killing a number of campers. The N shore of Hebgen Lake dropped 18 ft., portions of the highway fell into the lake, and Hebgen Dam was threatened. The slide blocked the river, forming Earthquake Lake, and crews hastily cut a spillway to release some of the pent-up water. The story is told at a visitor center just off the reconstructed highway and by a self-guided auto tour.

INTERPRETATION

Visitor center and *self-guided auto tour* at the Madison Earthquake Site, 8 mi. W of West Yellowstone on US 287.

Campfire programs at Cook City on US 212, E of Yellowstone NP. Fri.–Sat. only, in summer.

Recreation Opportunities Guide, looseleaf, can be seen at HQ and at the Bozeman and Livingston Ranger District offices. Information on camping, hiking, horse riding, hunting, fishing, gathering and identification, cross-country skiing and snowshoeing, etc.

ACTIVITIES

Camping: 37 campgrounds, 902 sites. Open season is generally June 1–Sept. 15. Unless gated and signed, campgrounds can be used after closing, without water or services. Campgrounds are seldom full. Those near West Yellowstone are closed to tent camping because of grizzly bears.

Hiking, backpacking: The Forest has 1,853 mi. of inventoried trails, of which 838 mi. are in the Absaroka-Beartooth and Lee Metcalf Wildernesses. Wilderness trails are generally serviceable. Almost half of the non-Wilderness trails are in need of repair or relocation. However, there are good trails in every part of the Forest, including 7 National Recreation Trails ranging from a quarter-mi. trail suitable for the handicapped to the 24-mi. Bridger Mountain Trail and 28-mi. Two-Top Snowmobile Trail. ROG pages for the principal trails have sketch maps, profiles, detailed descriptions, and information on attractions and considerations, length, difficulty, season, and destinations. Copies of selected pages are provided on request.

Hunting: Elk and mule deer are the chief big game species. Moose, bighorn sheep, mountain goat, black bear, and whitetail deer are hunted less intensively. Also hunting for sage, blue, and Franklin's grouse; chukar, wild turkey, and waterfowl.

Fishing: Sportsmen speak of the "legendary Madison," a blue-ribbon trout stream flowing W from Yellowstone NP. The Boulder also offers fine trout fishing. All fishing is for coldwater species. The Forest has over 1,000 mi. of fishing streams and 18,800 acres of lakes with fish. Not all lakes are productive; some at high elevations are barren.

Horse riding: Saddle horse and pack stock travel is increasingly popular, both in conjunction with hunting and fishing, and for summer recreation. The ROG has trail information and advice. A list of outfitters is available.

Boating: Hebgen Lake, Earthquake Lake, Hyalite Reservoir, major rivers.

Rafting, kayaking: Whitewater on the West Gallatin River, Yankee Jim

Canyon on the Yellowstone, Beartrap Canyon on the Madison. All served by outfitters.

Skiing: Ski areas at Big Sky and Bridger Bowl.

Ski touring. The ROG has pages on marked and groomed trails. Many other opportunities throughout the Forest.

PUBLICATIONS

Forest map. $1.

Absaroka-Beartooth Wilderness map. $1.

Information pages:

Camp and picnic areas.

Lee Metcalf Wilderness.

Absaroka-Beartooth Wilderness.

Occupied Grizzly Bear Habitat.

Climbers and Hikers Guide to the Bridger Range and Hyalite Peaks. 10 pp. Descriptions, maps.

Hiking and Climbing in the Gallatin National Forest. 14 pp. with maps.

Hiking, Climbing, Skiing, etc., Livingston Ranger District.

Ski Touring in the Gallatin National Forest.

Madison River Canyon Earthquake Area:

Leaflet.

Auto tour guide.

REFERENCES

Rudner, Ruth. *Bitteroot to Beartooth.* San Francisco: Sierra Club, 1985. Pp. 214–65.

Schneider, Bill. *The Hiker's Guide to Montana.* Billings, MT: Falcon Press, 1983. Pp. 184–206, 208–15, 222–36.

Turbak, Gary. *The Traveler's Guide to Montana.* Billings, MT: Falcon Press, 1983. Pp. 132–33, 195.

HEADQUARTERS: Box 130, Federal Building, Bozeman, MT 59715; (406) 587-5271.

RANGER DISTRICTS: Bozeman R.D., 601 Nikles, Bozeman, MT 59715; (406) 587-6920. Hebgen R.D., P.O. Box 520, West Yellowstone, MT 59758; (406) 646-7369. Big Timber R.D., P.O. Box A, Big Timber, MT 59001; (406) 932-5155. Livingston R.D., Route 62, Box 3197, Livingston, MT 59047; (406) 222-1892. Gardiner R.D., P.O. Box 5, Gardiner, MT 59030; (406) 848-7375.

MISSOURI HEADWATERS STATE PARK; MISSOURI HEADWATERS WILDLIFE MANAGEMENT AREA

Montana Department of Fish, Wildlife & Parks

2,165 acres; 523 acres are SP.

From Three Forks on I-90, 3 mi. E on US 10, then 3 mi. N on SR 286.

At Three Forks, the Gallatin, Madison, and Jefferson rivers come together to form the Missouri. This is flat land at about 4,000 ft. elevation. The rivers are broad, braided, meandering, slow-moving. The campground extends for about a mile along the Missouri banks.

The Wildlife Management Area has several tracts: the middle one at the confluence of the three rivers, including the State Park; Grey Cliff, 14 mi. up the Madison River; and Fairweather, 15 mi. down the Missouri. These lands were acquired to provide fishing access and developed as year-round habitat for pheasant and waterfowl. Development included planting feed crops. Surrounding lands are privately owned.

The sites are generally low-lying, brushy, with scattered willows and cottonwoods. Pheasants, ducks, and Canada geese use all three sites. Mule and whitetail deer are frequent visitors, moose appearing occasionally.

ACTIVITIES

Camping and picnicking are the primary visitor activities, followed by fishing. Few hunters use the areas.

Camping: 20 sites. May 15–Sept. 15.

Fishing: Trout. Judged "good, but rarely spectacular."

Boating: Ramp. The Toston Dam is about 15 mi. downstream.

NEARBY: Other Fishing Access Sites are on all four rivers.

HEADQUARTERS: Montana Department of Fish, Wildlife & Parks, Bozeman Regional Office, 8695 Huffine Lane, Bozeman, MT 59715; (406) 586-5419.

RED ROCK LAKES NATIONAL WILDLIFE REFUGE

U.S. Fish and Wildlife Service

40,300 acres, including 9,000 acres of water.

From Monida on I-15, just N of the ID border, E 28 mi. to Lakeview on unpaved road.

We don't recall another National Wildlife Refuge leaflet beginning with praise for wildflowers. That's but one of the unusual aspects of Red Rock Lakes. It's at higher elevation than most waterfowl refuges, about 6,600 ft., in the Centennial Valley, rising to over 9,000 ft. The Centennial Mountains on the S of the valley run W–E; most ranges of the region run N–S. The Refuge has camping; few federal refuges do. The entire Refuge has been proclaimed a National Natural Landmark. Many of its visitors come to fish, not to admire the birds, though there are many to admire.

It was established in 1935 to save the trumpeter swan. Killing swans for their feathers and meat had reduced the trumpeter population in the Lower 48 to 69 individuals. Two-thirds of them nested in the Centennial Valley. The Refuge provided safe and suitable habitat. By the 1950s there were enough swans to begin transplants, and populations were established in Nevada, Oregon, and South Dakota. The Alaskan trumpeter swan had not been in danger during this period.

The lakes and marshes of this high mountain valley grassland are amply supplied with water from snowmelt on the Centennials. Annual precipitation in the valley is about 20 in. At this elevation, much of this falls as snow, about 155 in. per year. The two largest lakes, Upper and Lower Red Rock, are each more than 3 mi. long, about 2 mi. wide. Swan Lake is about 1 1/2 mi. long. A cluster of ponds is at the E end of the Refuge.

The best time to see the Refuge is from May through Oct. The road from Monida is usually open by mid-Apr. but rough going until mid-May. The Refuge has no auto tour route, but there are about 26 mi. of roads. The road from Monida crosses the S side of the area, skirting Upper Red Rock Lake. Dirt roads extend up the W side of Lower Red Rock Lake, the farthest W, and among the ponds on the E side. Walking is permitted everywhere except the closed area on the E end from Oct. 1 to July 15. One of the best ways to see the Refuge is by canoe, but protection of nesting waterfowl requires that Upper Red Rock Lake be closed to boating until July 15, Lower Lake until Sept. 1. Boat motors are prohibited.

Plants: Wildflower blooming begins in May with pasqueflower. By July, according to Refuge literature, the valley becomes "a wildflower paradise." Noted are shootingstar, buttercup, sticky geranium, lupine, loco.

Birds: The spring migration is slow, and some migrants don't stop. Fall is more spectacular. This is a great nesting area, however, so there's much bird life to be seen May–Oct.

This population of trumpeter swans doesn't go south in winter. They seek open water here or nearby. Grain is provided at two of the ponds in winter, and over 300 swans gather when the weather is severe. Visitors can't be sure of seeing nesting swans and in any case are asked to stay at least 500 ft. away, but swans can be seen at camera range mid-July through Aug. at one of the small ponds.

A checklist of 258 species is available. A minority of the species are resident. Seasonally abundant or common species include western, eared, and pied-billed grebes; white pelican, double-crested cormorant, Canada goose, mallard, northern pintail, gadwall, American wigeon, northern shoveler; blue-winged, green-winged, and cinnamon teals; redhead, canvasback, lesser scaup, common and Barrow's goldeneyes, buffflehead, ruddy duck, common merganser, northern harrier; rough-legged, red-tailed, and Swainson's hawks; bald eagle, prairie falcon, American kestrel, great blue heron, sandhill crane, American coot, American avocet, killdeer, long-billed curlew, willet, Wilson's phalarope, common snipe, California and Franklin's gulls, Forster's and black terns, mourning dove, great horned owl, belted kingfisher, northern flicker, yellow-bellied sapsucker, hairy and downy woodpeckers, western wood-pewee, horned lark; barn, cliff, violet-green, and tree swallows; black-billed magpie, Clark's nutcracker, common raven, black-capped and mountain chickadees, dipper, red-breasted nuthatch, house and marsh wrens, American robin, Townsend's solitaire, mountain bluebird, ruby-crowned kinglet, water pipit, northern shrike, European starling. An addendum includes solitary and warbling vireos. Warblers: yellow, yellow-rumped, common yellowthroat, MacGillivray's, Wilson's. Western meadowlark; red-winged, yellow-headed, and Brewer's blackbirds; brown-headed cowbird, western tanager, Cassin's and rosy finches, pine grosbeak, pine siskin, lark bunting, dark-eyed junco. Sparrows: vesper, chipping, Brewer's, white-crowned, Lincoln's, song.

Mammals: Checklist available notes habitats where species occur. Common species include masked and water shrews, little brown myotis, pika, snowshoe hare, whitetail jackrabbit, yellowbelly marmot, Richardson ground squirrel, golden-mantled and pine squirrels, least and yellow pine chipmunks, northern pocket gopher, beaver, deer mouse; boreal redback, meadow, and longtail voles; muskrat, western jumping mouse, porcupine, shorttail and longtail weasels, mink, striped skunk, badger, red fox, coyote, bobcat, elk, mule and whitetail deer, moose, pronghorn.

ACTIVITIES

Camping: 2 campgrounds, 11 sites.

Hiking: Chiefly on unpaved roads. Nearby routes up the Centennials to the Continental Divide.

Hunting: Elk, deer, moose, pronghorn, waterfowl.

Fishing: Stream and lake. Cutthroat, rainbow, and brook trout; grayling, mountain whitefish.

Boating: Lakes. No motors. July 15 to freezeup on Upper Red Rock Lake, Sept. 1 to freezeup on Lower Red Rock Lake.

NEARBY: *Lima Reservoir,* in the Centennial Valley NE of Monida. Access by local roads N from the road to the Refuge. Largely surrounded by BLM land, the irrigation reservoir is about 11 mi. long, less than 1 mi. wide. It's supplied by the Red Rock River, flowing W from the Refuge. Good birding at times. No facilities.

PUBLICATIONS

Refuge folder with map.
Bird checklist.

Trumpeters.
Mammal checklist.
Regulations.
Camping information.

HEADQUARTERS: Monida Star Route, Box 15, Lima, MT 59739; (406) 276-3347.

RUBY MOUNTAINS
U.S. Bureau of Land Management
26,611 acres.

We usually omit sites without legal access even if we're told, as in this case, the intervening landowner tolerates passage. In 1987 BLM was seeking legal access. It's worth an inquiry to see if they succeeded. The range is E of Dillon.

The Ruby Mountains are a somewhat isolated range in SW Montana, about 12 mi. N–S, rising from sagebrush-grass prairie. Elevations range from 5,320 ft. on the E side to 9,391 ft. on Ruby Peak. A majority of the site is above 8,000 ft. About 80% of the site is forested, chiefly with Douglas-fir, lodgepole pine, Engelmann spruce, and limber pine. The high ridges and upper slopes have nearly pure stands of limber pine broken by small parks.

Terrain is generally steep and dissected, especially at the N end, which is drained by 20 major and minor canyons. The canyons provide secluded hiking routes. Between the ridges and rounded hills of the S end are two small perennial streams, streamside meadows, and aspen groves.

It's a scenic area, with free-standing rock walls, cliff faces, caves, talus slopes, and open grasslands with seasonal wildflowers. Views from the ridge include 13 mountain ranges, most of them in surrounding portions of the Beaverhead National Forest.

Although the site boundary is only about 2 mi. from SR 287, the area is usually deserted. Recreation visits are estimated at about 300 a year. Most of these visitors are hunters seeking elk, mule deer, and grouse. Except in hunting season, a hiker or backpacker could be sure of solitude.

The N end of the site has been recommended for Wilderness status.

HEADQUARTERS: BLM, Butte District, 106 N. Parkmont, Butte, MT 59702; (406) 494-5059.

ZONE 4

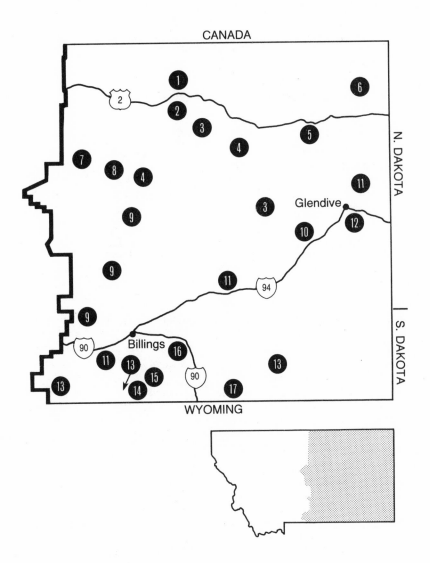

ZONE 4

Includes these counties:

Blaine	Phillips	Valley
Daniels	Sheridan	Roosevelt
Fergus	Petroleum	Garfield
McCone	Richland	Prairie
Dawson	Wibaux	Golden Valley
Musselshell	Rosebud	Custer
Fallon	Stillwater	Yellowstone
Treasure	Carbon	Big Horn
Powder River	Carter	

Zone 4 is the eastern half of Montana. Most of it is flat to rolling prairie, with isolated low ranges, hills, and buttes. The only high country is in the SW corner just N of Yellowstone National Park. Many travelers consider eastern MT featureless and dull. Those who look more closely often become enthusiasts.

Two of America's great rivers, the Missouri and the Yellowstone, cross the zone, meeting just across the North Dakota border. The Missouri has three principal sections: the Missouri Wild and Scenic River; Fort Peck Reservoir, surrounded by the Charles M. Russell National Wildlife Refuge; and the final section, attractive but overlooked. The Yellowstone is the longest free-flowing river in MT and one of the longest in the Lower 48. Both rivers have good to outstanding fishing; both are floatable; both attract wildlife.

Most of the zone is semiarid, receiving 12 to 14 in. of annual precipitation. However, the natural potholes that pock the prairies have been supplemented by several thousand man-made catchments. The result is an environment that attracts great numbers of nesting and migratory waterfowl and shorebirds. There are major concentrations of birds at the Bowdoin and Medicine Lake National Wildlife Refuges and their satellites. The C. M. Russell NWR is known chiefly for its big game and upland game birds.

In the S, several portions of the Custer National Forest offer opportunities for early and late season hiking. The Bighorn National Recreation Area has boat access in MT; for land travel one must enter it in WY. Just W of the NRA are the Pryor Mountains, wilderness country noted for herds of wild horses.

BIGHORN CANYON NATIONAL RECREATION AREA
National Park Service
34,879 acres in MT.

From Hardin on I-90, S on SR 313 to Fort Smith.

See entry in Wyoming Zone 2.

Yellowtail Dam, built by the U.S. Bureau of Reclamation, backed up Bighorn Lake, 71 mi. long, extending into WY. The E side of the NRA is roadless above the dam except for US 14A, which crosses the S end of the lake in WY. The only W side road extends from US 14A near Lovell, WY, to Barry's Landing in MT, about midway. HQ is at Fort Smith, MT, near the dam. One visitor center is at Lovell, another at Fort Smith. The only internal link between the two ends of the lake is by water.

The lake is in a narrow, winding canyon, with vertical walls up to 1,000 ft. high. Only at the S end does it open to widths of a mi. and more. From the Bighorn Mountains on the E, deeply incised canyons drain to the lake. Elevation at the lake is 3,600 ft.

In MT, visitor activity is limited almost entirely to the lake and the HQ area. There are no upland trails. The Crow Indian Reservation, which surrounds the NRA, does not welcome visitors. Winters are cold, springs usually cool and wet. Summers are hot and dry, and most visitors come then; the canyon is shaded and the water cool.

INTERPRETATION: *Yellowtail Visitor Center.* Exhibits feature Indian history and the dam.

ACTIVITIES

Camping: Campground with 24 sites at the Afterbay, below the dam. All year. Boat-in campground 5 mi. S of the boat ramp.

Fishing: Walleye, rainbow and brown trout, yellow perch, ling, crappie, catfish. Fishing in either state requires that state's license.

Boating: Ramp, fuel, and supplies at Ok-A-Beh, near dam. Boaters are asked to register. Boaters are advised to stay with a disabled boat, never to attempt to scale the canyon walls.

PUBLICATIONS
Leaflet with map.
Boating map.
Canyon Echos. Yearly newspaper.
Bird checklist.
Wildflower and shrub list.

List of publications on sale by Bighorn Canyon Natural History Association.

HEADQUARTERS: P.O. Box 458, Fort Smith, MT 59035; (406) 666-2412.

BIGHORN RIVER
Montana Department of Fish, Wildlife & Parks
About 68 river miles.

From Hardin on I-90: upstream access from SR 313, downstream from SR 47.

Below the Yellowtail and Afterbay dams, the Bighorn River flows N to the Yellowstone. Most of the silt the river once carried is now trapped in the reservoir, and many of the bars and islands nourished by silt have washed away. The altered conditions have made the river an outstanding trout fishery. Some wildlife species were deprived of habitat, but waterfowl and shorebirds are still abundant.

The first 44 mi. below the dam, by far the best trout waters, are within the Crow Indian Reservation. The Crow Tribe declared the river off limits to others but lost a bitter legal battle, the court ruling that the river bed is state property. Visitors must use only official access sites and stay within the high-water line.

Below the first camping and launch site in the Afterbay area of the Bighorn Canyon National Recreation Area, the state has 4 Fishing Access Sites, two within the Crow Reservation, two farther down. Camping is permitted at 3 of them.

The river is popular with fishermen and floaters, and traffic is often heavy on July–Sept. weekends. Most floating is between the Afterbay area and Two Leggins, an FAS at Mile 33, 8 mi. S of Hardin. Thereafter, traffic is lighter because of limited access and because the water is warmer, changing the character of the fishing.

ACTIVITIES

Camping: National Recreation Area campground at Afterbay. FAS camping at Miles 12 and 33 and at Manuel Lisa, near the Yellowstone confluence.

Hunting: Waterfowl, below the Crow Reservation.

Fishing: Famous for large trout. Below the Reservation, pike, sauger, sturgeon, catfish.

Boating: Ramps at Bighorn and Two Leggins for motorized craft.

Rafting: No rapids. The river can be floated by raft, kayak, or canoe, the principal hazards being weather, snags, and diversion dams.

REFERENCES

Fischer, Hank. *The Floater's Guide to Montana.* Billings, MT: Falcon Press, 1986. Pp. 15–18.

Sample, Mike. *The Angler's Guide to Montana.* Billings, MT: Falcon Press, 1984. Pp. 23–32.

HEADQUARTERS: Region 5, 1125 Lake Elmo Dr., Billings, MT 59105; (406) 252-4654.

BOWDOIN NATIONAL WILDLIFE REFUGE
U.S. Fish and Wildlife Service
15,500 acres.

7 mi. E of Malta, off old US 2.

On the Central Flyway, the Refuge is at the heart of a vast prairie pothole region through which pass great numbers of migrating waterfowl. The region is semiarid, receiving about 12 in. of precipitation per year. Before the Refuge was established, water from the spring runoff was not retained, and the remaining shallows became stagnant, frequently infested with botulism, deadly to waterfowl. Bowdoin was established in 1936. Dikes now retain water in 4 lakes, supplemented by water from the Milk River. Bowdoin is now a major breeding, resting, and feeding area. Ducks, geese, and shorebirds gather in the ponds and marshes.

Lake Bowdoin, largest of the impoundments, covers 3,700 acres. Three smaller lakes and semipermanent marshes total 2,675 acres, bringing the total wetlands area to almost one-half of the site. Other habitat types include 6,800 acres of native prairie, seeded nesting cover, and bush-shrub. Russian olive, caragana, chokecherry, cottonwood, and buffaloberry were planted to provide shelter and, for some animals, winter food. The site is virtually flat, with less than 80 ft. difference between its lowest point, 2,209 ft., and its highest.

Visitors are welcome on the Refuge roads. The 15-mi. self-guided auto tour route is graveled. Other roads may be impassable when wet. At times the tour route is so far from the wetlands that one needs a spotting scope. Other sections are on causeways and viewing is excellent. The tour route has no turnouts, and for much of the distance it would be difficult to allow another car to pass. This would be an annoyance if there were many visitors at one time, but in mid-July we were alone. During our visit we drove through great, dark, swirling clouds of mosquitoes, unbelievable numbers of them.

For waterfowl, early fall is the best time to come; up to 100,000 ducks and geese are attracted to Bowdoin. In Mar. and Apr. flocks of ducks and Canada geese return. Many nest, and the first broods appear in early May. In mid-July we found the birding excellent: many birds of many species. Deer, too, including a doe with fawn.

At the end of your tour, continue E on old US 2 until it joins the new route. Birding is good in ditches, wetlands, and fields.

Birds: Although the Refuge's primary mission is support of ducks and geese, many other species are attracted. Islands in Lake Bowdoin are nesting sites for white pelicans, double-crested cormorants, California and ring-billed gulls, and great blue herons. Franklin's gulls and black-crowned night-herons nest in the marshes. In summer the marshes are thronged with young and adult coots and eared grebes. Shorebirds are abundant, as are red-winged and yellow-headed blackbirds, black-billed magpies, and horned larks.

A checklist of 208 species is available. Seasonally abundant or common species, in addition to those named, include pied-billed grebe, American bittern, tundra swan; green-winged, blue-winged, and cinnamon teals; mallard, northern pintail, northern shoveler, gadwall, American wigeon, canvasback, redhead, lesser scaup, common goldeneye, bufflehead, common merganser, ruddy duck, northern harrier; Swainson's, red-tailed, ferruginous, and rough-legged hawks; American kestrel, prairie falcon, ring-necked pheasant, sharp-tailed grouse, sora, American coot, black-bellied plover, killdeer, American avocet, lesser yellowlegs, willet, spotted and least sandpipers, long-billed curlew, marbled godwit, long-billed dowitcher, common snipe, Wilson's phalarope, common and black terns, mourning dove, great horned and short-eared owls, common nighthawk, downy and hairy woodpeckers, northern flicker, willow flycatcher, eastern and western kingbirds, horned lark. Swallows: northern rough-winged, bank, cliff, barn. American crow, black-capped chickadee, house and marsh wrens, American robin, gray catbird, brown thrasher, Sprague's pipit, Bohemian and cedar waxwings, European starling; yellow and yellow-rumped warblers, common yellowthroat; rufous-sided towhee. Sparrows: American tree, chipping, clay-colored, Brewer's, savannah, grasshopper, song, white-crowned, Harris'. Lark bunting, dark-eyed junco, chestnut-collared longspur, snow bunting, western meadowlark, common grackle, brown-headed cowbird, hoary redpoll, American goldfinch.

Mammals: Whitetail deer are common; mule deer and pronghorn are seen occasionally. Other mammals include whitetail jackrabbit, mountain cottontail, Richardson ground squirrel, coyote, red fox, striped skunk.

ACTIVITIES

Camping: See entry for Nelson Reservoir State Recreation Area.

Hiking: All Refuge trails are open.

Hunting: Designated area. Waterfowl and upland game birds. No big game hunting.

NEARBY
Nelson Reservoir (see entry).
Four smaller Refuges are satellites of Bowdoin:
Black Coulee, 1,309 acres.
Creedman Coulee, 2,728 acres.
Hewitt Lake, 1,680 acres.
Lake Thibadeau, 3,868 acres.
They have no visitor facilities.

PUBLICATIONS
Refuge leaflet with map.
Auto tour guide.
Bird checklist.
Mammals checklist.
Refuge map.
Hunting map.

HEADQUARTERS: P.O. Box J, Malta, MT 59538; (406) 654-2863.

CHARLES M. RUSSELL NATIONAL WILDLIFE REFUGE
U.S. Fish and Wildlife Service
1,009,000 acres; 1,094,301 acres within boundaries.

Between US 191 on the W, SR 24 on the E. Various access routes from US 191 and US 2 on the N, SR 200 on the S.

Look at a map before you read further and try to imagine what you'd find here. The Refuge extends 125 air mi. upstream from the Fort Peck Dam. The reservoir appears to have backed up most of that distance. Its shape is dendritic, with dozens of large and small branches. The highway map shows Recreation Areas at several places on the shore. We imagined crowds of people coming here for fishing, cruising, water skiing, sailing, camping.

It's not like that, and it isn't easy to comprehend what it is like. One account says this area has changed but little since Lewis and Clark traveled up the Missouri. Another describes drastic, damaging changes.

The reservoir is rapidly filling with silt. At present the reservoir is about 90 mi. long, with a 1,600-mi. shoreline. There are 35 mi. of river between the W boundary and the reservoir. As the silt deposit continues, what was open water becomes river again, broad, shallow, braided. The first plants to appear on the silt islands may be washed away by the next flood, but others follow, and soon a grove of willows is trapping more silt, where cottonwoods take root. In the 1870s, steamboats carried cargo all the way up the Missouri to Fort Benton. In the 1980s, plans for a canoe trail below US 191 were abandoned because of shallows. Most power boating is based at Fort Peck.

It is probably the only National Wildlife Refuge where wildlife was officially subordinated to cattle. For forty years the Bureau of Land Management and the Fish and Wildlife Service shared management responsibility, BLM having the upper hand. Under this regime, cattle got most of the forage, overgrazing degraded the range, and wildlife declined. In 1975 the Secretary of the Interior gave BLM sole jurisdiction, only to be reversed by Congress. For the first time the Fish and Wildlife Service was in charge, although its mandate required that cattle be given a share. The cattlemen weren't about to retreat, and their Congressional delegation compelled FWS to abandon some of its plans. The battle continued in Congress, the Administration, and the courts while overgrazing continued to damage the range. When we visited in 1986, a new "decision" called for gradual livestock grazing reductions, beginning in 1987, achieving the final 33% reduction by 1991. That's a compromise, and it hasn't happened yet.

The Refuge's mission gives first priority to upland wildlife. The lengthy bird list includes many waterfowl, but they're visitors. Contrary to our expectations, the Refuge is not a significant waterfowl production area. Despite the dam, the deterioration of the range caused by overgrazing, and the disappearance of the bison, wolf, and grizzly bear, this is still a splendidly wild region. Doubts on that score are resolved by paying a visit.

The only paved roads are US 191, crossing the W end of the Refuge, and roads around Fort Peck at the E end. The 20-mi. auto tour route and a few roads to shoreline recreation sites are graveled. 700 mi. of other roads are described in the Environmental Impact Statement:

> Since many of the access roads on the refuge are built on gumbolike Bearpaw shale, any measurable precipitation, together with motorized use of these roads, is enough to turn them into impassable quagmires. Ruts created by vehicles during wet weather often do not heal from one year to the next. These ruts then provide channels for water runoff during subsequent rainfall, often leading to complete deterioration of the road . . .

For the first-time visitor seeking an introduction to this wild country, we suggest the auto tour route, which begins near the bridge on US 191. An entrance kiosk has maps and a tour guide. The road climbs high to provide a splendid view of the Missouri Breaks, then drops down to the shore. At Jones Island the visitor can follow a footpath among tall cottonwoods to the river's edge. Deer and elk are often seen, as well as many birds.

Most recreation is at the E end, around Fort Peck. Of the 109,907 visits to the NWR recorded in the most recent year, half were for camping, picnicking, swimming, boating, and waterskiing, 33% for fishing, 17% for hunting. Local residents predominate among those entering from Mosby and Jordan.

Elevation of the reservoir at normal pool is 2,246 ft. The surrounding prairies are 250 to 1,000 ft. higher. The river and its many tributaries have cut a strip 2 to 10 mi. wide into benches, steep-sided coulees, and spectacular badlands: the Missouri Breaks. Average annual precipitation is 12 to 13 in. Runoff is rapid. Winters are moderately cold, summers pleasant with some hot periods.

Plants: About 61% of the million-plus acres is sagebrush-greasewood-grassland. About 36%, chiefly in the W half, is dominated by the ponderosa pine-juniper type. The major part of the riparian plant community, critically important to wildlife, was inundated by the dam. What remains, in the W portion, is less than 1% of the total. Spring wildflowers, notably prairie coneflower, crocus, and wild rose, depend on rainfall, and the blooming season is often brief.

Birds: Checklist of 236 species available. Mid-Apr. through June, the green-up time, is the best season for birding. Upland sandpiper, mountain plover, long-billed curlew, burrowing owl, Sprague's pipit, chestnut-collared and McCown's longspurs, and clay-colored sparrow are of special interest. Sharp-tailed grouse is the most abundant upland game species; sharp-tailed and sage grouse both have dancing and strutting grounds. Other upland game species include ring-necked pheasant, turkey, and mourning dove. Species that are seasonally numerous include red-tailed hawk, northern harrier, common nighthawk, poor-will, eastern kingbird, horned lark, bank swallow, black-billed magpie, pinyon jay, American robin, mountain bluebird, Bohemian waxwing, western meadowlark; red-winged, yellow-headed, and Brewer's blackbirds; lark bunting, American goldfinch. 16 species of waterfowl are listed as seasonally abundant or common, but nearby refuges offer better viewing opportunities.

Mammals: No checklist. 45 species recorded. Mule deer is the most abundant big game species. Elk, once eliminated, were reintroduced; 1,300 to 1,500 inhabit the Breaks ecosystem, with the Refuge as part of their range. Pronghorn and whitetail deer occur in small numbers. Several attempts have been made to reintroduce bighorn sheep; a 1984 count reported 70.

Over a hundred scattered blacktail prairie dog towns are on the Refuge. Other mammals include bobcat, badger, coyote, striped skunk, whitetail jackrabbit, mountain and desert cottontail, raccoon, porcupine, beaver, mink, muskrat, various small rodents.

INTERPRETATION

Information kiosks stocked with brochures are at the beginning of the auto tour route, at Fort Peck, and at Jordan.

Museum maintained by the Corps of Engineers at Fort Peck includes paleontological displays.

Jordan Wildlife Station at Jordan can provide information.

ACTIVITIES
Camping: Corps of Engineers campground at Fort Peck. State Recreation Area on US 191 at the bridge. 7 other campgrounds, Corps and state. Camping is generally permitted anywhere on the Refuge; motor vehicles, otherwise restricted to roads, may drive to a campsite no more than 100 yards from a road.
Hiking: No developed trails. Few visitors hike.
Hunting: Deer, elk, pronghorn, grouse.
Fishing: Mike Sample calls the reservoir "one of the most diverse and challenging fisheries in the northern Great Plains." Northern pike, walleye, lake trout, sauger, channel catfish, paddlefish, turbot, yellow perch, black crappie, white crappie, a few smallmouth bass and trout. Refuge HQ says the fishing potential is not yet fully developed. Spawning is unsuccessful because of drawdowns.
Boating: Marinas at Fort Peck and Hell Creek. Ramps at 7 locations.

NEARBY: Several satellite waterfowl refuges are managed by the C. M. Russell. See entry: Hailstone, Halfbreed, Lake Mason, and War Horse.

PUBLICATIONS
Refuge leaflet.
Refuge map with text.
Auto tour guide.
Bird checklist.
Refuge history leaflet.
Mimeo pages:
  History.
  Reptiles and amphibians list.
Leaflet for satellite Refuges. (See entry, Hailstone National Wildlife Refuge.)

REFERENCE: Sample, Mike. *The Angler's Guide to Montana.* Billings, MT: Falcon Press, 1984. Pp. 196–201.

HEADQUARTERS: P.O. Box 110, Lewistown, MT 59457; (406) 538-8706.

CUSTER NATIONAL FOREST
U.S. Forest Service
1,112,477 acres in MT. Other units in North and South Dakota.

In the Beartooth Ranger District: Beartooth Unit is crossed by US 212 SW of Red Lodge. Pryor Mountain Unit is about 37 mi. S of Billings; access by local roads from US 310. Ashland R.D., E and S of Ashland, is crossed by US 212. Three units of the Sioux R.D. are in SE MT, about 40 mi. S of Baker; access by SR 7.

The Custer has 7 Ranger Districts with many parcels of land scattered over 3 states and 20 counties. They extend from the NE corner of Yellowstone NP to the SE corner of North Dakota, 670 mi. away. The 3 R.D.s in MT—Beartooth, Ashland, and Sioux—are largely forested. The 4 R.D.s in ND and SD are National Grasslands and outside the geographic scope of this book.

Beartooth Ranger District contains 2 units: Beartooth, 512,043 acres, and Pryor Mountain, 75,444 acres.

The *Beartooth Unit* extends from the NE tip of Yellowstone NP almost to Red Lodge, and from the WY border N to a point 20 mi. S of Big Timber. It adjoins the Gallatin NF on the W, and the Gallatin and Shoshone NFs on the S. The unit consists largely of the high plateaus, mountains, and deep valleys of the eastern part of the Absaroka-Beartooth Wilderness, rising to a chain of 12,000-ft. peaks in the SW.

The Absaroka-Beartooth Wilderness has 345,694 acres in the Custer NF, plus 599,640 acres in the Gallatin and Shoshone NFs. The Beartooth Mountains, in the Custer portion of the Wilderness, are MT's most rugged country. Two-thirds of the area is above timberline, 9,000 to 9,500 ft. High tundra plateaus, some covering several square miles; more than 300 high lakes; deep, sheer-walled canyons. In the SW, 12,799-ft. Granite Peak, highest in MT, is surrounded by others rising above 12,000 ft.: Glacier, Mystic, Tempest, Villard, and Peal, with more almost as high not far off. The Wilderness has more than 25 peaks above the 12,000 mark. Many have perpetual snowfields and active glaciers. At lower elevations, from 6,000 ft. to timberline, broad grass-sage meadows alternate with deep coniferous forest, species including lodgepole pine, Engelmann spruce, subalpine fir, Douglas-fir, and limber pine.

Typical vegetation includes rough and Idaho fescue, bluebunch wheatgrass, Columbia needlegrass, basin wildrye, lupine, sticky geranium, arrowleaf balsamroot, big sagebrush, tall larkspur, prairiesmoke, prairie junegrass.

This is MT's second largest Wilderness, next to the Bob Marshall, and it's said to have the largest expanse of alpine tundra S of Alaska. It has the third highest number of visitor-days per year of any National Forest Wilderness. Chief recreation activities are hiking, camping, and fishing.

Chief access to the Custer portion is through the Beartooth Face, by cherry-stemmed roads that penetrate the area from the NE and E, and from trailheads off the Beartooth Highway, US 212. Recreation trails follow the major streams. On the Custer portion of the Wilderness, two-thirds of the use is concentrated along streams and lakes within 7 mi. of the 8 primary trailheads. It occurs largely on weekends, and almost entirely in July–Aug. Winter use is on the increase but still less than 5% of the total. Campgrounds are near most trailheads.

One can roam freely off-trail on the plateaus, but they are separated by deep valleys and getting from one plateau to another may be a formidable challenge. Topo maps are the key to avoiding steep canyons and cliffs.

Annual precipitation in the high country is up to 80 in., with an average of about 50 in., most of this falling as snow. Winter snowfall of 200 in. is not unusual. Trails are seldom open before early July, and some lakes remain frozen until mid-July. Beartooth weather changes rapidly, and snow can fall any day of the year. Hikers and climbers are advised to consult weather forecasts and to be prepared for wet and cold. Blizzards have occurred in late July.

As for wildlife, no species checklists are available. Moose, elk, and mule deer use parts of the area for summer range. Mountain goat were introduced in the 1940s and have become established. Black bear are common; grizzlies are chiefly in the western portion. Whitetail deer are on the increase. Bighorn sheep inhabit the high elevations. Other mammals include coyote, mountain lion, lynx, bobcat, wolverine, beaver, badger, mink, weasel, pine marten, porcupine, marmot, skunk, red squirrel, ground squirrel, chipmunk, cottontail, snowshoe hare, shrews, voles, mice, and bats. Few mammals are seen on the barren ridges except pika and mountain goat. The Wilderness is within the habitat of the grizzly bear, and travelers should know how to avoid encounters.

Bird species mentioned include bald and golden eagle, blue and ruffed grouse, common raven, Clark's nutcracker, Steller's jay, American robin, mountain bluebird, northern flicker, pileated woodpecker, dipper. Several lakes are nesting and resting places for waterfowl.

Despite the heavy use of some areas, no permit or quota system has been adopted except for horse use. Generous limits have been placed on party size and numbers of stock. Shoreline camping is prohibited, and a campsite may be occupied for only 10 days. Visitors are advised to stop at HQ in Billings or the Ranger District office in Red Lodge for current regulations, maps, and advice.

Beartooth Face, 166,454 acres, is on both sides of Forest Road 71 W of Red Lodge. It extends from the the Wilderness eastward to the Forest border. The Beartooth Face, where the land descends from the high country to foothills and rolling grasslands, is the principal access to the Beartooth Unit, to Wilderness trailheads, and to 18 campgrounds. Seven stream valleys attract car campers, many of whom come to fish the lakes and streams.

Beartooth Highway, US 212, from Red Lodge to Yellowstone National Park, is one of America's most scenic drives. From 5,555 ft. elevation at the Red Lodge airport, it follows Rock Creek, then climbs rapidly by switchbacks to the high plateau country, much of which is above 10,000 ft. The road crosses the W summit at 10,947 ft., then drops by switchbacks some 1,000 ft. to Long Lake, eventually reaching and following the Clarks Fork of the Yellowstone to Cooke City and Yellowstone National Park. A major part of the route is within Wyoming's Shoshone NF, with the Absaroka-Beartooth

Wilderness to the N. The highway then turns into the Gallatin NF for a few miles before entering Yellowstone. The highway is open from June until closed by snow, usually in Sept.

Travelers on the Beartooth Highway should allow extra time, for there's much to see along the way. Many campgrounds are on the route: 6 in the Custer, 3 in the Shoshone, 2 in the Gallatin; they often fill early on summer weekends. Fishing is good in nearby lakes and streams. Trails offer opportunities for short strolls or extensive backpacking.

Beartooth Plateau, 46,650 acres in the Custer NF, 143,250 in the Shoshone, 17,900 in the Gallatin. The plateau is on both sides of the Beartooth Highway from the Custer NF boundary to Yellowstone NP. Trailheads are along the highway. On the N it adjoins the Absaroka-Beartooth Wilderness. Elevations range from 5,700 ft. near Red Lodge to 11,550 ft. on Mt. Zimmer, along the Yellowstone-Stillwater Divide. The dominant features of the area are near-level, treeless, alpine plateaus seasonally colorful with wildflowers and dotted with countless lakes. The plateaus are edged by rough, steep cliffs. Benchlands and drainages below the plateaus have dense stands of Engelmann spruce, subalpine fir, and lodgepole pine with patches of quaking aspen.

Climate ranges from semiarid near the mouth of Clarks Fork Canyon to subarctic above timberline, annual precipitation from 6 to 70 in. At high elevations, snow accumulations of 200 in. are common. Frost can occur in any season.

This is not a roadless area, but roads are few. The Sunlight Basin Road is a scenic route off SR 120 from Cody, ending at the Beartooth Highway. Some unpaved spurs radiate from US 212. The area has 165 mi. of designated trails, but off-trail hiking and horse riding are feasible. A National Recreation Trail is about 14 mi. long.

95 of the 127 lakes in the area have fish, chiefly rainbow and cutthroat trout, some lakes with grayling, whitefish, mackinaw, and mountain suckers, a few with golden trout. 150 mi. of fishable streams have trout populations. Streams are chiefly tributaries of Clarks Fork.

Campgrounds are often crowded on summer weekends. Trails to fishing lakes near the highway are heavily used. Ample opportunities for solitude are in the large areas reached by off-trail hiking.

Pryor Mountain Unit, 75,444 acres. About 9 mi. N–S, 14 mi. W–E, this area is about 6 mi. N of the WY border, NE of Warren. On the N is the Crow Indian Reservation. BLM's Pryor Mountain Wild Horse Range borders the SE corner. To the E is the Bighorn Canyon National Recreation Area. (See entries.)

The Pryors are an unglaciated island, largely of limestone, with elevations from about 3,300 ft. to 8,800 ft. Annual precipitation ranges from 7 in. at low elevations to 20 in. on the high slopes. Terrain includes dryland flats, heavily forested slopes, near-alpine meadows, many steep-walled canyons, numerous caves in the limestone.

Access is by graveled Forest Road 3085 that enters the NE corner from the Warren-Pryor road. 3085 passes the Sage Creek campground and turns S toward the BLM area. Forest Road 849 continues E past Big Ice Caves to a fine overlook, Dry Head Vista. Several other roads link the two sites. Beyond the graveled road, 4-wheel drive may be needed, and some stretches become quagmires in wet weather. Budget cuts have caused the Forest to close the Big Ice Caves. Despite lack of surface water, recreational use is gradually increasing, most visitors coming from nearby. Attractions are hunting, wild horses, and absence of crowds.

Ashland Ranger District, 436,210 acres, is E of the Northern Cheyenne Indian Reservation and is crossed by US 212.

The RD has two adjacent, irregularly shaped blocks, the western about 23 mi. N–S, 16 mi. E–W; the eastern about 43 mi. N–S, 11 mi. W–E. Otter Creek meanders between the two. The area is a rough, heavily eroded sandstone-shale plateau. Elevations range from 3,150 to 4,350 ft. Average annual precipitation is about 16 in. The general pattern of vegetation is ponderosa pine stands intermingled with grassland, but there are variations: broadleaf trees, shrubs, and grasses along creek bottoms; sparsely timbered dry slopes and ridges with exposed rock; shrub-grass associations on creek terraces and lower slopes.

Early homesteaders claimed much of the stream valley lands along the main tributaries of Otter Creek. To avoid trespassing, obtain a Visitor's Map at the Ashland Ranger Station.

An unpaved but passable road follows Otter Creek S from US 212. Numerous roads penetrate the site. Primary recreational use is deer and game bird hunting. The Red Shale campground is off US 212, 8 mi. E of Ashland; Cow Creek campground is reached by Forest Road 95 E from the S part of Otter Creek Road.

King Mountain Hiking and Riding Area is about 4 mi. N of Cow Creek Campground. *Cook Mountain Hiking and Riding Area* is about 6 mi. N of Red Shale Campground. King Mountain is about 8 mi. N–S. 1 to 4 mi. W–E. Cook Mountain is about 3 mi. N–S, 4 to 5 mi. W–E. These are wild, roadless, hilly areas at relatively low elevations.

Sioux Ranger District, 89,361 acres, is in three MT tracts, all in Carter County. 5 others are in South Dakota. The Ranger Station is at Camp Crook, SD.

The vast grasslands of this region are interrupted by these forested, sandstone buttes and hills rising 300 to 1,000 ft., visible for miles. The region is semiarid, annual precipitation about 14 in. These prairie islands offer numerous springs, shade, wildlife habitat, and solitude. Although they could not be called birding hot spots, they attract a respectable array of raptors and songbirds. They are remote from main travel routes, and recreational use is low. Hunting for deer, pronghorn, wild turkey, and other upland game birds attracts both local and out-of-state hunters.

INTERPRETATION (FOR ALL DISTRICTS)

A Recreation Opportunities Guide (ROG) has been developed for the Beartooth District, exclusive of Pryor Mountains. It has detailed information about campgrounds, trails, and other opportunities.

Maps and information are available at HQ and Ranger District offices.

ACTIVITIES

Camping:

Beartooth Unit	15 campgrounds	292 sites
Pryor Unit	2 campgrounds	26 sites
Ashland R.D.	3 campgrounds	25 sites
Sioux R.D.	6 campgrounds	54 sites

Season is generally June 1–Sept. 15, depending on snow; several have longer seasons. Camping out of season is permitted, without water or services.

Hiking, backpacking: Trail mileage by Districts was not available. Most trails are in the Absaroka-Beartooth Wilderness and on the Beartooth Plateau. The ROG has detailed information on the principal trails.

Hunting: Deer and upland game bird hunting in all Districts. Other big game hunting is chiefly in the Beartooth District.

Fishing: Lakes and streams of the Beartooth District.

Horse riding has become increasingly popular in the Beartooth high country. Some campsites and lake shores have been damaged by trampling. Check at the Ranger Station for a horse-use permit. A list of outfitters is available.

Boating: Campgrounds and boat ramps are on East Rosebud Lake, on the East Rosebud River, and Emerald Lake on the West Rosebud River. Both are on cherry-stem roads that penetrate the Absaroka-Beartooth Wilderness, SW of Columbus. East Rosebud Lake is about a mi. long, Emerald smaller. Campgrounds and ramps are also on Beartooth Lake and Island Lake on the Beartooth Highway in WY.

Rafting, kayaking: The Stillwater River, considered one of MT's best whitewater streams for kayaks, flows N through the Absaroka-Beartooth Wilderness, continuing NE to join the Yellowstone at Columbus. Few floaters carry their craft into the Wilderness. Some put in at the Woodbine Campground, on a cherry-stem road SW of Columbus. The first few miles are difficult, sometimes impossible. Further downstream, outside the Forest, are milder sections where canoes are practical. Forest HQ told us that the East and West Rosebud rivers are sometimes floated by kayak, folbot, or canoe.

Skiing: Red Lodge Mountain ski area. Late Dec. to late Mar.

Ski touring: Increasingly popular in all Districts. On the Beartooth, Lake Fork ski touring trail begins on Beartooth Highway 9 mi. from Red Lodge. Silver Run Ski Trail is off the West Fork of Rock Creek Road. Another trail runs through the Rock Creek Recreation Area.

PUBLICATIONS

Forest maps, Beartooth, Ashland, and Sioux R.D.s. $1 each.

Absaroka-Beartooth Wilderness map. $1.

Trail maps: Mystic Lake, Granite Peak; Red Lodge Area; Stillwater River/
Cooke City, West Fork Stillwater River; East Rosebud/Cooke City.
Lake Fork ski touring trails, sketch map.
Absaroka-Beartooth Wilderness. Folder, no map.
Snowmobile Policy.

REFERENCES

Rudner, Ruth. *Bitterroot to Beartooth.* San Francisco: Sierra Club, 1985.
Pp. 231–52.
Schneider, Bill. *The Hiker's Guide to Montana.* Billings, MT; Falcon Press,
1983. Pp. 231–39.
Turbak, Gary. *The Traveler's Guide to Montana.* Billings, MT: Falcon
Press, 1983. Pp. 80–81, 214–17.
Marcuson, Pat. *The Beartooth Fishing Guide.* Billings, MT: Falcon Press,
1985.

HEADQUARTERS: 2602 First Ave. N, P.O. Box 2556, Billings, MT 59013; (406)
657-6361.

RANGER DISTRICTS (MT ONLY): Beartooth R.D., Route 2, Box 3420, Red
Lodge, MT 59068; (406) 446-2103. Ashland R.D., P.O. Box 168, Ashland,
MT 59003; (406) 784-2344. Sioux R.D., Camp Crook, SD 57724; (605)
797-4432.

HAILSTONE, HALFBREED, LAKE MASON, AND WAR HORSE NATIONAL WILDLIFE REFUGES
U.S. Fish and Wildlife Service

These four waterfowl refuges are satellites of the Charles M. Russell NWR.
They have no reception or visitor facilities. Hailstone and Halfbreed are
closed to hunting.

Visitors are welcome, for birding, photography, and—at War Horse—
fishing. However, private and public lands are intermingled, and private land
should not be crossed without landowner permission.

It's advisable to inquire at the C. M. Russell NWR first for advice on access
roads, wetland conditions, and what's to be seen.

Hailstone NWR, 1,988 acres. 35 mi. W of Billings.

Established as a breeding ground for grouse and waterfowl. Hailstone Lake
covers 660 acres. Upland cover is sagebrush, greasewood, native grasses.
Some cropland. Open to hunting. No fish in the lake.

Halfbreed NWR, 3,886 acres. 5 mi. S of Hailstone NWR.

Excellent marsh and parts of two shallow lakes. Established chiefly as a
breeding and nesting area for migratory birds. When we visited, this was
private land, and landowner permission to enter was required, but federal
acquisition was pending. Inquire at CMR.

Lake Mason NWR, 16,670 acres. About 6 mi. NW of Roundup.

Lake Mason is over 2 mi. long, about 1 mi. wide, in the largest of several tracts of land scattered along Flat Willow Creek. The areas include open water, marsh, riparian habitat, and shortgrass prairie. The Refuge is a waterfowl and upland bird production area as well as a haven for migrants. The S portion of Lake Mason is open to public use.

War Horse NWR, 3,192 acres. NW of Winnett.

Three lakes are surrounded by land of mixed ownerships. Sagebrush-grassland uplands. Wild Horse Lake, 900 acres, holds water in 7 years out of 10. Yellow Water Reservoir has stocked rainbow trout. Bald eagles often feed at War Horse Lake when the ice goes out. High waterfowl populations attract hunters.

PUBLICATION: Leaflet describes all four NWRs.

HEADQUARTERS: c/o Charles M. Russell NWR, P.O. Box 110, Lewistown, MT 59457; (406) 538-8706.

JAMES KIPP STATE RECREATION AREA
Montana Department of Fish, Wildlife & Parks
465 acres.

On US 191 where it crosses the Missouri River, 63 mi. NE of Lewistown.

This is the final take-out for floaters on the Missouri Wild and Scenic River, at the western gateway of the Charles M. Russell National Wildlife Refuge (see entries). The drive from Lewistown is across open shortgrass prairie, after passing the Judith Mountains. Had our schedule allowed, we would have tried hiking in the Judiths. To the E of the highway, on BLM land, are moderate grassy slopes and ravines. It seemed quite possible to wander up the slopes into the trees, an easy and pleasant day hike. Several days later we learned that BLM is gradually developing a trail up Judith Peak.

The road drops down sharply into the Missouri Valley. These are the Breaks, heavily eroded, sandstone cliffs and bluffs, shallow, vertical-walled ravines. The Park is on the river in a grassy grove of cottonwoods, with aspen and willow.

The Refuge's self-guided auto nature trail begins just across the river.

Camping: 17 designated sites, a few informal. May 15–Dec. 1.

HEADQUARTERS: Region 4, Millegan Route, Great Falls, MT 59405; (406) 454-3441.

MAKOSHIKA STATE PARK
Montana Department of Fish, Wildlife & Parks
8,123 acres.

Immediately SW of Glendive, off Taylor Ave.

Makoshika is a scenic badlands park, occupying a choice portion of a 56,000-acre badlands area SE of Glendive. The region, a checkerboard of BLM, private, and state landholdings, is characterized by flat to rolling prairie, rough breaks, badlands, and river floodplains. The badlands are a landscape of colorful sandstone, clay, and shale, eroded into fanciful ridges, fluted slopes, pinnacles, caprocks, and hoodoos. Erosion has cut through layers of ancient rock, a 70-million-year record of geological history and the evolution of species. The Park and surrounding area are rich in fossils, including 10 species of dinosaurs and other creatures of the Cretaceous era, as well as fossils of trees and other plants. Once collected by visitors, these are now protected. Some can be seen at the Frontier Gateway Museum in Glendive.

Elevation is about 2,500 ft. The area is semiarid, annual precipitation 12 to 14 in., 90% in Apr.–Sept. Summers are warm, with showers and occasional thunderstorms. Winters are cool, with brief cold spells and an average snowfall of 28 in. The Park is very dry, with one small pond and no perennial streams.

Plants: The soft materials of the badlands are still eroding, providing few places for plants to become established. Some ponderosa pine and Rocky Mountain juniper grow on northern slopes and near coulee bottoms. Some draws have ash and boxelder. Most of the area is sparse grassland with sagebrush, greasewood, and rabbitbrush. Over 225 species of seasonal wildflowers have been identified, including pasqueflower, buttercup, phlox, vetches, sand lily, pussytoes, death camas, western wallflower, blue-eyed grass, evening primrose, bee plant, mariposa lily, sunflowers, yucca, coneflowers, goldenrod, eriogonum, asters.

Birds: No list has been compiled. Summering grounds for up to 50 turkey vultures. Also noted: sharptail and sage grouse, Hungarian partridge, mourning dove, meadowlark, black-billed magpie, mountain bluebird.

Mammals: No list has been compiled. Noted: whitetail and mule deer, bobcat, fox, coyote. Management is studying the possibility of reintroducing three former residents of the region: bison, bighorn sheep, and wild horse.

An all-weather road enters the Park in a canyon, climbs a big butte, then follows a ridge, ending at an amphitheater and overlook. Along this scenic route are a campground, picnic sites, and trailhead. A 4-mi. dirt road extends to an overlook near the SW corner, with a spur to another vista point.

The Park has no visitor center. An information station at the entrance has a supply of leaflets. A Park Ranger lives in a house at the entrance. The Park's literature is exceptionally good, including nature and hiking trail guides and a 48-page road guide.

About 80,000 people per year visit the Park, half in summer, the others equally divided between spring and fall. Most come from the local area, somewhat less than a third from out of state. They include rockhounds, geology buffs, and fossil hunters—although the hunters can hunt but not take.

Like most tourists, we had always driven through this part of MT as fast as the law allows. There's not much to stop for, other than a few Fishing Access Sites on the Yellowstone River. But travelers on I-94 who take a break here are likely to stay a while. Among the many fascinations of the badlands is the change of color, light, and shadow as the sun crosses the sky.

ACTIVITIES

Camping: One campground, 10 sites. May 1–Oct. 1.

Hiking: Kinney Coulee Trail, 1/2 mi., winds through a pine-juniper woodland to a coulee with unusual rock formations. Cap Rock Nature Trail makes a short descent into the badlands. Both have trail guides.

PUBLICATIONS

Park leaflet with map.
Cap Rock Nature Trail guide.
Kinney Coulee Hiking Trail guide.
Road Guide, 48 pp. $1.

HEADQUARTERS: P.O. Box 1242, Glendive, MT 59330; (406) 365-8596.

MEDICINE LAKE NATIONAL WILDLIFE REFUGE
U.S. Fish and Wildlife Service
31,324 acres of land and water.

Far NE MT. From US 2 at Culbertson, 24 mi. N on SR 16. See signs.

Approaching from the S, we were puzzled, but only briefly. At the Roosevelt-Sheridan county line, an impoundment on the left looked like part of the Refuge. Six mi. later, a sign directed us into an "interpretive area," a short loop beside a larger impoundment. We saw people fishing, many white pelicans, and several islands white with gulls, but no exhibits. Back on the highway we soon came to the turn for HQ and the auto tour route.

At HQ is a kiosk with leaflets and tour route guides, picnic tables nearby. The tour route wasn't planned for sightseeing. It's a good road but well away from Medicine Lake. We passed a few small ponds lively with ducks and saw many upland birds, including sparrows, lark buntings, and killdeer, but the viewing isn't great. Spur roads lead to lakeside fishing points. After about 8 mi. of this, at the E end of the tour, things became far more interesting. The route turns S over a causeway through marsh and open water, where the viewing is excellent. It then loops back to exit on a county road.

The S side of the lake has no public road. The lake, its islands, and the sandhills in the S central portion of the Refuge have been designated an 8,850-acre Wilderness. The entire Refuge is open to random foot travel, although wildlife management may require posting portions against access at certain times. Fishermen walk along the lake shore, and so did we.

Like the Bowdoin NWR (see entry), Medicine Lake is in the vast prairie pothole region, rolling plains with thousands of small wetlands that produce millions of ducks. After the Refuge was established in 1935, its productivity was increased by building dams, dikes, and other water control structures, by planting shelterbelts and by growing feed crops. The largest impoundment, Medicine Lake, covers 8,700 acres. 8 smaller lakes are within the main unit. Homestead Lake, which we passed 6 mi. back, covers 1,250 acres. The Refuge also administers 41 small, scattered waterfowl production areas in Roosevelt, Daniel, and Sheridan counties (see entry, Northeast Montana Wetlands).

Base elevation is 1,920 ft., the highest point 1,950. Annual precipitation is about 14 in., heaviest in May–June. Snowfall is light, about 30 in. per year. The Refuge is open all year. Lakes are usually frozen mid-Nov. to Apr.

Birds: A checklist of 221 species is available; at least 98 species are known to nest on the Refuge.

At one time a quarter-million waterfowl were attracted in spring and fall migrations. In 1987, as a consequence of 5 years of drought in NE MT, the estimate was lowered to 100,000. Blue-winged teal, gadwall, shoveler, lesser scaup, ruddy duck, and mallard are prominent, with smaller numbers of pintail, American wigeon, redhead, and canvasback. Combined, these species produced about 30,000 ducklings each year before the drought, about 18,000 in 1986. Restoration of a Canada goose population succeeded, and about a thousand goslings are produced annually. One of the largest white pelican rookeries is here, Big Island providing safe nesting; over 2,000 pelicans are usually produced annually. Other colonial nesters on the islands include double-crested cormorant, California and ring-billed gulls, and great blue heron. Grebes and many marsh and shore birds nest on the shoreline and other vegetation.

Thousands of sandhill cranes make a brief visit in late Oct. The Refuge is in the corridor used by the endangered whooping crane, which makes occasional visits.

In early spring, sharp-tailed grouse display their courtship dances. Ring-necked pheasant are commonly seen along the tour route; their number has increased as more cover was provided. Upland birds commonly seen in summer include burrowing and short-eared owls, lark bunting, Baird's and Le-Conte's sparrows, and chestnut-collared and McCown's longspurs.

Mammals: No checklist is available. 44 species have been observed. Whitetail deer and muskrat are commonly seen. Raccoons, foxes, and skunks prey on duck eggs.

The Medicine Lake and Bowdoin NWRs are in similar habitats, attracting mostly the same species. Both have tour routes on which the viewing ranges from poor to excellent. We can't compare foot travel in the two because the mosquitoes at Bowdoin would have left us bloodless in minutes had we left our vehicle. There's a public campground near Bowdoin, none near Medicine Lake.

ACTIVITIES

Hiking: Open terrain. Hike anywhere unless posted.

Hunting: Waterfowl, upland game birds, deer. Designated areas; special rules.

Fishing: Chiefly northern pike.

Boating: Cartoppers and canoes. No ramp. No motors.

PUBLICATIONS

Refuge leaflet with map.

Auto tour guide.

Bird checklist.

Fishing leaflet.

Guide to Northeastern Montana Wetlands.

HEADQUARTERS: HC-51, Box 2, Medicine Lake, MT, 59247; (406) 789-2305.

MISSOURI RIVER: FORT PECK DAM TO NORTH DAKOTA
Mixed ownerships
125 river miles.

S of US 2. Access by state and county roads.

From Fort Peck Dam to the border, the river meanders free-flowing, although the Corps of Engineers has plans. While the 149 mi. below Fort Benton are called the Missouri's last free-flowing section, this one seems to be forgotten. The Fort Peck Indian Reservation is on the N shore for about three-fourths of this distance. Other shoreline is mostly private land, with scattered bits of state and BLM holdings. Throughout this distance, there is no Fishing Access Site or other recreation facility.

Hank Fischer says this section of the river is primitive, floatable but rarely floated, rich in wildlife, the rough breaks country giving way to woodlands. It will, he wrote, "please the crustiest of river hermits."

Since no public agency has put a toe in the water yet, you're on your own.

REFERENCE: Fischer, Hank. *The Floater's Guide to Montana*. Billings, MT: Falcon Press, 1986. P. 81.

NELSON RESERVOIR STATE RECREATION AREA
Montana Department of Fish, Wildlife & Parks
228 acres of land; 4,500 acres of water.

From Malta, 17 mi. E on US 2, then 2 mi. N on county road.

One of the best fishing sites in eastern MT and the nearest public campground to the Bowdoin National Wildlife Refuge (see entry). The reservoir, almost 9 mi. long, is just S of the Milk River. It's surrounded by flat, open prairie at about 2,250 ft. elevation. BLM land adjoins the site. Two mi. W is Hewitt Lake, a satellite of the Bowdoin NWR.

ACTIVITIES
Camping: Informal sites. All year.
Hunting: Waterfowl. On the surrounding prairie: pronghorn, mule deer, pheasant, sharp-tailed grouse.
Fishing: Northern pike, walleye, yellow perch. Ice fishing.
Boating: Ramp.

HEADQUARTERS: Region 6, 437 Sixth Ave. N, Glasgow, MT 59230; (406) 228-9347.

NORTHEASTERN MONTANA WETLAND MANAGEMENT DISTRICT
U.S. Fish and Wildlife Service
9,000 acres of upland and wetland in 41 sites.
17,000 acres of easements.

Northeastern Montana.

These wetlands are part of a great pothole region extending nearly 2,000 mi. across the Prairie Provinces, from NE MT through the Dakotas and into Minnesota. About 90% of the duck production of North America takes place here.

BLM manages portions of the region. We talked with a BLM staff member who spoke rhapsodically about the pothole region around Malta. He came from mountainous New England, and at first this country seemed flat and featureless to him, as it does to many travelers along US 2.

"Beginning in spring, it comes alive!" he declared. The natural potholes have been enhanced by several thousand small catchments. In this semiarid environment, with annual precipitation of 12 to 14 in., these small basins that collect and retain water attract great numbers of waterfowl, shorebirds, and other wildlife.

Since the 19th century, in the name of "reclamation," at least half of the natural wetlands have been drained or filled for farming. (At one time, one federal agency was receiving appropriations for draining wetlands while another was receiving funds to restore them.) More than a million acres were thus lost to waterfowl production.

BLM has built thousands of catchments on the land it manages. In 1962 Congress approved use of funds collected by sale of duck stamps to purchase and protect marshes. The Medicine Lake National Wildlife Refuge can provide information about the 26,000 acres it administers. But the NWR and BLM combined have only a fraction of the region. In season, one can enjoy good birding by driving slowly on back roads, binoculars ready.

PUBLICATION: *Guide to Northeastern Montana Wetlands.* Folder with map.

HEADQUARTERS: Wetlands Manager, Medicine Lake NWR, Medicine Lake, MT 59247; (406) 789-2305.

PRYOR MOUNTAIN WILD HORSE RANGE
U.S. Bureau of Land Management
46,800 acres.

See entry, Bighorn National Recreation Area, in WY Zone 2. Proceed N on Bad Pass Highway from near Lovell, WY. Crooked Creek Road is on the left just before entering the NRA; this road is not for cars. From here N to Hough Creek, Bad Pass Highway is within the Wild Horse Range. For access from the N, see entry, Custer National Forest, Pryor Mountain Unit.

A large block of BLM land adjoins the National Recreation Area on the W. The Pryor Mountain Unit of Custer National Forest adjoins the BLM land on the N. The Wild Horse Range lies between Crooked Creek in the BLM area and Bighorn Canyon, occupying parts of both the BLM land and the NRA.

The site was designated in 1968 for the protection and management of wild horses. About 120 wild horses occupy the range, in three herds. Horses are captured and removed from time to time to limit herds to numbers the range can support.

A modest number of visitors use the BLM area for camping, hiking, hunting, horse riding, rockhounding, ski touring, and spelunking. More, though not a great number, use National Forest land on the N, which has better access. Most of these visitors come from nearby in 4-wheel-drive vehicles or pickup trucks. Visitors who want to see wild horses may find a herd along Bad Pass Highway in the NRA. We did.

Scenic values were rated "exceptional to moderate." Elevations range from 3,900 to 8,000 ft. Terrain ranges from almost flat in the S to deep, steep-walled canyons in the middle, rolling alpine hills in the N. There are numerous caves, isolated grassy plateaus, foothill slopes. Mystery Cave, attractive to spelunkers, is gated and locked because of its fragility; guided tours can be arranged June–Oct. if personnel is available.

Upper elevations have scattered stands of subalpine fir interspersed with meadows and plateaus. Midslopes are dominated by Douglas-fir, chiefly on N slopes, with fingers of open parks. Open areas have shrubs and grasses. Below this is a zone of mountain shrubs: Utah juniper, mountain-mahogany, big sagebrush, black sage, rabbitbrush, and grasses.

Climate is semiarid, annual precipitation from 5 to 30 in. Drainage is from the higher country on the N. The site has two perennial streams as well as permanent springs. Also, water accumulates in shallow limestone basins.

Large mammals on the site include mule deer, bighorn sheep, and black bear. Elk use the site periodically. Upland game birds include blue and sage grouse, ringnecked pheasant.

The site has no visitor facilities. Campgrounds are in the Bighorn Canyon National Recreation Area and Custer NF.

PUBLICATION: Information page and map.

HEADQUARTERS: BLM, Miles City District, P.O. Box 940, Miles City, MT 59301; (406) 232-4331.

TERRY BADLANDS
U.S. Bureau of Land Management
43,450 acres.

4 mi. W of Terry, across the Yellowstone River. From I-94, exit at Terry. About 1 1/2 mi. N on County Road 253, then 5 mi. W.

The described route leads to a signed overlook, which is as far as most visitors go. The badlands have many features shaped in sandstone by wind and water: bridges, tabletops, spires, and buttes. BLM's wilderness study noted "outstanding scenery."

The terrain is rugged, but exploring it on foot is feasible. Because of cattle grazing, the area has numerous old vehicle tracks, often following flat ridgetops. Access to the S portion is by an old railroad bridge 4 mi. W of Terry, now converted to automobile use. From the bridge, a road parallels the Yellowstone River and connects with the Calypso Trail that crosses the area SE–NW. Informal campsites can be found. The site has some petrified wood, and there are opportunities for rock and fossil collecting.

Roads within the site are impassable in wet weather.

HEADQUARTERS: BLM, Miles City District, P.O. Box 940, Miles City, MT 59301; (406) 232-4331.

TONGUE RIVER AND RESERVOIR
Montana Department of Fish, Wildlife & Parks
100-plus river miles.

SE MT. From Decker, near the WY border, 6 mi. N on SR 314, then 1 mi. E on county road to campground on reservoir. 4 mi. farther to second campground. Tongue River Road follows the river from the reservoir NE through Birney and Ashland to the Yellowstone River near Miles City.

Hank Fischer calls it "Probably the most overlooked float stream in Montana," despite easy paddling, excellent fishing, and fine scenery. We almost overlooked it. It's out of the way, yet readily accessible. A major difficulty is the lack of public access points. The state has a Recreation Area and a Fishing Access Site on the reservoir, then nothing until an FAS 12 mi. from Miles City, a gap of 90-odd mi. The river flows in a corridor between the Northern Cheyenne Indian Reservation and part of the Custer NF, but only private land adjoins it. There are a few highway bridges.

The reservoir, narrow and about 8 mi. long, is said to be an excellent warmwater fishery. Boating is limited to hand-launched craft. Elevation is about 3,250 ft.

The entire river valley is rather flat prairie. Annual precipitation is about 14 in.

REFERENCES
Fischer, Hank. *The Floater's Guide to Montana.* Billings, MT: Falcon Press, 1986. Pp. 101–03.

MONTANA ◄§ 302

Sample, Mike. *The Angler's Guide to Montana.* Billings, MT: Falcon Press, 1984. Pp. 207–09.

HEADQUARTERS: Region 7, 2004 Main, Miles City, MT 59301; (406) 232-4365.

UPPER MISSOURI WILD AND SCENIC RIVER
U.S. Bureau of Land Management

Of the 191 river miles in the Wild and Scenic River section of the Missouri River, well over half are in Zone 2, and the entry is there. The W & S section begins at Fort Benton, on US 87 in Zone 2, and extends E to the US 191 bridge at the W end of the Charles M. Russell National Wildlife Refuge (see entry).

YELLOWSTONE RIVER
Montana Department of Fish, Wildlife & Parks
671 river mi.; about 300 mi. in Zone 4.

Followed by I-90 and I-94 from Livingston to Glendive, then SR 16.

Rising in the mountains of Wyoming, flowing through Yellowstone Lake and the Grand Canyon of the Yellowstone, the river is free-flowing, undammed for its entire 671 mi. before entering the Missouri River just across the North Dakota line. After leaving Yellowstone NP, it passes through the Gallatin NF for about 12 mi. For the remainder of its course it is bordered almost entirely by private land, with only small, scattered tracts of state and federal holdings.

In Zone 4 it is never far from a major highway, passing many towns and cities. This was the route to the West, pioneered by explorers and trappers, followed by those who acquired and settled the riparian land.

It is, nonetheless, a river to be considered by outdoorsmen. The upper Yellowstone is famous for its trout fishing. In Zone 4 the current is slower, the stream broad and often braided; so this is warmwater fishing, for catfish, sauger, walleye, and paddlefish.

On maps the highway looks close, but it is seldom visible from the river. Afloat, one sees cottonwoods and willow thickets, bluffs and outcrops of yellow rock. The many islands and bars are habitat for waterfowl, shorebirds, beaver, mink, and muskrat.

The river can be floated. There's no challenging whitewater, and almost any maneuverable craft will do. The floater need not have high skill or great experience, but does need information and alertness. There are hazards: tricky currents, diversions, weirs, downed trees, and other obstacles.

Fishing Access Sites are well distributed along the entire length. We counted more than 20. They range from an acre to several hundred acres. Camping and launching are possible at most of them. We camped for a night at one, close to the water's edge, dining at a picnic table under a huge cottonwood. We had the site to ourselves. The only unnatural sound was the infrequent rattle of a car crossing a county bridge nearby.

Fishing access was not the only reason for acquiring riparian sites. River bottomland is essential to pheasant, whitetail deer, and waterfowl. Agricultural and industrial development were eliminating more and more of this habitat.

Seven Sisters, 365 acres. An example of multiple-purpose sites is Seven Sisters, the last FAS on the river in MT, acquired in 1974. It lies along 3/4 mi. of river channel and includes several sloughs. Riparian vegetation includes cottonwoods, buffaloberry, willow, red dogwood, Russian olive, snowberry, and rose, with grasses such as smooth brome, Kentucky bluegrass, Canada wild rye, quackgrass and cheatgrass. Oats and wheat have been planted. Cattails, rushes, and sedges grow in the sloughs.

The combination of water, food, and cover has attracted many waterfowl, including Canada goose, mallard, gadwall, pintail, green-winged and blue-winged teals, American wigeon, shoveler, wood duck, redhead, canvasback, lesser scaup, common goldeneye, ruddy duck, common and red-breasted mergansers. Also attracted is a substantial array of birds of prey, shorebirds, and passerines. Pheasant are abundant, sharp-tailed grouse common in fall and winter. Whitetail deer are present all year. Also noted: muskrat, beaver, mink, otter, badger, raccoon, coyote, red fox, striped skunk, bobcat. The site offers camping, hunting, fishing, and boat launching, as well as good wildlife observation.

PUBLICATION: *Treasure of Gold.* Floating guide, Billings to the Missouri. $1.

REFERENCES

Fischer, Hank. *The Floater's Guide to Montana.* Billings, MT: Falcon Press, 1986. Pp. 103–10.

Sample, Mike. *The Angler's Guide to Montana.* Billings, MT: Falcon Press, 1984. Pp. 142–64.

HEADQUARTERS: Region 5, 1125 Lake Elmo Dr., Billings, MT 59105; (406) 252-4654.

WYOMING

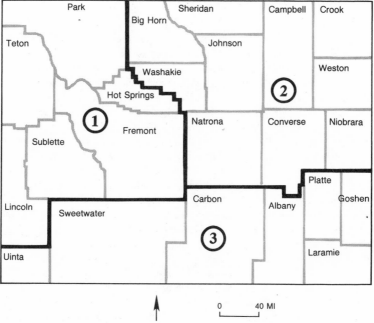

Park

Big Horn

Sheridan

Campbell

Crook

Teton

Johnson

Weston

Washakie

Hot Springs

② 2

Natrona

Converse

Niobrara

① 1

Fremont

Sublette

Lincoln

Carbon

Platte

Albany

Goshen

Sweetwater

③ 3

Uinta

Laramie

0   40 MI

↑
N
|

WYOMING

Wyoming is huge, wild, and young, with a diversity surprising to strangers. Even in midsummer few places are crowded. Solitude is easily found. Wyoming's wildernesses are more lightly used than those of any other state except Alaska.

Yellowstone National Park is the state's premiere attraction, followed by Grand Teton National Park. Both attract crowds in summer, but only to their developed areas. The National Forests have four times as much acreage. The 18 million acres of public domain include colorful badlands, vast areas of sand dunes, deep canyons, floatable rivers, ice caves, and more. The state's parks and wildlife areas have their own unique qualities, best known to local residents.

The two National Parks draw most of the out-of-state visitors. Most visitors to State Parks are Wyoming residents. When we asked about visitor activities in National Forests and the public domain—together covering two-fifths of the state—the standard answer was "hunting and fishing." Hiking, backpacking, bird watching, boating, rafting, climbing, and other "nonconsumptive" activities are gradually increasing, but few trails or backcountry destinations are heavily impacted. Hunting occurs in the fall. Fishermen go to the best streams and lakes. In midsummer we could always find an attractive place to hike or camp alone.

Wyoming's mean elevation is 6,700 ft. Even excluding the mountains, the average elevation in the S is well over 6,000 ft.; much of the N is 2,500 ft. lower. The highest point is 13,785-ft. Gannett Peak in the Wind River Range; the lowest, 3,125 ft., near the NE corner. Principal mountain ranges are the Wind River, Teton, Gros Ventre, and Absaroka in the NW, Bighorn in the N central, Laramie and Medicine Bow in the SE. These N–S ranges lie across the prevailing westerlies, intercepting moisture, so lands to their E are semiarid. The mountains are prominent, but the high plains cover more area.

The Continental Divide splits the state from NW to S central. The Snake River system drains to the Columbia River. The Green River, draining most of the SW, flows to the Colorado. In the N, the Yellowstone, Wind, Big Horn, Tongue, and Powder rivers flow N to the Missouri. The Platte, entering from the S, loops around the state's SE corner, exiting into Nebraska. The Belle Fourche, Cheyenne, and Niobrara rivers flow E. Wyoming has 20,000 mi. of rivers and their tributaries.

Dams intercept the flow of most large rivers. The largest impoundments are Flaming Gorge, Jackson, Boysen, Big Horn, Seminoe, and Pathfinder.

Hundreds of others range from 8,000 acres to small ponds. Yellowstone Lake is, by far, the largest natural water body. The high country is dotted with hundreds of clear alpine lakes.

Climate: It's cool. Temperature above 100° are seldom recorded outside the low elevations in the central and NE portions and along the E border. Summer nights are usually cool, even when days are hot. For most places away from the mountains, July mean minimum temperatures are 50 to 60°. Winter is a succession of cold waves.

In the mountains, cool often becomes cold. Midsummer readings below freezing are not unusual. Hikers in the high country are warned that snow can fall at any time. In winter, many valleys become pockets receiving cold air that drains from the mountains at night.

It's dry. Only on a few high slopes does annual precipitation exceed 18 in., and most of that is snow. Much of the SW receives less than 10 in., the eastern plains 12 to 16 in.

And it's windy. Prevailing winds of 10 to 15 mph are common.

Plants: Wyoming's geological history is a record of erosion. Soils are generally thin and poor. This aridity and scanty rainfall limit cropland to less than 4% of the state; most privately owned land is grazed. In the past, large areas were overgrazed, turned into dust, and abandoned.

Most of our earlier visits to Wyoming had been in summer, when the landscape had turned brown. In 1986 we arrived in May, at the end of an exceptionally wet spring. Everything was lush and green, spangled with countless wildflowers. Streams were over their banks, lakes full to overflowing.

Lodgepole pine, Engelmann spruce, subalpine fir, and Douglas-fir clothe many mountainsides.

Wildlife: Wyoming is world famous as big game country. At first we wondered why the Game and Fish Department makes little effort to attract hunters. Then we realized that professional outfitters and guides do it, advertising for clients not only in the United States but overseas. By law, a visiting hunter must hire a licensed guide to hunt in any Wilderness area. Big game includes elk, mule deer, bighorn sheep, moose, pronghorn, mountain lion, black bear.

Fishermen outnumber hunters. Some travel far to wet a line in such famous water as the Miracle Mile. Most are local residents who have favorite spots seldom visited by outsiders.

The great variety of habitats—deserts and wetlands, meadows and mountains, high plains and deep canyons—provides a diversity of species. The viewing is good, not just in backcountry but also along lightly traveled roads.

ROADS AND MAPS

The official highway map shows paved roads and a few graveled roads. That's about one-tenth of the total road mileage. Not shown are many county roads and the networks of National Forest and Bureau of Land Management roads.

For travel in a National Forest, buy the Forest map and ask for the Travel Map. The latter isn't as easy to read, but it has more current information on closures, road conditions, etc.

BLM has a fine series of ten recreation maps, numbered 5 through 14, covering the entire state except for the E tier. Numbers 1 through 4 haven't been published and apparently won't be. These maps show much detail: land ownership, back roads and trails, campgrounds, fishing and boating waters, scenic overlooks, historical trails, and more. We found this series best for general use, and most of our entries have a note such as "(BLM map 8)".

BLM also has a series of Surface Management Quads, 1/2 inch to the mile. It takes 110 quads to cover the state. Most users buy only one or two, for areas in which they have special interest.

Many back roads require 4-wheel drive or at least high clearance. Forest and BLM road maintenance funds permit current upkeep of only a minor fraction of the network. Several thousand miles receive no maintenance.

Rain can quickly make a good dirt road treacherous. Wyoming gumbo is notorious. The first rain turns the upper layer into an efficient lubricant over a hard base, so slippery that a car on one side of a high-crowned road may slide sideways into the ditch. As the mud deepens, ruts form that become rock-hard when dry. In desert areas such as the Killpecker Dunes, soft sand can trap a car.

Be cautious. Yesterday's road information may be incorrect today.

TRESPASS

Citizens have a legal right to use the BLM-managed public domain for recreation—if they can get to it. In some cases, the only access is across private land. Wyoming's trespass law is unusually restrictive. In most states, a landowner who wishes to exclude visitors must post boundaries. Not in Wyoming. Even though the boundary between private and public land is unmarked, you can be charged with trespass if you cross it.

The major issue is hunting. By using the trespass law, landowners control public access to thousands of acres of public land. Some charge hunters $100 a day for the privilege of crossing their land to hunt on public land. The members of one hunting club have exclusive use of a huge area of public land.

BLM acquires easements when it can, which isn't often. The law is being challenged in court. The state government is showing concern. Things may change, but don't count on it.

Even an irascible landowner won't shoot on sight. If you're hunting on his land, he may demand a fee or call the game warden and you'll pay a fine. If you're just bird-watching or hiking, he may warn you off, ignore you, or even say hello.

Our BLM advisors told us trespass isn't a problem in parts of western Wyoming where the landowners are large corporations rather than ranchers. We've been guided by their advice.

CONTINENTAL DIVIDE TRAIL

The Continental Divide enters Wyoming S of Encampment, in the Medicine Bow NF. It wanders NW through the Great Divide Basin, crossing private, state, and BLM land, to the Shoshone NF, then on through the Bridger-Teton NF and the SW corner of Yellowstone National Park. The trail is being planned. It will include some existing trails. Each year a few people hike or ride an approximation of the route. Each National Forest can provide current information.

OREGON AND MORMON TRAILS

Total length of these emigrant trails in WY was about 495 mi. Segments are now in private as well as public ownership. From Torrington, the route followed the North Platte River to the present site of Casper, then turned W and SW over hills to the Sweetwater River, following the river for 90 mi. Next the primary route headed SW to Fort Bridger, where the trails divided, the Oregon Trail heading N and NW to the border near Cokeville.

The routes of these and other historic trails are shown on the official WY highway map. Most traces of the trails have been obliterated in eastern WY, but ruts, graves, and artifacts can be seen in the W. Some segments are now roads. Along the route are landmarks such as Devil's Gate, Signature Rock, Independence Rock, and Register Cliff. Historical markers are at numerous points on public highways where they cross or overlook the trail.

A 1986 BLM management plan calls for placing markers at intervals along the entire length of the trails, and for managing the portions on public land to preserve them and provide for public use.

So many changes have occurred that most segments don't meet our definition of "natural area." Some do, however, especially along rivers and in high country.

Sections of the trail can be traveled now. We suggest inquiring at BLM offices in Casper, Rawlins, and Rock Springs.

The National Park Service has published two leaflets, "The Oregon Trail" and "The Mormon Pioneer Trail," with maps, description, etc. BLM offices may have them. Available from Pacific Northwest Regional Office, National Park Service, 2001 Sixth Ave., Seattle, WA 98121; (206) 442-5565.

CAVES

Wyoming has numerous caves, ranging from short crawlways to extensive complexes of rooms and passages. Many are on BLM land. We were asked not to pinpoint them. Inexperienced cavers risk drowning, hypothermia, falls, and entrapment. Some caves require skill and special equipment. Several of BLM's caves are gated and locked. Permits are issued to qualified parties. Cave information is available at BLM offices in Worland and Cody.

Many caves are described in *Caves of Wyoming* (see References). We were delighted by the names given to some of them: You're the Geologist, You Tell Me; Relatively Long Dark Ugly Tight Cave; God Awful Crack; Slimy Slick Pit; Creepy Crevice; Garbage Avalanche Pit; You-Can-Have-It Pit. Enticing!

HISTORY

We often regret these guides cannot include information on geology, archeology, and history. Space doesn't permit it. Wyoming's geology is complex. Forest Service and BLM archeologists have identified several thousand cultural sites and believe many more await discovery. Once one begins telling the stories of Lewis and Clark, the Oregon Trail, and Hole-in-the-Wall, there's no stopping.

A visitor can't escape history. Roadside markers remind travelers that pioneers passed this way. The road map marks their trails: Oregon, Mormon, California, Pony Express, and others. One can see the wheel ruts made by their wagons.

One soon becomes fascinated. Carved into this rock are the signatures of pioneers. Tens of thousands of emigrants struggled through this pass. And did you know Butch Cassidy survived, under another name, until 1937?

FEDERAL AGENCIES

U.S. FOREST SERVICE

Wyoming has four National Forests, bits of five others, and a National Grassland, a total of 9 1/4 million acres. They include the state's principal mountain ranges, the most extensive forests, hundreds of lakes and miles of rivers and streams. Over 3 million acres are Wildernesses. The Flaming Gorge National Recreation Area (see entry) is part of the Ashley NF.

Maps and publications are best obtained from each National Forest.

NATIONAL PARK SERVICE

The state has two National Parks (Yellowstone and Grand Teton) and two National Monuments (Devils Tower and Fossil Butte). The National Park system also includes the John D. Rockefeller Memorial Parkway, linking the two Parks, and the Bighorn Canyon National Recreation Area. Also the Fort Laramie National Historic Site, which is not an entry.

U.S. BUREAU OF LAND MANAGEMENT

Wyoming State Office
2515 Warren Ave.
Cheyenne, WY 82003
(307) 772-2425

BLM administers 17.8 million acres in Wyoming, more than one-fourth of the state. Most of this public domain lies between mountain ranges in the western two-thirds of the state, but there are also scattered tracts in the eastern third.

We have selected sites of special interest to outdoorsmen. Many, but not all, are Wilderness Study Areas.

We omitted sites without legal access. Sites that can be reached only with 4-wheel-drive or high-clearance vehicles were included only if they are too interesting to overlook. Sites managed as Wildernesses are closed to wheeled vehicles, so we considered access to trailheads or other suitable points on their borders.

U.S. FISH AND WILDLIFE SERVICE

Wyoming has 5 federal wildlife refuges. The largest is the National Elk Refuge at Jackson.

The 4 waterfowl refuges have few visitors, because of size and locations. Pathfinder is several tracts on Pathfinder Reservoir and is described in that entry. Seedskadee is off main travel routes but of interest to birders during the spring migration. Hutton is an attractive small refuge near Laramie. We were advised that the fourth isn't suitable for visitors.

STATE AGENCIES

WYOMING RECREATION COMMISSION

122 W. 25th
Cheyenne, WY 82002
(307) 777-7695

The commission administers 10 State Parks (one of which is about to be inundated), two Recreation Areas, two archeological sites, and a veterans' cemetery. When we first met with park officials, we thought only two or three of the parks would become entries. After our site visits, we included seven.

These seven recorded 2.5 million visitor-days in 1985, so they're crowded at times. But more than two-thirds of the visitors are Wyoming residents, and most of them come on weekends. We visited several of the parks on June weekdays and saw few visitors.

Park facilities are simple: no hookups or hot showers. Trail development is just beginning. Only Sinks Canyon and Guernsey have interpretive programs.

GAME AND FISH DEPARTMENT

5400 Bishop Blvd.
Cheyenne, WY 82002
(307) 777-7631

The department manages hunting and fishing sites. Its 30 Wildlife Habitat Management Units (WHMUs) range in size from 300 to 62,500 acres, totaling 258,000 acres. Most fishing sites provide access from a public highway to a parking place on shore, often with a launching ramp, sometimes enough room for RV camping.

Wyoming residents know where these sites are, at least those nearby. It's not easy for visitors to find them. The guidebooks once published by the department are out of print but we were told they'd be available again in 1988. The sites aren't noted on the official state highway map. If you know where to look, you can find most of the WHMUs on the BLM maps, but under other names, such as "Big Game Winter Range." We could find no publication listing Fishing Access Sites. Many of these access areas are identified by signs on highways.

Camping is permitted on most WHMUs, but we were asked to emphasize that there are no tables, fire pits, or water faucets, and usually a single privy. RVs were parked at several Fishing Access Sites we visited, but they weren't attractive as campsites.

We have entries for 11 WHMUs, selected for accessibility and their general attractiveness to outdoorsmen.

REFERENCES

PLANTS
Lanner, Ronald M. *Trees of the Great Basin.* Reno: University of Nevada Press, 1985.

BIRDS
Ryser, Fred A., Jr. *Birds of the Great Basin.* Reno: University of Nevada Press, 1985.

AMPHIBIANS AND REPTILES
Baxter, George Theodore. *Amphibians and Reptiles of Wyoming.* Cheyenne: Wyoming Department of Fish and Game, 1980.

HIKING AND BACKPACKING
Mitchell, Finis. *Wind River Trails.* Salt Lake City: Wasatch, 1975.
Sudduth, Tom and Sanse. *Wyoming Hiking Trails.* Boulder, CO: Pruett, 1978.
Wolf, James R. *Guide to the Continental Divide Trail: Wyoming.* Bethesda, MD: Continental Trail Society, 1986.

FISHING

Knapp, Kenneth J. *Wyoming Fishing Guide*. Jackson Hole, WY: Rising Trout Publishing, 1978.

CAVES

Hill, Chris, Wayne Sutherland, and Lee Tierney. *Caves of Wyoming*. Laramie: Wyoming Geological Survey, 1976.

GEOLOGY

Blackstone, A. L. *Traveler's Guide to the Geology of Wyoming*. Laramie: Wyoming Geological Survey, 1971.

Root, F. K. *Minerals and Rocks of Wyoming*. Laramie: Wyoming Geological Survey, 1977.

Hager, N. W. *Fossils of Wyoming*. Laramie: Wyoming Geological Survey, 1970.

ZONE 1

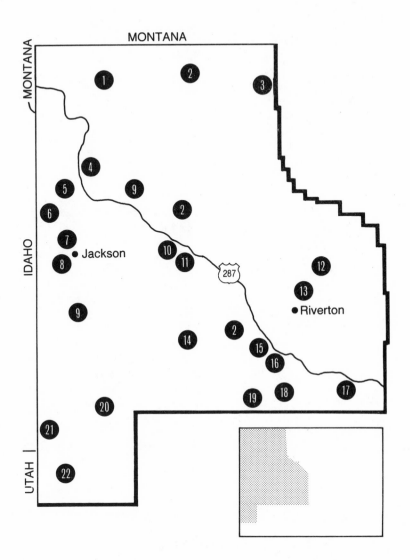

MONTANA

MONTANA

IDAHO

UTAH

① ② ③

④

⑤ ⑨

⑥ ②

⑦ • Jackson

⑧ ⑩ ⑪

287

⑫

⑬

• Riverton

⑨

⑭ ②

⑮

⑯

⑳ ⑱ ⑰

㉑ ⑲

㉒

ZONE 1

Includes these counties:

Park	Teton	Hot Springs
Lincoln	Sublette	Fremont

Here in the NW is Wyoming's highest and wildest country. Two National Parks, two National Forests, and adjoining Forests in Idaho and Montana form the largest block of unspoiled land in the Lower 48.

The main highways converge on the Parks: US 14/20 from the E, US 26/287 from the SE, US 187/189 from the S. The crowds follow the same routes, many travelers being unaware of the spectacular natural features along the way: several of the continent's principal glaciers, colorful badlands, cliffs rich with marine fossils, a vanishing river. So abundant are bighorn sheep around Whiskey Mountain that they are trapped for restocking other places. Ride a raft down the Snake River, or a sleigh among wintering elk.

The Wind River Indian Reservation occupies a large block on the map, second in size only to Yellowstone. Several highways cross it, including US 26 and US 287, with several towns along the way. We saw Indian faces but no effort to attract the tourist dollar, nor have we seen mention of a license to fish Reservation waters. The Indian population is less than 6,000.

BOYSEN STATE PARK
Wyoming Recreation Commission
19,885 land acres.

On US 20, N of Shoshoni. (BLM map 14)

The park land surrounds an 19,660-acre reservoir formed by damming the Wind River. On the N, it extends 2 mi. into the Wind River Canyon. Portions are within the Wind River Indian Reservation. Terrain is mostly rolling, arid plains, with occasional buttes, cut by a few intermittent streams and dry gulches.

At the N end are higher hills and bluffs. Here, below the dam, the scenic Wind River Canyon is 2,000 ft. deep, dividing the Owl Creek and Bridger mountains. US 20 runs through the canyon, a roadway blasted from solid granite, with three tunnels. The canyon is narrow, just wide enough for road, railroad, and river, which is about 30 ft. wide. The river flows N toward Thermopolis, becoming the Big Horn after it leaves the canyon.

The reservoir is subject to drawdowns, but we were told they don't interfere with recreation. Its shape is irregular, with drowned streams on both sides. Wildlife includes waterfowl, sage grouse, deer, pronghorn.

Most park visitors are from Wyoming, and most come on weekends for camping, picnicking, swimming, fishing, and boating.

On a weekday in June, we drove along the W shore. The all-weather road is gravel, rough in places. Spur roads to shoreline campsites were less well maintained; some we wouldn't wish to travel in wet weather.

We saw little to attract visitors on the W side. The land is rolling, treeless, windswept, no doubt dusty at times. We met no other cars, saw no one in the campgrounds, only two boats on the lake. The terrain off US 20 is much the same at the S end of the reservoir. At the N end are colorful hills. Most development, including marina, campgrounds, and park HQ, is here. Hills provide some shelter, but there are few trees. We thought the most attractive campsites were in the canyon below the dam, not on the reservoir.

ACTIVITIES

Camping: Campgrounds are scattered around the reservoir and in the canyon below the dam. 129 sites. All year. Campgrounds on the W shore are less in demand.

Fishing: Said to be excellent for trout, walleye, ling. Ice fishing. Below the dam: trout, yellow perch.

Boating: No hp limit. Marina on E side.

Swimming: No designated beach; no lifeguards.

ADJACENT: Sand Mesa Wildlife Management Unit (Wyoming Game and Fish Department, 17,949 acres). Before the dam was built, the Bureau of Reclamation acquired the land to be inundated and some bordering land. Included were several strips extending up Cottonwood, Muddy, and Fivemile creeks, as much as 16 mi. W from the reservoir. These are managed for waterfowl, upland game birds, and small game. Included are ponds and marshes as well as sagebrush-grasslands. Lake Cameahwait, 250 acres, offers camping and boating. Most visitors come for hunting and fishing, but hiking and birding are also possibilities. Camping is permitted. Several dirt roads lead into the area from the W side shoreline road, but except for the road to Cameahwait these are infrequently maintained.

PUBLICATION: Leaflet with map.

PARK HEADQUARTERS: Boysen Route, Shoshoni, WY 82649; (307) 876-2796.

BRIDGER-TETON NATIONAL FOREST

U.S. Forest Service
3,400,309 acres.

Western WY, adjoining Yellowstone and Grand Teton National Parks,
extending about 95 mi. S of Jackson. Crossed by US 14/20/16, US 287/26,
US 189/191, US 89.

When the Bridger and Teton National Forests were combined in 1973, they
became the largest National Forest outside Alaska. Lying on three sides of
Jackson Hole, the Bridger-Teton adjoins Yellowstone and Grand Teton Parks
and the Targhee National Forest on the W, the Shoshone National Forest on
the E. Together they comprise a gigantic block of splendid land, much of it
pristine wilderness.

The Forest has more than 1,500 lakes and 3,100 miles of streams, most of
them unpolluted and undisturbed, with some of the best fishing to be found
anywhere. Wildlife is abundant, with large populations of elk, moose, deer,
and bighorn. The Forest's size, natural riches, diversity, and proximity to two
popular National Parks attract many visitors: 1 3/4 million visitor-days in
1985. Although it has over 50 developed recreation sites, more than three-
fourths of Forest visitation is dispersed, away from these centers. Even so,
there are huge areas that receive few visitors, notably the Salt River and
Wyoming ranges and the Palisades area.

Most visitors come in summer. Hunting is the principal activity in the fall,
skiing and snowmobiling in winter. Campgrounds are generally open from
Memorial Day to Labor Day, but primitive camping is always available.

Topography is mountainous and complex. The Absaroka Range is on the
NE boundary. Much of the E boundary is the Continental Divide, on the crest
of the Wind River Range. The Gros Ventre Range is in the central portion,
in the SW the Salt River and Wyoming ranges. The highest terrain is on the
Wind River Range, with elevations up to 13,785 ft. On its W slopes is the
Bridger Wilderness, a region with more than a thousand lakes. In the NE
corner are high plateaus, ridges, and extensive mountain meadows along the
Yellowstone and Thorofare rivers, meandering through wetlands as they
approach their junction inside the Park. To the W, across the Divide, are
forested ridges interspersed with mountain meadows and grassy slopes. S of
Grand Teton National Park, the Snake River Range divides the Forest from
the Targhee National Forest. The Snake River Valley, E of the Range, is

mostly private land until the river turns W, where it becomes the Forest boundary. (BLM is contesting ownership of a strip along the river.)

For about 70 mi. S of the Snake River, the Forest is a rough oblong about 25 mi. wide. The Salt River and Wyoming ranges run N–S through this block, with Greys River between them. This region lies between the Great Basin and the Rocky Mountains, with elevations to 11,363 ft.

Almost 80% of the Forest is roadless. More than one-third has been set aside in three vast Wildernesses, and more roadless areas may be added to the Wilderness system. Seven sites in the Bridger Wilderness became so popular that restrictions had to be imposed, but it's not difficult to find solitude elsewhere.

Although most of the Forest is roadless, it has over 1,200 miles of roads, some all-weather, some requiring high clearance or 4-wheel drive. Many of the roads are in stream valleys.

Climate: Because of its terrain and range of elevations, the Forest has climates ranging from semidesert to alpine. Most of the area is above 7,000 ft. elevation and has a mean annual temperature below 32°F. Dec. and Jan. are coldest, with an average temperature below 10°. The frost-free period is brief: late June and early July. Mountain barriers are chiefly responsible for the wide range in average annual precipitation, from 14 in. at Jackson to over 60 in. on the Teton and Wind River mountains. There's enough snow for winter sports from around Thanksgiving until early Apr.

Plants: Two-thirds of the area is forested. Although logging yields several million board feet of timber annually, most stands are mature. Foresters concerned with timber production say the mature trees are deteriorating because of disease and insect infestation and should be clear-cut to make way for new growth. Many conservationists object to clear-cutting.

Sagebrush is the dominant plant on many of the lower slopes of the Wind River Range. Aspen marks the transition to forest, with lodgepole pine and some Douglas-fir above. North-facing slopes support lodgepole pine, spruce, and subalpine fir, interspersed with large meadows; most high mountain lakes are in this zone. Whitebark pine forest forms the transition between subalpine areas and true alpine vegetation. The high peaks are barren.

On the Salt River and Wyoming ranges, sagebrush grows at the lower elevations, with mountain-mahogany on the steeper, drier slopes. Douglas-fir and aspen are above the sagebrush, giving way to subalpine fir, with whitebark pine at the highest elevations.

The Forest has a variety of riparian communities, with such species as cottonwood, willow, cinquefoil, alder, dogwood, silver sage, sedge.

From valleys to tundra, the Forest has a rich array of wildflowers. No Forest checklist is available, but there are several wildflower guides to the region. Species include monkshood, yarrow, pussytoes, windflower, rock jasmine, columbine, heartleaf arnica, asters, milkvetch, balsamroots, Indian paintbrush, marsh marigold, thistles, clematis, larkspur, shootingstar, wallflower, eriogonum, gentians, scarlet gilia, globemallow, lupines, monkeyflowers, owl clovers, penstemons, phlox, phacelias, buttercups, cinquefoils, groundsels, valerians, speedwells.

Birds: 293 species recorded. A Jackson Hole checklist is available. Seasonally common species include common loon; horned, eared, western, and pied-billed grebes; double-crested cormorant, great blue heron, snowy egret, sandhill crane, black-crowned night-heron, white-faced ibis, trumpeter swan, American bittern, Canada goose, mallard, gadwall, pintail; green-winged, blue-winged, and cinnamon teals; American wigeon, northern shoveler, redhead, ring-necked duck, canvasback, lesser scaup, common and Barrow's goldeneyes, bufflehead, harlequin duck, ruddy duck, hooded and common mergansers.

Hawks include goshawk, sharp-shinned, Cooper's, red-tailed, Swainson's, rough-legged, ferruginous. Golden and bald eagles, northern harrier, prairie falcon, merlin, American kestrel. Blue, ruffed, and sage grouse; sandhill crane, sora, American coot, killdeer, common snipe, long-billed curlew, spotted and solitary sandpipers, willet, greater and lesser yellowlegs; least, stilt, and semipalmated sandpipers; long-billed dowitcher, marbled godwit, sanderling, American avocet, Wilson's phalarope. Gulls: California, ring-billed, Franklin's, Bonaparte's. Terns: Forster's, common, Caspian, black. Mourning dove. Owls: screech, great horned, pygmy, long-eared, short-eared, boreal, saw-whet. Poor-will, common nighthawk; broad-tailed, calliope, and rufous hummingbirds; belted kingfisher. Woodpeckers: Lewis', hairy, downy, black-backed, northern three-toed, northern flicker, yellow-bellied and Williamson's sapsuckers.

Eastern and western kingbirds. Flycatchers: willow, olive-sided, Hammond's, dusky, and western. Say's phoebe, western wood-pewee, horned lark. Swallows: violet-green, tree, bank, and cliff. Gray, Steller's, and pinyon jays; black-billed magpie, common raven, American crow, Clark's nutcracker, black-capped and mountain chickadees; white-breasted and red-breasted nuthatches, brown creeper, dipper; house, canyon, and rock wrens; long-billed marsh wren, gray catbird, sage thrasher, American robin, hermit and Swainson's thrushes, veery, western and mountain bluebirds, Townsend's solitaire, golden-crowned and ruby-crowned kinglets, water pipit, Bohemian and cedar waxwings, northern and loggerhead shrikes, European starling; solitary, red-eyed, and warbling vireos.

Warblers: orange-crowned, yellow, yellow-rumped, and Wilson's warblers. Northern waterthrush, red knot, pectoral and Baird's sandpipers, American redstart, house sparrow, western meadowlark; yellow-headed, red-winged, and Brewer's blackbirds; northern oriole, common grackle, brown-headed cowbird, western tanager; black-headed, evening, and pine grosbeaks; lazuli bunting. Finches: Cassin's, house, gray-crowned rosy, and black rosy. Common redpoll, pine siskin, American goldfinch, red crossbill, green-tailed towhee, lark bunting.

Sparrows: savannah, grasshopper, vesper, lark, sage, tree, chipping, Brewer's, white-crowned, white-throated, fox, Lincoln's, song. Dark-eyed junco, snow bunting.

Mammals: 74 species recorded. No checklist available. 1984 population estimates included 30,000 elk, 6,000 moose, 46,000 mule deer, 2,000 prong-horn, 1,000 black bear, 3,000 bighorn sheep, 20 mountain lion. Grizzly bear occur, but there is no recent population estimate. Reintroduction of gray wolf has been proposed.

Other species, excluding those considered rare, include shrews: masked, vagrant, dusky, dwarf. Northern water shrew. Bats: little brown, long-eared, fringed, long-legged, and small-footed myotis; silver-haired, big brown, hoary, Townsend, big-eared. Pika, whitetail jackrabbit, snowshoe hare, mountain and desert cottontails; least, yellow pine, and Uinta chipmunks; yellowbelly marmot, Richardson's and Uinta ground squirrels. Golden-man-tled and red squirrels, northern flying squirrel, whitetail prairie dog, northern pocket gopher, olive-backed and Great Basin pocket mice, Ord kangaroo rat, beaver, deer mouse, northern grasshopper mouse, bushytail woodrat. Voles: heather, redback, meadow, montane, longtail, sagebrush. Muskrat, western jumping mouse, porcupine.

Also coyote, red fox, black and grizzly bears, raccoon, marten, fisher, shorttail and longtail weasels, mink, badger, spotted and striped skunks, river otter, mountain lion, lynx, bobcat, bison.

FEATURES

Bridger Wilderness, 428,169 acres, in the Pinedale Ranger District. Extends about 90 mi. SE along the W side of the Wind River Range in a strip 5 to 13 mi. wide. Gannett Peak, 13,785 ft., is the highest point in Wyoming. Other peaks over 12,000 and 13,000 ft. are distributed along the entire length of the ridge. The Fitzpatrick Wilderness of the Shoshone National Forest is on the E side, but hikers seldom attempt the crossing on the few trails over passes above 11,000 ft. elevation.

The Wind River Range has 7 of the 10 largest glaciers remaining in the Lower 48. The Wilderness was sculptured by glaciers into a landscape with cirques, kettles, U-shaped valleys, hanging troughs, a landscape strewn with boulders on lower slopes. A remarkable feature of the Wilderness is its more than 1,300 lakes. Historically they had no fish, but stocking in the 1920s and 1930s established populations of trout in the principal lakes. Wildlife is abun-dant, including black bear but not grizzly.

Access is easy, from US 191 between Rock Springs and Jackson. Improved roads lead to more than a dozen trailheads with 600 mi. of wilderness trails. Accessibility and abundance of lakes have made this the most heavily used National Forest Wilderness in the region for hiking, backpacking, horsepack-ing, hunting, fishing, ski touring, and mountaineering.

Three of the trailheads—Green River Lake, Elkhart Park, and Big Sandy—

are best avoided by hikers who want solitude. Seven destinations have been heavily impacted; rules now limit group size and the number of stock used in these places. All groups and all parties using horses overnight must obtain permits, available at the Pinedale Ranger District. Others are asked to register, but entry is not yet limited. Rangers can suggest the least-crowded trails and destinations, and they can also suggest trails and destinations in other roadless areas where use is lighter.

A convenient route to the middle sector is NE of Boulder, through BLM's Scab Creek Wilderness (see entry).

Teton Wilderness, 585,468 acres, in the Buffalo Ranger District. Occupies almost the entire N portion of the Forest, on the S and E boundaries of Yellowstone National Park. The Forest is on the N and E boundaries of Grand Teton National Park; the Wilderness boundary is congruent or a short distance within. The Wilderness and Forest E boundary is on the Absaroka Range, with the Washakie Wilderness of the Shoshone National Forest on the other side.

The Continental Divide bisects the Wilderness, extending SE from Yellowstone and becoming the Wilderness SE boundary. The Yellowstone River flows NW on the E side of the Divide. Drainages on the W side include Pacific Creek and North and South Buffalo Forks, flowing to the Snake River.

Elevations are lower than in the Bridger Wilderness, 7,500 to 9,675 ft. on the W side, 8,000 to 12,165 ft. (on Younts Peak) on the E. A popular route crosses the Divide at Two Ocean Pass, 8,200 ft., so named because a creek divides here, one branch flowing eventually to the Atlantic Ocean, the other to the Pacific.

About 60% of the visitors come in summer for fishing, camping, and sightseeing. Almost all the rest are big game hunters. About 95% of the travel is by horseback, although backpacking is on the increase. The principal trailheads are on the W and SW.

The landscape is spectacular and unspoiled: high plateaus, forested ridges and slopes, mountain meadows, grassy slopes, creek valleys, riparian marshes, and lakes, although not as many lakes as in the Bridger. Popular features include South Buffalo Fork Falls, North Fork Falls, Big Springs on the Soda Fork, and Bridger Lake near the Yellowstone Park border. From Bridger Lake, the Thorofare Trail follows the Yellowstone River through the Park to Yellowstone Lake.

This is bear country, with grizzlies as well as black bear, so travelers should know how to avoid encounters. The Wilderness is summer range for part of the Jackson Hole elk herd. Big game species include moose and bighorn sheep. Fishing in most streams and lakes is excellent.

Gros Ventre Wilderness, 287,000 acres. About 6 mi. N of Jackson on US 26, just after crossing the Gros Ventre River, Gros Ventre Road runs NE along the river, which here is the boundary between Grand Teton National Park and the National Elk Refuge (see entry). In about 10 mi., after passing the small town of Kelly, the road enters the Forest and soon comes to the Gros Ventre Slide Geological Area. In 1925 a great section of mountainside broke away and roared down, part of it carrying 400 ft. up the other side of the valley. A lake was formed by the resulting dam. When the dam washed out two years later, it caused a disastrous flood. The scar left by the slide is still visible from far off. Three Forest Service campgrounds are along this road, which is unpaved beyond the slide area.

Numerous trails extend N and S from the river, most of them following watercourses. Ask about current trail conditions.

The *Palisades area,* a candidate for Wilderness status, is on both sides of the WY-ID border; about 82,000 of its 247,000 roadless acres are in the Bridger-Teton NF. The area is about 10 mi. SW of Jackson, within the large loop formed by the Snake River in WY and the Palisades Reservoir and Swan Valley in ID. The Snake River Range extends N–S through the area. Primary access is by US 26/89, SR 22, and the Wilson-Fall Creek Forest road, all connecting with Forest roads and trails. The Bridger-Teton portion has about 80 mi. of trails, little used and not well maintained.

Topography is mountainous, with deep canyons. Elevations from 6,000 to 10,000 ft. Lodgepole pine predominates on the lower slopes, with some subalpine fir, Engelmann spruce, and Douglas-fir. The spruce-fir mixture becomes dominant at higher elevations.

Although the scenery is not as spectacular as in nearby Parks and Wildernesses, it is diminished only by the contrast. The area has rugged terrain, abundant wildlife, and fine displays of seasonal wildflowers. Except in hunting season, few visitors come here. Backpackers rarely meet others on the trail.

The *Salt River Range* is another little-used, attractive area. Its 260,000 acres are essentially roadless. The range parallels the ID border, just E of US 89, S of Alpine. Elevations are from 6,000 to 10,000 ft. The range is cut by many steep, rugged, narrow canyons. It has several alpine lakes. N-facing slopes have Engelmann spruce and Douglas-fir. S-facing slopes have grasses, sagebrush, other shrubs. Grass, brush, and wildflowers dominate near the crest.

The area has about 250 mi. of trails. Off-trail hiking is often feasible. Maximum distance from surrounding roads is 3 to 6 mi. Big game hunting (elk, deer, and black bear) is the primary activity. There are opportunities for hiking and backpacking, camping, horse riding, snowmobiling, and ski touring, with little likelihood of meeting other visitors.

The *Wyoming Range* is a 400,000-acre roadless area E of and parallel to the Salt River Range, separated from it by the valley of Greys River. The N boundary is about 12 mi. S of Jackson. A 70-mi. National Recreation Trail extends along its entire length, on or near the crest. Lightly used, it is poorly maintained. Elevations range from 6,000 ft. to 11,363 ft. on Wyoming Peak. Many peaks along the ridge exceed 10,000 ft.

Benches at lower elevations rise to steep, rough slopes. The area has only a few small lakes. Vegetation is similar to that of the Salt River Range. Here, too, the principal activity is big game hunting in Sept.–Oct., with many opportunities for backpacking, fishing, horse riding, and ski touring in solitude.

Fremont Lake, NE of Pinedale, is the Forest's largest lake and second largest natural lake in WY, 12 mi. long, over 600 ft. deep. On a paved road, it has a campground and launching ramp. Several other lakes, 1 to 4 mi. long, are in this area, just outside the Bridger Wilderness boundary, with access by unpaved roads, some of which may require high-clearance or 4-wheel-drive vehicles.

ACTIVITIES

Camping: 39 campgrounds, 611 sites. All are open June through Aug., most on a limited basis in fall.

Hiking, backpacking: 2,856 mi. of trails. The system includes two National Recreation Trails: the Sheridan, 16 mi., and Wyoming Range, 70 mi. If the Continental Divide National Scenic Trail becomes a reality, more than 200 mi. will be here.

Most backcountry travel has been by horse, but hiking is on the increase, especially in the Bridger Wilderness.

Anyone planning more than an easy day hike should ask a District Ranger about trail conditions. Anyone visiting the high country should be prepared for bad weather. Snow and subfreezing temperatures are not unusual in summer.

Hunting: Chiefly big game: elk, deer, moose, pronghorn, bighorn sheep, mountain goat, black bear. See State Preface.

Fishing: Many lakes and streams. Chiefly cutthroat, brook, lake, and rainbow trout. A guide to Bridger Wilderness waters is listed in the Publications section.

Boating: Ramps on New Fork, Fremont, and Half Moon lakes. Cartoppers and canoes can be used on several others.

Rafting: Popular on the Snake River. Numerous outfitters. Only a few sections of the river are on or bordering Forest land. These include the Grand Canyon of the Snake, an exciting whitewater stretch.

Horse riding: Most trails are suitable for horse travel. Some trailheads and other locations have corrals and other facilities. WY Game and Fish Department will supply a list of licensed outfitters. Some special rules apply, especially in the Wildernesses.

Skiing: Three commercial ski areas are on National Forest land near Jackson and Pinedale.

Ski touring: Trails have been established in Cache Creek near Jackson and at the ski area near Pinedale. Many areas are suitable for cross-country travel, but check with the District Ranger for information on weather and avalanche conditions.

PUBLICATIONS
  Maps:
    Teton Division. $1.
    Bridger West Division. $1.
    Wyoming Wilderness map. $1.
    Teton Wilderness. $1.
    Bridger Wilderness (Pinedale R.D.). $1.
    Bridger Wilderness, showing areas with special restrictions.
    Travel Plan maps: Teton Division, Bridger W. Division, Bridger E. Division.
  Leaflet with map, information.
  Information pages:
    General Information.
    Recreational Activities.
    Bridger Wilderness.
    Teton Wilderness.
    Gros Ventre Wilderness.
  Bridger Wilderness pamphlet.
  A Guide to Bridger Wilderness Fishing Lakes.

REFERENCES
  Maughan, Ralph. *Beyond the Tetons.* Boulder, CO: Pruett, 1981.
  Sudduth, Tom and Sanse. *Wyoming Hiking Trails.* Boulder, CO: Pruett, 1978. Pp. 10–61; 86–123.
  Bonney, Orrin H. and Lorraine. *Field Guide to the Wind River Range.* Published by the authors, Moose, WY, 1975.
  Kelsey, Joe. *Climbing and Hiking in the Wind River Range.* San Francisco: Sierra Club Books, 1979.
  Mitchell, Finis. *Wind River Trails.* Salt Lake City: Wasatch, 1975.
  Lawrence, Paul. *Hiking the Teton Backcountry.* San Francisco: Sierra Club Books, 1973. Pp. 146–48 (trails from Grand Teton National Park).

HEADQUARTERS: P.O. Box 1888, Jackson, WY 83001; (307) 733-2752.

RANGER DISTRICTS: Kemmerer R.D., P.O. Box 31, Kemmerer, WY 83101; (307) 677-4415. Big Piney R.D., P.O. Box 218, Big Piney, WY 83113; (307) 276-3375. Greys River R.D., P.O. Box 338, Afton, WY 83110; (307) 886-3166. Jackson R.D. (Gros Ventre Wilderness), P.O. Box 1689, Jackson, WY 83001; (307) 733-4755. Buffalo R.D. (Teton Wilderness), Blackrock Ranger Station, P.O. Box 278, Moran, WY 83013; (307) 543-2386. Pinedale, R.D. (Bridger Wilderness), P.O. Box 220, Pinedale, WY 82941; (307) 367-4326.

DUBOIS BADLANDS
U.S. Bureau of Land Management
4,520 acres.

On the N side of the Wind River, across from US 287. From the E side of Dubois, an unimproved local road is the site's NW boundary, about 1 1/2 mi. from town. ORVs use part of the area, and ORV tracks may serve as hiking access routes.

We didn't visit this site, and opinions are divided. One BLM advisor said, "No more interesting than other badlands." Another called it outstandingly scenic, with colorful banding and unusual landforms. We might not have included the site were it hard to get to. This comment, from an enthusiastic visitor, persuaded us:

> I was skeptical about the "outstanding opportunities" at first because the unit is so small and so close to a major highway and developments. However, I was amazed to discover that by going just a few hundred yards into any of the draws you are quickly isolated from the noise and visual intrusions and enveloped in a wilderness world. Around every bend there are colorful natural sculptures, deer, bighorn sheep, golden eagles, or other surprises. It is truly an incredible area.

From near Dubois, the site extends about 5 mi. SE, close to the river but with only a short bit of frontage. Average width is about a mile. The enthusiastic visitor mentioned hiking up Mason, Byrd, and Windy Ridge draws. These ascend from the river in the SE half of the site. Presumably there is a hiking route along the river from Dubois.

The area can be seen from US 287.

HEADQUARTERS: Rawlins District, BLM, 1300 Third, Rawlins, WY 82301; (307) 324-7171.

FOSSIL BUTTE NATIONAL MONUMENT
National Park Service
8,200 acres.

Off US 30, 10 mi. W of Kemmerer. (BLM map 14)

A short distance from the highway, this site is well worth a stop. Most visitors come in July and Aug. The site is never crowded. We were the only visitors when we stopped, and the enthusiastic, well-informed ranger was delighted to show us about. The Monument occupies part of a geologic formation with an abundance of fossil fishes, as well as mammals, reptiles, shellfish, insects, bats, birds, and plants. Almost all the adjoining land is public domain.

The small visitor center has excellent exhibits plus an open workroom where one can see how fossils are found and prepared. One can also visit the fossil beds or, in fact, hike anywhere.

From an elevation of 6,800 ft., eroded badlands rise gradually to the base of the butte. The lowest layers are brightly colored: red, purple, yellow, and gray. Above, extending to the top of the butte, are the buff to white layers of the Green River Formation in which most of the fish fossils are found. Highest elevation is 8,084 ft.

The area is semiarid, with about 9 in. of annual precipitation, most of this falling as winter snow. Summer days are warm, nights cool.

Plants: A detailed plant list is available, Latin names only. Common names are used in a separate list of common flowers. The region is sage grassland, with scattered Douglas-fir and limber pine on high N-facing slopes, aspen in some ravines, willow thickets along intermittent streams. In addition to sagebrush, grasses are interspersed with such shrubs as rabbitbrush, snowbrush, greasewood, serviceberry. Seasonal wildflowers include mountain bluebell, arrowleaf balsamroot, phlox, larkspur, Indian paintbrush, scarlet gilia, sego lily, lupine, blazing star, western yarrow.

Birds: Birds said to be "abundant"; no list is available. Many species nest, including golden eagle.

Mammals: Common species are rodents, bats, plus whitetail jackrabbit, snowshoe hare, mountain cottontail, porcupine, coyote, bobcat, mule deer, moose, pronghorn. Elk are sometimes seen in winter.

Reptiles and amphibians: Include Utah tiger salamander, boreal chorus frog, leopard frog, eastern short-horned lizard, wandering garter snake.

INTERPRETATION

Visitor center has exhibits, talks, literature. *Open:* 9 A.M.–5 P.M. May–Sept.

Guided walks are offered on weekends. Schedules may vary from year to year. When we visited they included easy 1-hr. walks and more strenuous 3-hr. hikes.

Interpretive trail, 2 1/2 mi., with side loop to fossil quarry.

ACTIVITIES

Camping: Not permitted on the Monument grounds, but informal camping on surrounding BLM land. No water available at the Monument. The Monument has a picnic ground in an aspen grove.

Hiking: Few visitors venture beyond the visitor center and interpretive trail, but longer hikes are possible and rangers are glad to advise.

PUBLICATIONS
Leaflet.
General information: mimeo pages.
Checklists: plants, wildflowers, mammals, reptiles and amphibians, insect families.

REFERENCES
On sale at the visitor center:
Fish of Fossil Lake. $3.
Geological History of Fossil Butte National Monument and Fossil Basin. $3.
Poster: Fossil Butte/Fish. $1.

HEADQUARTERS: P.O. Box 527, Kemmerer, WY 83101; (307) 877-3450.

GRAND TETON NATIONAL PARK
National Park Service
310,520 acres.

N entrance from Yellowstone National Park via John D. Rockefeller Memorial Parkway. S entrance from Jackson on US 89/191/26. E entrance on US 287/26.

Magnificent scenery, hiking and backpacking on spectacular mountain trails, abundant wildlife, brilliant displays of wildflowers, lakes for boating and fishing, rafting on the Snake River, plus opportunities for horsepacking, climbing, and winter sports. Many people say this is their favorite Park.

We first saw the Tetons in 1963 and have returned a dozen times since. The changes in that time have been moderate. 1963 was the first year the Park had over 2 million visitors. Attendance peaked in 1978, then declined somewhat. The totals don't mean much, because they include travelers on US 26, which traverses much of the E side. Although a million people come in July–Aug., most drive through, pausing at overlooks to admire and photograph the magnificent mountains.

The Park, Yellowstone, five National Forests, and parts of three other National Forests, constitute the Greater Yellowstone Ecosystem, a contiguous natural area larger than Vermont, New Hampshire, Massachusetts, and Rhode Island combined. Trail systems have interconnections. Wildlife biologists must often consider the entire ecosystem.

The Park is about 36 mi. N–S and 10 to 22 mi. wide. The valley of the Snake River, generally called Jackson Hole, extends N–S. The magnificent Teton Range rises dramatically on the W side of the valley floor. Elevation of the floor is about 6,750 ft. Eight Teton peaks are higher than 12,000 ft.; the highest, the Grand Teton, is 13,770.

The visual drama is enhanced by the lakes at the base of the mountains. A dam on the Snake enlarged Jackson Lake. To the S are smaller lakes: Leigh, String, Jenny, Bradley, Taggart, and Phelps. Countless photographs have been taken with the Tetons reflected in the lake waters.

The main N–S highway extends from the N entrance on the E side of Jackson Lake, then E of the Snake River. Teton Park Road carries local traffic from the Moose entrance station to Jenny Lake and the S shore of Jackson Lake. There is a natural separation of those who come to enjoy the scenery from a distance and those who come to participate in it. Hiking or horse riding in the mountains, one is far removed from traffic and crowds.

Winter use of the Park is increasing. Through-roads are plowed. From the commercial slopes in Jackson, skiers turn to ski touring in the Park. Rangers lead snowshoe hikes.

The Teton Range is only about 40 mi. long, but every foot is splendid. The lower slopes are clad in evergreens and aspen. Above timberline is tundra, then snowy peaks and crags. At one viewpoint, the foreground is a meadow carpeted with lupine. At the next, the mountains are reflected in a placid lake. Another mile and one looks out over a beaver pond where a moose feeds in the shallows.

These relatively young mountains began thrusting upward 9 million years ago and are still rising. Marine fossils can be found high up. Subsequently, glaciers scoured away huge portions of the rock, cutting great cirques and gorges, filling the valley with an ice mass so deep it deposited glacial debris atop 7,593-ft. Signal Mountain. Fragments of the glaciers remain. Once, after backpacking for several days and eager to bathe, we waded, gasping, into a pond fed by a ribbon of meltwater dropping from a glacier.

Jackson Hole attracted sportsmen and tourists before 1900. The first dude ranch opened in 1908. Many tracts of public land in the valley passed into private ownership. When the National Park was established in 1929, it included only the main Teton Range and the glacial lakes at their base.

Local interests bitterly opposed expansion of the Park on the valley floor. Much of this was National Forest land, which cattlemen with grazing permits used as if it were their own. Guides and outfitters knew that National Park status would shut out hunting. On the shore of Jenny Lake, at the foot of the main peaks, was a growing cancer of gas station, cabins, dance hall, abandoned cars, and trash.

John D. Rockefeller, Jr.'s agents began buying land in 1927, acquiring more than 33,000 acres over the next 20 years. In 1943 President Franklin D. Roosevelt proclaimed a 210,000-acre Jackson Hole National Monument, including most of the federal land in the valley. Most of the Rockefeller land was donated to the government in 1949. The following year, Congress finally put it all together in the present National Park.

Compromises had to be made. Ranchers continued to graze cattle inside the Park. The new boundaries included many tracts of privately owned land, including ranches and guest houses. Congress would not permit acquisition from unwilling owners. Four decades later there are still 133 inholdings.

Jackson Hole Airport is the only commercial airfield inside a National Park. When the original field became inadequate for increasing traffic, Park supporters urged that a new airport be built elsewhere. James Watt, then Secretary of the Interior, granted a 50-year lease that permits expansion within the Park. The runway was extended to 8,000 ft. A larger terminal has been built. Park authorities try to persuade operators to limit the noise reverberating from the mountainsides, but they have little leverage.

Jackson Lake is controlled by the Bureau of Reclamation, which built the dam in 1911 and enlarged it in 1916 to supply irrigation water. Drawdown occurs in dry years. In 1985 the lake was drained 40 ft., to the natural lake level, to permit renovation of the dam. Refilling is scheduled for 1989–1990 at the earliest.

Grand Teton is the only National Park where hunting is permitted, another compromise made when the Park was created. Prospective hunters draw lots for a fixed number of elk permits. Those selected are deputized as park rangers, each allowed one kill.

Like all federal recreation lands, the Park shows the effects of budget cuts. Reduced trail maintenance was conspicuous in 1986. One of our favorite trails was impassable, blocked by dozens of wind-felled trees.

Climate: Average maximum temperatures exceed 65°F in June–Sept.; in July–Aug. the thermometer reaches 80° in more than half of the days. Summer nights are cool. Dec. and Jan. are the coldest months, with average daily maximums below freezing and minimums near zero. Dec. and Jan. also have the heaviest snowfalls, 38–39 in., about half of the 154-in. annual total. Snow makes up more than half of the average annual precipitation, rain in the warmer months about 10 in. Hikers soon learn that afternoon thundershowers are common in July–Aug. Storms come suddenly over the mountains, thunder echoing from the cliffs, dislodged rocks clattering down. Showers seldom continue more than 30 minutes. Blizzards, however, may last for several days, during which travel is inadvisable.

These temperatures were recorded in the valley. It's colder up above, and back in the canyons we have often found trails blocked by snow at the end of June.

Plants: Over 200 species of fungi and 921 species of vascular plants have been identified. No handout checklist is available, but the plant guide listed in the Publications section is excellent.

Subalpine fir, Engelmann spruce, whitebark pine, and limber pine are the predominant trees just below timberline. Aspen, Douglas-fir, and lodgepole pine are the principal species on the lower slopes and in the valley, with blue spruce, willow, and cottonwood along the streams. Riparian shrubs include bush willow, alder, and dwarf maple. Many visitors come for the fall colors, which are at their best about Oct. 1.

The most extensive plant community is sagebrush-grassland, a label that fails to suggest the succession of bright-colored wildflowers that often cover acres of the valley floor. The wildflower season is shorter in the alpine zone, but moss campion, spring beauty, globeflower, glacier lily, and alpine forget-me-not (the Park flower) are among the species rewarding energetic hikers.

Another fascinating and complex plant community is the wetlands, many of the ponds and marshes formed and maintained by beaver dams.

Among the wildflowers are evening primrose, beargrass, snowbrush ceanothus, white bog-orchid, phlox, columbine, marsh marigold, white campion, hairy golden-aster, salsify, blue flax, shootingstar, largeleaf avens, arrowleaf balsamroot, heartleaf arnica, monkeyflower, fireweed, Indian paintbrush, elephanthead, skyrocket gilia, asters, larkspurs, penstemons, phacelia.

Birds: The Park includes a variety of habitats, from alpine zone to river bottoms. Some excellent birding is along the rivers and floodplains and around the lakes. One of our favorite sites is Hermitage Point, S of the Colter Bay Visitor Center, an area of beaver dams, ponds, and marshes. Moose are usually present. A slackwater oxbow on the Snake River just E of Jackson Lake Junction offers good birding from a canoe. A large great blue heron rookery was active on our latest visit. Moose here, too. At Christian Pond we photographed a trumpeter swan nesting on a beaver lodge. We always see dippers near Hidden Falls.

293 species have been recorded. Checklist available. Seasonally abundant or common species include eared grebe, great blue heron, trumpeter swan, Canada goose, green-winged and blue-winged teals, mallard, northern pintail, gadwall, American wigeon, redhead, ring-necked duck, Barrow's goldeneye, bufflehead, common merganser, osprey, bald eagle, goshawk; Swainson's, red-tailed, and rough-legged hawks; American kestrel. Blue, ruffed, and sage grouse; American coot, killdeer, spotted sandpiper, common snipe, Wilson's phalarope, California gull, common nighthawk, calliope hummingbird, belted kingfisher. Woodpeckers: downy, hairy, yellow-bellied sapsucker, northern flicker. Olive-sided and dusky flycatchers, western wood-pewee. Swallows: tree, violet-green, bank, cliff, and barn. Gray and Steller's jays, Clark's nutcracker, black-billed magpie, common raven, black-capped and mountain chickadees, red-breasted and white-breasted nuthatches, house and marsh wrens, American dipper, ruby-crowned kinglet, mountain bluebird, Townsend's solitaire, Swainson's and hermit thrushes, American robin, water pipit, European starling, warbling vireo. Warblers: yellow, yellow-rumped, MacGillivray's, common yellowthroat, Wilson's. Western tanager, black-headed and evening grosbeaks, green-tailed towhee. Sparrows: chipping, Brewer's, vesper, savannah, song, Lincoln's, white-crowned, house. Dark-eyed junco; red-winged, yellow-headed, and Brewer's blackbirds; brown-headed cowbird, rosy and Cassin's finches, common redpoll, pine siskin.

Mammals: Checklist of 54 species is available. Since the Park was established, wild animals have gradually become accustomed to people. We see more wildlife in the Tetons now than we did in the 1960s.

Abundant or common species include the masked and vagrant shrews, little brown myotis, pika, snowshoe hare, least and yellow pine chipmunks, yellow-belly marmot, Uinta ground squirrel, golden-mantled and red squirrels, northern pocket gopher, beaver, deer mouse, several voles, muskrat, western jumping mouse, porcupine, coyote, black bear, marten, longtail weasel, badger, elk, mule deer, moose, pronghorn.

See entry: National Elk Refuge.

Reptiles and amphibians: Common species include western and common garter snakes, tiger salamander, western toad, western chorus frog, western spotted frog.

FEATURES

The mountains are the youngest of the Rockies. Formed by block faulting, they are steepest on their E side, the side seen from the valley. Blue-gray, with snow on upper slopes, they rise more than a mile above the valley's lakes and sagebrush flats, 33 of them above 10,000 ft. The Grand Teton is the highest. On the other side is some splendid wild country in the Targhee National Forest (see entry, Idaho Zone 4).

The canyons: The Tetons are impressive from a distance, more so from a canyon trail. Canyons have been cut between the peaks. Several of the canyons in the S half of the Park have good trails. The area between Webb and Leigh canyons on the W shore of Jackson Lake is a Protected Natural Area, designated to remain trailless. Access to trails in Webb Canyon and N is from the Rockefeller Parkway or the Targhee NF.

Cascade Canyon is the best known and most popular. Many hikers consider its trail the country's most spectacular. A shuttle boat crosses Jenny Lake frequently in summer. From the dock, it's an easy half-mile hike to Hidden Falls. The trail then climbs by switchbacks to Inspiration Point, which offers a sweeping view of the lakes, valley, and Gros Ventre Mountains. Now it's 3.6 mi. to the forks of Cascade Creek on a good, almost level trail beside a rushing stream, with Teewinot Mountain, the Grand Teton, and Mount Owen towering overhead. Pika and marmot are common on the talus slopes. We have often seen moose and bear. The right fork of the trail leads to Lake Solitude, then down Paintbrush Canyon to the Jenny Lake Trail. A vigorous hiker can make the 19.2-mi. loop in a day, if the divide isn't blocked by snow. Cascade Canyon offers backpackers and horsepackers access to the Teton Crest and Alaska Basin trails.

Other scenic canyon trails include those in Garnet, Death, Open, and Granite canyons.

The lakes: Jenny Lake has long been a favorite of visitors. Lines of prospective campers formed on summer mornings, becoming only slightly shorter when the tents-only policy was adopted. Jenny is the base for climbers. A trail circles the lake, but most mountain hikers prefer to take the ferry across. Several lakes are reached by easy hiking trails. At the base of the range, these include Leigh, String, Bradley, Taggart, and Phelps. On the E side are Two Ocean Lake and Emma Matilda Lake.

The rivers: The Snake is the largest of the Park's rivers, winding 40 mi. from N to S. Principal tributaries within the Park are Pacific Creek, Buffalo Fork, and the Gros Ventre River. The 27 mi. below the Jackson Lake Dam are cold, swift, and shallow, with riffles and some standing waves up to 3 ft. but no rapids within the Park. Floating the Snake is scenic, with good chances of seeing wildlife.

Signal Mountain is E of Jackson Lake. A good 5-mi. road climbs 1,000 ft. to the summit, with overlooks.

The Gros Ventre Slide and *Slide Lake* are outside the Park boundaries, up Gros Ventre Road, but nearly all who see them are Park visitors, and the great scar of the Slide is seen from many vantage points in the Park. In 1925 a great section of mountainside, 50 million cubic yards, suddenly roared down in the valley, damming the river. Two years later, the lake formed by the dam received heavy spring runoff and part of the dam washed out, releasing a flood that obliterated the small town of Kelly.

INTERPRETATION

Visitor centers at Moose and Colter Bay. Information, maps, museums, literature.

Teewinot, in tabloid newspaper format, provides current information about Park events and a schedule of interpretive activities, including guided walks, demonstrations, campfire programs, cruises, and canoe trips.

Self-guided trails are at Menor's Ferry, Cascade Canyon, Cunningham Cabin, Oxbow Bend, Colter Bay, Lunchtree Hill.

Summer seminars, with college credit, are offered by the Teton Science School. Field studies, informal lectures, some conducted while backpacking. Most are 5 days, others 2 to 9 days. Box 68, Kelly, WY 83011, (307) 733-4765.

ACTIVITIES

Camping: 5 campgrounds, 905 sites. At Jenny Lake, tents only. No reservations, but entrance stations and visitor centers report where space is available. In July–Aug., some campgrounds are full before noon, Jenny by 8 A.M. Space is usually available at the Gros Ventre campground.

Campground openings from May 10 to June 21, closings Sept. 10–Oct. 15; none all year. Limited winter camping in the parking area at the Colter Bay Visitor Center.

Other accommodations, concessioner-operated, including a trailer village, lodges, cabins, etc., are listed in the *Teewinot,* the Park newspaper.

Hiking, backpacking: Over 200 mi. of trails, some of which connect with the trail systems of adjacent National Forests and Yellowstone. Many short, easy trails to such destinations as Trapper, Bearpaw, Leigh, Bradley, and Taggart lakes, or a bit further to Emma Matilda, Two Ocean, Surprise, and Phelps lakes. Level trails on Hermitage Point, passing Swan Lake and Heron Pond.

Valley trails are usually snow-free by mid-June, mountain trails by mid- to late July.

A backcountry permit is required for overnight trips. Registration at the Jenny Lake Ranger Station is required for any climbing or off-trail hiking. Campfires are prohibited except at designated sites.

Mountain trails are rocky, requiring boots. Be prepared for afternoon thundershowers.

Fishing: Snake River cutthroat is the only native trout species. Introduced: rainbow, lake, brown, and brook trout and Rocky Mountain whitefish. Wyoming laws and license. Special Park regulations are available at visitor centers.

Horse riding: Horses are available at Jenny Lake, Jackson Lake Lodge, and Colter Bay. Breakfast and evening rides; guided pack trips. Unloading ramps are available at several trailheads. Riders must obtain regulations governing use of saddle and pack animals.

Boating: Cruises on Jackson and Jenny lakes. Rentals available on Jackson and Jenny. Ramps and marinas on Jackson. All private boats must be registered each season and carry a Park sticker. Motors permitted on Jackson, Jenny, and Phelps; limited to 7 1/2 hp on Jenny. Hand-propelled boats permitted on Jackson, Jenny, Phelps, Emma Matilda, Two Ocean, Taggart, Bradley, Bearpaw, Leigh, and String lakes. Most of the smaller lakes have no road access.

Rafting, kayaking: Several concessioners offer 5- and 10-mile float trips on the Snake River. Rafts, canoes, and kayaks are permitted. Although there are no rapids, the river has a maze of channels, and side channels are often blocked. Snags are common. The current is swift, and a steersman must make quick decisions. We have seen canoes hung up on snags and abandoned. The 4 1/2-mi. run from below the dam to Pacific Creek is recommended for beginners.

Winter activities include ski touring, snowmobiling, ice fishing, ice skating, and mountaineering. Registration and information at the Moose Visitor Center. Some areas are restricted. Severe storms are common, as well as temperatures as low as −40°F.

Ski areas in nearby National Forests.

Mountain climbing is a major activity. Climbers usually base at Jenny Lake, where there is a climbing school and where climbers must register.

ADJACENT

John D. Rockefeller, Jr., Memorial Parkway. (See entry.)

The National Elk Refuge adjoins the Park on the S. (See entry.)

The Targhee National Forest adjoins the Park on the W. (See entry, Idaho Zone 4.)

The Bridger-Teton National Forest adjoins the Park on the E. (See entry.)

PUBLICATIONS

When we submitted this entry to the Park for checking, we were advised that all their handouts were being revised. By the time this book is published, a new publications list should be available from Park HQ. The following list is therefore obsolete, but it indicates the scope of Park information.

Park leaflet with map.

Teewinot. Information on activities, information services, facilities, accommodations, etc.

Information pages:
Geologic history of Jackson Hole.
Historical sketch of Jackson Hole.
Travel information. (Air, bus, taxi, etc.)
Weather information.
Animal checklist.
Seeing wildlife in Grand Teton National Park.
Grand Teton's moose.
Grand Teton's elk.
Campground information.
Hiking and backcountry camping.
Hermitage Point trail map.
Saddle and pack animals. Regulations, map.
Fishing regulations.
Mountaineering in Grand Teton National Park.
Boating regulations.
Floating the Snake River.
Pamphlets:
Birds of Jackson Hole. (Provided by Wyoming Game and Fish Department.)
Cascade Canyon, a guide.
For a complete price list of Publications of the Grand Teton Natural History Association, write Moose, WY 83012. They include:
Grand Teton, Official National Park Handbook. $2.95.
Hiking and Climbing Map. $1.95.
Creation of the Teton Landscape. $4.95.
Birds of Grand Teton National Park. $5.95.
Plants of Yellowstone and Grand Teton. $5.95.
Large Mammals of Yellowstone and Grand Teton. $1.75.
Teton Trails. $1.50.

REFERENCE: *National Parkways Photographic and Comprehensive Guide to*

Grand Teton National Park. World-Wide Research and Publishing Company, 1224 West 30th, Casper, WY 82601. Was on sale at some Chevron stations.

HEADQUARTERS: P.O. Drawer 170, Moose, WY 83012; (307) 733-2880.

GREEN MOUNTAINS
U.S. Bureau of Land Management
Acreage indeterminate.

From Jeffrey City, 6 mi. E on US 287, then S on Green Mountain Road. (BLM map 7)

We wouldn't include this site if it weren't for the campground and the great view from Wild Horse Lookout. The natural environment has been scarred by clear-cutting, mining exploration, and roads. However, it's just off the highway.

The Green Mountains, about 12 mi. W–E, are one of several small ranges on the N perimeter of the Great Divide Basin. They rise about 2,500 ft. above their base. A map of the Green Mountain Loop Road is posted at the turnoff from US 287, with a notice that the road is closed, presumably because of snow, from Nov. 15 to July 1. Not always; it was open when we were there in early June, and we saw only patches of snow on the upper slopes. The road had a tendency to washboard but was quite passable.

The mountain are indeed green: grasses and shrubs with scattered juniper on the lower slope, conifer forest above.

The Cottonwood campground and Wild Horse Point picnic area are maintained by BLM. The BLM map shows trails leading S to the Continental Divide, but we didn't try them.

HEADQUARTERS: Rawlins District, BLM, P.O. Box 670, 1300 Third St., Rawlins, WY 82301; (307) 327-7171.

HONEYCOMB BUTTES; OREGON BUTTES
U.S. Bureau of Land Management
41,620 acres; 5,700 acres.

From SR 28 about 10 mi. SW of Atlantic City, 1 mi. beyond the Sweetwater River, S on County Road 4-74 about 8 mi. Honeycomb Buttes is on the E, Oregon Buttes on the W. (BLM map 10)

These adjacent roadless sites are in the central portion of the Red Desert complex (see entry). Instead of low, rolling dunes, they feature outstanding badlands topography with dramatic vertical relief. The buttes rise steeply from low sagebrush hills and greasewood flats. They have been eroded through brightly colored layers of green, red, white, yellow, gray, and other colors of sedimentary rock. Most of the erosion channels form deeply incised inverted V's, but occasional layers of harder rock cap these formations with horizontal shelves. The formations include cliffs, draws, and caves. Elevation of the surrounding flatlands is about 6,900 ft.

Honeycomb Buttes rise in a series of steps to the highest point, 8,431-ft. Continental Peak. Honeycomb Buttes has been proposed for Wilderness designation. Visitors are attracted by the striking formations, the sweeping view from Continental Peak, and opportunities to collect agate, jade, and petrified wood. The eroding buttes are barren.

The site has no perennial streams. Numerous intermittent streams flow during spring and early summer. Several springs are on the Oregon Buttes boundary, but visitors should bring a full water supply. Nine small reservoirs, built for livestock, are a resource for wildlife.

Oregon Buttes are a prominent landmark, rising 1,200 ft. above the desert floor. They have a variety of plant communities including limber pine stands, small stands of aspen, and wet meadows moistened by seeps. In the review process, one enthusiast commented, ". . . a national historic feature, an important recharge area for the desert, an exceptional wildlife area, and one of the most beautiful spots on the desert and in the state."

A few intermittent streams carry runoff in spring and early summer. Seven small reservoirs were developed for cattle.

Climate: Average daytime temperatures range from 60–65°F in July to 5–10° in Jan. Annual precipitation is about 10 in., slightly more than half of this falling as snow.

Plants: The area surrounding the buttes includes sagebrush hills and greasewood flats.

Birds: Excellent habitat for raptors, with golden eagle, prairie falcon, ferruginous hawk, and great horned owl noted.

Mammals: Pronghorn, mule deer, and elk are seasonally common. Mountain lion, bobcat, coyote, and swift fox have been seen, but only the coyote is common. Many wild horses.

HEADQUARTERS: Rock Springs District, BLM, Highway 191 North, Rock Springs, WY 82902; (307) 382-5350.

JOHN D. ROCKEFELLER, JR., MEMORIAL PARKWAY
National Park Service
82 road miles.

From West Thumb in Yellowstone National Park to the S entrance of Grand Teton National Park. (US 287/89)

The "82 miles" confused us, as it has others. The road distance between the two parks is only 7 1/2 mi. Most of the Parkway, designated by Congress in 1972, is within the parks.

The scenic corridor between includes 23,770 acres. On its W is the Targhee National Forest, on its E the Bridger-Teton NF. It is crossed by the Snake River. A commercial facility, Flagg Ranch, has cabins, motel, campground, restaurant, ski and snowmobile rentals, horseback and fishing trips. Trails lead into the Parks and Forests. A gravel road, not shown on the highway map, runs W into the Targhee, becoming Forest Road 261.

Camping: 1 campground, 24 sites. Mid-June to mid-Sept., depending on snow.

HEADQUARTERS: Grand Teton National Park, P.O. Drawer 170, Moose, WY 83012; (307) 733-2880.

LAKE MOUNTAIN
U.S. Bureau of Land Management
13,970 acres.

From La Barge on US 189, S 1 1/2 mi., then W on County Road 315, following La Barge Creek. From Mile 12 to about Mile 18, road is the SW site boundary. (BLM map 14)

The N boundary is the Bridger-Teton National Forest. Both BLM map 14 and the Forest map show primitive roads or trails entering the Forest along Sheep Creek at the NW corner and Deadline Ridge at the NE corner.

The site, within the Wyoming Range, contains steep-sided ridges and deep canyons. Elevations are from 7,400 to over 9,600 ft. Rock Creek, a perennial stream in the central portion, is the principal drainage. The mountainous terrain, with dense to moderate forest cover broken by meadowlike openings, is a scenic setting for a variety of recreational opportunities.

There aren't many visitors—chiefly weekend fishermen in summer and hunters in the fall. Except in hunting season, the site offers wilderness-quality hiking and riding with assurance of solitude.

Temperatures above 90°F are rare in summer, while subzero readings are common in winter. Average annual snowfall is more than 100 in. Average annual precipitation is about 12 in., rain falling chiefly in late spring and early summer.

Plants: About half of the area is sagebrush-grass community. Major shrubs include big sagebrush, bitterbrush, and rabbitbrush. Flowering plants include pussytoes, buckwheat, phlox, balsamroot, Indian paintbrush. Grasses include bluebunch wheatgrass, needle-and-thread, green needlegrass, spike and Idaho fescue. Hill slopes with adequate moisture support aspen with understory species that include snowberry, buffaloberry, currant; numerous wildflower species include bluebell, aster, lupine, columbine.

The conifer type at higher elevations is dominated by Engelmann spruce and Douglas-fir. Mountain shrubs on slopes and alluvial fans include curlleaf mahogany, big sagebrush, bottlebrush squirreltail, bluegrasses, snowberry.

Wildlife: The site includes critical winter habitat for elk, a few of which remain through the summer. Higher elevations are used by deer in summer, while part of the area is critical winter range. Most of the site is moose summer range; creek bottoms serve in winter. A few black bear are present. Beaver dams are seen along the Rock Creek drainage. Pika are fairly abundant on talus slopes.

Some waterfowl are attracted by beaver ponds. Game birds are sage, blue, and ruffed grouse.

Rock Creek is one of only two streams known to have "wholly pure" populations of Colorado River cutthroat trout in the Upper Green River drainage. Overfishing caused the Wyoming Game and Fish Department to close the stream in 1982.

HEADQUARTERS: Rock Springs District, BLM, P.O. Box 1869, Rock Springs, WY 82901; (307) 382-5350.

MCCULLOUGH PEAKS
U.S. Bureau of Land Management
24,570 acres.

N boundary is about 5 mi. S of Powell by local roads that may be impassable in wet weather. (BLM map 12)

Although this badlands area is dramatically scenic, BLM recommended against Wilderness designation. Reasons included the large areas of Wyoming already so designated, oil and gas potential, and limited public support. However, recreation opportunities are presently unimpaired, and they include public lands adjoining on the W, which lack wilderness characteristics but have about 6 mi. of frontage on the Shoshone River. The site consists largely of heavily eroded, vividly colored badlands on the N slopes of McCullough Peaks. Elevations range from 4,400 ft. at the NW corner to 6,400 ft. on the crest of the Peaks. Five major drainages branch into a maze of small, winding canyons, so that a hiker quickly has a sense of isolation.

Annual precipitation is about 7 inches, most of this falling in short but intense spring and summer thunderstorms. Runoff is rapid. Vegetation is scanty, consisting chiefly of sparse grasses, sagebrush, and saltbush, but sufficient to maintain wild horses, wintering mule deer, and transient populations of pronghorn and a few whitetail deer.

Other mammals noted include rodents, cottontail, jackrabbit, coyote, fox, and bobcat. Bird species include chukar and Hungarian partridge, golden eagle, prairie falcon, kestrel, red-tailed hawk, merlin, great horned owl.

BLM estimates annual visitation is "between a few hundred and a few thousand visitor-days per year." Summer heat limits recreation to spring, early summer, and fall.

HEADQUARTERS: Worland District, BLM, P.O. Box 119, 101 South 23rd, Worland, WY 82401; (307) 347-9871.

NATIONAL ELK REFUGE
U.S. Fish and Wildlife Service
24,700 acres.

E of US 26, between Jackson and Grand Teton National Park. (BLM map 13)

The Refuge was established in 1912 to protect the last large area of elk winter range in the Jackson Hole Valley—75% of the winter range in the Yellowstone-Jackson Hole region had been eliminated. The town of Jackson, ranches, and highways prevented the elk from using their traditional winter range.

Harsh winters in 1909, 1910, and 1911 caused a large part of the herd to die of starvation and caused many to raid ranchers' haystacks. In 1910 the Wyoming legislature provided $5,000 to feed hungry elk from haywagons. In 1911 Congress, responding to a request from the state, made an emergency appro-

341 ᚹᛏ ZONE 1

priation for feeding and ordered an investigation. The Refuge was established
the next year.

A few critics opposed the Refuge, calling it a "feed lot" that would make
the elk as dependent as animals in zoos. However, its carrying capacity has
been increased by irrigation and prescribed burning. The elk are fed when
deep or crusted snow prevents grazing. About 7,500 elk winter here. The
migration begins in late Oct. The elk begin returning north in late Apr. or
early May.

Summer visitors, driving from Jackson to the Grand Teton National Park,
can stop at a wayside overlooking Flat Creek, marshes, and grasslands. They
won't see elk, but the birding is usually good. We often see trumpeter swans,
sometimes with cygnets. From near Refuge HQ in Jackson (on Broadway St.,
1 mi. E of the town square) an unpaved road enters the S portion of the
Refuge. Off this road is the visitor center, open in winter only. Beyond it,
unpaved roads are open in summer.

Winter visitors can see elk from the highway or travel by horse-drawn
sleigh from the visitor center.

The Refuge borders US 20 to the Gros Ventre River, then follows the river
for about 10 mi., with Grand Teton National Park on the other side. On the
E, from the river to Jackson, is the Bridger-Teton National Forest.

The N half is dissected by steep rolling hills. Highest elevation is 7,200 ft.
The S half is relatively flat, with grassy meadows and marshes. A prominent
feature is Miller Butte, rising about 500 ft. above the valley floor. Flat Creek
nearly bisects the Refuge, flowing E–W, then turning S to parallel US 26.

Annual precipitation is about 15 in., most of it in winter and spring. Average annual snowfall is 1 to 2 ft.

Birds: A *Birds of Jackson Hole* checklist is available. Nearly 175 species
have been recorded. Species noted within the Refuge include great blue heron,
trumpeter and tundra swans, Canada goose, green-winged and blue-winged
teals, mallard, northern pintail, gadwall, American wigeon, redhead, ring-
necked duck, Barrow's goldeneye, bufflehead, common merganser, osprey,
bald eagle, goshawk, northern harrier; red-tailed, Swainson's, and rough-
legged hawks; American coot, sandhill crane, killdeer, long-billed curlew,
spotted sandpiper, common snipe, Wilson's phalarope, California gull, common nighthawk, belted kingfisher, black-billed magpie, long-billed marsh
wren.

Mammals: Checklist available. Species a visitor might see include Uinta
ground squirrel, beaver, deer mouse, voles, longtail weasel, porcupine, coyote,
badger, mule deer (winter), moose.

FEATURES

Tour route, 7 mi., through sagebrush, grassland, and butte country, not
wetlands. Unpaved road enters National Forest.

Sleigh ride, from visitor center in winter. Concession operated. Daily, late
Dec. through Mar., except Christmas Day.

ACTIVITIES

Hiking: Limited to Refuge roads. Hiking trail to the National Forest.

Hunting: Elk only. Special rules may change year to year. In 1986, 120 permits were issued weekly, in a 3-week season, by public drawing that applicants had to attend in person.

Fishing: Native cutthroat trout. Designated areas and seasons.

INTERPRETATION

Visitor center has exhibits, slide show, films, talks, literature. Open late Dec. through Mar., daily except Christmas, 10 A.M.–4 P.M.

Wayside exhibits on US 26 and Refuge Road.

Naturalist information and programs on request; consult HQ.

PUBLICATIONS

Leaflet with map.

History of the National Elk Refuge.

Elk of the National Elk Refuge.

Birds of Jackson Hole.

Mammals checklist.

Hunting information.

Fishing information.

HEADQUARTERS: P.O. Box C, Jackson, WY 83001; (307) 733-9212.

OCEAN LAKE WILDLIFE HABITAT MANAGEMENT UNIT

Wyoming Game and Fish Department
12,685 acres, including 6,100-acre reservoir.

About 17 mi. NW of Riverton, between US 26 and SR 134. (Shown on highway map.) Access roads from both. (BLM map 11)

Maintained primarily as habitat for waterfowl, upland game birds, and small game, the site is popular with nearby residents for boating, swimming, fishing, picnicking, and camping.

It provides both extensive wetlands and upland habitat, ranging from open water and wet marshes to arid sagebrush-grassland. Included are eight man-made and two natural ponds, in addition to Ocean Lake. Terrain is slightly rolling, a treeless region between the Owl Creek Mountains to the N and the Wind River Range to the W. Elevation at the lake is 5,234 ft.; highest point in the unit is only 136 ft. higher. The lake's deepest point is 31 ft.; more than half of the lake has depths less than 15 ft. Although the lake is the product of waste irrigation water, annual fluctuation is only about 18 in.

Average daily maximum temperature in July is about 88°F, average daily minimum in January about 5°F. Average annual precipitation is about 9 in., May–July being the wettest season.

The lake is popular all year. Total recreation is estimated at 40,150 visitor-days. Boating and water skiing account for 40% of the total, swimming 17%, fishing 15%, hunting 10%. Seven parking and camping areas are distributed around the lake's 18-mi. shoreline, so crowding seldom occurs.

Birds: Canada geese are management's first priority. Ocean Lake has a permanent population of 200–400, plus many more seasonal visitors. About 120 pairs nest on the lake, more in outlying areas. Goose population during migrations is 2,000–3,000. Mallards are the most abundant waterfowl species. Others common in spring and summer: pintail; green-winged, blue-winged, and cinnamon teals; redhead, gadwall, shoveler, ruddy duck, American wigeon, lesser scaup, bufflehead, red-breasted merganser, coot. Nesting and summer residents are chiefly mallard, teal, redhead, and coot. Early fall migrants are mostly teal and pintail, mallards coming later. Upland game birds are ring-necked pheasant and mourning dove. Common nongame species include eared and pied-billed grebes, white pelican, double-crested cormorant, great blue heron, American bittern, northern harrier, American kestrel, rough-legged and Swainson's hawks, great horned and short-eared owls, red-winged and yellow-headed blackbirds, long-billed marsh wren, upland plover; spotted, solitary, and least sandpipers; lesser yellowlegs, long-billed dowitcher, American avocet, Wilson's phalarope, California gull, killdeer, western meadowlark, horned lark, northern flicker, black-billed magpie, American robin.

Mammals: Include badger, striped skunk, red fox, coyote, raccoon, muskrat, cottontail, whitetail jackrabbit, whitetail prairie dog, Richardson ground squirrel, least chipmunk, deer and grasshopper mice, meadow vole, mule deer.

ACTIVITIES

Camping: 7 designated campgrounds. Water at only 1.

Hunting: Pheasant, waterfowl, mourning dove, cottontail.

Fishing: Said to be an excellent warmwater sport fishery: bass, walleye, pike, perch; some ling and crappie. Potential for commercial exploitation of rough fish.

Boating: Three ramps.

About 4 mi. of improved, all-weather gravel roads provide access to the popular shore sites. 36 mi. of other roads are rough and likely to be impassable when wet.

HEADQUARTERS: Wyoming Game and Fish Department, 5400 Bishop Blvd., Cheyenne, WY 82002; (307) 777-7631.

RAYMOND MOUNTAIN
U.S. Bureau of Land Management
32,936 acres.

Near the ID border, between US 30 at Cokeville and US 89. Best access is from SR 89 (US 89 on some maps) about 4 mi. N of Border; then E about 1 mi. BLM map 14 shows other low-standard roads. Local information is advised.

The site, about 19 mi. N–S, 4 mi. W–E, is in the Sublette Mountain Range. The Bridger-Teton National Forest boundary is 4 to 7 mi. away on the N and E. Elevations range from 6,250 ft. in drainage bottoms to 9,313 ft. The highest country is in the N: steep, rough mountains and hills. Lower, rounder hills are in the S sector. Nearly half of the terrain has slopes steeper than 80%.

The site is in essentially natural condition. Opportunities for backpacking, hunting, fishing, horse riding, climbing, ski touring, birding, and sightseeing are considered outstanding. Recreation use is estimated to be about 1,300 visitor-days per year. Two-thirds of this use is by hunters. Picnicking and fishing attract local visitors in the warmer months. Relatively few visitors come for hiking, backpacking, and horsepacking.

A cherry-stem road penetrates the site from the N about 6 mi. along Huff Creek to Huff Lake, a modest-size pond. A 200-acre private inholding is near the road's end.

Except for N-flowing Huff Creek, and Raymond Creek, which flows W, most streams flow S, some in steep-sided canyons. The Raymond Creek watershed occupies more than two-thirds of the site.

A 13,530-acre portion including the Raymond Creek and Huff Creek drainages has been given special protection as an Area of Critical Environmental Concern, as important to the survival of the Bear River cutthroat trout. This is also critical winter range for elk and deer.

Climate is cool, summer days rarely exceeding 90°F, subfreezing temperatures occurring up to 210 days per year. Annual precipitation averages 14 in., annual snowfall 100 in. Most rain falls in late spring and early summer.

Plants: Almost three-fourths of the site is in the sagebrush-grass plant community. Shrubs include big sagebrush, three-tipped sage, bitterbrush, rabbitbrush, and snowberry. Wildflowers include pussytoes, phlox, balsamroot, Indian paintbrush. Grasses include bluebunch wheatgrass, kingspike and Idaho fescues, needle-and-thread, Sandberg and Camby bluegrasses. Mountain shrubs occupy relatively dry slopes at higher elevations. Stands of curlleaf mountain-mahogany typify this community. Douglas-fir grows on high N-facing slopes, chiefly in the N sector. Engelmann spruce and subalpine fir are limited to the highest elevations, chiefly in the center of the site. Aspen grows on slopes where snow provides adequate moisture and in groves around springs.

Birds: Waterfowl are attracted to Huff Lake and beaver ponds on Raymond and Mill creeks; species include mallard, pintail, shoveler, American wigeon, gadwall, blue-winged and cinnamon teals. Raptors include red-tailed, ferruginous, sharp-shinned, and Cooper's hawks; golden eagle, goshawk, prairie falcon. Other species include sandhill crane, ruffed and blue grouse. Bald eagles have been seen in winter.

Mammals: The site is winter range for elk. Mule deer use the range in summer, to a more limited degree in winter. Moose are present all year.

ACTIVITIES

Camping: Most camping has been by hunters. Some use 4-wheel-drive vehicles to haul campers or trailers to Huff Lake or from W of the site up Raymond Canyon.

Hiking, backpacking: BLM map 14 shows a few trails in the S sector. Canyons offer routes for both hiking and horse riding. BLM says backpacking "occurs," but not much.

Hunting: Chiefly elk and deer.

Fishing: Considered good on Huff and Raymond creeks, but BLM estimates only 400 fisherman-days per year. Primary game fish is Bonneville or Bear River cutthroat trout, a genetically pure strain.

HEADQUARTERS: Rock Springs District, BLM, P.O. Box 1869, Rock Springs, WY 82902; (307) 382-5350.

RED CANYON BIG GAME WINTER RANGE
Wyoming Game and Fish Department
1,795 acres.

From Lander, 18 mi. S on SR 28. (BLM map 10)

The site is managed to provide winter habitat for elk. However, summer and fall visitors attracted by the scenery outnumber hunters 6 to 1. The road from Lander is driveable except for 4 unimproved miles that can be a problem when wet. Some sightseers pause here on their way to South Pass City, a site with much historical interest. Not that visitors are numerous; the average is about 8 per day, most of those coming on weekends.

About 15 mi. from Lander, a county road to the right runs through the canyon. This road is maintained summer and fall, closed at other seasons. From a high grassland bench E of SR 28, the terrain drops sharply to 6,100 ft. at Red Canyon Creek. The creek is an important tributary of the Little Popo Agie River.

Plants: Principal plant communities are sagebrush-grassland and mountain shrub-sagebrush-grassland. Cottonwood, aspen, and birch occur on the canyon floor.

Wildlife: Up to 600 elk use the area in winter, along with a few moose. Spring to fall mammals include pronghorn and a few black bear. Game birds include sage and blue grouse, chukar and Hungarian partridge, and pheasant. Numerous songbirds and raptors.

The site is closed to motor vehicles Dec. 1–Apr. 30.

HEADQUARTERS: Wyoming Game and Fish Department, 5400 Bishop Blvd., Cheyenne, WY 82002; (307) 777-7631.

SCAB CREEK WILDERNESS
U.S. Bureau of Land Management
7,636 acres.

From Boulder on US 187, E about 7 mi. on SR 353, then N on County 23-122 and BLM 5423, dirt roads, about 7 mi. Roads are narrow and rough. Most visitors have high-clearance vehicles, but ordinary cars can make it in dry weather. (BLM map 10)

BLM designated this site a Primitive Area in 1975 and has since given it special protection, including exclusion of motor vehicles. Now it has been proposed for Wilderness designation. It adjoins the Bridger-Teton National Forest on the N and E. The access road ends at the Scab Creek Campground, on the Wilderness boundary. This is a popular trailhead for backpackers and horsemen heading for the Bridger Wilderness lakes region.

The campground and trail have considerable use, estimated at 10,000 visitor-days per year. Summer visitors come for camping, hiking, fishing, rock climbing, or travel by foot or horseback into the Bridger Wilderness. Hunting attracts visitors in the fall. Winter activities include ski touring, camping, and wildlife viewing. The National Outdoor Leadership School uses the area.

The site is on the W-facing foothills of the Wind River Mountains. Terrain is characterized by steep, rocky, granite outcrops cut by glaciers and streams. The site has about 1/2 mi. of frontage on South Soda Lake, which is partially inside the Forest. The lake is about 1 1/2 mi. long and has no road access. Smaller lakes and ponds occur in glacial basins, chiefly in the N sector. Scab Creek crosses the N half of the site. Silver Creek and several intermittent streams also drain from the Forest through the site. Silver Creek Falls, one of the most spectacular in the Wind River Range, is in the SE corner. No maintained trail leads to the falls. BLM staff members found several fine viewpoints but reported most are accessible only by difficult off-trail hiking.

Elevations range from 7,400 ft. at South Soda Lake, in the NW corner, to 9,650 ft. near the Forest boundary. Summer temperatures rarely exceed 90°F; below-zero temperatures occur often in winter. Annual snowfall exceeds 100 in. Total annual precipitation is about 12 in.

Plants: Most of the site is covered by coniferous forest, with scattered areas of big sagebrush, bunch grass, and aspen. Wet meadows are a scenic feature as well as a special wildlife habitat. Principal tree species are lodgepole pine, limber pine, Douglas-fir, Engelmann spruce, and subalpine fir.

Wildlife: Abundant. Bird species include sage, blue, and ruffed grouse; some waterfowl, prairie falcon, bald eagle in migration. Mammals noted include elk, moose, mule deer, black bear, bobcat, mountain lion, coyote, badger, snowshoe hare, and possibly wolverine and lynx.

ACTIVITIES

Camping: Primitive campground at road's end.

Hiking, backpacking: Most hikers use the 2 1/2 mi. of trail from road's end to the Forest boundary. Another trail from the trailhead crosses the middle of the site to the Forest's Sage Basin pack trail; BLM plans to maintain this to a lower standard. The rugged terrain makes off-trail hiking difficult.

Hunting: Big game hunting is said to be excellent.

Fishing: Said to be excellent, but access is so difficult most fishermen continue on to the Forest lakes and streams. Scab Creek and Cutthroat Lake have cutthroat trout; Boundary Lake brook trout; Silver Creek rainbow, brook, and brown trout.

Horse riding: Trailhead is used by riders, summer and fall.

NEARBY: *Boulder Lake*—follow signs off SR 353 about 4 mi. E of Boulder. A good fishing lake with 2 primitive BLM campgrounds. Boating. Part of the lake is in the National Forest.

HEADQUARTERS: Rock Springs District, BLM, P.O. Box 1869, Rock Springs, WY 82901; (307) 382-5350.

SHOSHONE NATIONAL FOREST
U.S. Forest Service
2,433,029 acres; 2,466,587 acres within boundaries.

E of Yellowstone and Grand Teton National Parks. Extends S from the
Montana border to South Pass City. Crossed by US 212 in the far N; US
14/20/16 between Cody and Yellowstone National Park; and US 26/287,
through Dubois to both National Parks. (BLM maps 11, 12)

Most visitors to Yellowstone National Park pass through the Shoshone National Forest. The Forest's principal camping area is along US 14/20/16, the
route to Yellowstone's E entrance. A secondary area is on US 212, the Beartooth Highway, route to the Park's NE entrance. Recreation areas along these
well-traveled scenic routes account for a majority of the Forest's 1 million
visitor-days per year.

They are a small part of the Forest, which itself is part of a huge block of
rugged, mountainous, wild country in NW Wyoming. The block includes the
two National Parks, the Bridger-Teton National Forest, and the Wind River
Indian Reservation in Wyoming. It extends into Montana and Idaho.

The Forest offers attractive alternatives to the more heavily used Parks.
Hunters come for big-game hunting, which is forbidden in Parks. Wilderness
hiking trails are easily accessible and many are lightly used. Campsites are
available when Park campgrounds are full. On our most recent visit, Yellowstone's campgrounds were full, but there was ample room in Forest campgrounds along US 14/20/16.

Most of the Forest is still pristine, more than half of it in five Wildernesses.
Because of its rugged terrain, only about 6% of the Forest is suitable for
commercial timber production. About one-fourth of the area is at or above
timberline, generally above 10,000 ft. elevation.

Most of the Forest is within the Upper Missouri River Basin, subdivided
by the Wind, Bighorn, and Clarks Fork basins. It includes a part of the
Absaroka Range, the Wind River Range, and the Beartooth Plateau. Highest
point in the Forest, and in Wyoming, is 13,785 ft. atop Gannett Peak in the
Wind River Range. Lowest is 4,585 ft. at Clarks Fork Canyon, in the far N.

The Forest has 4,900 mi. of perennial streams, most of them free-flowing.
Heaviest runoff is May–July, peaking in June. Principal rivers are Clarks Fork
of the Yellowstone River, North and South Forks of the Shoshone, Greybull,
Wind, and Popo Agie. It has more than 500 mountain lakes, most of them
on the Beartooth Plateau or in the Fitzpatrick and Popa Agie Wildernesses
in the S.

Below 10,000 ft. elevation in the Absarokas are forested drainages and extremely steep mountainsides with high cliffs and talus slopes, as well as rounded ridges and open, grass-covered slopes. The Wind River Mountains have a mix of steep slopes and wide, rolling ridges, canyons, and rocky peaks. In the drainages are many waterfalls, cascades, pools, wetlands, and ponds.

Alpine areas are marked by rugged, rocky peaks, cirque basins, U-shaped canyons, talus slopes, and boulder fields, with snowfields and glaciers, the latter chiefly along the Continental Divide in the Wind River Range.

The Cody-Yellowstone corridor, 2 to 7 mi. wide, separates the two largest Wildernesses. To the S is the Washakie Wilderness, over 700,000 acres, adjoining Yellowstone Park and the Teton Wilderness of the Bridger-Teton National Forest. To the N is the North Absaroka Wilderness, over 350,000 acres, also adjoining Yellowstone. Trailheads are along the two main highways.

The Forest has 1,536 mi. of roads in nonwilderness areas, not counting U.S. highways and state-maintained roads. However, less than 20 mi. of the Forest system roads are paved, and less than 200 mi. of the others are rated "safe for car." Most unpaved roads are primitive; some are closed to vehicles for lack of maintenance. For hikers, these back roads supplement the Forest's 1,294 mi. of trails.

Climate: Topography and the 9,220-ft. range of elevations produce a wide range of climates. The general category is "continental mountainous." Annual precipitation ranges from 12 to 70 in. Higher elevations have the greatest precipitation, most of it falling as snow. Heavy snow on steep slopes creates potential for avalanches. Snowmelt combined with rain falling on snow in spring can produce floods.

Hiking in the high country is impossible or inadvisable before July because of snow-blocked trails and hazardous stream crossings. The optimum hiking season is short: July 10–Aug. 31. We asked about low-elevation trails and were told, "They're just routes to the high country."

At the nearest weather-reporting station, Cody, elevation 5,002 ft., average daily minimum and maximum temperatures in winter are 12 to 41°F, in summer 47 to 70°. It's colder at higher elevations. Severe thunderstorms are not uncommon.

Plants: Lists of plant species not available, but plant guides for Yellowstone and Grand Teton National Parks are applicable for comparable habitats.

Above 10,000 ft.: Low-growing alpine vegetation. Herbaceous species, mosses, lichens.

At 6,500 to 9,000 ft.: Coniferous forests, chiefly Douglas-fir and lodgepole pine. Engelmann spruce and subalpine fir at 8,000 to 10,000 ft. Interspersed are montane meadows. Sagebrush-grasslands communities also occur between 6,500 and 9,000 ft.

Riparian and wetlands species include willow, aspen, rose, big sagebrush, cottonwood, with grasses, sedges, and forbs.

These diverse habitats produce a great variety of seasonal wildflowers.

Among the many we saw were bluebell, marsh marigold, sticky geranium, Indian paintbrush, silky phacelia, lupine, dandelion, white phlox, heartleaf arnica, arrowleaf balsamroot.

Birds: No checklist is in print, but HQ has a computerized list. 230 species reported. Bird checklists and guides for the adjacent National Parks are applicable.

Mammals: No checklist is in print, but HQ has a computerized list. 72 species reported. Big game species include elk, mule deer, bighorn sheep, pronghorn, moose, black bear, whitetail deer, mountain goat, mountain lion.

A large area of grizzly bear habitat adjoins Yellowstone. Signs are posted along the Cody-Yellowstone corridor: "THIS IS GRIZZLY BEAR COUNTRY—INFORMATION AT VISITOR CENTER." The center offers advice on avoiding encounters. Some nervous lodge owners objected to the signs, fearing they'd scare customers away.

Presence of gray wolf is debated; sightings of a large canine have been reported. Some wildlife biologists are urging that the wolf be reintroduced in the Greater Yellowstone ecosystem.

FEATURES

Wildernesses occupy well over half of the Forest. Wilderness use is below the national average. The smaller Wildernesses, Fitzpatrick and Popo Agie, are the most popular, chiefly because of their many lakes and streams. Here most visitors travel on foot. Horse and outfitter use is characteristic of the larger North Absaroka and Washakie Wildernesses, where hunting is the chief interest. They have fewer natural attractions, such as lakes. Describing them, one forester said, "It's a long ways between nowhere."

Detailed information on access, trailheads, trails, and destinations is provided by the Recreation Opportunity Guide, available at HQ and Ranger Districts.

Fitzpatrick Wilderness, 198,838 acres, is S of US 26/287, a triangle between the Bridger Wilderness of the Bridger-Teton National Forest on the W and the Wind River Indian Reservation on the E. The area was formerly the Glacier Primitive Area and is so shown on the Forest map. The area has hundreds of mountain lakes and ponds and miles of perennial streams with rapids, pool, cascades, and waterfalls. The W boundary is on the Continental Divide, the crest of the Wind River Range, with peaks exceeding 13,000 ft. and several large glaciers.

The ridge bars access from the W, and the Reservation is closed, so the only access is from trailheads near Dubois in the N. For one of these, see the entry for Whiskey Basin.

Popo Agie Wilderness, 101,991 acres, is in a disjunct portion of the Forest on the S boundary of the Wind River Indian Reservation. The W boundary, like that of the Fitzpatrick, is on the crest of the Wind River Range, adjoining the Bridger Wilderness. Highest point is 13,400-ft. Wind River Peak; several others exceed 12,000 ft. The area has over 200 spectacular alpine and subalpine lakes, many streams, several waterfalls.

Absaroka-Beartooth Wilderness, 23,750 acres, lies N of US 212. It adjoins the far larger Absaroka-Beartooth Wilderness in Custer National Forest, Montana (see entry). This scenic high plateau attracts fishermen because of its many lakes and streams, hunters because of its abundant game, including elk, mule deer, moose, and mountain goat. At 9,000 to 10,000 ft. elevation, the boulder-strewn plateau is carpeted with tundra vegetation, flowering as snow melts, with a backdrop of bare crags and reddish-yellow peaks. The plateau is cut by deep canyons.

The Beartooth Highway is closed by snow from about Nov. 1 to about July 1. Snow can fall at any time, and the tundra is often wind-swept. Bring mosquito repellent.

North Absaroka Wilderness, 350,488 acres, occupies most of the area between US 212 and US 14/20/16. It adjoins Yellowstone National Park. The Absaroka ridge forms the boundary, with several peaks over 10,000 ft. Drainages in the N portion, many of them in steep canyons, converge toward the NE, emptying into Clarks Fork of the Yellowstone River. Those in the S drain to the North Fork of the Shoshone River.

Highest point in the Wilderness is Dead Indian Peak, 12,216 ft. (This is 15 mi. from Dead Indian Hill, Dead Indian Pass, Dead Indian Creek, and Dead Indian Campground, 8 mi. from Dead Indian Meadows.)

The Sunlight Creek Mining Region, excluded because of mines and roads, extends into the Wilderness from the E along Sunlight Creek to within 3 mi. of its western border. An all-weather road, SR 296 (FR 100 on the Forest map), provides access to campgrounds and Wilderness trailheads. Other Wilderness trails cross the area from N to S.

Washakie Wilderness, 703,981 acres, S of US 14/20/16, adjoins the Teton Wilderness of the Bridger-Teton NF and a wilderness region in the SE corner of Yellowstone National Park. Together these comprise one of the nation's largest blocks of wild land. The Absaroka ridge forms the Washakie's western boundary, with peaks over 11,000 ft. Peaks over 12,000 ft. are scattered throughout the area. The N portion is divided by the Wapiti Ridge; streams on one side flow to the North Fork of the Shoshone River, those on the other to the South Fork. Much of the S portion is drained by the South Fork and the Greybull River.

Large parts of the terrain are rough and barren, product of lava and volcanic ash, with many fossils. Vegetation is sparse. Good hunting for elk, deer, moose, black bear.

SR 291, SW from Cody, penetrates the area, following the South Fork, along which are many inholdings, as well as a campground and Wilderness trailheads.

INTERPRETATION

Visitor center on the Cody-Yellowstone road, near the Wapiti Ranger Station.

A former lookout tower just 2 mi. off the Beartooth Highway (US 212) is now an exhibit, manned by volunteers.

The Forest has no campfire programs, guided hikes, or other naturalist activities.

The Sinks Canyon State Park leaflet (see entry) includes a *Natural History Guide to the Loop Drive.* This 56-mi. auto tour route passes through the S portion of the Forest, S of Lander, E of the Popo Agie Wilderness. The State Park is at the Forest boundary S of Lander.

ACTIVITIES

The looseleaf Recreation Opportunities Guide (ROG) can be seen at HQ and any Ranger District office. It contains detailed information about all types of recreation. Each campground is described: location, elevation, season, types of sites, facilities, etc. Each Forest trail is described on a separate page with simple map, season of use, degree of difficulty, destinations, etc. The ROG has pages on hunting, fishing, wildflowers, wildlife, skiing, snowmobiling, rockhounding, horsepacking, boating. Visitors can obtain photocopies of pages.

Camping: 33 campgrounds, 542 sites. All campgrounds can be reached by paved or all-weather roads. Season is generally May 30–Labor Day, shorter for those at higher elevations. Campgrounds can be used out of season but have no water or services.

Hiking, backpacking: 1,294 mi. of trails, about 70% of them in Wildernesses. Outside the Wildernesses are hundreds of miles of primitive roads with little or no vehicle traffic. About 31% of the trails need reconstruction or relocation. Recent budgets have supported only a third of the required maintenance. Trails in regions with heavy snowfall and high runoff are difficult to maintain, and early-season hikers can expect rough spots. Trails in volcanic areas require stout boots.

Snow and runoff block high-country trails until early or mid-July. The optimum hiking season at high elevations is short, only about 6 weeks, considerably longer in the river valleys.

Horse riding: Horsepacking is the preferred way to reach the remote backcountry and travel on the steeper trails. Outfitters, guides, and dude ranches serve the area. Special rules apply in some Wilderness areas.

Hunting: Chiefly big game: mule deer, black bear, elk, mountain goat, whitetail deer, mountain lion, bighorn sheep, pronghorn. North Absaroka and Washakie Wildernesses are both considered prime hunting areas. Small game are not hunted extensively. Bird hunting is on the increase: sage, blue and ruffed grouse; snipe, mourning dove, some waterfowl.

Fishing: More than 1,000 mi. of perennial streams provide good trout habitat. Many high mountain lakes offer fine fishing. Game species include grayling, rainbow, brook, cutthroat, golden, and lake trout. However, some lakes are barren, and in others quality ranges from excellent to indifferent, so it's well to consult publications of the Game and Fish Department or other fishing guides.

Boating: No Forest lake is large enough for power boating. Few are close enough to roads for use of cartoppers.

Rafting: During runoff on the North Fork of the Shoshone River. Outfitters in Cody.

Ski touring is gaining popularity. Many opportunities on unplowed roads. See the ROG for special areas.

PUBLICATIONS
Forest map, N and S sections. $1 each.
Travel map.
Information pages:
General information.
Climate.
Hiking trails, Wapiti Ranger District.
Suggested Wilderness backpacking trails.
Wildlife.
Campgrounds.

REFERENCES
Sudduth, Tom and Sanse. *Wyoming Trails.* Boulder, CO: Pruett, 1978. Pp. 63–85, 124–47. (Trails in S portion of the Forest.)

HEADQUARTERS: 225 W. Yellowstone Ave., Cody, WY 82414; (307) 527-6241.

RANGER DISTRICTS: Clarks Fork R.D., 140 N. Ferris, Powell, WY 82435; (307) 754-2407. Greybull R.D., 2044 State St., Meeteetse, WY 82433; (307) 868-2379. Lander R.D., Highway 287 W., Lander, WY 82520; (307) 332-5460. Wapiti R.D., 225 W. Yellowstone Ave., Cody, WY 82414; (307) 527-6241. Wind River R.D., 209 E. Ramshorn Ave., Dubois, WY 82513; (307) 455-2466.

SINKS CANYON STATE PARK
Wyoming Recreation Commission
600 acres.

6 mi. SW of Lander on SR 131. (BLM map 10)

The V-shaped canyon begins on the NE slope of the Wind River Mountains, dropping from 7,200 ft. to 6,180 ft. within 4 mi. The Middle Fork of the Popo Agie River cascades down a boulder-strewn bed between steep to sheer rock walls. At The Sinks, the river plunges into a cavern, reappearing half a mile downstream in a large spring. It does, that is, when river flow is normal; we were there during a near-record runoff, far too much for the underground route to accommodate.

The Park occupies a 2-mi. strip of land within the canyon. SR 131 follows the river for 9 mi. to the boundary of the Shoshone National Forest. Here there is a parking area and trailhead, and SR 131 becomes a Forest road. This is part of a 56-mi. self-guiding natural history auto tour, which continues through the Forest to SR 28, returning to Lander by way of Red Canyon, a National Natural Landmark.

Plants: Vegetation on the sloping canyon sides shows the effects of microclimates. On the S-facing slope, which receives more solar radiation, are juniper, limber pine, sagebrush, and grasses. The moister N-facing slope has cottonwood, aspen, willow, Douglas-fir, and limber pine. Riparian areas have willow, cottonwood, and a myriad of wildflowers.

Birds: Shortly after our visit, a bird checklist was published. 94 species, keyed to season and habitat. Included are turkey vulture, goshawk; sharp-shinned, Cooper's, and red-tailed hawks; golden eagle, prairie and peregrine falcons, merlin, American kestrel, blue and ruffed grouse, chukar, spotted sandpiper, rock and mourning doves, great horned and saw-whet owls, poor-will, common nighthawk; broad-tailed, rufous, and calliope hummingbirds; belted kingfisher, northern flicker, yellow-bellied sapsucker, hairy and downy woodpeckers, willow and dusky flycatchers, western wood-pewee. Also violet-green, tree, and cliff swallows; gray, Steller's, and pinyon jays; black-billed magpie, common raven, American crow, Clark's nutcracker, black-capped and mountain chickadees, white-breasted nuthatch, brown creeper, dipper; house, canyon, and rock wrens; gray catbird, American robin; hermit, Swainson's, and gray-cheeked thrushes; veery, mountain bluebird, Townsend's solitaire, ruby-crowned kinglet, bohemian and cedar waxwings, northern and loggerhead shrikes, European starling, warbling vireo. Warblers: orange-crowned, yellow, yellow-rumped, MacGillivray's, Wilson's. Northern oriole, Brewer's blackbird, brown-headed cowbird, western tanager, black-headed and evening grosbeaks, lazuli bunting; Cassin's, house, and gray-crowned rosy finches; pine siskin, American goldfinch, red crossbill, green-tailed and rufous-sided towhees, dark-eyed junco. Sparrows: vesper, chipping, Brewer's, white-crowned, song.

INTERPRETATION

An exceptionally fine *visitor center* is at The Sinks, where the river usually vanishes. Exhibits, literature, well-informed rangers.

Two *nature trails,* one at the visitor center, a longer one near the SW campground.

355 ॐ ZONE I

ACTIVITIES
Camping: Two campgrounds, 30 campsites. June–Oct.
Hiking, backpacking: Chiefly in the National Forest.
Fishing: Trout.
Ski touring: Starting point for snowmobilers and skiers entering the Forest.

PUBLICATIONS
Leaflet with map, including auto tour guide.
Popo Agie Nature Trail guide includes plant and wildlife checklists.
Visitor Center Trail Guide.

HEADQUARTERS: 3079 Sinks Canyon Rd., Route 63, Lander, WY 82520;
(307) 332-6333.

SOUTH PARK WILDLIFE UNIT
Wyoming Game and Fish Department
636 acres.

From Jackson, 6 mi. S on US 26/89 to bridge over the Snake River. Site
is W of the bridge, on the N side of the river.

Like most travelers, we had passed this site numerous times without noticing
it. There are many other points of access to the Snake. S of here, the highway
stays close to the river. But this little park is attractive, convenient, and often
unoccupied.

The site was established as a winter elk feedground, and over 800 elk are
fed from December to mid-Apr. The site is almost entirely river bottomland
with a plant cover of grasses, forbs, and shrubs. A provisional list of 33 bird
species indicates good spring and summer populations, including a few waterfowl, nothing noteworthy except a few sightings of sandhill crane and the
possibility of osprey and bald eagle nest sites.

The Snake is a popular floating stream for rafts and kayaks. This 6-mi.
segment has numerous small islands. Whitewater trips begin 12 to 15 mi.
further S.

This site is closed Nov. 16–Apr. 30 to prevent interference with wintering elk.
Dates may be changed slightly depending on snow conditions.

HEADQUARTERS: Wyoming Game and Fish Department, 5400 Bishop Blvd.,
Cheyenne, WY 82002; (307) 777-7631.

SWEETWATER CANYON
U.S. Bureau of Land Management
9,056 acres.

From Atlantic City on SR 28, you'll need advice and BLM map 10.

BLM told us how to get there, but without a BLM map and someone to point the way the directions wouldn't work. The last road section may require 4-wheel drive, and then it's a half-mile hike to the canyon. We include such hard-to-reach sites only if they're special. This one is much as the pioneers saw it in the 1800s. The Oregon-Mormon Pioneer National Historic Trail forms parts of the site's northern boundary.

The central feature of this site is Sweetwater Canyon, 9 mi. long, about 350 ft. deep, a green oasis in the desert. Sweetwater River is a perennial stream flowing E. The canyon is surrounded by flat to gently rolling terrain with sparse sagebrush and grasses. The riparian canyon vegetation includes willows, conifers, and aspens. Elevation in the canyon is about 6,700 ft.

The area is all-year habitat for mule deer, critical winter habitat for moose and elk.

BLM has recommended 5,760 acres, including the canyon, for Wilderness status.

ACTIVITIES
Backpacking: Many good campsites for hikers along the river.
Fishing: Excellent brown and rainbow trout fishing.

NEARBY
The river continues flowing E, crossing US 287, passing well N of the junction of US 287 and SR 220, then crossing 220 and flowing into Pathfinder Reservoir. The river valley was the westward route of the Historic Trail. See the entry for Sweetwater Rocks in Zone 2.

HEADQUARTERS: Rawlins District, BLM, P.O. Box 670, 1300 Third St., Rawlins, WY 82301; (307) 327-7171.

TARGHEE NATIONAL FOREST
U.S. Forest Service
296,448 acres in WY; 1,557,792 acres in ID.

The WY acreage extends S from Yellowstone National Park to Teton Pass, between the ID border and the Grand Teton National Park's W boundary. Principal access is from ID.

See entry in Idaho Zone 4.

A strip from 2 to 7 mi. wide along the W boundary of the Park is the Jedediah Smith Wilderness. Several Park trails connect with trails in the Wilderness. Alaska Basin has been such a popular destination for backpackers and horsepackers going up Cascade and Paintbrush canyons that overnight use is restricted.

Also in WY is the Winegar Hole Wilderness, 10,600 acres, on the S boundary of Yellowstone National Park, separated from the Jedediah Smith Wilderness by a narrow corridor. Primary access is from Cave Falls campground at the end of Forest Road 582. Terrain is relatively flat. Numerous lakes, streams, wetlands, with extensive stands of lodgepole pine. Trailless except for one nonmaintained trail. Grizzly bear habitat.

Also in the WY portion is the Grand Targhee ski area.

HEADQUARTERS: 420 N. Bridge St., St. Anthony, ID 83445; (208) 624-3151.

WHISKEY BASIN
Wyoming Game and Fish Department; U.S. Bureau of Land Management
7,546 acres; 4,844 acres.

> From Dubois, 3 mi. SE on US 287, then S about 2.8 mi. on local roads, turning E for the lakes, W for the BLM site.

This area adjoins the Fitzpatrick Wilderness of the Shoshone National Forest (see entry). The Game and Fish Wildlife Habitat Unit features a chain of 2 small lakes on Torrey Creek. (The third, Torrey Lake, is on private land. Public access by boat ramp only; no bank fishing.) The access road is maintained for the 2.8 mi. from the highway, not beyond.

Foothills slope down to the N and E from the Wind River Mountains. Elevations are from 8,969 ft. down to 7,302 ft. The site includes rolling hills, talus slopes, glacial moraines, canyon rims, and level meadows. Torrey Lake is about 231 acres, Trail 120 acres, Ring 108 acres. Torrey Creek flows from the Forest. About 2 1/2 mi. of the creek are within the Unit.

More than three-fourths of the visitors, most of them from nearby, are attracted by the scenery. They come to picnic, camp, hike, and collect rocks. Fishermen outnumber hunters.

Part of the BLM site was proposed for Wilderness status because it adjoins and complements the National Forest's Fitzpatrick Wilderness. On the N, it drops off into Jakey's Canyon, offering spectacular scenery in solitude. The SE boundary is an old jeep trail to Ross Lake, now closed at the Wilderness boundary.

Together with adjoining acreage in the National Forest, these sites have the largest winter concentration of bighorn sheep in the country. Sheep are trapped here for translocation. Portions of the Game and Fish unit are closed Dec. 1–Apr. 30 to prevent disturbance of wintering wildlife. The entire Whiskey Mountain area is managed cooperatively by Game and Fish, Forest Service, and BLM under a joint wildlife management plan.

Plants: Much of the area has a cover of grasses or sagebrush-grass. About 2,000 acres are forested with Douglas-fir, limber pine, Engelmann spruce, and subalpine fir. Conifers are scattered through sagebrush-grass on steep slopes. Seasonal wildflowers include penstemon, phlox, knotweed, cinquefoil, dock, stonecrop, goldenrod, globemallow, dandelion, white clover, vetch, white violet, and death camas.

Birds: Waterfowl are fairly abundant and attract a few hunters. Seasonally common are Canada goose, mallard, common merganser, Barrow's goldeneye, pintail, shoveler, blue-winged and green-winged teals. Principal upland game birds are blue and ruffed grouse.

Mammals: Relatively large numbers of bighorn sheep winter here. From May to Nov. they are on Whiskey Mountain and other high slopes in the National Forest. Elk also winter. Mule deer are often seen, moose and black bear less frequently. Cottontail are abundant near buildings, red squirrel in timbered areas.

ACTIVITIES

Camping: The Game and Fish site has 6 parking areas; camping is permitted in 5. Sites have latrines.

Hiking, backpacking: The area is a trailhead for the Fitzpatrick Wilderness.

Hunting: More than half of the hunters come for sheep, others for elk, deer, and bear, few for waterfowl and small game.

Fishing: Lakes and stream. Rainbow, brown, brook, and lake trout; burbot, mountain whitefish.

Boating: Three launching ramps.

HEADQUARTERS: Wyoming Game and Fish Department, 5400 Bishop Blvd., Cheyenne, WY 82002; (307) 777-7631; Rawlins District, BLM, 1300 Third St., P.O. Box 670, Rawlins, WY 82301; (307) 324-7171.

YELLOWSTONE NATIONAL PARK
National Park Service
2,020,625 acres in WY; 167,623 acres in MT; 31,488 acres in ID.

N and S entrances on US 89; E and W entrances on US 20; NE entrance on US 212.

"Yellowstone, first of all National Parks, is splendid, unique, magnificent, awesome, spectacular—no superlatives suffice. It is also a much-abused National Park, the most commercialized, in some ways the most threatened."

That's how this entry began when we sent it to Park HQ for checking. We should have included "most controversial." We received a vigorous rebuttal from Public Affairs Officer Gregory Kroll, objecting to "commercialized" and much of what we said in the next few paragraphs.

John saw Yellowstone first in 1929, riding the concessioner's bus from the railhead to Old Faithful Inn and sightseeing by bus. He returned in 1930 driving a Model A Ford loaded with camping gear. There were no crowds.

We are dismayed by what has been done since then to accommodate growing crowds of visitors: acres of highway overpasses, loops, and intersections; more acres of parking; power lines hacked through forest. Concessioners operate 9 hotels and lodges, rental cabins, restaurants, bars, gift shops, groceries, gasoline stations, marinas, liveries, bus tours, cruise boats, snowcoach trips, snowmobile rentals, and more. They offer such features as Stagecoach Adventure, Old West Dinner Cookouts, and Water Scenicruise Mini-Voyages. As in other National Parks, the concessioners are politically powerful, often able to block changes that would benefit the public but might affect their own profits.

For years the National Park Service tried to meet growing demand with more bedrooms, campsites, parking areas, and shops. Spreading development threatened the Park's beauty and integrity. In peak season, campgrounds and parking at feature stops were overcrowded. Litter and vandalism increased. It seemed impossible to fulfill both primary mandates: preservation and public enjoyment.

Conflicts between visitors and wildlife multiplied. To keep bears and visitors apart, hundreds of bears were translocated or killed. The population of grizzly bears has been sharply reduced. Black bears, once common along roads and in campgrounds, today are seldom seen.

Present Park Service policy appears to recognize that limits must be fixed. Construction of new facilities has been slowed. Proposals to eliminate some commercial facilities and to limit the number of visitors have been vigorously opposed by those who value the tourist dollar.

To our description of the Park, Public Affairs Officer Kroll replied, in part:

"The present "figure-8" road system and the five present exit roads have been in existence since 1905. The subsequent, minimal alterations to traffic flow were built precisely to remove traffic from the park's finest features. . . . There is one overpass in the park and, at most, two to four total acres of intersections. . . .

"Consider for a moment what an earlier 20th-century visit to Yellowstone would have included. Not only was the Grand Loop just as it is today, there were more hotels and there were roads into pristine places like Pelican Valley and Heart Lake. There were open dumps and a paternalistic attitude toward the magnificent wildlife, including a predator control program and "bear feeding stations." Thermal features were curiosities and often treated with disregard. . . .

"Consider what is not here today. There is no hotel at Norris or on the rim of the Grand Canyon of the Yellowstone or at Yancy's Hole. There is no campground or swimming pavilion at Old Faithful, and the cabin ghetto, laundry, employee quarters, and other clutter is being removed. At West Thumb, the gas station, store, and dormitories have just been removed, and remaining facilities will be removed by the fall of 1987. The campground and cabins are already gone. . . . The tennis court and swimming pool beside Mammoth Terrace are gone, as is the golf course on the shoulder of Mount Everts. . . ."

We stand by our opening characterization of the Park—"splendid, unique, magnificent, awesome, spectacular"—and confess we hadn't missed the hotels and other intrusions now removed. We are not the only critics of the commercialization that remains, but most of the problem and controversy affects only 1% of Yellowstone's 2,219,805 acres. Yellowstone's backcountry, the other 99%, remains a largely pristine wilderness, seen by only a few visitors. Indeed, the number of backcountry campers has declined over the past 10 years.

Now Yellowstone is threatened by developments outside its borders. The Bridger-Teton, Targhee, Gallatin, Custer, and Shoshone National Forests border the Park. A huge geothermal area extends beyond Park boundaries. National Forests, unlike the Park, are open to mining, oil and gas extraction, and geothermal energy exploitation. Several million acres are under existing leases. Tapping geothermal energy would inevitably affect Yellowstone's geysers. The Yellowstone Coalition is urging the federal government to adopt a coherent policy for the entire Yellowstone ecosystem.

Yellowstone's operating funds have been cut. Less famous parks and forests are harder hit, but effects are evident here, such as unrepaired potholes in the roads. Trails aren't as well maintained. Rangers, especially ranger-naturalists, aren't seen as often.

The Grand Loop. Covering about 3,400 sq. mi., Yellowstone encompasses several broad, forested volcanic plateaus. Elevations range from 5,314 ft. where the Yellowstone River exits near Gardiner, on the N, to 11,358 ft. at Eagle Peak in the SE corner. Alpine scenery is less common here than in other Rocky Mountain parks, but there is spectacular high country in the Absarokas on the E and in the Washburn and Gallatin ranges.

The Park has the world's greatest system of thermal phenomena: geysers, boiling springs, and fumaroles. It has nine major geyser-hot springs basins and over a hundred clusters of hot springs. Reports of these phenomena by early explorers and trappers led to the Washburn-Langford-Doane expedition and establishment of the Park.

The Grand Canyon of the Yellowstone is second in size to the Grand Canyon of the Colorado. Yellowstone Lake is the largest body of water above 7,500 ft. in North America: 139 sq. mi. in area with a 110-mi. shoreline.

The Park has 5 principal entrances, on the N, NE, E, S, and W. Each leads to the 142-mi. Grand Loop that circles the central plateau.

People come to Yellowstone to see its unique features: Old Faithful, Norris Geyser Basin, the Grand Canyon and falls of the Yellowstone River, Obsidian Cliff, Mount Washburn, Mammoth Hot Springs, Tower Falls, Firehole River, and other features along the 300 mi. of roads. This is where the crowds are.

Come out of season if you can. Crowds begin to arrive in mid-June. July is the peak month, Aug. not far behind. In mid-Sept. we found the Park well populated but not congested; on Saturday afternoon we booked into Old Faithful Inn with no reservation. Craig Pass, between Old Faithful and West Thumb, was closed by snow next morning, open by afternoon. If you must come in midsummer, get up early. Crowds at the feature attractions are lightest near dawn and sunset.

"Yellowstone, the Ultimate Winter Experience," proclaims a leaflet from TW Services, a major concessioner. The winter season, from mid-Dec. through mid-Mar., offers what Park literature describes as "a beautiful and rewarding experience, but one that needs much planning and preparation." Visitors travel to lodges at Old Faithful or Mammoth Hot Springs by snowcoach or snowmobile, then tour by snowcoach, drive rented snowmobiles on unplowed roads, or go cross-country on skis. Some conservationists criticize Park management for allowing winter use, disturbing wildlife in what had been a quiet season. However, motorized snow vehicles are confined to designated unplowed roads.

The Backcountry. Roads divide the Park into 10 backcountry roadless areas of 12,000 to 483,000 acres. The larger areas adjoin National Forest Wildernesses, comprising the largest wilderness areas in the Lower 48.

Some 60 major trailheads are on Park roads. Trails enter from surrounding public lands at 30 points on the boundary. The backcountry has over 1,000 mi. of trails, most of them suitable for either foot or horse travel.

Day hikers need no permits; backcountry travelers do. They must camp in designated sites; permits include site reservations. Special restrictions apply where bear activity is a greater than usual hazard, and where camping might disturb nesting eagles or ospreys. Permits are issued not more than 48 hrs. in advance. These and other rules, more stringent than in most other Wildernesses, help keep the backcountry pristine.

Surprisingly, Yellowstone's backcountry is relatively little used. Of every

1,000 Yellowstone visitors, only 7 spend a night in the backcountry. The number of backcountry visitors has declined over the past decade.

Climate: Summers are short (mid-June to mid-Aug.). Temperatures are usually in the mid-40s in early morning, rising to the 70s in the afternoon. Brief afternoon thundershowers are common. Nights are cool, in the 30s at higher elevations to the mid-40s in lower elevations. Occasional freezes, even at lower elevations.

By the middle or end of Aug., frost and freezing temperatures can be expected at higher elevations; at lower elevations, morning temperatures in the 30s occur. Between early Sept. and Nov., morning readings are generally in the teens and 20s throughout the Park. Afternoon readings decline from the 60s and upper 50s to the 40s and 30s.

Winters are harsh, cold and snowy. At sunrise temperatures average from below zero in the higher areas to about 10° in lower areas, sometimes dropping to 40 or 50 below zero. A ranger told us of a night when the hot water expelled by Old Faithful froze in midair and fell tinkling to the ground. Snow depths usually peak in Mar.

From Mar. to mid-May temperatures begin to moderate, with morning temperatures at lower elevations in the teens and 20s, and 5 to 10 degrees colder at higher elevations. Afternoon temperatures begin to rise above freezing early in Mar., reaching the 50s by mid-May.

Patches of snow can be found on the highest peaks throughout the summer. The ice on Yellowstone Lake usually breaks up by the end of May. Snowfalls may begin again in early fall, with increasing frequency and accumulation through the late fall. During the winter, snow occurs several times a month, with little or no melting. Snow cover can be extremely deep, with snowshoes or skis necessary for backcountry travel.

From mid-May to mid-June, rapidly warming temperatures bring heavy snowmelt, high water in streams and lakes, and hazardous backcountry stream crossings.

Plants: 80% of the Park is forested. Principal tree species include lodgepole pine, aspen, Engelmann spruce, Douglas-fir, subalpine fir, whitebark and limber pines, Rocky Mountain juniper. No plant checklist is available, but numerous publications describe the Yellowstone flora. See References.

Common wildflowers include beargrass, blue and death camas; sego, leopard, and glacier lilies; coralroot and calypso orchids, spring beauty, columbine, marsh marigold, Oregon grape, globeflower, lupine, pricklypear cactus, low larkspur, yellow pondlily, monkshood, wild rose, stonecrop, cinquefoil, wild geranium, serviceberry, fringed gentian, fireweed, yellow violet, blazingstar, evening primrose, penstemon, Indian paintbrush, scarlet gilia, wild phlox, alpine forget-me-not, fleabane, mule ears, butter-and-eggs, elephanthead, heartleaf arnica, monkeyflower, balsamroot.

Birds: Checklist of 225 species available. Seasonally abundant, common, and "locally common" species include white pelican, trumpeter swan, great blue heron, Canada goose, mallard, gadwall, pintail, green-winged teal, American wigeon, lesser scaup, Barrow's goldeneye, bufflehead, common merganser, red-tailed and Swainson's hawks, bald eagle, osprey, American kestrel, blue grouse, American coot, killdeer, common snipe, spotted sandpiper, ring-billed gull, common nighthawk, northern flicker, yellow-bellied sapsucker, hairy woodpecker. Also violet-green, tree, and cliff swallows; gray jay, black-billed magpie, common raven, Clark's nutcracker, mountain chickadee, red-breasted nuthatch, dipper, rock wren, American robin, hermit thrush, mountain bluebird, ruby-crowned kinglet, water pipit, northern shrike, European starling, warbling vireo; yellow and yellow-rumped warblers, common yellowthroat; yellow-headed, red-winged, and Brewer's blackbirds; northern oriole, Cassin's finch, pine grosbeak, pine siskin, green-tailed towhee, dark-eyed junco. Sparrows: savannah, vesper, chipping, Brewer's, white-crowned, song.

Mammals: In the early days of the Park, it was policy to kill predators—wolves, mountain lions, and coyotes. The wolf was eliminated, and reintroduction is under consideration. (Some believe a few wolves are in the Park.) The bison population, once reduced to about 50, is now about 2,000. Elk thrive, despite disruption of their seasonal migration routes.

Wildlife viewing along the main roads isn't as exciting as it was years ago, when "bear jams" disrupted traffic. Some species have sought quieter places. But one can count on seeing bison and elk, with a fair chance of seeing mule deer and moose. On our most recent visit, we saw three elk with calves swim the Madison River. Nearby, we photographed swans at close range. We often see coyotes in early morning. Marmot, golden-mantled squirrel, chipmunk, Uinta ground squirrel, and red squirrel are common. So are beaver, though one seldom sees them by day.

Other species checklisted include shrews, bats, marten, fisher, weasels, mink, skunks, wolverine, badger, river otter, red fox, lynx, bobcat, northern flying squirrel, northern pocket gopher, several species of mice and voles, muskrat, porcupine, pika, whitetail jackrabbit, snowshoe hare, cottontail, pronghorn, bighorn sheep.

FEATURES

We will not describe the Park's most spectacular features: Old Faithful, Midway Geyser Basin, Fountain Paint Pots, Firehole and Gibbon falls, Norris Geyser Basin, Obsidian Cliff, Mammoth Hot Springs, Tower Falls, Mt. Washburn, Grand Canyon of the Yellowstone, Upper and Lower falls, and Yellowstone Lake. They have been described and depicted in countless publications, including those of the Park.

The other 99% of the Park also has special features: geysers, fumaroles, hot springs, waterfalls, cascades, canyons, and more. Their scale is more modest, but one can enjoy them in solitude. Backcountry travelers see more wildlife than motorists do.

A map of the Park shows us many places we haven't been and want to see, such as the SE corner, a trek better undertaken by horse than on foot.

INTERPRETATION

Visitor centers are at Mammoth Hot Springs (open all year), Old Faithful (open mid-Apr.), Norris (mid-May), Fishing Bridge (mid-May), and Grant (early June.)

Self-guiding trails with leaflets at Upper Geyser Basin, Fountain Paint Pots, Norris Geyser Basin, Mammoth Hot Springs Terraces, Grand Canyon, Mud Volcano.

Campfire programs, nature walks, and other interpretive activities are scheduled each year. Information is available at visitor centers and ranger stations.

The Yellowstone Institute, sponsored by the Yellowstone Library and Museum Association, offers 2- to 6-day courses in geology; history, art, and literature; photography, plant life, and zoology, with many field trips. (Yellowstone Institute, P.O. Box 117, Yellowstone National Park, WY 82190; (307) 344-7381.)

ACTIVITIES

Camping: 12 campgrounds; about 2,000 sites. Mammoth is open all year. Others open May 1–June 24, close Sept. 3–Oct. 31. No reservations. 7-day limit July 1–Aug. 24; 30 days otherwise. Demand exceeds supply July–Aug., and sites in the most popular campgrounds are occupied before noon; queues sometimes form at dawn. Reservations can be made at a concessioner trailer park at Fishing Bridge: (307) 344-7311.

(The same concessioner operates hotels and cabins.)

Campsites are usually available at National Forest campgrounds outside the E and NE entrances. The nearest commercial facilities outside the Park are at Gardiner, MT (N entrance), West Yellowstone, MT (W entrance), and between the S entrance and Grand Teton National Park.

Hiking, backpacking: Many short trails, shown on the Park leaflet map and with well-marked trailheads, offer easy hiking in scenic areas. More challenging day hikes have such destinations as the peaks of Mt. Washburn and Mt. Holmes, Shoshone Geyser Basin, and Heart Lake Geyser Basin.

The longest trail begins in the Bridger-Teton National Forest, enters the SE corner of the Park, then follows the E side of the Yellowstone River, Yellowstone Lake, and the E side of the river again to Canyon, then continues near the river to the North Entrance. Many other trails are in the roadless areas.

Backcountry use permits are required for overnight hikes. Apply in person, not more than 48 hours in advance. Camping is permitted only at the places and times specified in the permit. Backpack stoves are recommended; fires are permitted only at designated sites.

Off-trail hiking is discouraged and usually difficult. Backpackers are expected to carry topo maps and compass and to know how to use them. They are also expected to know the hazards and problems of backcountry travel—streams in flood, lightning, hypothermia, bear encounters, giardia, biting insects—and how to cope with them. They are also expected to know the rules on waste disposal.

Horse riding: Conducted morning and afternoon rides are offered by the concessioner; reservations at Park Activities Desks.

Horsepacking, a traditional way to see the backcountry, requires a permit, which specifies route and campsites. Special rules govern party size, management of stock, and camping practices.

Fishing: State licenses are not required; a Yellowstone Park fishing permit is required. The management objective is to maintain a natural, self-sustaining fish population, chiefly for the benefit of eagles, ospreys, pelicans, otters, grizzly bears, and other wildlife dependent on this food supply. Stocking was discontinued more than 30 years ago. Regulations governing open season, protected species, closed waters, catch and length limits, tackle, and bait may be changed from year to year. Some waters are designated for catch-and-release.

The number of fishermen, many returning year after year, suggests that the rules are not considered unduly onerous.

Boating: All boaters must have Yellowstone Park permits. Power boats are permitted on most of Yellowstone Lake and Lewis Lake. The southern arms of Yellowstone Lake have no-wake zones and zones limited to hand-propelled craft. Boating is prohibited on all Park streams and rivers, except that hand-propelled craft may use the channel between Lewis and Shoshone lakes.

Yellowstone Lake is exposed to sudden high winds, and the water is extremely cold. Power boaters are urged to seek shelter quickly if winds rise. Canoeists are urged to wear life jackets and stay close to shore.

Small boats, but not canoes, can be rented at Bridge Bay marina.

Some backcountry campsites are accessible by boat.

Ski touring: No special regulations other than permits required for overnight trips. Most skiers enter the park by snowcoach or snowmobile. Snowcoaches operate from mid-Dec. through the first week of Mar. Ski trails are mapped in the Old Faithful, Mammoth Hot Springs, and Canyon areas. Most trails are not groomed.

Snowmobiling: Rentals available outside the Park and at Mammoth Hot Springs. Snowmobiles are restricted to marked portions of unplowed roads; no off-road travel. Usual season begins mid-Dec., declines in late Feb. as roads are plowed, ends in late Mar.

PUBLICATIONS

Leaflet with map.

Information pages: general information: climate, roads, transportation, accommodations, services, campgrounds, activities, regulations, etc. Winter season information.

Leaflets:

Yellowstone, a Natural Ecosystem.

Birds of Yellowstone.

Wildlife of Yellowstone.

Boating.

Fishing regulations.

Horse packing.

Bicycling.

Beyond Road's End; a Backcountry User's Guide.

Hazards in Yellowstone.

Fatigue.

Grizzly.

Old Faithful ski trails.

Skiing the Canyon Area.

Skiing the Canyon Rims.

Mammoth Area Ski Trails.

Tower Area Ski Trails.

List of books, maps, and pamphlets.

Yellowstone Institute Field Courses.

Concessioner publications:

Activities schedule.

Winter Guide to Yellowstone Country.

2 Parks, 2 Seasons.

Yellowstone, the Ultimate Winter Experience.

Snowmobile Yellowstone's Winter Wonderland.

Winter Bus and Snowcoach Schedule.

REFERENCES

The Yellowstone Library & Museum Association publishes an extensive list of books, maps, and pamphlets that can be ordered by mail or purchased at the Park (P.O. Box 117, Yellowstone National Park, WY 82190; 307-344-7381). Many other references, some long out of print, can be found in libraries. We list here only a few current publications pertaining to Yellowstone's backcountry:

Marschall, Mark. *Yellowstone Trails, A Hiking Guide.* Yellowstone Library and Museum Association, 1978; rev. 1984.

Bartlett, Richard A. *Yellowstone—a Wilderness Besieged.* Tucson: University of Arizona Press, 1985.

Shaw, Richard J. *Plants of Yellowstone and Grand Teton National Parks.* Salt Lake City: Wheelwright Press, 1981.

Bach, Orville E., Jr. *Hiking the Yellowstone Backcountry.* San Francisco: Sierra Club Books, 1972.

Chittenden, Hiram C. *The Yellowstone National Park.* Norman: University of Oklahoma Press, 1982.

Mitchell, Ron. *50 Eastern Idaho Hiking Trails.* Boulder, CO: Pruett, 1979. Pp. 8–9.

HEADQUARTERS: P.O. Box 168, Yellowstone National Park, WY 82190; (307) 344-7381.

ZONE 2

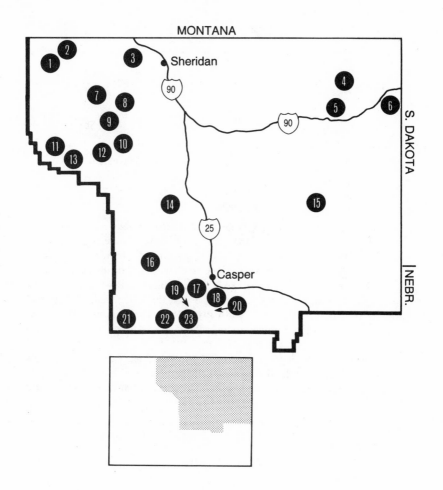

ZONE 2

Includes these counties:

Big Horn   Sheridan   Washakie
Crook   Johnson   Converse
Weston   Natrona
Niobrara   Campbell

North central and northeast Wyoming are framed by mountains: the Bighorns on the W, Black Hills on the E, Laramie Range on the S. Between the mountains is a vast expanse of high plains, sometimes flat, more often carved by erosion into hills, buttes, escarpments, badlands, and dendritic drainages.

W of the Bighorn Mountains, the N-flowing Bighorn River is dammed in Montana, the pool backing up beyond US 14A; this is the Bighorn National Recreation Area. In the S, the North Platte River curves around the N end of the Laramie Range, dammed to form Pathfinder, Alcova, and other reservoirs.

In the zone are the Bighorn National Forest and a piece of South Dakota's Black Hills NF. Near the Black Hills is the first National Monument: Devils Tower. Entries describe some delightful hiking trails, unusual badlands, and a sprawling National Grassland that has an impressive bird checklist.

ALCOVA RESERVOIR
Natrona County Parks and Pleasure Grounds
2,223 water acres.

From Casper, 32 mi. SW on SR 220. (BLM map 7)

This is one of the most attractive reservoirs on the North Platte River. Much of the surrounding landscape is rugged, with colorful rock formations, including perched rocks, boulder-strewn hillsides, cliffs, bluffs, outcrops, in shades of red, brown, gray, and green. Sagebrush flats, cottonwood in draws, juniper on hillsides; and, when we visited, abundant wildflowers. A scenic drive follows the E side of the reservoir, for the most part at a distance, winding around small canyons, with spur roads to the shore. 14 mi. from Alcova Dam, the drive joins County 408, the route from SR 220 to Pathfinder Dam, 7 mi. farther S. One can turn back or take 408, a less scenic route back to the highway.

The Natrona County leaflet calls this "one of the most popular recreation areas in southern Wyoming." There is a cluster of commercial development near the dam; Lake Alcova Park is a resort community of SR 220 on the N shore; but on the drive around the reservoir we encountered only two other cars.

The U.S. Bureau of Reclamation built the dam. The impoundment is about 3 1/2 mi. long. Surrounding land is a mix of federal, state, and private. Natrona County has provided camping and boating developments.

NEARBY

Fremont Canyon of the North Platte is between Alcova and Pathfinder reservoirs. It is crossed by the scenic drive. Stop at the bridge for a fine view. Vertical walls about 200 ft. high. Raptors nest.

Grey Reef Reservoir is a 182-acre storage basin just below Alcova on SR 220. Fishing, canoeing. Put-in for float trips (see entry, North Platte River, Alcova to Casper).

Pathfinder Reservoir (see entry).

ACTIVITIES

Camping: 4 campgrounds; undesignated sites.

Hiking, backpacking: It's fine hiking country, so open no trails are needed; scenic; splendid solitude. Hot in summer, though.

Fishing: Rainbow and brown trout, grayling.

Boating: Marina, ramps.

HEADQUARTERS: 4621 CY Avenue, Casper, WY 82604; (307) 234-6821.

AMSDEN CREEK WILDLIFE UNIT
Wyoming Game and Fish Department
4,147 acres.

From Dayton on US 14, 3 mi. W on local roads. (BLM map 5)

US 14, from Dayton to Greybull, is one of Wyoming's most scenic highways, crossing the Bighorn Mountains. At Burgess Junction, 14 Alternate offers a scenic route to Lovell and the Bighorn National Recreation Area (see entry).

The primary mission of the Amsden Creek unit is to provide winter forage for 300 elk, but some visitors come just for the scenery in Tongue River Canyon. An all-weather road follows Tongue River for about 1 1/2 mi. The river is rated a "fishery of national importance," for rainbow, brown, and brook trout and mountain whitefish. The river is near the S boundary of the site. A foot trail continues into the adjacent Bighorn National Forest (see entry). Amsden Creek, near the N boundary, also offers good fishing. More than three-fourths of the visitors come for fishing, sightseeing, hiking, or camping.

The unit is about 2 mi. N–S, 3 1/2 mi. W–E. Elevations rise from 4,260 ft. near the SE corner to 7,130 ft. on the W. The E portion has rolling, open hills, divided by a N–S timbered ridge. The W portion is more rugged, with steep, often timbered slopes, rising to the Bighorns.

Plants: One-third of the site, chiefly the steep mountain slopes, is coniferous forest, with ponderosa pine the dominant species, scattered limber pine. Perennial forbs and grasses, and quaking aspen with forbs and grasses each cover about one-fifth of the area.

Wildlife: 275 to 325 elk use the area from Nov. to May, as do about 250 mule deer and 20 whitetail deer. About 6 mountain lion and 4 black bear include this site in their territories. Game birds include sharp-tailed and blue grouse, ringneck pheasant, Hungarian partridge, wild turkey, and mourning dove. Small game includes cottontail and snowshoe hare.

Camping: Three primitive campgrounds.

A part of the unit is closed in winter to prevent disturbance of wildlife.

HEADQUARTERS: Wyoming Game and Fish Department, 5400 Bishop Blvd., Cheyenne, WY 82002; (307) 777-7631.

BIGHORN NATIONAL FOREST
U.S. Forest Service
1,107,670 acres; 1,115,172 acres within boundaries.

N Central WY, extending S from the Montana border. Crossed by US 14, Greybull to Sheridan; US 14 A, Lovell to Burgess Jct.; and US 16, Worland to Buffalo. (BLM maps 5, 12)

The Forest is a single block in N central WY. It extends about 70 mi. N–S, 30 mi. W–E, occupying most of the Bighorn Mountain Range.

The Bighorns are an isolated range rising from rolling plains country at about 4,000 ft. elevation. Near the western Forest boundary, the land rises suddenly to a gently sloping plateaulike shoulder at 7,000 to 9,000 ft. elevation. Above this are rolling timbered ridges and drainages, rising to the foot of the barren granite peaks of the main ridge. The steepest country is in the S half of the Forest, where the highest point is 13,165-ft. Cloud Peak.

The mountains look formidable from a distance, snow-capped, with active glaciers, elevated more than 9,000 ft. above the surrounding plains. Only two roads cross the ridge. However, the Bighorns are gentler and more accessible than the rugged Absarokas to the W. Broad valleys ascend to alpine meadows, fine open terrain for hiking, horse riding, ski touring, and snowmobiling. Over most of the Forest, the climate is milder, the season longer, although there's plenty of snow in winter, 150 to 200 in. per year at 9,000 ft. elevation and above.

Plenty of water, too. The surrounding plains are semiarid, but the mountains intercept moisture. The Cloud Peak Wilderness, occupying the highest country, has several hundred fishing lakes ("We haven't yet counted them."), and many more lakes, reservoirs, and ponds are scattered, chiefly in the S half of the Forest. Principal streams include Goose Creek, Tensleep Creek, Tongue River, Clear Creek, Shell Creek, Little Bighorn River and Paintrock Creek. Most snow melts between May 15–June 15, but the highest trails, on Cloud Peak, aren't accessible to hikers until July.

Annual visitor-days total about 1.5 million. Many of the visitors are Wyoming residents who enjoy hunting, fishing, snowmobiling, and ORV travel. Many remote areas are most easily accessible by ORV. Although regulations limit motorized vehicles to roads and trails in most areas, the terrain encourages violations and enforcement is difficult. Dispersed recreation, outside of developed sites and not including wilderness visits, makes up more than half of the total.

In addition to US 14, Alt. 14 and 16 (all fine scenic drives), the Forest has 1,497 mi. of roads. Most of these are local roads, often unmaintained or closed to vehicles except when Forest operations require, but available for hiking. There are also 630 mi. of trails, many within or adjacent to the Cloud Peak Wilderness. Except within the Wilderness, most trails can be used by motorized vehicles such as trailbikes.

The Forest has only one Wilderness, Cloud Peak, managed as a Primitive Area until it was designated Wilderness by the Wyoming Wilderness Act of 1984. Until then, wilderness visits accounted for only about 5% of total recreation visitor-days, but the designation may attract more visitors.

The principal campgrounds, especially those scattered along the two main roads, are often full on summer weekends, not mid-week. Those on all-weather and dirt spur roads are slower to fill. In any case, one can camp almost anywhere, and even car campers should have no difficulty finding attractive sites.

Climate: Annual precipitation ranges from 10 to 40 in., one-half to two-thirds of it falling as snow. Local thunderstorms are common in summer. The W side is drier than the E. On the upper slopes, average snow depth in May is from 1 to 81 in., averaging 47 in. Cloud Peak, Blacktooth, and several others in the central portion of the range have perennial snowfields.

Recorded temperature extremes are 90°F and −42°. July is the warmest month, Jan. the coldest. In the high country, freezing temperatures can be encountered in any month.

Plants: About 60% of the area is forested. Major species are lodgepole pine, Engelmann spruce, and Douglas-fir. The principal plant communities are:

Alpine tundra. Above 10,000 ft. Low-growing perennial grasses, sedges, forbs, dwarfed shrubs. Many colorful wildflowers follow snowmelt. Much of this community is in the Cloud Peak Wilderness. Stunted conifers commonly occur between 9,000 and 10,000 ft.

Lodgepole pine. 6,000 to 9,000 ft. Dominant species in the subalpine forest, occupying 30% of the Forest land area, much of it area previously logged or burned.

Engelmann spruce, subalpine fir. 6,000 to 9,000 ft. Though it now occupies only half as much subalpine acreage as lodgepole pine, this association would become dominant if the forest were left undisturbed.

Douglas-fir. Only 5% of the Forest, but often dominant on steep, N-facing slopes at lower elevations.

Aspen. Scattered patches, most noticeable when displaying its brilliant fall colors.

Grasslands and meadows. Almost one-fifth of the Forest, interspersed with other plant communities.

Sagebrush. About one-tenth of the Forest, at lower elevations.

A list of 65 wildflower species is available, arranged by color but not season or habitat. Among them: Red, pink, reddish-purple: shootingstar, twinflower, Indian paintbrush, fireweed, vetch. White: globeflower, marsh marigold, death camas, mariposa lily, starflower. Blue: forget-me-not, little larkspur, pasqueflower, blue flax. Yellow: buttercup, cinquefoil, heartleaf arnica, dandelion, arrowleaf balsamroot.

Birds: 276 species recorded. Checklist available. Seasonally abundant or common species include eared, western, and pied-billed grebes; double-crested cormorant, great blue heron, Canada goose, mallard, gadwall, pintail, green-winged and blue-winged teals, American wigeon, northern shoveler, redhead, lesser scaup; red-tailed, rough-legged, and ferruginous hawks; American kestrel, sharp-tailed grouse, ring-necked pheasant, American coot. Also killdeer, common snipe, spotted and Baird's sandpipers, long-billed dowitcher, Wilson's phalarope, ring-billed gull, rock and mourning doves, great horned owl, common nighthawk, northern flicker, downy woodpecker, eastern and western kingbirds, least flycatcher, western wood-pewee; tree, rough-winged, barn, and cliff swallows. Also black-billed magpie, American crow, pinyon jay, warbling vireo. Warblers: orange-crowned, yellow, yellow-rumped, common yellowthroat, yellow-breasted chat, Wilson's. Western meadowlark; yellow-headed, red-winged, and Brewer's blackbirds; common grackle, brown-headed cowbird, evening grosbeak, Cassin's and house finches, American goldfinch, lark bunting. Sparrows: house, vesper, lark, tree, chipping. Oregon junco.

Mammals: 54 species recorded. Checklist available. Species include bats: little brown, small-footed and long-eared myotis, silver-haired, spotted, big brown. Masked, vagrant, and water shrews. Least chipmunk, yellowbelly marmot, red squirrel, northern flying squirrel, northern pocket gopher, deer mouse, bushytail woodrat, several voles, western jumping mouse, striped skunk, pika, snowshoe hare, whitetail jackrabbit, mountain cottontail, Ord kangaroo rat, beaver, muskrat, porcupine, coyote, red fox, mountain lion, lynx, bobcat, wolverine, river otter, badger, fisher, martin, mink, longtail and shorttail weasels, moose, elk, mule and whitetail deer, Rocky Mountain bighorn sheep, pronghorn, black bear, raccoon, coyote.

Bighorn sheep were abundant when the mountains were named but are no longer. From a remnant population of 30 in the Forest in 1950, the population increased to 185 in 1973, then declined again to about 25. Antelope population has also declined to about 35, whitetail deer to about 15, while moose numbers have gradually increased. Estimated populations of the principal big game species in 1984 were 14,400 mule deer, 6,200 elk, 310 black bear, 260 moose.

Reptiles and amphibians: 18 species recorded. Checklist available shows habitats. Species include tiger salamander, Plains spadefoot toad, western boreal toad, chorus and leopard frogs, snapping and painted turtles, western spiny softshell, northern sagebrush and short-horned lizards. Rubber boa, yellow-bellied racer, bull snake, milk snake; red-sided, Plains, and western terrestrial garter snakes; western prairie rattlesnake.

FEATURES

Cloud Peak Wilderness, 195,500 acres, in the S central part of the Forest, extends for 30 mi. along the highest part of the Bighorn Range, including 13,175-ft. Cloud Peak. The lower slopes, up from 8,000 ft. elevation, have an attractive mix of spruce-pine forest, open meadows, streams, and wetlands. The Wilderness has several hundred lakes, many of them with excellent fishing, and over 50 mi. of fishing streams. (New totals haven't been compiled since Congress added to the Wilderness.)

Trailheads on both sides of the area give access to over 100 mi. of maintained trails. Most trailheads are near campgrounds accessible by car, others at the end of 4-wheel-drive tracks used chiefly by hunters. Until recent years most visitors have been hunters and fishermen. Since 1980 their number has been stable, while the number of hikers has increased from 7,700 to nearly 45,000. Most visitors travel on foot. Horseback users in 1984 numbered 7,850.

Snowshoes are needed to enter the area in early June. Late that month the lower slopes are accessible, though drifts remain on trails. The best season for backpacking is July 15–Sept. 15. High temperatures then are in the 60s and 70s, with nights dropping down as low as the 20s. Rain or snow may fall at any time in the high country.

From *Owen Creek,* on US 14 about 5 mi. S of Burgess Junction, an all-weather road runs E and S to campgrounds and Wilderness trailheads. This gravel road, known as the Red Grade Road, continues down the steep E face of the Bighorn Range to the town of Big Horn.

Shell Creek Canyon and Falls are on US 14 near the W boundary. The creek has cut a deep granite gorge, with falls and cascades. Several trails and 4-wheel-drive roads are in the area, as well as two campgrounds.

Tensleep Canyon is on US 16 just inside the W boundary. The main road has been cut into the steep canyon wall. We camped at Leigh Creek and hiked past a fish hatchery up the dirt road on the opposite side of the canyon. Quiet and scenic.

Bucking Mule Falls National Recreation Trail follows the rims of Devil's Canyon through pine-spruce forest. An 11-mi. hike, featuring a 250-ft. waterfall. In the NW corner of the Forest. The end of the Devil's Canyon road and Porcupine Campground are the principal trailheads. Nearby, on Sheep Mountain Road, is *Medicine Wheel,* a prehistoric 75-ft. wheel formed with rocks, with a 3-ft.-high hub and 28 spokes. Who made it and why are debated.

Little Bighorn River, often called "Littlehorn," flows NE about 16 mi. from about 2 mi. N of US Alt. 14 to the NE corner of the Forest. The canyon is used by livestock operators to drive cattle to high summer ranges, and it is used today by hikers, horsemen, hunters, and fishermen. Portions of the river, free-flowing and pristine, have been determined to be eligible for study for inclusion in the Wild and Scenic River system. In the N portion, the canyon's sheer cliffs are 1,600 ft. high. Steep talus slopes extend from cliffs to the river. Upstream, the terrain is gentler, with lower cliffs and small gorges. Near the headwaters, the stream meanders through meadows. Access is by road (in the S only), 4-wheel-drive route, and foot trails in the canyon and along the rim.

Tongue River has also been found eligible for study for inclusion in the Wild and Scenic River system. The river flows E from the Bighorns, generally close to US 14A, through a broad, scenic plateau. Beyond Burgess Junction the river is generally 2 or 3 mi. N of US 14. Here it has cut a canyon with sheer walls 1,000 ft. high. A gravel road runs SW from Dayton to the mouth of Tongue Canyon, near the Forest boundary. The canyon is accessible to hikers, horsemen, and trailbikers by the Tongue River Trail. Riparian plants include balsam poplar, quaking aspen, and narrowleaf cottonwood. The canyon portion of the river is a Blue Ribbon Stream, a fishery of national importance, with native cutthroat, rainbow, brook, and some German brown trout. The river has rapids, riffles, and pools. Most of it (except Box Canyon) is floatable in the spring runoff, but most rafting begins at the parking lot at the canyon's mouth and continues downstream, outside the Forest. Most of the visitors coming from Dayton to the lower canyon stop at Tongue River Cave.

Caves: The ROG has descriptions of 101 caves. Except for Tongue River Cave, the longest is 474 ft. Many others are shallow, some just open pits; a number are hazardous. Entering any cave without information is foolhardy.

Tongue River, with 6,500 ft. of passages, is one of the most visited caves in the state and distressingly vandalized.

INTERPRETATION

No visitor center, nature trails, campfire programs, or other interpretive activities, except exhibits at Shell Falls and interpretive signs at the Medicine Wheel Archeological Site.

A looseleaf Recreation Opportunities Guide (ROG) can be seen at Headquarters and Ranger Districts. Prepared about 1977, it has not been kept up to date, but much of the information is still valid.

ACTIVITIES

Camping: 38 campgrounds, 462 sites. Four are open all year. For others, opening dates range May 15–July 1, closing Sept. 1–Oct. 31. When closed, some campgrounds may be gated; others can be used, without water and services. One can camp almost anywhere in the Forest.

Hiking, backpacking: Of the 630 mi. of trails, a few in the Cloud Peak area have heaviest use, chiefly southern entry points at Hunter Corrals on the E, West Tensleep Lake on the W. Trails in the N half of the Forest generally have lighter use. The ROG describes some trails.

Hunting: Chiefly big game: moose, elk, mule deer, black bear. Small game includes cottontail, snowshoe hare, whitetail jackrabbit. Upland game: blue, ruffed, and sage grouse.

Fishing: The ROG has charts showing lakes, fish species, and access. Brook, brown, cutthroat, golden, and rainbow trout; grayling.

Horse riding: The ROG has trail information. HQ has no list of outfitters but can usually handle inquiries.

Boating: Meadowlark Lake is the only one where power boats can be used, and it's only about a mile long. Hand-powered craft can be used elsewhere, but only Sibley Lake on US 14 and a few others have car access.

Downhill skiing: Two small ski areas: Big Horn and Meadowlark. Both have lifts and a variety of slopes. Both are family day-use areas. We were advised that Big Horn might not continue operations.

Ski touring: Plenty of snow and favorable terrain. Excellent ski touring opportunities. A few maintained trails at Sibley Lake, Willow Park, and Pole Creek. Usual season: Nov.–Apr.

PUBLICATIONS

Forest map. $1.
General information (mimeo pages).
Bird checklist.
Travel map.

REFERENCE: Bonney, O. H. and L. G. *Guide to Wyoming Mountains and Wilderness Areas.* Chicago: Sage Books, Swallow Press, 1977.

HEADQUARTERS: 1969 S. Sheridan Ave., Sheridan, WY 82801; (307) 672-0751.

RANGER DISTRICTS: Tensleep R.D., 2009 Big Horn Ave., Worland, WY, 82401; (307) 347-8291. Tongue R.D., 1969 S. Sheridan Ave., Sheridan, WY 82801; (307) 672-0751. Buffalo R.D., 381 Main St., Buffalo, WY 82834; (307) 684-7981. Medicine Wheel R.D., P.O. Box 367, 142 E. Third St., Lovell, WY 82431; (307) 548-6541. Paintrock R.D., P.O. Box 831, 1220 N. 8th St., Greybull, WY 82426; (307) 765-4435.

BIGHORN CANYON NATIONAL RECREATION AREA
National Park Service
30,739 acres in WY, 34,879 in MT. (BLM map 12)

Visitor center is at Lovell on US Alt. 14. Bad Pass Highway, SR 37, 2 mi. E of Lovell, is access to the S end of the NRA.

Also see entry in MT Zone 4. There is no direct link between the two ends of the Area except by water, so we provide separate entries.

From N of Sheridan, take US 14, then US Alt. 14 at Burgess Junction, scenic routes over the Bighorn Mountains through the Bighorn National Forest (see entry). The route has some 10% grades. Soon after descending to semiarid flatlands one comes to a wayside exhibit:

BIGHORN CANYON NATIONAL RECREATION AREA
YELLOWTAIL WILDLIFE HABITAT AREA
Before you is Bighorn Lake. Yellowtail Dam at Fort Smith, Montana, backs up the Bighorn River 71 miles to this point. . . . Fluctuations in river flow and differing demands will cause extreme changes in lake elevation. At this location a 30-foot change in water level could move the lake shore 5 miles. At normal pool, the surface is 12,685 acres.

Continue on to the handsome visitor center, just outside Lovell, which has exhibits, publications, and a helpful Ranger.

The two ends of the lake are relatively open. The central portion is constricted in Bighorn Canyon. Travel in the NRA is almost entirely by water. Bad Pass Highway, the blacktop road on the W side, runs N, crossing the Shoshone River, entering the NRA in about 6 mi. It winds through a hilly desert landscape in tones of gray, tan, and red. Vegetation is sparse, chiefly sagebrush and snakeweed.

The NRA is a relatively narrow strip through the Crow Indian Reservation, where travel is restricted to members of the tribe except on public roads. Bighorn Canyon is on the E, the Pryor Mountain Wild Horse Range (see entry in MT Zone 4) on the W. For 17 mi. along Bad Pass Highway, the Wild Horse Range overlaps the NRA. This area is frequented by one of the three wild horse herds. We saw more than a dozen horses and a herd of seven bighorn sheep, most of them juveniles.

The first turnoff is for Horseshoe Bend, principal recreation center. Here the predominant landscape color is terracotta, with formations resembling dunes. There is a modest marina, a launching ramp, store, snack bar, and a campground on a bare, windswept hillside. On September 9 concessions were closed for the season, but we could have launched or camped.

Continuing N, the road enters Montana, where the next turnoff is for the Devil's Canyon Overlook. Here is a splendid, dramatic view of the area. The valley appears to be about 3 mi. wide, rim to rim. The canyon itself is a narrow, meandering slot, up to 2,200 ft. deep, with vertical rock walls.

The road ends a few miles further, at Barry's Landing, which has a launching ramp and primitive campground.

There are no hiking trails, but the Ranger can suggest hikes, destinations including the Wild Horse Range. Most recreation is water-based. Boaters can cruise for hours, often in seclusion. A boat-in camp is a mile N of Barry's Landing. Fishing is said to be excellent at times, including ice fishing.

The NRA has yet to attract large numbers of visitors. We were there late in the season and saw no one on land or water.

NEARBY: Yellowtail Wildlife Unit (see entry).

INTERPRETATION
Visitor center has exhibits, film, literature, information.
Campfire programs at Horseshoe Bend, Fri.–Sat., Memorial Day to Labor Day.
Auto tour cassette tape available at the visitor center.
Crooked Creek Nature Trail, 1/3 mi. Self-guiding; leaflet.

ACTIVITIES
Camping: Two campgrounds, 156 sites, seldom if ever full. Season officially May 1–Nov. 1, but one could camp at other times, without water.
Fishing: Chiefly walleye. Also brown and lake trout, sauger, ling, perch. Ice fishing at Horseshoe Bend.
Boating: Boaters are asked to sign in and out, carry day and night signaling devices, stay with their boats in case of breakdown; the canyon walls can't be climbed.
Swimming: Lifeguard, in season, at Horseshoe Bend.

PUBLICATIONS
Leaflet with map.
Canyon Echoes. Guide to the NRA.
Boating information.
Checklist of area birds.

List of common flowers and shrubs, with blooming seasons.
Weather information.

HEADQUARTERS: P.O. Box 458, Fort Smith, MT 59035; (406) 666-2412. Visitor Center: P.O. Box 487, Lovell, WY 82431; (307) 548-2251.

BLACK HILLS NATIONAL FOREST
U.S. Forest Service
In WY: 175,401 acres.
In SD: 1,060,671 acres.

Two blocks, N and SE of I-90 at Sundance. Access by local roads.

This is South Dakota's only National Forest, except for scattered bits of Montana's Custer. It occupies that state's only mountains, their highest point 7,242 ft. Despite the modest elevations, many roads, and numerous inholdings, the Forest has much to offer visitors: scenic drives, deep forests, small lakes, streams with cascades and waterfalls, unique rock formations, even a 10,700-acre Wilderness. Within or adjacent to the Forest are Wind Cave National Park, Custer State Park, Jewel Cave National Monument, and Mount Rushmore National Memorial.

Part of the WY acreage consists of several dozen small fragments, some as small as 40 acres. The two largest blocks have many inholdings. The N block, 25 mi. N–S and 3 to 10 mi. W–E, is on the Bear Lodge Mountains. Three small campgrounds are in this block, one of them on a small lake. All three are at elevations below 5,000 ft. and are open all year. The Forest map shows no trails in this block, which is within the Bearlodge Ranger District.

The acreage SE of Sundance adjoins the main body of the Forest, across the state line. The Forest map shows no campgrounds or trails in WY, but attractive campgrounds are across the border.

PUBLICATION: Forest map. $1.

HEADQUARTERS: Box 792, Custer, SD 57730; (605) 673-2251.

RANGER DISTRICTS: Bearlodge R.D., Forest Service Building, Sundance, WY 82729; (307) 283-1361. Elk Mountain R.D., 640 South Summit, Newcastle, WY 82707; (307) 746-2783.

BOBCAT DRAW
U.S. Bureau of Land Management
17,150 acres.

W of Worland on SR 431. We're not sure how far, and the landmarks aren't on the BLM map, so we suggest inquiring in Worland for the Murphy Draw Road; a BLM sign is on the N side. Go toward Squaw Teats; 2-wheel drive is adequate in dry weather. Badlands can be seen from SR 431. (BLM map 12)

Badlands are common on the public lands of the Bighorn Basin. In selecting sites for entries, we look for special features. The badlands of this area are among the most unique and spectacular. The primary reason is the presence of erosion-resistant rock layers sandwiched between layers of easily eroded materials. The resulting differential erosion has produced an endless array of fanciful formations: arches, windows, hoodoos, goblins, mushrooms, and castles.

These shapes occur in the central and southern portion of the area, in pockets among deep, sharp furrows cut into jagged, angular ridges. The bare ridges are predominantly reddish, often intermixed with layers of vivid purple, off-white, blue, and gray. A BLM enthusiast proclaimed it "better than Badlands National Park!"

On the W are broad, benchlike, grass-covered ridges separated by deep, wide drainage. The E side opens into the broad bottomland at the confluence of Bobcat Draw and Timber Creek. At the N edge is the flat, sandy drainage of Fifteenmile Creek, seen on the highway map just NW of Worland.

Elevations range from 4,600 ft. in the E and S drainage bottoms to 6,200 ft. on the summit of Squaw Teats. The climate is dry, less than 10 in. of annual precipitation. Winters are cold, summers hot.

Wildlife is limited by lack of water, but mule deer, pronghorn, wild horse, and small mammals are present, as well as raptors.

The site has no facilities or developed trails. Old bladed tracks offer some hiking routes, but travel is not difficult over much of the site. A BLM advisor suggests backpacking into the area, making camp, and sightseeing at leisure, studying plants, wildlife, and fossils. There is no water.

HEADQUARTERS: Worland District, BLM, 101 S. 23rd, Worland, WY 82401; (307) 347-9871.

CEDAR MOUNTAIN
U.S. Bureau of Land Management
21,570 acres.

On the E side of the Bighorn River, across from Kirby on US 20. About 5 mi. S of Kirby, Black Mountain Road crosses the river. In about 1 mi., turn N about 4 mi. to S boundary of the site. (BLM map 11.) *The last 4 mi. is a private road; landowner permission is required to drive through.*

We rarely include sites that lack public access. Although this site has interesting features, we would not include it but for its 1 1/2-mi. frontage on the Bighorn River and the fact that permission has been granted to visitors. Public land tracts on the river are rare. The mountain rises to 5,500 ft. from 4,200 ft. elevation at the river. The S face is an impressive rock escarpment. Along the river, bluffs are cut by deep drainages. Vegetation is mostly sagebrush-grassland, with a belt of juniper on the mountain. Climate is dry. Streams are ephemeral.

The site has no facilities. Open country and old bladed trails make hiking feasible on the mountain and along the river. Visitation is estimated to be less than 500 visitor-days per year. Because of summer heat, most visitation is in spring and fall. Some cross-country skiing occurs when snow cover is sufficient.

Hunting: Mule deer, gray and chukar partridge.

HEADQUARTERS: Worland District, BLM, 101 S. 23rd, Worland, WY 82401; (307) 347-9871.

DEVILS TOWER NATIONAL MONUMENT
National Park Service
1,347 acres.

From I-90 at Moorcroft or Sundance, 7 mi. N on US 14.

This was the first National Monument, proclaimed by Theodore Roosevelt in 1906. Its central feature, the Tower, is a plug, the core of an ancient volcano, rising 867 ft. above its base. The flat top measures 1 1/2 acres, the bottom diameter 1,000 ft. Vertical striations on the Tower gave rise to a Kiowa legend that attributes them to a clawing bear.

Plains and mountains meet here: the grasslands of the rolling plains to the W, pine forests of the Black Hills to the E. Lowest point in the Monument is 3,847 at the Belle Fourche River, which flows N from Keyhole State Park (see entry), forms a part of the Monument's S boundary, then crosses the SE corner. The Monument is surrounded by privately owned land.

Entering on the E side of the roughly square site, the Monument road turns SW past a prairie dog town and Park headquarters, then loops to the N, E, and S, ending at the visitor center, 3 mi. from the entrance. From here a 1 1/2 mi. trail circles the Tower.

The Tower was first climbed in 1893. About 1,000 visitors make the ascent each year. More than 120 routes have been defined. Climbers must register.

Plants: Tree species include ponderosa pine, cottonwood, oak, chokecherry. Wildflowers are seasonally abundant in the sagebrush-grassland community; checklist available.

Birds: 90 species recorded. Checklist available. Noted: bald and golden eagles; prairie falcon, American kestrel, turkey vulture, meadowlark, mountain bluebird, nuthatch, black-billed magpie, western flycatcher, yellow-rumped warbler, black-capped chickadee, hairy woodpecker, grouse, wild turkey.

Mammals: Include whitetail and occasional blacktail deer, raccoon, squirrel, chipmunk, skunk, porcupine, prairie dog.

INTERPRETATION

Visitor center has exhibits, talks, literature. Open May–Sept. 8 A.M.–4:45 P.M., to 8:45 P.M. June–Aug.

Campfire programs: June–Aug.

Guided hikes: June–Aug.

Climbing demonstrations daily, in season.

ACTIVITIES

Camping: 49 sites. All year. After Sept., restroom facilities are at the Administration Building, 1/4 mi. away.

Hiking: Four trails, 1 1/4 to 2 3/4 mi., display the site's several life zones: forest, meadow, river valley.

PUBLICATIONS

Leaflet with map.

The Devils Tower Natural History Association (Devils Tower, WY 82714) has a publications price list. By mail, add $1; $2 for orders over $5. Included:

Bird checklist. $.10.

Flower checklist. $.10.

Geology of Devils Tower. $.40.

Devils Tower Handbook. $3.00.

HEADQUARTERS: Devils Tower, WY 82714; (307) 467-5370.

HELLS HALF ACRE
Natrona County Park and Pleasure Grounds
320 acres.

45 mi. NW of Casper on US 20/26. (BLM map 6)

In 1930, Wyoming highways were unpaved. Wet, they became slippery gumbo. One June day, two dozen motorists took refuge here in a roadside restaurant to wait out a storm. When the sky cleared, we overlooked the nearby canyon, often called a miniature Grand Canyon, a colorful array of dramatic formations: cliffs, towers, spires, caves, fins, and figures. It's only about a hundred feet deep, and one can scramble down to the canyon floor.

We stopped here again in the early 1980s. We didn't know it then, but it had become a county park in 1935. What we saw was a motel and store, restaurant, service station, and bare campground. They're a concession and still there. The canyon was unchanged except for the scars of trailbikes.

We were glad to learn that trailbikes are now banned from the canyon, although enforcement isn't easy. The county leaflet says, "It is the only natural geological phenomenon of its kind in the United States." It's worth a stop.

HEADQUARTERS: 4621 CY Avenue, Casper, WY 82604; (307) 234-6821.

HONEYCOMBS
U.S. Bureau of Land Management
21,000 acres.

From US 16 about 8 mi. W of Tensleep, S about 4 mi. on BLM's Blue Bank Road. (BLM maps 5, 6)

W of Tensleep, US 16 crosses an extensive area of badlands. The formations at Honeycombs are more dramatic and colorful. The central area of sharply eroded, strongly dissected badlands is surrounded by rolling to steep hills. In part of the area, the formations resemble large, closely spaced beehives. Other formations include towers, spires, cliffs, and buttresses. Soil colors range from reds, pinks, and purples to shades of brown and tan, hues changing with the angle of the sun.

This desert environment receives only 7 in. of precipitation annually, most of it in late spring and summer thundershowers. Winters are cold.

The 21,000-acre Wilderness Study Area is roadless. Blue Bank Road is the E boundary. Tracks along other parts of the perimeter require 4-wheel drive. Old bladed trails within the unit, made for mineral exploration, are eroding and revegetating, but some are useful for hiking.

The lack of water limits wildlife populations, but the site is both winter and year-round habitat for pronghorn, mule deer, a few elk, and sage grouse.

Recreation use includes sightseeing from cars, hiking, hunting, and rock-hounding. Estimated use is less than 500 visitor-days per year.

HEADQUARTERS: Worland District, BLM, 101 S. 23rd, Worland, WY 82401; (307) 347-9871.

JACKSON CANYON
U.S. Bureau of Land Management
4,500 acres.

From Casper city limits, 5 mi. SW on SR 220. (BLM map 7) The canyon, a night roosting area for about 60 bald eagles from Dec. through Mar., is off limits; the birds are not to be disturbed. However, BLM and the Murie Audubon Society collaborated in developing a bird-watching turnoff, with plaques for raptor identification.

KEYHOLE STATE PARK
Wyoming Recreation Commission
6,256 land acres; 9,418 water acres.

From I-90 W of Sundance, exit at Pine Ridge interchange, then 8 mi. N.

We first marked this "no entry," then reconsidered. It's the only large water body within a hundred miles. Usually, not always, it has good boating and fishing.

The reservoir is about 8 mi. long, irregular in shape, with many bays. It was formed in 1952 by damming the Belle Fourche River. The W end is in flat grassland. The E is at the W end of the Black Hills, with rolling rangeland, forested hills, low cliffs on the N shore. A narrow belt of Park land surrounds the reservoir. Almost all neighboring land is private.

Semiarid climate. Winters are cold, summers often hot. Winds are strong, averaging 12 mph.

Most developments are at the E side: campgrounds, motel, marina, boat club, cafe, and swimming beach. Other shoreline is undeveloped and available for hiking. We were told there would be no objection to backpacking or boat camping, but almost no one does either.

More than 80% of the visitors are WY residents, most others from nearby South Dakota. Principal activities are camping, fishing, picnicking, swimming, boating, and water skiing.

Water level fluctuates. Relatively small changes have marked effects on the surface area. A drop of 9 ft., which is not unusual, shrinks the surface area by almost one-third. Although the water level usually remains high during the summer recreation season, dry years do occur; in the summer of 1985, the level dropped to 23 ft. below full pool. The shallowest areas are in the S and W. Park developments are mostly in the E, which is less affected by moderate changes. With a 23-ft. drop, however, most ramps are unusable and recreation areas are far from the water's edge.

ACTIVITIES

Camping: 7 campgrounds, 70 sites. All year.

Fishing: WY state records for northern pike and walleye. Brown trout, bass, crappie, channel catfish.

Boating: Marina; ramps.

NEARBY: Devils Tower National Monument; Black Hills National Forest. (See entries.)

PUBLICATION: Leaflet with map.

HEADQUARTERS: Inyan Kara Route, Moorcroft, WY 82721; (307) 756-3596.

MEDICINE LODGE CANYON

U.S. Bureau of Land Management, Wyoming Game and Fish Department, Wyoming Recreation Commission
12,127 acres.

From Worland, N on US 16/20 to Manderson, then E on SR 31 toward Hyattville. Just outside Hyattville, left on Alkali-Cold Springs Road; right on Cold Springs Road. In 4 mi., see sign, "Medicine Lodge Habitat Unit." 1 1/2 mi. on gravel road. (BLM map 5)

We gave this site high marks and hope to return. The canyon is spectacular, up to 1,000 ft. deep. A delightful trail follows the stream in Dry Medicine Lodge Canyon up to the Bighorn National Forest. At the mouth of the canyon is an attractive streamside campground maintained by the Wyoming

Recreation Commission. Here also is the Medicine Lodge State Archeological Site, featuring many well-preserved petroglyphs. Most of the land in and around the canyon, up to the Bighorn National Forest boundary, is public domain. Game and Fish Department has responsibility for wildlife management.

The trail is in Dry Medicine Lodge Canyon. It hadn't been recently maintained, and there's at least one washout, but what we saw of it presented no difficulties. Wet Medicine Lodge Canyon, forking off to the E, has no trail.

Elevations of the area range from 4,800 to 8,800 ft. Average annual precipitation at the lower elevations is about 5 in., about 14 in. at the Forest boundary. Snow cover is common at the upper elevations Nov. through Apr.

Plants: Most of the area surrounding the canyon is semiarid sagebrush-grassland. S-facing canyon slopes support grasses and mountain-mahogany. N-facing slopes have Douglas-fir forest interspersed with open areas of sagebrush, mountain-mahogany, and grasses. Forest cover increases at the higher elevations, with lodgepole, limber, and ponderosa pine as well as Douglas-fir. Willow, cottonwood, boxelder, maple, snowberry, serviceberry, and other riparian growth along the creek is so dense in places one can't see the rushing water from the trail.

Wildlife: The area is critical elk winter range. Portions are critical deer winter range. Some elk and deer remain through the summer, as well as bighorn sheep. Other mammals include black bear, mountain lion, and cottontail. Game birds include chukar, sage and blue grouse, wild turkey, pheasant.

ACTIVITIES

Hiking, backpacking: The lower canyon can be hiked in spring, before the high country is open. Later this is a route into the National Forest, with trails to the Cloud Peak Wilderness. Although the route is quite suitable for horses, we were told there are few riders except in hunting season.

Fishing: Rainbow, brown, brook, and cutthroat trout.

Most of the unit is closed from Dec. 1 to June 1 to prevent disturbance of wintering wildlife.

NEARBY: Paint Rock Canyon (see entry).

HEADQUARTERS: Worland District, BLM, 101 S. 23rd, Worland, WY 82401; (307) 347-9871. Region 2, Game and Fish Dept., Box 988, Cody, WY 82414; (307) 587-3434.

MIDDLE FORK POWDER RIVER
U.S. Bureau of Land Management
48,400 acres.

Inadvisable to travel without BLM quad map or topo. From Kaycee on SR 192 just off I-25, SW about 27 mi. Up to Outlaw Cave the roads are rough, but a passenger car can make it in dry weather. Beyond, you need pickup or 4-wheel drive. (BLM map 6 shows the area but not in enough detail to serve as a road map.)

This remote, rugged area was seldom visited except by hunters until books and films retold its history, featuring Butch Cassidy and the Hole-in-the-Wall Gang. Although notorious, the Hole-in-the-Wall isn't much to look at. Scenically the area's principal feature is the Middle Fork Canyon, sometimes called Outlaw Canyon.

About 20 mi. W of I-25, the Red Wall, over 30 mi. of bright red sandstone cliffs, rises vertically from the floor of an open, grassy valley. About 300 ft. high, 45 mi. N-S, it was a barrier to travel except at a few breaches. One is the Hole-in-the-Wall, another where the Middle Fork Powder River has cut through. West of the Red Wall is the gently sloping flank of the Bighorn Mountains.

Middle Fork Canyon runs W–E, up to 1,000 ft. deep, with steep, almost vertical walls. Massive, colorful rock outcrops are broken by a few tributary canyons, the largest of them Bachaus Creek, entering from the S. Several primitive roads end at the canyon rim, where there are several trailheads for hiking routes to the canyon floor. Elevation at the rim is about 7,500 ft. Vegetation above the canyon is chiefly open grass and shrublands with sparse trees.

Annual precipitation is about 14 in., most of it Apr.–July rainfall. Summers are warm here, but none of the people who know the canyon said it becomes too warm for summer hiking. The hiking season extends from mid-May through most of Sept., although snow is possible in early fall.

As recreational interest in the area increased, BLM joined with state and private landowners to design an 85,000-acre Middle Fork Planning Area, including the adjacent 10,158-acre Ed O. Taylor Wildlife Unit of the Game and Fish Department, which provides winter range for elk, year-round habitat for bighorn sheep and mule deer. Other wildlife of the area includes pronghorn, cottontail, snowshoe hare, red squirrel; ruffed, blue, and sage grouse; chukar and Hungarian partridge, wild turkey, mourning dove, some waterfowl.

The area attracts more fall hunters than any other portion of the Casper BLM District. The Game and Fish Department calls the Middle Fork a fishing stream of national importance, and the number of fisherman visitors is increasing. ORV activity was disrupting trout spawning in Bachaus Creek, but BLM seems to have brought this under control. Except in hunting season, hikers should have no difficulty in finding solitude.

PUBLICATION: *The Middle Fork Powder River Management Area* (folder).

HEADQUARTERS: Casper District, BLM, 951 N. Poplar, Casper, WY 82601; (307) 261-5101.

MUDDY MOUNTAIN
U.S. Bureau of Land Management
12,000 acres.

About 12 mi. S of Casper. Cross Casper Mountain on SR 251 and continue on gravel road to Muddy Mountain area. (BLM map 7)

The area is closed from the first heavy snowfall until June to protect an elk calving area and prevent road and trail damage.

At 8,315 ft. elevation, Muddy Mountain is 3,200 ft. above the city, markedly cooler on a hot day, snowier in winter. Land ownership in the area is a mix of federal, state, and private. Until the 1960s, logging and cattle grazing were the chief activities, with hunting in the fall. Logging roads attracted increasing numbers of campers and hikers. In 1967, BLM designated 1,260 acres for recreation. In the 1970s, BLM invited state and private landowners to participate in developing recreation plans for a 45,000-acre area. Recreation was becoming the principal land use, and visitor traffic was causing environmental damage. Also, some visitor activities were conflicting, cross-country skiers complaining about snowmobilers and vice versa.

The mountain has areas of conifer forest, other areas recovering from recent logging, and shrub-grassland range. There are no perennial streams. The E end of the mountain is winter range for elk, all-year habitat for mule and whitetail deer. The critical wildlife habitat was closed to vehicle traffic. Some roads with serious erosion problems were closed. Elsewhere motor vehicles were limited to established roadways. Separate areas were set aside for snowmobiling and skiing.

BLM completed a gravel access road, picnic areas, and two campgrounds, only one of which has a well. Some maintenance work was performed on existing trails. As public use has increased, however, BLM's recreation budget has been reduced. Some recreation pressure on Muddy Mountain has been relieved by development of the Natrona County Mountain Parks (see entry).

ACTIVITIES
Camping: 2 campgrounds; informal sites.
Hiking, backpacking: No trail map is available.

Recent infestation of mountain pine beetle has caused serious tree loss.

HEADQUARTERS: Casper District, BLM, 951 N. Poplar, Casper, WY 82601; (307) 261-5101.

NATRONA COUNTY MOUNTAIN PARKS
Natrona County Parks and Pleasure Grounds
12,000 acres.

S of Casper, on or near SR 251. (BLM map 7)

We seldom include county parks, but these can't be overlooked. Some of the parks on and around Casper Mountain are developed for intensive use, but they include acres protected from development and a network of summer and winter trails.

Ponderosa Park, 2,640 acres, on County Road 506, has rugged canyons, old-growth ponderosa pines, small streams, meadows and sagebrush flats, abundant wildlife. Hiking, ski touring, snowmobiling.

Casper Mountain Park, on SR 251, is a complex of 12 tracts totaling 550 acres, linked by roads and trails. Mountain scenery, meadows and timbered areas, streams, ponds, wildlife. A popular picnic area. One 15-site campground. Features include a Braille trail.

Beartrap Meadow Park is small and heavily used. Many group picnics in summer. A network of ski trails begins here.

Rotary Park, 7 mi. S of Casper off SR 251, features a handsome waterfall, canyon, and 6 mi. of scenic trail.

PUBLICATION: Leaflet with map.

NEARBY: Muddy Mountain (see entry).

HEADQUARTERS: 4621 CY Ave., Casper, WY 82604; (307) 234-6821.

NORTH PLATTE RIVER—TRAPPER ROUTE CANOE TRAIL
U.S. Bureau of Land Management, state, and local agencies.
45 river miles.

Between Alcova and Casper, paralleling SR 220.

The North Platte River enters WY from Colorado SW of Laramie. It flows N, then E and SE past Casper, Glenrock, and Douglas, leaving the state near Torrington. The route was used by Indians, explorers, and trappers. This entry covers the 45 mi. from Alcova Reservoir to Casper. Here the river meanders through farm and rangeland, a quiet float trip.

Several public land sites are distributed along this route. Five have parking and other improvements. All sites are small, totaling only 200 acres. Other riparian land is privately owned. Along the river, red signs mark the private land where boaters mustn't go ashore without permission; blue signs, the public land. Highway signs mark the public areas.

River flow is regulated by upstream dams. Low water is usually in late winter to mid-Apr. Thereafter depth is usually sufficient to permit use of small motors, if one is alert for sandbars. Floating the 45 mi. takes about 15 hours.

Wildlife: Birding along the river is good, species including waterfowl, shorebirds, raptors, grouse, songbirds. Mammals often seen include mule deer, antelope, badger, beaver, muskrat, rabbit, bobcat.

Camping: Permitted at Grey Reef, near Alcova, the upstream put-in, and at two BLM sites downstream. BLM has closed one site because of drinking, litter, and vandalism by nonboaters and may have closed the other.

PUBLICATION: Leaflet with map.

HEADQUARTERS: Casper District, BLM, 951 N. Poplar, Casper, WY 82601; (307) 261-5101.

PAINT ROCK CANYON
U.S. Bureau of Land Management
2,770 acres.

Same route as to Medicine Lodge Creek Canyon (see entry). On Cold Springs Road, see BLM sign for Lone Tree Trail. (BLM map 5)

Paint Rock and Medicine Lodge canyons join near Hyattville. Both canyons are scenic routes to the Bighorn National Forest. Both creeks offer good fishing.

Paint Rock is a narrow canyon, about 5 mi. long, on the W slopes of the Bighorn Mountains. It begins where Paint Rock Basin narrows, 1 1/2 mi. below the National Forest boundary, and ends at Paint Rock Valley. Canyon depth is 400 to 900 ft. Many smaller canyons enter from the sides. The creek is perennial and clear, with many riffles and pools. Numerous springs and seeps flow or drip from the canyon walls. Fauna and flora are similar to those in Medicine Lodge Canyon. Access to Medicine Lodge Canyon is on public land. The most convenient access to the lower end of Paint Rock Canyon is across private land. BLM has an agreement with the landowner to permit visitors to cross, on foot only, May–Oct. Most visitors come to fish, and most are WY residents.

Lone Tree Trail enters Paint Rock Canyon from public lands along the canyon's N rim, providing foot access without crossing private land.

HEADQUARTERS: Worland District, BLM, 101 S. 23rd, Worland, WY 82401; (307) 347-9871.

PATHFINDER RESERVOIR
U.S. Bureau of Land Management, U.S. Fish and Wildlife Service, Natrona County Park and Pleasure Grounds
10,000 water acres.

From Casper, about 36 mi. W on SR 220, then about 8 mi. S on County Road 409. (BLM map 7)

This reservoir on the North Platte River is about 28 mi. long, up to 3 mi. wide, with several narrow necks. It is linked to Alcova Reservoir downstream (see entry) by Fremont Canyon. At 5,850 ft. elevation, it is 500 ft. below the Seminoe Reservoir to the S (see entry in Zone 3). Between them is the "Miracle Mile," one of WY's outstanding trout fisheries. In semidesert country, the reservoir is surrounded by low hills except on the E, where the Pedro Mountains rise to 8,316-ft. Pyramid Peak. Reservoir elevation is 5,850 ft.

It has a shoreline of over a hundred mi., most of it accessible only by boat or on foot. Most surrounding land is federal. County Road 409 leads to the dam and nearby campground and launching area at the NE end. The shoreline on the N and W is roadless. The BLM map shows a dirt road near the E shore; we were advised not to drive it. Access to the S end is also difficult. Cars in good condition can travel the dirt road beyond Seminoe State Park in dry weather, but pickups and 4-wheel drives are recommended.

The Pathfinder National Wildlife Refuge of the U.S. Fish and Wildlife Service occupies 16,807 acres in 4 tracts. The largest tract surrounds the Sweetwater Arm, NW of the dam, where the pool extends up the Sweetwater River. Two smaller bits are on the W side of the main body, the fourth at the S end. The Refuge has no facilities and no resident personnel. HQ is 200 mi. away, in CO.

Natrona County operates the campground and boating facilities. No other developments are on the reservoir. When we visited on a June weekday, the campground had few tenants and only 2 boats were on the lake. Even on busy weekends, however, boating activity is concentrated within a few miles of the ramp. Further S, one can easily find solitude for cruising or boat camping.

Birds: The reservoir is an important feeding, resting, and nesting area for waterfowl. 163 species recorded. No printed list is available, but the Hutton Lake NWR (see entry in WY Zone 3) has a printed, classified list that can be used as an approximate guide to the abundant and common species found here.

An island has a large breeding colony of white pelicans. Once there were 24 pelican colonies W of the Rockies. Now there are only 8, so these are given special protection. Fishermen and boaters are asked not to cruise near the island or go ashore. Game and Fish Department patrols are maintained.

Waterfowl, wading birds, and shorebirds found here include common loon; horned, eared, western, and pied-billed grebes; white pelican, double-crested cormorant, great blue heron, great and snowy egrets, black-crowned night-heron, American bittern, white-faced ibis, whistling swan, Canada and snow geese, mallard, gadwall, northern pintail; green-winged, blue-winged, and cinnamon teals; American wigeon, northern shoveler, redhead, ring-necked duck, canvasback, lesser scaup, common and Barrow's goldeneyes, bufflehead, ruddy duck, hooded and common mergansers, American coot, long-billed curlew, common snipe. Sandpipers: spotted, solitary, Baird's, least, stilt, western. Also willet, long-billed dowitcher, marbled godwit, sanderling, American avocet, Wilson's phalarope.

Mammals: Bats include little brown myotis, big brown, western big-eared, Mexican and big free-tailed. Mice: northern grasshopper, western harvest, deer, house. Pocket mice: Wyoming, Plains, silky, hispid. Long-tailed and meadow voles, meadow jumping mouse, masked shrew, Ord kangaroo rat; Richardson, thirteen-lined, and spotted ground squirrels; golden-mantled and rock squirrels, whitetail prairie dog, least and Colorado chipmunks, whitetail jackrabbit; eastern, desert, and mountain cottontails; bushytail woodrat, raccoon, beaver, muskrat, porcupine, mink, longtail weasel, spotted and striped skunks, mink, badger, red and kit foxes, coyote, bobcat, elk, mule deer, pronghorn.

Reptiles: Refuge notes horned lizard, tiger salamander, bull snake, prairie rattlesnake.

ACTIVITIES

Camping: Natrona County campgrounds at Pathfinder Mountain and Bishops Point; no designated sites. All year. Primitive sites on "Miracle Mile" S of the reservoir. One can camp almost anywhere in the area except within the Refuge.

Hiking: The BLM map shows numerous trails extending from both sides of the reservoir. These are almost certainly tracks of ranch vehicles, but adequate for foot travel, and off-trail hiking is feasible. Our BLM advisor said the uplands aren't especially interesting.

Hunting: Waterfowl, sage grouse, cottontail, deer, pronghorn.

Fishing: Brown, brook, and rainbow trout; walleye pike.

Boating: Ramp. No fuel or services.

PUBLICATION: Refuge HQ issues a map of the reservoir.

HEADQUARTERS: Casper District, BLM, 951 N. Poplar, Casper, WY 82601; (307) 261-5101. Natrona County: 4621 CY Ave., Casper, WY 82604; (307) 234-6821 Pathfinder NWR, P.O. Box 457, Walden, CO 80480; (303) 723-8557.

PRYOR MOUNTAIN WILD HORSE AREA
U.S. Bureau of Land Management

This site adjoins and overlaps the Bighorn Canyon National Recreation Area (see entry), along the NRA access road N of Lovell. Most of the acreage is in Montana. See entry in MT Zone 4.

RENNER WILDLIFE HABITAT MANAGEMENT UNIT
Wyoming Game and Fish Department
16,548 acres.

11 mi. N of Tensleep, E of the county road to Hyattville. (BLM map 5)

Game and Fish manages the site to improve winter range for big game, chiefly mule deer. However, the great majority of visitors are local fishermen, attracted by 72-acre Renner Reservoir.

On the lower W slopes of the Bighorn Mountains, the unit has elevations rising from 4,400 to 7,600 ft. Cedar Mountain and Ziesman Canyon are in the W sector; Renner Reservoir is at the upper end of the canyon. Two steep, rugged canyons, Salt Trough and Red Dick, cut N–S through the central and E sectors.

The site is crossed by 32 mi. of unimproved dry-weather roads; a short all-weather road serves the headquarters. It has no facilities, but a parking area and latrine are planned for the reservoir.

Plants: Most of the area has a cover of sagebrush and shortgrass, with scattered pinyon-juniper and a few stands of ponderosa. A plant list has been compiled, including an array of seasonal wildflowers.

Wildlife: About 300 elk and 1,500 mule deer winter in the area. Other mammals include coyote, whitetail prairie dog, Ord kangaroo rat, least chipmunk, meadow vole, deer mouse, mountain cottontail, red squirrel, and badger. Black bear and mountain lion have been reported. Upland game birds include sage grouse, chukar, dove. The list of other birds includes American wigeon, mallard, American coot, golden eagle, northern harrier, American kestrel, turkey vulture, yellow-breasted chat, magpie.

ACTIVITIES
Camping: No campground, but sites can be found.
Hunting: Chiefly elk, deer, grouse, partridge, cottontail.
Fishing: Reservoir. Largemouth bass.

NEARBY
Bighorn National Forest (see entry). Attractive campsites are in Tensleep Canyon, E of Tensleep on US 16.
Medicine Lodge Wildlife Habitat Management Unit (see entry) has a campground.

HEADQUARTERS: Wyoming Game and Fish Department, 5400 Bishop Blvd., Cheyenne, WY 82002; (307) 777-7631.

SWEETWATER ROCKS
U.S. Bureau of Land Management
32,575 acres.

On the N side of the Sweetwater River valley, near the junction of US 287 and SR 220. No easy access. On the W side: From Jeffrey City, 7 mi. E on US 287; then NE 4 mi. on Agate Flat Road, BLM road 2004, which skirts the W end of the area. (BLM map 7)

The Sweetwater Rocks can be seen from two BLM wayside interpretive exhibits: Devil's Gate, on SR 220 about 14 mi. NE of the junction, and Split Rock, on US 287 about 10 mi. NW of the junction. Both sites overlook the Sweetwater River valley, which is private land. Both exhibits feature the history of the valley, route of the Emigrant Trail. The Devil's Gate exhibit also overlooks Sun Ranch, first open-range ranch in the region.

Beyond the river are the great masses of the Sweetwater Rocks, extending about 18 mi. W–E. The Rocks are decomposing granite uplifts forming gigantic slabs, domes, and piles of broken rocks. Terrain is rugged and mountainous, the rocks cut by numerous draws and rather large pockets.

Recreation opportunities include rock climbing and scrambling, rock-hounding, hiking and backpacking, hunting. There are no established trails. One advisor said it's difficult to find a campsite because most of the level land is private. Another assured us that the numerous pockets offer adequate places to camp.

Vegetation on the slopes is generally sparse. Scattered trees include Douglas-fir, juniper, limber pine, and aspen. In the moister pockets, sagebrush and grasses grade into dense stands of limber pine, juniper, and aspen. Most, but not all, of the open grassy meadows and expanses of sagebrush at the foot of the rocks are on private land.

The more accessible western portion is crossed by Lankin Creek and a strip of private land. Principal feature is Lankin Dome. Popular with rock climbers, it is said to be reminiscent of Devils Tower. Elevations range from 6,200 ft. at the W boundary to 7,700 ft. atop the Dome. Highest point in the area is 8,508-ft. McIntosh Peak, nationally known to climbers, a training site for the National Outdoor Leadership School. Contiguous on the N are large areas of public land. BLM map 7 shows trails or tracks through these areas, some leading N into the Granite Mountains.

Principal feature of the eastern portion is 7,843-ft. Savage Peak. Some of the land on the lower E slopes is private.

Information was not available on wildlife. Birding was said to be outstanding, although no list is available. Pronghorn is the principal game species.

HEADQUARTERS: Rawlins District, BLM, P.O. Box 670, 1300 Third St., Rawlins, WY 82301; (307) 327-7171.

THUNDER BASIN NATIONAL GRASSLAND
Medicine Bow National Forest
U.S. Forest Service
572,372 acres.

NE Wyoming. Crossed by SRs 116, 450, and 59. Some National Grasslands, notably those in Colorado, attract large number of birders. That doesn't seem to be the case here, although the bird checklist of 200 species indicates there is much to see. Indeed, this appears to be one of the most productive bird-watching areas in the state, especially in the Upton-Osage area, which has many small ponds.

The area is flat to rolling, with elevations generally between 4,500 and 5,000 ft. Average annual precipitation is 12 to 14 in., creating a semiarid environment with a grassland community easily damaged by overgrazing. Homesteaders settled on tracts far too small for successful cultivation or cattle ranching. Many homesteads were abandoned, but uncontrolled grazing continued. Years of drought turned the region into a dust bowl.

In the 1930s, the federal government acquired many distressed or abandoned tracts. The Forest Service mission is to restore the land to productivity, encouraging neighboring landowners to do the same. Cattle and sheep now graze the area under permit. Oil and gas wells and coal, uranium, and bentonite mines are common.

The tracts of federal land are a patchwork. Many federal tracts are surrounded by fenced private land and thus inaccessible. Most roads are unpaved, and many become impassable in wet weather. Visitors are advised to stop at the Ranger District office for advice on travel routes and points of interest.

Birds: The Medicine Bow National Forest Recreation Opportunities Guide (ROG) has a bird checklist available for photocopying. Species observed on the National Grassland include Canada goose, mallard, pintail, gadwall, American wigeon, shoveler; blue-winged, green-winged, and cinnamon teals; redhead, canvasback, ring-necked duck, greater and lesser scaup, common goldeneye, bufflehead, ruddy duck; common, hooded, and red-breasted mergansers; common loon; western, horned, pied-billed, and eared grebes; double-crested cormorant, great blue heron, black-crowned night-heron, American bittern, white-faced ibis, mountain and semipalmated plovers, killdeer, long-billed curlew, marbled godwit, willet, greater and lesser yellowlegs. Sandpipers: upland, solitary, spotted, stilt, semipalmated, pectoral, Baird's, least, western. Long-billed and short-billed dowitchers, Hudsonian godwit, Wilson's and northern phalaropes, American avocet. Gulls: California, ring-billed, herring, Franklin's, Bonaparte's. Common, black, and Forster's terns.

Also turkey vulture, golden and bald eagles. Hawks: goshawk, Cooper's, sharp-shinned, northern harrier, rough-legged, ferruginous, red-tailed, Swainson's, Harlan's. Prairie falcon, merlin, American kestrel, peregrine falcon. Owls: great horned, short-eared, burrowing, snowy, barn.

Also poor-will, common nighthawk, belted kingfisher, yellow-bellied sapsucker, northern flicker; red-headed, hairy, and downy woodpeckers; eastern, western, and Cassin's kingbirds, Say's phoebe. Flycatchers: least, dusky, Traill's, western wood-pewee. Horned lark. Swallows: barn, cliff, violet-green, rough-winged, tree, bank. Blue and pinyon jays, black-billed magpie, Clark's nutcracker, American crow, common raven, black-capped chickadee; white-breasted, red-breasted, and pygmy nuthatches; house and rock wrens, catbird, brown and sage thrashers. Wood, Swainson's, and hermit thrushes; American robin, mountain and western bluebirds, ruby-crowned kinglet, water pipit, bohemian and cedar waxwings, northern and loggerhead shrikes, European starling; solitary, red-eyed, and warbling vireos. Warblers: black-and-white, yellow, yellow-rumped, Townsend's, yellowthroat, MacGillivray's, Wilson's, American redstart. Orchard oriole, bobolink, western meadowlark; yellow-headed, red-winged, and Brewer's blackbirds; brown-headed cowbird, northern oriole, common grackle, black-headed grosbeak, lazuli bunting, gray-crowned rosy finch, rufous-sided towhee. Sparrows: savannah, grasshopper, vesper, chipping, clay-colored, Brewer's, Baird's, lark, sage, tree, Harris', white-crowned, song. Lark and snow buntings, dark-eyed junco, McCown's and chestnut-collared longspurs, red crossbill; house, purple, and black rosy finches.

No list of mammals is available. Pronghorn are abundant.

HEADQUARTERS: Thunder Basin R.D., Medicine Bow National Forest, 809 South 9th, Douglas, WY 82633; (307) 358-4690. (For National Forest HQ, see entry in Zone 3.)

TRAPPER CANYON
U.S. Bureau of Land Management
7,200 acres.

Trapper Creek appears on the highway map near Shell on US 14. Access is by BLM roads N from Hyattville. Inquire at Worland BLM office. (BLM map 5)

It isn't easy to get there, and hiking within the 13-mi. canyon is extremely difficult. There is no developed trail. Travel is by game trails and rock scrambling. Those who have been there say it's worth it.

It's one of the most spectacular canyons on the W slope of the Bighorn Mountains. The immediately surrounding area is uninhabited. BLM's wilderness inventory gave it the highest possible scenic rating, citing dramatic cliffs, spires, massive rock outcrops, rich color combinations, a clear, cascading stream, and great variety of vegetation. The site has been recommended for Wilderness designation.

Near-vertical cliffs rise from talus slopes. At its mouth the canyon is about 500 ft. deep, 800 ft. between rims; here most of the rise is cliffs, with only short talus slopes at their base. Near its middle, the canyon is 1,200 ft. deep, with half of the depth in talus slopes. Near the E end, the canyon becomes shallower and much wider. Only one significant canyon enters from the S. Several on the N side are hanging canyons, ending in drop-offs.

Near the upper end, the stream vanishes underground in several places, reappearing downstream. It's called "a stream of outstanding natural beauty."

Elevations range from 4,700 ft. at the W end to 8,400 ft. at the E. Annual precipitation is 10 to 18 in. Snow often restricts use of access roads mid-Dec. through Apr.

Plants: Above the rim, sagebrush-grasslands predominate. The mountain-mahogany/juniper plant community is present on N-facing slopes at lower elevations and on S-facing slopes throughout. Higher N-facing slopes have Douglas-fir, with some juniper and limber pine. Riparian vegetation has dense growth of currant, gooseberry, grapevine, chokecherry, cottonwood, alder, aspen, grasses, and forbs, often so dense as to obstruct passage.

Wildlife: Several hundred elk and deer use the area as winter range, and some remain through summer. Bobcat, mountain lion, and black bear have been reported. Birds include blue and sage grouse, chukar, nesting golden eagle and prairie falcon. Bald eagle and peregrine falcon have been sighted.

ACTIVITIES

Fishing: Game and Fish rates the stream Class 3, fishery of regional importance. Brown, rainbow, and cutthroat trout.

Spelunking: The lower entrance of Great Expectations Cave is within the site. This is the second deepest cave in the United States, and one of the most hazardous. The entrance is gated, and permits are issued only to qualified spelunkers.

HEADQUARTERS: Worland District, BLM, 101 S. 23rd, Worland, WY 82401; (307) 347-9871.

YELLOWTAIL WILDLIFE UNIT
Wyoming Game and Fish Department
19,424 acres.

Near Lovell on US Alt. 14. One unit is along the Shoshone River to its mouth at Bighorn Lake. Access is by SR 37, 2 mi. E of Lovell, the route to the Bighorn Canyon National Recreation Area (see entry). The second is S of US Alt. 14, along the Big Horn River and the upper end of Bighorn Lake; local roads on both sides. (BLM map 12)

According to Game and Fish, "The diversity of nongame birds on the unit would probably equal that of any other area in the State." The site is managed primarily for upland game birds and waterfowl. Most visitors come for pheasant hunting or fishing. For birders visiting the National Recreation Area, this site is a useful side trip.

Prior to construction of Yellowtail Dam, the federal government acquired the land to be inundated and the bordering lands that are now within the National Recreation Area. These two tracts were assigned to the Wyoming Game and Fish Department for conservation and management of wildlife species.

The upper end of Bighorn Lake is shallow. A 1-ft. drop in lake depth can move the shoreline several hundred feet. The US Alt. 14 bridge crosses "lake" or "river," depending on current water level.

Lowest elevation is about 3,600 ft.; highest, 3,900, on hilltops. Average annual precipitation is about 7 in. Mean monthly temperatures are 18°F in January, 72° in July. Recorded extremes are −51° and 112°. Occasional snowfalls are light, seldom remaining on the ground for more than a few days.

Plants: The Wildlife Unit includes arid shrublands, irrigated farmland, marshes, river bottomlands, open water, and—at times of low water—expanses of dry lake bed. The lake shore is sparsely vegetated, but both rivers have dense riparian growth. The site has few tree species, chiefly juniper, poplar, cottonwood, Russian olive, and salt cedar, but a wide variety of shrubs, grasses, forbs, and aquatic species.

Birds: Upland game birds include ring-necked pheasant, mourning dove, and wild turkey. Chukar, Hungarian partridge, sage and sharp-tailed grouse are rare. Principal waterfowl include Canada goose, snow goose, mallard, pintail, gadwall; green-winged, blue-winged, and cinnamon teals; American wigeon, shoveler, canvasback, redhead, bufflehead, ruddy duck, wood duck, greater and lesser scaup, Barrow's and common goldeneyes; red-breasted, hooded, and common mergansers; western and pied-billed grebes, white pelican, whistling swan, double-crested cormorant.

Others include turkey vulture, goshawk; Cooper's, sharp-shinned, rough-legged, and red-tailed hawks; merlin, northern harrier, American kestrel, prairie and peregrine falcons, osprey, golden and bald eagles. Also snowy egret, great blue heron, black-crowned night-heron, American bittern, Virginia rail, sora, common snipe, American coot, American avocet, killdeer, marbled godwit, spotted sandpiper, willet, greater and lesser yellowlegs, long-billed dowitcher, Wilson's phalarope, common snipe, ring-billed gull, common tern.

Also screech, great horned, long-eared, short-eared, and snowy owls; black-billed cuckoo, common nighthawk, belted kingfisher, northern flicker; red-headed, hairy, and downy woodpeckers; white-throated swift, eastern and western kingbirds, western wood-pewee, olive-sided flycatcher, horned lark; barn, violet-green, tree, and bank swallows; pinyon jay, black-billed magpie, common raven, American crow, black-capped and mountain chickadees, rock and house wrens, long-billed marsh wren, gray catbird, brown thrasher, American robin, Townsend's solitaire, mountain bluebird, Bohemian and cedar waxwings, northern and loggerhead shrikes, European starling, western meadowlark; red-winged, yellow-headed, and Brewer's blackbirds; common grackle, brown-headed cowbird, northern oriole, western tanager, evening and blue grosbeaks, lazuli bunting, Cassin's and house finches, American goldfinch, rufous-sided towhee, slate-colored junco. Warblers: yellow, yellow-rumped, common yellowthroat, yellow-breasted chat. Sparrows: house, tree, chipping, white-crowned, song.

Mammals: Mule and whitetail deer are common, as well as cottontail, whitetail jackrabbit, beaver, muskrat, mink, longtail weasel, raccoon, coyote, striped skunk, and bobcat.

ACTIVITIES

Camping: Camping is permitted in the 7 parking areas.

Fishing: Reservoir and rivers. Brown and rainbow trout, walleye pike, sauger, yellow perch, black crappie, ling, channel catfish, black bullhead.

HEADQUARTERS: Wyoming Game and Fish Department, 5400 Bishop Blvd., Cheyenne, WY 82002; (307) 777-7631.

ZONE 3

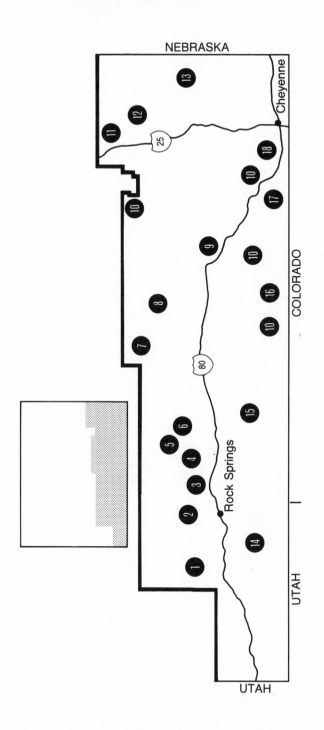

ZONE 3

Includes these counties:

Uinta	Sweetwater	Goshen
Albany	Platte	
Laramie	Carbon	

The zone is a strip across the entire S of the state. Most of the W half is semiarid, with less than 12 in. of precipitation per year. In the W half are the N end of the Flaming Gorge Reservoir, several badlands, the Red Desert Complex, and the Killpecker Dunes (see entry, Sand Dunes). In the E half are the Medicine Bow and Laramie ranges, both in the Medicine Bow National Forest. The North Platte River, flowing NE, is dammed to form the Seminoe and Pathfinder reservoirs. When it re-enters the zone, flowing SE to Nebraska, it is dammed to form the Glendo and Guernsey reservoirs.

ADOBE TOWN
U.S. Bureau of Land Management
85,710 acres.

> Get guidance from BLM! SW of Rawlins. Bitter Creek exit from I-80. S on Sweetwater County Road 19. After crossing Shell Creek at Eversole's ranch, go 3 to 4 mi. and bear left. The road heads SE; Adobe Town rim is directly E. (BLM map 9)

One couldn't ask for a more isolated and desolate wilderness. Getting to the area can be an adventure in itself; travel within it is a challenge. Don't try it without advice from the BLM office. Blazing desert heat makes summer visits unwise. Those who like badlands will love it here.

A high desert plateau has been deeply carved by wind and water into dramatic, colorful, often grotesque formations. Elevations range from 6,500 to 7,000 ft., with rims, buttes, and escarpments. In Monument Valley, chimneys, haystacks, and banded cliffs topped by castle shapes rise from stabilized dunes. Small canyons, draws, and washes offer shade and shelter from winds and primitive campsites with no near neighbors.

Precipitation is scanty: 7 to 9 in. a year. Vegetation is mostly big sagebrush, saltbush, and black greasewood, with sparse grasses and forbs. Bands of wild horses, as well as pronghorn and mule deer. Other wildlife includes coyote, bobcat, cottontail, and other small mammals, together with raptors, other birds, and species of snakes and lizards typical of high desert.

HEADQUARTERS: Rawlins District, BLM, 1300 Third St., P.O. Box 670, Rawlins, WY 82301; (307) 324-7171.

ALKALI DRAW; SOUTH PINNACLES
U.S. Bureau of Land Management
27,816 acres.

From Point of Rocks on I-80, E and N on County Road 4-15. In about 18 mi., 4-15 turns right. Continue about 10 mi. to a V. Branches to left and right are the S boundary of the South Pinnacles area. In 3 mi. on left fork, Alkali Draw area is on the left. (BLM map 9)

"Some might consider this desolation," a BLM evaluator commented. Others prize the area as one of the few extensive, undisturbed remnants of the Red Desert, with its vast expanse, constant winds, emptiness, and colorful rock formations, including some hoodoos. Several of the geological layers have fossil snails, clams, and leaves. (See entry, Red Desert Complex.)

The Alkali Draw area is a complex of rims, draws, and wide basins, a few mi. E of the Continental Divide. Long mountain ridges, none high, rise from the basins. Alkali Draw and its tributaries drain to the E from Bush Rim and 8,683-ft. Steamboat Mountain, creating a washboard topography. Most of the area is between 7,000 and 7,500 ft elevation. Alkali Rim, in the SW, is a striking blue rock escarpment.

The South Pinnacles area to the E is generally flatter, but with some bluffs, ridges, rimrock, and small canyons. A rimrock area of rough, rocky crags and an interesting escarpment run W–E across the site.

Plants: Big sagebrush and grass are the dominant vegetation, with saltbush and greasewood common.

Wildlife: The area is good habitat for wild horse, mule deer, elk, and pronghorn. Large prairie dog towns attract raptors.

HEADQUARTERS: Rock Springs District, BLM, Highway 191 North, Rock Springs, WY 82902; (307) 382-5350.

CURT GOWDY STATE PARK
Wyoming Recreation Commission
1,960 land acres.

21 mi. W of Cheyenne on SR 210, Happy Jack Road.

The Park isn't a prime natural area, but it's a pleasant stop if you're traveling this way, and it has an addition that is fenced and undeveloped except for a trail. The two units, 1/4 mi. apart, each surround a reservoir. Granite (189 acres) is at the end of the short, paved entrance road. Crystal (136 acres) is on an all-weather road about 1 1/2 mi. to the SE. The reservoirs are fed by a pipeline from the Snowy Range. Both supply water to Cheyenne; swimming is not allowed.

In the foothills of the Laramie Mountains, this is rolling terrain with many granite outcrops, some resembling towers, others stacks of giant blocks. Elevations are from 6,969 to 7,700 ft. Much of the area is open grassland, with pinyon pine on slopes and some ponderosa forest. Pockets of aspen provide brilliant fall colors. When we visited in September, the prominent wildflowers were aster, milkweed, blackeyed Susan, and sunflower.

Developments are scattered around the lake: campsites, picnic shelters, fireplaces, latrines. Some sites are in wooded draws away from the shore. The arrangements seemed pleasantly informal and uncrowded. Drinking water is supplied by hand pumps.

When we visited, the drawdown at Granite seemed to be about 20 ft., but the exposed shore was a sandy slope firm enough for a pickup truck to drive on to launch a boat.

We saw trails leading back into the hills, but the country is open enough for bushwhacking. ORVs had scarred some hillsides; signs now prohibit off-road driving.

SR 210 continues W to the Laramie Division of Medicine Bow National Forest (see entry). It was being paved when we were there.

Birds: Recorded species include pintail, mallard, blue-winged and green-winged teals, golden and bald eagles, unspecified hawks, turkey vulture, mourning and rock doves, nighthawk, western kingbird, unspecified woodpeckers, chickadee, mountain bluebird, western tanager, American crow, American robin, black-billed magpie, brown-headed catbird, meadowlark.

ACTIVITIES
Camping: 3 campgrounds, 78 sites. All year.
Boating: Hand-propelled craft only on Crystal; no restriction on Granite.

PUBLICATION: Leaflet with map.

HEADQUARTERS: 1319 Hynds Lodge Rd., Happy Jack Route, Cheyenne, WY
82009; (307) 632-7946.

ENCAMPMENT RIVER CANYON
U.S. Bureau of Land Management
3,380 acres.

2 mi. S of Encampment by local road branching left from SR 70. Signed.
(BLM map 8)

The site lies between Encampment and the Hayden Division of Medicine Bow
National Forest. It offers a splendid hiking route into a Wilderness area on
the Forest. It's a popular day hiking and picnicking area for local residents,
but trail use is light on weekdays, and dense riparian vegetation in the canyon
is effective screening.

Measuring only 3 mi. W–E and 2 N–S, the site straddles two narrow, deep,
rugged gorges, the canyons of the Encampment River and Miner Creek. The
canyons have striking rock outcrops and steep talus slopes. A foot trail in the
Encampment River Canyon connects, through an easement, with a continuation in the Forest. Sagebrush is common on open slopes, with scattered stands
of limber pine, aspen, cottonwood, and lodgepole pine.

Wildlife is abundant. Bighorn sheep were reintroduced and are often seen,
frequently close enough for photography. The site is important winter habitat
for mule deer and elk.

ACTIVITIES
Camping: A BLM campground is at the canyon mouth. Backpackers can
find suitable sites along the river.
Fishing: Said to be good when the river isn't high.

HEADQUARTERS: Rawlins District, BLM, 1300 Third St., Rawlins, WY 82301;
(307) 324-7171.

FERRIS MOUNTAINS
U.S. Bureau of Land Management
20,495 acres.

Pickup or 4-wheel drive needed, and advice from BLM. The area is E of
Lamont on US 287, N of the Continental Divide, on Cherry Creek. (BLM
map 7)

We include few sites that require 4-wheel drive for access. This is one of the exceptions. In S central WY, a series of small mountain ranges extends WNW–ESE just N of the Continental Divide. The Ferris Mountains, one of the series, are about 15 mi. long. They offer a wilderness experience uncommon in this part of the state, with a longer snow-free season than in higher country.

They're not for an easy afternoon stroll. Elevation rises from 6,580 ft. near the highway to 10,037 at the summit of Ferris Peak, where there's a register for visitors to sign. Terrain is extremely rugged, with deep canyons and steep slopes. There are no established trails, but much of the site is open country, and hikers can find feasible routes, including some drainages. The planned Continental Divide National Scenic Trail may cross the area.

Hunters seem to be the chief visitors, although the latest estimate for them was only 1,150 visitor-days per year. Some campers and hikers use the site. Small brook trout can be caught in Cherry Creek, within the livestock exclosures.

The Ferris range is a scenic attraction along the highway, visible for miles. A limestone outcrop several miles long makes a prominent white band on the southern flank. From a distance, the mountains look forested, but some slopes are covered by shrubs, grasses, and forbs. To the S are sand dunes and hay meadows; to the N gently rolling sagebrush plains. Sagebrush-grassland typifies the site's lower elevations, with cottonwood and willow in drainages. Douglas-fir predominates below the 8,000-ft. elevation in the SW and W. Lodgepole pine has revegetated a large old burn, while lodgepole and aspen have filled some openings. Upper slopes have scattered patches of limber and ponderosa pines, Engelmann spruce, and subalpine fir. Several of the canyons have perennial streams, none large enough to maintain a significant fishery.

Average annual precipitation is about 11 in. Nov.–Feb. are the driest months, Mar.–May the wettest.

Mammals: Elk were reintroduced in the 1960s and have increased to a present population of over 100. Pronghorn number 1,200 to 1,850, mule deer about 240, bighorn sheep 6 to 12. Other large mammals include occasional moose, black bear, and mountain lion. Small mammals include desert and mountain cottontail, snowshoe hare, red squirrel.

Birds: Species noted include blue and sage grouse, mourning dove, prairie falcon, golden eagle, Swainson's and Cooper's hawks.

HEADQUARTERS: Rawlins District, BLM, 1300 Third, Rawlins, WY 82301; (307) 324-7171.

FLAMING GORGE NATIONAL RECREATION AREA
Ashley National Forest; U.S. Forest Service
95,517 acres in WY; 94,308 acres in UT.

S of Green River. Access in WY from SR 530 (W side) and US 191 (E side). (BLM map 9)

In UT, the NRA is embedded in the NE corner of the 1.3-million-acre Ashley National Forest. Flaming Gorge Dam, in the canyon of the Green River near Dutch John, UT, created a 66-sq.-mi. reservoir extending 91 mi. N, almost to Green River. In UT, much of the reservoir is confined within the winding, vertical redrock canyon walls of the Green River. Near the WY border, it broadens. From here N the NRA land area is a narrow strip, only 1 to 2 mi. back from each shore, with some inholdings. The WY environment is desert: low hills, shale badlands, desert shrubs. Elevation at high water is 6,040 ft.

Since the dam was completed in 1964, Flaming Gorge has become a major area for water-based recreation. Although more than half the 91-mi. length of the lake is in WY, most development and activity are concentrated in UT. Of the NRA's 22 campgrounds, only 2 are in WY. Also in WY are 2 primitive boat ramps.

Most of the WY shoreline is undeveloped and far from any road. The only recreation complex on the W shore is at Buckboard Crossing, off SR 530 about 25 mi. S of Green River This has a marina, visitor contact station, campground with trailer facilities and water, and a store. A boat ramp is about 6 mi. S. Firehole is the only campground on the E side, reached by a paved road; a boat ramp is about 11 mi. S. Each side has a few unpaved routes to the lake shore.

The WY portion of the reservoir isn't as scenic as the UT portion, with its deep, colorful gorges. However, many people find a lake in the desert visually dramatic. This one can be enjoyed in solitude. Boat traffic in the WY portion is light. One can often cruise for miles without sighting another craft.

N of Buckboard Crossing, the land surrounding the reservoir includes many private holdings. From there S to the UT border, lands bordering the NRA are almost entirely BLM.

The principal visitor season begins in mid-May, peaks in July–Aug. Campgrounds are closed for the season by mid-Sept. However, it's easy to find an informal campsite on Forest or BLM land.

ACTIVITIES
Camping: 2 campgrounds; 88 sites.

Fishing: Rainbow, brown, and lake trout. Ice fishing is popular.

Boating: The water is cold in spring and fall, and the lake is subject to sudden strong winds. Boaters are advised to wear life jackets at all times and to head for shore promptly when the wind rises. Running out of fuel can become a serious problem in the WY portion of the lake, where traffic is light.

PUBLICATION: Leaflet with map.

HEADQUARTERS: Ashley National Forest, Flaming Gorge R.D., Manila, UT 84046; (801) 784-3445.

GLENDO STATE PARK
Wyoming Recreation Commission
9,930 land acres; 12,500 water acres.

4 mi. E of Glendo.

Glendo and Guernsey (see entry) are reservoirs on the North Platte River, close together, both surrounded by State Parks; but they are not alike. Glendo is six times as large—5 water bodies connected by necks. About 18 mi. long, it has a 78-mi. shoreline. Much of it can be seen from I-25, which parallels the W shore, or SR 319, which is closer to the shoreline. The Park is a narrow strip of land surrounding the reservoir.

We found Guernsey more attractive because of its rugged, rocky shoreline, forested slopes, and limited development. Much of Glendo, especially on the S and W, is surrounded by low, treeless hills. But Glendo's size and irregular shape offer greater possibilities for boaters and fishermen.

Glendo is among Wyoming's most heavily used State Parks, chiefly for water-based recreation. However, most development is clustered at the SE end of the reservoir. Much of the shoreline is inaccessible except by boat, and it's possible to enjoy a degree of isolation for boating or boat camping.

The low hills give little protection from wind, and the wind does blow, averaging 12 mph, often stronger for several consecutive days. The climate is semiarid, with 9 to 16 in. of precipitation per year. Snowfall is between 35 and 65 in. Winters are long and cold. Summers usually have several periods of high temperatures. Elevation is about 4,700 ft.

Birds: 155 species recorded, 49 of them requiring shoreline or marsh habitat.

ACTIVITIES

Camping: 7 campgrounds; 165 sites. All year.

Hiking: No trail system, but the open country is hikable.

Fishing: Said to be good. Rainbow and brown trout; walleye, yellow perch, channel catfish.
Boating: Marina, ramp, rentals. No hp limit.
Swimming: No protected beach.

ADJACENT: The Game and Fish Department provides fishing access to 1 1/2 mi. of river below the Glendo dam. Fishing is best July–Aug. One primitive campground.

PUBLICATION: Leaflet with map.

HEADQUARTERS: P.O. Box 398, Glendo, WY 82213; (307) 735-4433.

GUERNSEY STATE PARK
Wyoming Recreation Commission
6,538 land acres; 2,100 water acres.

1 mi. NW of Guernsey, off US 26.

This site delighted us. Our visit was at a good time, a June weekday; we saw only one other camper. It had been a wet spring, and the landscape was green, dotted with a multitude of wildflowers.

The reservoir, formed by a dam on the North Platte River, is irregular in shape, about 7 mi. long. Much of shoreline is bordered by cliffs, rock layers of cream and brown, some reddish. Elsewhere the land is gently rolling. The terrain and the reservoir's age—it was completed in 1928—give it the appearance of a natural lake.

One reason for our delight is discovering that the Park was developed by the Civilian Conservation Corps. Here, as in many other Parks, the CCC left monuments to an era we hope will come again. At Guernsey they built, with stone, shelters, a visitor center, culverts, and other structures, which have served for half a century with little maintenance. Even the dioramas and other exhibits in the visitor center look bright and fresh. The center also has a slide film, literature, and other information. The Park is listed on the National Register of Historic Places.

The film informed us that the CCC built 34 mi. of hiking trails here. The two pleasant employees manning the center said they knew of no trails. The Park leaflet shows several trails on the W side of the lake. We found old trails, unmarked and unmaintained but still hikable. Several had been scarred by ORVs. Later we learned there have been no funds for trail maintenance.

A good paved road follows the E shore of the lake, and most of the limited development is along this road: headquarters, visitor center, and campgrounds. The campgrounds are small, scattered, and informal. We parked our RV for the night at the water's edge. A gravel "Skyline Road" is high above the opposite shore, with spurs to the shoreline. The NW portion of the lake is roadless.

For management reasons, the lake is drained down at the end of each July and refilled in Aug., so fishing is insignificant.

ACTIVITIES
Camping: 7 campgrounds; 142 sites. All year.
Boating: Ramp. No hp limit.
Swimming: No designated area, but many visitors swim.

PUBLICATION: Leaflet with map.

HEADQUARTERS: P.O. Box 429, Guernsey, WY 82214; (307) 836-2334.

HUTTON LAKE NATIONAL WILDLIFE REFUGE
U.S. Fish and Wildlife Service
1,968 acres.

From Laramie, about 6 mi. SW on SR 230, then S about 3 mi. on County Road 37, crossing the Laramie River.

This small Refuge is a quiet, accessible place to observe waterfowl and shore and wading birds. It has a cluster of 5 ponds, the largest about 1/2 mi. across. Elevation is 7,150 ft., about the same as Laramie. The setting is rolling grasslands, the Laramie Plains. There are no facilities or resident personnel. HQ is in Walden, CO. Surrounding land is privately owned.

The ponds are accessible by unpaved Refuge roads. Drive on them cautiously, especially after wet weather. Hiking is permitted, and although there are no trails the terrain is favorable.

Birding is best in the spring migration, next best in fall.

Birds: Checklist of 176 species available, classified by abundance and season. Seasonally abundant or common species include eared, western, and pied-billed grebes; great blue heron, snowy egret, black-crowned night-heron, American bittern, white-faced ibis, Canada goose, mallard, gadwall, northern pintail, green-winged and blue-winged teals, American wigeon, shoveler, redhead, canvasback, lesser scaup, bufflehead, ruddy duck, common merganser, turkey vulture, Swainson's hawk, golden eagle, northern harrier, American kestrel, Virginia rail, sora, American coot, killdeer, common snipe; spotted, least, and stilt sandpipers; willet, lesser yellowlegs, long-billed dowitcher, American avocet, Wilson's phalarope, California gull, Forster's and black terns, mourning dove, common nighthawk, ash-throated flycatcher, Say's phoebe, horned lark, bank and cliff swallows, black-billed magpie, brown creeper, sage thrasher, American robin, mountain bluebird, yellow warbler, western meadowlark; yellow-headed, red-winged, and Brewer's blackbirds; gray-crowned rosy, black rosy, and brown-capped rosy finches; lark bunting, dark-eyed junco. Sparrows: house, savannah, vesper, lark, chipping, white-crowned, Lincoln's, song.

Mammals: Bats: little brown myotis; northern grasshopper, western harvest, and deer mice; Wyoming and hispid pocket mice, meadow vole, meadow jumping mouse, masked shrew, Richardson and thirteen-lined ground squirrels, whitetail prairie dog, least chipmunk, whitetail jackrabbit, desert cottontail, raccoon, muskrat, mink, longtail weasel, striped skunk, coyote, mule deer, pronghorn.

No camping, hunting, or fishing.

PUBLICATIONS
Map.
Bird checklist.

HEADQUARTERS: P.O. Box 457, Walden, CO 80480; (303) 723-8557.

MEDICINE BOW NATIONAL FOREST
U.S. Forest Service
1,090,352 acres; 1,402,684 acres within boundaries.

The *Medicine Bow Division,* 519,483 acres, and *Hayden Division,* 338,737 acres, are on the Colorado border W of Laramie. The *Pole Mountain Division,* 52,819 acres, is SE of Laramie. The *Laramie Peak Division,* 179,313 acres, is N of Laramie. They are described individually in this entry. The *Thunder Basin National Grassland,* 572,372 acres, also part of the Forest, is described in a separate entry in Zone 2.

The Medicine Bow doesn't have the vast, unbroken area one finds in National Forests farther W. The four Divisions include two large blocks of land, several of modest size, and several dozen scattered bits. Little of this land is pristine. An extensive road network records past and present uses. An inventory of roadless areas found none larger than 31,300 acres. The 1984 Wyoming Wilderness Act established three new Wildernesses, Platte River, Huston Park, and Encampment River, but together with the older Savage Run Wilderness these total just under 80,000 acres, 7% of the Forest. By contrast, the Bridger-Teton NF has more than 1.3 million Wilderness acres, almost 40% of the total Forest acreage.

The Medicine Bow has much to offer, however. It includes the Medicine Bow Range, which towers to more than 12,000 ft. elevation, as well as the Laramie and Sierra Madre ranges. The high country is dotted with over a hundred glacial lakes. The Forest has some of Wyoming's finest fishing waters, as well as an abundant wildlife. Along its several scenic highways are numerous attractive trails for day hiking, as well as pleasant campgrounds, many of them on lakes.

Many visitors to Wyoming drive through the Medicine Bow without pausing. Most of those who know and enjoy its best features come from nearby communities, chiefly Laramie and Cheyenne, and from northern Colorado and western Nebraska. When we asked if any areas were overused, the answer was no, but a few picnic area and campgrounds are usually full on pleasant weekends.

The Forest has 3,601 mi. of roads. The state maintains SRs 130, 210, 230, and 70. Other roads are unpaved and maintenance funds are inadequate. Many roads are impassable in wet weather. Some require high clearance or 4-wheel drive. Some are closed seasonally. About 400 mi. will be closed and revegetated. The Forest Travel Map shows current travel conditions.

Climate: Average annual precipitation is about 15 in. at the lowest elevations, over 40 in. in alpine areas, much of the latter falling as snow. On the high slopes, 3 to 7 ft. of snow accumulate in winter, with deeper drifts and wind-scoured bare rock. Summer high temperatures are about 80°F at low elevations. Winter lows in alpine areas reach −40°.

High winds are common in some areas, chiefly near mountain passes and canyons. Average summer velocities are 10 to 15 mph, rising to 20 to 30 mph in winter.

Plants: Almost half of the Forest, 452,000 acres, is dominated by lodgepole pine, much of it in pure, even-aged stands. At higher elevations, Engelmann spruce and subalpine fir occupy about 164,000 acres. 49,000 acres of ponderosa pine are mostly in the Laramie Peak Division. Aspen, which typically appears in burned areas, occupies about 85,000 acres. Above timberline are about 12,000 acres of alpine vegetation: grasses, forbs, low shrubs, stunted trees. Other important plant communities are mountain shrub, sagebrush, meadow, grassland, and riparian.

Seasonal wildflowers include sand, snow, and sego lilies; wild iris, marsh marigold, buttercup, pasqueflower, Rocky Mountain columbine, larkspur, monkshood, penny cress, western wallflower, stonecrop, saxifrage, wild rose, bitterbrush, cinquefoil, mountain-mahogany, serviceberry, lupine, purple vetch, wild geranium, wild flax, pricklypear, fireweed, evening primrose, kinnikinnick, shootingstar, phlox, scarlet gilia, penstemon, harebell, twinflower, snowberry, browneyed Susan, groundsel, easter and mountain daisies, aster, arnica, gaillardia, goldenrod, sunflower.

Birds: The ROG has a checklist of 136 species, without notes on abundance or seasonality. Included: mallard; green-winged, blue-winged, and cinnamon teals; ring-necked duck, turkey vulture. Hawks: sharp-shinned, goshawk, Cooper's, red-tailed, Harlan's, Swainson's, ferruginous. Northern harrier, golden and bald eagles, osprey, prairie falcon, merlin, American kestrel. Blue and sage grouse, white-tailed ptarmigan, wild turkey, mourning dove, black-billed cuckoo. Owls: screech, great horned, pygmy, great gray, long-eared, short-eared, saw-whet. Poor-will, common nighthawk, white-throated swift. Hummingbirds: black-chinned, broad-tailed, rufous, calliope. Belted king-fisher, northern flicker, yellow-bellied and Williamson's sapsuckers; hairy, downy, black-backed three-toed, and northern three-toed woodpeckers. Horned lark. Flycatchers: willow, alder, gray, western, olive-sided, western wood-pewee. Swallows: violet-green, tree, bank, rough-winged, barn, cliff. Jays: gray, blue, Steller's, pinyon. Black-billed magpie, common raven, Clark's nutcracker. Black-capped and mountain chickadees; white-breasted, red-breasted, and pygmy nuthatches; brown creeper, dipper, gray catbird, brown and sage thrashers, American robin, hermit and Swainson's thrushes, veery, mountain bluebird, Townsend's solitaire, golden-crowned and ruby-crowned kinglets, water pipit, northern and loggerhead shrikes; solitary, red-eyed, and warbling vireos. Warblers: orange-crowned, yellow, yellow-rumped, ovenbird, MacGillivray's, common yellowthroat, yellow-breasted chat, Wilson's, American redstart. Western meadowlark; red-winged, rusty, and Brewer's blackbirds; brown-headed cowbird, western tanager. Black-headed, pine, and evening grosbeaks; lazuli bunting. Finches: house, Cassin's, gray-crowned, black rosy. Pine siskin, red crossbill, green-tailed and rufous-sided towhees, Oregon and gray-headed juncos. Sparrows: vesper, lark, sage, tree, chipping, clay-colored, Brewer's, Harris', white-crowned, fox, Lincoln's, song.

(The list includes species occurring on the Thunder Basin National Grassland.)

Mammals: No checklist. 77 species recorded, including redback and long-tail voles, dwarf shrew, deer mouse, western jumping mouse, Richardson ground squirrel, golden-mantled squirrel, chipmunk, cottontail, prairie dog, beaver, raccoon, muskrat, porcupine, badger, yellowbelly marmot, skunk, weasel, coyote, mountain lion, black bear, mule and whitetail deer, elk, prong-horn, bighorn sheep.

Hayden Division is on the CO border and is crossed by SR 70 between Baggs and Encampment. This Division extends along the Continental Divide on the N end of the Sierra Madre Range. Most of the ridge is above 9,000 ft. until it drops down into the Great Divide Basin, beyond the Forest boundary. Highest point in the Division is 11,004-ft. Bridger Peak. Lowest is 7,400 ft. at the Encampment River, near the point where SR 70 enters the Forest. No roads within the Division are paved. SR 70 is all-weather. From near its E entrance, another all-weather road drops S to the CO border, entering the Routt NF. Several campgrounds are along these roads. The Division has a modest network of dirt and primitive roads, some requiring 4-wheel drive, on which are several backcountry campgrounds. The trail network links with that of the Routt NF in CO.

The W slopes are largely covered with quaking aspen and brush, product of old fires. Drainage is to the Little Snake River. The E side has extensive stands of lodgepole pine and Engelmann spruce. Drainage is to the North Platte River.

FEATURES

Encampment River Wilderness, 10,400 acres. The Encampment River flows N from CO through the Division and on past the town of Encampment to join the North Platte River. The Wilderness straddles the river, a strip less than a mile wide in the S, broadening to almost 5 mi. wide near the N boundary, where it includes several tributaries. Its principal feature is a scenic canyon trail, easily accessible from Encampment. (See entry, Encampment River Canyon.)

Huston Park Wilderness, 31,300 acres. S of SR 70, in the Sierra Madres, straddling the Continental Divide. Drainages are to the Little Snake and North Platte rivers. Elevations to above 10,000 ft. Vegetation includes quaking aspen interspersed with open parks and brush. Higher elevations and the E side of the Divide are dominated by Engelmann spruce and lodgepole pine. Best access is from Lost Creek Campground on SR 70. No developed trailheads.

Lakes: Five lakes and reservoirs. Only one, Hog Park, is large enough for motorized boats.

Medicine Bow Division is on SR 130, W from Laramie. Several all-weather routes provide access to the N and S portions. The Division, largest of the four, is on the CO border, where it adjoins both the Routt and the Arapaho and Roosevelt National Forests. From the border, it extends N about 40 mi. in a block about 20 mi. wide. SR 130, the Snowy Range Highway, offers good access, with campgrounds, overlooks, and picnic sites.

It lies on both sides of the N–S Medicine Bow Range, locally called the Snowy Range, which has many peaks over 10,000 ft. elevation. Highest is 12,013-ft. Medicine Bow Peak. Most of the area is above 8,000 ft. In this high country, snowbanks persist well into summer. It has more than a hundred glacial lakes, ranging in size from potholes to a hundred acres. Perennial streams flow W and E to the North Platte, which loops over the N end of the range. Up to timberline, slopes are forested with Engelmann spruce, ponderosa pine, Douglas-fir, subalpine fir, limber pine, cottonwood, and quaking aspen.

FEATURES

This Division offers the greatest variety of natural features and attracts the most visitors.

Savage Run Wilderness, 15,260 acres, is on the W side of the Medicine Bow Division. It isn't the highest part of the area, with elevations from 8,000 to 10,000 ft., but it met Wilderness criteria, being roadless and in natural condition. A portion of its boundary is an all-weather road. Steep-sided canyons are at the lower elevations, rising to rolling plateaus.

The Savage Run Trail, 12 mi., parallels Savage Run Creek. The western 3 mi. are on moderate sagebrush slopes, followed by 9 mi. through virgin timber. Well-marked trailheads are on the N and S sides.

Platte River Wilderness, 22,363 acres, plus additional acreage in the Routt National Forest of CO. The North Platte River enters the Routt National Forest 4 mi. S of the WY border. In WY, it continues in the Wilderness, flowing through North Gate Canyon, leaving the National Forest near Six Mile Gap Campground, 18 mi. from the Routt access. This segment of the river is a popular whitewater float trip. Primary access from Pelton Creek, Pike Pole, Pickaroon, and Six Mile Gap campgrounds.

Lakes: About a hundred alpine lakes and reservoirs. Two are large enough for motorized boats.

SR 130, the Snowy Range Highway, is a fine scenic route across the Snowy Mountains. Beginning in a lodgepole forest, it climbs through spruce forest to the Alpine Zone. Wildflowers are spectacular from early June through July. Libby Flats Observation Site, near the pass, offers a good view of Medicine Bow Peak and high points in CO. Several mountain lakes and campgrounds are nearby. Closed in winter, it usually opens on Memorial Day.

Pole Mountain Division is SE of Laramie. I-80 crosses its W edge. SR 210, a paved road, is a scenic alternative between Cheyenne and Laramie. Smallest of the four, the Division is about 11 mi. N–S, 9 mi. W–E. The highest point, 9,053-ft. Pole Mountain, is surrounded by forested rolling hills. The original ponderosa pine forest was cut and burned. Now it's a young open forest of lodgepole pine with aspen groves and immature Douglas-fir on N-facing slopes.

Although less dramatically scenic than the larger Divisions, it has canyons with interesting geologic features, streams with beaver dams. Its accessibility and network of all-weather roads attract many campers and picnickers from nearby Laramie and Cheyenne.

FEATURES

Devils Playground is one of several geologic features along Crow Creek, in the SW corner of the Pole Mountain Division. From SR 210, just inside the Forest boundary, SW on Forest Road 700. Huge granite boulders have been stacked in fantastic formations. The area includes Turtle Rock, Vedauwoo

Glen, and the Vedauwoo Campground. This is a popular weekend spot for residents of Laramie and Cheyenne and can become crowded in good weather.

Laramie Peak Division is SW of Douglas, via SRs 91 and 94. The Forest map is essential in finding campgrounds and other features. The Division consists of more than a hundred scattered fragments, some as small as 40 acres, the largest an irregular block about 16 mi. by 4 mi. Other landholdings are an equally scattered mix of BLM, state, and private land. Many acres of Forest land are inaccessible because private owners control rights-of-way.

The Division is of interest, none the less, located in the Laramie Mountains, with rugged and rocky slopes bordered by open grass and sagebrush, mountain parks, and deep valleys. Many slopes have stands of ponderosa and limber pine and Douglas-fir. Elevations range from 5,500 ft. to 10,272-ft. Laramie Peak. Several others are above 9,000 ft. These high, sharp, rocky peaks are linked by narrow ridges. Between the rugged breaks are attractive mountain parks and deep valleys. Many of the slopes have stands of ponderosa and limber pine, subalpine fir, and Douglas-fir.

Several all-weather roads cross or penetrate the area, as well numerous primitive and 4-wheel-drive routes. There are three campgrounds.

FEATURES
Laramie Peak can be ascended by trail from Friend Park, W of Wendover. The roads in this area are unpaved but should be suitable for cars in dry weather. A campground at Friend Park isn't shown on the Forest map.

La Bonte Canyon, reached by Forest Road 658, is one of the most scenic in the Division. Steep canyon sides with patches of aspen and conifers. Many deer and elk, some bighorn sheep.

The ROG has descriptions of several scenic drives in the Division, up to 140 mi.

INTERPRETATION (for all Divisions)
The Forest has no visitor center, campfire talks, or other interpretive programs.

The looseleaf Recreation Opportunities Guide (ROG) can be consulted at HQ or any R.D. office. Pages describing trails, campgrounds, etc., can be photocopied.

ACTIVITIES
Camping: 31 campgrounds; 437 sites. Season is determined by snow. Pole Mountain and Laramie Peak areas open by May 1, although subfreezing nights occur through mid-June. Sites above 9,500 ft. may be blocked by snow until early July. Season for most campgrounds is June–Sept. Campgrounds on SR 130 (Medicine Bow Division) E of Snowy Range Pass are generally full on weekends, often mid-week. The ROG has detailed information for each campground.

Hiking, backpacking: The Forest has only 296 mi. of managed trails. Most trails are short, suitable for day hiking. Only three areas are extensive enough for backpacking: the Savage Run and Huston Park Wildernesses and the Snowy Range.

Hunting: The Forest is considered a prime hunting area for elk, mule deer, pronghorn, and bighorn sheep. Some of the best hunting is in the Medicine Bow Division.

Fishing: The Forest has 1,748 mi. of perennial streams. Blue-ribbon waters of the North Platte and Encampment rivers are said to have some of the state's best rainbow and brown trout fishing. 83 lakes and reservoirs offer 1,417 acres of fishing opportunity. Most are in the Medicine Bow Division. The ROG has a 16-page list of fishing waters with locations, information on stocking, etc.

Horse riding: The ROG has information on outfitters and trails suitable for horse use.

Boating: Most lakes are small. Motors are allowed on Lake Owen and Rob Roy Reservoir in the Medicine Bow District, Hog Park Reservoir in the Hayden District. Hand-propelled boats can be used on 15 other lakes in the Medicine Bow District, 3 others in the Hayden.

Rafting: From the Routt NF access to Six Mile Gap Campground, the North Platte is hazardous whitewater with no exit in North Gate Canyon. Visitors are advised to use a commercial outfitter. Rafting season is unpredictable, but usually late May–late June. Beyond Six Mile, the river is suitable for canoes, flat-bottom boats, and small rafts; flow is usually sufficient in June and July.

Skiing: Snowy Range Ski Area, privately operated, off SR 130 W of Centennial. Open Wed.–Sun., Nov.–Apr. 12 runs; lifts.

Ski touring: Groomed trails at the Snowy Range Ski Area; Happy Jack Road (off I-80 in the Pole Mountain Division).

PUBLICATIONS

Forest map. $1.

Savage Run Wilderness leaflet with map.

Maps of the Encampment River, Huston Park, and Platte River Wildernesses. (These are not hiking guides.)

HEADQUARTERS: 605 Skyline Drive, Laramie, WY 82070; (307) 745-8971.

RANGER DISTRICTS: Brush Creek R.D. (N portion of Medicine Bow Division), 212 S. First, Saratoga, WY 82331; (307) 326-5258. Laramie R.D. (S portion of Medicine Bow Division), 605 Skyline Drive, Laramie, WY 82070; (307) 745-8971. Hayden R.D., P.O. Box 185, Encampment, WY 82325; (307) 327-5481. Laramie Peak R.D., 809 S. Ninth, Douglas, WY 82633. Thunder Basin R.D. (see entry for Thunder Basin National Grassland in Zone 2), 809 S. Ninth, Douglas, WY 82633; (307) 358-4690.

NATURAL CORRALS
U.S. Bureau of Land Management
1,116 acres.

From Point of Rocks on I-80, E and N about 8 mi. on County Road 4-15 to the Jim Bridger power station. In about 2 mi. turn W toward Superior. At 3 1/2 mi., take right fork; in about 2 1/2 mi., track to left enters the site. The last 2 1/2 mi. require 4-wheel drive when wet. (BLM map 9)

Two aspects of this scenic site attract visitors, most of them local: ice caves, and the legend that Butch Cassidy's loot was hidden here.

The site's geological past produced an impressive jumble of huge volcanic boulders. The "caves," which do have ice all year long, are spaces under the pile. One can crawl a considerable distance before emerging. No one has found any loot. (Caution: Volcanic rocks are abrasive.)

The area was used by Indians at least 7,500 years ago, according to archeologists who have studied the artifacts, and there are indications of its use as a natural corral.

It has been given protection as an Area of Critical Environmental Concern and nominated for the National Register of Historic Places. School groups often come here.

NEARBY
Where County Road 4-15 turns N, about 2 1/2 mi. E of Point of Rocks, Ten-Mile Marsh is on the E, a wetland attractive to waterfowl.

Also see entry: Alkali Draw; South Pinnacles.

HEADQUARTERS: Rock Springs District, BLM, Highway 191 North, Rock Springs, WY 82902; (307) 382-5350.

PATHFINDER RESERVOIR
See entry in Zone 2.

RED DESERT COMPLEX
Mixed ownerships
4,500,000 acres.

Generally, between Rock Springs and Rawlins, N of I-80. (BLM map 9)

Some atlases don't recognize the Red Desert. The U.S. Geological Survey places the Red Desert Basin as a modest subunit of the Great Divide Basin, N of the town of Red Desert on I-80. Others use it as a convenient label for what the highway map shows as a vast unroaded area in northern Sweetwater County, sprinkled with such names as Alkali Flat and Chain Lakes Flat. More detailed maps show a network of roads and apologies for roads, none paved, some requiring 4-wheel drive.

The area has no towering, snow-clad mountains or endless green forests, but it has great diversity: blowing sand dunes, colorful buttes, volcanic plugs, miles-long escarpments, sagebrush flats, barren playas. The road network is there because of cattle ranching, oil and gas drilling, and other economic activities.

To provide samples of this complex, we have entries for several roadless, relatively undisturbed tracts of public land identified in BLM's wilderness inventory process. See entries in Zone 3 for

Sand Dunes; Buffalo Hump
Red Lake; Alkali Basin-East Sand Dunes
Honeycomb Buttes; Oregon Buttes
Alkali Draw-South Pinnacles

RED LAKE; ALKALI BASIN-EAST SAND DUNES
U.S. Bureau of Land Management
9,515 acres; 12,800 acres.

From Table Rock on I-80, N about 30 mi. on County Road 4-21. (BLM map 9)

These roadless areas, separated by the gravel county road, are part of the Red Desert (see entry) and include a portion of the Killpecker Dunes.

Red Lake, a playa, rarely has any water. The area consists of rolling sand dunes, most of them active, with a range of elevations of only 200 ft. The stabilized dunes are vegetated with big sagebrush, saltbush, grasses, and forbs.

The Alkali Basin-East Sand Dunes area is more of the same, with only a 100-ft. range of elevation and a higher proportion of barren, active dunes.

Wildlife is typical of the Red Desert: wild horse, pronghorn, coyote, bobcat, small mammals.

Why come here? Many people would find it hot, barren, and uninteresting. But in the wilderness review process, one enthusiast called it "an attractive combination of dunes, sage-covered hills . . . offers outstanding recreational opportunities." Another found it to be "a giant open-air sandbox providing a unique opportunity for unabashed play." We suggest playing in spring or fall, not summer.

HEADQUARTERS: Rock Springs District, BLM, Highway 191 North, Rock Springs, WY 82902; (307) 382-5350.

SAND DUNES
U.S. Bureau of Land Management
38,480 acres.

From Rock Springs, about 10 mi. N on US 191 (US 187 on older maps). Right on Tri-Territory Rd., County Road 4-17. Across railroad tracks, road turns N. At intersection, left on 4-16 about 6 mi; site boundary is on the right. Be alert for patches of soft sand. 4-17 continues E to an ORV area. (BLM maps 9 and 10)

The Killpecker Sand Dunes extend from the Eden Valley eastward across Wyoming to Nebraska, shaped by westerly winds blowing through a natural funnel. In many places they are vegetated and stabilized, seen as hills rather than dunes. The site described here is at the heart of the largest active dune fields in North America, with dunes up to 200 ft. high constantly changing as sand is blown eastward.

Hiking into the dunes is strenuous but rewarding. Wandering among the dunes, one quickly has the feeling of being isolated and lost. Indeed, without a compass and with a heavy overcast obscuring the sun, one could become disoriented. We suggest having compass, BLM map, and advice from BLM's Rock Springs office, to be sure of finding the area's most unique and astonishing feature. It takes a 5 or 6 mi. hike across the dunes to see it.

At the base of many of these desert sand dunes are pools of water, some crystal clear and as much as 8 ft. deep! We saw photos of visitors swimming. The water source is as unusual as the occurrence. The phenomenon depends on fairly constant westerly wind. Winter snow and ice, accumulating on the lee sides of the living dunes, are covered by blowing sand. Insulated by the sand, the eolian ice-cells persist into warm weather, melting slowly into the pools. The clear pools have little aquatic life, but others, muddy and murky, are well populated with insects, salamanders, and tadpoles, miniature ecosystems based on algae and grasses. The water also attracts other wildlife.

Prevailing winds average 15 mph. Much higher wind speeds occur in late winter and spring. Average annual precipitation is 8 to 10 in. Average daytime temperatures range from 60–65°F in July to 10–15° in Jan.

Average elevation of the site is 6,800 ft. The largest dunes are over 200 ft. high. Highest point, in the N, is 6,970 ft.

Plants: Barren dunes cover about three-fifths of the site. Among the dunes are small wet and dry meadows. Other dunes have been stabilized by vegetation, chiefly the sagebrush-grass community, including rabbitbrush, grasses, and forbs.

Birds: Limited numbers of waterfowl use the ponds for nesting as well as resting and feeding. Shorebirds are spring and fall visitors.

Mammals: Mule deer and Wyoming's only herd of desert elk occupy the site in summer. Some deer remain through the winter. Pronghorn occupy the S portion of the site. Other species noted include Ord kangaroo rat, coyote, red fox, mountain lion, bobcat. About 100 wild horses were present at the most recent count.

ORV operators have been the principal recreational users of the area. Because ORVs do irreparable damage to desert vegetation, BLM attempts to restrict them to the barren dunes. 16,280 acres have been recommended for Wilderness designation, which would exclude all motor vehicles. ORVs would continue to use other parts of the dune area, here and farther E.

ADJACENT AND NEARBY

Boar's Tusk is a prominent landmark just outside the S boundary, a volcanic plug, its top at 7,095 ft. elevation.

Buffalo Hump is a 10,300-acre roadless area on the W boundary. The sites are separated by a railroad line. The SE portion of the area has the same characteristics as Sand Dunes.

Cedar Canyon, 2,560 acres, is small, attractive, with features that caused it to be declared an Area of Critical Environmental Concern. School groups come here for nature study. Interpretive signs. An annual university study site for its archeological and biological features. En route to the Sand Dunes, about 10 mi. beyond the RR crossing on Tri-Territory Road, turn right at the sign. Cars can drive the first 4 mi., but it may be necessary to walk the last 1 1/2 mi. because of soft sand.

The canyon isn't deep, but its orientation produces a microclimate moister than the surrounding area, and thus a richer vegetation, including limber pine and juniper. Many petroglyphs, some of 19th-century Shoshone origin. Cliffs are a nesting area for many raptors. Deer and elk winter range.

White Mountain Petroglyphs. Follow directions to Cedar Canyon, but at sign 10 mi. N of railroad crossing turn left instead of right. Indian artwork incised in sandstone cliffs.

HEADQUARTERS: Rock Springs District, BLM, Highway 191 North, Rock Springs, WY 82902; (307) 382-5350.

SEEDSKADEE NATIONAL WILDLIFE REFUGE
U.S. Fish and Wildlife Service
14,376 acres.

From Green River, W on I-80 to the LaBarge-SR 372 exit. N 28 mi. on
SR 372 to the HQ turnoff. (BLM map 9)

"Who comes here?" we asked. "Very few," was the reply. "Some dedicated
birders from Green River and Rock Springs. Local hunters in the fall."

The Refuge is a 35-mi. strip along the Green River. The Fontenelle Dam,
built upstream in the 1950s, dried the sloughs and marshy oxbows on which
many waterfowl depended. The Refuge was established to mitigate the loss.
River water is diverted to maintain marshes. Now the Refuge is an important
feeding, resting, and nesting site on the E edge of the Pacific Flyway. Whooping cranes from Grays Lake are among the visitors.

Spring is the time for birding, Apr. and May the peak months. There's no
tour route, and road conditions are variable, especially after rain. When we
visited, some roads were under water because of exceptionally high releases
from the dam. Stop at HQ. They'll tell you where the action is.

No facilities are here; bring food and water, and be sure to have enough
gasoline to get back to Green River.

The Green River Basin, open, rolling, semiarid country, had been sadly
damaged by years of overgrazing, sheep depleting the forage available to mule
deer, pronghorn, and moose, as well as bottomland vegetation used by waterfowl as food and cover. Refuge management has improved food supply for
waterfowl, and bottomland vegetation has made some recovery. Today,
within the Refuge, typical bottomland vegetation includes grasses with stands
of cottonwood, willow, and brush.

Birds: The name *Seedskadee* meant "river of the prairie hen" in Shoshone,
and sage grouse are still here in numbers, most visible in dry summers when
they come out of the sagebrush for water. Canada geese have nested along
the river for decades. Checklist of 227 species available. Species abundant or
common include eared, western, and pied-billed grebes; great blue heron,
white pelican, white-faced ibis, whistling swan, Canada goose, mallard, gadwall, northern pintail; green-winged, blue-winged, and cinnamon teals;
American wigeon, northern shoveler, redhead, ring-necked duck, canvasback, lesser scaup, common goldeneye, ruddy duck, common merganser,
red-tailed and rough-legged hawks, golden eagle, northern harrier, prairie
falcon, American kestrel, sage grouse, American coot, killdeer, common
snipe, spotted and stilt sandpipers, long-billed dowitcher, marbled godwit,
Wilson's phalarope, ring-billed and Franklin's gulls, mourning dove, great

horned owl, northern flicker, Say's phoebe, willow flycatcher, horned lark. Swallows: violet-green, tree, bank, barn, cliff. Black-billed magpie, American robin, mountain bluebird, European starling, western meadowlark; yellow-headed, red-winged, and Brewer's blackbirds; brown-headed cowbird. Sparrows: house, vesper, Harris', white-crowned. Dark-eyed junco.

ACTIVITIES

Fishing: The Green River is an outstanding trout fishery, when water conditions are right.

Rafting: Class I water; no rapids. Suitable for raft, canoe, kayak. A 16-mi. float trip is possible in spring and summer. Ask at Fontenelle Dam about put-in. Boat camping is not permitted on the Refuge.

No camping on the Refuge. Bureau of Reclamation campgrounds are 2 and 6 mi. upstream.

PUBLICATIONS
Leaflet with map.
Bird checklist.

HEADQUARTERS: P.O. Box 67, Green River, WY 82935; (307) 875-2187. (Mail address; HQ is on the Refuge.)

SEMINOE RESERVOIR; SEMINOE STATE PARK
Wyoming Recreation Commission
3,821 land acres; 6,560 water acres.

From Sinclair on I-80, 33 mi. N on paved county road.

The county road crosses open range, then enters the canyon of the North Platte River. Canyon walls are sloping, not high, layers of sedimentary rock chiefly in shades of brown, dotted with sagebrush and juniper. We saw a few more colorful formations. The river is winding, 60 to 80 ft. wide, floatable, no rapids. Along the road are many pullouts where one can camp, picnic, or fish.

Seminoe Dam is below the confluence of the Medicine Bow and North Platte Rivers, backing the pool up both. The main body plus the North Platte arm is about 18 mi. long. The site is in the Seminoe Mountains. Elevation at the dam is 6,358 ft. Highest point in the mountains, outside the Park boundary, is 8,948 ft. Just to the NE are the Bennett Mountains, which include an abruptly rising mountain wall on the S and small canyons on the N. Hillsides around the reservoir are moderate to steep, some grassy hills, many rock outcrops. The reservoir lies across the Killpecker Sand Dunes, a belt extending across WY. Blowing sand has created several swimming beaches, as well as a sandbar extending out into the lake.

Federal land surrounds the reservoir, with a dozen or so private inholdings. The paved road is on the W side. Seminoe State Park includes 4 lakeside recreation areas reached by spur roads. Spurs to South and North Red Hills, the two principal sites, are well-maintained gravel. 4-wheel drive is advised for the others. We saw several dirt tracks to the shore, where several parties were camping in undesignated sites. Most had pickups, but a few bold individuals made it with ordinary cars. The E shore is generally inaccessible by land except with 4-wheel drive.

Most visitors come for fishing and boating, though we saw a few campers without boats. Hunters camp here in the fall. Most of the surrounding area is public domain. Hiking is possible, but few visitors hike.

Upland vegetation is typical of high desert, including yucca, greasewood, sagebrush, and salt sage, with willow and marsh grasses in draws, pinyon pine and juniper on mountain slopes. Wildlife includes elk, mule deer, bighorn sheep, porcupine, prairie dog, coyote, skunk, bobcat, and mountain lion. We saw a dozen pronghorn near the county road and on the lake shore. Waterfowl include nesting Canada goose.

NEARBY: Just N of Seminoe Dam is the "miracle mile" of the North Platte, famous for trout fishing. The road beyond Seminoe State Park is unpaved, and we were advised not to try it except in dry weather. The road from the N is longer and no better. The dam can't be crossed by car or on foot.

ACTIVITIES
Camping: 3 campgrounds; 47 sites. All year. Many informal sites, and boat camping is possible.
Hiking, backpacking: On adjoining BLM lands.
Fishing: Rainbow and brown trout, walleye.
Boating: Ramps.

PUBLICATION: Leaflet with map.

HEADQUARTERS: Box 367, Sinclair, WY 82334; (307) 324-6955.

SPRINGER WILDLIFE UNIT
Wyoming Game and Fish Department
1,911 acres.

From Torrington, US 85 and SR 154 to Yoder, then 2 mi. S.

This isn't a prime destination for the out-of-state visitor, but it's worth a look if you're passing on US 85, especially during spring and fall waterfowl migrations, or if you want a quiet, overnight primitive campsite.

The 364-acre Springer Reservoir and 180-acre Bump-Sullivan Reservoir are used for irrigation and often show marked drawdown by fall. The small Wellnitz Ponds nearby may dry completely in years of low rainfall. The fluctuation markedly affects waterfowl nesting. In spring and fall migrations, 25,000 to 100,000 ducks and 5,000 to 10,000 Canada geese use the area. In good years, Springer can hold 10,000 geese and 25,000 or more ducks from November through January.

Both reservoirs can be reached by graded, gravel roads off the Yoder-Hawk Springs road, as well as by ungraded dirt roads that should be avoided when wet.

Springer attracts an average of about 15,000 visitor-days per year, for boating, swimming, fishing, and picnicking.

ACTIVITIES
Camping: In 6 parking areas. One has seasonal closure.
Hunting: Pheasant, dove. Special rules and seasons for goose and duck.
Fishing: Low water levels have affected all game fish except bullheads.

Closed to vehicles after Memorial Day.

NEARBY
Table Mountain Wildlife Unit, 1,716 acres, 6 mi. W of US 85 on local road 1 mi. N of Downar Bird Farm. Year-round habitat for Canada geese and ducks, this is also a good birding site. Undulating to rolling grassland. Nine small impoundments total 189 acres. More than 25,000 ducks and 2,000 geese pause during spring migration; some remain and nest. About twice that number of ducks have been counted in the fall migration beginning in Aug. Camping in 3 parking areas.

Closed to vehicle access during pheasant and waterfowl seasons.

HEADQUARTERS: Wyoming Game and Fish Department, 5400 Bishop Blvd., Cheyenne, WY 82002; (307) 777-7631.

WICK BROTHERS WILDLIFE HABITAT UNIT
("Medicine Bow Elk Winter Range" on BLM map.)
Wyoming Game and Fish Department
12,135 acres.

From 1 mi. NW of Arlington, 1 mi. SW on Sand Lake Road. Or from I-25 NW of Arlington, S from Wagonhound exit. (BLM map 8)

This site offers opportunities for quiet streamside camping and easy day hiking, close to I-80. It adjoins the N boundary of Medicine Bow National Forest (see entry). Sand Lake Road continues as Forest Roads III and 101 to Sand Lake and Deep Creek Campground. Several primitive roads and foot trails link the two sites.

The site is managed to provide winter habitat for elk. Several hundred winter here from late Nov. through Apr. Public use is light, about 2,500 visitor-days per year. Hunting and fishing each account for about 1,000. Other visitors come to camp, hike, and observe wildlife.

This is the northern edge of the Medicine Bow Mountain Range. From 7,200 ft. at the N boundary of the unit, rolling hills give way to rugged foothills as the terrain rises to 8,770 ft. at the Forest boundary. Principal streams are Wagonhound and Foote creeks, flowing NE. Three ponds, each smaller than an acre, are stocked.

Climate is semiarid, most of the unit receiving 15–19 in. of precipitation annually. Most of the vegetation is grassland, sagebrush-grassland, or mountain shrub-sagebrush-grassland, with about 1,000 acres of wet meadow.

Wildlife: Deer are common all year, pronghorn May–Nov. Bear have been seen along creek bottoms. Game birds are blue and sage grouse, and mourning dove. A few waterfowl visit until the ponds freeze.

ACTIVITIES

Camping: In 4 parking areas. 2 have latrines.
Fishing: Rainbow, brook, and brown trout.

HEADQUARTERS: Wyoming Game and Fish Department, 5400 Bishop Blvd., Cheyenne, WY 82002; (307) 777-7631.

INDEX

ABOUT THE AUTHORS

THE PERRYS, long residents of the Washington, DC., area, moved to Winter Haven, Florida, soon after work on these guides began. Their desks overlook a lake well populated with great blue herons, anhingas, egrets, ospreys, gallinules, and wood ducks, a nesting pair of bald eagles, and occasional pelicans, alligators, and otters.

Jane, an economist, came to Washington as a congressman's secretary and thereafter held senior posts in several executive agencies and presidential commissions. John, an industrial management consultant, left that work to spend ten years with the Smithsonian Institution, involved in overseas nature conservation.

They have hiked, backpacked, camped, canoed, and cruised together in all fifty states. They have written more than fourteen books and produced two dozen educational filmstrips, chiefly on natural history and ecology.

Their move to Florida marked a shift from international to local conservation action. They hold various offices in county Sierra Club and Audubon Society groups and the Coalition for the Environment. John is a trustee of the Florida Nature Conservancy.

The guide series keeps them on the road about three months each year, living and working in a motor home, accompanied by Tor II, a black Labrador.